THE NIV®

Standard

LESSON COMMENTARY

2005–2006

edited by

RONALD L. NICKELSON

published by
Standard Publishing

Jonathan Underwood, Senior Editor

Carla J. Crane,
Production Manager

Twelfth Annual Volume

Standard

P U B L I S H I N G

Bringing The Word to Life™

CD-ROM AVAILABLE

The *Standard Lesson Commentary*® is available separately in an electronic format. This compact disk contains the full text of the King James *Standard Lesson Commentary*® and *The NIV Standard Lesson Commentary*®, a variety of preparation resources powered by the Libronix Digital Library System, and a collection of presentation helps that can be projected or reproduced as handouts. Ask for the *Standard Lesson eCommentary* (#06006) at your local Christian bookstore or directly from Standard Publishing.

System Requirements: Windows XP/2000/ME/98; Pentium 133 MHz processor (300MHz recommended), 64 Meg RAM (128 recommended); 60 Meg Available Hard Drive Space; 2x or better CD-ROM drive.

If you have any questions regarding the installation, registration, or activation of this CD-ROM, please contact Logos **Customer Service** at **(800) 875-6467.**

If you have problems with the CD, *Technical Support* is available by telephone at *(360) 679-4496,* by e-mail at *tech@logos.com,* or online at *www.logos.com/support.*

© 2005
STANDARD PUBLISHING
a division of STANDEX INTERNATIONAL Corporation
8121 Hamilton Avenue, Cincinnati, Ohio 45231
Printed in U.S.A.

In This Volume

Special Features

Fall Quarter 2005
You Will Be My Witnesses

Writers

Lesson Development..............James Lloyd (1-4), Dennis Gaertner (5-13)
Verbal Illustrations ....Charles R. Boatman
Discovery Learning......................Ronald G. Davis
What Do You Think? ....A. Eugene Andrews
Why Teach This Lesson? ....Vicki Edwards

Winter Quarter 2005–2006
God's Commitment—Our Response

Writers

Lesson Development ....Lloyd Pelfrey (1-4), Harvey Bream (5-9), Mark Krause (10-13)
What Do You Think? ....Kenneth Beck (1-4), Richard Baynes (5-13)
Discovery Learning ....Ronald G. Davis (1-9), Alan Weber (10-13)
Verbal Illustrations A. Eugene Andrews (1-4, 10-13), James B. North (5-9)
Why Teach This Lesson? ....Charles R. Boatman (1-4, 10-13), Harvey Bream (5-9)

Spring Quarter 2006
Living in and as God's Creation

Writers

Lesson Development.....................David Marvin (1-4), J. Michael Shannon (5-9), Mark Krause (10-13)
Verbal Illustrations ....Charles R. Boatman
Why Teach This Lesson? ....Ronald G. Davis
Discovery Learning....Richard A. Koffarnus (1-4, 10-13), Ronald G. Davis (5-9)
What Do You Think? ....Kenneth Beck (1-4), Tom Lawson (5-9), Mark Moore (10-13)

Summer Quarter 2006
Called to Be a Christian Community

Writers

Lesson Development ....Kenny Boles (1-4), Tom Thatcher (5-13)
Verbal Illustrations ......A. Eugene Andrews (1-9), Terry Bowland (10-13)
Why Teach This Lesson?..................Mark Krause
Discovery Learning ....Alan Weber (1-9), Ronald G. Davis (10-13)
What Do You Think?..................Jeffrey Snell (1-9), Kenneth Goble (10-13)

Index of Printed Texts, 2005–2006

The printed texts for 2005-2006 are arranged here in the order in which they appear in the Bible. Opposite each reference is the page number on which the lesson that treats the passage begins in this volume.

Cumulative Index of Printed Texts

A cumulative index for the Scripture passages used in *The NIV Standard Lesson Commentary®* for September 2004–August 2006 is presented here for your convenience.

How to Say It

The following pages list some of the names and other hard-to-pronounce words used in the lessons of this edition of *The NIV Standard Lesson Commentary*® along with a phonetic pronunciation guide for each. In each lesson is an abridged version of this list that includes only the words used in that lesson.

Abednego. Uh-BED-nee-go.
Achaia. Uh-KAY-uh.
Aegean. A-JEE-un.
Aesop. EE-sup.
Agur. AY-gur.
Ahaz. AY-haz.
Alexandrians. Al-ex-AN-dree-unz.
Al-Qaeda. Al KAI-duh.
Amphipolis. Am-FIP-o-liss.
Ananias. An-uh-NYE-us.
Annas. AN-nus.
Antioch. AN-tee-ock.
Apollo. Uh-PAH-low.
Apollonia. Ap-uh-LOW-nee-uh.
Apollos. Uh-PAHL-us.
Aquila. ACK-wih-luh.
Areopagus. Air-ee-OP-uh-gus.
Aristobulus. Uh-RIS-toe-BU-lus .
Assyria. Uh-SEAR-ee-uh.
Azotus. Uh-ZO-tus.

Baal Peor. Bay-al-PE-or.
Babylon. BAB-uh-lun.
Babylonians. Bab-ih-LOW-nee-unz.
Barachel. BAR-uh-kel.
Bathsheba. Bath-SHE-buh.
Berea. Buh-REE-uh.
Bildad. BILL-dad.
Bithynia. Bih-THIN-ee-uh.

blasphemous. BLAS-fuh-mus.
Buzite. BEW-zyet.

Caesarea Maritima. Sess-uh-REE-uh Mar-uh-TEE-muh.
Caiaphas. KAY-uh-fus or KYE-uh-fus.
Caligula. Kuh-LIG-you-luh.
Candace. CAN-duh-see.
Capernaum. Kuh-PER-nay-um.
Carthage. CAR-thij.
Cassini-Huygens. Kuh-SEE-nee HOI-genz.
caveat emptor (Latin). KA-vee-at EMP-ter.
Cenchreae. SEN-kree-uh.
Cephas. SEE-fus.
Chloe. KLO-ee.
Cilicia. Sih-LISH-i-uh.
Claudius Caesar. CLAW-dee-us SEE-zur.
Cleopas. CLEE-uh-pass.
Cornelius. Cor-NEEL-yus.
Cretan. CREE-tun.
Crispus. KRIS-pus.
Cyrenians. SIGH-REE-nee-unz.

Damascus. Duh-MASS-kus.
Delphi. DEL-fi.

Dietrich Bonhoeffer. DEE-trick BON-huh-fur.
Dionysius. Die-oh-NISH-ih-us.
dynamis (Greek). DOO-nuh-mis.

Edomites. EE-dum-ites.
Elihu. Ih-LYE-hew.
Eliphaz. EL-ih-faz.
Elisha. E-LYE-shuh.
Elymas. EL-ih-mass.
Emmaus. Em-MAY-us.
Ephesus. EF-uh-sus.
Epimenides. Ep-ih-MEN-ih-deez.
Ethiopian. E-thee-O-pee-un.
Eunice. U-NYE-see or U-nis.
eunuch. YOU-nick.
euthanasia. you-thuh-NAY-zhuh.

Gaius. GAY-us.
Galatia. Guh-LAY-shuh.
Galileans. Gal-uh-LEE-unz.
Gallio. GAL-ee-o.
Gamaliel. Guh-MAY-lih-ul or Guh-MAY-lee-al.
Gerizim. GAIR-ih-zeem or Guh-RYE-zim.
Gnostics. NAHSS-ticks.
Goliath. Go-LYE-uth.

Hannah. HAN-uh.
Herod Agrippa. HAIR-ud Uh-GRIP-puh.
Herod Antipas. HAIR-ud AN-tih-pus.
Herod Archelaus. HAIR-ud Are-kuh-LAY-us.
Herodians. Heh-ROE-dee-unz.
Hymeneus. Hi-meh-NEE-us.

Iconium. Eye-KO-nee-um.
Immanuel. Ih-MAN-you-el.
Isthmian. IS-me-unh.

Jochebed. JOCK-eh-bed.
Josephus. Jo-SEE-fus.
Joses. JO-sez.
Judaism. JOO-duh-izz-um or JOO-day-izz-um.
Judas Iscariot. JOO-dus Iss-CARE-ee-ut.
Judea. Joo-DEE-uh.

koinonia (Greek). koy-no-NEE-uh.
Korah. KO-rah.

Lechaeum. Lek-uh-EE-um.
Lemuel. LEM-you-el.
Libertines. LIB-er-teens.
Lucius Annaeus Seneca. LOO-shuss Uh-NEE-us SEN-uh-kuh.
Lydia. LID-ee-uh.
Lystra. LISS-truh.

Macedonia. Mass-eh-DOE-nee-uh.

Machiavelli. **MA-key-uh-VEH-lee**.
Magdalene. MAG-duh-leen or Mag-duh-LEE-nee.
Magnificat. Mag-NIF-ih-cot.
Mao Tse-tung. Mau dzuh-DUNG.
Meshach. ME-shack.
Messiah. Meh-SIGH-uh.
Miletus. My-LEE-tus.
Moabite. MO-ub-ite.
Mosaic. Mo-ZAY-ik.
Mysia. MISH-ee-uh.

Nabataen. NAB-uh-**TEE**-un.
Napoleon Bonaparte. Nuh-POL-yuhn BO-nuh-**PART**.
Nazareth. NAZ-uh-reth.
Nazarite. NAZ-uh-rite.
Neapolis. Nee-AP-o-lis.
Nebuchadnezzar. NEB-yuh-kud-**NEZ**-er.
Nicodemus. NICK-uh-**DEE**-mus.
Niebuhr. NEE-burr.

Onesimus. O-NESS-ih-muss.

Pamphylia. Pam-FILL-ee-uh.
Pentecost. PENT-ih-kost.
Pharaoh Akhenaton. FAIR-o (or FAY-roe) Ock-NAW-tun.
Pharisees. FAIR-ih-seez.
Philetus. Fuh-LEE-tus.
Philippi. Fih-LIP-pie or FIL-ih-pie.
Phrygia. FRIJ-e-uh.
Pilate. PIE-lut.
Pisidia. Pih-SID-ee-uh.
Pontus. PON-tuss.
Potiphar. POT-ih-far.
proselytes. PRAHSS-uh-lights.

Quaternions. kwa-TER-nee-unz.

Sabeans. Suh-BE-unz.
Sadducees. SAD-you-seez.
Salome. Suh-LO-me.
Samaritan. Suh-MARE-uh-tun.
Samothracia. Sam-o-THRAY-shuh.
Sanhedrin. SAN-huh-drun or San-HEED-run.
Sebaste. Seh-BAS-tee.
Septuagint. Sep-TOO-ih-jent.
Shadrach. SHAY-drack or SHAD-rack.
shalom (Hebrew). shah-LOME.
Sheba. SHE-buh.
Shechem. SHEE-kem or SHEK-em.
shekel. SHEH-kul.
Simeon. SIM-ee-un.
Søren Kierkegaard. SO-ren KIR-kuh-gard.
Stephanas. STEF-uh-nass.
Suetonius. Soo-TOE-nee-us.
Sychar. SIGH-kar.

Tarsus. TAR-sus.
Tertullian. Tur-TULL-yun.
Thyatira. THY-uh-**TIE**-ruh.
Troas. TRO-az.
Trophimus. TROFF-ih-muss.
Tyrannus. Ty-RAN-nus.

Zacchaeus. Zack-KEY-us.
Zarephath. ZAIR-uh-fath.
Zebedee. ZEB-eh-dee.
Zeus. Zoose.
Zophar. ZO-far

Fall Quarter 2005

You Will Be My Witnesses

(Acts)

Special Features

Lessons

See 2008/09 Acts 2:1-17

Unit 1: In Jerusalem

Unit 2: In All Judea and Samaria

See 2008/09 Act 6:1-15

See 2008/09 Act 9:1-19
Acts 13:1-12

Unit 3: To the Ends of the Earth

About These Lessons

"Ripples in a pond" is a good analogy for this quarter's lessons. On the Day of Pentecost, the church was born and began to spread outward from Jerusalem. Those ripples travel across both geography and time to reach us now. We not only experience those ripples personally, we help send them on!

Sep 4
Sep 11
Sep 18
Sep 25
Oct 2
Oct 9
Oct 16
Oct 23
Oct 30
Nov 6
Nov 13
Nov 20
Nov 27

Times Such as These

Have you noticed that no one seems to have figured out what to call this particular decade? The 1990s were known as "the nineties," the 1980s were "the eighties," and so forth. But to call our current decade "the zeroes" just doesn't sound quite right! "The nulls" sounds even worse.

Yet every decade, whatever we eventually call it, should be known as a time of growth for God's people—both spiritually for the individual and numerically for the church. This is the will of God. It has been his will for centuries. It shall continue to be his will until Jesus returns. It is stressed in this year's lessons.

Our lessons for the fall quarter sketch the rapid growth of the first-century church. By the power of the Holy Spirit, the church expanded to countless thousands in about 30 years. Jesus wants his church to grow just as rapidly today.

The winter lessons begin by showing us the foundation for the later growth of the church: the coming of Christ. Following our Christmas lessons, we move to the Pastoral Epistles to focus on personal spiritual growth.

The spring lessons take us to the Wisdom Literature of the Old Testament. Our spiritual growth depends on understanding how God expects us to think and act.

Summer will find us back in the New Testament. The letters 1 and 2 Corinthians are painful to read, for they were written to a church in big trouble. But spiritual and numerical growth depends on being able to address serious problems in a Christ-honoring way. These two letters have much to teach us still.

Times such as these—meaning the years we're living in right now and the problems they carry with them—demand such lessons, don't they?

International Sunday School Lesson Cycle
September, 2004—August, 2007

YEAR	FALL QUARTER (Sept., Oct., Nov.)	WINTER QUARTER (Dec., Jan., Feb.)	SPRING QUARTER (Mar., Apr., May)	SUMMER QUARTER (June, July, Aug.)
2004-2005	The God of Continuing Creation (Bible Survey)	Called to Be God's People (Bible Survey)	God's Project: Effective Christians (Romans, Galatians)	Jesus' Life, Teachings, and Ministry (Matthew, Mark, Luke)
2005-2006	"You Will Be My Witnesses" (Acts)	God's Commitment— Our Response (Isaiah; 1 and 2 Timothy)	Living in and as God's Creation (Psalms, Job, Ecclesiastes, Proverbs)	Called to Be a Christian Community (1 and 2 Corinthians)
2006-2007	God's Living Covenant (Old Testament Survey)	Jesus Christ: A Portrait of God (John, Philippians, Colossians, Hebrews, 1 John)	Our Community Now and in God's Future (1 John, Revelation)	Committed to Doing Right (Various Prophets, 2 Kings, 2 Chronicles)

"Creation"	"Call"	"Covenant"	"Christ"	"Community"	"Commitment"

Christ for All!

by Ronald L. Nickelson

What "type" of Christianity do you believe in? There seem to be three choices that are proposed these days. Many people believe in an *exclusive* Christianity. Under this idea, salvation is exclusively for those who make a confession of faith in Jesus Christ as they follow the biblical plan of salvation.

Others, however, think that that idea is much too rigid. They propose instead that we should believe in an *inclusive* Christianity. The idea here is that people can be saved by Christ without placing faith in him or without ever even hearing of him. Such people can still be saved by Christ and only by Christ (so the theory goes) as long as they respond positively to whatever light of God's revelation that they are aware of.

Still others hold what is called a *pluralistic* view. Under this idea, Christianity may be "right for me," but other religions are equally "right for others." We can be saved by Christ, but (so the theory goes) others can be be saved by Muhammad or Buddha just as well.

This quarter's lessons should leave no doubt: the Christianity that the Holy Spirit established on the Day of Pentecost is an *exclusive* Christianity. Those who spread the gospel of Jesus Christ in the first century "in Jerusalem, and in all Judea and Samaria, and to the ends of the earth" (Acts 1:8) lived and died for this belief. Peter, John, Stephen, Paul, Philip, Priscilla, and Aquila are New Testament names familiar to many of us. As we see them labor for the gospel this quarter, we definitely will not get the idea that they think that faith in Jesus is one option among many!

UNIT 1. IN JERUSALEM

Lesson 1: The Spirit Comes. "Well begun is half done," so the old saying goes. Talk about a great beginning! An international crowd is on hand in Jerusalem on the Day of Pentecost when the Holy Spirit comes to mark the beginning of the church. A vital part of the message that day is that Jesus is "both Lord and Christ." This lesson's Key Verse of Acts 2:38 will come to fruition time and again throughout the book of Acts.

Lesson 2: The Believers Share. Many recognize that *true community* is an important foundation for their lives. The most important community in the world is the church. The earliest fellowship of believers was a marvel to behold, as that group "had everything in common." What an enduring example for us! Having everything in common begins with having a common Savior: Jesus Christ.

Lesson 3: Peter and John Heal a Lame Man. The healing of the man in Acts 3 is the first healing miracle recorded in that great book of the church's history. This valuable lesson enriches us when we allow it to point us to something far more valuable than physical healing—namely, the spiritual wholeness that comes only through God's Son.

Lesson 4: The Church Is Bold. Courage and conviction are human traits that seem to go in and out of style with the passing of time. Sometimes those traits are sadly misdirected, as in the cases of violent religious extremism today. Peter and John show us the right kind of boldness. It is a boldness that pushes the gospel forward in a way that honors God. The Holy Spirit stands ready to give boldness to us as well.

SEPTEMBER

UNIT 2. IN ALL JUDEA AND SAMARIA

Lesson 5: Stephen Is Faithful to the End. The pages of history are stained with the blood of Christian martyrs. After the church was established on Pentecost, the first recorded martyr was Stephen. Honoring God can exact a very high price! Yet Stephen and others died for their conviction of truth: Jesus is the Christ, the Son of the living God.

Lesson 6: Philip Preaches in Samaria. The stoning of Stephen marked the outbreak of persecution against the church. But God turned that evil into victory as "those who had been scattered preached the word wherever they went" (Acts 8:4). In so doing, evangelists such as Philip crossed racial and cultural barriers with the gospel.

Lesson 7: Philip Teaches an Ethiopian. Although many longtime Christians "ought to be teachers" by now, they have yet to progress beyond the "milk" to the "solid food" of God's Word (Hebrews 5:12). Philip was not one of those. When someone needed an explanation of Scripture, he was ready. With the eternal destinies of others at stake, how can we not be ready as well?

Lesson 8: God Welcomes Gentiles. Cornelius, a Gentile, was a man who knew something about God. Cornelius apparently realized the importance of prayer and helping the poor. He understood this without ever having heard the gospel. But that knowledge and practice wasn't enough. Cornelius still needed Christ.

Lesson 9: Peter Escapes Prison. Peter was thrown in prison, probably awaiting execution, for preaching the gospel. His fellow Christians were somewhere outside the prison gates. He was surrounded by pagan soldiers guarding him. And yet Peter was not abandoned. God was always with him. God is always with us, too. We are never alone.

UNIT 3. TO THE ENDS OF THE EARTH

Lesson 10: Paul Meets the Lord. Jesus Christ has the power to transform lives. Nowhere is this more evident than in the life of Saul of Tarsus (renamed Paul). It is unlikely that any of us will have a "Damascus Road experience" as he had. That will be God's choice, not ours. Jesus certainly has the power to change lives in other ways. For instance, he may very well change our lives by opening our hearts to the printed account of Paul's shocking experience.

Lesson 11: Lydia Demonstrates Faithfulness. The gospel expands fastest when believers are committed to serving in any way they can. This can mean inconvenience. Before we complain too much about our inconveniences, however, remember one thing: it was quite inconvenient for Jesus to come to earth and die on a cross! May God give each of us the heart of Lydia as we serve in the manner we are gifted.

Lesson 12: Priscilla and Aquila Serve Together. Sometimes Christians work alone to spread the gospel. One good example of this occurred when Philip taught the man from Ethiopia. More often it is teamwork that wins the day. A shining example of how much a good team can accomplish is the combination of Priscilla and Aquila as they serve alongside Paul. May this couple always be a model to us.

Lesson 13: Paul Says Good-Bye. The Christian life has its "downs" as well as its "ups." Sad good-byes are part of our earthly sojourn. Yet we can draw strength from fellow believers in such times. Sad good-byes also challenge us to lift our thoughts to the time when all Christians will be together for eternity, never to be parted from one another again.

CHRIST FOR ALL, AND CHRIST EXCLUSIVELY

This quarter's lessons offer us one example after another of the nature of the gospel message and how it spread. Behind the convictions of the first-century believers lie some powerful truths. Consider the following:

> But small is the gate and narrow the road that leads to life, and only a few find it (Matthew 7:14).

> I am the way and the truth and the life. No one comes to the Father except through me (John 14:6).

> Salvation is found in no one else, for there is no other name under heaven given to men by which we must be saved (Acts 4:12).

The first two of these three passages are from the lips of Jesus during his earthly ministry. The third was spoken by Peter as he was filled with the Holy Spirit in the presence of the men who had sentenced Jesus to death (part of the context of lesson 4). When we place these three texts alongside the options of *exclusive* Christianity, *inclusive* Christianity, and *pluralistic* Christianity that we mentioned at the outset, which of the three options appears to be correct?

Only *exclusive Christianity* can be correct! Jesus Christ came to redeem all humanity from sin, but we must place our faith specifically in him and in him alone. Matthew 7:14; John 14:6; Acts 4:12 and a host of other texts require this. Our 13 lessons for the quarter demonstrate time and again the beliefs and actions of the earliest Christians in this regard. They did not waver, and neither should we.

Lesson Planning Page

List the aims here, either directly from the lesson or revised to suit your individual needs.

LESSON AIMS

Begin with an opening activity like the illustration from the beginning of the lesson, "Into the Lesson" from the Discovery Learning page, a discussion question, or some other appropriate opener.

GETTING STARTED

List in order the activities you will use. These include discussion questions, activities from the discovery learning page and the reproducible page—as well as key points from the commentary section.

LESSON DEVELOPMENT

I.

II.

III.

How will you bring the lesson to a climax, stressing the key point and desired action steps?

CONCLUSION & APPLICATION

Dismiss the class with an activity that reinforces the Bible lesson.

CLOSING ACTIVITY

The Gospel Spreads
to Jerusalem, Judea, and Samaria

SYRIA

• Tarsus

• Damascus

MEDITERRANEAN SEA

GALILEE

• Caesarea

• Samaria

JUDEA

• Jerusalem

• Gaza

The Gospel Spreads

to the Rest of the World

MACEDONIA

ACHAIA

Corinth

Cenchrea

Philippi • Neapolis

SAMOTHRACE

Troas

ASIA

Ephesus

PHRYGIA

GALATIA

Lystra

Derbe

MEDITERRANEAN SEA

JUDEA

Jerusalem

SYRIA

THE SPIRIT COMES

WHY TEACH THIS LESSON?

The subject of the third person of the Trinity, as the Holy Spirit is sometimes called, is a source of endless fascination. While it's tempting to focus on the spectacular phenomenon that occurred as God's Holy Spirit was poured out on the Day of Pentecost, the learner must not miss the bigger picture of what this means to us. The new covenant we have with God through Christ's sacrifice allows us to have the continual presence of God's Holy Spirit. This presence is a vital link in our relationship with God the Father and the Son. God's empowering Spirit is now available to all Christians.

Church tradition can be interesting to study with regard to the Holy Spirit, but Bible study is the most important thing. Today's lesson moves us behind 20 centuries of human study about the Spirit to the time when the Spirit manifested himself to inaugurate the church. We will see the presentation of the first gospel message. We will see what a proper response to accepting that message looks like. Finally, we will see the Spirit-led believers of the first-century church establish a unique and influential fellowship. This is still our pattern for today.

INTRODUCTION

Some churches possess the following cornerstone: Founded in Jerusalem A.D. 30. Wherever a church is located and regardless of when its building was constructed, it is good that its people remember the very first church. Today's lesson describes that wonderful day when the church was born. It was a day of miracles that changed history.

A. BIRTHDAY CELEBRATIONS

Pharaoh celebrated his birthday with a great feast (Genesis 40:20). Herod celebrated his same way, but on that dark day he gave his own gift—the head of John the Baptist (Mark 6:21-29). People from all walks of life love to celebrate birthdays. Europeans and Americans celebrate birthdays with family dinners and parties where presents are given. Christians celebrate Jesus' birth by giving to others. Christians remember Pentecost as the birthday of the church.

B. LESSON BACKGROUND

The Old Testament predicted deliverance in terms of people flocking together as sheep in a pen (Micah 2:12, 13). The prophet Joel, though, gave the greatest of all prophecies of Christ's church. Joel saw Judah devastated by a terrifying locust plague (Joel 2:1-11). Yet God promised to remove the plague and pour out his blessings if the people repented (Joel 2:12-27). But as he looked into the distant future, Joel said that God planned to do more than restore crops. He also promised to pour out his Spirit (Joel 2:28, 29).

Centuries later, just before he returned to Heaven, Jesus told his disciples that he would send them the promised Holy Spirit. They were to remain in Jerusalem

DEVOTIONAL READING:
PSALM 16

BACKGROUND SCRIPTURE:
ACTS 2

PRINTED TEXT:
ACTS 2:1-8, 36-42

LESSON AIMS

After participating in this lesson, each student will be able to:

1. Recount the events of the Day of Pentecost that accompanied the birth of the church.

2. Explain how the power of the Holy Spirit helped bring the church into being.

3. Identify one way of helping his or her church remember its first-century origins.

KEY VERSE

Peter replied, "Repent and be baptized, every one of you, in the name of Jesus Christ for the forgiveness of your sins. And you will receive the gift of the Holy Spirit."   —Acts 2:38

until they were clothed with power from on high (Luke 24:49). Shortly thereafter, God fulfilled his promise and poured out his Spirit. Peter explained, "This is what was spoken by the prophet Joel" (Acts 2:16).

I. EARTH-SHAKING EVENT (ACTS 2:1-8)

Earthquakes are frightening beyond words. They can kill tens of thousands and wipe entire cities off the map. For example, one of the deadliest earthquakes of the twentieth century obliterated the sleeping city of Tangshan, China, in 1976, killing more than 240,000 people. But some events, especially the one in our lesson today, shake the earth in a good way.

A. PENTECOST GATHERING (v. 1)

1. *When the day of Pentecost came, they were all together in one place.*

God wants his people to gather in public worship. *The day of Pentecost* was one of the special days in Old Testament times that reminded Israel how God had blessed them (see Exodus 23:14-17). Feast days helped sweep away differences as the tribes gathered to praise God and offer sacrifice for sin.

Pentecost, also called The Feast of Weeks (Exodus 34:22; Deuteronomy 16:9-11), was held seven weeks and a day (fifty days) after the Passover Sabbath (Leviticus 23:15, 16). It marked the completion of the barley harvest. Two loaves were waved symbolically before the Lord, while animal sacrifices were presented as sin and peace offerings (Leviticus 23:17-20). It was a single day of joy for the blessings of the harvest.

What a wonderfully symbolic day for the birth of the church! Jesus compared God's Word with seed (Matthew 13:1-23). As a farmer scatters seed and later harvests a crop, so also the seed of God's Word grows in human hearts and produces an abundant harvest of souls. Jesus indicated that what we may call "fields of people" are just waiting to be harvested (John 4:35). As the Day of Pentecost dawns in A.D. 30, thousands of souls are about to be gathered in from those fields. As events unfold, we will see this particular Pentecost to be a day of great spiritual harvest.

When the text says *they were all together in one place,* we may wonder exactly who *they* are. Some say that it is the 120 believers mentioned in Acts 1:15. It is more likely, though, that this refers only to the apostles, since that group was just mentioned in Acts 1:26. Jesus promised that this baptism of the Spirit was to be upon them (Acts 1:5).

WHAT DO YOU THINK?

God is a God of purpose, and he definitely had a purpose for selecting Pentecost as the day on which the church began. What principles can the church learn from this today?

B. HOLY SPIRIT POWER (vv. 2-4a)

2-4a. *Suddenly a sound like the blowing of a violent wind came from heaven and filled the whole house where they were sitting. They saw what seemed to be tongues of fire that separated and came to rest on each of them. All of them were filled with the Holy Spirit.*

The Old Testament pictured God's Spirit as a mighty force that caused people to walk in God's laws (Ezekiel 36:27), brought new life (Ezekiel 37:14), empowered leaders (Judges 3:10), and inspired prophets (Micah 3:8). Now God's Spirit is about to be poured out in a new way.

Two symbols describe this outpouring of the Spirit: *wind* and *fire.* The original word for spirit could mean "breath" or "wind," depending on context. God's presence is like a great wind (2 Samuel 22:16). Scripture does not say that those present feel a physical wind. Rather, it says they hear *a sound like the blowing of a violent wind* that *came from heaven and filled the whole house.*

Fire is also used as a symbol of God's presence (see Exodus 19:18). As *the Holy Spirit* fills the apostles, it appears as if *tongues of fire* rest over them. The fire is divided into separate flames.

The word *filled* is used when the Spirit empowers God's people for service (Acts 9:17) and inspires people with important messages (Acts 4:8). God is about to give an important message. See also Luke 24:49.

C. HOLY SPIRIT MIRACLE (vv. 4b-8)

4b-8. . . . and began to speak in other tongues as the Spirit enabled them. Now there were staying in Jerusalem God-fearing Jews from every nation under heaven. When they heard this sound, a crowd came together in bewilderment, because each one heard them speaking in his own language. Utterly amazed, they asked: "Are not all these men who are speaking Galileans? Then how is it that each of us hears them in his own native language?"

A great number of people are in Jerusalem at Pentecost. Thousands come from all over the world. Acts 2:9-12 lists 15 countries or other localities. These are described as *every nation under heaven.* This sweeping language is often used to describe the known world of the day or the territory of earth's leading empire (in this case the Roman Empire).

The people hear the message in their native languages. They are *amazed* because the apostles are simple Galileans and are not from a metropolitan area where they might have greater opportunity to learn other languages. The crowd perhaps recognizes the speakers as *Galileans* by their unique accent or dialect (compare Matthew 26:73).

Most of the crowd this day could understand the apostles if they had spoken in Greek. But the Spirit empowers the apostles to speak in the peoples' *native* languages for a reason: God wants to show everyone that the apostles speak for God and that their message is true. This miracle also makes it clear that their message is for all nations. The Holy Spirit will continue to empower the early church with the ability to speak in tongues and do other amazing things (1 Corinthians 12:1-11).

II. LIFE-CHANGING MESSAGE (ACTS 2:36-42)

Peter began his sermon by noting that the prophet Joel had predicted this great event (Acts 2:14-22). He reminded the crowd that although God worked great miracles through Jesus, they handed Jesus over to wicked men who crucified him. God reversed their decision by raising Jesus from the dead just as the Scriptures had predicted (Acts 2:23-35). The apostles are witnesses. They had seen Jesus alive and had watched him ascend to Heaven to sit at God's right hand. Peter now proclaims Jesus' death and resurrection.

A. MESSAGE CENTERS ON JESUS (v. 36)

36. "Therefore let all Israel be assured of this: God has made this Jesus, whom you crucified, both Lord and Christ."

This is the end of Peter's great sermon. Seven weeks earlier, Peter denied even knowing Jesus (Mark 14:66-72). Jesus forgave him and put him back to work (John 21:15-19). Peter is now a different man, filled with courage and power.

This message is often called the first complete gospel sermon because it is the first public announcement of the significance of Jesus' death, burial, resurrection, and ascension. By these things God made Jesus *both Lord and Christ.* The Scriptures had predicted that the Messiah would do all these things (Psalms 2, 16, 22;

Isaiah 53). The word *Lord* indicates the one having authority and sovereign power. The word *Christ* means "anointed one, the one chosen by God."

B. Message Cuts to Hearts (v. 37)

37. When the people heard this, they were cut to the heart and said to Peter and the other apostles, "Brothers, what shall we do?"

This gospel message penetrates the soul like a sword (Hebrews 4:12). This sword of the Spirit (Ephesians 6:17) is designed to stab the old man of sin and bring about godly sorrow. In this case the people are *cut* to the very core of their being. People in the crowd are sorry that they had rejected Jesus. Even though they had not driven the nails into his hands and feet, they had either agreed with those who did (Luke 23:21) or else they had approved of the crucifixion by their silence. They are sorry, but they know that this is not enough. So they ask the apostles what they should *do*.

A Place Without Hope

Jason Roemer gives us this interesting insight into his childhood. He says, "I can remember my grandmother warning me when I was up to no good. . . . 'You don't want to end up on Alcatraz, do you?'"

From 1934 to 1963, Alcatraz was the end of the line for the worst of America's convicted felons. If the U.S. federal prison system could keep them nowhere else, they went to Alcatraz—"the Rock." George "Machine Gun" Kelly and Al Capone were among its infamous residents. Located in San Francisco Bay, Alcatraz offered tantalizing views of "the outside world" just over a mile away. Alcatraz was maximum security, and the 50-degree water added to the idea that escape attempts were futile. This imprisonment was not only physical but psychological as well!

Many in Peter's audience on Pentecost may have felt their actions had committed them to a "spiritual Alcatraz." The message had convicted them of murdering God's Son—the promised Messiah! With all hope seemingly gone, how could they ever break out of this spiritual prison? This terrible dilemma was expressed in their hopelessly pained question, "What shall *we* do?"

All of us have put ourselves in a similar position—our sins have locked us into a prison of alienation from God. There is no escape from this prison by our own effort. But the message of the gospel is that there is hope! Jesus said, "I am alive for ever and ever! And I hold the keys of death and Hades" (Revelation 1:18).   —C. R. B.

C. Message Offers Forgiveness (vv. 38, 39)

38, 39. Peter replied, "Repent and be baptized, every one of you, in the name of Jesus Christ for the forgiveness of your sins. And you will receive the gift of the Holy Spirit. The promise is for you and your children and for all who are far off— for all whom the Lord our God will call."

The word *repent* means "a change of mind that leads to a change of life." Instead of denying, excusing, or justifying their sins, the people must turn from them. Peter also appeals for submission to baptism. Several important New Testament texts discuss the meaning of baptism. Romans 6:4 says, "We were therefore buried with him through baptism into death." (See also Colossians 2:12; Galatians 3:27; and 1 Peter 3:21, among others.) In the text at hand, baptism is closely connected with repentance.

The Bible also makes it clear that the Holy Spirit is at work when people are converted to Christ (see Titus 3:5, 6). God's Spirit renews us as we are washed and raised to newness of life. Ananias told Saul, "Now what are you waiting for? Get up, be baptized and wash your sins away, calling on his name" (Acts 22:16).

WHAT DO YOU THINK?

Simon Peter's presentation of the gospel was a long way from where he had been just five weeks earlier when he denied Jesus. What a tremendous change! In what ways do you see God continuing to make significant changes in people's lives today? In what ways can you and your church become a source of transformation for those in your sphere of influence?

WHAT DO YOU THINK?

One school of thought says that it is not necessary for one to repent or change one's way because this involves human effort, and we are not saved by human effort. What would you say to someone who claimed to be a Christian but had obviously not repented of sin?

Peter indicates that when people turn to Jesus Christ and away from sin, God promises *forgiveness* of sins and *the gift of the Holy Spirit.* The most important thing that people can do once they reach the age where they know that they have sinned against God is to have those sins forgiven.

The wonderful thing is that God is not only willing to forgive sins, he is also willing to help us deal with sin in our lives. So the Holy Spirit, among other things, gives life from the dead and empowers us to overcome sin each day. This is the gift of the Holy Spirit.

The Holy Spirit also gives spiritual gifts (1 Corinthians 12:11). The apostle Paul indicates that not everyone has the gift of speaking in tongues or other miraculous gifts (1 Corinthians 12:29-31). But all Christians have the gift of the Holy Spirit promised by Peter. The wonderful gift of the Holy Spirit empowers God's people to live lives that please him. With the gift of the Spirit, Christians have the power to put off the works of the flesh and to bear the fruit of the Spirit (Galatians 5:22-25).

D. MESSAGE URGES RESISTANCE OF EVIL (v. 40)

40. With many other words he warned them; and he pleaded with them, "Save yourselves from this corrupt generation."

The word translated *corrupt* means "perverse and rebellious." The Israelites who rebelled against God were called "a warped and crooked generation" (Deuteronomy 32:5). Christians must shine like stars in a world darkened by sin and keep themselves "from being polluted by the world" (James 1:27).

E. MESSAGE PRODUCES THE CHURCH (vv. 41, 42)

41, 42. Those who accepted his message were baptized, and about three thousand were added to their number that day. They devoted themselves to the apostles' teaching and to the fellowship, to the breaking of bread and to prayer.

Sorrow over sin now turns to gladness as people find God's grace. What a moment! *Three thousand* people are *baptized!* Their decision changes their lives—and their eternity. They now steadfastly do things that they had not done before.

For one thing, they heed the *apostles' teaching* (or doctrine). Jesus had promised that the Holy Spirit would guide the apostles "into all truth" (John 16:13). The apostles now pass some of those truths along as they teach about Jesus' dying for sins and rising from the dead (compare 1 Corinthians 15:3-8). Only Jesus brings forgiveness of sins and eternal life. They teach people to seek salvation through him, who will judge the world. That life-changing message, preserved in the pages of the New Testament, is the very center of the Christian faith. Pure doctrine is important!

Those who are *added to* them also remain steadfast in *fellowship.* Christians share in the privilege of belonging to the greatest family on earth and working together to spread the good news. When Christians pool their money, time, and energy to this great task, we can say they are "fellowshiping" in the gospel (Romans 15:26; 2 Corinthians 8:4; 1 John 1:7). Christians also have a fellowship of suffering with Christ (Philippians 3:10).

In this passage, *the breaking of bread* could refer either to an ordinary meal or to the Lord's Supper (compare 1 Corinthians 10:16; 11:24). Just which idea the author has in mind here is a matter of some debate. At the very least, we should think that these meals are to involve some kind of close Christian fellowship since fellowship has just been discussed. (See also Acts 2:46 in next week's lesson.)

HOW TO SAY IT

Corinthians. Ko-RIN-thee-unz.
Deuteronomy. Due-ter-AHN-uh-me.
Ephesians. Ee-FEE-zhunz.
Ezekiel. Ee-ZEEK-ee-ul or Ee-ZEEK-yul.
Galileans. Gal-uh-LEE-unz.
Jerusalem. Juh-ROO-suh-lem.
Leviticus. Leh-VIT-ih-kus.
Micah. MY-kuh.
Pentecost. PENT-ih-kost.
Pharaoh. FAIR-o or FAY-roe.

DAILY BIBLE READINGS

Monday, Aug. 29—God's Spirit Will Be Poured Out (Joel 2:23-29)

Tuesday, Aug. 30—God Is Always with Us (Psalm 16:5-11)

Wednesday, Aug. 31—The Holy Spirit Comes (Acts 2:1-13)

Thursday, Sept. 1—Peter Speaks to the Crowd (Acts 2:14-21)

Friday, Sept. 2—Peter Speaks About the Crucified Jesus (Acts 2:22-28)

Saturday, Sept. 3—Peter Speaks About the Risen Christ (Acts 2:29-36)

Sunday, Sept. 4—Three Thousand Are Baptized (Acts 2:1-8, 37-42)

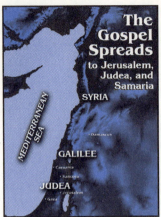

The Gospel Spreads
to Jerusalem, Judea, and Samaria

SYRIA

MEDITERRANEAN SEA

GALILEE

JUDEA

Visual for Lesson 1. *Keep this map posted throughout Lessons 1 through 9 to set a framework for your students.*

The new converts also remain steadfast in *prayer.* Whether it be individual prayers or prayers of Christians who join their hearts together when making requests to God, these Christians realize just how important prayer is to their new relationship with God. Great churches today are the ones, whether large or small, that continue to remain steadfast in these same areas.

A PORTABLE CHURCH

Many of us have become numb to news of religious structures around the world being blown up by radicals. So it was a welcome bit of news a couple of years ago when British designer Michael Gill announced a way to "blow up" churches in a constructive way: he has developed a vinyl minicathedral that can be inflated in just three hours!

Gill's Web site www.inflatablechurch.com shows the details. The inflatable "building" stands 47 feet high at the peak of the steeple, and there are fake stained-glass windows in its gothic arches. The designer says one of the advantages of the inflatable church building is that it can be taken wherever there are people who want a church service. He hopes his invention will restore interest in the church in England—a nation where church attendance has been falling off for many years.

We don't know whether Peter's sermon took more or less than three hours on the Day of Pentecost, but the power of the Spirit built a church in short order on that day. Three thousand people responded to a message that offered hope to those who so recently had given assent to the execution of the Messiah. The church that resulted was a "portable church." The new Christians had come to Jerusalem from all over the Roman world, and they would soon be taking their faith—and the church—with them wherever they went. Shouldn't we be doing the same?   —C. R. B.

CONCLUSION

What a beginning the church had! And the Holy Spirit continues to work in mighty ways yet today. The following list shows us how important it is never to forget or minimize our relationship with the Holy Spirit.

1. The Spirit inspired God's Word, so we must obey it without hesitation (2 Peter 1:21).
2. Our bodies are the temple of the Holy Spirit, so we must not gratify the desires of the sinful nature (1 Corinthians 6:19; Galatians 5:16).
3. The Spirit gives us the most personal of relationships with God, so we must trust God with a childlike faith (Galatians 4:6).
4. The Spirit seals us for "the day of redemption," so we must not grieve the Spirit (Ephesians 4:30).
5. The Spirit makes people alive from the dead, so we must walk in newness of life and put to death the waywardness of the body (Romans 8:13; Titus 3:5).
6. The Spirit helps us to bear the fruit of the Spirit, so we need to walk with the Spirit (Galatians 5:22-25).
7. The Spirit helps us with our prayers, so we must pray in faith without doubting (Romans 8:26; James 1:6).
8. The Spirit raised Jesus from the dead and will resurrect us, so we must live in hope (Romans 8:11).
9. The Holy Spirit inspired Peter with the gospel message. That message is still just as powerful as ever and still changes lives. The church, born by the Spirit's power, still moves throughout the world for good. Have you let God's Spirit transform your life?

Discovery Learning

This page contains an alternative lesson plan emphasizing learning activities. Classes desiring such student involvement will find these suggestions helpful. The next page is a reproducible activity page to further enhance discovery learning.

LEARNING GOALS

After participating in this lesson, each student will:

1. Recount the events of the Day of Pentecost that accompanied the birth of the church.

2. Explain how the power of the Holy Spirit helped bring the church into being.

3. Identify one way of helping his or her church remember its first-century origins.

INTO THE LESSON

Decorate your class's assembly space with birthday items: balloons, streamers, a "Happy Birthday" banner, and perhaps a cupcake with a candle for each learner. If your personal budget allows, get half-dollars from your bank to give to each arriving student; perhaps put a small stick-on bow on each half-dollar and say, "Happy Birthday" as you distribute the coins. Once every one arrives and someone asks, "Whose birthday is it?" say, "The Church! Today's study is of the founding of Christ's church in Jerusalem in the first century." If no one says so, tell the group that the half-dollar represents the 50 days when Pentecost follows Passover.

INTO THE WORD

Either hand out birthday party invitations or let your class fold a piece of paper to be filled in as if it were a party invitation. Tell them you want the class to look at today's text and suggest elements of an invitation that God could have sent for the birthday of Christ's church. Suggest they consider such things as the actual event being celebrated, time, place, appropriateness of gifts, whether to R.S.V.P., special events at the party, special guests to be expected, special dress/costumes. Give an example or two of what they could include, such as "R.S.V.P.," with an asterisk explained as, "Repent if you please"; "Baptismal clothes recommended"; "No gifts, please; gifts will be distributed." (See also the "You're Invited!" activity on page 24.)

After a few minutes, ask for volunteers to say what they have included. Ask for clarification for any entry that needs it.

INTO LIFE

If you distributed half-dollars at the beginning of class, you may want to suggest that students pass these along to others during the week with an explanation of their significance.

If your congregation has a badge maker, prepare one for each learner with this design: a cross separating the circle into four parts, a 1 in the upper left segment, a 21 in the lower right. Distribute these and give this explanation:

> I want to be a first-century Christian in the twenty-first-century culture. I look to the first-century New Testament for twenty-first-century direction.

Suggest that students be prepared to give a similar explanation to anyone who asks about the significance of the badge as it is worn.

The lesson writer's "Conclusion" is a "So what?" list of the important roles the Holy Spirit continues to offer in our lives. Prepare a three-column work sheet ahead of time for distribution to your students. (If you use the student book, this is included there.)

Put the following entries in column one, which is headed "The Holy Spirit at Work": (1) The Spirit inspired God's Word; (2) Our bodies are the temple of the Holy Spirit, who is within us; (3) The Spirit gives us the most personal of relationships with God; (4) The Spirit seals us for the day of redemption; (5) The Spirit makes people alive from the dead; (6) The Spirit helps us to bear the fruit of the Spirit; (7) The Spirit helps us with our prayers; (8) The Spirit raised Jesus from the dead.

Column two, headed "So We Must," will have these entries: (A) Flee sexual sin; (B) Live in hope; (C) Don't Grieve the Spirit; (D) Obey the Spirit without hesitation; (E) Pray in faith, not doubting; (F) Trust God with a childlike faith; (G) Walk with the Spirit; (H) Walk in newness of life and put to death the misdeeds of the body.

Third column, headed "Scripture Affirmation," will have these entries: (I) Romans 8:11; (II) Romans 8:26; (III) 1 Corinthians 6:19; Galatians 5:16; (IV) Galatians 4:6; (V) Galatians 5:22-25; (VI) Ephesians 4:30; (VII) Romans 8:13; Titus 3:5; (VIII) 2 Peter 1:21.

Direct students to connect affirmations in column one with consequences in column two and with Scripture in column three. Discuss correct connections, per the lesson writer's conclusion. (Alternative: Use the Sermon Outline and Notes activity on page 24.)

You're Invited!

Which of the following texts might, in some way, be considered an "invitation" to the church's birthday event? Why do you say so?

Jeremiah 31:31-34

Joel 2:28-32

Matthew 16:16-19

Sermon Outline and Notes

If Peter had been using a PowerPoint® presentation for his sermon as recorded in Acts 2, what might it have looked like?

What would his basic outline be?

     This message centers on the person of _____ (v. 36).

     This message brings about _____ (v. 37).

     This message offers _____ from sin (vv. 38).

     This message urges its listeners to resist this _____ world (v. 40).

     This message produces a great _____ (vv. 41, 42).

What graphics or animations could be added to such a presentation today? Sketch a few below.

(Suggested words to fill in: *Jesus, repentance, forgiveness, corrupt, church.*)

THE BELIEVERS SHARE

LESSON 2

Sep
11

WHY TEACH THIS LESSON?

John Ortberg refers to a study headed by a Harvard scientist that tracked 7,000 people over nine years. People who had poor health habits (smoking, obesity, etc.) but who had strong social ties lived significantly longer than isolated people with great health habits. Ortberg concludes, "It is better to eat Twinkies® with good friends than to eat broccoli alone" (*Everybody's Normal Till You Get to Know Them*, Zondervan, 2003).

If relationships are important to our physical well-being, what about the spiritual? The infant, first-century church, empowered by the Holy Spirit, shows us a great harmony of pure fellowship. The ideal of the earliest church remains the model for Christians today. Harmonious fellowship impressed the people of the first century. If we allow the Holy Spirit to unite us in an other-centered, love-fueled community for Christ, we will affect our culture, too. God will make sure of that.

INTRODUCTION

A. DIVISION AND UNITY

Saber-toothed cats roamed North America during the Ice Age. Their seven-inch-long canine teeth made them feared predators. An article in *National Geographic* included a photograph of the remains of two such cats that died while locked in mortal combat. One had bitten into the leg of the other so hard that his teeth became locked in the leg bone, thus dooming both.

One cannot help but wonder how humanity avoids extinction when it is so divided by hatred, prejudice, lust for power, and fear. The world is divided sharply by race, religion, and social standing. These differences are so intense that solutions seem impossible.

Many attempts have been made to unify the human race. Various empires have attempted it through military might. The atheist Robert Owen (1771–1858) tried to create a more perfect society through education and the abolition of social classes and personal wealth. Jim Jones's attempt to create a perfect society in Guyana ended with deception, murder, and mass suicide in 1978. All of these attempts missed the real problem: sin.

The human race has a sin problem that we simply cannot solve or circumvent on our own. That is why all human attempts to unite people end in failure sooner or later. But God can do what we cannot. God can solve the deepest problems of the human race, beginning with the sin problem. Revelation 7:9 indicates that Heaven will be enjoyed by people from all families, tribes, languages, and nations. The message of Christ breaks down barriers and unites people regardless of their many differences. Christ destroyed the barrier between Jew and Gentile and united them under a common Savior within his church (Ephesians 2:11-18). If God can unite groups once marked with such hostility, he can overcome any barrier that divides humanity.

DEVOTIONAL READING:
ROMANS 8:9-17

BACKGROUND SCRIPTURE:
ACTS 2:41-47; 4:32-37

PRINTED TEXT:
ACTS 2:43-47; 4:32-35

LESSON AIMS

After participating in this lesson, each student will be able to:

1. Describe the various ways the earliest Christians shared their lives with each other.

2. Explain how God's Word, Christian love, and corporate worship give the church a strong foundation.

3. Plan a class project to help a needy family in the church.

KEY VERSE

When the apostles in Jerusalem heard that Samaria had accepted the word of God, they sent Peter and John to them.
—Acts 8:14

LESSON 2 NOTES

B. LESSON BACKGROUND

The book of Acts covers a span of about 30 years, beginning in A.D. 30. Today's lesson (as last week's) takes us into the earliest part of that time span. We will see the great unity enjoyed by the very first church. This will be a lesson in how we can succeed as they did.

I. EMPOWERED CHURCH (ACTS 2:43-47)

A. MIRACLES AND AWE (v. 43)

43. Everyone was filled with awe, and many wonders and miraculous signs were done by the apostles.

After communities are devastated by a tornado or an earthquake, people often walk around dazed, not knowing what to do next. The great outpouring of the Spirit, the powerful message of salvation by Peter, and the overwhelming number of conversions in a single day shakes Jerusalem to its foundations. But what happened on the Day of Pentecost was only the beginning. Jerusalem continues to be rocked by aftershocks that bring fear and awe upon every soul.

While some shake with fear as they realize that they had rejected and killed the Messiah, the fear that is mentioned here is that of respect, reverence, and *awe*. God continues to shake Jerusalem by empowering the apostles to do great miracles. The miracles are *wonders* because those who witness them are filled with great amazement. They are signs because they point people to the truth about Jesus (compare John 14:11). Peter had made the bold statement that God made Jesus "both Lord and Christ" (Acts 2:36). Now *the apostles* prove the truth about Jesus by miracles. Many of these undoubtedly include the same kinds of healing miracles that Jesus had performed while on earth (example: Matthew 4:23).

It is a good thing to have godly fear (see Proverbs 1:7). Reverent awe of God is appropriate for Christians (compare Luke 5:26; 7:16). If the church had more people who feared the Lord, the church would be morally and spiritually stronger.

B. GIVING AND RECEIVING (vv. 44, 45)

44, 45. All the believers were together and had everything in common. Selling their possessions and goods, they gave to anyone as he had need.

These verses have been used as a basis by communal groups and certain cults to encourage people to bring all of their possessions together in one place where everyone can live together and share one another's belongings equally. These two verses also have served as the basis for the belief of some that the first-century Christians practiced an early form of communism or socialism. But such ideas miss the point. Passages such as Acts 2:46 and 1 Corinthians 11:22 indicate that those Christians still had individual homes. It would be physically impossible for thousands of people suddenly to start living in one location in Jerusalem.

The fact that these earliest Christians have all things *in common* indicates that they share their possessions by going so far as to sell property and give as everyone has *need*. This is well illustrated in Acts 4:32-37. There we read of Barnabas voluntarily selling a field and bringing the proceeds to give to the apostles. This allows the apostles to distribute the money as appropriate.

This is the generosity that marks the early church. It is not mandatory, however. Peter makes it clear to Ananias in Acts 5:4 that the property he owned was his to do with as he pleased. Today, various forms of government require that people give up some (or all) of what they have so that the state can redistribute it.

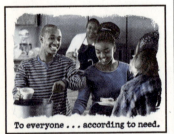

To everyone . . . according to need.

Visual for Lesson 2. *God calls us to meet needs. In this regard, use this visual to reinforce the importance of the question at the top of the next page.*

The early Christians love one another so much that they want to help those in need. No sacrifice is too great for this.

God helps the needy, and Christians must be like-minded (1 John 3:17). This is one of the first lessons that the early Christians learn, and they learn it quite well. They really do love one another!

UTOPIA?

In introducing today's lesson, we mentioned Robert Owen, a famous atheist of the nineteenth-century. (He debated Alexander Campbell in 1829 on the legitimacy of Christianity.) Although Owen's theology was flawed, his concern for the poor and needy was not. In England he proposed limiting common laborers to a 48-hour, 6-day work week, with no decrease in pay. Neither political nor industrial leaders were ready for this.

In America he bought the whole town of Harmony, Indiana, to give life to his dreams. In this town—renamed New Harmony—there would be a community of goods, no religious activities, and no competition in the production of goods. It was assumed that everyone would contribute mutually for the good of all. But within a year, this would-be utopia began to fail. It had no spiritual base for its founder's reforms.

Robert Owen found what all such social reformers from ancient times to modern Marxists have discovered: without the change of heart that faith brings, there will never be a utopia. On the other hand, the fledgling church of Christ proved that social change can occur when the transforming power of the gospel renews the human heart. Their example stands as a challenge to us of what love can do.

—C. R. B.

C. FELLOWSHIP AND WORSHIP (vv. 46, 47a)

46a. Every day they continued to meet together in the temple courts.

These early Christians are so excited about their newfound faith that they cannot stay apart from one another. They are motivated by love to come together *every day* for worship and fellowship. Three thousand people will find it difficult to *meet* anywhere else but on the grounds of *the temple* complex. Acts 3:11; 5:12 indicate that they may be gathering in Solomon's colonnade, which runs along the east side of the outer court.

Sadly, people sometimes let the things of this world and the responsibilities of life crowd worship and fellowship from their schedules. They lose that excitement that they had when they first became Christians. They feel no great loss when they skip church, having lost the wonder and joy of Christianity. In his book *Recapture the Wonder,* Ravi Zacharias notes that, "Wonder enriches you when you take time to reflect and ponder the greatness of our faith in Jesus Christ" and that "Wonder is retained by pondering." Unfortunately, he observes, "Thinking is a dying discipline in a society that throbs with activity."

Deliberately scheduling Bible study—the kind that really makes us think—helps us recapture the wonder of those feelings we had when we first came to Christ. In addition to Sunday (Lord's Day) Bible enrichment programs, some churches offer small-group studies during the week. Christians can value these opportunities.

46b. They broke bread in their homes and ate together with glad and sincere hearts.

Many churches today enjoy fellowship meals. But fellowship is not limited to such activities. Here we see how the early Christians meet in one another's homes. There they share meals and enjoy one another's company. They enjoy that "singleness of heart" that sets them apart from the rest of the world. (See

WHAT DO YOU THINK?

One of the marks of the Lord's church is the concern expressed toward one another, especially to those in need. How can we meet needs of other believers in our church and in our area more effectively?

HOW TO SAY IT

Ananias. An-uh-NYE-us.
Barnabas. BAR-nuh-bus.
Cephas. SEE-fus.
dynamis (Greek). DOO-nuh-mis.
Ephesus. EF-uh-sus.
Jerusalem. Juh-ROO-suh-lem.
Messiah. Meh-SIGH-uh.
Pentecost. PENT-ih-kost.

WHAT DO YOU THINK?

Jesus prayed for the unity of his followers in John 17:20, 21. In Ephesians 4:3, Paul encourages Christians to make every effort to maintain unity. How can the church continually maintain the unity Paul commanded and for which Christ prayed? Why is it important to recognize the difference between unity and uniformity?

also Acts 5:42; 20:7.) This is not the kind of thing that can be "forced." It just happens as a natural outflowing of love.

Christians are part of the greatest family in the world. It seems as natural as breathing for people who love one another—people who enjoy a common faith and a common salvation—to invite each other to their homes for food and fellowship. It helps bind together those who "have received a faith as precious as ours" (2 Peter 1:1). In modern society, people are often too busy with worldly activities to engage in this kind of fellowship. People get home after work, shut the garage door with an electric opener, and "cocoon" for the rest of the evening. Year after year they miss out on one of the real pleasures of the Christian life, opportunities that bind the church together.

ENTHUSIASTIC FELLOWSHIP

"Mr. and Mrs. Smith" were a Christian couple who had been active members for several years in an old, declining church. This church had lost its vision. It was content to keep doing what it had always done until it died. Mrs. Smith herself had been plagued for years with debilitating health problems that robbed her of her vitality and crushed her formerly lively spirit.

Then the Smiths moved to a new community. There they found fellowship in a congregation with a willingness to try new ways to reach the lost. This church had a program of enthusiastic missionary outreach and an abundance of small-group Bible studies. Other fellowship groups opened their homes for meals together. The congregation swept up the Smiths into its open arms.

A strange thing began to happen: Mrs. Smith's health problems got no better, but her spirits began to lift. As the vitality of the new congregation found its way into her life, the clinical depression she had fought for years no longer held her in its death grip. Although she felt no better physically, she got involved in a way she had not been for many years. Enthusiastic concern of others for her as well as her newfound opportunities for service changed her life.

Timeless principles that made the Jerusalem church so alive still work. When God's people respond to the gospel with enthusiasm, he works to change lives!

—C. R. B.

47a. . . . praising God and enjoying the favor of all the people.

The old saying "You can't please everyone" is true, but these Christians impress their community as a whole. It will be clear in the next two chapters, however, that not everyone is truly pleased with them. The religious leaders will arrest Peter and John and threaten them. However, when people are helping, sharing, loving, and caring for one another, even the hardest sinners in the community have to take notice and be impressed. This *favor of all the people* must make many unbelievers listen again to the gospel message as more and more respond to it.

D. GROWTH AND BLESSING (v. 47b)
47b. And the Lord added to their number daily those who were being saved.

So the church continues to grow *daily*. Many churches today have a tradition of making people wait until some future time before they can be baptized. But the earliest Christians proclaim the message of salvation each day and baptize without delay (compare Acts 8:36-38; 16:33). The earliest Christians see opportunities to bring people to salvation on a daily basis.

Not only do they succeed by making a strong witness to the community, they also are successful in God's eyes. The Lord, after all, is the one who ultimately saves. Titus 3:5 says, "He saved us, not because of righteous things we had done,

WHAT DO YOU THINK?

Why is it significant to understand that it is the Lord who adds to the church? How should this fact affect the life of the church?

but because of his mercy. He saved us through the washing of rebirth and renewal by the Holy Spirit." God places the names of those who were *saved* in the Lamb's book of life (Revelation 21:27).

II. SUCCESSFUL CHURCH (ACTS 4:32-35)

A. GREAT UNITY ACHIEVED (v. 32)

32. All the believers were one in heart and mind. No one claimed that any of his possessions was his own, but they shared everything they had.

The wonderful unity that these early Christians enjoy is nothing short of remarkable. We know that it is impossible to force people to love one another. True love is something that flows naturally because of the relationship people have with God—a relationship that affects all other relationships of life.

This attitude should always be present among Christians (see Galatians 6:10). God places before us each day opportunities to do good. The trouble is that many people do not keep their eyes open for such opportunities, or else they ignore them when they see them. Christians are a part of a wonderful household of faith. When each looks out for ways to do good, a marvelous unity is enjoyed, a unity that serves as a solid foundation for everything else that happens in the church.

But Christ expects even more than this. "Do nothing out of selfish ambition or vain conceit, but in humility consider others better than yourselves" (Philippians 2:3). Christ thought of us more than he thought of himself. If that were not the case, he would never have gone to the cross. But he did. Christians who consider other people's needs to be more important than their own have reached a stage of spiritual maturity that pleases God greatly.

B. GREAT MESSAGE PROCLAIMED (v. 33)

33. With great power the apostles continued to testify to the resurrection of the Lord Jesus, and much grace was upon them all.

Christians watch out for the physical needs of one another, but the church's primary mission is to provide witness *to the resurrection of the Lord Jesus* to the world. "For what I received I passed on to you as of first importance: that Christ died for our sins according to the Scriptures, that he was buried, that he was raised on the third day according to the Scriptures, and that he appeared to Peter, and then to the Twelve. After that, he appeared to more than five hundred of the brothers at the same time" (1 Corinthians 15:3-6a).

Paul calls the gospel "the power of God for the salvation of everyone who believes" (Romans 1:16). Preachers are fond of pointing out that the word *power,* both in that passage and in the text before us, is the Greek word *dynamis* from which we derive the English word *dynamite.* But that connection is only surface deep. Dynamite is destructive, while the power of God's great grace is a healing force. Everyone in the city of Jerusalem in A.D. 30 knows that Jesus had been crucified. But when God raised Jesus from the dead, God proved "with power" that Jesus is his Son (Romans 1:4). The message of the resurrection is proclaimed *with great power* by *the apostles.* Thousands find this eyewitness testimony irresistible. As a result, their lives are changed for all eternity.

Surely God's great *grace* is poured out upon the church! God's continuing blessing is seen in the way the first-century church grows numerically, in the way that he answers prayers, and in the way that Christians grow spiritually in the grace and knowledge of the Lord Jesus. Churches that fulfill the royal law of loving one another (James 2:8) will find God blessing them with the riches of his grace.

WHAT DO YOU THINK?

How can the power of the gospel most forcibly be made known in the church and world today? How well is our church doing in this regard?

What Do You Think?

Gifts from those in the church were brought and laid at the feet of the apostles. Why is it a good idea that gifts are brought to those in positions of authority in the church?

C. Great Love Shown (vv. 34, 35)

34, 35. There were no needy persons among them. For from time to time those who owned lands or houses sold them, brought the money from the sales and put it at the apostles' feet, and it was distributed to anyone as he had need.

Again, Luke (the author of the book of Acts) refers to the great acts of generosity of these earliest believers in Christ. Two new things are here mentioned. First, no Christian lacks for the basic necessities of life. No member of this great congregation of believers can tolerate seeing a fellow believer lack food, clothes, or shelter.

Again, this does not mean that the Christians are selling absolutely all that they own because of the simple fact that they are still meeting in their homes and breaking bread from house to house. God expects people to take care of their own households. So God would not expect a person to move his own family out onto the street.

The apostle Paul has something to about this. He writes that anyone who does not take care of his immediate family has "denied the faith" (see 1 Timothy 5:8). So we see a balance by combining these ideas. Immediate family comes first, but not to the point that our own selfishness means that others lack basic necessities. (The rich young ruler was told to "sell everything" in Luke 18:22 because of a problem that was specific to him.)

The other thing we learn is that when people sell property and give the proceeds to the church, they allow the leadership to make distribution to the ones in need. As the church grows, other people will be selected to oversee this task and accomplish it efficiently (Acts 6:1-6). The Scriptures also tell us that the first-century church maintains a list of widows to help (1 Timothy 5:9, 10). God expects his people to take care of their own family members first. But when someone has no family, or when a family is destitute or has some special need, then Christians will do what they can to assist.

Many Christians today miss out on an important way of glorifying God when they believe that the government will always step in to help. Have we Christians lost our powerful witness to the community by failing to help others? Have Christians forgotten that the Lord taught that "it is more blessed to give than to receive"? (See Acts 20:35.) Think what an impact the church would have on the world if it sought to recapture this spirit of love and unity that permeated the earliest church!

CONCLUSION

Reproducing the doctrine and message of the first-century church in the twenty-first century is a worthy goal. Many congregations strive to restore the worship and teaching of those early believers. While that is good, such efforts fall short if Christians do not reproduce the heart and love of those early Christians as well. Unfortunately, the congregations of the first century would find themselves challenged in this regard all too soon (examples: 1 Corinthians 1:10; 11:17-22; Galatians 5:15; Titus 3:10).

The case of the church at Ephesus proves that resisting false doctrine isn't enough (see Revelation 2:1-7). Jesus prayed for the unity of believers (John 17). The apostles encouraged it (Ephesians 4:3). The first-century church at Jerusalem lived it. A key to this unity is mutual love expressed through action (1 John 3:16-18). No wonder the earliest church was a thing of great power that brought new life to an entire city! Churches today must realize that such unity will continue to empower the church and will cause it to enjoy the favor of God.

Discovery Learning

This page contains an alternative lesson plan emphasizing learning activities. Classes desiring such student involvement will find these suggestions helpful. The next page is a reproducible activity page to further enhance discovery learning.

LEARNING GOALS

After participating in this lesson, each student will to:

1. Describe the various ways the earliest Christians shared their lives with each other.

2. Explain how God's Word, Christian love, and corporate worship give the church a strong foundation.

3. Plan a class project to help a family in the church.

INTO THE LESSON

As students arrive, divide them into two groups with separate seating. Use some artificial criterion, such as those carrying something from those empty-handed or those wearing black shoes from those wearing shoes of color.

Have an artistic member of the class draw a simple outline of an "old-fashioned" church building from the perspective of looking at it toward the front entrance. A simple steeple with a cross atop it and arched windows will help the image convey "church." For the gable, use double lines to mark it off, then divide it into ten parts. Across the foundation have a similar double-lined section divided into nine spaces.

Say, "The lesson writer uses two key words in his outline for today's study. Guess a letter included in either of these two words—one has ten letters, one has nine—and I will write it in appropriately. As soon as you think you know either of the words, say it, and I will write it in." The word to be written into the ten gable spaces is *successful*. The word for the nine foundation spaces is *empowered*. Once both words are identified say, "The successful church is an empowered church—empowered by God with love, through worship and fellowship."

Next, say, "I am going to give you two minutes to write down factors that make us different from one another." If they need help getting started, suggest answers such as age, birthplace, and different learning styles. At the end of the two minutes, have the student who has the most entries read his or her list. Afterward, ask others to tell items on their lists that went unnamed. Comment simply, "Many things differentiate us. Today's text and study highlights the factors that unify us in the church."

INTO THE WORD

Give each learner the following list of six unifying factors for a group: Common Emotions, Common Beliefs, Common Assets, Common Worship, Common Sense of Grace, and Common Leadership. Ask students to put verse numbers from today's text next to each unifying factor to show which factor is illustrated in that passage. For example, Acts 2:43 (fear/awe unifies them, and they all looked to the apostles as leaders) would be cited with the Common Emotions factor.

Give students time to work their way through the text and make their decisions, and then go through them unifying factor by factor and ask for verse notations. If students differ, have them explain their choices. Though a variety of possibilities exist, here is one printed text choice for each of the common factors: Emotions, 4:34 (love); Beliefs, 4:33 (Jesus' resurrection); Assets, 2:44 ("everything"); Worship, 2:47 ("praising God"); Sense of Grace, 4:33 ("much grace was upon them all"); Leadership, 4:35 (money turned over to the apostles). Ask the class if they can identify other unifying factors for a functioning group.

Acts 2:44 summarizes the thrust of today's study. Go around your group and have each person say that verse: "All the believes were together and had everything in common." Hearing it over and over should fix the idea in their memories. At the end say, "The church's togetherness (unity) and its commonality (fellowship) are always the secret of a successful church."

(Alternative: pass out copies of the "Built Right" activity [page 32] for each student to work on as he or she enters class; use the results as lead-in to the lesson.)

INTO LIFE

In the early days of the Jerusalem church, members were willing to sell some of their possessions in order to fund the needs of others. Discuss the possibility and logistics of a "class garage sale" with the income to be given to the congregation's benevolence fund or to a needy family of the class's choice. It may be preferable to suggest individual families have their own garage sales and make anonymous contributions.

Consider also organizing a work crew of volunteer class members to go into homes of the less fortunate or physically limited for home repairs and maintenance. Projects can be as simple as painting a room. Distribute copies of the "It's Great" activity (page 32) as thought-provoking homework for the week ahead.

Built Right

What elements in today's text in Acts 2 and 4 reflect essential foundation stones for a successful church? Write them in the blocks below this drawing of a church building.

It's Great!

The lesson writer suggests that a successful church, as shown in Acts 4:32-35, has great unity, a great message, and great love. Rate your own congregation on the scale of 1 (low) to 10 (high) on all three attributes. After each one, write your personal commitment to move your church a notch closer to matching the Jerusalem church's score of 10 on all three attributes.

Great Unity   1————————5————————10

     My commitment:

Great Message   1————————5————————10

     My commitment:

Great Love   1————————5————————10

     My commitment:

PETER AND JOHN
HEAL A LAME MAN

WHY TEACH THIS LESSON?

Many of the people of his town wrote him off—he was just a crippled beggar to them. That's all he would ever be. That was reality. Yet God seems to specialize in taking "obvious reality" and showing it for the confusion that it is. Thus the power of Jesus' name raised to his feet the man who had been paralyzed.

We, too, can be quick to write a person off. We can be quick to consider a problem too big to resolve. Yet God loves reversals. In our lesson, John and Peter looked at the man who was crippled. Perhaps they had passed him many times before. But this time they saw a person to reach out to in the name of Jesus.

This lesson may strike us in various ways. Some may realize that they, like the man with the disability, are asking for pocket change instead of reaching for new life. Others, although lacking the miraculous ability that Peter and John had, may realize that they can still touch the world with what they *do* have.

INTRODUCTION

A. PROBLEMS WITHOUT HUMAN SOLUTIONS

This world appears to have problems with no solutions. According to the World Health Organization, malnutrition affects close to 800 million people. Hunger plays a major role in the deaths of 14,000 children every day. Access to health care is a major concern for many. Terrorism continues to threaten world security. Even the best diplomats lack long-term solutions. So many problems!

The story is told of a captain who ran from the battlefield. "General, the enemy is too numerous. We cannot hope to win!" he exclaimed. But the general responded, "Captain, we are not here to count the enemy but conquer them. And conquer them we must." God expects the same thing, and he provides the power to do so. Human wisdom and strength cannot win the day, but God can help his people win even the most difficult battles of life.

B. LESSON BACKGROUND

Today's lesson demonstrates that God's power can solve problems that seem to have no solution. The power to change the world rests not in human ingenuity. Rather, it rests in God and in his message.

That message can change the world one life at a time. Some changes are instantaneous and miraculous while others take much longer to unfold. We see both categories in the pages of Scripture. But God, on his own timetable, wins the victory. We're now only three lessons into our study in Acts, but already we have seen God's power and his victories time and again. Today it's time to see one more. A great miracle is about to prove the truth of Christianity yet again. It all begins with a meeting that no one planned and was on no one's daily schedule.

DEVOTIONAL READING:
LUKE 7:18-23

BACKGROUND SCRIPTURE:
ACTS 3

PRINTED TEXT:
ACTS 3:1-16

LESSON AIMS

After participating in this lesson, each student will be able to:

1. Retell the story of Peter and John's healing of the man who was crippled.

2. Summarize Peter's claim that Jesus deserves the glory for healing.

3. Participate in a time of prayer for people to be healed physically and spiritually in Jesus' name.

KEY VERSE

By faith in the name of Jesus, this man whom you see and know was made strong.
—Acts 3:16a

LESSON 3 NOTES

I. INCIDENTAL MEETING (ACTS 3:1-3)

A. TWO MEN GOING TO PRAY (v. 1)

1. One day Peter and John were going up to the temple at the time of prayer—at three in the afternoon.

Perhaps *Peter and John* had been preaching earlier in the day. They now walk together to *the temple* at *the time of prayer,* which was at 3:00 P.M. The rhythm of temple practice revolves around sacrifice and prayer at set times (see Exodus 29:38, 39; Numbers 28:4, 8; Psalm 141:2; Ezekiel 46:13-15). Jesus' death made animal sacrifices obsolete (Hebrews 9:11-15; 10:1-12), but it is still appropriate for Peter and John to pray. They may have opportunity to share Christ with others who are there.

Christians still need regular times of prayer. Daniel was an extremely busy man, but he was not too busy to pray (see Daniel 6:10). Modern Christians tend to allow busy schedules and entertainment opportunities to crowd out prayer time. Christians can learn much from Peter and John who, in spite of being very busy teaching thousands of Christians who are new in the faith, still understand their deep need for prayer.

B. ONE MAN IN DESPERATE NEED (vv. 2, 3)

2, 3. Now a man crippled from birth was being carried to the temple gate called Beautiful, where he was put every day to beg from those going into the temple courts. When he saw Peter and John about to enter, he asked them for money.

Peter and John arrive at one of the gates of the temple complex. Modern scholars have tried to determine exactly which *gate* is called *Beautiful,* but this is very difficult. The Jewish historian Josephus suggests that it is made of Corinthian bronze. He describes it as a thing of exquisite workmanship, being of greater value than the gates plated with silver and set in gold.

As Peter and John prepare to enter the *temple,* a certain *man crippled from birth* asks them for *money.* He is over 40 years old (Acts 4:22). It is hard for many to imagine what it would be like to deal with such a long-term problem. Perhaps he was taught to beg even as a little child.

One cannot help but wonder if this man is now all alone in the world. Perhaps his parents are dead. If he has brothers and sisters, they may consider him to be too much of a burden. Perhaps all he has are two or three people who pity him enough to help him to the temple where he can beg for money. One of the entrances to the temple is an ideal location for this.

Those who are challenged physically sometimes feel isolated, lack self-respect, and are unable to enjoy life. They even find themselves rejected by their own family members, who consider them a burden or do not know how to help them.

On the other hand, people find it difficult to know what to do when they meet those who ask for money. Most people want to be generous and help those in need, but many are reluctant to give because they know that some misrepresent themselves and their need. Many find such moments uncomfortable, but Peter sees this an opportunity to help this man.

II. UNEXPECTED ANSWER (ACTS 3:4-6)

A. ORDINARY EXPECTATION (vv. 4, 5)

4, 5. Peter looked straight at him, as did John. Then Peter said, "Look at us!" So the man gave them his attention, expecting to get something from them.

WHAT DO YOU THINK?

Judaism had designated times for prayer. This is still true in many world religions today. Christianity does not have standardized times for prayer, but rather we are encouraged to pray continually (1 Thessalonians 5:17). In addition to that, do you think it is a good idea to have set times for concentrated prayer? Why, or why not?

The beggar asks *Peter* and *John* for money in the same way that he has asked countless others. The *man* evidently has begged for so long that it has become a routine. Perhaps he has his head down, feeling embarrassed or ashamed to beg for a living.

Some probably give him coins without pausing even for a moment to offer a kind word. Others perhaps hurry right on by, neither wanting to be bothered nor wanting others to notice their stinginess. Some even may have seen this man so often that he just blends into the background and goes unnoticed. But Peter and John stop and tell the man to *Look at us!* So he looks up, hoping for a gift.

B. Extraordinary Gift (v. 6)
6. Then Peter said, "Silver or gold I do not have, but what I have I give you. In the name of Jesus Christ of Nazareth, walk."

What comes next is startling, to say the least! For that one instant, the man's face must fall with disappointment when he hears that they have no money. After all, he needs *silver* and *gold* to buy his next meal. But Peter wants to give him something better: the ability to *walk* by the power of *Jesus Christ of Nazareth*. As the Son of God, he was chosen by the Father to be the Savior of the world. His power can make the lame to walk.

Many of us today cannot say *silver and gold I do not have* because we do indeed have money. Christians with financial resources have an obligation to be generous and share with others in need (see 1 John 3:17, 18).

But even if a person has no money, people still have so much to give. How much does it cost to pray for someone who is in desperate need? How much does it cost to bring a word of comfort to a neighbor who has lost a family member? How much does it cost to share the good news of God's grace to someone who is lost? So much can be done that costs nothing. A "cup of cold water" can be a powerful help at times (Matthew 10:42). God blesses all Christians so that each may bless others who are faced with seemingly impossible problems. When we help others in the name of Jesus, God will bless (compare Acts 3:16; 4:10).

Better Than Expected

At the turn of the millennium just a few years ago, the African nation of Congo was in a war that would go on for years with a steadily rising death toll. Some authorities say only 10 percent of the victims were killed in battle; the rest died from starvation and disease. Adding to the tragedy is the case of the people who died at the hands of their priest!

In late 2003 in the small town of Bosobe, a priest promised his congregation that he would give them salvation. Marauding militias used terror, rape, and murder as the means to maintain power in that war-torn country. So one can understand the desire for salvation, whether temporal or eternal. The priest promised his people they would find salvation by drinking a potion he gave them. Of the 100 who drank it, 64 died from the poison it contained. What they got was far from what they expected!

What a different situation for the man in today's text. He didn't expect salvation, only money to help maintain his misery-filled life. What he got instead was healing and wholeness. God will judge the priest in the Congo for what he did to those who trusted him. But we can be sure of God's pleasure in what Peter and John did for the man who was crippled. We may not be able to perform miracles, but we can offer the gospel, which is the most important thing. One measure of our Christian lives is that we offer to those who need our help something more and better than what they expect.
—C. R. B.

Daily Bible Readings

Monday, Sept. 12—Jesus Tells of His Healing Power (Luke 7:18-23)

Tuesday, Sept. 13—The Twelve Receive Power to Heal (Luke 9:1-6)

Wednesday, Sept. 14—Jesus Rebukes a Demon (Luke 4:31-37)

Thursday, Sept. 15—A Beggar Asks for Money (Acts 3:1-5)

Friday, Sept. 16—A Man Is Healed (Acts 3:6-10)

Saturday, Sept. 17—Peter Speaks to the People (Acts 3:11-16)

Sunday, Sept. 18—Peter Tells the People to Repent (Acts 3:17-26)

What can you offer others?

a word of encouragement
call someone who is feeling down
send thank-you notes
give compliments
pray for others

a smile
introduce yourself to church visitors
be friendly to those you meet on the street

a helping hand
offer babysitting services
prepare a meal
offer your talents
offer a ride to appointments or church

"Silver and gold have I none; but such as I have give I thee" (Acts 3:6).

Visual for Lesson 3. *Use the question on this poster to challenge your students to think beyond themselves.*

III. AMAZING MIRACLE (ACTS 3:7-10)

A. HEALING AND STANDING (v. 7)

7. Taking him by the right hand, he helped him up, and instantly the man's feet and ankles became strong.

Notice that the man doesn't initially stand on his own. Instead, Peter takes the man's *right hand* and lifts him up. This perhaps helps the man overcome a moment of uncertainty. Peter's command to rise up and walk undoubtedly seems incredible. He has never once taken a step, so Peter takes the initiative to help *him up.*

This is a true miracle that goes far beyond everyone's imagination. The healing is instantaneous and complete. This man immediately receives strength in his *feet and ankles,* so he rises to walk. After 40 years of atrophy, the deteriorated muscles suddenly come alive.

Not to be overlooked is the fact that this man has no experience in walking. A toddler has to learn to keep balance, falling many times while taking those first steps. But this man immediately walks—and more (see next).

B. WALKING, LEAPING, AND PRAISING (v. 8)

8. He jumped to his feet and began to walk. Then he went with them into the temple courts, walking and jumping, and praising God.

Isaiah 35:6 describes the joys of the redeemed by predicting how the lame would leap like a deer. Has this man become so discouraged that he thinks he has no reason to go into the temple and thank God? (Compare Leviticus 21:16-23.) After all, he sat begging while others entered to pray. Now he also goes inside. This somber time of prayer is interrupted by a man who is *jumping* into the air and shouting praise to God for a great blessing!

C. RECOGNITION AND AMAZEMENT (vv. 9, 10)

9, 10. When all the people saw him walking and praising God, they recognized him as the same man who used to sit begging at the temple gate called Beautiful, and they were filled with wonder and amazement at what had happened to him.

Now people react quite differently toward this man. He no longer blends into his surroundings. They can ignore him no longer. He is a walking and talking testimony to the power of Almighty God. No one doubts his identity or the miracle that has taken place. The joy and praise is contagious and spreads quickly through the crowd.

IT'S CATCHING!

Have you noticed you can make yourself yawn just by thinking about it? At some time, someone probably has said to you, "Stop that yawning! You're making me do it, too." What is there about yawning that seems to be so contagious?

People even from the time of Aristotle (who lived more than three hundred years before Christ) were aware of the contagious nature of yawns. As you would expect, modern psychologists have studied the phenomenon also. Although babies yawn even in the womb, yawning apparently doesn't become contagious until about age two, when a child begins to recognize himself in a mirror. Some believe yawning has something to do with our self-perception and how we relate to others. It may be a subconscious way for us to show empathy for others.

Now think about how other behaviors affect us. It is hard not to feel some excitement when someone else is demonstrating ecstatic joy or enthusiasm, whether it is over their football team scoring a touchdown or as they are telling us some good personal news they have just received. This is what was taking place with the

---

WHAT DO YOU THINK?

The full and instantaneous healing of the man who was disabled brings us joy when we read of it. But this account may have a different effect on someone who prays for healing but does not receive it. How should one respond when the healing sought does not come? Be sure to consider 2 Corinthians 12:7-9 in your answer.

WHAT DO YOU THINK?

When God works, praise follows. How can we praise God for his mighty works? Why should we do so?

man who had just been healed of his lameness. As he jumped for joy and praised God for what had happened to him, the crowd who saw him was also caught up in a spirit of wonder and excitement. Does anyone ever get amazed and excited because of how we rejoice in God's blessings? —C. R. B.

IV. POINTED SERMON (ACTS 3:11-16)

A. LARGE CROWD GATHERS (v. 11)

11. *While the beggar held on to Peter and John, all the people were astonished and came running to them in the place called Solomon's Colonnade.*

Solomon's colonnade is a covered porch on the east side of the temple. This was a familiar area to Jesus (see John 10:23), and it will remain a popular meeting place for the earliest Christians (Acts 5:12). *People* run to this area as the man who had been lame holds tight *to Peter and John.*

B. GOD GETS THE CREDIT (vv. 12, 13a)

12, 13a. *When Peter saw this, he said to them: "Men of Israel, why does this surprise you? Why do you stare at us as if by our own power or godliness we had made this man walk? The God of Abraham, Isaac and Jacob, the God of our fathers, has glorified his servant Jesus.*

The first time that this lesson writer had contact with a homeless person, money was given along with an invitation to go to church. The man's reply was startling: "What has God ever done to make me thankful?" Nothing seemed to reach that man. This sermon by *Peter,* though, has far greater success.

Peter undoubtedly sees utter amazement in the eyes of those who gather around him and the *man* who had been lame. People are often drawn to charismatic persons who claim to have God's power or who seem to be spiritual giants. Paul and Barnabas will have to deal with this later while performing an identical miracle (Acts 14:8-13). But the apostles refuse to take credit for the miracles. Peter immediately points people to *God* and to his Son *Jesus.*

Notice that Peter calls God the *God of Abraham, Isaac and Jacob, the God of our fathers.* This reminds the people of the covenant God made with Abraham and his descendants. The apostles proclaim that Jesus fulfills these promises. "If you [whether Jew or Gentile] belong to Christ, then you are Abraham's seed, and heirs according to the promise" (Galatians 3:29). In fact, each of the following blessings is said specifically to be a fulfillment of the promise God made to Abraham and the fathers: Jesus' birth (Luke 1:68-75); his resurrection (Acts 13:32, 33); the conversion of sinners (Acts 3:24-26); justification through faith (Romans 4:16-18; Galatians 3:8); the gift of the Holy Spirit (Galatians 3:14); and the plan to bring people to Christ (Galatians 3:26-29).

C. PEOPLE ARE ACCUSED (vv. 13b-15)

13b-15. *"You handed him over to be killed, and you disowned him before Pilate, though he had decided to let him go. You disowned the Holy and Righteous One and asked that a murderer be released to you. You killed the author of life, but God raised him from the dead. We are witnesses of this.*

Peter now reminds the people of their guilt regarding the death of Jesus. Surely their memories are still fresh with regard to those horrible events of just several weeks previous! *Pilate,* the Roman governor, knew that the religious leaders were jealous of Jesus' popularity (Matthew 27:18). His custom was to release a prisoner during Passover, so he planned to release Jesus. But the leaders and their supporters demanded that he release Barabbas, who had committed murder in

HOW TO SAY IT

Barabbas. Buh-RAB-us.
Barnabas. BAR-nuh-bus.
Corinthians. Ko-RIN-thee-unz.
Isaiah. Eye-ZAY-uh.
Josephus. Jo-SEE-fus.
Nazareth. NAZ-uh-reth.
Pilate. PIE-lut.

WHAT DO YOU THINK?

Servants of God are often given praise for the good things they do. When this happened to Peter, he immediately deflected the attention away from himself and pointed to God. What cautions should we take to be sure all the glory goes to God?

Prayer

Father, may we never hinder Jesus, the prince of life, from bringing new life to our souls. May we know that his great power can heal, give eternal life, and bless abundantly. In Jesus' name, amen!

an uprising against Rome (Mark 15:7). Peter sees irony in the fact that they chose *a murderer* over *the author of life*—someone who takes life rather than gives it.

Peter also makes it clear that God can reverse even the most horrible decisions people can make. Daniel had been thrown into the lions' den, but God reversed the decision by stopping the mouths of the lions. Daniel was rewarded instead of being eaten alive (Daniel 6). Joseph was sold as a slave by his own brothers, but God reversed their decision and Joseph became a great man in Egypt (Genesis 41:41).

But the greatest example is the one in our text. Humanity's sin problem was so great that people even murdered God's Son, who came to give abundant life. God reversed that decision by raising Jesus from the dead. God brought about his greater plan by working through human weakness.

Peter uses two arguments to convince the crowd about Jesus. First, he makes it clear that eyewitnesses of Jesus' resurrection are present. Peter and John saw Jesus alive after being crucified (John 20:19, 20; 21:1). The second reason is given next.

D. Jesus Granted the Healing (v. 16)

16. *"By faith in the name of Jesus, this man whom you see and know was made strong. It is Jesus' name and the faith that comes through him that has given this complete healing to him, as you can all see."*

Peter also states that the man who had been lame is living proof that Jesus is alive because he was healed in Jesus' name. This miracle proves everything Peter has to say about Jesus.

Peter shows great boldness by proclaiming Jesus to the very ones who had been instruments of his death. A few weeks earlier, Peter's fear had caused him to stay behind locked doors (again, John 20:19). Now he boldly lifts Jesus up to this crowd because he wants them to know that the greatest problem of the human race is not physical pain or suffering (see Acts 3:17-26, not in today's text). The greatest problem is sin.

Sin cripples every soul. Those without Jesus are even worse off than the man who was crippled had been. But all can be healed by God's power and can receive joy, peace, forgiveness of sins, and eternal life by the one who is the prince of life.

What Do You Think?

God always has been able to take the worst of situations and bring good from them. He promises his people that he will do so (Romans 8:28). How has God demonstrated his power to bring good out of a bad situation in your life? in your church?

CONCLUSION

The world is filled with people whose situations seem hopeless. Bill and Gloria Gaither, the authors of many wonderful Christian songs, had gone through some difficult times. Bill had been seriously ill. Gloria sat in a dark room experiencing torment and fear and thinking about what an awful world this is. They were expecting a baby, but she wondered, "Who in their right minds would bring a child into a world like this?"

Then something happened. The panic and fear turned to calm and assurance as she remembered the empty tomb of Jesus. She knew she could have that baby and face the future with optimism and trust because Jesus lives. As a result, she wrote that marvelous song, "Because He Lives." It speaks of facing the future without fear.

The world is filled with seemingly insurmountable problems, but none are so great that God cannot help us to face them all. The facts of Jesus' resurrection and the indwelling Holy Spirit help deal with grief, discouragement, temptation, suffering, pain, and loss as we look to eternity.

Thought to Remember

The living Jesus still heals.

Discovery Learning

This page contains an alternative lesson plan emphasizing learning activities. Classes desiring such student involvement will find these suggestions helpful. The next page is a reproducible activity page to further enhance discovery learning.

LEARNING GOALS

After participating in this lesson, each student will be able to:

1. Retell the story of Peter and John's healing of the man who was crippled.

2. Summarize Peter's claim that Jesus deserves the glory for healing.

3. Participate in a time of prayer for people to be healed physically and spiritually in Jesus' name.

INTO THE LESSON

Begin class with a time of prayer, but recruit a class member to interrupt the prayer soon after you have begun by jumping up and shouting, "Praise the Lord! He's a mighty God!" repeatedly as he or she leaps about the room. As students react, say, "This is exactly what happened in the events described in Acts 3. At a reverent, quiet hour of prayer in a worship assembly, someone dared interrupt with shouts and dances. Let's take a closer look at that marvelous and interesting story."

(As an alternative to this and the first activity under *Into the Word*, hand out copies of "An Upper-Case Summary" from the reproducible page for students to work on as they enter class.)

INTO THE WORD

Display the following words as a list: *a, about, and, and, heal, Jesus, John, lame, man, Peter, preach, then, who, was.* Say to your class, "If you reorganize these 14 words correctly, you will have a one-sentence summary of the story told in Acts 3." Give students some time to think. If they need a clue, say, "Peter is the first word." If they need more help, say, "Jesus is the last word—in more ways than one!" The complete sentence is "Peter and John heal a man who was lame and then preach about Jesus."

Label this next activity, "Peter Did It." Give your students the following list of sentences (here alphabetized by the second word in each). Ask students to put them in chronological order. (Verse answers are provided in parentheses—do not give those.) Peter accompanied a friend to the temple (1); Peter accused his audience, without hesitation (14); Peter admitted he had no money (6); Peter affirmed the resurrection of Jesus and claimed to be a witness (15); Peter asked for the beggar's atten-

tion (4); Peter assumed that some of his audience were at the early morning "trial" of Jesus before Pilate (13); Peter corrected the view that the healing power was his and John's (12); Peter credits the God of the Old Testament for working this miracle to honor Jesus (13); Peter expressed his surprise that such a miracle would create marvel (12); Peter helped the man to stand (7); Peter indicated the great power in Jesus' name and faith in Jesus (16); Peter invoked the name of Jesus to heal the man (6); Peter reached the Solomon's porch area of the temple (11); Peter heard a request for a monetary gift (3).

INTO LIFE

Say to your class, "Medications are a major factor in the life of many adults. Though the curse of sin and death remains on the earth, God's grace has allowed mankind to discover a wealth of pharmaceutical realities he created in the beginning. Make a list of what you think are the greatest medicinal discoveries." After a list is compiled, invite the class to join you saying in unison, "Praise God for _____," filling in each entry on your list in turn. Comment that, "All too often we take for granted the marvelous blessings God has given us."

Nearly everyone has a physician who has helped him or her with disease and pain. But doctors, like most professionals, seldom receive words of encouragement from their patients. Hand out blank thank-you cards and recommend that students jot their doctor a quick note to the effect, "I thank God that you dedicated yourself to the healing art. May he strengthen you for your service. May his wisdom aid yours each day." If students seem a bit hesitant, indicate that sending the note anonymously could work as well as signing it.

Draw the class to a close by distributing the "Time to Pray" clock from the reproducible page. Explain how students can use it for the week ahead. Then say, "Though physical healing is much to be valued and prayed for, spiritual healing is all the more critical."

Use this observation to move to a time of group prayer. After naming those in need, use these words to close the prayer: "God, we know that all die because of sin, so we are coming to pray for those who are still dead in sin. Heal them by your gospel. Provide that Christian 'physician' who can prescribe salvation. In the name of the great physician, amen."

An Upper-Case Summary

As you read the following summary of today's text in Acts 3, note the incorrectly capitalized letters. Transfer each of the incorrectly capitalized letters, in sequence, to the lines below, and then you will have a one-sentence capsule of the whole chapter.

When Peter and John aPproached thE temple aT prayer timE, an interRuption stopped them. A mAn who couldN't walk askeD for a gift. Without Judging him, Peter Offered a word of disappointment, tHen hope. "I have No money," Peter said," but I Have something bEtter. In the nAme of Jesus, stand and waLk!"

By God's power, the man sTood, and everyone Heard him cry, "PraisE God! I caN walk!"

As they Passed into the poRtico of the tEmple, a large crowd gAthered. Peter then fulfilled his apostoliC role. He spoke once again of CHrist's power and grace.

__ __ __ __ __ __ __ __ __ __ __ __ __ __ ,

__ __ __ __ __ __ __ __ __ __

Time to Pray

Peter and John had it right: it is good to have planned prayer times in one's daily schedule. Plan a day of prayer when you make a concerted effort to stop every hour on the hour and pray for the physical and/or spiritual healing of 12 specific individuals or groups. Consider ailing individuals in your class or congregation but also other groups such as service organizations or evangelism/mission teams related to your congregation. Write the 12 names on the lines radiating from the clock's hour designations. Start and finish at the hour of your choice.

THE CHURCH IS BOLD

LESSON 4

WHY TEACH THIS LESSON?

When official channels move too slowly, sometimes an enterprising scientist may release a discovery directly to the public via mass media. There are dangers in this because new theories and innovations may not have been thoroughly tested. But once some new cure or invention has been "made public," even the powerful people who oppose it are forced to reckon with the claim.

The religious officials thought they had stifled the radical teacher Jesus when they crucified him. But then a middle-aged man, crippled from birth, started jumping all over the temple courts. Jesus' disciples—uneducated, uncredentialed men—are healing and giving credit to their master. The city is abuzz with praises and talk of Jesus. As a result, persecution begins.

Various kinds of persecution against Christians are still prevalent. Today's lesson encourages us to pray, as the disciples did, for God-given boldness to speak the name of Jesus. Some things are just too good to keep quiet.

INTRODUCTION

A. SOBERING PERSECUTION

In *The World Christian Encyclopedia*, David Barrett estimates that just under 70 million Christians have died for their faith during the first 2,000 years of church history. But of that number, 45 million (almost two-thirds) were killed during the twentieth century alone. Barrett includes a map that indicates that a significant portion of the world remains "highly dangerous" to Christians.

As frightening as that may be, it does not even take into account the many Christians who have been persecuted without being killed. Some countries forbid Christian literature. Others deny employment to Christians. Many Chinese Christians have to worship secretly. Even in America some parents refuse to allow their children to be baptized or to enter Christian service. Not to be forgotten are those who are forbidden to read a Bible or pray in a public place or are harassed because of their faith. Paradoxically, it seems that the more "tolerant" society becomes, the more intolerant it is to Christians.

B. LESSON BACKGROUND

Last week we saw Peter and John on their way to pray when they were interrupted by an opportunity to heal a man who was crippled. As we will see today, Peter and John would never make it to their intended time of prayer. Jesus warned his disciples that they would be hated and persecuted as their master had been (Matthew 10:22). Today's lesson records the first known persecution against the church after its birth on the Day of Pentecost. Peter and John had healed a man in Jesus' name. The crowds were amazed and listened as they proclaimed the resurrection of Jesus. Those in authority opposed their message, but the apostles overcame fear. The boldness of Peter and John presents a strong example for Christians yet today.

DEVOTIONAL READING:
EPHESIANS 6:10-20
BACKGROUND SCRIPTURE:
ACTS 4:1-31
PRINTED TEXT:
ACTS 4:1-4, 23-31

Sep
25

LESSON AIMS

After participating in this lesson, each student will be able to:

1. Retell Peter and John's bold proclamation of the gospel in spite of persecution.

2. Discuss the depth of the apostles' faith in relation to their boldness.

3. Write a prayer asking God for boldness in witnessing for Jesus.

KEY VERSE

Now, Lord, consider their threats and enable your servants to speak your word with great boldness.   —Acts 4:29

LESSON 4 NOTES

I. BOLD WITNESS (ACTS 4:1-4)

A. CONFRONTATION (v. 1)

1. The priests and the captain of the temple guard and the Sadducees came up to Peter and John while they were speaking to the people.

Peter and John now face opposition at the hands of some of the very men who had crucified Jesus only a short time earlier. Many *priests* serve in the temple. *The captain of the temple guard* commands what may be thought of as a temple police force. Judas Iscariot had betrayed Jesus into the hands of "the chief priests and the officers of the temple guard" (Luke 22:4). It was they who had arrested the Lord (Luke 22:52).

The Sadducees also opposed Jesus. They had been relentless in their attempts to undermine his ministry. They joined with the Pharisees in testing Jesus by asking for a sign from Heaven when he already had performed numerous signs (Matthew 16:1). They had asked questions, hoping to use Jesus' words against him (Mark 12:18-27). The Sadducees deny the resurrection of the body (Matthew 22:23; Acts 23:8), so when they hear Peter and John teaching the truth of this doctrine (Acts 3:15), they are alarmed.

This particular Jewish party originated sometime after the Jews returned from the Babylonian captivity (536 B.C.). The Jewish historian Josephus tells us they are aristocratic and that most of their supporters are wealthy. People in general do not follow them, but they exercise great authority.

The phrase *came up to Peter and John* may seem harmless. But as the story unfolds, we will see the true intent. The captain of the temple may think that the apostles are inciting a riot. But the fact that the priests and Sadducees come with them indicates that the temple leaders are upset mostly at the apostles' teaching.

B. MESSAGE (v. 2)

2. They were greatly disturbed because the apostles were teaching the people and proclaiming in Jesus the resurrection of the dead.

We noted in our previous discussion that the Sadducees deny *the resurrection* of the body. The apostles proclaim that the healing had been done in Jesus' name, the same Jesus they had crucified, but whom God had raised from the dead (Acts 3:15, 26). The miracle and the message of resurrection now threaten the very existence of the Sadducees. If God had raised Jesus' dead body from the grave, then the Sadducees' teaching is in error. Thus they have to exercise their authority quickly and show the people "who's boss." If they fail, they could lose control of the masses.

It is essential to remember that the resurrection of Jesus is central to the message of the early church. It is impossible to explain the great success of the early church without the truth of the resurrection of Christ. But this message of resurrection is the very thing that the enemies of the church resist (Matthew 28:11-15). They have to know that Jesus' resurrection is the one element that either proves or disproves the apostles' message. If Jesus is still in the tomb, then all of this is for nothing (1 Corinthians 15:4, 12-19). But if Jesus is alive, then everything he ever taught is true, and all that *the apostles* are *teaching* is also true.

C. IMPRISONMENT (v. 3)

3. They seized Peter and John, and because it was evening, they put them in jail until the next day.

Peter and John are arrested. The fact that the opponents in verse 1 seize them seems to indicate that these two are manhandled as they are put *in jail*. In spite

WHAT DO YOU THINK?

The apostles were confronted by many enemies of the gospel. How do we tell the difference between an enemy who is not interested in truth and an enemy who may be won over by the truth?

of all of the good that they have accomplished, they are treated as common criminals (compare Luke 22:52).

Evening means that it is about sunset, or roughly 6:00 P.M. Since Peter and John had arrived at the temple at about 3:00 P.M. and the miracle took place right away, these two must have preached to the crowd for the better part of three hours. Thus it takes some time for the authorities to move against them. The authorities spend the night preparing charges and planning their next move once they have these two *in jail.*

Comparing and contrasting the arrest of these two apostles with the arrest of Jesus is interesting. Peter and John are arrested in broad daylight, surrounded by hundreds of people. The people know what happened, so the authorities proceed with discretion. Jesus, on the other hand, was arrested in a remote location in the middle of the night. He was given a hasty, nighttime trial that probably was illegal in its format.

D. RESULT *(v. 4)*

4. *But many who heard the message believed, and the number of men grew to about five thousand.*

Some will always oppose the gospel and deny the truth of God's Word. But that does not stop *the message* of Christ from changing people's lives. Through the power of the Holy Spirit, the church cannot but succeed when the message of Jesus is proclaimed to a lost world. And it will succeed even in the midst of opposition.

The authorities can throw Peter and John in prison, but they cannot stop their message. It is the custom in that part of the world to count only the *men* (compare Matthew 14:21; 15:38). What that means is that the church is much larger than *five thousand.* It is now possibly no more than two or three months after the Day of Pentecost, when the number of believers in the Jerusalem area swelled from 120 (Acts 1:15) to three thousand (Acts 2:41). Thus the number five thousand shows how rapidly the church is growing and how it succeeds, even in the midst of persecution.

II. CONFIDENT ATTITUDE (ACTS 4:23-28)

A. GOD'S POWER *(vv. 23, 24)*

23, 24. *On their release, Peter and John went back to their own people and reported all that the chief priests and elders had said to them. When they heard this, they raised their voices together in prayer to God. "Sovereign Lord," they said, "you made the heaven and the earth and the sea, and everything in them.*

Some interesting things happen in Acts 4:5-22 (not in today's text). Peter and John are released, but not before they were brought before the Jewish Supreme Court, the Sanhedrin (Acts 4:15). The *elders,* rulers, and teachers of the law assembled for the trial. Even Annas and Caiaphas, the high priests who had condemned Jesus, were present (Acts 4:5; compare John 18:12-14).

These two had demanded that Peter and John tell them, "By what power or what name did you do this?" (Acts 4:7). In no uncertain words, Peter replied that this miracle had been done in the name of Jesus Christ of Nazareth. Peter reminded those religious leaders that they had crucified him, but God had raised him from the dead (Acts 4:10).

Peter went on to proclaim that salvation is found in Jesus alone (Acts 4:12). Their enemies noted the courage of the two (Acts 4:13), but could not deny what they said because of the great miracle they had performed. Instead of being

WHAT DO YOU THINK?

Persecution is often the result of prejudice. In what ways are prejudice and bias against Christianity still evident in today's culture? How should we respond?

WHAT DO YOU THINK?

In about A.D. 197, Tertullian said, "the blood of martyrs is the seed of [the church]." This means that when persecution comes, the church characteristically moves forward with growth and effectiveness. In what ways have you seen opposition result in the growth of the church?

HOW TO SAY IT

Abednego. Uh-BED-nee-go.

Annas. AN-nus.

Babylonian. Bab-ih-LOW-nee-uhn.

Caiaphas. KAY-uh-fus or KYE-uh-fus.

Goliath. Go-LYE-uth.

Josephus. Jo-SEE-fus.

Judas Iscariot. JOO-dus Iss-CARE-ee-ut.

Meshach. ME-shack.

Nazareth. NAZ-uh-reth.

Pentecost. PENT-ih-kost.

Pharisees. FAIR-ih-seez.

Sadducees. SAD-you-seez.

Shadrach. SHAY-drack or SHAD-rack.

Tertullian. Tur-TULL-yun.

changed by the truth as thousands already had been, they simply admitted that they could not deny that a miracle had happened—but they refused to believe that it had anything to do with Jesus (Acts 4:14-16). They were determined to stop the apostles from speaking further in that name (Acts 4:17).

The apostles, though, said that they would never stop speaking about what they had witnessed (Acts 4:20). This caused a dilemma for the authorities. They wanted to punish them, but they were afraid of the people. Unable to agree on the form of punishment, they tried to frighten them with threats before releasing them (Acts 4:21).

As soon as they are released, the two men report to their fellow believers what had happened. The most appropriate thing that they can do at this point is to pray, which they do *together*. They begin by acknowledging God as the one who is the great creator of the universe (Genesis 1:1). In the midst of persecution it is important to remember that God is the one with supreme power and authority.

B. GOD'S WORD (vv. 25, 26)

25, 26. *"You spoke by the Holy Spirit through the mouth of your servant, our father David:*

> *"'Why do the nations rage*
> *and the peoples plot in vain?*
> *The kings of the earth take their stand*
> *and the rulers gather together*
> *against the Lord*
> *and against his Anointed One.'*

The first two verses of Psalm 2, written by *David*, are quoted. Earlier, Peter had referred to David as a prophet who predicted Jesus' resurrection (Acts 2:25-31). The second psalm is one of the most important prophecies of the messianic work of Jesus because it predicts his persecution, resurrection, and glorification. The early church often referred to this psalm (see Acts 13:32, 33; Hebrews 1:5; 5:5; Revelation 2:27). The phrase *take their stand* brings to mind how Goliath stood to defy God's people (1 Samuel 17:8). He learned the hard way that God does not take such insolence lightly.

C. GOD'S PURPOSE (vv. 27, 28)

27, 28. *"Indeed Herod and Pontius Pilate met together with the Gentiles and the people of Israel in this city to conspire against your holy servant Jesus, whom you anointed. They did what your power and will had decided beforehand should happen.*

The identity of those mentioned in verses 25 and 26 is now revealed. The Gentile rulers include the Roman governor *Pilate*, under whose orders Jesus was tortured and crucified mercilessly. *The people* include Israelites, led by King *Herod*, who shared in the responsibility for Jesus' death. They had dared to do these things to God's *holy servant Jesus*.

Nothing is outside God's knowledge or authority. God had already revealed the suffering of the Messiah by David one thousand years before it happened. God also revealed it by other prophets such as Isaiah, who prophesied over seven centuries before Jesus' death. It was God's predetermined counsel that the Messiah must suffer (Luke 9:22). Jesus could not save humanity from sin unless he took the punishment of sins upon himself. His suffering paid the price that God had set for sin's punishment. This is what purchases our salvation for eternity.

THE POWER OF CONFIDENCE

Several Hollywood personalities have proclaimed boldly their faith in Scientology. On the other hand, few show-business personalities are known for their faith in Christ. For many, God simply is not part of their lives. This fact was indicated clearly in a recent article in the *Los Angeles Times Magazine.* One "romantic leading man" said, "I don't know if I believe in God." A well-known character actor said (somewhat wistfully, it would seem), "I don't believe in God now. I can still work up an envy for someone who has faith. I can see how that could be a deeply soothing experience."

Further, an actress famed for her role in Star Wars (her Web site unabashedly labels her "a cultural icon") said, "I love the idea of God, but it's not stylistically the way I function." Another leading lady puts it this way: "I like all religions, but only parts of them."

Does anyone see a common denominator in these statements? Could it be that when people are idolized by the public, they begin to believe their press notices and thus have no room in their lives for the real God? Think of how different Peter and John were: they had seen God at work in Christ and in their lives. As a result, they had absolute confidence in God's ability to protect them in the present and to shape their future. This kind of confidence gives hope!   —C. R. B.

III. FEARLESS DETERMINATION (ACTS 4:29-31)

A. DETERMINED IN SPITE OF THREATS (v. 29)

29. "Now, Lord, consider their threats and enable your servants to speak your word with great boldness.

The apostles are determined now more than ever to continue preaching the good news of Jesus Christ. One of the remarkable parts of this story is how the apostles do not pray that persecution might end. They realize that persecution can end only if God's people end their witness. Only when the church no longer presents Jesus as Savior will the church cease to be persecuted.

The apostles know that they must continue preaching the gospel, so they ask that God would make them bold. Peter has no desire to cower in fear as he once did when he denied even knowing Jesus (Matthew 26:69-75; John 20:19). The apostles leave the persecutors in God's hands. The apostles intend to continue doing God's will.

B. DETERMINED TO SHOW GOD'S POWER (v. 30)

30. "Stretch out your hand to heal and perform miraculous signs and wonders through the name of your holy servant Jesus."

The apostles also request that God's mighty *hand* continue to work through them. This again acknowledges that the power does not come from themselves. If miracles are accomplished, it is God at work. They pray that other miracles may be performed as *signs* pointing people to Jesus and as *wonders* causing people to be amazed at the power of his *name.* These miracles are not mere acts of kindness to people who need physical healing. These miracles have a much larger purpose: they establish the truth of the gospel.

C. DETERMINED TO PREACH GOD'S WORD (v. 31)

31. After they prayed, the place where they were meeting was shaken. And they were all filled with the Holy Spirit and spoke the word of God boldly.

God responds to the prayer in a mighty way when the house shakes as though moved by an earthquake (compare Exodus 19:18; Isaiah 6:4). Those present are again *filled with the Holy Spirit* as on the Day of Pentecost. The Holy Spirit mani-

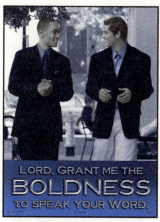

Visual for Lesson 4. *Refer to this photograph as you introduce the next question below.*

WHAT DO YOU THINK?

Boldness was a mark of the first-century church. In what ways will our boldness be similar to and different from the boldness of first-century believers? What is the difference between boldness and foolhardiness?

WHAT DO YOU THINK?

The role of the Holy Spirit is much debated today. How should we express our understanding of the Word of God in this regard? When do our attempts at dialogue on the role of the Holy Spirit do more harm than good?

PRAYER

Father, many are lost and are dead in sin. Make us bold so that we will proclaim your Son as the Savior of the world. May our friends and neighbors know of the power in Jesus' name to forgive and to save and to give hope. Give [list a specific name], who serves in a dangerous area of the world, boldness to preach Jesus. In Jesus' powerful name, amen!

THOUGHT TO REMEMBER

"I have chosen you out of the world. That is why the world hates you" (John 15:19).

fests himself in such a way that the apostles are assured that God loves them and wants to help them. This causes them to go out into the world with renewed confidence. It is God who gives them the boldness that they requested in verse 29.

SHAKING THE HOUSE

The United States of America of the early 1800s was an irreligious nation in certain ways. Christians found themselves disenchanted with the rigid control of the faith by professional clergy and how the church had divided into warring sects. But a movement was under way that would shake the house of American religious expression. Its effects are seen to this very day. It was called the Second Great Awakening, lasting from the 1790s to the 1840s.

The tone of the change that was underway was set a half-century earlier by Samuel Davies in the original Great Awakening, perhaps dated from the 1730s to the 1770s. In one sermon Davies called Christians to unity: "My brethren, I would now warn you against this wretched, mischievous spirit of party. . . . A Christian! A Christian! Let that be your highest distinction!"

As in apostolic times, when the followers of Christ have followed courageously, prayed fervently, and spoken boldly, God has "shaken the house" and changed the world. We must pray that God will do it again . . . and again!   —C. R. B.

CONCLUSION

God's people must be bold. God told Joshua to be strong and courageous as a leader of God's people (Joshua 1:6, 7). Shadrach, Meshach, and Abednego, Daniel's friends, courageously obeyed God's Word even though it meant being thrown alive into a furnace of fire (Daniel 3). David testified that even if an army attacked him he would not fear (Psalm 27:3).

Christians must be courageous as we live in this world. The Word of God encourages us not to be frightened by those who oppose us, but to stand united in defense of the faith (Philippians 1:27, 28).

The apostle Peter is the one we see speaking in today's lesson. He will come to experience much persecution over several decades of ministry. Toward the end of his life, he can still challenge us to refuse to conform to the evil desires of the world and to fear no one but God. The world may think it strange that we do not live immoral lives as they do. They may even heap abuse on us, but we still courageously live lives that please God (1 Peter 1:13-16; 4:2-5).

The Word of God encourages us to live boldly as strangers in this world, living such good lives among the pagans that they will see our good deeds and glorify God (1 Peter 2:9-12). We remember that even if we suffer for doing what is good, we must not be afraid because God will bless us (1 Peter 3:13-15).

We also remember the bold example of Jesus, who refused to speak evil of those who mistreated him (1 Peter 2:21-23). We can rejoice when we are insulted because of the name of Christ. God is pleased when we face persecution boldly and continue to do good (1 Peter 4:12-19).

The apostle John was Peter's companion before the Sanhedrin. While exiled on Patmos years later, he encouraged the church not to fear suffering (Revelation 2:10). Yes, persecution is real to every believer. No one knew this better than Paul: "Everyone who wants to live a godly life in Christ Jesus will be persecuted" (2 Timothy 3:12). Jesus warned, "If they persecuted me, they will persecute you also" (John 15:20). But let us never forget that like the apostles we can, "approach the throne of grace with confidence, so that we may receive mercy and find grace to help us in our time of need" (Hebrews 4:16). Let us pray for boldness that Jesus Christ will be exalted.

Discovery Learning

This page contains an alternative lesson plan emphasizing learning activities. Classes desiring such student involvement will find these suggestions helpful. The next page is a reproducible activity page to further enhance discovery learning.

LEARNING GOALS

After participating in this lesson, each student will:

1. Retell Peter and John's bold proclamation of the gospel in spite of persecution.

2. Discuss the depth of the apostles' faith in relation to their boldness.

3. Write a prayer asking God for boldness in witnessing for Jesus.

INTO THE LESSON

Display the following on the board as class begins. Use a two-column format: Key Words and Verses. Under the Key Words heading have these three scrambled words: *bdlo, aeeflrss,* and *cdefinnoti;* under the Verses heading, have Acts 4:1-4; Acts 4:23-28; and Acts 4:29-31. After the words are deciphered (*bold, fearless,* and *confident*), ask, "Is this the order in which these three characteristics arise? Or should the order be different? That is, does boldness precede confidence and confidence precede fearlessness? Or is another sequence more accurate?"

Let your class discuss and decide. You may want to add the other words of the lesson outline: bold witness, confident attitude, and fearless determination.

INTO THE WORD

Form three discussion groups and give them the following directions.

Group One: Read Acts 4:1-4 and answer the following: Acts 2 describes a large assembly in the temple area in which Jesus was preached as the Christ without opposition; why would the religious leaders react so swiftly and violently on the occasion in Acts 4? How do you suppose the witnesses of Peter and John's arrests reacted? Why would the temple leaders put Peter and John in prison and delay a trial simply because it was late in the day? Didn't they try Jesus at night?

Group Two: Skim Acts 4:5-22, which is not part of today's text. Answer the following: What was the gist of Peter's address to the Jewish leaders? Why did the leaders put Peter, John, and the healed man out of the assembly before deliberating? Why did they let them go?

Group Three: Read Acts 4:23-31 and answer the following. Why would the Christians recite the story of Jesus' arrest and condemnation in their prayer? What elements of their prayer do you find worthy of imitation in contemporary Christians' prayers?

Allow time for reading and discussion. Then ask group representatives to answer their questions for all.

Say to your class, "The incident in Acts 4 notes things that still are opposed strongly around the world. What 'controversial' issues are included in the text that even today are considered 'fighting words'?"

If the class is slow to respond, ask, "What is there in verse 2 that continues to elicit denials and even anger?" (The answer is that in Jesus there is resurrection from the dead.) If the group needs further help, ask, "What is it in verse 27 that stirs anger, and even violence, as seen in Mel Gibson's film on the death of Christ?" (The answer deals with who were responsible for having Jesus killed. Verse 27 rightly includes all who are a party to the sin.) Your class may well see and highlight other doctrines that face almost immediate and constant attack.

(For an alternative, have three groups complete the "Praying a Psalm, Matching a Psalm" activity on the reproducible page, then compare answers.)

INTO LIFE

Note that one secret of the early church's success in prayer was that they "raised their voices together in prayer to God" (v. 24). The unity of purpose and desire is critical. Have your class stand around the room in a circle holding hands as a reflection of the unity you have in Christ. Distribute to volunteers the following short, single-sentence prayers, to be said aloud in any order: "Make us one, Lord"; "Give us boldness, Lord"; "You are God, O Lord"; "See our enemies, Lord"; "Help us speak, Lord"; "Shake us, Lord, from lethargy"; "Fill us with the Spirit, Lord"; "Take our fears, Lord"; "Deepen our faith, Lord."

Distribute copies of the following self-rating scale that uses the lesson writer's outline. (This in included in the student book.) Indicate to learners that they should respond to each statement with *always, usually, most of the time, occasionally,* or *never.* "In matters of my faith in Jesus Christ, (1) I make a bold witness; (2) I have a confident attitude; (3) I have fearless determination." Along this same line, you can pass out the "A Question of Boldness" activity on the reproducible page for students to work through personally outside of class.

Praying a Psalm, Matching a Psalm

Acts 4:24 reports that the Christians who had gathered together prayed when they heard the thrilling story of Peter and John's release by the Sanhedrin. They used a psalm of David in their prayer. Match the following occasions with a psalm that could be appropriate in a prayer for God's help in each situation. (Answers are at the bottom.)

PSALM	OCCASION
1	___ 1. When materialism threatens to lure you in
8	___ 2. When you feel like God is not there for you
13	___ 3. When ungodly friends keep pestering you to join them in sin
22	___ 4. When you find yourself neglecting time spent in studying God's Word
73	___ 5. When a bickering group to which you belong comes together in unity
119	___ 6. When you feel the comforting presence of God and his strength
133	___ 7. When you feel like coworkers or others are "out to get you"
140	___ 8. When you are feeling rather small in the grand scheme of things

A Question of Boldness

Would you consider the contemporary church to be bold or timid? How can any timidity be explained?

What about your own personal approach to the world as a person of faith? Where on this continuum would you place yourself?

TIMID————————————————————————————BOLD

What commitment will you boldly make to move yourself closer to the *bold* end?

Psalm matching answers: 1. 73; 2. 22; 3. 1; 4. 119; 5. 133; 6. 13; 7. 140; 8. 8

STEPHEN IS FAITHFUL TO THE END

LESSON 5

WHY TEACH THIS LESSON?

While on the surface it might look discouraging to read about a faithful Christian dying unjustly at the hands of a violent mob, the value of today's lesson is actually encouragement. In *The Hiding Place*, Nazi concentration camp survivor Corrie ten Boom recalls words of comfort her father taught her.

"Corrie . . . when you and I go to Amsterdam—when do I give you the ticket?"

"Why, just before we get on the train."

"Exactly. And our wise Father in Heaven knows when we're going to need things, too. Don't run out ahead of him, Corrie. When the time comes that some of us will have to die, you will look into your heart and find the strength you need—just in time."

Stephen's legacy to us is assurance that God will give us what we need to remain faithful to him—even in death. We may wonder, sitting untested in times of calm, how we would stand up to the pressure of persecution. Stephen shows us how to be bold. God will empower us to do any task he calls us to.

INTRODUCTION

A. HANDLING THE HARDSHIPS

Stories abound of people who face hardships in life. Sometimes we wonder how we would hold up if life delivered some of the catastrophic blows that some people must handle. We eagerly listen to some hint of the source of their strength and then ask whether we have developed this in ourselves.

Max Cleland led a typical all-American life in high school, starring in sports and receiving the title of most outstanding senior. At the age of 24 he volunteered for combat duty in Vietnam. Just one month before returning home, Cleland discovered a grenade that had been dropped accidentally. Moving quickly to snatch it away, he was thrown backward by its explosion. He looked down to find his right hand and right leg missing and his left leg badly mangled. When Cleland recovered from his triple amputation, he recalled two things: the apostle Paul had said that hope "does not disappoint us" (Romans 5:5), and General George S. Patton, Jr. had said, "Success is how high you bounce when you hit bottom."

So when Cleland returned to civilian life, he entered politics, learned to drive a car specially equipped for him, and traveled extensively to mobilize support for veterans' causes. At age 34 he became the youngest man ever to head the Veterans Administration. Later he was elected to be a senator from Georgia. Max Cleland summarizes his experience this way: "Life doesn't revolve around an arm and a leg. People look at you the way you look at yourself."

Today's lesson presents a servant of God who faced a catastrophic blow as well. It was a blow that led directly to his death. The story of God's servants is

DEVOTIONAL READING:
ISAIAH 6:1-8

BACKGROUND SCRIPTURE:
ACTS 6:8–7:60

PRINTED TEXT:
ACTS 6:8-15; 7:54-60

Oct
2

LESSON AIMS

After participating in this lesson, each student will be able to:

1. Describe the stoning of Stephen and the events that led up to it.

2. Contrast the fearful retreat of some Christians with the courageous leadership of Stephen.

3. Write a eulogy for Stephen based on the text.

KEY VERSE

Stephen, a man full of God's grace and power, did great wonders and miraculous signs among the people.
—Acts 6:8

stained with the blood of prophets and apostles who paid the price for speaking the truth, and today's lesson presents this reality in especially vivid detail. The story is not a pretty one, but one that Bible students need to face squarely because the days of persecution for believers are not over.

B. Lesson Background

The book of Acts begins the story of the earliest church by focusing on developments within Jerusalem. The theme of "witnesses in Jerusalem, and in all Judea and Samaria, and to the ends of the earth" (Acts 1:8) demands that this book present a sketch of the activities of the Jerusalem church. So the narrative begins with events that occurred on the Day of Pentecost (Acts 2:1-41), providing plenty of information regarding the power behind this dynamic Jerusalem fellowship.

Then in chapters 3 through 5 of Acts come snapshots of the ministry of the Jerusalem church. These focus especially on the powerful actions of God and the way the apostles used those events to proclaim Christ.

Acts 6 begins with a description of the necessity of choosing those of Greek background to serve in the Jerusalem church (Acts 6:1-7). In the process we see two dynamic preachers of the gospel whose ministries Luke (the author of the book of Acts) describes in some detail. These preachers are Stephen (6:8–8:3) and Philip (8:4-40). Stephen's preaching leads to his execution at the hands of the Sanhedrin, establishing him as the first martyr for Christ on record. Philip's willingness to preach the gospel leads him to great success among the Samaritans and to the inquisitive traveler from Ethiopia (next two lessons).

In the book of Acts, the inspired author carefully documents how the first preachers of the gospel, whether apostles or servants in the Jerusalem church, faced their opponents and problems with courage. They refused to compromise the truth about Jesus Christ.

I. POWER AND OPPOSITION (ACTS 6:8-15)

The book of Acts introduced Stephen in 6:3, 5 as one chosen by the Jerusalem church to "wait on tables" (v. 2). Acts now continues the focus on Stephen by describing his ministry as a preacher of the gospel.

A. Ministry of Power (v. 8)
8. Now Stephen, a man full of God's grace and power, did great wonders and miraculous signs among the people.

Stephen is obviously *a man* who has God's full approval. For the first time in the book of Acts, we see *great wonders and miraculous signs* performed by someone who is not an apostle. The miracles probably consist of healing and exorcisms (see Acts 3:1-10; 5:14-16). Perhaps the laying on of the apostles' hands conveys this *power* (see Acts 6:6). Stephen's miraculous ministry is not one of self-promotion. Rather, Hebrews 2:3, 4 notes that miracles were performed by the apostles and earliest Christian preachers as a way of confirming the truth of the gospel. Modern examples of healers or miracle workers who seem to seek personal profit from their "power" demonstrate that they do not understand a ministry like Stephen's.

B. Source of Opposition (vv. 9, 10)
9. Opposition arose, however, from members of the Synagogue of the Freedmen (as it was called)—Jews of Cyrene and Alexandria as well as the provinces of Cilicia and Asia. These men began to argue with Stephen,

How to Say It

Alexandrians. Al-ex-AN-dree-unz.

blasphemous. BLAS-fuh-mus.

Cilicia. Sih-LISH-i-uh.

Cyrene. Sigh-REE-nee.

Ethiopia. E-thee-O-pee-uh.

Jerusalem. Juh-ROO-suh-lem.

Leviticus. Leh-VIT-ih-kus.

Pentecost. PENT-ih-kost.

Pharisees. FAIR-ih-seez.

Sadducees. SAD-you-seez.

Samaritans. Suh-MARE-uh-tunz.

Sanhedrin. SAN-huh-drun or San-HEED-run.

synagogue. SIN-uh-gog.

Now for the first time in the book of Acts we see *opposition* to the gospel coming from a source other than the Sanhedrin, though the source is still a Jewish one. *The Synagogue of the Freedmen* describes a Jewish house of worship composed of former slaves, or descendants of slaves, who had been liberated from their bondage. Freedmen are plentiful in the Roman world, and they come from every nationality. These freedmen are *Jews* who had once lived in *Cyrene* or *Alexandria* in northern Africa, as well as the provinces of *Cilicia and Asia.* The apostle Paul himself could have participated in this synagogue because he was a Jew from Cilicia (Acts 22:3).

Whether more than one synagogue is in view here is a matter of some debate. In any case, the dispute *with Stephen* may have started with the point that his ministry is being conducted in the name of Jesus Christ. The Jewish leadership in Jerusalem does not want the believers teaching in that name (see Acts 4:17).

10. . . . but they could not stand up against his wisdom or the Spirit by whom he spoke.

Stephen was recognized previously in Acts 6:3 as one "full of the Spirit and wisdom." Whatever arguments Stephen's critics try, they are unable to dislodge him from the truth of Christ. This is true both in terms of his accuracy in using Old Testament reflections on the Messiah as well as in the power of his words, as will be seen in Acts 7. Truth is its own defense. Believers who exemplify Christ in their lives and speak the truth accurately will be powerful witnesses for the Lord.

C. CHARGE OF BLASPHEMY (vv. 11-14)

11. Then they secretly persuaded some men to say, "We have heard Stephen speak words of blasphemy against Moses and against God."

When Stephen's antagonists cannot overturn his arguments, they resort to falsehoods. The foundational accusation is that Stephen's words contradict both *Moses* and *God.* Since the Law of Moses was given by God, these charges easily could have centered on Jewish institutions sanctioned in the Law of Moses and, therefore, inspired by God. The word *blasphemy* in a Jewish context makes the guilty person worthy of death (compare Leviticus 24:16; Matthew 26:62-66). Yet Stephen continues to perform his ministry without flinching, knowing that the critics are accusing him of speaking *against God.*

12. So they stirred up the people and the elders and the teachers of the law. They seized Stephen and brought him before the Sanhedrin.

The Sanhedrin, composed of 71 members, represented both the Sadducees and the Pharisees, two major parties within Judaism. Jerusalem is the council's seat of power, not only in religious matters but also in civil affairs. The council exercises its power under the watchful eye of Rome. Some of the members of the Sanhedrin hearing the case against Stephen undoubtedly were also present at the hearing of Jesus.

13. They produced false witnesses, who testified, "This fellow never stops speaking against this holy place and against the law.

False witnesses are set forward in order to seal Stephen's condemnation. Just as in the trial of Jesus, those witnesses who testify against him are interested primarily in twisting his words rather than quoting him fairly (see Matthew 26:60). Now their charges take on a more specific reference than in Acts 6:11. The phrase *this holy place* is a reference to the place where they are hearing the charges. The Sanhedrin meets in court session in the temple complex, so this charge from the false witnesses involves accusations that Stephen is speaking against the temple of God.

WHAT DO YOU THINK?

Stephen's testimony was one that could not be refuted. How can we witness in such a way today? Why is it important to do so?

WHAT DO YOU THINK?

The first-century enemies of the gospel did all they could to undermine the integrity of the people of God. In what ways have you seen people discredited today? Why is this done?

Visual for Lesson 5. *This collage can be a discussion starter on things that challenge our faithfulness.*

Threats against sacred sites can draw the death penalty in the Greco-Roman world. This was equally true for the Jews of Old Testament times (see Jeremiah 26:1-11). In addition, the Old Testament law of God provided for animal sacrifices, so anything Stephen said about Christ as the perfect sacrifice (compare Hebrews 9:13-28) could be twisted to mean that Stephen is undermining God's law.

14. "For we have heard him say that this Jesus of Nazareth will destroy this place and change the customs Moses handed down to us."

The Sanhedrin protects the temple, and the party of the Sadducees provides most of the leadership that operates that facility. To do away with the temple would mean doing away with their professions. In John 11:48 we heard the Sanhedrin members say of Jesus, "If we let him go on like this, . . . the Romans will come and take away both our place and nation." In that passage, *place* can refer to the temple. The temple is the engine that drives the economy of Judea. It supplies jobs for thousands of construction workers, priests, and attendants. Thus the misguided Sanhedrin probably is not trying to protect the religion of Israel as much as it is protecting its own economic security. The charge of changing *the customs Moses handed down to us* is similar to the accusation against Paul in Acts 21:21.

D. DEMEANOR OF AN ANGEL (v. 15)

15. All who were sitting in the Sanhedrin looked intently at Stephen, and they saw that his face was like the face of an angel.

Stephen's fearless *face* exhibits something like one who had been in the presence of God—as in the case of angels. Without a doubt, this servant of God demonstrates a courage that would be impossible without help from the Lord. God is powerful in this man's life, and his fortitude before the authorities proves it.

How many modern "heroes of the faith" can we name today? How many believers are standing courageously against those who want to stop the preaching of the gospel? We hear stories about persecuted Christians in a variety of countries around the world. Even in our own culture there are those who suffer for their testimony. This reality will be with us as long as people walk in the darkness and do not want to hear the truth because their deeds are evil (John 3:19).

II. TESTIMONY AND TORMENT (ACTS 7:54-58)

Acts 7:1-53 (not in our text for today) describes in detail Stephen's lengthy address to the Sanhedrin. In his review of Old Testament history, Stephen does not introduce any new facts. But in selecting the accounts that he does, he demonstrates a long history of Jewish rebellion against the will of God. He also demonstrates the important point that God does not require a sacred place, like the temple, for relating to his people (Acts 7:48).

A. FURY OF THE SANHEDRIN (v. 54)

54. When they heard this, they were furious and gnashed their teeth at him.

This Sanhedrin might be called a particularly bloodthirsty one. Not only had they crucified Jesus, they had also punished the apostles (Acts 5:17-40). Now this same body is ready to deal a crushing blow to the ministry of Stephen. The members of the Sanhedrin are *furious,* and they demonstrate this with *their teeth*—perhaps by grinding them together in some visible or audible way. Compare Psalm 37:12.

B. VISION OF GLORY (vv. 55, 56)

55, 56. But Stephen, full of the Holy Spirit, looked up to heaven and saw the glory of God, and Jesus standing at the right hand of God. "Look," he said, "I see heaven open and the Son of Man standing at the right hand of God."

Stephen does not throw insults at his accusers, but turns his gaze heavenward. As he does, he catches a heavenly vision of the Lord *Jesus* Christ. He is not sitting at the right hand of God, as is usually the description (see Matthew 26:64; Mark 16:19; Luke 22:69), but is *standing at the right hand of God.* Perhaps he is standing to welcome the first Christian martyr. Perhaps he is standing to fulfill the image in Daniel 7:9-16 of the one standing in the presence of the Ancient of Days.

Whatever the case, this is a heavenly vision brought to Stephen at the very moment of his fatal torment. It echoes the heavenly encouragement often delivered to saints at the moment of their trials (see Acts 4:31; 22:17-21; 23:11; 27:23-26). As Peter's confession of Christ was revealed to him by the Father (Matthew 16:16, 17), so Stephen confesses because of what is revealed to him. He can do so because he is *full of the Holy Spirit,* while those who torment him are full of the rage of the evil one.

This statement of Stephen serves as a confession of faith. In seeing Jesus standing at the right hand of God, Stephen uses the words *Son of Man* to describe him. This is the same phrase Jesus used to describe himself so often (example: Mark 8:31). It is a title that can be traced to Daniel 7:13, 14. Note also that in Acts 7:59 (below), Stephen identifies the Lord as Jesus.

C. ACTION OF MOB (vv. 57, 58)

57, 58. At this they covered their ears and, yelling at the top of their voices, they all rushed at him, dragged him out of the city and began to stone him. Meanwhile, the witnesses laid their clothes at the feet of a young man named Saul.

The sentence of death is passed upon Stephen without the benefit of a fair trial. The Sanhedrin takes into its own hands the administration of capital punishment, a penalty that is reserved for the Romans to carry out (compare John 18:31). In the case of Stephen, the council members are too furious to worry about the rule of law. They are in "lynching mode" now. Luke (the author of the book of Acts) is careful to note the presence of *Saul,* a fact that Saul himself (renamed Paul) will point out as he speaks to a crowd in Acts 22:20.

WHEN THE TRUTH HURTS

For more than a half-century, critics of the Roman Catholic church have claimed that the pope and the church aided the Nazi extermination of six million Jews during World War II. That church has denied vociferously those claims. However, the Roman Catholic church backtracked somewhat in 1998 when the Vatican published a document entitled, "We Remember: A Reflection on the Shoah." (The word *Shoah* means "horror" and is the Hebrew word for the Holocaust.)

The Vatican admitted that the document was an "act of repentance." It confessed "the errors and failures of . . . sons and daughters of the Church" that contributed to the Holocaust. Although expressing the church's "deep sorrow for the failures of her sons and daughters in every age," the paper stopped short of criticizing the actions (or inactions) of church officials.

Of course, it is always easy to look back and say, "This is what should have happened." But it is hard to admit one's sins, and the frequent reaction to unsettling truth is equivocation or even outright denial. The knife-edge of truth cut Stephen's persecutors to their hearts and enraged them to the point of murder. How do we react when the truth "finds us out"?

—C. R. B.

III. PRAYER AND DEATH (ACTS 7:59, 60)

With his last words, Stephen does not accuse his tormentors. Instead, he prays for them.

A. APPEAL TO JESUS, PART 1 (v. 59)

59. While they were stoning him, Stephen prayed, "Lord Jesus, receive my spirit."

This is a prayer of faith, uttered with Stephen's dying breath. Even as the stones are crushing the life from him, he places his destiny in the hands of God. As he does, he prays just as Jesus did from the cross—that God would receive his spirit (Luke 23:46).

B. APPEAL TO JESUS, PART 2 (v. 60)

60. Then he fell on his knees and cried out, "Lord, do not hold this sin against them." When he had said this, he fell asleep.

Stephen's final words are for his tormentors, just as was true of Jesus, who asked his Father to forgive those who were crucifying him (Luke 23:34). The courage to suffer such persecution without becoming angry toward those who are bringing the suffering is quite amazing. Think about how often we have turned to vengeance for lesser offenses!

When Stephen refuses to condemn his enemies, he demonstrates a heart filled with the grace of God. It is a heart driven by faithfulness to God's cause. The book of Acts describes his death in the same way that other New Testament verses describe death for the Christian—like falling asleep (see 1 Thessalonians 4:13-18). Like sleep, it is temporary. Stephen knows where his eternal home is.

"FRAMING" ONE'S RESPONSE

An original, early 1900s gilded picture frame by Herman Dudley Murphy is worth more than $250,000—for a picture frame measuring only 3 by 4 feet! A simple nineteenth-century frame of 5 by 5 inches recently sold for $1,500. Edouard Manet (ed-WARD mah-NAY), the nineteenth-century French impressionist painter, once said, "Without the proper frame, the artist loses 100 percent." He was saying that even a great painting is diminished significantly if it is not viewed in the context of the proper frame. To make the point, an expert on the Antiques Roadshow TV program described putting an 1890s portrait in a 1960s-era frame "like dressing up a pig in a tutu."

Think of the "spiritual frame" in which Stephen places his death as the first Christian martyr. Where have we previously heard the sentiments of his dying prayer? Faced with the worst his tormentors could do to him, Stephen "framed" his response to their evil actions in the dying words of his Lord.

His thoughts are in keeping with Jesus' instructions in the Sermon on the Mount: rather than returning "an eye for an eye," demonstrate the presence of God in your heart by an attitude of forgiveness. Stephen's example shows us how to put a frame of Christlikeness around our lives and thus increase the value or our witness immensely!

—C. R. B.

CONCLUSION

Like Stephen, there are courageous servants of God today who stand up and speak the truth even when the pressure is against them. In some countries Christians are targeted because they are not in the majority, and they pay a heavy price for their faith. In other cultures there are believers who take courageous positions for Christ at work and in the home. Let us be sure to honor those whose testimonies for Christ cost them so much.

Discovery Learning

*This page contains an alternative lesson plan emphasizing learning activities. Classes
desiring such student involvement will find these suggestions helpful. The next page
is a reproducible activity page to further enhance discovery learning.*

LEARNING GOALS

After participating in this lesson, each student will be able to:

1. Describe the stoning of Stephen and the events that led up to it.

2. Contrast the fearful retreat of some Christians with the courageous leadership of Stephen.

3. Write a eulogy for Stephen based on the text.

INTO THE LESSON

As students arrive, hand them each a small rock. As class begins, ask this simple question: "What can you do with a rock?" Expect such answers as "Build with it"; "Throw it into a stream to splash"; "Use it as decoration in a flower bed"; "Put it in a fish tank"; "Pave a dirt road or path with it"; "Mix it with other materials to make concrete."

If no one suggests, "Stone someone with it," then bridge to today's study by saying, "There is one other use for a rock prescribed in the Old Testament: stone some-one to death with it. That is the use we see in today's text when Stephen is martyred by angry listeners."

INTO THE WORD

Because this is a lesson in which truth meets opposi-tion and lies, use the following true-false quiz (included in the student book) to draw attention to the printed text. Answers and explanations are in parentheses.

1. Until the incident in today's text, Stephen had had a quiet ministry among the Christians. (*False; he was busy doing "great wonders and miraculous signs."*)

2. Stephen's initial opposition came from the temple leaders. (*False; his disputers and accusers were from a par-ticular synagogue, the Freedmen.*)

3. Unable to resist the wisdom of his words, Stephen's accusers had to agree they were true. (*False; they were not able to dissuade him by argument, but they re-fused to believe his affirmations about Jesus.*)

4. The men from the synagogue decided to find false witnesses to indict Stephen. (*True; v. 11.*)

5. Stephen's accusers charged him with blasphemy against Moses, against God, against the temple, and against the Law. (*True; vv. 11, 13.*)

6. Stephen was hunted down, manhandled, and dragged off to the Sanhedrin. (*True; after hearing Stephen,*

the men from the synagogue stirred up common people, the Jewish elders, and the teachers of the law—they forced him to appear before the Sanhedrin. See v. 12.)

7. For a second time, Stephen's accusers used false witnesses against him. (*True; vv. 11, 13.*)

8. The foundational accusation against Stephen was that he was claiming Jesus was the Christ. (*False; their charge reflects the false indictment of Jesus that he would de-stroy the temple [see Matthew 26:61] and that he was going to change Moses' Law.*)

9. Stephen's face glowed, as did Moses' face after Sinai as recorded in Exodus 34:29-35. (*True, although there is no such comparison in the text.*)

10. The decision to kill Stephen was purely a logical and legal one: blasphemers were to be killed. (*False; the decision appears to have been made in a jealous and emo-tional rage [see v. 54], although Leviticus 24:11-16 did pre-scribe stoning for blasphemy.*)

11. Stephen is the only person in the Bible said to have been able to look into Heaven itself. (*False; see Isa-iah 6 and Revelation 1 for two other examples.*)

12. Without approval of the Roman authorities, the Jewish leaders pushed Stephen violently outside the temple and city and stoned him. (*True; Stephen's murder was done in a blind rage, so no thought of proper authority was even considered.*)

13. Stephen died in anticipation of being with Jesus and with forgiveness on his lips. (*True; see vv. 59, 60. This is a model for any who serve Jesus.*)

(For an alternative, make copies of the "Truth, Oppo-sition, Consequences" exercise from the reproducible page for students to work on in small groups.)

INTO LIFE

See if your church office or local Christian bookstore can provide you bulletins designed for a funeral. Give each learner one (or simply a piece of paper folded) and give this direction: "You have been asked to deliver the eulogy for Stephen's funeral as held by the Jerusalem Christians. Put your notes of what you want to say into this memorial bulletin."

After a bit of time, ask class members to read their eu-logies. The exercise entitled "The Best Way to Die" from the reproducible page can be a thoughtful lead-in for writing and delivering the eulogies, time permitting.

Truth, Opposition, Consequences

Stephen's story is a common one: truth meets opposition and the consequences can be deadly. Connect two letters from the two columns below and write a word to the right that is a factor in or consequence of the fatal battle between truth and falsehood. An example would be <u>S</u>A<u>T</u>AN, using the S from the first column and the T from the second column.

```
T          O
R          P
U          P          _____
T          O
H          S          _____
M          I
E          T          _____
E          I
T          O          _____
S          N
                      _____
```

The Best Way to Die

In Acts 7:59, 60, Stephen demonstrates the best way to die. It has two components. One has to do with personal hope. The other has to do with personal grace. Fill in the two statements here:

"Lord Jesus, _____ _____ _____."
　　　　　　　(a belief in eternity)

"Lord, do not _____ _____ _____ _____ _____."
　　　　　　　(a character of forgiveness)

Do I share Stephen's doctrine and maturity? Where do I need to improve in either matter?

PHILIP PREACHES IN SAMARIA

WHY TEACH THIS LESSON?

When you pick up the phone to call for technical support for your computer, you may find that the person on the other end is in India. When you check your e-mail, you may find a message from a person who lives across the ocean. Stopping at a restaurant or bank may put you in touch with people from a different nation and culture, some of whom may have had little or no exposure to the gospel message.

When you meet such folks, it is all too easy to assume that those who sound or look a certain way are Muslims, Buddhists, etc. Some of them may indeed be adherents to such false religions. But people can change! Today's lesson shows a people who had been impressed by a magician, but recognized a greater power working through Philip. Like Philip, we are to share the good news with those who have been exposed to false ideas, praying that they will recognize the truth.

INTRODUCTION

A. TAKING CHRIST WHERE PEOPLE ARE

An astute observation (attributed to George MacLeod) puts a lot of things in perspective: "I simply argue that the cross be raised again at the center of the marketplace as well as on the steeple of the church. I am recovering the claim that Jesus was not crucified in a cathedral between two candles, but on a cross between two thieves; on the town garbage heap; at a crossroad so cosmopolitan that they had to write his title in Hebrew and in Latin and in Greek . . . and at the kind of place where cynics talk smut, and thieves curse, and soldiers gamble. Because that is where he died. And that is what he died about. And that is where churchmen ought to be, and what churchmen ought to be about."

What this writer says reminds us that we have work to do for Christ. This is a work that emphasizes content over cosmetics and Christ over self. It is a work that takes the gospel beyond the church walls rather than simply being contained within them. It is a work that may be uncomfortable. In today's lesson Philip shows us that we should take up this work regardless of how uncomfortable it may be.

B. LESSON BACKGROUND

Last week we studied the martyrdom of Stephen. That event unleashed a tidal wave of persecution upon the Jerusalem church (Acts 8:1). Jerusalem believers were scattered everywhere like seed borne on the wind, many of them traveling north to cities such as Tyre, Damascus, and Antioch. Those Christians were not safe anywhere they went, because Saul began tearing the church apart. Distant cities were within his reach (Acts 8:3).

Nevertheless, the book of Acts makes clear that these believers left their homes, carrying the gospel wherever they went. As a result, the areas north of Jerusalem began to hear the gospel. New converts began showing up in every city.

DEVOTIONAL READING:
ACTS 19:1-10
BACKGROUND SCRIPTURE:
ACTS 8:4-25
PRINTED TEXT:
ACTS 8:4-17

LESSON AIMS

Oct 9

After participating in this lesson, each student will be able to:

1. Summarize Philip's ministry in Samaria.

2. Explain how Philip helped break down cultural barriers by preaching to the Samaritans.

3. Support his or her church's efforts at cross-cultural evangelism.

KEY VERSE

When the apostles in Jerusalem heard that Samaria had accepted the word of God, they sent Peter and John to them.
—Acts 8:14

LESSON 6 NOTES

WHAT DO YOU THINK?

Being "scattered" means that the Christians of the early church were willing to suffer persecution for their faith in order to continue to proclaim the gospel. What does this say about the trustworthiness of the gospel? How should this affect our stand for the gospel today?

DAILY BIBLE READINGS

Monday, Oct. 3—Jesus Teaches in Judea (Matthew 19: 1-12)

Tuesday, Oct. 4—Healing in Jericho (Matthew 20:29-34)

Wednesday, Oct. 5—Zacchaeus Welcomes Jesus (Luke 19:1-10)

Thursday, Oct. 6—Jesus Meets a Samaritan Woman (John 4:1-10)

Friday, Oct. 7—Water Gushing Up to Eternal Life (John 4:11-15)

Saturday, Oct. 8—Philip Preaches in Samaria (Acts 8: 4-13)

Sunday, Oct. 9—Peter and John Preach in Samaria (Acts 8:14-25)

I. MINISTRY OF PHILIP (ACTS 8:4-8)

A. PROCLAMATION (vv. 4, 5)

4. Those who had been scattered preached the word wherever they went.

Stephen's ministry continued the theme of "witnesses in Jerusalem" (Acts 1:8). Now Luke (the author of the book of Acts) shows us how the gospel begins to spread like ripples in a pond. Jesus' command to be witnesses "in all Judea and Samaria" (again, 1:8) is thus being fulfilled.

The word is a reference to the gospel of Jesus Christ (see Acts 6:4; 16:6; 2 Corinthians 4:2). In a Jewish context, the idea is one of explaining from the Old Testament Scriptures that the Christ had to suffer and rise from the dead (compare Acts 17:3).

Philip has been mentioned already in Acts 6:5. His preaching enables the Samaritans to understand Christ as sent by God in fulfillment of Old Testament prophecies. As the believers scatter outward from Jerusalem, they take with them this good news about Jesus Christ to whomever will listen.

A CHURCH ON THE MOVE

The first European settlers in North America could have dreamed neither of how vast the continent was nor of how their descendants would move ever westward. The U.S. Census Bureau keeps track of this migration in America, and every 10 years announces the hypothetical "human center of gravity" of the nation.

In 1790 that population center was Chestertown, Maryland. The center has been moving in a westerly direction ever since. By 1890 the center was Greensburg, Indiana. By 2000 it was in Edgar Springs, Missouri, about 100 miles southwest of St. Louis, where the Jefferson National Expansion Memorial commemorates the historic migration. The memorial and its Gateway Arch symbolize the city's role as "Gateway to the West" in the days following the Louisiana Purchase during Thomas Jefferson's presidency.

The first Christians could not have known it at the time, but Philip's mission to Samaria would start a massive shift in the church's "population center." Lacking perspective, some probably took a dim view of extending the gospel to Samaritans and Gentiles. Others, however, rejoiced. Today, Christianity's population center is shifting from the northern hemisphere to the southern, where eager ears are hearing the gospel gladly. God moves to where people seek him. Like those first Christians, we can resist or we can rejoice. Which will it be?   —C. R. B.

5. Philip went down to a city in Samaria and proclaimed the Christ there.

Philip conducts his ministry outward from Jerusalem. The land where the Samaritans live originally had rested squarely in the middle of the tribes of Israel in Old Testament times. When the Assyrians invaded and took captive great portions of the Israelite population in 722 B.C., *Samaria* was left desolate. The few Jews who were left behind in Samaria struggled against the pressures to blend with their neighbors. Ultimately, intermarriage diminished the distinctive Jewish identity of much of this population (2 Kings 17). Beyond this, the Samaritans constructed their own rival temple at Mount Gerizim (see John 4:20).

The Jewish religious leadership in Jerusalem accused the Samaritans of losing their faith, and, as a result, a level of hatred grew. This hatred sometimes moved Samaritans and Judean Jews to separate themselves from one another (see John 4:9). It is to these despised neighbors to the north that Philip travels to preach the gospel.

We aren't really certain which *city in Samaria* is in mind here. Some possibilities include Sebaste, Gitta, Sychar, or the old capital city of Shechem. No one knows for sure. In any case, Philip's ministry takes him to a territory and a people despised by the Jews in Jerusalem.

Today's lesson finds in Philip's ministry to the Samaritans an example of how we are to share the gospel beyond our own borders. His willingness to travel to Samaria with the gospel of Christ inspires us to carry the same gospel to parts of our world that we may find uncomfortable. How will we answer the call of Christ to be witnesses to the Samaritans in our world?

B. RESULT (vv. 6-8)

6. When the crowds heard Philip and saw the miraculous signs he did, they all paid close attention to what he said.

Here the book of Acts speaks of *miraculous signs* and preaching in a way that reveals the connection between them. Miracles are intended to draw attention to the message of Christ (compare John 14:11). The Samaritans see the miracles in Philip's ministry, and this causes them to take seriously his preaching. The wording indicates their authentic response to the truth of Christ, as they give heed to what they hear. Their response to the Word is more than just a passing, superficial attention, such as may be true of mere entertainment. They are serious in attending to the demands of Philip's message.

7. With shrieks, evil spirits came out of many, and many paralytics and cripples were healed.

The powerful miracles consist of healings and exorcisms, as is true elsewhere in Acts (see 5:16; 19:11-19). The presence of *evil spirits* is mentioned frequently in the Gospels and Acts, and the reality of the spirit world should not surprise us. Paul writes that our struggle is "not against flesh and blood, but against the rulers, against the authorities, against the powers of this dark world and against the spiritual forces of evil in the heavenly realms" (Ephesians 6:12). Modern Christians must deal with the reality of Satan and his power, whether this power is demonstrated in overt demonic activity or in more subtle forms of temptation to sin.

8. So there was great joy in that city.

This *joy* is the outcome of the acceptance by the Samaritans of the Word of Christ brought by Philip. The book of Acts frequently notes the joy and gladness that come with salvation through Christ (see 2:46; 8:39; 13:48). Sharing the good news means sharing a joy that will never fade away.

II. CONVERSION OF SIMON (ACTS 8:9-13)

A. SIMON'S REPUTATION (vv. 9-11)

9, 10. Now for some time a man named Simon had practiced sorcery in the city and amazed all the people of Samaria. He boasted that he was someone great and all the people, both high and low, gave him their attention and exclaimed, "This man is the divine power known as the Great Power."

This certain *man, named Simon,* is a person who uses some kind of *sorcery,* or magic, to boost his own reputation. He is at the point where people refer to him as *someone great* or even a *divine power.* And he obviously welcomes the adulation.

In the ancient world, sorcerers usually employ various magical arts such as astrology, divination, incantations, and potions for practicing their "profession." In the Old Testament, God expressly forbade such practices (see Leviticus 19:26; Deuteronomy 18:10, 14; 2 Kings 17:17; 21:6). Even so, sorcery was common among pagans (see Exodus 7:11; Daniel 2:2). Later in Acts will come a reference

WHAT DO YOU THINK?

Though we may not be able to perform miracles to gain a hearing, what are some things that Christians can do today to be an influence?

WHAT DO YOU THINK?

Where the work of God is done and the Word is proclaimed, joy results. How is the joy in your church? How is the joy in your life?

to another magician named Bar-Jesus or Elymas (Acts 13:6-12), but unlike here that case is cast in a negative light.

11. They followed him because he had amazed them for a long time with his magic.

It seems that Simon has retained sole possession of the stage in Samaria for quite some *time*. His impact is probably felt at all levels of that society. So the book of Acts records the face-off between the ministry of Philip and the influence of Simon. What happens when the gospel is carried to cultures where lesser religious powers are served? Will the Samaritan people stick with Simon, or will they now follow Christ?

B. SIMON ABANDONED (v. 12)

12. But when they believed Philip as he preached the good news of the kingdom of God and the name of Jesus Christ, they were baptized, both men and women.

Philip's preaching reaches through the haze of Simon's deception. As a result, *both men and women* believe the message of Christ and accept the invitation to be *baptized*. This statement demonstrates that the gospel of Jesus Christ conquers the powers of evil and falsehood when it is *preached* truthfully. Acts 19:14-16 will show, on the other hand, what can happen when the gospel is preached falsely. Our text shows clearly that the Samaritans respond with authentic faith when they hear the news of Jesus Christ. This point is important for what follows.

C. SIMON BELIEVES (v. 13)

13. Simon himself believed and was baptized. And he followed Philip everywhere, astonished by the great signs and miracles he saw.

The ultimate victory comes when *Simon himself* accepts the gospel message and submits to baptism. Luke (the author of Acts) uses the same language of conversion that is seen elsewhere. On the Day of Pentecost, for example, Peter told the audience to repent and be baptized, and the text follows with the news that about 3,000 were indeed baptized (Acts 2:38-41). In the same way, Simon *believed and was baptized;* his new faith then moves him to support the ministry of *Philip*. There apparently is no such thing as an "unbaptized Christian" in the first-century church.

WHAT DO YOU THINK?

Those won to the gospel in the New Testament era often came out of very pagan backgrounds. How can the church today affect a pagan culture for Christ? Which things are primary, and which are secondary? Why?

III. MINISTRY OF PETER AND JOHN (ACTS 8:14-17)

A. NEWS SPREADS (v. 14)

14. When the apostles in Jerusalem heard that Samaria had accepted the word of God, they sent Peter and John to them.

Reports of conversions in *Samaria* come as wonderful news. This story would make headlines today. In Jerusalem there must be amazement and perhaps even some skepticism. So the apostles in Jerusalem respond immediately. Their decision is to send *Peter and John* northward to see the situation with their own eyes.

B. PRAYER OFFERED (vv. 15, 16)

15. When they arrived, they prayed for them that they might receive the Holy Spirit,

The apostles' first action upon arrival is prayer. They need to make sure that the new believers receive the same gift of *the Holy Spirit* that was bestowed on the Day of Pentecost.

This language about receiving the Holy Spirit is surprising on the surface because earlier in Acts the preaching of Peter connects the reception of the Holy Spirit with baptism (Acts 2:38). The Samaritans had not only believed, but they also had been baptized. Their conversion looks authentic in light of the language of Acts (see comments above at 8:6), so why have they not yet received the Holy Spirit? And what does this account imply about the reception of the Holy Spirit today? One thing that should be noticed immediately is that the reception of the Spirit is connected here with prayer. Prayer is linked elsewhere with the authentic conversion of a person to Christ (see Acts 9:11; 10:2).

16. . . . *because the Holy Spirit had not yet come upon any of them; they had simply been baptized into the name of the Lord Jesus.*

This parenthetical verse begins to offer an explanation for the absence of *the Holy Spirit* with regard to the Samaritans after their baptism. To take this verse to mean that they were baptized improperly creates a problem since the baptism of the Samaritans in *the name of the Lord Jesus* matches the plea "be baptized . . . in the name of Jesus Christ" in Acts 2:38. We must read the next verse to move toward a solution.

C. HOLY SPIRIT RECEIVED (v. 17)

17. *Then Peter and John placed their hands on them, and they received the Holy Spirit.*

The Samaritans had not *received the Holy Spirit* because they simply had been baptized, rather than being baptized and having the apostles' hands laid on them. When this is accomplished, they do indeed receive the Holy Spirit.

But this verse raises an important question: Why is the laying on of the apostles' *hands* required for receiving the Holy Spirit in this case while there is no mention of the same thing on the Day of Pentecost? This is a difficult question and several answers have been proposed. Some argue that the Holy Spirit's coming is unpredictable and that in the case of the Samaritans (and later the Ephesian believers—see Acts 19:1-6), the laying on of an apostle's hands is necessary for unknown reasons.

Another theory proposes that the laying on of the apostles' hands isn't for the indwelling of the Holy Spirit that all Christians receive, but is for bestowal of certain spiritual gifts, such as speaking in tongues. This theory is tied in with what Simon sees and how he reacts in Acts 8:18-24. When he sees the result of the laying on of the apostles' hands, he is impressed sufficiently that he wants to pay money to have the same power (v. 18). It's not that he wants the Holy Spirit to dwell within him (so the theory goes), but rather he wants the ability to lay hands on people and have them receive the visible signs of the Spirit's presence in terms of miraculous spiritual gifts. Thus when the text comments that the Samaritans only had been baptized (v. 16), the meaning under this theory is that without the laying on of the apostles' hands they could not receive the miraculous gifts from the Spirit.

Yet another idea says that the key lies in the religious and cultural differences between Samaritans and Jews. Perhaps the Samaritans were willing to give Philip a fair hearing because he was a Grecian Jew (see Acts 6:1, 5) rather one of the "pure blood" Jews that the Samaritans despise. Under this theory, the Samaritans are thus willing to accept Philip's message, but they also need to see that "salvation is from the Jews" (John 4:22); this requires Peter and John—two "pure blood" Jews—to come and lay hands for receiving the Holy Spirit. Thus God in his wisdom provides both (1) a messenger whom the Samaritans will listen to (meaning Philip) and (2) a way for the Samaritans to see where salvation truly lies. One happy result should be that racial and cultural antagonism between Jewish Christians and Samaritan Christians would then disappear.

Visual for Lesson 6. *Use this chart to demonstrate that the book of Acts is a book about conversions.*

HOW TO SAY IT

Antioch. AN-tee-ock.

Assyrians. Uh-SEAR-e-unz.

Damascus. Duh-MASS-kus.

Elymas. EL-ih-mass.

Gerizim. GAIR-ih-zeem or Guh-RYE-zim.

Samaritans. Suh-MARE-uh-tunz.

Sebaste. Seh-BAS-tee.

Shechem. SHEE-kem or SHEK-em.

Sychar. SIGH-kar.

Tyre. Tire.

PRAYER

Lord of the nations, help us to remember that there are people of every race and culture who are ready to become your children. But they can do so only if we will take the gospel of salvation to them. We confess that we have not always had the heart to do this as we ought. May the Spirit give us such a heart today. We pray through Christ, amen.

THOUGHT TO REMEMBER

The gospel is meant for all the world, including those parts that do not look just like home.

WHAT DO YOU THINK?

What signs can indicate that someone in the church is seeking personal glory instead of God's glory? How do we keep from falling into this trap?

Whichever theory is best (even if it's a theory not mentioned here), our text highlights the unique role of the apostles. While they are alive, their function as representatives of Christ is crucial in many settings.

"SAY THE MAGIC WORD"

Parents often find they have difficulty getting their children to be polite. The basic niceties of society do not seem to come naturally to children. They must be coerced, instructed, and sometimes begged into doing and saying what will later be expected of them as civilized adults. "Please" and "thank you" are two phrases that most of us have found to be helpful in smoothing the occasionally rough waters of social discourse.

Some parents have found that getting a child to say "please" when asking for something comes easier when it is called a "magic word." So the phrase "say the magic word" becomes a frequent parental refrain until the "magic word" becomes a natural part of the child's vocabulary. Of course, the parent is speaking figuratively rather than of magic as we may normally think of it. Most children realize this, too.

But curiously, some Christians have fallen into the trap of thinking in terms of "magic words" when trying to solve the interpretation difficulty of verses 16 and 17, as noted above. Some Christians speculate that the new believers in Samaria had not been baptized "properly"—that is, without the "right words" having been said over them. Acts 2:38 calls for baptism in the name of Jesus Christ, and Matthew 28:19 calls for baptism in the name of "the Father and of the Son and of the Holy Spirit."

Quibbling about such variations in the words said at baptism misses the point. Paul does not say in Romans 6 that baptism's power lies in "saying the magic words," but in uniting our wills and spirits with the death and resurrection of Christ. No magic here! It is the power of God.   —C. R. B.

CONCLUSION

Philip's courageous trip to preach to the Samaritans opened doors for God's grace. When modern believers determine to preach the gospel beyond their own cultural borders, God is honored. Surprising results can come, as missionaries will attest. What mission fields are waiting for us to respond to today?

Whatever mission field God calls us to—whether it be a far-off land or our own places of work—we should not be surprised at setbacks. We see a setback in Acts 8:18-23, just after the close of today's text. There Simon was so impressed by what he saw that he wanted to pay money for the same power.

Simon's offer can be connected easily with his former profession as a sorcerer. His wish to captivate an audience surfaced again, and he could think of no better way to acquire the ability of Peter and John than to pay for it. The reception of the Spirit by his fellow Samaritans was connected with power. Thus Simon was moved somehow to make his unseemly offer.

Simon may have thought that he could pay for a trade secret, but the apostle Peter was not amused. Peter's subsequent curse on both Simon and his money amounts to some of the harshest words in Scripture: "May your money perish with you, because you thought you could buy the gift of God with money!" (Acts 8:20).

Without flinching, Peter then went on to cite the source of the problem: "your heart is not right before God" (v. 21). The problem of sin starts, as always, with the condition of the heart. It is an issue of standing in a right relationship with God.

Discovery Learning

This page contains an alternative lesson plan emphasizing learning activities. Classes desiring such student involvement will find these suggestions helpful. The next page is a reproducible activity page to further enhance discovery learning.

LEARNING GOALS

After participating in this lesson, each student will:

1. Summarize Philip's ministry in Samaria.

2. Explain how Philip helped break down cultural barriers by preaching to the Samaritans.

3. Support his or her church's efforts at cross-cultural evangelism.

INTO THE LESSON

Display five concentric circles labeled simply, "Moving Out." As class begins, write in each circle (beginning in the middle) one of the following words: *community, state, nation, continent,* and *world.* Ask the class to name a missionary or missions organization working in each of the places designated. Write in responses. When completed, say, "Today's text is a record of the church moving out just as Jesus had directed. The spread of the gospel had started in Jerusalem and Judea; now it's time for it to move out—out to Samaria."

A good map of New Testament Palestine will be very useful in this lesson. Display one, if available.

INTO THE WORD

Copy the following script for an "Interview with Simon of Samaria." Prior to class, recruit a volunteer to read the part of Simon. Ask the class to follow along in the text to distinguish which details are recorded in the biblical account and which ones are literary license.

Teacher (T in following): Simon, what was there about Philip's preaching of Christ that so appealed to you?

Simon (S in following): I must admit, the words kind of came and went, but when I saw the miracles he did—wow! They were the real deal.

T: Which miracles impressed you the most?

S: Compared with my tricks, all of them. But when I saw evil spirits running away and cursing, and when I saw people who couldn't walk made whole, I struggled to believe it. I am familiar with trickery, you know.

T: What was the general mood in your city?

S: Since the Romans arrived, there was a dark pall. But Philip brought a sunshine of the Spirit. Such joy!

T: Did you really have the people fooled?

S: Fooled? Oh, yes. They all thought I was someone great. They believed anything I said.

T: Why were you baptized, Simon?

S: Philip's message promised a new life. Honestly, I was tired of my old one—a life of deceit.

T: What was your impression of Peter and John when they arrived from Jerusalem?

S: They looked ordinary—Galileans, if my ear was correct. But they were far from ordinary. And their prayer was simple—a simple request for us to receive the Holy Spirit. God honored them. With a light touch of the hand, the Holy Spirit was given. What a gift!

[Optional: create additional script here for Acts 8:18-23, not in today's lesson text.]

T: It is good to see you today, Simon.

S: Let me ask your believers (turning to class) to pray for one another. All of us have sin in our hearts. We need one another.

INTO LIFE

Have a general class discussion about "sorcerers today." Ask these questions: (1) Who are individuals you would call "sorcerers of modern culture"? Why would you label them this way? (2) How do you explain the apparent abilities to act as spiritual mediums? (3) In what sense could these modern-day sorcerers be considered "seekers of truth"? How could such a person be approached with the truth of the gospel?

Ask the class to respond to the following characteristics to see if they are "Like Simon." (This activity is also in the student book.) Say, "Most of us resemble Simon of Samaria at different points in our lives. Respond to the following characteristics as a self-evaluation : pretending to be more than we are; accepting praise unworthily; using sin to get attention; hanging around with the 'popular crowd'; (the next are optional) expecting money to buy the most valuable things; being publicly humiliated by appropriate correction; hypocritically expressing faith.'" (If you prefer to have your students compare themselves to Philip instead of Simon, use the "Reasons Not To" exercise on the reproducible page.)

Return to the concentric circles idea used at the beginning of the lesson. Write in names of Christians whom your congregation or class supports who are working in each area. Ask volunteers to pray for each as they are written in. Use the "Reaching Hands" exercise on the reproducible page to stimulate discussion on how your church can reach those in these circles.

Reasons Not To

Many Christians seem to be looking for reasons not to "move out" in evangelism. Which of the following "reasons not to" could Philip have used when he came to Samaria (Acts 8)? Put a *P* next to reasons that Philip could have used. Which reasons have you used? Put an *I* next to these.

___ It's too risky. (My friend was just killed trying.)

___ These people don't deserve the gospel.

___ I'm an outsider; I don't even belong here.

___ The devil appears too strong here.

___ There are individuals who may resent my interference.

___ They already have their own beliefs and religions.

___ I'm by myself; the real leaders are back home.

___ What if someone sees only the financial advantages of godliness?

___ I'm not an apostle or preacher; I'm just a lowly servant.

___ What if the "wrong sorts" accept the gospel?

Reaching Hands

In which of the following cross-cultural evangelism opportunities do you think your congregation should be involved, if it is not so already?

___ Starting a worship service for a group of another language

___ "Mothering" a congregation in another cultural neighborhood

___ Sponsoring children of another culture for daily needs and Bible teaching

___ Distributing New Testaments in other languages

___ Committing to a series of short-term missions trips to another culture

___ Supporting a Christian family for ministry to another culture

___ Having a Christian from another culture serve on your church's staff for a year

___ Providing facilities for the teaching of another language to your members

___ Encouraging your high school seniors to consider cross-cultural mission work

___ Designing a hospitality program for international students in your community

Give your congregation a score of 10 points for each of the opportunities it now offers from the above list. Does it get a passing score? What recommendations could you make to your church's leadership? How can you help?

PHILIP TEACHES AN ETHIOPIAN

LESSON 7

WHY TEACH THIS LESSON?

Have you ever been making plans when you were interrupted by, well, life itself? Philip was intent on sharing God's message. But he obviously was busy doing something when God revealed unique plans for him. With God's redirection, he ended up running alongside a chariot—no small expenditure of effort and enthusiasm! Obedience was Philip's hallmark; fruitful witness followed.

It is unlikely that we will receive direct instructions from an angel as Philip did. But if we are ready and willing the share the Word with people, God will send seeking souls in our direction. Staying tuned to the gentle nudges of the Holy Spirit's call in this regard will take sensitivity and flexibility. We can learn from both Philip and Christians today who are open to God's "steering," no matter how it comes about.

INTRODUCTION

A. PERFECTLY QUOTED SCRIPTURE

Dave Veerman describes how his family determined to learn the Bible by memorizing one verse each week. His daughters were ages ten and six, so this pace seemed about right. Dave and his wife, Gail, kept the verses on cards where they could be easily seen, recited, and discussed. While at home one evening, the parents heard the girls fighting. One yelled, "I hate you!" and the other responded in a similar manner.

Dave relates that he did not wish to jump headlong into the fray, so he called one of his daughters by name and asked her what the verse was for the week. He hoped that the recitation of the verse in question would serve to quiet the fight by its implication.

Dave heard his daughter Kara promptly quote 1 John 4:11, which speaks of the importance of loving one another, but then the girls went right back to fighting. So Dave tried the same tactic with the other daughter, Dana. The results were the same. Before intervening personally, Dave and Gail couldn't help but laugh.

Human nature is fascinating, isn't it? The religious leaders of the first century A.D. knew the Old Testament Scripture inside out. They could quote it word for word and with passion. They believed it. Yet they were somehow unable to apply it as God intended. They didn't see how it applied to Jesus. As a result, those leaders killed Jesus and launched a persecution of the church. Yet God knows how to bring about the spread of the gospel in the midst of such an evil plan.

B. LESSON BACKGROUND

In Acts 6–8 the theme of witnesses in Jerusalem transforms into the theme of witnesses in all Judea and Samaria as the persecution breaks out (compare Acts

DEVOTIONAL READING:
ACTS 11:19-26
BACKGROUND SCRIPTURE:
ACTS 8:26-40
PRINTED TEXT:
ACTS 8:26-38

LESSON AIMS

After participating in this lesson, each student will be able to:

Oct
16

1. Retell how Philip used Scripture to teach the Ethiopian about Jesus.

2. Explain how Philip's use of the Old Testament is a model for us today.

3. List Scriptures that can be used to help someone make a decision for Christ.

KEY VERSE

Then Philip began with that very passage of Scripture and told him the good news about Jesus. —Acts 8:35

LESSON 7 NOTES

6:7 with 8:1). Stephen and Philip, two chosen in Acts 6:1-6 to serve, become key figures. Luke (the author of the book of Acts) depicts Stephen's ministry as resulting in a hearing before the Sanhedrin that leads to his martyrdom (6:8–8:1). Philip's ministry follows that tragedy and involves the conversion of the Samaritans (8:4-25). His witness to the Ethiopian official comes next (today's lesson).

Both Stephen and Philip faithfully proclaimed Christ wherever they went. Stephen's faithfulness ended in execution. Philip's faithfulness took him to witness to people of different cultures. God was glorified in both cases.

In this part of the record of Acts, events reveal a theme not reflected in the longer title *The Acts of the Apostles*. Stephen and Philip were not apostles at all. The Bible thus presents the diligent work of believers other than the apostles. As a matter of fact, the growth of the earliest church depended very much on non-apostles who took seriously their duty to preach Christ.

Today's lesson reminds us that we are the ones God desires to use for helping people come to understand salvation. Philip's example demonstrates that we should be ready with answers to the questions that lead to salvation.

I. PREACHING TO THE ETHIOPIAN (ACTS 8:26-29)

A. ANGELIC DIRECTIVE (v. 26)

26. *Now an angel of the Lord said to Philip, "Go south to the road—the desert road—that goes down from Jerusalem to Gaza."*

God clearly blessed Philip's preaching to the Samaritans (Acts 8:6). But *Philip* has more work to do as *an angel of the Lord* commands a journey southward. *The road* that leads *to Gaza* is not necessarily a *desert road* in the sense that it runs through sand dunes and sagebrush. The term speaks of the fact that the area is uninhabited.

B. ETHIOPIAN TRAVELING (vv. 27, 28)

27, 28. *So he started out, and on his way he met an Ethiopian eunuch, an important official in charge of all the treasury of Candace, queen of the Ethiopians. This man had gone to Jerusalem to worship and on his way home was sitting in his chariot reading the book of Isaiah the prophet.*

Philip's quick reaction to the divine commission is seen in the phrase *he started out*. Acts indicates more than once this kind of obedience to an opening for preaching (see 9:20; 16:10). This is as it should be. The response of any believer to the command of God to go and tell someone of Christ should be immediate and decisive. Even so, the Bible records instances of God's people hesitating at times (examples: Exodus 4:13; Acts 9:13, 14).

The person that Philip meets on the road is a man of Ethiopia. This location is in Africa, just south of Egypt, where there are large Jewish communities. It is not unreasonable to think of this man as being Jewish, returning to Ethiopia from *Jerusalem*, where he had worshiped at the temple. Eunuchs in the time of the apostles are officials in the palaces of kings and queens. Because most kings possess harems, male servants often were emasculated to prevent them from molesting the women in the royal entourage. In some situations, however, the term *eunuch* applies to officials regardless of their physical condition. If the term *eunuch* here indicates that this man carries the physical disability of his position when he travels to Jerusalem, then his condition carries with it some noticeable social barriers (see Deuteronomy 23:1). His role in the palace is under Queen *Candace*, a dynasty name that is transferred to several women who occupy the Ethiopian throne.

WHAT DO YOU THINK?

Whether it is Abraham, Jonah, or Philip, God is in the business of calling his people to arise and go. In what ways is God calling you as an individual to take his message into the world? How is God calling your church to go into the world?

WHAT DO YOU THINK?

Philip's response to God's command was immediate obedience. Often we fail to obey at once. Why are we often reluctant to go when God's call is clear?

This man's reading material that day is the Bible, and he has zeroed in on a passage from *the book of Isaiah*. Most likely this document is in scroll form. Since such scrolls are always copied laboriously by hand, they are expensive. Thus this *Ethiopian* is a man of some means.

C. SPIRIT'S COMMAND (v. 29)

29. The Spirit told Philip, "Go to that chariot and stay near it."

Philip receives guidance from God each step along the way, whether by an angel of the Lord or by the Holy *Spirit*. God's plan in evangelism is to bring the believer together with the unbeliever so that the gospel can be shared. Philip's role, as seen in the verses that follow, is to preach and teach Christ. And that is the role for believers today.

II. ANSWERING BIBLE QUESTIONS (ACTS 8:30-35)

A. PHILIP'S QUESTION (v. 30)

30. Then Philip ran up to the chariot and heard the man reading Isaiah the prophet. "Do you understand what you are reading?" Philip asked.

Philip's obedience to the command of God is evident again as he runs to the side of the Ethiopian. It is rare for a Jewish man to display such a lack of dignity, but nevertheless it is mentioned a few times in the Bible (see Luke 15:20; 19:4; 24:12). The Ethiopian is *reading* the prophet *Isaiah* with great interest. So *Philip* starts the conversation by asking him about what he is reading. What a perfect opening for sharing Christ!

Philip raises the same question that can be raised whenever we have the chance. A lot of people have Bible questions. Philip opens the conversation by asking if the Ethiopian understands what he is reading from Isaiah, a Bible book that can produce plenty of questions!

B. ETHIOPIAN'S INVITATION (v. 31)

31. "How can I," he said, "unless someone explains it to me?" So he invited Philip to come up and sit with him.

The Ethiopian official is puzzled about what he is reading and he is ready for some answers. Philip's question results in an invitation to come closer for a dialogue. Believers should prepare themselves for opportunities such as this one (see 1 Peter 3:15). Why should such a chance be missed because we are not ready?

C. ISAIAH'S PREDICTION (vv. 32, 33)

32, 33. The eunuch was reading this passage of Scripture:

> *"He was led like a sheep to the slaughter,*
>   *and as a lamb before the shearer is silent,*
>   *so he did not open his mouth.*
> *In his humiliation he was deprived of justice.*
>   *Who can speak of his descendants?*
>   *For his life was taken from the earth."*

At this point in the record of Acts, we learn exactly which passage from Isaiah is creating the questions for the Ethiopian. This quotation comes from Isaiah 53:7, 8 as found in the Septuagint (which is the Greek translation of the Hebrew Bible as produced in the two centuries preceding the birth of Christ). The New Testament writers often draw upon the Septuagint for quotations.

"Philip opened his mouth, and began at the same Scripture, and preached unto him Jesus" (Acts 8:35).

Visual for Lesson 7. *Use this artwork to remind your students of the church's main task.*

WHAT DO YOU THINK?

Being sent by God obviously requires some level of knowledge of the Word of God. What things should we know? Why?

HOW TO SAY IT

Azotus. Uh-ZO-tus.

Caesarea. Sess-uh-REE-uh.

Candace. CAN-duh-see.

Ethiopian. E-thee-O-pee-un.

eunuch. YOU-nick.

Isaiah. Eye-ZAY-uh.

Judea. Joo-DEE-uh.

Mediterranean. MED-uh-tuh-
     RAY-nee-un.

Philippian. Fih-LIP-ee-un.

Pilate. PIE-lut.

Samaria. Suh-MARE-ee-uh.

Samaritans. Suh-MARE-uh-
     tunz.

Sanhedrin. SAN-huh-drun or
     San-HEED-run.

Septuagint. Sep-TOO-ih-jent.

Thessalonians. THESS-uh-LO-
     nee-unz.

WHAT DO YOU THINK?

How can we be effective instruments of God as Philip was?

This section of Isaiah is part of the Servant Songs. Isaiah contains four of these songs in which the prophet describes a coming "servant of the Lord" who will represent the living God, but will be tormented for doing so. They are found in Isaiah 42:1-9; 49:1-13; 50:4-11; and 52:13–53:12.

The question that had intrigued godly people for centuries was the identity of the servant in these songs. Even among the ancient Jews there was a belief that these verses appear to describe the coming Messiah, although few could comprehend the idea of God's chosen One having to suffer. So the question of the Ethiopian is not surprising.

D. ETHIOPIAN'S QUESTION (v. 34)

34. The eunuch asked Philip, "Tell me, please, who is the prophet talking about, himself or someone else?"

The Ethiopian wants to know what nearly every Bible scholar wants to know: Is Isaiah describing *himself* in his ministry as a prophet of the Lord? Is he describing the nation of Israel, which is sometimes referred to as the Lord's servant (example: Isaiah 49:3)? Or is Isaiah describing the coming ministry of the Messiah?

The Ethiopian's request of *tell me, please,* conveys a certain intensity. Philip now has the perfect opportunity to speak the truth of God.

E. PHILIP'S RESPONSE (v. 35)

35. Then Philip began with that very passage of Scripture and told him the good news about Jesus.

Philip's answer to the Ethiopian's question is to instruct *about Jesus.* This, of course, tips off modern readers as to the identity of the servant in this passage from Isaiah. Philip's instruction undoubtedly informs the Ethiopian about the facts of Jesus' life, crucifixion, and resurrection. Judging from the other passages in Acts, the discussion probably includes details about Jesus' miracles, his innocence of wrongdoing, his hearings before the Sanhedrin and before Pilate, and his resurrection appearances (see Acts 2:22-33; 13:23-31).

These are the facts about the gospel of Christ that should be close to the heart and on the tip of the tongue of every Christian. These are the things we believe about Jesus, and because we believe we find salvation through him. How can we ever justify ourselves if we cannot inform people of at least this much when they ask us questions about the Bible?

DO YOU UNDERSTAND?

The National Institute for Literacy says that America has a higher percentage of illiterate adults than either Canada or several nations of Europe. More than 20 percent of American adults cannot read well enough to apply for a good job (or keep it if they get hired). These 45 million-or-so Americans are unable to read a children's story or help with their children's education.

As troubling as these statistics are, they pale in comparison with the problem of biblical illiteracy. A little over a year ago, a candidate for the U.S. presidency did what politicians often do: he tried to make voters think he was more religious than his off-the-campaign-trail behavior indicated. To validate his profession of "being religious," he named the book of Job as his favorite book in the New Testament! Perhaps he simply misspoke, but his gaffe is symptomatic of a problem in modern culture. This problem is particularly troubling within the church itself. What some politely call a "diversity" in doctrinal viewpoints among Christians is described more accurately as "a crisis of biblical illiteracy" (Barna Research, "Religious Beliefs Vary Widely by Denomination," June 25, 2001).

The Ethiopian's problem was not really one of illiteracy—scriptural or otherwise. As a Jew, he could read, and he knew the Scriptures to a point. What he needed was someone to help him understand the Scriptures beyond the confines of the Old Testament. Specifically, he needed to be able to identify himself with Israel's hope—the Messiah. Would you have been biblically literate enough to lead that man to Christ as Philip did?   —C. R. B.

III. RESPONDING TO THE GOSPEL (ACTS 8:36-38)

A. QUESTION ABOUT BAPTISM (v. 36)

36. As they traveled along the road, they came to some water and the eunuch said, "Look, here is water. Why shouldn't I be baptized?"

This verse surely implies that the instruction about Jesus to this point has included teaching about baptism as a response to the gospel message (see Acts 2:38; 22:16). Archaeologists have located a couple of places along this route where springs of water can be found. Thus it would not have been difficult for *the eunuch* to notice one of these and pose this question to Philip.

B. SUBMITTING TO BAPTISM (vv. 37, 38)

[37. Philip said, "If you believe with all your heart, you may." The eunuch answered, "I believe that Jesus Christ is the Son of God."]

You will notice that this verse is a footnote in the NIV.® That's because it does not appear in the earliest manuscripts. Nevertheless, it is safe to assume that Philip's preaching emphasizes the need for the Ethiopian to put his faith in *Christ,* just as is true in Paul's preaching (see Acts 16:31; 18:8).

38. And he gave orders to stop the chariot. Then both Philip and the eunuch went down into the water and Philip baptized him.

The language of the baptism implies immersion as the mode, since there would be no reason to go *down into the water* unless an immersion is intended. We should notice that baptism is presented here as elsewhere in the New Testament: it accompanies the faith of a person who has accepted the claims of Christ as being true. Notice that there is no hint of the need for a probationary period in which the believer is tested or trained prior to the baptism. Just as in the case of the Philippian jailer (Acts 16:33), the Ethiopian can be *baptized* immediately on the basis of his faith in Christ.

Every modern believer has the tools for witnessing as Philip does in this situation. The Bible offers all of the information about the ministry of Christ, how he suffered and died but rose on the third day to bring the hope of everlasting life. The Bible also provides the information needed for becoming a Christian. There is no reason for modern believers not to be as prepared as Philip when the opportunity comes to lead someone to Christ.

EXPECTED RESPONSE, EXPECTED SUBMISSION

What do we see while we stand in the checkout lane of our local grocery store? Racks of tabloids picturing the latest antics of the world's celebrities! On TV we see their fans follow them nearly everywhere, screaming and shrieking when they see their idols. It does seem almost idolatrous, doesn't it? Some may think this kind of attitude toward celebrities began with the fans of the Beatles or Elvis. Yet some of us remember when teenaged "bobby-soxers" swooned at the sight of the young Frank Sinatra!

Regardless of when the phenomenon began, it is now what we expect to see. For example, when a popular entertainer appeared in court a couple of years ago to

DAILY BIBLE READINGS

Monday, Oct. 10—Jesus Teaches About Responding to Others (Matthew 5:38-42)

Tuesday, Oct. 11—Jesus Teaches About Signs (Matthew 12:36-42)

Wednesday, Oct. 12—Jesus Teaches Nicodemus About Rebirth (John 3:1-15)

Thursday, Oct. 13—Jesus Rebukes the Pharisees and Scribes (Matthew 15:1-9)

Friday, Oct. 14—Jesus Asks the Pharisees a Question (Matthew 22:41-46)

Saturday, Oct. 15—Philip Meets the Ethiopian Official (Acts 8:26-31)

Sunday, Oct. 16—Philip Proclaims the Good News (Acts 8:32-40)

PRAYER

God of truth, make us bolder, we pray, to share the truth of salvation. You have revealed that truth to us, and we must share it. We pray in the name of the one who brought truth to light for all of us. In Jesus' name, amen.

WHAT DO YOU THINK?

After his baptism, the Ethiopian rejoiced (v. 39). Unfortunately, some Christians lose that initial joy of salvation. How can we maintain our joy?

THOUGHT TO REMEMBER

God will use you in his service to the extent that you have prepared yourself to be used.

enter his plea on a criminal charge, thousands of his fans gathered outside the courthouse. Some had been up all night in a bus convoy to be there for the occasion; others had even flown in from Japan and Europe! He did not disappoint them: after the hearing, he climbed atop his limousine and invited the screaming multitude to his nearby mansion for a celebration.

We worship the God of the universe, not entertainers. And yet the expected response to hearing the gospel is both calmer and more thoughtful. The book of Acts tells us of convert after convert who entered the waters of baptism in humble submission as God was working in their hearts. This is still the response that God expects of those who come to him in faith. —C. R. B.

CONCLUSION

As is true at the beginning of this narrative, the event closes with divine guidance: the baptism of the Ethiopian was followed by the Spirit of the Lord taking Philip away (Acts 8:39). Philip disappeared from sight.

The phrase *took Philip away* implies a supernatural action that removed Philip from the spot of the baptism. The Greek word for *took away* is the same word as found in 1 Thessalonians 4:17, where Paul writes that at the appearance of Christ the believers who are alive will be caught up together to meet the Lord in the air. In Philip's case, this is not some kind of "rapture," of course. But the snatching away was both sudden and miraculous. Perhaps the Ethiopian searched behind a sand dune or two, but Philip was gone just as suddenly as he had arrived.

Even so, the Ethiopian went on his way rejoicing (v. 39). This notation is the way that Acts refers to the commitment after the baptism. When people are converted to Christ, the book of Acts usually does not merely describe belief and baptism. A statement usually is supplied to show readiness to follow Christ after the baptism. In the case of the Ethiopian it is going his way rejoicing. In the case of the converts on the Day of Pentecost, "they devoted themselves to the apostles' teaching and to the fellowship, to the breaking of bread and to prayer" (Acts 2:42).

We may also think of Simon and Lydia. After Simon was converted to Christ, "he followed Philip everywhere, astonished by the great signs and miracles he saw" (Acts 8:13). After Lydia was converted to Christ, she invited the apostles to her home (Acts 16:15).

But the account before us also testifies to the fact that God was not finished with Philip's ministry. After disappearing from the side of the Ethiopian, Philip appeared at Azotus on the Mediterranean coast and then at Caesarea by the sea, King Herod's lavish city. Philip will not be mentioned again until Acts 21:8, some 20 years later, in the same city of Caesarea.

Philip's ministry gives modern Christians a reason to ask whether we have prepared ourselves for moments such as Philip faced. Have we learned enough about the life and ministry of Jesus that we could help lead someone to salvation? Are we prepared to speak to someone about how Jesus died on the cross, was buried in the tomb, and rose on the third day?

Safety officials often warn us that every family should prepare an exit strategy from their homes before a catastrophe occurs, because it is much too late to react when the crisis comes. By the same token, every believer should prepare a witnessing strategy for answering questions that may lead to salvation. We should learn what God's will is for sinners who ask, "what shall we do?" as was asked on the Day of Pentecost (Acts 2:37). We should be prepared to answer as the apostles answered such questions.

Discovery Learning

This page contains an alternative lesson plan emphasizing learning activities. Classes desiring such student involvement will find these suggestions helpful. The next page is a reproducible activity page to further enhance discovery learning.

LEARNING GOALS

After participating in this lesson, each student will be able to:

1. Retell how Philip used Scripture to teach the Ethiopian about Jesus.

2. Explain how Philip's use of the Old Testament is a model for us today.

3. List Scriptures that can be used to help someone make a decision for Christ.

INTO THE LESSON

Display a toy rubber duck sitting beside a clear glass bowl of water. As class begins, ask, "What old saying does this scene represent?" When someone suggests, "like a duck out of water," say, "Certain things belong together. A duck in the water is as happy as . . . well, a duck in the water. God knew that a traveling Ethiopian official and a certain Christian evangelist belonged together. He made the arrangements. Let's see the story in today's text in Acts 8."

INTO THE WORD

Call this activity, "Surprise or No Surprise." Give each learner a copy of the 11 statements below (which also appear in the student book) and ask them to decide if the truth in these statements is in any way surprising. Direct them to put surprise or no surprise before each statement and be prepared to give a rationale for their choices. (Some brief explanatory notes are given in parentheses after each statement.)

1. God knows the precise location of the Ethiopian official—in the desert. (*No surprise, for God knows all.*)

2. An Ethiopian has been to Jerusalem to worship. (*No surprise, for many Jews lived in North Africa, and perhaps this man was a convert.*)

3. An Ethiopian has a scroll of the book of Isaiah. (*Surprise, because such scrolls were rare and valuable. He may have purchased it for his queen.*)

4. A treasurer for the queen of Ethiopia can read the language of the scroll. (*No surprise; this was a Greek version of the Old Testament, and Greek was a nearly universal language among the educated.*)

5. A Jewish man runs to catch up with a traveler. (*Surprise, in that Jewish men generally would not run, considering it undignified; but no surprise in that Philip was

obeying God's specific command.*)

6. The Ethiopian official does not understand fully what he is reading. (*No surprise, for even Old Testament scholars debated the messianic passages—and still do!*)

7. Philip recognized what the man was reading as coming from the book of Isaiah. (*No surprise, for a devout Jew would be on very familiar terms with the writings of the Old Testament.*)

8. Isaiah pictured a Messiah who did not defend himself with power. (*No surprise to those of us who understand the nature of the Messiah from this side of the cross, but perhaps a big surprise to a Jew of the earlier era.*)

9. The travelers find water in a desert. (*No surprise; this desert place simply means uninhabited, and several seasonal streams flow from the hill country to the sea.*)

10. The official asks to be baptized. (*No surprise, for baptism is part of the gospel presentation in the book of Acts.*)

11. Philip baptizes the Ethiopian. (*No surprise, for that is part of what he was sent to do.*)

[Of course, students may have a different view on some of these; let them express their views and give their rationale.]

INTO LIFE

Establish two discussion groups and give each group one of the following two case studies to analyze.

Case #1. A stylist working on your hair has on the counter a book about angels. As she works, she says, "I'm just not sure whether that book is right about angels or not. Some of it is pretty weird stuff." What Bible texts and occasions would you suggest to identify revelation about angels and their ministry?

Case #2. A rider gets on the bus and seats himself beside you. He is reading one of the contemporary best-sellers on the end times. After you comment, he says, "This stuff is so strange—I wonder if any of it is true." What Bible texts do you refer to in response?

Allow time for groups to discuss their scenarios. Then ask each to read its case to the whole class and list their answers. You can enrich the discussion by giving each group a copy of the "The Evangelism Triangle" exercise (on the reproducible page) to consider alongside their cases. Distribute "Evangelism Heart" to students as they leave as a thinking exercise in the week ahead.

The Evangelism Triangle

On the simple map to the right, write in Jerusalem, Caesarea (which seems to be Philip's home base), and Gaza. Jerusalem represents the place of worship; Caesarea represents one's home; Gaza represents the place of daily affairs.

In the space to the left, draw in a triangle and label the three points *home, church,* and *opportunity.* Briefly describe how God calls you from your home and from church assemblies to meet others at the point of opportunity for evangelism.

Evangelism Heart

Read the statements below about the Christian's obligation to spread the gospel. How are you doing? For each statement give yourself a *5* if you are fully in line with the truth. Give yourself a *1* in areas where you need much improvement.

_____ 1. There is no reason for modern believers not to be prepared as Philip was to lead someone to Christ when the opportunity arises.

_____ 2. Believers should not miss a chance for evangelism because they have not studied their Bibles to have answers to Bible questions.

_____ 3. The growth of the church (both in the first century and in the twenty-first century) depends very much on ordinary believers who take seriously their duty to share Christ.

_____ 4. The response of any believer to the command of God to go and tell someone of Christ should be immediate and decisive.

_____ 5. Facts about the gospel should be close to the heart and on the tip of the tongue for every Christian.

You Will Be My Witnesses

Unit 2: In All Judea and Samaria

(Lessons 5-9)

GOD WELCOMES GENTILES

WHY TEACH THIS LESSON?

Occasionally we hear strong opinions about buying foreign products. Some people base their objections on bitter memories of hardships and atrocities from past wars. Others have strong feelings about possible loss of income or opportunity for themselves or for fellow citizens as jobs go overseas to foreign workers.

But are not all Christians "foreigners" in a very real sense? My daughter carries a "green card" from a recent youth convention. Those who live in the United States will recognize green card as describing a form of identification for people who live there but are not citizens. The "green card" my daughter carries is supposed to remind her that Christians are aliens here since we are citizens of a world not yet visible to us. Today's lesson should remind us that while there are nearly 200 independent sovereign states, over five dozen dependent areas, and six disputed territories in the world, there are but two kinds of people: those who have received God's grace through Christ and those who still need to.

God wants us to see every person from every nation as someone he loves. That makes our response clear: we are to view every person as someone who needs to hear of God's love personally. Cultural barriers can seem daunting, but love is stronger. Today's lesson should be a constant reminder of this fact.

INTRODUCTION

A. HEARTS FULL OF PREJUDICE

Daniel "Chappie" James, Jr. (1920–1978) was the first African-American to attain the rank of four-star general in the U.S. armed forces. There were many bumps along the way. At a speech given in Philadelphia in 1976, General James recalled a certain incident of racism in his life.

After being promoted to full colonel, James was wearing his military uniform with pride as he walked down a sidewalk in his hometown one day. Suddenly, two men confronted him and ripped the rank insignia from his shoulders. The men heaped verbal abuse on James, saying insulting and racist things. They told him that no person of his race could possibly be a colonel in the United States Air Force.

But America had looked past skin color in promoting James ever higher in rank. The fact is, James had done a superb job in position after position. He deserved his promotions on merit.

Many in our world still struggle to look past racial, ethnic, and cultural dividing lines. But God has no such difficulty. His impartiality is not based on our merit but is based on the fact that all humans are created in his image. Today's lesson shows how God sent the apostle Peter to offer salvation across the dividing line between Jew and Gentile—an unbridgeable chasm to the thinking of many in the first century. The courage of Peter's actions in preaching to Cornelius should guide us to consider our own behavior toward people of other cultural or racial backgrounds.

DEVOTIONAL READING:
ACTS 13:44-49

BACKGROUND SCRIPTURE:
ACTS 10:1-48

PRINTED TEXT:
ACTS 10:1-20

LESSON AIMS

After participating in this lesson, each student will be able to:

1. List the events leading up to Peter's visit with Cornelius.

2. Discuss the prejudices that Peter and Cornelius had to overcome.

3. Acknowledge a personal struggle with prejudice and determine one way to overcome it.

Oct 23

WHAT DO YOU THINK?

Why is prejudice so prevalent? What are some forms of prejudice that we need to be aware of?

KEY VERSE

While Peter was still thinking about the vision, the Spirit said to him, "Simon, three men are looking for you. So get up and go downstairs. Do not hesitate to go with them, for I have sent them."
—*Acts 10:19, 20*

LESSON 8 NOTES

WHAT DO YOU THINK?

Does God hear the prayers of lost (unsaved) people? Why, or why not? How can this text be used to help answer this question? [Consideration of Lamentations 3:44; James 4:3; and 1 Peter 3:7 may enrich your discussion.]

DAILY BIBLE READINGS

Monday, Oct. 17—Cornelius Has a Vision (Acts 10:1-8)

Tuesday, Oct. 18—Peter Has a Vision (Acts 10:9-16)

Wednesday, Oct. 19—Cornelius's Men Call on Peter (Acts 10:17-22)

Thursday, Oct. 20—Peter Visits Cornelius (Acts 10:23-33)

Friday, Oct. 21—Peter Shares the Good News (Acts 10:34-43)

Saturday, Oct. 22—Gentiles Receive the Holy Spirit (Acts 10:44-48)

Sunday, Oct. 23—Peter Explains How Gentiles Also Believed (Acts 11:1-15)

B. LESSON BACKGROUND

Jesus commissioned the apostles to be his witnesses "in Jerusalem, and in all Judea, and Samaria, and to the ends of the earth" (Acts 1:8). The first seven chapters of Acts describe the way that witness was presented in Jerusalem from events on the Day of Pentecost (chapter 2), to the healing of the man who was lame (chapter 3), to the ministries of Stephen (6:8–8:1) and Philip (8:4-40).

After the martyrdom of Stephen, the believers were scattered from Jerusalem, preaching the gospel wherever they went. Conversions of people to Christ are presented from both the Jerusalem period before the death of Stephen and the period afterward in which the witnesses go to all Judea and Samaria. The succession of converts includes people such as the Samaritans (8:4-25), the Ethiopian (8:26-40), and Saul of Tarsus (9:1-31). Human logic tells us that at least some of those included would be unlikely believers in Christ. But Acts 10 presents a convert much more unexpected.

Jews and Gentiles in the Roman world looked at each other with much suspicion. Gentiles found Jewish beliefs and customs to be confusing and narrow-minded, while Jews thought of Gentiles as pagan and immoral. Some Gentiles, however, became convinced that the God of the Jews was good and true. In some cases, these Gentiles converted to Judaism, becoming what was known as *proselytes*. The book of Acts mentions that the worshipers on the Day of Pentecost included such proselytes (2:11).

In other cases, Gentiles did not convert fully to Judaism, but engaged in worship with Jews and lived by many of the requirements of the Law of Moses. These worshipers were referred to as *God-fearers* and are also mentioned in Acts. When Paul stood to speak in the synagogue at Antioch of Pisidia, he directed his words to the "Men of Israel and you Gentiles who worship God" (13:16). When the missionary speakers began proclaiming the gospel of Christ, such synagogue worshipers were ripe for conversion to Christ.

One other factor that is essential for understanding the account about Cornelius is the political situation in Palestine. Rome ruled the Mediterranean area, but they did not consider Jerusalem to be the capital city of Judea. Instead, Caesarea Maritima (or "Caesarea by the sea") was where Roman rule was established, some sixty miles northwest of Jerusalem. (Note: This Caesarea is different from Caesarea Philippi, so don't get the two confused.)

I. VISION OF CORNELIUS (ACTS 10:1-8)

A. DEVOUT CORNELIUS (vv. 1, 2)

1. At Caesarea there was a man named Cornelius, a centurion in what was known as the Italian Regiment.

Cornelius has not been mentioned to this point in the book of Acts. Though nothing about the name itself is revealing, the mention of his home in *Caesarea* and his position as a *centurion* communicates to us that this man is a Gentile. Caesarea, a beautiful Gentile city, was rebuilt by Herod the Great from about 22 to 10 B.C. to honor Caesar Augustus.

A centurion commands a cohort, which is a subunit of a Roman legion. Legions consist of about 6,000 troops, and each centurion commands between 80 and 100 men. The *Italian Regiment* is a name that the soldiers use to describe this particular cohort, a practice not uncommon for Roman soldiers. Centurions are respected for their dedication to their responsibilities.

2. He and all his family were devout and God-fearing; he gave generously to those in need and prayed to God regularly.

The description of Cornelius now includes matters related to his spiritual life. Being *devout and God-fearing* suggests that he lives in a way that is consistent with the Law of Moses, even though he is not a full proselyte or convert. His charitable gifts and his prayer life show where his heart truly lies. His faith in God is not a selfish faith. Luke (the author of the book of Acts) describes other Gentiles in somewhat similar ways in Acts 13:50; 16:14; 17:4, 17; and 18:7.

B. HEAVENLY VISITOR (vv. 3-6)

3. One day at about three in the afternoon he had a vision. He distinctly saw an angel of God, who came to him and said, "Cornelius!"

Cornelius now experiences *a vision* from the Lord similar to such visions elsewhere in the Bible. The surprise in this, of course, is that Cornelius is a Gentile. The word *distinctly* describes how clear the vision is when Cornelius experiences it. *An angel of God* is evident enough that Cornelius cannot miss him.

The mention of the time *three in the afternoon* is important. It is at this same time that Peter and John were going to the temple in Acts 3:1. It is one of the three times of prayer in the temple: early morning, afternoon, and sunset. So Cornelius, the Gentile God-fearer, stands in God's presence in prayer (see Acts 10:30) at the same time of day that dedicated Jewish worshipers are in prayer as well.

4. Cornelius stared at him in fear. "What is it, Lord?" he asked.

The angel answered, "Your prayers and gifts to the poor have come up as a memorial offering before God.

Who cannot sympathize with *Cornelius* in his reaction of *fear* in seeing *the angel*? Fear is the reaction to an appearance of the heavenly visitors in several places in the Bible (examples: Matthew 28:5, 8; Luke 1:11, 12; 2:9).

In the midst of his fear, Cornelius expresses awareness that this is indeed no ordinary visitor. The angel himself confirms this in responding that *God* has taken note of Cornelius's *prayers and gifts to the poor*. The idea of a *memorial offering before God* is somewhat similar to wording in Leviticus 2:2 and Philippians 4:18. The sincere acts of devout truth-seekers such as Cornelius are not ignored in Heaven. His acts of faithfulness have found acceptance with God, who looks at the heart. Even with all of Cornelius's devotion, however, he still needs the salvation that only Christ can bring.

5, 6. "Now send men to Joppa to bring back a man named Simon who is called Peter. He is staying with Simon the tanner, whose house is by the sea."

Joppa is another coastline city, located about 30 miles to the south of Caesarea. Acts prepares us for this command from the angel by reporting at the end of Acts 9 that Peter had decided to stay with *Simon*, who is a *tanner* (9:43). A tanner works with animal skins for a living, so having a *house* that is *by the sea* serves as a help to the tanning process because of the water needed. Thus Peter is staying in a house where there will be constant exposure to the dead carcasses that Jews know will bring defilement (see Leviticus 11). Perhaps this environment helps to explain the content of the vision that God brings to Peter (see below).

When Peter retells this story later in Acts, he summarizes the words of the angel as telling Cornelius that Peter would bring "a message through which you and all your household will be saved" (Acts 11:14). As is true in the account of Philip and the Ethiopian (Acts 8:26-40), God's way of evangelism is to bring a human messenger into contact with the one who needs the message. Thus the angel, instead of bringing the message of salvation directly to Cornelius, commands him to send for Peter, who will bring the gospel message.

WHAT DO YOU THINK?

In ancient times as now, various religions of the world have specific times set aside for prayer. Is this important for modern Christians? Why, or why not?

[handwritten note:]
Prayer Time
1. Early morning
2. Afternoon 3pm
3. Sunset

HOW TO SAY IT

Antioch. AN-tee-ock.
Caesarea Maritima. Sess-uh-REE-uh Mar-uh-TEE-muh.
Caesarea Philippi. Sess-uh-REE-uh Fih-LIP-pie or FIL-ih-pie.
Cornelius. Cor-NEEL-yus.
Ethiopian. E-thee-O-pee-un.
Gentiles. JEN-tiles.
Jerusalem. Juh-ROO-suh-lem.
Leviticus. Leh-VIT-ih-kus.
Mediterranean. MED-uh-tuh-RAY-nee-un.
Philippians. Fih-LIP-ee-unz.
Pisidia. Pih-SID-ee-uh.
proselytes. PRAHSS-uh-lights.
Samaritans. Suh-MARE-uh-tunz.
synagogue. SIN-uh-gog.
Tarsus. TAR-sus.
Tyre. Tire.

This principle should guide our thinking today when it comes to evangelism. The church's mission should focus on sending messengers with the gospel, even to people of other races and cultures. See Matthew 28:19, 20.

HEARING VOICES

What are some of the symptoms of insanity? If you said "hearing voices," you have given a typical answer. "Hearing voices" is sometimes used as a defense in criminal cases in which the defendant claims to have heard a voice telling him or her to kill someone else.

Now a new invention can make us hear real voices in a unique way. It is an ultrasound device, able to send a focused beam of sound to a single person hundreds of feet away. The marketing industry is already rejoicing over the sales potential of the invention. A large discount store chain and a popular fast food outlet have begun testing the device. So if you hear a tiny voice whispering in your ear, "Buy Brand X coffee" or "Supersize your order," and no one around you hears it, relax. You are not going crazy!

Peter and Cornelius were neither insane nor "hearing voices." God sent a messenger to each of them so both sight and sound could confirm the message. Each of them saw, heard, and responded positively. We may never get a message in that same way, but God still speaks to us through his Holy Word, the Bible. When we open its pages and read, our response should be as positive and immediate as theirs.
—C. R. B.

C. RELAYED MESSAGE (vv. 7, 8)

7, 8. *When the angel who spoke to him had gone, Cornelius called two of his servants and a devout soldier who was one of his attendants. He told them everything that had happened and sent them to Joppa.*

And so the drama continues to unfold! For reasons unknown to us, the angel did not tell Cornelius to go to Joppa personally. Rather, Cornelius is to "send men" (v. 5), so that's exactly what he does.

II. VISION OF PETER (ACTS 10:9-16)

A. PRAYER, HUNGER, TRANCE (vv. 9, 10)

9, 10. *About noon the following day as they were on their journey and approaching the city, Peter went up on the roof to pray. He became hungry and wanted something to eat, and while the meal was being prepared, he fell into a trance.*

As the messengers from Cornelius travel on their day-long journey, *Peter* is exercising his faith just as Cornelius had. *Noon* is not a "normal" hour for prayer for Jews, but it shows us that Peter isn't locked into a ritualistic pattern for prayer.

Peter's choice of the rooftop for prayer reminds us of the flat-roofed structures of homes in that area. This place allows Peter *to pray* quietly with the benefit of cool breezes from the sea. But while waiting for *the meal* to be *prepared,* Peter falls into *a trance.* Thus the experience of Peter parallels that of Cornelius (see Acts 10:3, above). The will of God is to be once again revealed through a trance or a vision. Peter is about to be enlightened with regard to God's plan for Gentiles.

B. ANIMALS, REPTILES, BIRDS (vv. 11, 12)

11. *He saw heaven opened and something like a large sheet being let down to earth by its four corners.*

Peter's vision begins with the opening of *heaven,* an indication that the point of the trance will be a message from God. This point is emphasized in the direction from which the *large sheet* is coming, that is, *down* from Heaven to the *earth.*

WHAT DO YOU THINK?

Even today there can be a tendency to hold to legalistic righteousness. Why is there often a preference to hold to legalistic requirements instead of to the freedom found in Christ?

12. It contained all kinds of four-footed animals, as well as reptiles of the earth and birds of the air.

On the sheet is a multitude of various animals. They represent food to a hungry man. The designations *four-footed animals,* and *reptiles,* and *birds of the air* matches rather closely a similar description in Genesis 6:20.

C. COMMAND, REPLY, REBUKE (vv. 13-16)

13. Then a voice told him, "Get up, Peter. Kill and eat."

There is no mystery about the source of the *voice.* The opened heavens and direction of the sheet make clear that the voice is from the Lord. His voice comes to Peter as a command to *kill* one of these animals and prepare a meal.

14. "Surely not, Lord!" Peter replied. "I have never eaten anything impure or unclean."

Peter knows he is addressing the Lord, and his first words are a reaction to the thought of eating *unclean* animals. The Law of Moses divided animals into the categories of "clean" and "unclean." Leviticus 11 presents details about the distinction between these animals. That passage closes with the divine command that the people of God should not defile themselves with any of the unclean animals (11:43). Clean animals, as defined in that passage, are acceptable for eating and offering sacrifices to the Lord. This issue has nothing to do with hygiene. To eat unclean animals is to reject the authority of God and to make oneself defiled before him.

Peter's reaction is an honest one. He is horrified at the thought of making himself unclean before the Lord. He refuses to eat anything common in this regard. This reaction should be remembered not only in terms of Peter's sense of defiling himself, however, but also in Peter's sense of what Gentiles are doing to themselves when they eat unclean animals.

15, 16. The voice spoke to him a second time, "Do not call anything impure that God has made clean." This happened three times, and immediately the sheet was taken back to heaven.

With the *second* and third sound of the Lord's voice comes not only an emphasis of the original point, but an additional principle. This principle relates to food, but applies directly to Peter's views about Gentiles. God has cleansed animals, so Peter should stop thinking of them as unclean or *impure.* This same principle surfaces in Mark's Gospel. After Jesus declared all foods clean, the next event in Mark is the visit of Jesus to a Gentile woman in the vicinity of Tyre (Mark 7:19, 24-30).

Once the vision is completed, *the sheet* is taken up again into *heaven,* and this part of Peter's lesson is over. As events unfold, however, the point that the vision makes will not be lost on Peter. Later, in the home of Cornelius, Peter will say that he learned from the vision that he should not avoid contact with Gentiles because God does not show favoritism (Acts 10:34, 35).

III. COMMISSION FOR PETER (ACTS 10:17-20)

A. MEN INQUIRE (vv. 17, 18)

17, 18. While Peter was wondering about the meaning of the vision, the men sent by Cornelius found out where Simon's house was and stopped at the gate. They called out, asking if Simon who was known as Peter was staying there.

Full understanding does not come instantly for *Peter.* But notice how God has arranged the timing of things: he begins to provide the answer in the form of visitors from *Cornelius* at the very time when Peter is trying to comprehend the

WHAT DO YOU THINK?

As God called on Peter to lay aside his prejudices or biases, he calls upon all of us to do so as well. In what ways might God be calling on you to overcome your prejudices or biases today?

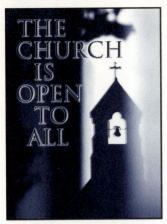

Visual for Lesson 8. *Start a discussion by turning this statement into a question: "Is our church open to all?"*

PRAYER

God of love and mercy, help us to reach those of every nation who need your saving grace. Encourage us to be ready for them with the gospel of Christ. Through Christ we pray, amen.

THOUGHT TO REMEMBER

We have no right to build smaller doors for the kingdom than God originally designed.

vision. The note that they are standing before *the gate* indicates a typical first-century courtyard.

B. SPIRIT DIRECTS (vv. 19, 20)

19, 20. While Peter was still thinking about the vision, the Spirit said to him, "Simon, three men are looking for you. So get up and go downstairs. Do not hesitate to go with them, for I have sent them."

Peter is still on the roof considering the meaning of *the vision* when the Lord steps in again. This time it is the voice of the Holy *Spirit* that tells Peter that the visitors are part of the divine plan. He is *to go with them* without question. To do so will mean that Peter is setting aside some of the ancient Jewish prohibitions against contact with Gentiles, as God intends. To go to Caesarea with these strangers will mean lodging in a Gentile home, and perhaps sitting down to a meal with Gentiles. Neither idea is appealing to a Jew who seeks to live according to the Law of Moses.

So it is that the voice of the Spirit interrupts Peter's thought process to send him to a destination where the gospel of Christ is needed. Peter needs to know that the journey ahead will come in connection with the mission of Christ. As is true in so many places in Acts, God directs his servant so that he comes into contact with those who need salvation (see Acts 8:26; 13:1-3; 16:9).

BREAKING TRADITION

What comes to mind when I say, "traditional wedding"? This will depend on one's culture. For most western Christians, at least, it means a church wedding. Traditional weddings may also include a white bridal gown, a few attendants, and a reception featuring a multitiered wedding cake (again, depending on culture).

One of the strangest nontraditional weddings ever was held on August 10, 2003. The bride, Ekaterina Dmitriev, said her vows while looking at a television screen in Houston's Johnson Space Center. The groom, Yuri Malenchenko, was wearing a bow tie with his space suit while orbiting 240 miles overhead in the international space station. The groom's mother cried—that's traditional—but it was because she thought the whole thing was unnecessary sensationalism!

When Peter answered God's call, he was, in a sense, officiating at a nontraditional wedding. Cornelius, a Gentile, was becoming part of the church, the bride of Christ. This was contrary to the traditions Peter had known all his life. In a changing world, we sometimes must be willing to give up our traditions in order to reach the lost. So we must ask: Which of our traditions stand in the way of others who need Christ?

—C. R. B.

CONCLUSION

Peter's trip from Joppa to see Cornelius was not without controversy. Peter's actions will invite disapproval when, in Acts 11:1-18, he is called upon to answer to the charge of entering the home of a Gentile: "the circumcised believers criticized him and said, 'You went into the house of uncircumcised men and ate with them'" (vv. 2b, 3). Peter ably defends himself, and all agree that he did the right thing.

For too long believers have permitted the "Gentiles" of modern culture to remain those who are untouched with the gospel. Peter's vision tells us today that God disapproves when we pick and choose those members of society whom we think deserve the kingdom of God. All races and ethnic groups should hear the gospel. The Spirit is sending us to our own "Gentile city." How will we answer that call?

Discovery Learning

This page contains an alternative lesson plan emphasizing learning activities. Classes desiring such student involvement will find these suggestions helpful. The next page is a reproducible activity page to further enhance discovery learning.

LEARNING GOALS

After participating in this lesson, each student will be able to:

1. List the events leading up to Peter's visit with Cornelius.

2. Discuss the prejudices that Peter and Cornelius had to overcome.

3. Acknowledge a personal struggle with prejudice and determine one way to overcome it.

INTO THE LESSON

Decorate your classroom with flags of various nations to represent the church's move to incorporate the Gentiles. Also display a large, face-shaped oval on the board. Label it, "The Ugly Face of Prejudice." Ask the class to suggest features on such a face. To get them started, sketch an eye and say, "an eye that looks down on others." Other possibilities include, "an ear that hears selectively," "an ear that hears only one tongue or dialect," "a mouth filled with criticism," and "an upturned nose of snobbery." Conclude by saying, "It is truly an ugly face."

(As an alternative, hand out copies of the "Pride and Prejudice" activity from the reproducible page to students as they walk in. They will naturally begin talking about the activity as other students arrive.)

INTO THE WORD

Collect the following objects: Italian flag, toy sword, bag of coins, a clock set to 3:00, a leather object, a fancy dinner napkin, stuffed animals (two or three), a dirty rag, and a math flashcard bearing "3 x 1." Randomly display the items.

Then say to the class, "Before we read today's text, I want you to see some objects I have brought. After the reading, we will come back to them." Have a good oral reader read the text, and then ask, "How can you relate each of these objects to things in the text?"

Let the class make suggestions. One possible relationship for each is given here: the flag represents Cornelius's home and army band; the sword represents his rank as centurion; coins represent his generosity; the clock represents 3:00 P.M.; the leather object represents Simon the tanner; the napkin represents Peter's hunger; the stuffed animals represent the contents of the sheet from Heaven; the dirty rag represents the concept of un-

clean; the math flashcard represents the three times God gave the same message.

Prepare flashcards for the following words: *name, nationality, vocation, location, diet, piety, family, generosity, prayer, revelation, worship, sanctification.* Show these words one at a time and then say, "Some of these words are things that sometimes create prejudice while some are things that should eliminate prejudice. Let's separate these words into the two groups. Help me decide which words often are associated with prejudice and which words are likely to alleviate prejudice."

The first five words are factors often accompanying prejudice; the other seven are matters that should help alleviate or eliminate prejudice. Ask the class, "In what verse(s) do you see these words or ideas represented?"

Though a variety of responses may be accepted, here is a possibility for each: *name* and the fact that Latin, Greek, and Hebrew names are all included in the text; *nationality* and Cornelius being a Roman; *vocation* regarding the occupations of Cornelius and Simon; *location* and the prejudices that accompany country differences; *diet* and the Jewish dietary law; *piety* and Cornelius's devoutness; *family* and the fact Cornelius's whole house followed his example; *generosity* and the willingness to give to the needy; *prayer* and the submission to God that bespeaks equality; *revelation* and the need of both Cornelius and Peter for God to speak; *worship* and the fact that Cornelius's prayers and gifts to the poor received God's commendation; *sanctification* and the fact that God can make clean in the manner that he chooses.

(Use the "Hard Questions" exercise from the reproducible page as an alternative learning experience.)

INTO LIFE

Say, "Because of our life experiences, most of us carry some intrinsic prejudices that we have not allowed the Spirit to remove. I want us to have a time of silent prayer in which I will suggest areas of possible prejudice. If one of these areas is a hidden issue within you, stop and pray that God's Spirit will be given free rein as you seek to leave that prejudice behind. Let us pray."

In your prayer list various factors that result in prejudice. End with this: "God, we know that You are the creator of all. Help us to value all people redemptively as you do. In the name of Jesus, amen."

Hard Questions

Why questions usually have complex answers. What do you think are adequate answers for these questions based on the incident in Acts 10:1-20?

Why did God choose a Gentile soldier as worthy of the gospel message?

Why had Cornelius become attracted to the religion of the Jews?

Why did God send an angel rather than simply sending Peter?

Why was Cornelius afraid when he received the vision?

Why was Peter staying in the house of a tanner with all its unclean elements?

Why would Peter get distracted by hunger in the middle of a time of prayer?

Why did God use the descending sheet filled with animals to communicate his will?

Why would God portray the visual images three times?

Why would Peter still be in doubt when Cornelius's envoys arrived?

Why does this incident of Peter and Cornelius merit a whole chapter in Acts?

Pride and Prejudice

How prevalent are the following views? To the left of each view put a *1* by those views almost universally held; put a *5* if you think it is an almost non-existent view.

____Physically disabled people are likely to be mentally disabled also.

____People with body odors very likely live a life of little or no self-control.

____Immigrants should stay in their home countries.

____Poorer neighborhoods are unlikely candidates for the gospel.

____Men are generally less capable mentally than are women.

____The church is primarily a blue-collar experience.

____Women are more sensitive than men; thus, they are more likely to respond to the gospel.

____People in my home country are generally superior to the peoples of other nations.

____Advocates of religions other than Christianity are more stubborn and less reasonable.

____Rich people sense no real need for the gospel.

What is your own position in relation to each statement? At the end of each sentence, rate yourself from "fully accept" (*1*) to "fully reject" (*5*).

You Will Be My Witnesses

Unit 2: In All Judea and Samaria
(Lessons 5-9)

PETER ESCAPES PRISON

LESSON 9

WHY TEACH THIS LESSON?

We pray for sunny weather. When it arrives we say, "I'm glad the warm front finally came through." We pray for healing. When health is restored, we say, "Isn't medicine wonderful?" We know we have a supernatural God, but most of us don't expect a miracle every day, even on days we pray for one.

Peter was shackled to guards. That was his reality. He wondered if the angel who jabbed him in the side was a dream. His friends were praying all through the night, yet the news of Peter's escape struck them as fantastical. Condemned men walking around, gates opening by themselves—there's no earthly explanation for such things!

This lesson presents a vivid reminder that even while we are "shackled" to this present world, there is another world that is invisible to us. There is a God beyond it all. We don't notice him breaking the rules of our natural world on a regular basis (the rules that he himself established). Yet he still has the power to command angels to our rescue, to open gates without our touch, to answer prayers in ways we may not expect.

INTRODUCTION

A. FACING DANGERS

We usually feel quite secure as we fly, don't we? But back in the 1930s it may not have been so safe. In *A Treasury of Humor*, Eric Johnson relates the following set of instructions from one of the first manuals for stewardesses—now called flight attendants: (1) Keep the clock and altimeter wound up. (2) Carry a railroad timetable in case the plane is grounded. (3) Warn the passengers against throwing their cigars and cigarettes out the windows. (4) Keep an eye on passengers when they go to the lavatory to be sure they don't mistakenly go out the emergency exit.

The dangers that these instructions guard against no longer exist, thankfully! But that doesn't mean that there are no longer any dangers associated with flying. Today we're always on the alert for terrorist attacks, for example. This kind of threat was virtually unknown in the 1930s. So one set of dangers has been replaced by another.

Today's lesson lets us observe how the first-century Christians faced certain dangers. The dangers we face as twenty-first-century Christians may be somewhat different, but the question is the same: How courageous are we when opponents spring up to hinder our witness for Christ? The example of the apostle Peter presses us to answer that question honestly and to take stock of our faith in God's ability to protect us.

B. LESSON BACKGROUND

The apostles were natural targets as soon as the persecution of believers began. Luke (the author of the book of Acts) reports that they stayed in Jerusalem in

DEVOTIONAL READING:
PSALM 46

BACKGROUND SCRIPTURE:
ACTS 12:1-17

PRINTED TEXT:
ACTS 12:1-16

LESSON AIMS

After participating in this lesson, each student will be able to:

1. Relate the sequence of events of Peter's imprisonment and escape.

2. Explain how prayer can lead to God providing escape from a seemingly impossible situation.

3. Identify a Christian in another country—perhaps a missionary supported by the church—who is in prison for preaching the gospel and pray together for God's intervention.

Oct
30

KEY VERSE

Suddenly an angel of the Lord appeared and a light shone in the cell. He struck Peter on the side and woke him up. "Quick, get up!" he said, and the chains fell off Peter's wrists.　—Acts 12:7

spite of the pressure against the Christians (see Acts 8:1). Life could not have been easy for this hardy band. The martyrdom of Stephen brought a strong initiative from Jewish authorities to stamp out this group known as "the Way" (see Acts 24:14). Jesus had called them to be his witnesses (Acts 1:8), but he never promised them that they would not suffer. Acts is a record of how the witness of the gospel spread throughout Jerusalem, then through Judea and Samaria, and to the world. In telling this story, Acts also relates some of the ways that the gospel was opposed, especially by Jewish authorities.

Today's lesson is a good time to remember that Palestine in the days of the apostles was still dominated by Roman rule. At times the Romans governed Palestine with proconsuls, or governors. At other times they used client-kings. (Sometimes they used both at once.) A client-king had authority only as Rome dictated. But if the king was governing efficiently in the eyes of Rome, then he had freedom to govern as he wished.

The Herodians were client-kings. Herod the Great (of Matthew 2:1-12) was shrewd in his political maneuvers. This gave him a prominent role as king in Palestine (37 B.C. to 4 B.C.). His sons, Herod Archelaus (see Matthew 2:22), Herod Philip (Luke 3:1), and Herod Antipas (Matthew 14:1, 2), each shared in rule over Palestine after the death of their father. The following generation of Herodians produced Herod Agrippa I, the Herod in today's lesson.

I. PETER'S ARREST (ACTS 12:1-4)

A. HEROD'S PERSECUTION (vv. 1, 2)

1. *It was about this time that King Herod arrested some who belonged to the church, intending to persecute them.*

This particular *King Herod* is Herod Agrippa I, the son of Aristobulus, who was a son of Herod the Great. The latter years of Herod the Great's reign were marked by jealousy, suspicion, and intrigue concerning potential rivals to his throne. So he had his son Aristobulus (among others) executed.

But the son of Aristobulus survived and was reared and educated in Rome. There he came into contact with Romans such as Claudius and his nephew Gaius, later to become emperors. Gaius (that is, Emperor Caligula) granted him this kingship in Palestine in about A.D. 37. When Claudius comes to power after Gaius (Caligula) is assassinated, he extends the authority of Herod Agrippa even further.

Herod Agrippa I, like all the Herods, certainly is capable of ruling with blood on his hands. His reasons for arresting *some who belonged to the church* in order to *persecute them* are not mentioned, but verse 3 (below) offers one of the motives for this violence.

2. *He had James, the brother of John, put to death with the sword.*

This *James*, son of Zebedee, is the one frequently mentioned in the Gospels in company with Peter and *John* (see Matthew 4:21). This is not the James who is a half-brother of Jesus and important to the leadership of the church later (see Acts 15:13-21; Galatians 1:19; 2:9).

The death of the James mentioned here is the first martyrdom of the Twelve, since Stephen was not an apostle. The use of *the sword* represents death by beheading. The authority of Herod to administer capital punishment comes with his status as client-king under Roman dominion. This one-sentence notation about James lacks so many details that we would find interesting. How do the apostles handle this frightening new persecution? How does the family of James deal with it? What impact does it have on the church in Jerusalem?

WHAT DO YOU THINK?

Persecution of Christians is still prevalent in our world, though not much is heard about it in the media. Why are modern Christians often apathetic or ignorant of this? What can be done to raise the awareness of this tragic practice?

B. HEROD'S PLANS (vv. 3, 4)

3. When he saw that this pleased the Jews, he proceeded to seize Peter also. This happened during the Feast of Unleavened Bread.

The Herods are not respected in Jerusalem because they are of Nabataen, rather than Jewish, heritage. For this reason they spend much of their time considering how to deal with a sometimes hostile Jewish populace. In this case, King Herod perceives the Jewish approval of the execution of James and determines that executing *Peter* will also gain approval.

The time of year, noted as *the Feast of Unleavened Bread*, corresponds with March–April. This seven-day event connects with the Passover feast (Exodus 23:15; 34:18; Deuteronomy 16:1-8; Luke 22:1). Since we know from sources outside the Bible that this King Herod dies in A.D. 44—an event that is described in Acts 12:23—we can assume that the arrest of Peter occurs around A.D. 43.

This arrest shows us the motivation for Herod's further action as one of seeking Jewish approval as it is timed with this feast. It is possible that Herod selects this timing to be parallel to the time of Jesus' own trials and crucifixion some 13 or 14 years previously, but this is just a guess.

4. After arresting him, he put him in prison, handing him over to be guarded by four squads of four soldiers each. Herod intended to bring him out for public trial after the Passover.

Peter is guarded by *four squads* with *four soldiers* in *each* squad—a total of 16. This number of squads corresponds to the four watches of the night and is an indication that Peter's guard is a full-time one. Herod's intent is to bring Peter *out for a public trial* following *Passover*.

HISTORY REPEATING ITSELF

George Santayana (1863–1952) wrote, "Those who cannot remember the past are condemned to repeat it." His statement is understood more clearly in its popularized form, "Those who will not *learn* from the past . . . ." History proves this truth. The war once called "the war to end all wars" is now known simply as World War I. In the 90 years since that war, World War II and many smaller wars have followed because political leaders are still sinful and humanity hasn't yet learned how to deal with the problem. So we keep repeating the past.

The Herods didn't learn the lesson either. As is the case with so many others, their perverted ambition got in the way. Agrippa probably looked back at the popular support that Herod Antipas enjoyed when he agreed with Pilate's execution of Jesus. Ignoring the fact of Jesus' resurrection, Agrippa may have thought Jesus' death at Passover made it an auspicious time to kill James. When he saw the public favor he gained by that evil act, he thought to do the same with Peter. But he wasn't counting on God's intervention. Evildoers ignore the lessons of the past.

Christians should remember the other side of the equation: If we learn the lessons of biblical history, we will find that righteousness eventually prevails and those who practice it are blessed. It may not happen immediately, but God always keeps his promises.

—C. R. B.

II. PETER'S ESCAPE (ACTS 12:5-11)

A. APPEARANCE OF THE ANGEL (vv. 5-7)

5. So Peter was kept in prison, but the church was earnestly praying to God for him.

Imprisonment in the Roman world usually means that the prisoner is condemned to die already or that hearings are scheduled. Unlike modern systems, prisoners generally are not held for long periods of time.

WHAT DO YOU THINK?

For every tyrant that falls, there seem to be two to take his place. Such rulers thrive by oppressing others. How should the church respond?

DAILY BIBLE READINGS

Monday, Oct. 24—Peter Heals One and Revives Another (Acts 9:32-42)

Tuesday, Oct. 25—Jesus Is Tempted (Luke 4:1-13)

Wednesday, Oct. 26—Jesus Prays in Gethsemane (Matthew 26:36-46)

Thursday, Oct. 27—Jesus Dies on the Cross (Mark 15: 33-37)

Friday, Oct. 28—James Is Killed and Peter Imprisoned (Acts 12:1-5)

Saturday, Oct. 29—An Angel Frees Peter from Prison (Acts 12:6-11)

Sunday, Oct. 30—Peter Tells the Others What Happened (Acts 12:12-17)

WHAT DO YOU THINK?

Ephesians 6:18 and 1 Thessalonians 5:17 encourage prayer at all times and in all situations. How can your church improve its prayer life for the work of God's kingdom?

WHAT DO YOU THINK?

We may find it amazing that Peter was able to sleep in a situation such as this! How can someone be at peace when his or her life seems to be crumbling all around?

The book of Acts presents an interesting contrast: while Peter is locked up in prison, *the church is praying.* Note that nothing is said about the content of their prayers. It does not say, for example, that the church is praying for Peter's release. Perhaps they are, perhaps not. With the martyrdom of Stephen and James on their minds, their prayers most likely include a request for Peter to have courage to face the persecution coming against him. In fact, it is an act of courage for the church to assemble under these circumstances.

6. The night before Herod was to bring him to trial, Peter was sleeping between two soldiers, bound with two chains, and sentries stood guard at the entrance.

Peter's faith is obvious: on the very *night before* his probable execution he is *sleeping* peacefully while surrounded by guards! The *two soldiers* mentioned are the ones to whom Peter is chained. The other two soldiers (from this particular shift of four soldiers) stand *guard at the* door.

7. Suddenly an angel of the Lord appeared and a light shone in the cell. He struck Peter on the side and woke him up. "Quick, get up!" he said, and the chains fell off Peter's wrists.

Our text now describes a prison escape like no other! The fact that the initiative is from God and not from *Peter* is emphasized. *An angel of the Lord* arrives in the cell and the *light* shines, perhaps similar to the night of Jesus' birth when the glory of the Lord shone around the shepherds (Luke 2:9). Peter's sleepiness is another emphasis in the account. He is far too sleepy to engineer his own escape, and the angel even has to tell him how to get dressed (next verse).

B. INSTRUCTIONS FROM THE ANGEL (vv. 8-11)

8. Then the angel said to him, "Put on your clothes and sandals." And Peter did so. "Wrap your cloak around you and follow me," the angel told him.

The angel's instructions to *Peter* about getting dressed are a reminder of the clothing styles of the day. Putting on his *clothes* means that Peter will wrap around his waist a wide cloth belt. Binding up the *sandals* consists of wrapping the long leather straps around the calf. Peter has dressed himself countless times before, of course, so the fact that the angel must give instructions indicates how sleepy Peter is. He certainly is too sleepy to mastermind his own escape!

9. Peter followed him out of the prison, but he had no idea that what the angel was doing was really happening; he thought he was seeing a vision.

Peter is sure that his senses are fooling him. "I must be dreaming," he undoubtedly thinks. His groggy condition does not allow him to consider any of this as real. Nevertheless, he obeys the instructions of *the angel* and walks out of the cell.

10. They passed the first and second guards and came to the iron gate leading to the city. It opened for them by itself, and they went through it. When they had walked the length of one street, suddenly the angel left him.

The *guards* are apparently in a deep sleep, perhaps brought on by the Lord (compare Matthew 28:4). Of course, all of this is done by the power of God alone. The entire episode is more properly thought of as a "release" than an "escape," because Peter could do none of it himself. *The angel* eventually disappears, his task finished.

11. Then Peter came to himself and said, "Now I know without a doubt that the Lord sent his angel and rescued me from Herod's clutches and from everything the Jewish people were anticipating."

Now, for the first time, *Peter* realizes for sure that this is reality and not a dream. His rescue is from Herod, who exercised authority in executing James.

Peter also is rescued from the *people* because it is the *Jewish* leadership who approved that execution (see 12:3, above). In the book of Acts, frequently there are Jewish voices behind the decision of a ruler under Roman dominion who passes judgment or makes a decision concerning believers. See Acts 18:12; 19:32-41; 24:1-4; 25:1-5.

III. PETER'S RETURN (ACTS 12:12-16)
A. ARRIVAL AND PRAYER (v. 12)
12. *When this had dawned on him, he went to the house of Mary the mother of John, also called Mark, where many people had gathered and were praying.*

In verse 5 we saw that the church was *praying*. Now we learn one of the locations for this prayer. The mention of *John, also called Mark,* introduces a personality who will appear as a missionary traveler with Paul (Acts 13:5). Here we learn that his *mother* is a certain *Mary,* and that she owns a *house* in Jerusalem large enough for the believers to meet for prayer. Most people in the ancient world do not venture from their homes at night, so these believers are demonstrating dedication in being absent from their own homes to attend this prayer meeting.

B. KNOCK AND ANSWER (vv. 13, 14)
13, 14. *Peter knocked at the outer entrance, and a servant girl named Rhoda came to answer the door. When she recognized Peter's voice, she was so overjoyed she ran back without opening it and exclaimed, "Peter is at the door!"*

Peter's knocking, which perhaps goes on for several minutes, endangers him further. The soldiers might be close behind. This house is a large one, since an *outer entrance* is mentioned. *A servant girl named Rhoda* answers the knock. Her reaction is somewhat amusing. She cannot believe this is really Peter even though she personally hears his *voice*. She is so stunned that she dashes back inside without even letting *Peter* in!

C. CRITICISM AND AMAZEMENT (vv. 15, 16)
15. *"You're out of your mind," they told her. When she kept insisting that it was so, they said, "It must be his angel."*

This verse often brings forth the criticism that the church in Jerusalem does not have enough faith. This criticism says that here they are praying for Peter's release, and when he is released they do not believe it. In other words, they cannot accept the answer to their own prayers.

The problem is that Acts does not say they were praying for Peter's release. Their reaction to the news that *Peter* is standing at the door is more consistent with the notion that they fully expect Peter's execution, and that they are praying that he will meet the trial with faith. Thus the theory of those present that this is Peter's *angel*.

16. *But Peter kept on knocking, and when they opened the door and saw him, they were astonished.*

Luke (the author of the book of Acts) heightens the drama of Peter's release by reporting that he *kept on knocking* at the gate. All this noise out on the street does nothing at all to contribute to Peter's safety! Nevertheless, Peter's release is secured by a power greater than all of Herod's forces.

When believers place their trust in the Lord to face dangerous times, the will of God always wins out. This is not to guarantee that every believer will escape the sword. We could ask the family of the apostle James about that! But whether

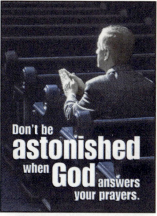

Visual for Lesson 9. *Use this visual as you discuss the astonishment mentioned in verse 16.*

WHAT DO YOU THINK?

How have you experienced God's deliverance in your life? How can you tell the difference between God's deliverance and the successes that we have by our own power?

HOW TO SAY IT

Aristobulus. Uh-RIS-toe-BU-lus.

Caligula. Kuh-LIG-you-luh.

Claudius. CLAW-dee-us.

Deuteronomy. Due-ter-AHN-uh-me.

Gaius. GAY-us.

Herod Agrippa. HAIR-ud Uh-GRIP-puh.

Herod Antipas. HAIR-ud AN-tih-pus.

Herod Archelaus. HAIR-ud Are-kuh-LAY-us.

Herodians. Heh-ROE-dee-unz.

Judea. Joo-DEE-uh.

Nabataen. NAB-uh-TEE-un.

Samaria. Suh-MARE-ee-uh.

PRAYER

Almighty God, we trust this day in you, because your power is superior to all the forces on earth that want to harm Christians. We ask for the courage of Jesus who made the good confession before Pontius Pilate and faithfully spoke your truth. In Jesus' name, amen.

THOUGHT TO REMEMBER

God lets us participate in his victories, and the evil one is reminded constantly that his days are numbered.

saints are spared paying the ultimate price or are forced to yield up this earthly existence at the hands of some evil power such as Herod, the promise of Acts is that the Word of God will run free.

This victory of God's truth will come no matter what attempts are made to silence the messengers of Christ. In fact before chapter 12 of Acts closes, the evil king who murdered the apostle James and tried to eliminate the voice of the apostle *Peter* must accept death himself. He can find no escape because his death is brought on by the same Lord who opened the prison doors for the apostle Peter (see again Acts 12:23).

By this point, the believers understand that this is indeed *Peter* and not an angel. Now they recognize that God has performed a miraculous work, and they are as *astonished* as at any time when powerful deeds of God are seen. This reaction is exactly the one that is recorded so often in the Gospels when people witnessed the miracles of Jesus (Luke 7:16; 9:43; etc.).

MORE THAN ONE KIND OF PRISON

How to Break Out of Prison is the cleverly misleading title of John Wareham's recent book. One day a week, the author goes to Rikers Island prison in New York to teach a class of inmates how to change the negative thinking that put them there. Wareham has discovered that executives of large corporations sometimes use those same kinds of negative thinking patterns! The result is that they short-circuit their careers and destroy their family lives.

Although written for corporate executives, the book's principles apply to the lives of us all. Wareham discusses the ways we can get stuck in doing things one way. It may never occur to us that new ways of performing a given task might allow us to work more productively. Ironically, we may even strongly resist when someone suggests a different approach! (It even happens in churches, doesn't it?) Wareham calls this a "mental prison" that can confine our lives and restrain our potential as surely as stone walls and steel bars.

The church's amazement at Peter's escape surprises us at first. Was this what they were praying for or not? Their disheartenment had become a prison! But as we think about it, we begin to realize that prisons of stone and steel (or of doubt and discouragement) cannot confine God. Has *our* church ever tried to limit God in the prison of our negative thinking?   —C. R. B.

CONCLUSION

Today's passage does not guarantee that all believers will escape the hands of their tormentors. Church tradition holds that Peter eventually will embrace his own martyrdom in Rome.

If victory means expecting to escape the trials that come against us, then modern Christians will be sadly disappointed. What is guaranteed is that even though all earthly forces may assemble against the Word of God, they cannot prevail. Victory for God's truth is assured. Evil kings can try to silence God's messengers, but the Lord will break the chains and spring open the doors so that the truth can run free.

Our role as witnesses gives us the privilege of participating in this universal victory over the evil one. So when God chooses to intervene on our behalf and snap the chains or spring open the doors, we should never accept these actions selfishly. It is not because we have attained a special holiness that God moves on our behalf. But because we serve faithfully as his messengers, we gain the joy of experiencing the victories that come. How great the ultimate victory will be when Jesus returns!

Discovery Learning

This page contains an alternative lesson plan emphasizing learning activities. Classes desiring such student involvement will find these suggestions helpful. The next page is a reproducible activity page to further enhance discovery learning.

LEARNING GOALS

After participating in this lesson, each student will to:

1. Relate the sequence of events of Peter's imprisonment and escape.

2. Explain how prayer can lead to God providing escape from a seemingly impossible situation.

3. Identify a Christian in another country—perhaps a missionary supported by the church—who is in prison for preaching the gospel and pray together for God's intervention.

INTO THE LESSON

Say, "Today's text introduces one of the Bible's bad guys. Listen to the following statements and identify which 'Bible bad guy' is in mind."

1. "I had a wonderful world to live in, but I killed my brother in a fit of anger." (*Cain*)

2. "I was God's choice to lead his people as their first king, but my own will negated his choice." (*King Saul*)

3. "Gifted by God, I let my lusts and pride overcome me. I ended up blinded, then dead." (*Samson*)

4. "I had such an egocentric view that God caused me to go mad and live like an animal, eating grass." (*Nebuchadnezzar*)

5. "Hearing about someone being born to become king was enough for me to act. Young boys had to die!" (*Herod the Great*)

6. "I acted just like my grandfather. I would do almost anything to appease the Jews I ruled over." (*Herod Agrippa I*) If no one guesses number six, identify him as the bad guy in today's text.

(As an alternative, say, "Today's text introduces one of the Bible's good guys who was thrown in prison. On this listing, identify other 'Good Guys in Prison.'" Use the exercise with that title from the reproducible page.)

INTO THE WORD

Distribute paper and pens. Say, "I want you to do something you probably haven't done since first grade: trace an outline of your hand." Let them do so.

Next, say, "Now as I read our text a verse at a time, write something a person either does with his or her hand or a use of the hand in the text that could be in-ferred." Read verse 1 and give an example: use the hand to attack another person. Here are other examples from today's text: use a weapon to kill another (v. 2); eat ceremonial foods (v. 3); keep a person confined (v. 4); lift in prayer (v. 5); hold restraints such as chains (v. 6); touch or shake someone (v. 7); put on clothes (v. 8); open doors or gates (v. 10); knock (v. 13); gesture dramatically to convince someone you are telling the truth (v. 15); point (to where Peter was at the door; v. 14).

Class members may suggest other uses. If they need help, ask them a question such as, "What did the angel do to Peter, as verse 7 records?"

As an alternative way to get students to look at the text, say, "Because the stories in Acts are of real people in real history, we see the full range of human emotions. Look at Acts 12:1-16 and identify a verse wherein each of the following emotions and behaviors (given in alphabetical order) are shown or implied": astonishment (v. 16); curiosity (v. 9); faith (v. 11); fear (generally); gladness (v. 14); grief (v. 2); hope (v. 5); hostility (v. 1); irritation (v. 15); patience (v. 5); persistence (v. 16); pleasure (v. 3); shock (v. 7); surprise (v. 7); unity of purpose (v. 12).

Your students may suggest other possibilities. (A related activity is included in the student book; however, the words are scrambled.)

INTO LIFE

As a group, make a short list of Christians who struggle with difficult life circumstances. After a list of four or five is made, ask for that same number of volunteers to invite several class members into their homes for a short prayer meeting to pray for one of those specific situations during the coming week. Before closing, give volunteers time to arrange such a meeting with others. Use the following words as a reminder: "Assembling in someone's home for the purpose of praying for someone in distress is simply part of following the example of the first-century church, as in today's text."

(Alternative: If you would rather use a hypothetical list, use the "What to Pray" reproducible exercise.)

If time permits, make a list of elements that would be appropriate for such prayers: the faith of the person in distress, the comfort of that person's family, the opportunity of that person to witness to the gospel, a growing sense of compassion within the praying group, etc.

Good Guys in Prison

The Bible records several instances of righteous men being unjustly imprisoned. Peter, in today's text in Acts 12, is only one such example. On the first line provided, identify each of the Bible heroes being described. Then tell what God did for each of them.

_____ Doing the right thing in freeing a young lady from her demon got me and my friend in trouble with her owners. But God _____. *(Acts 16:16-26)*

_____ Falsely accused of sexual assault, I was locked away and nearly forgotten. But God _____. *(Genesis 39:6-23; 41:41)*

_____ My crime was praying, praying to the wrong God, praying at the wrong times. But God _____. *(Daniel 6:6-16)*

_____ Preaching what sounded to some like a treasonous message got me thrown into a pit. But God _____. *(Jeremiah 38:1-13)*

What to Pray

The lesson writer suggests that the Christians were surprised when Peter showed up freed from prison because they probably were not praying for his freedom, but rather for his faith. What would you consider to be an appropriate prayer for Christians caught in the following circumstances?

A young mother whose husband offers no support: emotional, financial, or in matters of faith

A young couple who seem to be addicted to credit and the things it will buy

A teenager caught in the depression and futility of dark rock music

A middle-aged couple in the whirlpool of "keeping up with the Joneses"

A preaching minister who is beginning to like the power of being "the chief bishop" of his congregation

The discouraged wife of a terminally ill husband who has been incapacitated for months

PAUL MEETS THE LORD

LESSON 10

WHY TEACH THIS LESSON?

In his book *Rumors of Another World*, Philip Yancey speaks of "smoltification," a process that takes place in salmon before they migrate to the sea. Besides a multitude of behavioral changes, each fish changes to a silvery color, becomes more streamlined, and develops a greater tolerance for sodium and potassium. Through this process, the salmon actually changes from a bottom dwelling, territorial fresh water fish to a creature of the open sea. While some learners will have experienced a gradual progression toward faith early in life, others may have made dramatic transformations, like the salmon—like Saul.

When we look at the people with whom God has put us in close proximity, we should never decide someone is "too far gone" to become a believer. Dramatic conversions happen today. Also, when we look at our own lives, we can be sure that God can transform us dramatically if we are willing to let him. As with the salmon, the changes God makes in us will prepare us to inhabit our next home.

INTRODUCTION

A. ZERO TOLERANCE

College basketball fans know the name of Bobby Knight, the former coach of the Indiana University basketball team. His reputation was built not only on winning, but also on a manner of handling the press that was direct and sometimes tactless. At times he also exhibited a red hot temper during games that he coached. When the university officials grew tired of repairing damage caused by Knight's outbursts, they established a zero-tolerance policy with him.

After the policy was announced, Knight soon violated it, and he was fired. Someone said afterward that it is good that God does not establish a zero-tolerance policy toward us, or who would be able to stand in the judgment?

Today's lesson about the conversion of Saul of Tarsus challenges us to remember that the gospel is more powerful than our sin. God's policy toward us does not rule us out after one slip. Instead, God confronts us with the gospel of grace.

B. LESSON BACKGROUND

The book of Acts specializes in unlikely conversions. Philip preaches to a Samaritan sorcerer named Simon and converts him to Christ (Acts 8:4-13). Peter preaches the gospel in the home of the Gentile Cornelius and converts him to Christ (Acts 10:25-48). Paul preaches the gospel to some skeptical intellectuals in Athens and converts some of them to Christ (Acts 17:16-34).

What an impact the gospel of Christ can have! A main theme of Acts is witnessing "to the ends of the earth" (Acts 1:8), and these preachers carried out that mission. Saul of Tarsus (later called Paul, beginning in Acts 13:9) is a vital part of this story. He began to persecute the church fiercely after the martyrdom of Stephen (Acts 8:1-3). We may say that the church was under a terrorist attack, and that the attack came from a tormentor who created a climate of fear (Acts 9:1).

DEVOTIONAL READING:
ACTS 9:23-31
BACKGROUND SCRIPTURE:
ACTS 9:1-31
PRINTED TEXT:
ACTS 9:3-18

LESSON AIMS

After participating in this lesson, each student will be able to:

1. Summarize Saul's conversion experience.

2. Explain the significance of Saul's conversion.

3. Praise God for one specific way his or her life has been changed by knowing God.

Nov
6

KEY VERSE

Immediately, something like scales fell from Saul's eyes, and he could see again. He got up and was baptized. —Acts 9:18

LESSON 10 NOTES

WHAT DO YOU THINK?

From a human perspective, some people seem too far from the truth to be reachable. Why are we often hesitant to take the gospel to those who seem so far from belief? What can your church do to correct this situation?

Saul of Tarsus had participated in the execution of Stephen by guarding the coats of those who were throwing the stones (Acts 7:58–8:1; 22:20). Saul's authority to round up Christians in Damascus included letters from the high priest, who presided over the Sanhedrin (Acts 9:2). This authority has been called into question because the Sanhedrin, based in Jerusalem, normally did not exercise authority over synagogues as far away as Damascus. Acts does not, however, elaborate on the content of these letters from the high priest. They may not have been documents with legal authority, but letters recommending that the synagogues take action against believers in Jesus. Such recommendations would carry much weight for those who respected the temple leadership in Jerusalem.

Saul's conversion was a landmark event in the life of the church. Acts highlights the event by presenting the full account three times—in Acts 9:1-19; 22:1-21; and 26:1-18—with some variation in details. Today's lesson explores the first of these accounts in Acts and examines the effects of the powerful gospel of God's grace on a sinful life.

I. HEAVENLY VOICE (ACTS 9:3-9)

A. LIGHT FROM HEAVEN (v. 3)

3. As he neared Damascus on his journey, suddenly a light from heaven flashed around him.

Saul probably walks the 150 miles from Jerusalem to *Damascus*. This is a city of great historical significance, mentioned more than 40 times in the Old Testament. The journey takes about a week to complete, so there can be no doubt about Saul's commitment to arresting Christians.

The expression *a light from heaven flashed around him* is similar to the description in Luke 2:9, which tells us of the appearance of the angels to the shepherds in the field on the night of Jesus' birth. There the light is specifically "the glory of the Lord." The brilliant light in the passage before us bathes Saul in its brightness. He is about to receive a message from the Lord.

B. VOICE FROM THE LORD (vv. 4-6)

4. He fell to the ground and heard a voice say to him, "Saul, Saul, why do you persecute me?"

Saul's reaction to the blinding light is to fall *to the ground*. The *voice* is from Jesus (see v. 5, next). Calling *Saul* by name twice seems to emphasize that the words are meant for him alone. The question put to Saul involves his actions against the believers, but the words are personal: *why do you persecute me?* When Saul persecutes Christians, he is persecuting Jesus. Jesus makes the same point in his parable about the sheep and the goats when he says that God will announce at the judgment that what was done or not done for the brothers was, in fact, done or not done to Jesus himself (Matthew 25:31-46). Saul is about to learn that hurting Christians means hurting Jesus.

5. "Who are you, Lord?" Saul asked.

"I am Jesus, whom you are persecuting," he replied.

Saul's first reaction is to call very respectfully for the identity of the voice. The use of the word *Lord* in his question does not necessarily mean that he is confessing Jesus as Lord just yet. The term can also be translated "sir."

Jesus then reveals how contrary to the will of God is Saul's campaign against the believers. Later in life the apostle will acknowledge this when he admits that he did not deserve to be called an apostle because he persecuted the church (1 Corinthians 15:9). Yet he will maintain that he persecuted believers because of

WHAT DO YOU THINK?

How can we, even as Christians, be guilty of persecuting Christ today? How do we avoid this?

ignorance and that he found forgiveness through the grace of the Lord (1 Timothy 1:12-14).

6. *"Now get up and go into the city, and you will be told what you must do."*

The Lord's instructions are to go into *the city* of Damascus, where Saul is headed anyway. The parallel account in Acts 26:16-18 includes instructions that describe the ministry that Saul will be called to fulfill (also in Acts 9:15, 16). Here the Lord's words include an allusion to the visit by Ananias (see 9:10-18, below).

C. SURPRISE OF SAUL'S COMPANIONS (vv. 7-9)

7. *The men traveling with Saul stood there speechless; they heard the sound but did not see anyone.*

Saul's fellow travelers do *not see* the one speaking to *Saul*. They do not comprehend what is happening. Acts 22:9 offers us a similar description.

8, 9. *Saul got up from the ground, but when he opened his eyes he could see nothing. So they led him by the hand into Damascus. For three days he was blind, and did not eat or drink anything.*

Saul's blindness reduces him to helplessness. But his refusal to *eat or drink* is an indication of his humiliation at hearing the words of Jesus on the road. He is humbled at the judgment pronounced by Jesus, because he now realizes that he has been persecuting the people of God. Fasting in the Bible is connected frequently with sorrow. David fasted after his sin with Bathsheba and the sickness of his son (2 Samuel 12:13-23). Nehemiah fasted because of his sorrow over the disgraceful condition of Jerusalem (Nehemiah 1:4). Saul's fasting probably indicates his sorrow for his own sin and his repentance before God.

Thus the book of Acts shows us the image of the fierce persecutor of the church brought to his knees before the Lord whom he persecuted. The powerful gospel reaches into Saul's heart. The knowledge that Jesus is really the Messiah will capture Saul completely. His transformation is about to begin.

Modern believers should not be surprised about the powerful impact of Christ on wayward sinners. We can all think of examples of people who came face to face with Christ, and the change was dramatic. The truth of Jesus Christ still operates with this power today. No wonder we are called to be witnesses of this truth (Acts 1:8)!

II. FAITHFUL MESSENGER (ACTS 9:10-16)

A. COMMAND TO ANANIAS (vv. 10-12)

10. *In Damascus there was a disciple named Ananias. The Lord called to him in a vision, "Ananias!"*

"Yes, Lord," he answered.

Using the term *disciple* to describe *Ananias* reminds us that early Christians are often referred to by this term (see Acts 11:26, 29; 14:20, 28). Ananias is a follower of Christ because he has accepted the gospel as true and has identified himself with those who acknowledge Jesus as Lord.

Ananias's response to the voice of God is similar to what Eli instructed young Samuel to offer when he heard God's voice. The boy was told to respond with, "Speak, for your servant is listening" (1 Samuel 3:10). When Isaiah heard the voice of the Lord in the vision in the temple, he responded with "Here am I. Send me!" (Isaiah 6:8). Ananias answers in a way that demonstrates obedience.

11, 12. *The Lord told him, "Go to the house of Judas on Straight Street and ask for a man from Tarsus named Saul, for he is praying. In a vision he has seen a man named Ananias come and place his hands on him to restore his sight."*

HOW TO SAY IT

Ananias. An-uh-NYE-us.
Athens. ATH-unz.
Bathsheba. Bath-SHE-buh.
Cornelius. Cor-NEEL-yus.
Damascus. Duh-MASS-kus.
Gentile. JEN-tile.
Isaiah. Eye-ZAY-uh.
Jerusalem. Juh-ROO-suh-lem.
Messiah. Meh-SIGH-uh.
Nehemiah. NEE-huh-MY-uh.
Samaritan. Suh-MARE-uh-tun.
Sanhedrin. SAN-huh-drun or
    San-HEED-run.
synagogue. SIN-uh-gog.
Tarsus. TAR-sus.

WHAT DO YOU THINK?

How can you determine whether or not someone has had a real encounter with God—or is this even our prerogative? What are the results of coming into contact with God in a personal way?

WHAT DO YOU THINK?

God does not always use the high-powered evangelist or gifted communicator to reach the lost. He wants to use all his people for this purpose. Who is God calling you to reach with the gospel right now? How will you do it?

In the case of *Ananias,* the voice of the Lord speaks for the purpose of sending a disciple on a mission, as with Isaiah. This particular Ananias is not known elsewhere in the New Testament. He is not an apostle or a prophet, but apparently an "ordinary" believer who now receives an active role in the drama of Saul's conversion. Acts 22:12 describes Ananias as a Jew devoted to following the Law of Moses and highly respected among other Jews in the city.

Even the address for finding *Saul* is included. The description of Saul being in prayer implies that his heart is ready for receiving the Word of the Lord. The vision presents a summary of what Ananias is to do when he comes to see Saul. Ananias will say and do even more than what is noted briefly here, as the book of Acts makes clear.

Straight Street runs east and west through the city. This street is a colonnaded thoroughfare enclosed with gates at both ends. Of course, the irony that Saul of Tarsus is now ready to walk the "straight and narrow" pathway cannot be missed (compare Matthew 7:14). The disciple named *Judas* mentioned here is unknown elsewhere in the New Testament.

B. CONCERNS OF ANANIAS (vv. 13, 14)

13, 14. *"Lord," Ananias answered, "I have heard many reports about this man and all the harm he has done to your saints in Jerusalem. And he has come here with authority from the chief priests to arrest all who call on your name."*

This fearful reaction from *Ananias* certainly is easy to understand, given the reputation of Saul for locking up Christians as prisoners (9:2). The letters carried by Saul from the chief priests, though not legally binding on the synagogues north of Jerusalem, would carry authority because of the high level of respect for the Jerusalem leadership. The words of Ananias seem to imply that he has heard *reports* about Saul, but has not been involved personally in the persecution *in Jerusalem.* Thus he is probably not one of those believers scattered from Jerusalem (Acts 8:1). His mention of *your name* is a reference to the name of Jesus, as in verse 15 (below).

Ananias does not speak these words out of disrespect for the Lord's command, but as a natural reaction of fear. There are times in the service of the Lord that fear of those who will do bodily harm is a factor in deciding when and where to serve. Paul's preaching in several cases is adjusted according to the dangers of angry opponents (see Acts 13:51; 14:20; 19:30).

WHAT DO YOU THINK?

The "fear factor" is a major reason Christians fail to reach out to others with the gospel of Christ. How can this fear be overcome?

THE MEANEST MAN ALIVE

George Foreman is best known today as a smiling pitchman for his line of barbecue grills. Yet there was a time when many considered him the meanest man alive. His brute strength and ugly disposition made him a greatly feared boxer, and he became heavyweight champion in 1973. Then on March 17, 1977, Foreman lost a fight he should have won easily. That night, in his despair, he turned to Christ and quit boxing. A boxing historian calls the event "one of the greatest turnarounds in history in terms of persona and likability."

Foreman returned to boxing ten years after his conversion because he needed money to support the recreational center he had started for poor urban youth. In one of the greatest comebacks in boxing history, he became heavyweight champion of the world in 1994 at age 45! Today he is a preacher at a small church in Houston, supported largely by the profits from his grill business.

It is hard not to see at least a faint parallel between the "before" and "after" pictures of George Foreman and Saul of Tarsus. Ruthlessness had characterized the earthly careers of both. Yet Christ is the one who can turn such lives around—for eternity. Christ works in the lives of sinful, mean, and surly people to remake them in his loving image. How much work does God still have to do in us?   —C. R. B.

C. ANSWER FOR ANANIAS (vv. 15, 16)

15, 16. But the Lord said to Ananias, "Go! This man is my chosen instrument to carry my name before the Gentiles and their kings and before the people of Israel. I will show him how much he must suffer for my name."

The Lord speaks in order to ease the anxiety of *Ananias.* God's purposes for Saul are revealed so that Ananias can understand that there is a divine use for this life that had created such havoc for the church. Saul will be a *chosen instrument* (figuratively, a favorite water jug or a special vase) for the master in a way similar to Old Testament Israel as a chosen possession (see Exodus 19:5; Deuteronomy 7:6; 26:18). Ananias cannot miss the point that the Lord has very important plans for Saul.

Bearing the *name* of the Lord *before the Gentiles* and *kings* foreshadows certain events, as seen in Acts 24 and 25. Then there will be times when Saul (later renamed Paul) stands before Jewish audiences, *the people of Israel,* as well (Acts 13:13-52). These accounts present specific instances of Paul's own sufferings for the gospel. The tormentor will become the tormented. This news convinces Ananias to risk his life to go and stand in the same room with Saul.

What a transformation the church is about to witness in the life of Saul of Tarsus! This should convince modern believers that the gospel has more power to transform lives than we can possibly imagine. Later Saul (Paul) will refer to himself as "the worst" of sinners (1 Timothy 1:15). If God can transform terrible sinners, how much more can we expect him to do so with the sinners we know?

III. CONVERTED TORMENTOR (ACTS 9:17, 18)

A. VISIT FROM ANANIAS (v. 17)

17. Then Ananias went to the house and entered it. Placing his hands on Saul, he said, "Brother Saul, the Lord—Jesus, who appeared to you on the road as you were coming here—has sent me so that you may see again and be filled with the Holy Spirit."

The laying on of *hands* is important in Acts (see Acts 8:17; 13:3; 19:6). The identification of *Jesus* as *Lord* here corresponds to a major truth in Acts: Jesus is both Lord and Christ (Messiah, or "anointed one"; Acts 2:36; 10:36; 11:17; 28:31). Ananias presents a truth to Saul that Saul already has come to accept because of his experience *on the road* to Damascus.

RELUCTANT HEROES

Tom Brokaw's 1998 best-seller, *The Greatest Generation,* touched a sympathetic nerve. In 1984 Brokaw had gone to Normandy to do a documentary on the D-Day invasion forty years earlier. That daring invasion would be a turning point in World War II. Brokaw said, "There, I underwent a life-changing experience." The book is the product of that experience. It tells the story of a generation of Americans who grew up during the Depression of the 1930s and the war years of 1941–1945. As one critic phrased it, Brokaw told the story of a "generation [that] was united not only by a common purpose, but also by common values."

In four dozen or so interviews, Brokaw puts together a story of commitment to doing what was required, regardless of the cost. He doesn't gloss over their faults; he reports their racism and prejudices as well as their virtues. But as French/English author Hilaire Belloc said of this generation's efforts, "They died to save their

How has Christ transformed your life?

Visual for Lesson 10. Point to these two photos as you ask, "What was life like for you 'before' and 'after' you placed faith in Christ?"

Prayer

Lord of grace and mercy, we ask today that you remind us of the potential within each sinner we know. Help us to think of him or her as ready for the truth of Jesus Christ. Let us look upon each as a potential "Paul," and not as a "Saul." As we do, may we see ourselves the same way. We pray in Christ, amen.

Thought to Remember

The worst sinner is capable of becoming the best Christian.

country and they only saved the world!" We owe an unfathomable debt to these reluctant heroes who "only" did what had to be done.

Ananias was also such a person. While fearing what the cost might be to himself, he did what had to be done and went to see Saul. The world was changed as a result of that visit. A sense of duty coupled with trust in God can be the most powerful force in the world. —C. R. B.

B. Baptism of Saul (v. 18)

18. Immediately, something like scales fell from Saul's eyes, and he could see again. He got up and was baptized.

In verse 17, Ananias stated that his reasons for coming were twofold. First, he came to Saul so that he could receive his sight back; this happens when something like scales, or a flaky layer of substance, falls from Saul's eyes. The second objective for Ananias is that Saul might receive the Holy Spirit; this is accomplished when Saul is baptized. Verses 17 and 18 demonstrate the connection between baptism and the reception of the Holy Spirit (compare Acts 2:38; Titus 3:5).

"The rest," we may say, "is history." Saul becomes a dynamo for Jesus because the power of the gospel turns him from a persecutor of Christ to a preacher of Christ.

A New Way of Seeing

Michael May was 3 years old when an accident left him blind in his left eye and barely able to see light in the right one. He describes that partial vision as "like looking through a windshield that's completely iced over." He worked at having as normal a life as possible. May even become an expert skier and helped to develop a Global Positioning System receiver that works with the Braille method. Four corneal transplant attempts were unsuccessful. Then, 43 years after the accident, donor stem cells from an adult cornea and a fifth transplant succeeded.

After regaining his vision, he found that the ability to see is almost as much in the brain as it is in the eye. Because the accident happened when May was so young, his adult brain had to train itself to recognize objects in a way the rest of us do automatically and without thinking. He said, "I need to see something for the tenth time before it sinks in what it is. It's like learning a language. You have to build up the vocabulary."

Saul's experience was somewhat like this. But we're not talking about his loss and recovery of physical sight. The problem was long-term spiritual blindness. His temporary physical blindness in Damascus opened the eyes of his heart, we could say, and he began learning a whole new spiritual language. He didn't immediately become the person we know as the apostle Paul. It took several years for him to sort out what he began to see spiritually. In what ways are our experiences like Saul's? —C. R. B.

CONCLUSION

Think of the believers you know of who could have been described as the worst of sinners. What differences do you now see? How do you explain these differences? Those who knew Saul of Tarsus were amazed at the difference after he met the Lord. When he began preaching in the synagogues after his baptism, those who heard about it could not believe the change (see Acts 9:21).

The gospel of Christ still has power to transform lives. That power has never dimmed. Our obligation is to reach out with this gospel to the worst of sinners. Who knows what surprises we will see!

Discovery Learning

This page contains an alternative lesson plan emphasizing learning activities. Classes desiring such student involvement will find these suggestions helpful. The next page is a reproducible activity page to further enhance discovery learning.

LEARNING GOALS

After participating in this lesson, each student will:

1. Summarize Saul's conversion experience.
2. Explain the significance of Saul's conversion.
3. Praise God for one specific way his or her life has been changed by knowing God.

INTO THE LESSON

Distribute the "Spoken to by Name" reproducible exercise to your early arrivers as they walk in. This will focus the conversation leading up to the start of class.

Recruit several class members—ideally spanning a wide age range—to recount their conversions to Christ. Suggest that they include details such as the people who influenced them, the specific occasion of confession and submission, the sudden changes in the way they behaved and how others behaved toward them, and other matters they consider significant.

At the end of their accounts say, "All of us have some vivid memories of the occasion when we first named Jesus as Lord. Today's study is of one whose life was turned around completely in a series of startling events."

INTO THE WORD

Recruit three good readers to assist with this activity. Say, "Our text today records the occasion of Paul's call to faith and ministry. Two other times Paul recites the occasion when he was being challenged regarding his ministry: before the Jews in Jerusalem and before King Agrippa in Caesarea. Our readers are going to read the three texts in a comparison format. Listen for common elements; listen for variations."

Prepare the following list in advance for your three readers. Instruct them to alternate reading to the class, as implied by the lists.

9:1, 2	22:4, 5	26:9-11
9:3, 4	22:6, 7	26:12-14
9:5, 6	22:8	26:15
9:7, 8	22:9-11	26:16
9:9-14, 17	22:12, 13	26:17, 18
9:15, 16, 18	22:14-16	[none]
9:19, 20	[none]	26:19, 20

As class members note variations, remind them that the three accounts were given with different purposes to different audiences. Note these purposes: the first account is God's revelation of the events; the second account is Paul's defense and explanation of his ministry to angry Jews who had assumed Paul had brought Gentiles into the temple; the third account is Paul's defense of himself before a political ruler as to why he is under arrest and why he has appealed to Caesar's court.

Another activity for examining today's text is to "interview" three of the minor characters in the story: Judas of Straight Street, with whom Paul was staying upon arrival in Damascus; the (hypothetical) wife of Ananias; and one of Paul's fellow travelers from Jerusalem. (The "Confusion" reproducible exercise is similar to this.)

After a reading of the text, ask the class to develop questions they would like to have these three characters answer if they were available for an interview. Share the following examples: for Judas, "What did Saul tell you when he was brought in blind to your house?"; for the wife, "Had your husband ever gotten up and run out in such a way as he did on the occasion he went to Saul?"; for one of Saul's fellow travelers, "What exactly did you see and hear on the road when Saul fell to the ground?" As the questions are developed, ask what the questioner thinks the answer may be.

Say to your class, "Ananias is called disciple in verse 10 of our text. Which title do you prefer for your relationship to Christ: child of God, believer, Christian, disciple, saint? Why do you prefer that choice?" Give opportunity for various choices and explanations.

INTO LIFE

Say, "God declared Saul to be his chosen vessel for a special purpose (Acts 9:15). When you look around our congregation, whom do you see who especially seems to be called for a specific purpose in God's kingdom?"

Collect several small ceramic vases, such as those sold in dollar stores. Provide one for each learner. Ask each to choose a name from the list the class compiled and write a short thank-you note. The note can be as simple as, "I thank God that he is using you as a chosen vessel for____." Roll the completed note and insert it into the small vase. Ask an older children's class to deliver the "vessels" to the people intended. (Alternative: use the "Changed" reproducible exercise to write a thank-you note to God.)

Spoken to by Name

On rare occasions in the Bible, God spoke to individuals by name. Both Saul and Ananias received that honor in today's text, Acts 9. Before you look up the following Scriptures, decide who else God spoke to. Write down your responses and read the Bible texts below to confirm or correct your choices.

_____   _____   _____   _____
Exodus 3:4   1 Samuel 3:6   1 Kings 19:13   Matthew 1:20

Confusion

Saul was not the only person confused on his journey from Jerusalem to Damascus. His fellow travelers were obviously startled and confused as well. What questions do you believe ran through their minds? Fill in the thought balloons with possible questions.

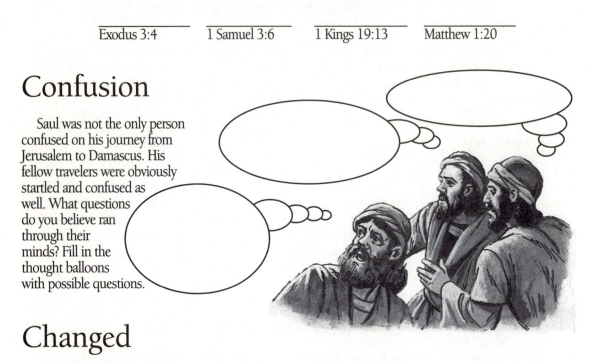

Changed

Few individuals have made the dramatic changes in beliefs and lifestyle that Saul did. But for each of us who has named Jesus as Lord and has begun submitting to his will, changes have been made. What are some of the ways you have seen your own life change? Use the space below to express your thanksgiving to God for helping you make those changes.

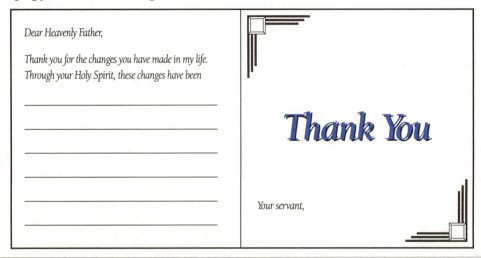

Dear Heavenly Father,

Thank you for the changes you have made in my life. Through your Holy Spirit, these changes have been

_____

_____

_____

_____

Thank You

Your servant,

LYDIA DEMONSTRATES FAITHFULNESS

LESSON 11

WHY TEACH THIS LESSON?

Take a minute to make a mental list of all the stuff you need to do this week. What's on your list? Perhaps things like attend church, go grocery shopping, see a movie, rake the leaves, clean out the gutters, winterize the car, eat out, and prepare a Sunday school lesson. Did "offer hospitality to someone" make it onto your list? Probably not!

Our problem is that offering hospitality seems a bit foreign—it's just something that's expendable given the requirements of an already busy schedule. Yet, according to the Bible, offering hospitality is not a suggestion, but a command (see Romans 12:13; 1 Peter 4:9). In today's lesson we see how someone's desire to serve and open her home superseded her inconvenience, her schedule, and even her safety.

This lesson gives us an example of hospitality that we can emulate today. Whether we open our homes, share a meal, a snack, or a conversation, hospitality is giving of oneself to another. It's an important way we can share God's love. A hospitable person is readily receptive to others.

INTRODUCTION

A. CONGRESS ON HOSPITALITY

A well-known professor has issued a challenge to the church that must be taken seriously. He was summoning the church to a national congress on hospitality. He says that it could be held in Minneapolis near the Betty Crocker® Kitchens, and could perhaps borrow the Pillsbury Doughboy® as its symbol. After all, he says, there is truth to the old slogan, "Nothing says lovin' like something from the oven."

His point is to remind believers that the world of Jesus was a world where hospitality meant "love of strangers." Yet he charges that too often people who visit our churches feel unwelcome. They are not greeted enthusiastically. They are not even noticed. It is as if we think a one-line greeting in the Sunday bulletin covers the need adequately.

But, says the professor, hospitality breaks down barriers and helps to build bridges. For those who are tempted to shrug off this call for a congress on hospitality because other evangelistic outreaches are planned, the professor points out that hospitality does not conflict with outreach, but rather complements it. To invite someone in for coffee, to offer to baby-sit, to take a meal to a sick mother—all of these show that Christians care. And people will listen to someone who cares.

Then he concludes by saying that he withdraws his call for a congress on hospitality! Instead, he says we should invite a few lonely folks into our homes. There we can show them genuine Christian hospitality. This, too, is the love of Christ.

DEVOTIONAL READING:
ACTS 16:25-34
BACKGROUND SCRIPTURE:
ACTS 16
PRINTED TEXT:
ACTS 16:6-15, 40

LESSON AIMS

After participating in this lesson, each student will be able to:

1. Retell the account of Lydia's conversion.

2. Compare and contrast the importance of hospitality in the ancient and modern worlds.

3. Plan two class hospitality events: one for believers and one for unbelievers.

WHAT DO YOU THINK?

How can our church become a "congress of hospitality"?

Nov
13

KEY VERSE

When she and the members of her household were baptized, she invited us to her home. "If you consider me a believer in the Lord," she said, "come and stay at my house." And she persuaded us. —Acts 16:15

B. Lesson Background

By the time the reader of Acts meets Lydia, the preaching of the gospel has traveled from Jerusalem to all Judea and Samaria and onward to the Gentile world. Acts 1:8 predicted this. As the book of Acts unfolds, we see examples of conversions at each stage of the story. In Jerusalem there are conversions of people such as the audience at Pentecost (2:38-41) plus a large number of priests (6:7). Beyond the city limits of Jerusalem there are the conversions of the Samaritans (8:4-25), the Ethiopian (8:26-40), Saul of Tarsus (9:1-19), and Cornelius (chapter 10). Well outside the boundaries of Judea and Samaria, there are the conversions of the Philippian jailer (16:16-34), the Corinthians (18:7, 8), and more.

Beginning in Acts 13:1, the missionary travels of the apostle Paul are the focus of the book. The church in Antioch commissioned Paul and Barnabas to carry the gospel beyond that Syrian city to the regions of Cyprus (a large island), Pisidia, Pamphylia, and Galatia. We often refer to this as Paul's first missionary journey (Acts 13:1–14:28). On the next missionary journey (Acts 15:36–18:22), Paul and Silas visited the previous locations, but then pushed farther west toward Roman Asia.

It is at this point in the second missionary journey of Paul that we arrive at today's lesson. The example of the convert named Lydia challenges modern believers to think of hospitality as part of faithful obedience in service to Christ. The year is perhaps A.D. 50, and it has been some 16 years since Paul's conversion (last week's lesson).

I. GUIDANCE FROM THE SPIRIT (ACTS 16:6-10)

A. Spirit's Prohibition (vv. 6, 7)

6, 7. Paul and his companions traveled throughout the region of Phrygia and Galatia, having been kept by the Holy Spirit from preaching the word in the province of Asia. When they came to the border of Mysia, they tried to enter Bithynia, but the Spirit of Jesus would not allow them to.

The missionary journeys of *Paul* are usually aimed at the larger Roman cities. For this reason, cities like Antioch of Syria, Ephesus, and Corinth are prominent in the account of Paul's work. The regions of Phrygia and Galatia are locations in which Paul and Barnabas had established churches on the first missionary journey. Now Paul and Silas seek to spread the gospel beyond what was accomplished previously.

On the route that Paul and Silas are traveling, *Asia* is located to the west and *Bithynia* to the north. For reasons unknown, *the Spirit* communicates to the missionaries that these destinations are off limits.

The travelers obey the direction they receive. Since traveling west or north is prohibited, they move in a northwesterly direction toward Troas and beyond.

B. Man from Macedonia (vv. 8-10)

8. So they passed by Mysia and went down to Troas.

We can only wonder what the travelers think as they are led to restrain their preaching when *Mysia* is such a logical target. *Troas* is close to the ruins of the ancient city of Troy and is located on the eastern coastline of the Aegean Sea. This port city is an important link in the Mediterranean network of commercial activity. Finding a Roman sailing vessel headed for other destinations will not be difficult. Paul will revisit this important city at a later time (see Acts 20:5, 6; 2 Corinthians 2:12).

What Do You Think?

We often go forward with our plans when they may be against what the Holy Spirit desires. How does the Spirit say no to plans we make that are out of line with the will of God? How has the Spirit said no to some of our church's plans?

9. During the night Paul had a vision of a man of Macedonia standing and begging him, "Come over to Macedonia and help us."

Macedonia is a province brought under Roman control by 146 B.C. Made famous during the Greek period by Philip II, father of Alexander the Great, Macedonia contains well-known cities such as Philippi and Thessalonica. *During the night*, Paul sees what is often called the Macedonian *vision*. What distinguishes the man in Paul's vision as being from Macedonia is not specified, but the invitation is clear.

In saying *help us*, the assistance that the *man* calls for is to hear the gospel of Christ. When we send the gospel to people who have not heard it, we are offering the best possible help that we can give!

10. After Paul had seen the vision, we got ready at once to leave for Macedonia, concluding that God had called us to preach the gospel to them.

The quick response of *Paul* to *the vision* reflects his readiness to obey the will of the Lord. We can wonder at the arrangements that Paul needs to make in going down to the docks, waiting for a Roman commercial vessel sailing in the direction of Macedonia, and contacting the ship's captain in order to pay for passage. But the book of Acts skips over all of these details. What is primary is that Paul moves quickly to obey the call from *God*.

The use of the term *we* in this verse is an example of sections in Acts where the narrative takes on a first-person perspective. These "we sections" are found in Acts 16:10-17; 20:5–21:18; and 27:1–28:16. Because the rest of Acts uses the third-person in speaking of what "he" did or "they" did, the use of *we* in these sections is best explained by concluding that the author (namely Luke, the companion of Paul) becomes a participant in these events.

"If Only . . . "

"For of all sad words of tongue or pen, The saddest are these: 'It might have been.'" These words of John Greenleaf Whittier (1807–1892) have a pathetic ring to them that most of us can relate to. Who among us has not said, "If only I had done such and such, things might be better now"?

Sometimes the issues are larger than personal. When Prime Minister Neville Chamberlain returned from Germany after meeting with Adolf Hitler in September 1938, he informed the British nation that the recently signed accord represented "the desire of our two peoples never to go to war with one another again. . . . My good friends, this is the second time in our history that there has come back from Germany to Downing Street peace with honor. I believe it is peace in our time."

But less than two years later, Nazi Germany's air force had begun a lengthy bombardment of Britain. How many British citizens must have said, "If only we had not listened so naively to Mr. Chamberlain, we might have been spared the results of Nazi treachery!"

On the other hand, Christians in the Western world will never complain, "If only Paul had not followed the Spirit's leading, things would be better now." The hand of God was at work, and there is nothing to regret. Because Paul went where the Spirit led, Christianity became the dominant force in Western history for 2,000 years!
—C. R. B.

II. CONVERSION OF LYDIA (ACTS 16:11-14)
A. Arrival in Philippi (vv. 11, 12)
11. From Troas we put out to sea and sailed straight for Samothrace, and the next day on to Neapolis.

Paul and his companions immediately followed the leading of the Spirit. But, like Gideon in Judges 6, we often want further confirmation before obeying. Why are we this way? How can we more readily follow the Spirit's leading?

Chart of Conversions

Lesson 1	Acts 2:1-8, 36-42	Three thousand souls accepted Christ at Pentecost.
Lesson 2	Acts 2:43-47; 4:32-35	"The Lord added to the church daily such as should be saved" (2:47).
Lesson 4	Acts 4:1-4, 23-31	Many who heard Peter and John's message believed and the number of men grew to about 5,000.
Lesson 6	Acts 8:4-17	Philip preached in Samaria. Men and women were baptized—including Simon.
Lesson 7	Acts 8:26-38	Philip taught an Ethiopian eunuch who believed and was baptized.
Lesson 8	Acts 10:1-48	The conversion of Cornelius and those of his house.
Lesson 10	Acts 9:3-18	The conversion of Saul.
Lesson 11	Acts 16:6-15, 40	Lydia and her family were baptized.
Lesson 12	Acts 18:1-4, 18-21, 24-28	Priscilla and Aquila taught Apollos about baptism into Jesus Christ.

Visual for Lesson 11. *Use this chart to demonstrate that the book of Acts is a book about conversions.*

WHAT DO YOU THINK?

Many like Lydia believe that God exists and so they worship him. How should the church respond to unchristian "God-fearers"? Who are the unsaved God-fearers in our community?

Samothrace is a small island-city, rising about 5,500 feet above sea level, off the eastern coast of Macedonia. *Neapolis* serves as the port city for Philippi, which is located about ten miles inland. The sea voyage takes only a day, implying that the wind is favorable for the journey. Later, the same journey going in the opposite direction will take five days (Acts 20:6).

12. From there we traveled to Philippi, a Roman colony and the leading city of that district of Macedonia. And we stayed there several days.

Philippi is a major Roman city with a rich history. Named after Philip II, the city came under Roman control in 168 B.C. It is not the capital city of *Macedonia*, but rather is considered a leading city in one of the four districts into which Macedonia is divided. It became a colony (in 42 B.C.) because of its allegiance to Rome and its desire to be patterned after the Imperial City itself. Philippi is populated with retired Roman soldiers and not many Jews. The ministry lasts certain days, which may mean a stretch as short as a week.

B. RESPONSE OF LYDIA (vv. 13, 14)

13. On the Sabbath we went outside the city gate to the river, where we expected to find a place of prayer. We sat down and began to speak to the women who had gathered there.

Paul's usual pattern is first to go to the local synagogue when beginning a ministry in a new city (see Acts 13:14; 14:1; 18:4). In Philippi, however, the procedure is different as the travelers go to a place by a *river.* This may be a reference to the Gangites River, about a mile from town.

The gathering here of certain *women* for *prayer* on *the Sabbath* probably indicates that there is no synagogue in Philippi. Speaking with the women from a seated position places Paul in the role of a rabbi teaching his audience (compare Luke 4:20, 21).

14. One of those listening was a woman named Lydia, a dealer in purple cloth from the city of Thyatira, who was a worshiper of God. The Lord opened her heart to respond to Paul's message.

The description of *Lydia* as one who worships *God* means that she is Jewish, a convert to Judaism, or a God-fearing Gentile. Perhaps she and the others meet outside of the city because the city authorities consider her religion a threat.

Her profession indicates status and wealth, since *purple cloth* frequently is sold to royalty in the ancient world. The trade is often associated with *the city of Thyatira* in the Roman province of Asia (compare Revelation 2:18). Verse 15 (next) substantiates her status and wealth because her house is large enough to provide lodging for the missionaries.

In spite of the independence and wealth of Lydia, her *heart* is ready for the message of Christ. Her heart is *opened* up by the Lord as Paul speaks the word of God; she responds to the gospel. The phrase that describes God's actions in the heart of Lydia is important. There are some Christians who believe that God alone determines who responds to the gospel. Their position is that God opens up hearts as he determines to do, and hearers have no responsibility in the matter. This doctrine, when carried to its logical end, amounts to salvation against one's free will.

Though this verse makes clear that the Lord takes action in Lydia's heart, it does not rule out Lydia's own freewill faith as important in the process. This verse does not say, for example, that the Lord gave Lydia faith and repentance.

Accepting Christ depends both on the action of God in revealing to us the truth and on our personal, freewill initiative in accepting that truth. Paul talks about how we should work out our own salvation, but at the same time it is God who works in us to act according to his will (Philippians 2:12, 13). The Bible makes clear that God holds people responsible for their beliefs and actions. The Lord opens Lydia's heart to respond, but she must still respond to the truth by her own volition.

How revealing is this event when it comes to our understanding of evangelism! When we pray for those who need to accept Christ, we are praying to the Lord who opens hearts. But people with open hearts still need to hear the gospel from someone who takes the time to proclaim it. This group of women welcome into their circle some visitors from a distant land, and, without knowing it, they are bringing into their circle the message of the Christ who came to offer salvation to all.

III. HOSPITALITY OF LYDIA (ACTS 16:15, 40)

A. BAPTISM OF LYDIA'S HOUSEHOLD (v. 15)

15. *When she and the members of her household were baptized, she invited us to her home. "If you consider me a believer in the Lord," she said, "come and stay at my house." And she persuaded us.*

Paul's words to the women beside the river apparently include a discussion of the need to submit to baptism. Throughout the book of Acts, the story is the same with people who are converted to Christ. Typically, their faith and baptism are mentioned specifically. The Samaritans who listened to Philip's preaching believed and *were baptized* (8:12). The same is true of the Philippian jailer and his family (16:31-33). The Corinthians who listen to Paul's preaching also believe and are baptized (18:8). Lydia's conversion follows the same pattern.

After her baptism, Lydia makes a proposal that must not be overlooked. The book of Acts consistently offers a description of the heart of the person after baptism, and this is true with Lydia as well. In the case of the Ethiopian, he left rejoicing (Acts 8:39). The Philippian jailer is filled with joy, but also brings the missionaries into his house and prepares a meal for them (16:34). Part of Lydia's response after her baptism is her insistence that Paul and his companions *come and stay at* her *house.*

This invitation should be understood in the proper context. It would not have been considered a moral issue because there are likely both men and women who already live in Lydia's house as servants. But it may be a dangerous arrangement for Lydia because of potential resistance from a community that may be opposed to the gospel. The fickle mob that opposes the progress of the gospel can be seen at Ephesus (Acts 19:28). Lydia can invite the missionaries to stay in her home, but she cannot guarantee what the reaction of the neighbors will be. Her invitation, more than just an inconvenience to her busy schedule, is an act of courage.

UNSUNG HEROES

Almost everyone knows the name Lance Armstrong. We also know about his courageous recovery from cancer several years ago and how he became a record-setting Tour de France bicyclist. But has anyone here ever heard of Floyd Landis? Landis was one of Armstrong's teammates for the 2003 Tour de France in which Armstrong won his fifth straight victory. Seven months before the race, Landis broke his hip in a training accident. He had hip surgery again just two months before the big race.

In the intricate strategy of bicycle racing, a champion's victory is due almost as much to his teammates' skills in protecting him from the challenges of other teams

HOW TO SAY IT

Aegean. A-JEE-un.
Amphipolis. Am-FIP-o-liss.
Antioch. AN-tee-ock.
Apollonia. Ap-uh-LOW-nee-uh.
Athens. ATH-unz.
Berea. Buh-REE-uh.
Bithynia. Bih-THIN-ee-uh.
Cornelius. Cor-NEEL-yus.
Cyprus. SIGH-prus.
Ethiopian. E-thee-O-pee-un.
Galatia. Guh-LAY-shuh.
Lydia. LID-ee-uh.
Macedonia. Mass-eh-DOE-nee-uh.
Mysia. MISH-ee-uh.
Neapolis. Nee-AP-o-lis.
Pamphylia. Pam-FILL-ee-uh.
Phrygia. FRIJ-e-uh.
Pisidia. Pih-SID-ee-uh.
Samothrace. SAM-o-thrays.
synagogue. SIN-uh-gog.
Syrian. SEAR-ee-un.
Thessalonica. THESS-uh-lo-NYE-kuh.
Thyatira. THY-uh-TIE-ruh.

WHAT DO YOU THINK?

In this age of easy access to restaurants and motels, is "in-home" hospitality really all that important? Why, or why not?

PRAYER

Lord, may the gospel of Christ open not only our eyes to the truth, but our doors to the cause of preaching the gospel. We pray this through Christ who opened his heart for us, amen.

THOUGHT TO REMEMBER

Sometimes to open a door is the best way to open a heart.

as it is to his own strength and stamina. This is where Landis came in. The determination of the "little guy" helped the champion to win the prize, while Landis finished in 77th place.

Lydia was also such a person. Paul's name appears 128 times in Acts (in the original Greek), while Lydia is named only twice. But she helped "the champion" succeed by her largely unsung contribution. True faith is demonstrated by a willingness to serve where needed even when others have the spotlight. Lydia's hospitality to Paul is an example of this. Her love for the cause of Christ prompted her quiet help to Paul in his ministry. How many of us practice this unobtrusive, but still vitally important, proof of our faith?　　　　　—C. R. B.

B. PAUL'S FAREWELL TO LYDIA (v. 40)

40. After Paul and Silas came out of the prison, they went to Lydia's house, where they met with the brothers and encouraged them. Then they left.

The dangerous situation in Philippi erupted in persecution for *Paul and Silas* when the evil spirit was thrown out of the slave girl and her owners objected to the loss of their profit (Acts 16:19-21). Paul and Silas were beaten and thrown into jail as a result (16:22, 23).

Following the events of Acts 16:24-34, the city officials decided to release them and send them out of the city quietly (16:35, 36). The forthcoming travels will take the missionaries on to such places as Amphipolis, Apollonia, Thessalonica, Berea, Athens, and Corinth (chapters 17 and 18). Thus the gospel will spread despite persecution.

Before departing from Philippi, Paul and his companions feel compelled to stop again at the home of Lydia, whose generous hospitality has been so welcome a short time before. This also gives them a chance to see *the brothers*. This is a reference to the new church that is meeting in the city of Philippi, probably in Lydia's home.

Once again the hospitality of Lydia steps to center stage. The chance for the missionary travelers to see their fellow Christians requires a place for the meeting. Lydia's home is not only open to the missionaries, but also to the entire church. This fact implies that she has a large home by first-century standards. Whatever the risk from her pagan neighbors, Lydia is devoted to helping those who travel to preach the gospel of Christ.

CONCLUSION

Lydia's example sets the pace for modern believers who want to use their resources in ways that advance the cause of Christ. One of the best resources a believer has is often his or her own home.

Using our homes for the work of the gospel means considering our homes as gifts given to us by the Lord. As with God's other gifts, it means dedicating our homes to the glory of God and then opening our doors to opportunities that arise. Perhaps these opportunities will come in the form of missionaries who need a place to stay while on furlough. Or perhaps the church will need a place for young people to gather. Or perhaps a troubled family will need some temporary shelter.

In all of these cases, believers in Christ can make their hospitality a witness for the gospel of Christ. This is the reason for commands such as Hebrews 13:2: "Do not forget to entertain strangers, for by so doing some people have entertained angels without knowing it." What an important way to demonstrate faithfulness!

Discovery Learning

This page contains an alternative lesson plan emphasizing learning activities. Classes desiring such student involvement will find these suggestions helpful. The next page is a reproducible activity page to further enhance discovery learning.

LEARNING GOALS

After participating in this lesson, each student will be able to:

1. Retell the account of Lydia's conversion.

2. Compare and contrast the importance of hospitality in the ancient and modern worlds.

3. Plan two class hospitality events: one for believers and one for unbelievers.

INTO THE LESSON

Prepare 11 index cards with the following sets of letters front and back respectively: H and E; O and V; S and A; P and N; I and G; T and E; A and L; L and I; I and S; T and M; Y and an exclamation point. Display the cards so that the word *hospitality* is spelled. (One way to display the cards would be to attach them to the wall with reusable adhesive.)

Say, "Our study today is a lesson about hospitality and its results. But it is also a lesson about another Christian responsibility. Behind each of these cards is another letter. Try to guess the letters that will reveal the second Christian responsibility we will examine in today's lesson. As you correctly guess a letter, I will turn over the corresponding card." Allow students to suggest letters until someone correctly identifies the word *evangelism.* Then say, "Lydia's hospitality provided an excellent opportunity for evangelism. It always does."

INTO THE WORD

Display a wall map or PowerPoint® computer image that highlights the geography of today's study. Seeing the important cities of the first-century Roman world will help students understand the culture as well as the geography.

Present the class the following quiz (also found in the student book) and direct them to answer each question with a verse number from today's text in Acts 16:6-15, 40. (Answers are given in parentheses.)

___1. What was Lydia's source of livelihood? (v. 14)

___2. Who comforted whom when Paul and Silas were finally released from imprisonment? (v. 40)

___3. Where did Jewish believers assemble in Philippi? (v. 13)

___4. Does the Holy Spirit ever say no to good plans? (vv. 6, 7)

___5. What did Lydia and others in her household do when they accepted Jesus? (v. 15)

___6. Did anyone else in Paul's company have his same dream of a man in Macedonia? (v. 10)

___7. What kind of sailing weather did Paul encounter from Troas to Neapolis? (v. 11)

___8. The man of Macedonia called for help; what is the best help anyone can be given? (vv. 9, 10)

If your congregation has a woman who enjoys drama, recruit her to give the following monologue as Lydia. Be sure to give her a copy of the monologue early enough for advance preparation.

"When Paul and Silas were arrested, the news came back to me immediately. Philippi is not the kind of city where such an event escapes notice. Those rascals using that poor girl with a demon's voice would not lose their profit quietly, you understand. Paul and Silas were my honored houseguests. I first thought, Lydia, you must rush down to the jail and see what you can do. But Cleotus, my beloved servant, said, 'Mistress, to do so is dangerous. You must not go!' All we could do was pray and wait to see the outcome.

"My mind returned to that Saturday evening by the river. Devoted women from all over Philippi were there to pray and worship, for we had no synagogue hall. When strangers arrived, we were leery, but Paul's words clearly were from God.

"We were in the right place. When Paul pictured the death and resurrection of Christ, his instruction to be baptized brought no objections.

"I was exultant. Everything seemed so new. My house is large, but it had the lonely emptiness of business. So I invited Paul and his company to stay with us. What a blessed time we had!"

INTO LIFE

Divide your class into two groups: the "Jailers" and the "Lydias." Note that both the jailer and Lydia hosted Paul in their homes at the time of their conversions. Ask the "Jailers" to plan a kindness event for unbelievers (perhaps taking treats to a fire station, etc.). Ask the "Lydias" to plan an event for believers (perhaps taking Christian widows and widowers out for a luncheon). As an alternative, use small groups to work through the two lists from the reproducible page.

A Congregational Kindness List

Which of these kindnesses does your congregation provide as part of its overall ministry? Place a check-mark to the left of each kindness your church does.

___ A family dinner on the occasion of a funeral
___ A house for a missionary family on furlough
___ A "welcome to the neighborhood" gift for new residents
___ A dinner invitation plan for worship service visitors
___ A church pantry for needy families
___ A program matching senior adults to young families for social occasions
___ A temporary shelter for needy young mothers and their children
___ A welcome center at your church building for new attenders
___ Study groups that meet in members' homes
___ A benevolent fund for families who lose a home to fire or other damage
___ Maintenance services for those unable to maintain their homes
___ A clothing closet for those in need

A Personal Action List

Go back to the list above and put a check mark out to the right of the kindnesses that your congregations does not currently provide, but that you wish they did.

Which would you be willing to help organize? Write your initials by that one and immediately write a proposal to your church's leadership, as below.

To the leadership of my church,

I think Christ would be honored if we were to add the following hospitality-related ministries.

1. _____
2. _____
3. _____

Furthermore, I volunteer to help with or lead these ministries.

Signed, _____

PRISCILLA AND AQUILA SERVE TOGETHER

LESSON 12

WHY TEACH THIS LESSON?

In his book *Frames of Mind*, Howard Gardner proposes that there are 8 distinct types of human intelligence, which we all possess in varying degrees. David Kiersey categorizes human temperaments into 16 groups in his book *Please Understand Me II*. Organizations often use findings such as these to create teams of people whose talents complement each other. Further, these studies show what many would say is obvious: no one person excels in all areas.

God has made each of us to be a unique combination of personality, passions, and talents. While society often rewards individual achievement, there are many endeavors that benefit from, or even depend on, a pooling of effort, resources, and abilities. In short, we need each other. It is divine design. Today's lesson shows Christians sharing their abilities to support and encourage each other while spreading the gospel. In the 20 centuries that have passed, the lessons of teamwork should be ever new.

INTRODUCTION

A. TEAMWORK

Two men were riding a bicycle built for two, and they came to a big, steep hill. It took a great deal of struggle for the men to complete the stiff climb. When they got to the top, the man in front turned to the other and said, "That sure was a hard climb." The fellow in back replied, "Yes, and if I hadn't kept the brakes on all the way we certainly would have rolled down backward."

I wonder how many of us have the brakes on with God? Progress is always more difficult when half the team refuses to cooperate. The body of Christ depends on the cooperation of all its members. Only then can Christ's work be accomplished fully in the church.

Today's lesson brings Priscilla and Aquila to the forefront as a married couple whose ministry spanned several cities in the Roman world. Their example reminds us of the cooperation required for effective ministry for Christ.

B. LESSON BACKGROUND

The ancient Jews who lived outside their homeland of Palestine came to be called the Diaspora. Such Jews could be found in cities such as Rome, Alexandria in Egypt, and Antioch of Syria. The term Diaspora came from the idea of scattering seed. Since the days of the Assyrian and Babylonian captivities (the eighth through sixth centuries before Christ), the Jews had been scattered widely outside of Palestine.

Priscilla and Aquila were Diaspora Jews who became Christians. Diaspora Jews were not always popular in Roman society. Romans looked with suspicion

DEVOTIONAL READING:
LUKE 10:1-11

BACKGROUND SCRIPTURE:
ACTS 18:1–19:10

PRINTED TEXT:
ACTS 18:1-4, 18-21, 24-28

LESSON AIMS

After participating in this lesson, each student will be able to:

1. Tell how Paul, Priscilla, and Aquila demonstrated the benefits of teamwork in spreading the gospel.

2. Identify modern-day examples of Christian teamwork.

3. Plan a specific way to minister cooperatively for Christ.

WHAT DO YOU THINK?

Synergy is combined action. Combined, cooperative efforts produce greater results than separate, individual efforts. How can the church use the principle of synergy?

KEY VERSE

Because he was a tentmaker as they were, he stayed and worked with them.

—*Acts 18:3*

Nov
20

on Jewish religious practices, and they loathed the Jewish contention that there was but one God.

From time to time, conflicts surfaced between Jewish and Roman elements within society, as happened during the reign of Claudius Caesar, who reigned A.D. 41–54. The Roman historian Suetonius describes how Claudius expelled the Jews from the city of Rome because of riots between Jews and Gentiles, which apparently were caused by disputes about someone called Chrestus. Most scholars take this name as a reference to Christ and believe that Claudius wanted the Jews to leave because of their supposed role in the instigation of this trouble. The date for this decree was A.D. 49 or 50. The Roman leadership of the time really didn't see Christianity as a separate religion, but as an offshoot or variation of Judaism.

So Jewish residents such as Priscilla and Aquila were forced from their homes. Conditions in the Roman world were relatively favorable to travelers, so Jews driven from Rome did have options. The commercial centers of the Mediterranean world were connected by a network of roads, and travelers moved along these thoroughfares on a regular basis. Roman shipping lanes crisscrossed the Mediterranean Sea, so travelers could journey from Rome to any site in an eastward direction in a matter of a few weeks.

Today's lesson picks up the story of Aquila and Priscilla in Acts 18. They enter the narrative of Paul's travels because of his encounter with them in the city of Corinth.

I. MINISTRY WITH PAUL (ACTS 18:1-4)

A. PAUL ARRIVES IN CORINTH (v. 1)

1. After this, Paul left Athens and went to Corinth.

The phrase *after this* refers to the events of Acts 17:16-34. Paul's departure from *Athens* comes after his address before the Areopagus on Mars' Hill. *Paul* is leading a missionary tour, which had begun in Antioch of Syria (Acts 15:35, 36). He had left Silas and Timothy behind in Berea while he moved on without them to Athens and *Corinth* (17:14, 15). Even so, there is some traveling back and forth by Silas and Timothy (see Acts 18:5; 1 Thessalonians 3:1). The year is most likely A.D. 50.

Corinth is an important Roman city. It is located on an isthmus some 40 miles west of Athens. Corinth has access to harbors on both sides of the city: Lechaeum on the west and Cenchrea on the east. Corinth thus commands a powerful position for commercial activity with its access to the Roman sea-lanes. The Romans had even developed a quick way to move ships across the isthmus on a track, thus saving the voyage around the dangerous southern coastline.

With its mixture of cultures and pagan religions, Corinth offers the same moral conditions that one would expect in larger commercial cities today. Paul wants to see the gospel take root in this pagan city.

B. PAUL RECEIVES ASSISTANCE (vv. 2-4)

2, 3. There he met a Jew named Aquila, a native of Pontus, who had recently come from Italy with his wife Priscilla, because Claudius had ordered all the Jews to leave Rome. Paul went to see them, and because he was a tentmaker as they were, he stayed and worked with them.

For the first time in the New Testament, *Aquila* and *Priscilla* make their appearance. They may have been Christians before coming to Corinth from *Rome*, though nothing specifically is said about this. The emperor *Claudius* made no

WHAT DO YOU THINK?

Corinth was a major cultural and commercial center of its day. Should the church be more aggressive in reaching major cities instead of focusing so much on suburbs, exurbs, and rural settings? Why, or why not?

distinction between Jews who were believers in Jesus and those who were not when issuing his edict.

Paul arrives in Corinth with no means for earning an income except for his trade. If he carries any funds from the church that commissioned him in Antioch, these do not appear evident in the account of Acts. The arrival of Silas and Timothy from Macedonia probably provides some support from these churches because after their appearance, Paul turns from tentmaking to full-time preaching (Acts 18:5).

Fortunately for Paul, Jewish families of the day are very careful to equip their male children with a trade for life. That trade is tentmaking in the case of Paul. The phrase can include various kinds of leather-working, including the fashioning of tents, awnings, and coverings. Whatever prayers Paul offers for daily needs in Corinth are answered by the God who matches Paul with these fellow tentmakers.

4. Every Sabbath he reasoned in the synagogue, trying to persuade Jews and Greeks.

During the time that he spends tentmaking, Paul's pattern is to preach part-time by using *synagogue* meetings as his opportunity to reach the worshipers for Christ. Synagogues in the Diaspora include not just Jewish worshipers, but also Gentile worshipers called "God-fearers," who had not received circumcision.

Paul's entire effort in Corinth is off and running because of the help of Aquila and Priscilla. This couple provides the right amount of help to Paul for his preaching. It is possible that their leather-working shop is also the meeting place for the believers at Corinth.

II. MINISTRY IN EPHESUS (ACTS 18:18-21)

A. DEPARTURE FOR EPHESUS (v. 18)

18. Paul stayed on in Corinth for some time. Then he left the brothers and sailed for Syria, accompanied by Priscilla and Aquila. Before he sailed, he had his hair cut off at Cenchrea because of a vow he had taken.

Paul's ministry *in Corinth* lasts at least 18 months (see Acts 18:11). This verse comments on the end of that period, as *Paul* decides to move on. So he says good-bye to the Corinthian brothers and sails back *for Syria.* That is the Roman province that includes Antioch, his ultimate destination (Acts 18:22). *Priscilla and Aquila* leave Corinth with him because Paul has plans for their continuing work for the Lord.

Before boarding the sailing vessel, Paul has his head shaved *at Cenchrea,* the eastern port city for Corinth. The vow is probably a kind of Nazirite vow (see Numbers 6:1-21), which in some cases can be taken for a period of 30 days. Paul's act may be either the beginning or the conclusion of the *vow.* If it's the beginning of the vow, Paul may be shaving his head in order to take his *hair* with him to the temple in Jerusalem.

Upon arrival there, he may intend to throw it into the fire of a burnt offering, thus bringing the vow to completion. Such an action on Paul's part illustrates his firm connection with his Jewish heritage, even after his conversion to Christ. Naming the name of Jesus does not prevent him from participating in Jewish ceremonies at the temple (see also Acts 21:17-26).

Priscilla and Aquila's willingness to uproot and accompany Paul for an uncertain future speaks to their devotion and faith. Did they volunteer or did Paul ask them to accompany him? There is no way to know, but one easily imagines the idea springing almost spontaneously as the three discuss Paul's future labors.

WHAT DO YOU THINK?

Today we use the term tentmaker *to describe missionaries and others in ministry who are self-supporting in their work. When should this be a pattern for ministry today, if ever?*

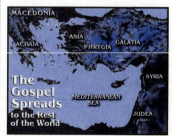

Visual for Lesson 12. *Use this map to help your students see the broader framework for Lessons 10 through 13.*

B. Arrival in Ephesus (v. 19)

19. They arrived at Ephesus, where Paul left Priscilla and Aquila. He himself went into the synagogue and reasoned with the Jews.

At this point Paul's plans for traveling to and through *Ephesus* become clear. Stopping there on his way to Syria, his message to the *synagogue* worshipers would be similar to his presentation in synagogues at Antioch of Pisidia (Acts 13:13-41) and Thessalonica (Acts 17:1-4).

Paul's plans for *Priscilla and Aquila* also become clear as he leaves them in Ephesus for further ministry. Here again the cooperation of this couple as a team working for Christ is important. They evidently listen to Paul's encouragement about leaving Corinth and traveling to Ephesus, setting up their leather-working business there, and working for the cause of Christ. Whatever the sacrifice to them personally, Aquila and Priscilla are willing to bear it in order to present their witness for Christ.

C. Departure from Ephesus (vv. 20, 21)

20, 21. When they asked him to spend more time with them, he declined. But as he left, he promised, "I will come back if it is God's will." Then he set sail from Ephesus.

Paul has a schedule set in his mind. So when some in *Ephesus* want him to stay longer, he declines in favor of moving on. Whatever reason Paul has for not staying, he promises to return to Ephesus. This is a promise he keeps on that third missionary journey (Acts 19). Apparently it is more important for Priscilla and Aquila to remain in Ephesus than to accompany Paul to Syria.

UNWELCOME GUESTS

Newspaper advice columns often carry letters from readers whose relatives come to visit and overstay their welcome. But humans aren't the only ones who have unwelcome guests. Pristine Lake Davis, in California's northern Sierra Nevada, has had some unwanted visitors for a couple of decades. Someone had introduced illegally a foreign fish species, namely the northern pike.

Pike are a popular game fish elsewhere, but these vicious predators have been killing off native species in Lake Davis. The fear is that the pike will wipe out the native trout as well as salmon downstream. Wildlife officials have poisoned the lake and used dynamite, nets, traps, and electric shocks—all to no avail. The pike still thrive, proving that visitors can cause trouble regardless of their species!

The apostle Paul was not that kind of guest. He had stayed with Aquila and Priscilla during the many months he had ministered in Corinth. They moved with Paul to Ephesus, and they begged him to continue as their guest when he announced other plans. To have found such a bond, they must have shared with him an affinity of personality as well as involvement in the same trade. More important, they also shared a firm commitment to the ministry of the gospel. That is the strongest basis for a lasting friendship, as well as for being a welcome guest.

—C. R. B.

III. MINISTRY WITH APOLLOS (ACTS 18:24-28)

A. Preaching of Apollos (vv. 24, 25)

24. Meanwhile a Jew named Apollos, a native of Alexandria, came to Ephesus. He was a learned man, with a thorough knowledge of the Scriptures.

This verse introduces us to *Apollos.* His background is Jewish, and he hails from *Alexandria* in Egypt, a city well known for its large Jewish community. The fact that he has *a thorough knowledge of the Scriptures* tells us that he is a scholar.

What Do You Think?

What is the value in a husband-wife team ministry? What are the drawbacks?

How to Say It

Achaia. Uh-KAY-uh.
Antioch. AN-tee-ock.
Apollos. Uh-PAHL-us.
Aquila. ACK-wih-luh.
Areopagus. Air-ee-OP-uh-gus.
Athens. ATH-unz.
Berea. Buh-REE-uh.
Cenchrea. SEN-kree-uh.
Claudius Caesar. CLAW-dee-us SEE-zur.
Ephesus. EF-uh-sus.
Judaism. JOO-duh-izz-um or JOO-day-izz-um.
Lechaeum. Lek-uh-EE-um.
Nazarite. NAZ-uh-rite.
Pisidia. Pih-SID-ee-uh.
Pontus. PON-tuss.
Suetonius. Soo-TOE-nee-us.
synagogue. SIN-uh-gog.
Syria. SEAR-ee-uh.
Thessalonica. THESS-uh-lo-NYE-kuh.

His arrival in Ephesus comes between the time of Paul's departure for Syria and Paul's return several months later (compare Acts 19:1).

25. He had been instructed in the way of the Lord, and he spoke with great fervor and taught about Jesus accurately, though he knew only the baptism of John.

Although he is a scholar, Apollos comes to Ephesus with some deficiencies. He apparently knows some accurate things *about Jesus* already. But when it comes to the subject of Christian baptism, he does not know more than *the baptism of John*. Thus his teaching about baptism lacks reference to those promises that come after Jesus' resurrection, such as forgiveness of sins and the gift of the Holy Spirit (see Acts 2:38; 22:16). John's baptism was designed to be temporary (Acts 19:1-5).

B. Instruction of Apollos (vv. 26-28)

26. He began to speak boldly in the synagogue. When Priscilla and Aquila heard him, they invited him to their home and explained to him the way of God more adequately.

Aquila and *Priscilla* hear the preaching of Apollos in Ephesus. Given all of the deficiencies they notice in his preaching, they could merely avoid him entirely. But instead, they take him *to their home* as they gently lead him to understand the facts about Jesus Christ. Nothing is said about the baptism of Apollos, but it is reasonable to assume that their teaching is followed by his baptism into Christ (compare again Acts 19:1-5).

Here again the example of this couple should encourage us to think of how cooperation can contribute to effective ministry. Both husband and wife are ready to be used by God in a private teaching ministry.

INFLUENTIAL PEOPLE

Michael Hart's book *The 100: A Ranking of the Most Influential Persons in History* may surprise us. He ranked Muhammad No. 1, Isaac Newton No. 2, and Jesus No. 3. Anticipating our objections, Hart said he would have ranked Jesus first if all the people who today identify themselves as Christians actually followed Jesus' teachings more substantially. Hart believes that modern Muslims show more of the influence of Muhammad in their lives than Christians do of Christ in theirs. Hmmm!

After we have recovered from our shock, we may take solace in the fact that Hart's list is a secular evaluation. Muhammad created a geographic empire; Jesus did not.

Not one of us is likely to make it into anyone's book about the 100—or 1,000 or even 10,000—most influential people in history. But that is not nearly as important as the kind of influence we can have on the people close to us. Aquila and Priscilla are good examples of this truth. In mentoring Apollos, their influence reached many others through the ministry of that man.

In a way that really counts, Aquila and Priscilla were influential people! We can be, too, if our concern is more for Christ than for worldly recognition. Can you think of someone whom you might mentor in the faith?   —C. R. B.

27. When Apollos wanted to go to Achaia, the brothers encouraged him and wrote to the disciples there to welcome him. On arriving, he was a great help to those who by grace had believed.

Apollos moves on *to Achaia*, the province in which Corinth is prominent. Paul's ministry had finished there several months before, and now Apollos is ready to add his influence. The believers in Ephesus *wrote* letters to the Christians in Achaia to encourage them to accept Apollos as a preacher of the truth.

WHAT DO YOU THINK?

What do we learn from the account of Aquila and Priscilla about how to approach those who have an incomplete or false knowledge of Scripture? Give an example of a time when you did not follow the pattern of Aquila and Priscilla; explain what happened.

PRAYER

Father of all believers in Jesus, we ask you today to remind us that we belong to your family. We ask that all rivalry, jealousy, and triumphalism against other Christians will disappear in favor of the unity and peace that comes to your people wherever Jesus is truly honored as Lord. Through Christ who adds us to his church we pray, amen.

THOUGHT TO REMEMBER

May the voices of Christians working together for Christ blend as one.

Paul later comments on the work of Apollos by remarking that he (Paul) had planted the seed in Corinth, "Apollos watered it, but God made it grow" (1 Corinthians 3:6). It was the ministry of Priscilla and Aquila that made this "watering" possible.

28. For he vigorously refuted the Jews in public debate, proving from the Scriptures that Jesus was the Christ.

Apollos's preaching method of showing by the Scriptures that *Jesus was the Christ* is consistent with the method of the apostles. Think about Peter's sermon on the Day of Pentecost (Acts 2:1-36), which drew from Psalm 16:8-11; 110:1; and Joel 2:28-32 to prove that Jesus is both Lord and Christ. Compare also Paul's sermon in the synagogue of Antioch of Pisidia (Acts 13:16-41). There he presented a grand review of Old Testament history as a backdrop for the Messiah—Jesus Christ. The preaching of Apollos follows this method of establishing proof as he engages the Jews publicly.

Even so, the strength in the words of Apollos is not just his factual knowledge. He speaks with power. He himself is convinced utterly that Jesus is the Christ. When Jewish audiences hear him, they are presented with authoritative persuasion to reach the same conclusion. And behind this powerful preaching stands the solid, low-key ministry of Aquila and Priscilla!

CONCLUSION

In three different cities—Rome, Corinth, and Ephesus—Priscilla and Aquila worked in the ministry of Christ. Their work in Rome may have contributed to the order from Claudius Caesar to expel the Jews from the city. That's speculation, however. We know for certain that this couple went back to that great city as witnesses for Christ (Romans 16:3-5a).

The work of this couple in Corinth enabled the apostle Paul to survive in a difficult situation without income and without friends. Priscilla and Aquila turned their business into something of a support system for mission work, and their home into a place for believers to meet. Their work in Ephesus exemplified what it means to guide someone who needs more of the truth into a productive ministry for the Lord.

The New Testament presents Priscilla and Aquila working together. Whether referred to as Priscilla and Aquila (see Acts 18:18; Romans 16:3) or as Aquila and Priscilla (see Acts 18:2; 1 Corinthians 16:19) seems to make no difference. This couple consistently appears united in their service to Christ.

These two accomplish things together that could not have been accomplished apart. The fact that Priscilla's name can appear first in some cases has been noticed by scholars, who sometimes take it to mean that she had a prominence in the church separate from her husband. Yet the fact that their names can be interchanged may tell us that their cooperation was so complete that who received the credit meant nothing to them or anyone else, as long as the work was accomplished.

Whether thinking of husbands and wives or best friends who serve Christ side by side, the team of Priscilla and Aquila is a model for modern believers. Their unity in service is something we should imitate, especially when it comes to presenting Christ before a pagan society. Our efforts to influence the world for Christ will be hampered if our service is fractured, sporadic, and individualistic. When our faith operates consistently and cooperatively with believers who share our love for the Lord, the world will take note that we have been in the presence of Jesus.

Discovery Learning

This page contains an alternative lesson plan emphasizing learning activities. Classes desiring such student involvement will find these suggestions helpful. The next page is a reproducible activity page to further enhance discovery learning.

LEARNING GOALS

After participating in this lesson, each student will be able to:

1. Tell how Paul, Priscilla, and Aquila demonstrated the benefits of teamwork in spreading the gospel.

2. Identify modern examples of Christian teamwork.

3. Plan a specific way to minister cooperatively for Christ.

INTO THE LESSON

As your early arrivers walk in, hand out one (or more) of the three reproducible exercises. They can work on these and have some preliminary discussions before class starts.

Provide paper and pens for students when it's time to begin, and ask them to make a list of all the places they have lived. After a few minutes, ask students to compare their lists. Give a small prize (such as an atlas from a dollar store) for the one who has lived in the most places.

Next, say, "We think of our modern society as a highly mobile one. But the Roman Empire had a transient population as well. Priscilla and Aquila are noted to have lived in Pontus, Rome, Corinth, and Ephesus—some places more than once. Of course, God does care where you live; but more importantly he cares about what you do where you live. Priscilla and Aquila did the right thing wherever they were."

INTO THE WORD

Prepare index cards with the questions and answers below. Place either a question or an answer on each card. (Use only one answer or one question per index card. Do not put questions and answers on the same cards.) Randomly distribute the cards; keep one card for yourself if you have an uneven number of students.

Q: Where was Paul before he came to Corinth? A: Athens.

Q: Why had Priscilla and Aquila left Rome? A: The emperor had ordered all Jews out of the city.

Q: Why did Paul initially associate with Priscilla and Aquila? A: All were tentmakers.

Q: What was the plan for evangelism in Corinth? A: To instruct in the synagogue.

Q: Where did Paul go after he left Corinth? A: To the city of Ephesus.

Q: Why did Paul cut off his hair before sailing for Syria? A: He had taken a vow of some sort.

Q: What was the shortcoming in Apollos's religious education? A: He knew only of the baptism of John, not of baptism into Christ.

Q: Where did Paul leave Priscilla and Aquila as he traveled on to Syria? A: At Ephesus.

Q: What did Paul do in the synagogue at Ephesus? A: He reasoned with the Jews about Christ.

Q: Where was Apollos from? A: Alexandria in northern Africa.

Q: Where did Aquila and Priscilla hear Apollos's teaching? A: In the synagogue at Ephesus.

Q: How did Aquila and Priscilla deal with Apollos's incomplete doctrinal understanding? A: They took him aside privately and taught him the complete gospel.

Q: What was Apollos's plan when he left Ephesus? A: He wanted to visit the churches in Achaia.

Q: By what means did the Ephesian Christians commend Apollos to the believers in Achaia? A: They gave him a letter of recommendation.

Once the cards are distributed, say, "Circulate among yourselves until you find the question or answer that is a pair with your card." After pairs are made, ask students who are paired up to read their questions and answers. Then ask the group to identify the verse where the information is found.

INTO LIFE

Provide your class with the names and addresses of missionary couples that your congregation supports. Ask for volunteers to write thank-you letters to them during the next week, commending them for their cooperative effort in spreading the gospel. If there is one missionary couple that your class is especially close to, consider collecting a special offering to send them as an "Aquila and Priscilla award" and as a thank-you.

If your congregation has a preacher whose wife faithfully serves the congregation with him, present the "Aquila and Priscilla award" to them. (The gift could be matching leather wallets in honor of Aquila and Priscilla's craft in leather.) Invite the preacher and his wife to the beginning of your class next Sunday and make the presentation with a reference to your study of the ministry team of Aquila and Priscilla.

Moving with the Gospel

Believers of the first century moved about freely in the Roman world. In today's text ten places are included. Write in the four province names (Achaia, Italy, Pontus, Syria) on the lines at their location. Then write in the six city names (Alexandria, Athens, Cenchrea, Corinth, Ephesus, Rome) at the dots.

Two Are Better Than One

For a biblical statement on the advantage of two working together, look at Ecclesiastes 4:9-12 and fill in the blanks appropriately here.

"Two are better than one, because they have a _____ _____ for their _____: If one _____ _____, his friend can help him _____. But pity the man who falls and has _____ _____ to help him _____! Also, if two _____ _____ together, they will keep _____. But how can one keep _____ alone? Though one may be _____, two can _____ themselves. A cord of _____ _____ is not quickly broken."

Still True

Which of the following Christian ministries is probably better if two people do them together rather than one person alone? Why?

_____ Make hospital visits

_____ Greet church visitors at the door

_____ Ask another for forgiveness for a slight or grievance

_____ Take a gift to parents of a newborn

_____ Baby-sit for a young couple to free them for time together

_____ Teach a class of children

_____ Counsel a person with a problem

_____ Visit a widow to help with house maintenance

_____ Present the gospel in someone's home

_____ Deliver food gifts to the needy on special occasions

PAUL SAYS GOOD-BYE

WHY TEACH THIS LESSON?

Some say life is not a sprint but a marathon. Perhaps life is truly more like a *relay*. We live and work and minister in a place for a time, then changes come. Job, life stage, or situational changes force us to let go of the people and/or work we've invested in, hopefully leaving others to carry on in our stead. The critical, sometimes difficult part of the relay is the passing of the baton. In today's lesson, that's what we see Paul doing: passing the baton to the faithful believers he was leaving behind. Change was about to take place.

Many things have been said about the idea of change. Some of those observations are whimsical, some are ironic, and some are serious. Samples include, "Change is inevitable, except from a vending machine"; "There is nothing permanent except change"; and "You must welcome change as the rule, but not as the ruler." Although most of us find change to be challenging, we can choose to bless others with words of encouragement and empowerment as we traverse the passages of our lives. We can look at beginnings and endings as opportunities to strengthen others in our highly transient, unpredictable world. Today's lesson has some important things to say about how to handle change in a godly way.

INTRODUCTION

A. COMFORT FOR THE GRIEVING

In his book *Helping the Hurting*, Philip Yancey tells a story about the famous composer Ludwig van Beethoven (1770–1827), a man who was not known for social grace. Because of deafness later in life, Beethoven found conversation difficult and humiliating. When he learned of the death of a friend's son, Beethoven hurried to the house, overcome with grief. He had no words of comfort to offer, but he saw a piano in the room. For the next half hour he played the piano, pouring out his emotions in the most eloquent way he could. When he finished, he left. The friend later remarked that no one else's visit had meant so much.

We may contrast that remark with the words of Job to the friends who thought they were helping: "miserable comforters are you all" (Job 16:2). Believers are sometimes faced with challenging times that include grief and sadness. Spiritual leaders must learn to use their words to help the sorrowing find comfort and perspective. Paul's words to the Ephesians accomplished this purpose.

B. LESSON BACKGROUND

During his third missionary journey, Paul was headed for Jerusalem but planning to go to Rome as well (Acts 19:21). He had established new churches in territories such as southern Galatia, Asia, Macedonia, and Achaia. Many had been baptized into Christ, and churches had grown stronger in spite of the persecution they often faced. Paul's journeys were carried out with the help of several traveling companions. Frequently he depended on coworkers to provide leadership in his absence.

DEVOTIONAL READING:
ACTS 20:31-35
BACKGROUND SCRIPTURE:
ACTS 20:17-38
PRINTED TEXT:
ACTS 20:17-28, 36-38

LESSON AIMS

After participating in this lesson, each student will be able to:

1. Recall the main points of Paul's final talk with the Ephesian elders.

2. Identify some of the "sad good-byes" that Christians experience today.

3. Write a letter of encouragement to a fellow Christian who lives in a foreign country.

KEY VERSE

Keep watch over yourselves and all the flock of which the Holy Spirit has made you overseers. Be shepherds of the church of God, which he bought with his own blood.
—Acts 20:28

Nov
27

The book of Acts records much of this activity, but many of the details must be collected from the letters of Paul. Among the churches he established, the evidence tells us that at least some congregations formed a very close bond with the apostle. (See Philippians 4:10-20 and 1 Thessalonians 2:1-16.) Today's text will show us that Paul also developed a close relationship with the Ephesians elders.

I. GOOD-BYE, WITH MEMORIES (ACTS 20:17-21)

A. CALL FOR THE EPHESIAN ELDERS (v. 17)

17. From Miletus, Paul sent to Ephesus for the elders of the church.

Miletus (also in 2 Timothy 4:20) is a city of Asia located on the coast of the Aegean Sea. It is about 30 miles south of *Ephesus*, meaning that messengers will have to be *sent* to call for the Ephesian *elders*. The distance is about two days to walk, thus the round-trip requires four days or so. In spite of the inconvenience of the distance, Paul wants to see these elders again, and they are more than happy to meet him in Miletus.

Paul's Ephesian ministry is recorded in Acts 19. That ministry included the re-baptism of the disciples of John the Baptist, the defeat of the Jewish exorcists, and the riot energized by the silversmiths. Paul's ministry at Ephesus occupied a great deal of his time (see Acts 19:10). These elders had served with Paul in all kinds of circumstances, and he is grateful for his relationship with them.

Paul's reasons for summoning the elders rather than traveling to Ephesus to see them probably have to do with the delays that may occur should he return to that place. People had rioted during his last visit there (see Acts 19:23-41)! Yet sensing the difficulties before him, Paul wants to make arrangements to meet with these special believers for this occasion.

B. REFLECTIONS ON MINISTRY (vv. 18-21)

18, 19. When they arrived, he said to them: "You know how I lived the whole time I was with you, from the first day I came into the province of Asia. I served the Lord with great humility and with tears, although I was severely tested by the plots of the Jews.

Paul's first words to the Ephesian elders when they were come to him are a reminder of shared experiences in ministry. Paul's reference to *the first day* he came into *Asia* takes us back to Acts 18:19-21. He had left Corinth with Priscilla and Aquila and had arrived in Ephesus to preach and teach briefly. He then left for Jerusalem and Antioch of Syria, returning later to spend many months in Ephesus (Acts 19:8-10; 20:31).

Paul's mention of *humility* and *tears* calls attention to his style of ministry. When he reminds the Thessalonians of his ministry with them, he points out that he had used neither flattery nor coveted praise, but had ministered among them as gently as a mother cares for her young (1 Thessalonians 2:4-9). This often included working to pay his own bills (see also 1 Corinthians 9:12-18). Similarly, he now reminds the Ephesian elders that he has not ministered in a selfish way, looking for what advantage he could gain for himself. His ministry was marked by tears for their progress, giving the glory to God. His attitude in ministry is always that he and his coworkers are merely instruments through which God accomplishes his work (see 1 Corinthians 3:5-9).

The phrase *the plots of the Jews* reminds us that trouble from Jewish opponents seems to follow Paul wherever he goes. He was stoned at Lystra (Acts 14:19). At Thessalonica Jews rounded up some men of low repute to attack the house where Paul was staying (Acts 17:5). In Corinth the Jewish elements of the popu-

Achaia. Uh-KAY-uh.

Aegean. A-JEE-un.

Asia. AY-zha.

Caesarea. Sess-uh-REE-uh.

Colossians. Kuh-LOSH-unz.

Corinth. KOR-inth.

Corinthians. Ko-RIN-thee-unz.

Ephesians. Ee-FEE-zhunz.

Ephesus. EF-uh-sus.

Ezekiel. Ee-ZEEK-ee-ul or Ee-ZEEK-yul.

Galatia. Guh-LAY-shuh.

Gallio. GAL-ee-o.

Lystra. LISS-truh.

Macedonia. Mass-eh-DOE-nee-uh.

Miletus. My-LEE-tus.

Silas. SIGH-luss.

Thessalonians. THESS-uh-LO-nee-unz.

Thessalonica. THESS-uh-lo-NYE-kuh.

Tyrannus. Ty-RAN-nus.

Tyre. Tire.

lation initiated an action that placed Paul in front of Gallio, proconsul of Achaia (Acts 18:12). Even in Ephesus he met resistance from Jews, which moved him to begin a ministry in the lecture hall of Tyrannus (Acts 19:9, 10).

20, 21. *"You know that I have not hesitated to preach anything that would be helpful to you but have taught you publicly and from house to house. I have declared to both Jews and Greeks that they must turn to God in repentance and have faith in our Lord Jesus.*

Paul speaks with confidence that he has not robbed the Ephesians of any part of the truth during his months of preaching. His efforts included both public preaching and teaching in private settings. His target is not only *Jews,* but also *Greeks* (Gentiles; compare Acts 18:6). His ministry in Ephesus gave him an opportunity to preach to both Jews and Gentiles.

Paul sketches the content of his gospel as *repentance* toward God, and *faith* toward our *Lord Jesus* Christ. Though Paul's letters emphasize faith more frequently than repentance, both of these themes can be found (see, for example, Romans 1–3). Repentance emphasizes sorrow for sin as one turns away from evil; faith focuses on the commitment of the heart to Christ.

This review of Paul's history with the Ephesians reminds those elders of their common bond. Their shared experiences give Paul a high degree of respect that make his words more powerful. When believers want to express comfort to people facing grief, the words will be more powerful if they come from someone whose life has been intertwined with those who are listening.

II. GOOD-BYE, WITH COMMITMENTS (ACTS 20:22-24)

A. ANTICIPATION OF SUFFERING (vv. 22, 23)

22, 23. *"And now, compelled by the Spirit, I am going to Jerusalem, not knowing what will happen to me there. I only know that in every city the Holy Spirit warns me that prison and hardships are facing me.*

Paul feels *compelled by the Spirit* to go back *to Jerusalem.* It is a trip he must take! In his letter to the Romans (probably written during the time mentioned in Acts 20:1-3), he urges the believers to pray for this trip because he sensed danger ahead (Romans 15:31). In the text before us, he makes clear that difficult challenges are coming on this journey to Jerusalem and that he has been warned of this by *the Holy Spirit.*

The cities that Paul has in mind here are not named. But later in Acts, warnings will come from people in cities such as Tyre and Caesarea (Acts 21:3, 4, 8-11). Paul mentions the Holy Spirit because the warnings he receives are often directed at him by people who are moved by the Spirit to speak such messages.

B. COMMITMENT TO A CAUSE (v. 24)

24. *"However, I consider my life worth nothing to me, if only I may finish the race and complete the task the Lord Jesus has given me—the task of testifying to the gospel of God's grace.*

The warnings, however, do not diminish Paul's determination to continue his ministry for Christ. His attitude about his life is that he has given himself to *the Lord* to be crucified with Christ (Galatians 2:20). Therefore whatever life he has belongs to Christ. His focus is on serving Christ, not on preserving his own *life.* Therefore, he will not be discouraged at the warnings regarding dangers to come.

Instead, Paul is determined to finish his course with joy. His choice of terms here refers to the course set out for the runners of a *race.* Paul uses athletic terminology elsewhere in his letters (see 1 Corinthians 9:24; 2 Timothy 4:7).

WHAT DO YOU THINK?

Paul's preaching included a call to repentance. Why is repentance necessary? How can your church do a better job of calling people to repent?

WHAT DO YOU THINK?

Paul spent much of his ministry in bondage. Why would God allow such a tremendous preacher of the Word to be restricted by captivity? What bondage are you experiencing that can be beneficial to God's kingdom in the long run?

WHAT DO YOU THINK?

Even in the face of more persecution, Paul kept pressing forward in his ministry. How is this focus a model for us today? How are our struggles in the faith similar to and different from those of Paul?

This ministry of Paul is his because the Lord Jesus Christ *has given* it to him. Such language takes the listener back to Paul's experience on the road to Damascus (Acts 9:1-19). There Jesus revealed to Paul that he was chosen for the purpose of carrying the *gospel* to both Jews and Gentiles. Paul will refer to this moment as his commissioning from the Lord into this ministry (see Acts 26:12-18). So Paul expresses his sentiments to the Ephesian elders by reminding them of his commitments to the Lord and to his ministry. Just because he will not be present with them does not mean that he has forgotten his calling.

There are always times in life when parting from friends or coworkers will mean offering words of encouragement. Paul's use of his own example of dedication should inspire us to consider how our own dedication to Christ lifts others in times of sadness. Speaking about our love of Christ and his ministry to those facing sadness, loss, or grief can sometimes help friends take heart for the future.

THE PRIORITIES OF LIFE

The Guinness Book of World Records is an amazing collection of human endeavors. These endeavors can be serious, whimsical, significant, or ridiculous. If any human activity can be counted or measured, be assured that someone has done it and it is certified by Guinness. For example, Sammy and Billy Kishek spent several years (sometimes working 11 hours a day) and $15,000 creating a ball of rubber bands big enough to make it into the record book. At last count the ball was 5 feet high and weighed 2,700 pounds—and it was still growing!

The nearest known competitor of the Kishek brothers is no longer a threat. The competitor's 2,500-pound rubber band ball made the Guinness Book in 2002. In celebration the *Ripley's Believe It or Not* TV show dropped the ball from an airplane a mile above the Arizona desert to see how high it would bounce. It didn't; it just made a cloud of dust and a crater, exploding in the process.

With a great variety of things to which we might commit our lives, rubber band balls should be pretty low on our list. How much different Paul's priority was! Regardless of cost to freedom and life, he was prepared to fulfill the mission God had given him. As a result, his name is in God's book, which is much better than being in the Guinness book. What is *our* greatest priority in life?   —C. R. B.

III. GOOD-BYE, WITH CHALLENGES (ACTS 20:25-28)

A. FAITHFULNESS IN PREACHING (vv. 25-27)

25. "Now I know that none of you among whom I have gone about preaching the kingdom will ever see me again.

The danger that lies ahead in Jerusalem is great indeed! The narrative moves forward in the next chapter with details about Paul's arrest there (Acts 21:33), followed by his hearings, leading to this imprisonment in Rome (Acts 28:16). This is indeed a touching moment as Paul confesses this conviction in clear language to his friends from Ephesus. With their love and respect for Paul, how can they not be affected emotionally by his words?

26, 27. "Therefore, I declare to you today that I am innocent of the blood of all men. For I have not hesitated to proclaim to you the whole will of God.

Paul's language calls upon the Ephesians to "mark this down." He has fulfilled his duty to serve as a watchman on the city wall, as the prophet Ezekiel described his own job (Ezekiel 33:1-6). He had seen the danger and had warned the people of Ephesus with every ounce of strength he could generate. He had declared all the counsel of God so that every listener would know God's *will*.

Paul implies that he could have shunned this effort by speaking only what was safe or popular for him to speak. He calls upon the Ephesians to remember that he did not limit his words to the "safe" things. Rather, he had spoken the entirety of God's truth fearlessly. Thus he is innocent *of the blood* of any who will be destroyed when judgment day comes because they did not heed his gospel call.

THE POWER OF INTEGRITY

Abraham Lincoln consistently tops the list of "greatest American presidents." More recent presidents always come near the top, their numbers buoyed up by the public's general disdain of history, but Abraham Lincoln stays at number one.

Why do you think this is the case? Consider the nickname history has given him: "Honest Abe." Those two words summarize our image of him: "honest"—a man of integrity; "Abe"—a man of the common people. While crowds today may be drawn to flamboyant TV and movie celebrities whose self-serving antics provide fodder for the tabloids and other media, the person Americans hold in highest esteem was an unpretentious man of high moral principles.

The name of the apostle Paul was not on any public opinion poll. As we have seen with presidential polls, such fame is largely illusory. But Paul's place in history has stood the test of time. It is due to the factors he mentions to the elders in Ephesus: humility, compassion, consistency in purpose, and steadfastness during troublesome times. These traits of character endeared Paul to them and to Christians in every age since.   —C. R. B.

B. CHALLENGE TO LEADERS (v. 28)

28. "Keep watch over yourselves and all the flock of which the Holy Spirit has made you overseers. Be shepherds of the church of God, which he bought with his own blood."

So Paul leaves the Ephesian elders with a challenge to imitate his own ministry. First he challenges them to pay attention to themselves as elders. If they don't guard their own lives, who will? To Timothy, a leader at Ephesus, Paul will expand this discussion by saying, "Watch your life and doctrine closely. Persevere in them, because if you do, you will save both yourself and your hearers" (1 Timothy 4:16).

Paul also urges the elders to remember the importance of watching over *the flock*. This describes the teaching needed by the church to grow in faith. The apostle Peter echoes something of the same thing in 1 Peter 5:1-3. Paul's reference in the verse before us is especially to the threat of false teachers, as in his other writings such as Ephesians 5:6, 7 and Colossians 2:8.

As these elders present doctrine that nourishes the church, they should remember that they are not the owners of the church. Christ Jesus purchased the church with his own blood when he died on the cross. Paul's farewell to the Ephesian elders (*overseers*) is thus an appeal to continue to minister as if they were handling a precious possession bought with Christ's blood—which they are! Those who give their lives to shepherding the flock of God can influence fellow believers by accepting this challenge as their own.

FAMOUS LAST WORDS

People's last words give insight into their character. Consider these last words: P. T. Barnum asked, "How were the receipts today at Madison Square Garden?" Poet Dylan Thomas said, "I've had 18 straight whiskies, I think that's the record." As Joan Crawford's housekeeper prayed, the actress said, "Don't you dare ask God to help me."

Some people express their despair at what awaits them. The writer Thomas Hobbes said, "I am about to take my last voyage, a great leap in the dark." "Lord,

"Take heed therefore unto yourselves, and to all the flock, over the which the Holy Ghost hath made you overseers, to feed the church of God, which he hath purchased with his own blood." (Acts 20:28).

Visual for Lesson 13. *Refer to this photograph as you ask, "What are some ways that the people of the church are to be cared for?"*

PRAYER

Lord of all hope and comfort, help us this day to realize the power of our words when times are difficult. When people need to see in us a reason to trust you through hardships, may we have the strength to show them the way. In Christ, amen.

WHAT DO YOU THINK?

In the church we often have to say good-bye to members who move away. What are some ways we can do this effectively?

THOUGHT TO REMEMBER

Words of faith and courage can make good-byes easier to bear.

WHAT DO YOU THINK?

Paul was aware of the pain that his words brought to the Ephesian elders. He therefore spoke words of encouragement as well. How can we be more ready to offer such words? At what times should we be ready to do this?

help my poor soul" were Edgar Allan Poe's last words. The Emperor Vespasian, perhaps speaking sarcastically, said, "Woe is me. Methinks I'm turning into a god." Leonardo da Vinci's last words may surprise us: "I have offended God and mankind because my work did not reach the quality it should have."

Then there are the distinctly Christian farewells. Author Joseph Addison said, "See in what peace a Christian can die." Thomas à Becket, Archbishop of Canterbury who was martyred at the instigation of King Henry II, said, "I am ready to die for my Lord, that in my blood the Church may obtain liberty and peace."

Paul's words in our text were not his dying words, but they were the last words some of his colaborers would hear from him. They were a fond good-bye and a challenge to faithfulness. When the time comes for our farewells or last words, we can do no better. —C. R. B.

IV. GOOD-BYE, WITH PRAYER (ACTS 20:36-38)

A. KNEELING IN PRAYER (vv. 36, 37)

36, 37. When he had said this, he knelt down with all of them and prayed. They all wept as they embraced him and kissed him.

Kneeling in prayer is an expression of seriousness and humility (Ephesians 3:14), since standing in prayer is more often the posture used (Luke 18:9-14). Paul's friends are not only ready to pray with him, they also express their deep feelings in the form of tears. This is a farewell that touches everyone who loves and respects him. They show this by throwing their arms around him and kissing him on the cheeks.

Working for Christ can form bonds that are closer than family. These spiritual brothers of Paul are now parting with someone dear to them, and they cannot resist expressing their heartfelt love. Believers should never be ashamed of expressing their sadness and comfort in visible ways.

B. SADNESS OF PARTING (v. 38)

38. What grieved them most was his statement that they would never see his face again. Then they accompanied him to the ship.

There is no avoiding the sadness of Paul's message. The emotional reaction to it is inspired by the news that this could be his final contact with *them*. Obviously there is concern for his coming hardships, the persecutions, and the suffering for his faith. But as they say good-bye at the ship, they understand that they are looking into the eyes of Paul for the final time.

So Paul's departure from Miletus is sad but not lonely. His Christian friends surround him with their love and support. At the same time, Paul does not leave these Christian friends before forcing them to ponder their future without his personal leadership. Even in his final moments with these friends, his focus is not on his own sufferings but on what he hopes that they will do in the ministry for Christ.

CONCLUSION

When times are difficult it is important that Christian leaders share words that keep the church focused on the things of God. Paul's words were spoken at a moment when believers saw gloomy times coming. But his words and example gave them courage. What opportunities will we have to speak words that bring comfort and courage? Can we use our words to lift the spirits of those whose faith may be threatened or overwhelmed? Our words can inspire faith and dedication in those who are weak and vulnerable. May the Lord help us to find ways to build up the church in times of distress.

Discovery Learning

This page contains an alternative lesson plan emphasizing learning activities. Classes desiring such student involvement will find these suggestions helpful. The next page is a reproducible activity page to further enhance discovery learning.

LEARNING GOALS

After participating in this lesson, each student will be able to:

1. Recall the main points of Paul's final talk with the Ephesian elders.

2. Identify some of the "sad good-byes" that Christians experience today.

3. Write a letter of encouragement to a fellow Christian who lives in a foreign country.

INTO THE LESSON

Put a variety of verbal farewells on classroom display from several different languages; for example, "good-bye," "vaya con Dios," "adieu." If you have class members who know other languages, call them ahead of time and add their farewell expressions to your list.

As class begins, ask class members, "How do some of these expressions call for the blessing of God on the one being greeting?" (Good-bye represents the English "God be with you"; *vaya con Dios* is simple Spanish for "go with God"; *adieu* is French representing "to God.") After explanations, say, "Today's study is of a poignant good-bye that the Christians of Ephesus and Paul experienced. A desire for God's presence and blessing is always appropriate when Christians part."

INTO THE WORD

Divide your class into three groups (six groups if you have more than 24 students). Give the first group(s) this assignment: "Luke records Paul's initial ministry in Ephesus in Acts 19. Skim that chapter and develop a summary of Paul and the Spirit's ministry in that city. You will be asked to review that history before the other groups give their reports."

Give the second group(s) this assignment: "Look at today's text in Acts 20:17-38. Paul is meeting, advising, and encouraging the elders of the Ephesian church. Make a list of attributes that are overt or implied in those elders. Identify verses where you see the characteristics. For example, they were overseers (v. 28); they were teachable (v. 20). When you give your report to the class, list the attributes, but ask the class to identify the relevant verses."

Give the third group(s) this assignment, "Look at today's text in Acts 20:17-38. Paul is meeting, advising, and encouraging the elders of the Ephesian church. Make a list of attributes that are overt or implied in the apostle Paul. He represents what all preaching ministers should be like. For example, he is demonstrative (v. 37); he is unprejudiced (v. 21). When you give your report to the class, list the attributes, but ask the class to identify relevant verses."

Give each group at least eight minutes to work. Then ask groups (in the order you passed out the assignments) to report. If you have two groups working on the same assignment, ask for one to begin the summary and the other to finish it or else alternate between groups. (A similar activity is included in the student book.)

Your class can encourage the elders of your church with a "thinking of you"-type card. You may want to make such cards available; most Christian bookstores can provide boxed quantities. (One with a picture of Jesus as the good shepherd would be especially suitable, with today's Key Verse added and personalized with a note of thanks.) For example, begin with "Dear brother _____," then quote Acts 20:28, then add a personal note of thanks.

INTO LIFE

Ask the class to develop a list of sad good-byes that we experience in life. If the group is slow to respond, give some examples: good-bye to a retiring minister; good-bye to a trusted family business that goes out of business; good-bye to a church family moving to a different community. After the list is made, ask the class to suggest an appropriate word to be given in each situation.

Provide a list of seven e-mail (or regular mail) addresses of Christians serving in foreign lands. Discuss with your class the appropriate words of encouragement that could be shared with each of the people on the list of addresses that you are providing.

Encourage students to send an e-mail per day to one of the seven names provided. Ask those who use regular mail to select one person to send an air letter and use the same encouraging words. (A similar activity is included in the student book.)

As an alternative, use the "Personal Omission" exercise from the reproducible page. Close the class by distributing the "Personal Admission and Submission" exercise from that page. Discuss as time permits.

Personal Omission

Probably some beloved brother or sister has "gotten away" to a new city or a new congregation without your first having said something that needed to be said. Identify two such individuals/families in your life and make notes that you will put into a letter to be mailed this week.

Personal Admission and Submission

In Acts 20:24 Paul makes one of the grandest statements of life purpose ever made by a human:

I consider my life worth nothing to me, if only I may finish the race and complete the task the Lord Jesus has given me—the task of testifying to the gospel of God's grace.

That is a challenge worthy of each of us, especially as this is the end of our study for the quarter. If you can say the same about your own life purpose, sign your name and date this commitment:

```
"What Paul says in Acts 20:24
    applies to me, too!"


Signed, _____

        November _____, 2005
```

Winter Quarter 2005–2006

God's Commitment—Our Response

Special Features

Lessons

Unit 1: God's Redeeming Love

Unit 2: God's Gifts of Leadership

Unit 3: Faithful Followers, Faithful Leaders

About These Lessons

Have you ever had the unsettling experience of committing yourself to planning an elaborate event, only to have people ignore your invitation? The God of the universe has committed himself to making big plans for us. But he expects a response! This quarter's lessons show us why and how.

Dec 4

Dec 11

Dec 18

Dec 25

Jan 1

Jan 8

Jan 15

Jan 22

Jan 29

Feb 5

Feb 12

Feb 19

Feb 26

God's Plans for Humanity

by Lloyd Pelfrey

A Christian businessman in south-central Illinois was often associated with this statement: "If God is your partner, make your plans big." Almost a century ago, a similar sentiment was offered: "Make no little plans; they have no magic to stir men's blood and probably themselves will not be realized. Make big plans; aim high in hope and work."

The lessons for the next three months provide a study of God's plans for humanity. These are big plans! Our study of them will involve passages concerning God's prophecies about the Christ who was to come. We will also study God's expectations for those who respond favorably to his gracious designs.

The plans begin in the Old Testament. There we discover the basic theme is that Someone is coming! God will send his anointed one (Messiah) for the spiritual benefit of all. The first promises are found in the book of Genesis, and they continue on through the Minor Prophets. God's preparations for the promised one included individuals and nations. This divine determination for sending the Messiah was made before the creation of the world (1 Peter 1:20).

DECEMBER

GOD'S REDEEMING LOVE

British statesman William Gladstone remarked in 1878 that "National injustice is the surest road to national downfall." The fall of great nations is normally accompanied by injustices among the leaders and their people. In **Lesson 1** we will see the prophet Isaiah predict that one aspect of the Messiah's work will be to bring judgment and justice. Nations and individuals can receive the promised blessings only as justice is applied throughout their lives.

Lesson 2 teaches us about strength. When it seems that no one cares, there is a temptation simply to quit. It is in such circumstances that God's people find strength in the redemptive work of the Messiah. The fact that the Lord has demonstrated his concern in the past provides a renewed determination for his people to encourage one another today. Together we can handle the tribulations, trials, and testings of life.

Lesson 3 starts us in Isaiah 53. That grand passage prophetically depicts the suffering of the Messiah for the sins of others. The lesson text also includes part of the Gospel of Luke. Attention there is given to the famous expression of Mary during the time that she visited Elizabeth (who was to be the mother of John the Baptist). In the midst of her unusual circumstances, Mary expressed confidence in God. Her expression of praise included reflections on her blessings and the mighty acts of God through the centuries.

Lesson 4 combines a prophecy in Isaiah about the ministry of Jesus with the passage in Luke that proclaims that the Savior is born. Angelic messengers brought the good news. The shepherds from the Bethlehem area then set the example as they made known to others the good things that they had seen and heard. How appropriate it is that our study takes place on the day when we traditionally celebrate the Savior's birth!

JANUARY

GOD'S GIFTS OF LEADERSHIP

Leaders of any group or organization must be concerned about the next generation. If they're not, then their groups will die off! **Lesson 5** shows us Paul's concerns in this regard. We will see the apostle describe to Timothy his own experiences, and then encourage his son in the faith to follow his example in fighting the good fight. Sadly, not everyone remains true to the affirmations that they made about following Jesus, and Paul cites examples for Timothy to note. The first Sunday of a new year is a good time to consider how we will pass the mantle of church leadership to future generations.

Prayer is the emphasis in **Lesson 6**. Again we take our text from Paul's first letter to Timothy. There the apostle's exhortation is for Timothy—and indeed everyone—to pray. One major consideration is that such prayers are to be for governmental leaders. The spiritual qualities of presidents, prime ministers, and others in authority should always concern us. But the real purpose in such prayers is to allow the followers of God to be able to live in peace as they fulfill their obligations to God and humanity.

Lesson 7 focuses on leaders in the church. In this focus Paul sets forth the qualities that the church should expect elders and deacons to exhibit as they serve. Genuine leaders have genuine faith. Their lives may be noted as positive examples both in and out of the church. To have leaders with anything less than what the apostle describes is not only disappointing, but also harmful to the body of Christ.

Teaching is also a major part of the work of the church. Jesus emphasized this in Matthew 28:20 as a part of the Great Commission. **Lesson 8**, from 1 Timothy, gives us Paul's perspectives on teaching. He sounds warnings that there will be teachers who promote false doctrine. Such falsehood has its origins in evil spirits and demons who deceive. Teachers in the church must be examples in all aspects of their lives. The task of teaching is of the utmost importance, for eternal destinies are at stake.

Lesson 9. The last Sunday in January 2006 continues our study of church leadership. The tasks of leaders necessarily include maintaining proper relationships, and Paul offers needed cautions in this regard. A further thought concerns duties to see that the needs of the others (especially widows) are met. Warnings and advice about the lives of leaders and prospective leaders enrich this lesson.

FAITHFUL FOLLOWERS, FAITHFUL LEADERS

Every Christian is grateful for being a child of God. Many have a spiritual heritage that has helped to shape their lives. **Lesson 10** advances into 2 Timothy, where Paul reminds Timothy of two people whom he must remember: a godly mother and grandmother. They guided him spiritually in his formative years. Not every believer has such a benefit, but every Christian has someone who taught him or her in the faith.

The apostle goes on to warn Timothy about being ashamed; Paul reminds his younger colleague that he (Paul) was never ashamed of the gospel of Christ. Timothy must not be timid concerning his faith in Christ. Key tasks for Timothy will be to develop the virtues of love and personal discipline.

Contention causes tensions, and **Lesson 11** gives advice about quarrelsome words. The rhyme from school days that words do not hurt is simply not true. What a person says is important! Words may become a blessing to others or they may severely damage the church and its members.

The text is again from 2 Timothy, which includes a caution about handling the Word of God correctly. The abuse of what God's Word really says is a major factor in producing division. The lesson concludes with advice on responding to those who have been a part of the opposition. The goals are to treat them gently, lead them to repentance, and instill a knowledge of the truth.

Albert Schweitzer (1875–1965) wrote, "Example is not the main thing in influencing others. It is the only thing." **Lesson 12** emphasizes the importance of selecting a good mentor to be one's example of a godly life. This mentor-apprentice methodology always has been in God's plan for us. We see it stated forcefully in Deuteronomy 6:7, 8, one of the famous passages of the Bible. The concept is repeated in the final charges by the aged apostle to his son in the faith. There is also a vivid reminder that the crowns of righteousness are for all who eagerly await the return of the Savior.

Lesson 13, the final lesson of the quarter, is somewhat of a review. As such, it reinforces Paul's thoughts concerning attitudes and actions of Christians. The text is Paul's letter to Titus. There we see that every leader must live and teach the truth of the Word. There can be no disharmony between what is taught and what is done.

A GREAT COMMITMENT, A GREAT RESPONSE

The quarter begins with God's initiative in promising that the Christ would come into the world. It concludes with words of instruction for leaders and other followers of the Christ, who has indeed come. His redemptive work by necessity demands that every one who hears the gospel must respond. The response is either to reject or accept the Son of God. That's the theme of these lessons: "God's Commitment—Our Response." As we grow in maturity and leadership skills, we continue to respond to him.

The World of Paul, Timothy, and Titus

ASIA

Timothy was in Ephesus when he received both letters from Paul.

• Ephesus

Titus was on Crete when he received his letter from Paul.

CRETE

• Troas

MACEDONIA

• Philippi
• Thessalonica

Paul wrote 1 Timothy from Macedonia.

• Corinth

MEDITERRANEAN SEA

Paul wrote 2 Timothy from Rome.

• Rhegium

• Syracuse

ADRIATIC SEA

• Puteoli

ITALY

• Rome

SICILY

MALTA

Mary's Song
(Luke 1)

WHAT MARY DOES

WHAT GOD DOES

WHAT OTHERS DO

Glorifies the Lord (46); Rejoices in God (47)

Call Mary blessed (48)

Sees Mary's humble state (48)

Does great things (49)

Is merciful (50)

Shows strength (51)

Scatters the proud (51)

Puts down the mighty (52)

Exalts the humble (52)

Fills the hungry (53)

Sends the rich away empty (53)

Helps his servant Israel (54)

Remembers to be merciful (54)

JUSTICE FOR ALL

LESSON 1

WHY TEACH THIS LESSON?

"That's not fair!" is a common complaint of children. Instilled in our natures is this sense that life ought to be fair. However, it doesn't take long for us to recognize that life isn't fair. Some are born into poverty, some into wealth; some are born with good genes that provide superior intelligence, health, athleticism, and beauty; others have genes of a more ordinary nature.

But that doesn't—and shouldn't—keep us from seeking fairness or justice. States, provinces, and nations incorporate this dream for justice into their mottoes, such as "Justice for All" (the District of Columbia). The motto of Canada's Prince Edward Island implies the same lofty goal: "The Small Under the Protection of the Great." The French Revolution raised the banner of Liberte, Egalite, Fraternite (freedom, equality, brotherhood—all of which imply justice). And, of course, the pledge of allegiance to the United States flag calls for "liberty and justice for all."

The human race keeps looking futilely for justice because we turn away from the only source where justice will ever be truly found. Today's lesson points us to that source.

INTRODUCTION

A. "JUSTICE FOR ALL!"

To hear the word *justice* may bring to mind the aspects of deserved reward or punishment. The definitions may also have these facets: rightness, lawfulness, to exercise a proper power and authority to maintain what is right. When all the facets of justice are considered, it is plain why only God's plan can bring "justice for all." When differing levels of government are falling over themselves to outdo each other in abandoning absolutes, it becomes evident that what is really needed is godly justice. Only then can the singing about peace in the Christmas carols bring the desired results.

Occasionally, a news item appears that does not pass the "sniff test" for justice. The story may be of a robber who was injured by the defensive actions of the intended victim. The robber then sues the victim and receives much more than the robbery would have gained for him. A recent article has this comment: "You may . . . have to compensate those who would have harmed you on your property!"

John Jay, an early justice of the U.S. Supreme Court, wrote, "Justice is indiscriminately due to all, without regard to numbers, wealth, or rank." Some of the high-visibility court trials in recent years have demonstrated that those with wealth can afford very capable attorneys who are more likely to win in the justice system. Wealth, however, is not the only factor. In the past it often seemed that the person's race, country of origin, etc., produced miscarriages of justice.

One of the symbols of justice is "The Blind Lady." You've seen her with her eyes covered as she holds a sword in one hand and the scales of justice in the

DEVOTIONAL READING:
ISAIAH 41:8-13

BACKGROUND SCRIPTURE:
ISAIAH 41, 42

PRINTED TEXT:
ISAIAH 42:1-9

LESSON AIMS

After participating in this lesson, each student will be able to:

1. Describe how the servant demonstrates justice.

2. Explain how the figures of speech concerning the servant are fulfilled in the New Testament.

3. Suggest one specific way to promote God's justice in the coming week.

KEY VERSE

"I, the Lord, have called you in righteousness; I will take hold of your hand. I will keep you and will make you to be a covenant for the people and a light for the Gentiles." — Isaiah 42:6

LESSON 1 NOTES

other. Combining the ideas of the blindfold and the scales suggests that the true courts of justice are blind to prejudice. But what about the sword? As one thoughtful observer put it, "Justice that does not bear a sword beside its scales soon falls into ridicule" (perhaps by Charles de Gaulle, 1890–1970).

B. LESSON BACKGROUND

Each of the four lessons for December has selections from the book of Isaiah, and the final two lessons of the month will also have passages from the Gospel of Luke. The book of Isaiah is usually dated over the period of 740–700 B.C. Isaiah lived and wrote during the reigns of four kings of Judah (see Isaiah 1:1). Isaiah's task was formidable, for King Ahaz was one of the worst kings of ancient Judah. The idolatry that he introduced marked the beginning of the end for that nation (2 Chronicles 28:1-4). Godly Hezekiah succeeded Ahaz, but his personal righteousness could not tip the scales of justice away from the sentence that the people deserved for their idolatry.

Although Assyria was the dominant power in his day, Isaiah prophesied that the nation would eventually fall to the Babylonians (Isaiah 39:5-7). Nebuchadnezzar and his Babylonian army ultimately destroyed Jerusalem and the temple in 586 B.C. As Isaiah begins chapter 40, the entire nature of the book changes. The prophet writes to provide comfort for people who will be in exile, and he instructs them to leave Babylon with joy when the opportunity comes (48:20).

But Isaiah also prophesies even greater deliverance. In so doing, he uses four poems about a special servant of the Lord who would come. (See Lesson 7 from the fall quarter.) These poems give new dimensions to the one who already had been the subject of earlier prophecies. (See especially Isaiah 7:14; 9:1-7; and all of chapter 11 for those prophecies.) Sections of each poem are noted in the New Testament as being fulfilled in Jesus.

I. DISCLOSING THE SERVANT (ISAIAH 42:1)

A. SELECTION OF THE SERVANT (v. 1a, b)

1a. "Here is my servant, whom I uphold,
     my chosen one in whom I delight;

Matthew 12:18-21 cites the first four verses of Isaiah 42. This is the longest quotation in the Gospel of Matthew from the Old Testament. We may take note of the larger context by observing that several chapters in this part of Isaiah challenge the idols to do what God can do. The verses before Isaiah 42:1 present vivid contrasts to what God sets forth in today's text. The word *see* occurs in 41:29 and seems to be addressed to the images that are "wind and confusion" (41:29). God now introduces his *servant*, and the difference is dramatic!

Some have thought that the use of the word *servant* is intended to show the humility of the one sent. Jesus certainly was meek (see Matthew 11:29), but this is not the text for it. In royal circles it is a great honor to be the servant of a king.

The fact that this servant is fully endorsed by the Lord is expressed in three ways. First, God states that he will *uphold* him. The thought is that the servant will be sustained by God. Enemies will not prevail against the servant. Second, this servant has been specially appointed by God. Finally, he is the one *in whom* God finds a special joy. This is but a preview of the statements made by God at the baptism and the transfiguration of Jesus (Matthew 3:17; 17:5).

B. SPIRIT FOR THE SERVANT (v. 1c)

1c. " . . . I will put my Spirit on him

WHAT DO YOU THINK?

Culture can influence our understanding of the Bible. In Isaiah 42:1 we may cringe at references naming the coming Messiah as a servant. How do we tend to view servanthood today vs. how that idea may have been understood in Isaiah's day? Why is this distinction important?

The presence of the *Spirit* is also mentioned in Isaiah 11:2 and 61:1. The latter passage will be cited centuries later by Jesus at the synagogue in Nazareth. He will note that the passage is fulfilled that day (Luke 4:17-21).

C. SIGNIFICANCE OF THE SERVANT (v. 1d)

1d. " . . . *and he will bring justice to the nations.*

Achieving *justice* always has been difficult. One of the Ten Commandments warns about giving a false testimony (Exodus 20:16). This judicial feature is a part of God's judgment for all humanity; it is not restricted to Old Testament Israel. These messages are found throughout the prophetic writings. They affirm that even though other nations will be severely judged, God also promises that they would have the opportunity to know the one true God.

II. DESCRIBING THE SERVANT (ISAIAH 42:2-4)

A. HIS DISPOSITION (vv. 2, 3a)

2. *"He will not shout or cry out,*
     or raise his voice in the streets.

The word *not* is very vivid in the original Hebrew; it is emphasized by being the first word in the sentence in the ancient text. This is the first of seven uses of this word into the first part of verse four, although they don't all show up in English as *not*.

The use of the word *not* may seem to give a negative implication, but this is not the case. It emphasizes the peaceful approach that characterizes Jesus' ministry to those who receive his teaching. Jesus could, however, use a whip (John 2:15), overturn tables, and prohibit anyone from using the temple for a shortcut (Mark 11:16).

This servant is not going to *raise his voice* in a boisterous way so as to drown out others by sheer volume. Physically, however, his voice will have tremendous power by the way he will be able to preach to thousands. His quiet manner is enhanced by the power of the message. The Son of God will not need to publicize himself with excessive noise. He will not force his way on anyone.

3a. *"A bruised reed he will not break,*
     and a smoldering wick he will not snuff out.

A bruised reed is one that has been bent or broken over. It is normally considered to be useless, and it is therefore despised. In this case it represents those who may be considered as outcasts, but Jesus welcomes them also. It may also represent one who is hurting, struggling with sin or sorrow. The church is a place where all are to be welcomed and given genuine love, either tender or tough as the situation warrants.

The *smoldering wick* is one that is not really producing light as it should. It is almost spent, simply useless, and ready to be discarded—but it can be restored! The flax or wick can be trimmed, and the oil in the lamp replenished. Then the flame is renewed to its intended brightness. So lives that have been almost spent can be restored if they choose to be; but first the message must be communicated to them.

B. HIS DUTIES (vv. 3b, 4)

3b. *"In faithfulness he will bring forth justice;*

This is the second time in the passage that the word *justice* is used. In verse 1 it was announced that God's judgments are for all nations. This time the emphasis is on the truthfulness of the justice of God.

VISUALS FOR THESE LESSONS

The visual pictured in each lesson (e.g., page 130) is a small reproduction of a large, full-color poster included in the Adult Resources *packet for the Winter Quarter. The packet is available from your supplier. Order No. 292.*

WHAT DO YOU THINK?

The secular world sometimes identifies Christians by all the things we will "not" do. Do you think this is fair? Why, or why not?

WHAT DO YOU THINK?

Drawing on Isaiah 42:3 and other passages, what differences do you see between the judgment found in human courts and that which will occur in the final judgment? How can we explain this difference to unbelievers? Why is it important to do so?

In faithfulness carries the idea of administering justice with fidelity. In an age when truth and fidelity are considered relative, it is interesting to compare how many times the word *truth* occurs in the New Testament. Jesus is the truth (John 14:6). Those who hold to his teaching will know the truth and be set free (John 8:31, 32). God's Word is the "word of truth" (Ephesians 1:13; 2 Timothy 2:15; James 1:18). This truth must be spoken in love (Ephesians 4:15). The balance between love and truth must be a foundation of personal relationships, especially in those situations when the truth of the Word is presented to those who are lost.

4. " . . . *he will not falter or be discouraged*
     till he establishes justice on earth.
          In his law the islands will put their hope."

The final two uses of the Hebrew for *not* occur in this verse, although only one shows up in English. The words that they modify, namely *falter* and *discouraged*, are fascinating, for they are words from the previous verse. There they were translated as "smoking" and "bruised." In other words, the servant will burn brightly and will not be broken. He will understand when others experience these things.

The purpose of his coming is again set forth: to establish *justice* so that those who have placed their confidence in him will not be disappointed. God's plans will come to fruition! This is the type of Savior that everyone should desire.

III. DECLARATIONS TO THE SERVANT (ISAIAH 42:5-9)

A. POWER OF GOD (v. 5)

5. *This is what God the LORD says—*
     he who created the heavens and stretched them out,
          who spread out the earth and all that comes out of it,
     who gives breath to its people,
          and life to those who walk on it:

The final five verses of this servant poem or song express assurances to the servant. They also provide insights into the actual ministry that Jesus will have centuries later while on earth.

In an Old Testament context, we recall that each nation tended to have its own god or gods. Sometimes a god's sphere of influence was limited to a single city. Not so with the God of Israel! He is the one who *created the heavens* and *spread out the earth*. That concept was used by Jonah to identify his God to pagan sailors (Jonah 1:9). During and after the exile in Babylon, it becomes a custom to refer to God as the "God of heaven" (Ezra 1:2; 7:12; Daniel 2:37, 44).

In this section of Isaiah (chapters 40–48), one of the main points is to contrast the one true God with the idols—idols that had to be made (Isaiah 44:17), had to be carried (45:20), and that cannot move and will not answer (46:7). The God of Israel, by contrast, is the one who created the stars and calls them by name (40:26). It is the power of this God that is behind the promise of sending a servant who will bring justice to all.

The latter part of the verse gives another great truth. It states that *God the Lord* is the one who provides *breath* and *life*. The life principle does not exist in the earth itself, nor is it a result of a lightning strike. Life is the gift of God.

B. PROTECTION OF GOD (v. 6a)

6a. "*I, the LORD, have called you in righteousness;*
     I will take hold of your hand."

The coming of the servant will be no accident, for *the Lord* is the one calling him as a part of his redemptive purposes. He will come *in righteousness*, thus re-

WHAT DO YOU THINK?

In what ways is the servant establishing "justice on earth" yet today? What are some things we can do to help bring this about?

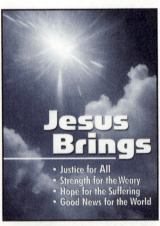

Jesus Brings
- Justice for All
- Strength for the Weary
- Hope for the Suffering
- Good News for the World

Visual for Lesson 1. *Use this visual as a discussion starter on the topics of justice, strength, hope, and good news.*

flecting all the standards of ethics, morals, and conduct that a holy God has by his very nature.

The servant has the assurance that he will be protected so as to fulfill his mission. To *take hold of* the *hand* expresses a constant affirmation of security and safety. The Savior who comes into the world will be protected from the wrath of Herod and from early attempts to end his life. Finally, however, he has to die for the sins of humanity. At that moment the Lord will express that he has been forsaken (Matthew 27:46), but this also is part of God's plan.

C. PURPOSES OF GOD (vv. 6b, 7)

6b. *"I will keep you and will make you*
    to be a covenant for the people
    and a light for the Gentiles,

Two aspects of the servant's mission are stated, and most students consider that there are two distinct recipients. The word *people* is a prophetic term for those who belong to God, and in this case it refers to the people of Israel (compare Hosea 2:1, 23). The other entity to receive a blessing is *the Gentiles.*

Two terms are used to depict the purposes of the servant. They are *covenant* and *light.* Just as Jesus is light, so also in this passage he is portrayed as a covenant. He is the very foundation and essence of the New Covenant.

The ancient Hebrew mind is fully aware of the implications of covenants. The word is first used in the covenant God made with Noah after the flood, and then to the patriarchs, the nation of Israel, and with David. In such covenants God makes promises that he will keep, but conditional factors often play an important part. Humans can lose the benefits unless they keep their part. It is necessary both to accept and then to keep a covenant that God offers.

We may also note that this verse seems to be behind the statement of Simeon at the dedication of Jesus. Simeon rejoiced that his eyes had seen the salvation that God had prepared: "a light . . . to the Gentiles and for glory to your people Israel" (Luke 2:30-32).

7. *" . . . to open eyes that are blind,*
    to free captives from prison
    and to release from the dungeon those who sit in darkness."

Jesus will cause *blind* eyes to see during his time on earth. But here figurative language means that the servant will eliminate spiritual blindness and *darkness,* bringing freedom from the *prison* of sin.

RESTORED TO USEFULNESS

In the field of mortuary science, there exists the practice known as restorative arts. The goal of this work is to restore a dead body to an appearance closely resembling the person while living. To perform restorative arts successfully involves learning principles of color theory in pigments, principles of cosmetology, as well as a consideration of normal complexion types and deviations from those. Yet long before there was any such thing as restorative arts, there was God, the greatest restorer of all.

Think about it: God takes what is dead—what appears to be of no value—and restores it by the power of his Son, Jesus. God's restoration process comes as he works on people's hearts through his Word and the Holy Spirit. Seemingly useless people with nothing to offer are restored by the gospel; those who are dead in their sins are restored by the sanctifying power of God's Spirit to new life and purpose.

God is such a powerful restorer! The church as a whole and Christians as individuals seek to be his agents of restoration. Instead of labeling others as beyond help

DAILY BIBLE READINGS

Monday, Nov. 28—An Eastern Victor Is Roused (Isaiah 41:1-7)

Tuesday, Nov. 29—God Will Strengthen Israel (Isaiah 41:8-13)

Wednesday, Nov. 30—God Will Care for the People (Isaiah 41:14-20)

Thursday, Dec. 1—God Is Greater Than Babylon's Deities (Isaiah 41:21-29)

Friday, Dec. 2—My Servant Will Bring Forth Justice (Isaiah 42:1-9)

Saturday, Dec. 3—Sing Praise to God (Isaiah 42:10-17)

Sunday, Dec. 4—Blind and Deaf to God's Instruction (Isaiah 42:18-25)

WHAT DO YOU THINK?

Few seem open to hearing the idea that they live in spiritual darkness! How does Christ's compassion toward those who rejected him serve as a model for us in this regard?

HOW TO SAY IT

Ahaz. AY-haz.

Assyria. Uh-SEAR-ee-uh.

Babylonians. Bab-ih-LOW-nee-unz.

Ephesians. Ee-FEE-zhunz.

Ezra. EZ-ruh.

Gentiles. JEN-tiles.

Hezekiah. Hez-ih-KYE-uh.

Hosea. Ho-ZAY-uh.

Isaiah. Eye-ZAY-uh.

Judah. JOO-duh.

Nazareth. NAZ-uh-reth.

Nebuchadnezzar. NEB-yuh-kud-NEZ-er.

synagogue. SIN-uh-gog.

PRAYER

Almighty God, just as you have demonstrated your compassion to us, we resolve today to make a difference in the lives of others by acts of justice and benevolence in the name of the servant whom you sent. In Jesus' name, amen.

THOUGHT TO REMEMBER

Each person decides if he or she will receive God's justice or God's mercy—mercy given only to those who accept the servant of the Lord as personal Savior.

and hope, it is our task to be ministers of reconciliation and restoration. Through the power of the Holy Spirit, that's exactly what God expects of us.　　　—A. E. A.

D. PREEMINENCE OF GOD (vv. 8, 9)

8. "I am the LORD; that is my name!
　　I will not give my glory to another
　　or my praise to idols.

The personal *name* of *the Lord* is behind all that is being promised. That name had a special significance at the time that Moses was called (Exodus 3:13, 14). Exodus 34:14 says that God is a jealous God. This is jealousy in the right sense: there are no real rivals to the one God. *Idols* are worthless.

9. "See, the former things have taken place,
　　and new things I declare;
　before they spring into being
　　I announce them to you."

The former things, those that had been prophesied in the past, are fulfilled as predicted in the course of time. The Lord proclaims new blessings long *before they* are accomplished. It is indeed a blessing today for us to know that these really were predictive prophecies. The discovery of the Dead Sea Scrolls with copies of the book of Isaiah proves that God truly had spoken these things centuries ahead of time. They came to pass just as he said. Fulfilled prophecy is a guarantee of truth; it is a vital part of the Christian's guarantee of eternal life.

GUARANTEED PROTECTION

People spend a lot of money on security and safety. Alarm systems to prevent theft of cars and laptop computers are considered necessities by many. There are systems designed for detecting smoke or carbon monoxide levels in our homes. Bars on the windows and multiple dead bolts on the doors are common in high crime areas.

Celebrities, for their part, have personal bodyguards. So do political figures. This is especially true of heads of state, who are constantly under the watchful eye of trained protectors. For years there has been screening of bags and people at airports. In a post–September 11 world, this security has been heightened. We all want to feel secure, don't we? Yet we know all too well that earthly security is never perfect.

The only perfect security comes from God. His promise of "new things" is, among others, a promise of eternal security. "I am making everything new" (Revelation 21:5). This "newness" is for those who are his children of righteousness. The newness includes the fact that "there will be no more death . . . for the old order of things has passed away" (Revelation 21:4). This protection is available to all who call upon the name of Jesus and submit themselves to what his Word has to say. Jesus is with his people as protector, now and forevermore.　　　—A. E. A.

CONCLUSION

Jesus came to the earth to bring justice. Some of its applications may include the influences that Christians have had in their homes, at work, and in their communities. It also includes the larger scene as described in Matthew 25:31-46 when the nations will be judged. But the criteria that are mentioned there are challenging: they are acts of benevolence to those brothers in need! When we do such things, we demonstrate our faith in Christ by what we do (James 2:14-26). It is the responsibility of each Christian to resolve to do his or her part in bringing "justice for all."

Discovery Learning

*This page contains an alternative lesson plan emphasizing learning activities. Classes
desiring such student involvement will find these suggestions helpful. The next page
is a reproducible activity page to further enhance discovery learning.*

LEARNING GOALS

After this lesson, each student will be able to:

1. Describe how the servant demonstrates justice.

2. Explain how the figures of speech concerning the servant are fulfilled in the New Testament.

3. Suggest one specific way to promote God's justice in the coming week.

INTO THE LESSON

Wear a black robe (symbolizing a judge) to class. Carry a gavel and a large book. Strike the gavel onto the table and declare, "Hear ye! Hear ye! Justice for all."

Display the following fill-in-the-blanks activity to highlight the lesson titles and themes for the first four lessons of this series: ___ for ___; ___ for the ___; ___ for the ___; ___ ___ for the ___. Display also this list of words: *all, good, hope, justice, news, strength, suffering, weary, world.* Say, "Fit the words into the blanks without looking at the lesson materials. What I said when I struck the gavel is a clue to one of the phrases."

INTO THE WORD

After introducing the lesson with the opening activity, distribute to each student an index card with one of these letters: *S, E, R, V, A, N, T.* Duplicate each letter, as necessary, to have enough cards for everyone. Give these directions: "For the letter you have been given, identify a descriptive word (or words) that characterize the servant in today's text in Isaiah 42:1-9. Also note a verse or verses from today's text where each descriptive word is noted or implied." Give this example: "For the letter *S* one may note 'Spirit-filled,' based on verse 1."

Here are a few possibilities that you may suggest: S—successful (v. 4); E—excellent (v. 1); R—righteous (v. 6); V—valued (v. 1); A—anticipated (v. 4); N—nurturing (v. 3); T—true (v. 6).

Say, "When God speaks to the servant, he reveals the special relationship they share." Divide the class into three sections. Ask the first section, "What do you see characterizing the servant and the Father's special relationship?" Expect such responses as "loving support," as seen in verses 1 and 6. Ask the second section, "What elements of that relationship does the individual Christian share with the Father?" Expect such responses as the loving support we also receive, as seen in 1 John

3:1. Ask the third section, "What attributes of the servant must one adopt to enable such a relationship with the Father?" Expect such responses as "submission to his will," as seen in Romans 12:2.

Next, divide the class quickly into seven groups of people seated next to each other. Say, "Several of the images in our text bring to mind specific examples of what Jesus-the-servant and his disciples did, as recorded in the Gospels and in Acts." Then give each group one of the following phrases/verse numbers from Isaiah 42: (1) v. 2; (2) v. 3a; (3) "a light for the Gentiles," v. 6; (4) "to open eyes that are blind," v. 7a; (5) "I am the Lord; that is my name", v. 8; (6) "new things do I declare," v. 9; (7) v. 4b, regarding the islands placing hope in him.

Say, "Quickly select a good New Testament example of the fulfillment of your assigned verse." Allow for a variety of responses, but these are possibilities: (1) the whole tenor of Jesus' ministry; (2) one of Jesus' rescues of someone nearly lost to Satan's power, such as the Gadarene demoniac; (3) the Greeks coming to Jesus, as recorded in John 12:20, 21; (4) the healing of the blind man of John 9; (5) Jesus' designation of himself as "I am" in John 8:58; (6) the people's conclusion at the end of the Sermon on the Mount in Matthew 7:28, 29; (7) Paul and Barnabas's work on the island of Cyprus as recorded in Acts 13:4-12.

Alternative: Use small groups (or the class as a whole) to complete the "God and His Servant and His Servants" activity on the reproducible page.

INTO LIFE

Say, "Today's lesson shows us that God has a special concern for justice. At the final judgment, he will establish complete justice to eliminate injustice for eternity." Then give to each student a three-inch slip of paper, which you have prepared in advance, printed with the word *INJUSTICE.*

Say, "When you see or read of an injustice this week at work, home, or in the news, decide what you can do to help correct that injustice. After you take the action, tear off the letters IN from INJUSTICE from your slip of paper. Then pray that God will see justice done in all circumstances." [Use the "Smoking Wicks and Broken Stems" activity from the reproducible page as an alternative (or additional) *Into Life* commitment.]

God and His Servant and His Servants

When Isaiah, by the Spirit, reveals the relationship between God and the Servant Messiah, he also reveals God's relationship to anyone who becomes his servant. To the left of each statement, identify a Bible verse(s) from Isaiah 42:1-9 that relates to that statement. To the right of each statement, write a sentence prayer regarding your own relationship to God as his servant. To help get your started, the first statement has been completed for you.

v. 1 God upholds his servant.   Thank you, Father, for daily strength.

___ God expects righteousness in his servant.   _____

___ God expects to be the one and only.   _____

___ God expects his servant to be a light.   _____

___ God expects his servant to stand for justice.   _____

___ God's servant will live in quiet effectiveness.   _____

___ God's servant recognizes him as creator of all.   _____

Smoking Wicks and Broken Stems

Look at verse 3 of Isaiah 42. Write the name of a person on the smoldering lamp who is only weakly maintaining his faith and witness. On the stem write the name of a person who is broken and at risk of "drying up" spiritually.

Decide <u>how</u> and <u>when</u> you will serve these two people with the grace and kindness of God's servant.

How?   When?

STRENGTH FOR THE WEARY

LESSON 2

WHY TEACH THIS LESSON?

Today's lesson begins with a reminder that this season can be a tiring time of the year. The frantic pace of modern life takes its toll in other ways also: many are forced by their jobs to stay "connected" at all times. Cell phones, pagers, and wireless laptop computers keep many from ever getting away from life's pressure cooker. Some even impose these burdens on themselves to feel important.

This lesson reminds us that Christ experienced pressures and troubles we will never be forced to encounter. Since Christ's work means peace with God, we can face life stresses with better perspective. Isaiah's "suffering servant"—Jesus Christ—can provide the strength that will help us overcome.

INTRODUCTION

A. CHEERY OR WEARY?

Christmas is two weeks away. For many it seems that much of the cheeriness is gone, for they are exhausted with the preparations.

A church paper gave the lament of one young preacher about a planned outing for his wife and himself. They intended to purchase all the necessary Christmas gifts within a set period of time and within a certain cost limit. The results were that the shopping expedition took five times longer than anticipated and cost twice as much as their agreement. In the end they were weary, not cheery.

The title of today's study is "Strength for the Weary," but is this the weariness described above? We would have to be *very careful* to think through the question before answering. The Messiah did indeed come to comfort his people and to provide comfort for the poor in heart. Isaiah 40:31 affirms that those who wait or hope in the Lord will renew their strength, and that they can run or walk without being weary or faint. In context, that passage may refer to the people to be exiled in Babylon. When they receive word that they can return to their homeland, the excitement would invigorate them. Good news is definitely a factor in providing "strength for the weary." And the message of Christmas is definitely *good news!*

Returning to our story about the weary preacher and his wife, we should note that physical weariness can lead to spiritual defeat. Comfort for both physical and spiritual weariness can come from prayer, by the examples of how other Christians handle stresses, or through the genuine love and compassion of those who minister personally in the name of Christ. Comfort and strength are also available through today's lesson as we reflect anew on God's plan to save us.

B. LESSON BACKGROUND

The background for this lesson is approximately the same as for the previous study. We already noted the fact that there are four servant poems or servant

DEVOTIONAL READING:
ISAIAH 49:7-13
BACKGROUND SCRIPTURE:
ISAIAH 49–50
PRINTED TEXT:
ISAIAH 49:5, 6; 50:4-11

LESSON AIMS

After participating in this lesson, each student will be able to:

1. Recite at least two purposes that Isaiah prophesied for the Messiah to fulfill.

2. Tell how Jesus fulfilled those prophecies.

3. Prepare an explanation of how the shame Christ underwent saves us.

KEY VERSE

Because the Sovereign Lord helps me, I will not be disgraced. Therefore have I set my face like flint, and I know I will not be put to shame.   —Isaiah 50:7

songs in Isaiah (42:1-9; 49:1-13; 50:4-11; 52:13–53:12; see also Lesson 7 for the fall). The previous lesson, from Isaiah 42, was the first of such poems. Today's lesson offers verses from the next two. In the fullness of time, the Son of God would come to earth. The ultimate purpose was to provide freedom from the weight of sin. Thus does Jesus give strength for the weary for eternity.

I. COMMISSION OF THE SERVANT (ISAIAH 49:5, 6)

A. STATED BY THE SERVANT (v. 5)

5. And now the LORD says—
>   he who formed me in the womb to be his servant
> to bring Jacob back to him
>   and gather Israel to himself,
> for I am honored in the eyes of the Lord
>   and my God has been my strength—

The speaker is the *servant*, and several features of his special commission are given. First, there is an awareness that *the Lord* has a divine plan. Second, it is stated figuratively that this plan always has been in the mind of God. *In the womb* makes this affirmation in a common figure of speech (see also Isaiah 49:1).

The commission is that he is to return *Jacob* to the Lord. Jacob is another term for *Israel* (see Deuteronomy 33:10). Jacob later came to be used to refer to Judah, the southern part of divided Israel (Jeremiah 5:20; Lamentations 2:2).

While the exiles in captivity may read this and interpret it as a return from Babylon, its ultimate meaning is much greater. The emphasis here (and in the next verse) indicates a spiritual return by the people of Israel. It is sin that will cause the Babylonian captivity, and God's primary concern is spiritual reform.

The identification of the servant has been much debated. The apostle Paul applies the final part of the next verse to his work in going to the Gentiles (Acts 13:47) and makes it a messianic command. This is in accord with the traditional view that the word *servant* applies to the Messiah. This concept means that the reference to the servant as *Israel* in verse three of this poem could be providing yet another name for the Messiah. Similar to Jacob of old (Genesis 32:22-32), Jesus wrestled to a victory in his service for God (Luke 22:44).

The servant's determined faithfulness guarantees that his mission will be accomplished. He will therefore be exalted *in the eyes of the Lord.*

We may also note that the title for this lesson has an application here. In prophetic fashion the servant states that *God* is the source of his *strength.* Psalm 46:1 contains a similar statement, that God is "our refuge and strength."

B. STATED BY THE LORD (v. 6)

6. . . . he says:
>   "It is too small a thing for you to be my servant
>   to restore the tribes of Jacob
>   and bring back those of Israel I have kept.
> I will also make you a light for the Gentiles,
>   that you may bring my salvation to the ends of the earth."

Parents today often encourage their children to advance to a higher level of achievement. Here, the Lord, God the Father, uses that concept in language that we can understand. The servant's mission is enlarged beyond the people *of Israel.* It also must include *the Gentiles.* It is this prophecy that shows that much more than a physical return from Babylonian captivity is in view. It is this verse that Paul cites to justify his going to the Gentiles (Acts 13:47).

A Light to the Gentiles

"I the LORD have called thee in righteousness, and will hold thine hand, and will keep thee, and give thee for a covenant of the people, for a light of the Gentiles."
—Isaiah 42:6

Visual for Lesson 2. *Start a discussion with this visual as you ask "How are we part of Jesus' ministry of light?"*

God had told the people of Israel through a prophet that they, of all the families of the earth, were the only ones chosen by him (Amos 3:2); yet God's ultimate plan includes all peoples. The text before us is intended to give instruction not only to encourage the servant but also to tell Israel to be ready to implement the promise of *salvation* to the extremities *of the earth.* This is to happen at the appointed time in God's plan of redemption. The concept of the Messiah as developed by the ancient rabbis did not include the thought that he would be *a light for the Gentiles.* Their faulty concept produced much tension in the early church, as we see in Acts 11:1-3.

LIGHT ATTRACTS

We are all familiar with the ability of light to attract. Sometimes this is a positive thing, sometimes negative. Insects attracted to a light can be pests as they enter our homes. But an airport searchlight that brings an airplane to a safe arrival is a very positive attraction. In many communities there are very large displays of Christmas lights at this season of the year. This too can be either positive or negative.

In a positive sense, such lights at Christmas can witness to the one who is the "light of the world": Jesus, who came as a baby born in Bethlehem. In a negative sense, such lighting displays can merely be witness to the extravagance of the one putting them up. You've probably noticed that the displays seem to get more elaborate every year. No longer does decorating a single evergreen in the front yard suffice. It's as if every tree demands its own ropes of light, wrapping trunks as well as branches. The same trends that lead to conspicuous consumption in other areas also make Christmas lights more abundant.

As we put up Christmas lights in our homes and churches this year, may those lights point to the source of true light and not to our own cleverness or extravagance. Our Christmas lights will attract in either a positive or a negative way. The choice is ours. —A. E. A.

II. COMFORT BY THE SERVANT (ISAIAH 50:4, 5)

A. TONGUE TO TELL (v. 4a)

4a. The Sovereign LORD has given me an instructed tongue,
    to know the word that sustains the weary.

The printed text moves to the third servant poem in the book of Isaiah. The subject changes from the larger mission of the servant to personal aspects of his task. Overall, it examines his personal responsibilities in speaking, listening, suffering, and showing determination. Many of the prophets of ancient Israel are threatened, abused, imprisoned, and put to death because they faithfully proclaim the message they received (Acts 7:52). Jesus' experiences will be very similar hundreds of years after Isaiah writes. Jesus may come as the precious babe in the manger, but eventually he will be fully aware of the temptations, trials, and rejections that exist on this planet.

Moses predicted that someday there would be a prophet like himself (Deuteronomy 18:15). Various comparisons may be made between Moses and Jesus, but there is one contrast especially interesting here: Moses claimed that he lacked eloquence and could not speak (Exodus 4:10); the servant, on the other hand, declares that the *Lord has given* him a *tongue* that is capable and ready to speak. He will be taught, evidently, by God and man (Luke 2:40, 52). He will know what needs to be said, and he will say it.

The ministry of Jesus will produce weariness for him. It will be tiring to speak to thousands, to know that people are seeking to be with him for the wrong reasons, and to tolerate the quarrels of the disciples. At such times the Word of God

WHAT DO YOU THINK?

Many Jews of the first century seemed to have overlooked the ancient promise that the coming servant would be a light to the Gentiles. How have we been guilty in allowing our own expectations and experiences to color our understanding of Scripture? How do we guard against this?

WHAT DO YOU THINK?

How will you allow God to relieve your own weariness?

from what we call the Old Testament will bring strength to him. He is the one who brings us strength in season through his Word today.

B. EAR TO LISTEN (vv. 4b, 5)

4b. He wakens me morning by morning,
    wakens my ear to listen like one being taught.

This commentary is being written in the evening, and the alarm must be set to one of those early hours—my designated slot for a prayer vigil in the *morning.* Jesus did not need an alarm clock; God the Father could awaken him each morning and begin the day's interactions. The figure of speech is fascinating: the *ear* also is awakened so as to be alert to this special instruction from on high.

5. The Sovereign LORD has opened my ears,
    and I have not been rebellious;
    I have not drawn back.

It fills the mind with wonder to speculate on what God the Father and God the Son shared whenever Jesus prayed. The Son imposed limitations on himself when he gave up the glories of Heaven temporarily (Philippians 2:7). Minimal records are given of these prayers (Mark 14:36), but they must have been times of intense mental interchange between the heavenly Father and the Son.

WHAT DO YOU THINK?

What are some ways to keep our ears open to God's leading? How would we guard against mistaking our own desires for God's voice?

The response of the servant when God opens his *ears* is a great example. He does not resist; he is not *rebellious.* The servant Son listens, obeys, and does not turn *back* from his appointed mission. He is fully aware that the things before him will lead to rejection, physical torture, public shame, and humiliation. But he continues to have an ear that is open to his Father.

III. COMPOSURE OF THE SERVANT (ISAIAH 50:6-9)

A. IN SUFFERING (v. 6)

6. I offered my back to those who beat me,
    my cheeks to those who pulled out my beard;
    I did not hide my face
    from mocking and spitting.

A local church had a candlelight service on Christmas Eve. The theme was "From the Manger to the Cross." The emphasis that December night is the same as that of this verse. The gradual intensification of the servant's mission tells of things that take place before he reaches the cross. This poem is the servant's own predictive statement of what he will endure over 700 years after Isaiah writes these words.

The New Testament writers record that God's servant underwent the torture of being scourged or flogged (Matthew 27:26; Mark 15:15; John 19:1). The Gospels also record the mockery and *spitting* that the servant comes to endure (Matthew 27:27-31; Mark 15:16-20).

WHAT DO YOU THINK?

How can suffering actually help to define a person's ability to lead?

The divine prophecy states that Jesus *did not hide* his *face* from these things. Matthew records Jesus as saying that he could call 12 legions of angels, but he was determined that the Scriptures be fulfilled (Matthew 26:53, 54).

B. IN STANDING FIRM (vv. 7-9)

7. Because the Sovereign LORD helps me,
    I will not be disgraced.
    Therefore have I set my face like flint,
    and I know I will not be put to shame.

The servant expresses an emphatic confidence that the *Lord* will sustain him. In this he sets the example that has been followed through the centuries. Psalm 46:1, a favorite passage of many, agrees: "God is our refuge and strength, an ever-present help in trouble." Every Christian who is struggling with weariness—physical, emotional, or spiritual—must occasionally be reminded of this fact. The problem may persist, but strength for coping comes.

The conviction of the servant shows real determination with the phrase *set my face like flint*. One of the famous sermons of history is entitled "The Christ of the Flint Face." It is connected with a statement in Luke 9:51 where Jesus is said to set "his face to go to Jerusalem" (*King James Version*). There he eventually is to face brutal torture and an agonizing death. (Compare Paul's own statement in Acts 20:22.)

The result is that the servant is confident that the disgrace of failure will not be in his experiences. His actions always will be pleasing to the Lord. While reproach may be cast upon him, he will never suffer the humiliation of failure in his mission.

8. He who vindicates me is near.
　　Who then will bring charges against me?
　　Let us face each other!
　Who is my accuser?
　　Let him confront me!

The language changes to a court scene, and the servant expresses several things. First, he is aware of the nearness of God. Second, it is his vindication that is the only thing that matters. Third, the servant dares anyone to bring an accusation against him. The servant may suffer, but he has confidence in the ultimate court of justice.

9. It is the Sovereign LORD who helps me.
　　Who is he that will condemn me?
　They will all wear out like a garment;
　　the moths will eat them up.

The servant again declares that it is the *Lord* who is the source for his strength. And again he challenges anyone to *condemn* him or prove him guilty in any way.

The final words of the servant give the end of those who would presume to sentence him. The figure of *a garment* is used to show the outcomes. Clothing is a valuable commodity in primitive cultures (see Joshua 7:21). But clothing usually suffers destruction from use (wears out) or from insects such as *moths*. So will the enemies of the servant be destroyed.

IV. COUNSEL ON BEHALF OF THE SERVANT (ISAIAH 50:10, 11)

A. TO THOSE WHO ACCEPT HIM (v. 10)

10. Who among you fears the LORD
　　and obeys the word of his servant?
　Let him who walks in the dark,
　　who has no light,
　trust in the name of the Lord
　　and rely on his God.

The words of the *servant* come to an end. But the poem continues with an exhortation and a warning on behalf of the servant who will someday come to earth.

One question about this verse and the next is the identity of the speaker. Is it Isaiah, or is it the Lord? In the final analysis it is God. The exhortation here is

HOW TO SAY IT

Amos. AY-mus.
Babylon. BAB-uh-lun.
Deuteronomy. Due-ter-AHN-uh-me.
Gentiles. JEN-tiles.
Isaiah. Eye-ZAY-uh.
Israel. IZ-ray-el.
Jacob. JAY-kub.
Jeremiah. Jair-uh-MY-uh.
Joshua. JOSH-yew-uh.
Messiah. Meh-SIGH-uh.
Philippians. Fih-LIP-ee-unz.

addressed to anyone who reveres *the Lord* and who is obedient to *his servant*. This serves as a reminder that it is the fear of the Lord that is foundational to true wisdom (Proverbs 9:10).

Involved in such obedience is a recognition that the person has previously walked in darkness and has had *no light* for the journey of life. Now the plea is to *trust* in *the Lord* and be determined to have continual faithfulness.

TRUST FOR THE JOURNEY

As we start out on a trip, there are many things in which we place our trust. We trust in our automobile to give us good service. We trust the traffic enforcement officers to maintain the laws of the highway so the journey will be safe. We trust that the gas stations will be open for the purpose of refueling and restaurants will be open for food. The map we read we trust to be accurate. We are confident that the road signs point the right direction.

Our walk with God also demands trust. On this spiritual journey, we depend upon God's protection that he will build a hedge of safety around us. We depend upon spiritual nourishment from the encouragement of others and a refueling and renewing by the Holy Spirit. The Word of God is our road map, and we can be sure that following this will never lead us down a wrong road.

Before we start out on a journey, it's best to plan ahead. The same is true for our spiritual journey. Time spent with God in prayer and Bible reading at the beginning of the day puts us on the right road. Times of encouragement as we interact with fellow Christians provide fuel for the journey. God has promised that he will never abandon those who belong to him. It is only He, who can be trusted to provide guidance, protection, and strength for our journey toward eternity.   —A. E. A.

B. TO THOSE WHO REJECT HIM (v. 11)

11. But now, all you who light fires
and provide yourselves with flaming torches,
go, walk in the light of your fires
and of the torches you have set ablaze.
This is what you shall receive from my hand:
You will lie down in torment.

A warning is given to the many who are self-sufficient in trying to provide their own *light* for life. It is easy to accept the world's lie that we can take care of ourselves, protect ourselves, and handle life if we have health, wealth, and good luck. Many choose to light *fires* that they kindle for themselves.

God makes a promise that from his *hand* such people will be compelled to *lie down* in anguish. Make sure you're not one of those!

CONCLUSION

The verdict is clear: there is strength for the weary! We tap in to the ultimate source of that strength by fearing the Lord and obeying his voice (v. 10, above). The factor of obedience must not be overlooked. Many people desire physical blessings in abundance from God, but there are few attempts to live faithfully in obedience to God's commands. Should God be expected to strengthen the weary who live in flagrant disobedience to him?

The Sermon on the Mount ends with the familiar account of the two builders (see Matthew 7:24-27). One built on the rock, and the other built on sand. Jesus said that building on the rock means hearing his words and obeying them. To obey God brings with it a certain assurance and joy that give strength to live for God every day.

Discovery Learning

This page contains an alternative lesson plan emphasizing learning activities. Classes desiring such student involvement will find these suggestions helpful. The next page is a reproducible activity page to further enhance discovery learning.

LEARNING GOALS

After participating in this lesson, each student will be able to:

1. Recite at least two purposes that Isaiah prophesied for the Messiah to fulfill.

2. Tell how Jesus fulfilled those prophecies.

3. Prepare an explanation of how the shame Christ underwent saves us.

INTO THE LESSON

Display the following as class begins: "What makes one WEARY?" Ask students to suggest answers using the letters of the word. For example, for *W, work* is a possibility. If students seem to be stuck at points, some additional examples include *worry, exercise, emotions, argument, anxiety, running, yearning, yelling.* At the end of the activity, point out the lesson title, "Strength for the Weary" and draw attention to today's text.

INTO THE WORD

The lesson outline uses *commission, comfort, composure, counsel.* There are 33 letters in those words. Divide the words so that you have the number typically in your class. For example, if you usually have 15 students, divide the words into these 15 sets: *CO, MM, IS, SI, ON, CO, MFO, RT, CO, MP, OS, URE, CO, UN, SEL.* Put each combination on a separate card. Mix the cards and give one to each student.

Say, "To discover an emphasis in today's lesson, find others whose letters, when combined, make a key word related to the text." Encourage students to stand and "mill around" for this activity. If they need help, say that each word begins with *CO.* After students gather into their four groups (because there are four words), assign each a sitting area for the discussion to follow.

Put the four-part lesson outline on display. Give one of the following discussion stimulus assignments to each of the appropriate groups.

Commission—As the servant speaks in Isaiah 49:5, what insight does he show into God's eternal plan? What confidence does he express in God? What do we understand God's eternal plan to be? As the Lord speaks in Isaiah 49:6, how does he state his eternal purpose? What would be surprising in God's declaration to Isaiah's first hearers? What special relationship do we as Christians have to the servant's purpose? How do we fulfill the servant's purpose?

Comfort—Look at Isaiah 50:4, 5. What essential difference do you see between Moses as God's servant and the servant of Isaiah? What examples from the Gospels come to mind of Jesus saying the right thing at the right time? How and what did the Father speak to the Son in his earthly state? What is the servant's response to the Father's instructions? How far are we from affirming the servant's vow of Isaiah 50:5 for ourselves?

Composure—Read Isaiah 50:6-9. What similarities do you see between the servant's description of the way he reacts to persecution and the way Christ reacted after his arrest? What is commendable about the nonresistance of the servant to his enemies? How does one develop a similar composure in the face of such attacks?

Counsel—Read Isaiah 50:10, 11. What are the two secrets to a godly life? In what sense does a person without God walk in darkness? How does self-sufficiency cause a multitude of sins? In what way does a person have no more than sparks when trying to light his or her own path?

Allow time for groups to present conclusions. If you want to focus specifically on the weariness/comfort idea, use the two exercises on the reproducible page.

INTO LIFE

Next, divide your class into six groups where they are already seated. Say, "Verse 10 of Isaiah 50 has a grand question and God's grand answer for the weary." Assign each group one of these segments of the verse: "Who among you fears the Lord?"; "and obeys the word of his servant"; "Let him who walks in the dark"; "who has no light?"; "trust in the name of the Lord,"; "and rely on his God." Say the part of the verse relevant to each group, and let them repeat it. Then ask the groups to say the parts in sequence three times as quickly as they can.

Finally, ask, "What words to the weary will you use personally this week?" Suggest that verse 10 holds the answers: fearing, obeying, trusting, and relying. Distribute small pieces of paper. Say, "Write down the verse and carry it with you this next week as 'defense against world-weariness.'" You can also suggest that some may wish to put their notes where they will see it each day rather than carry it.

A Word for the Weary

For each scenario below, use your Bible knowledge (or a Bible concordance) to write a "word that sustains the weary" (Isaiah 50:4).

1. A minister has worked diligently for five years to develop the congregation's evangelistic outreach but to little success. He is discouraged.

2. A lady has been teaching preschoolers nearly every Sunday for 10 years. She is burned-out.

3. A teenager has lost her mother and both grandparents to death in only a short time. She is depressed.

4. For over 20 years a wife has tolerated a husband who moves from job to job and place to place. She is overwhelmed.

5. A student minister regularly overextends himself by being "too available" to the church's youth. He is exhausted.

Wings for the Weary

Isaiah 40:31 is one of God's grand encouragements to his servants. Connect the following phrases in the correct order. Then replace the words *those* and *they* with the word *I*. Also replace *their* with *my*.

and not be faint

in the Lord

they will walk

on wings like eagles

they will soar

those who hope

they will run

will renew their strength

and not grow weary

HOPE FOR THE SUFFERING

LESSON 3

Dec
18

WHY TEACH THIS LESSON?

Theologians and ordinary Christians alike have long struggled with the question "What place does suffering have in the life of one who trusts God?" Today's lesson doesn't answer that question, but rather it helps us understand that a Christian may enjoy hope even in the midst of his or her suffering. Each member of the class can bring to the discussion an experience of hurt: the unremitting pain of terminal cancer, the loss of a job, the heartbreak of a child's or grandchild's turning away from the Lord, the emotional agony of divorce, etc. Through it all we remember that no one knows more about suffering than Jesus. His suffering for sin's penalty makes our suffering bearable in light of eternity.

INTRODUCTION

A. HOPE DEFINED

Hope sometimes has been defined as "confident expectation" or a "union of desire and expectation." By its very nature, the concept of hope is restricted to those who are alive (Ecclesiastes 9:4).

The Christian has the great joy of having a living hope that has been guaranteed by the resurrection of Jesus Christ. That hope looks forward to an inheritance that is reserved in Heaven (1 Peter 1:3, 4). That hope sustains the believer, regardless of the trials that may come in this life. That hope serves as an anchor of the soul to those who find refuge in the promises of God (Hebrews 6:18, 19).

Hope is a part of that famous trilogy of faith, hope, and love. Each serves an important role in defining the Christian experience.

B. HOPE AT CHRISTMAS

The celebration of the Savior's birth has the concept of hope associated with it in many ways. For children it is usually what they expect to receive as gifts. Sometimes those hopes are fulfilled, but often those hopes are unrealistic.

Christmas also is associated with a certain nostalgia that family members should attempt to be together. People often hope (sometimes unrealistically) that travel plans, weather, and schedules will permit such reunions.

Many families indeed will be together for Christmas in a few days. But one or more family members may be absent because of death in the past year. The lesson for the day is entitled "Hope for the Suffering," and some will be hurting because of those deaths. In Christ, however, they are able also to express the confident hope of being able to be reunited with Christian loved ones. The Christ whose arrival we celebrate at Christmas is the one who brings this hope.

C. LESSON BACKGROUND

Passages from Isaiah and Luke are the texts for this lesson. The first three verses of Isaiah 53 are a part of the fourth servant poem or servant song. (See the discussion of these four in our previous two lessons.) The poem at issue today

---

DEVOTIONAL READING:
ROMANS 12:9-16

BACKGROUND SCRIPTURE:
ISAIAH 53; LUKE 1

PRINTED TEXT:
ISAIAH 53:1-3; LUKE 1:46-55

LESSON AIMS

After participating in this lesson, each student will be able to:

1. Compare and contrast the predictions of Isaiah 53:1-3 with Mary's song.

2. Explain why the suffering-servant concept is important to understanding the significance and joy of Christ's birth.

3. Express Mary's joy in a personal way.

KEY VERSE

"His mercy extends to those who fear him, from generation to generation."   —Luke 1:50

begins at Isaiah 52:13 and continues to the end of Isaiah 53. Polycarp, a Christian writer of the second century, refers to Isaiah 53 as "the golden passional of the Old Testament." This is the passage that has given rise to the phrase *suffering servant*. A prophetic view of the substitutionary death of the Messiah is clearly shown in the poem. Isaiah 53 is quoted at least six times in the New Testament. (See Matthew 8:17; Luke 22:37; John 12:38; Acts 8:32, 33; Romans 10:16; and 1 Peter 2:22.) There are 30 or so other references to it that are not direct quotations. What an important passage this is!

The Gospel of Luke, for its part, gives careful attention to the birth of Jesus, which occurs some 700 years after Isaiah writes. The occasion of the passage from Luke for today's lesson is Mary's visit to Elizabeth, a relative. Elizabeth was with child herself, and that child would come to be known as John the Baptist. Mary's response to Elizabeth's blessing is sometimes called The Magnificat, following the Latin translation.

I. DESPISING THE SERVANT (ISAIAH 53:1-3)

As indicated above, this servant poem actually began at Isaiah 52:13. The word *servant* appears in Isaiah 52:13 and 53:11. This is the longest of the four servant songs or servant poems.

A. DECLARATIONS ABOUT THE SERVANT (v. 1)

1. *Who has believed our message*
    and to whom has the arm of the Lord been revealed?

Isaiah is the speaker, and the word *our* may refer to the collective statements of all that the prophets had made about the Messiah's coming. It even could include the actual statements to be made by the Messiah himself during his ministry. The two questions are rhetorical. In this context they become affirmations that God's servant does not enjoy positive responses by his people (see John 1:11).

God's communication to his people is said to be done in two ways. The first is by what is said (*message*). The second is what is done by *the arm of the Lord*. That is a figure of speech to refer to the mighty acts of God. It therefore includes the miracles that Jesus will perform. This is the interpretation that John 12:37, 38 gives to this verse. Romans 10:14-17 establishes that faith comes by hearing the message. Yet Romans 10:16, which quotes Isaiah 53:1, tells us of those who reject the message. Some people hear and know, but their lives show that they do not believe in the Messiah who was born in Bethlehem.

B. DESCRIPTIONS OF THE SERVANT (v. 2)

2. *He grew up before him like a tender shoot,*
    and like a root out of dry ground.
   He had no beauty or majesty to attract us to him,
    nothing in his appearance that we should desire him.

The phrasing for *he grew up before him* clearly shows a distinction between God the Son and God the Father as the servant grows up before (in the sight of) the Lord. The statement *grew up* is predictive prophecy that requires some 700 years to come to completion. Yet on God's timeline it is indeed completed!

Two words from agriculture are used to describe the servant. They are *shoot* and *root*. Both words reflect qualities in the Messiah that do not make him attractive to those who will prefer a militaristic Messiah who would make Israel to be supreme among the powers of the world.

Another figure of speech is that this growth will be from *dry ground*. Thus it would appear to be weak and of no value. To the casual observer, it is not something to be desired.

Jesus' kingdom is not of this world, and the preconceived notions of many will not match what Jesus will have to say. There are prophecies that the Messiah will be a branch and out of the roots of Jesse, the father of David (Isaiah 4:2; 11:1). But many ancient Jews hope that the branch will turn into a mighty cedar.

Many also prefer that their leaders be handsome or attractive physically, don't they? David, Jesus' ancestor, had this quality (see 1 Samuel 16:18). When Jesus arrives following this prophecy, it will seem that he does not have the kind of physical attributes that compels instant endorsement from those who see him.

C. DISDAINING THE SERVANT (v. 3)
3. He was despised and rejected by men,
     a man of sorrows, and familiar with suffering.
   Like one from whom men hide their faces
     he was despised, and we esteemed him not.

The words *despised and rejected* are forceful ways of showing an intensity in the disfavor that Jesus is to receive during his earthly ministry. Jesus will not be just disregarded or ignored. Rather, he will be rejected and renounced deliberately. It has been said that unreturned love is one of the cruelest experiences that a person can have. When applied to the way that many have shown a total disregard for the love of God, it takes on gigantic proportions and implications. This has eternal consequences.

RISING ABOVE REJECTION

In the summer of 1807, Robert Fulton's crude little steamboat was prepared to move up the Hudson River on its maiden voyage. Critics called the boat Fulton's Folly. But we know now that this was no folly, it was no fluke. Fulton rose above his critics. As a result his boat became the predecessor to today's large ocean liners.

It is easy to cast doubt, isn't it? Parents are guilty at times of stifling creativity in their children. The road of life is littered with people who have been told that they would never amount to anything—and believed it. But there are always the overcomers, those who refuse to listen to the naysayers. Such people go on to greatness.

The ultimate example of this is Jesus, although his greatness is like no other. He was loathed by many. And his way is still rejected today by the masses. But Scripture reminds us that "the stone the builders rejected has become the capstone" (1 Peter 2:7).

Just as God has raised Jesus to the place that is above all, so he continues to exalt his will and his way in the world. The example of Jesus, the supreme overcomer, encourages us to serve our Lord and seek to promote his will in a critical, hostile world. Jesus himself will help us. What appears folly to the world will in the end be the triumph of the plan of God.   —A. E. A.

II. DELIBERATIONS BY MARY (LUKE 1:46-55)

In keeping with the season, Isaiah 53 leads us to think on the coming of the infant Jesus. We approach him in this lesson through his mother Mary. She is at the house of Elizabeth as we pick up the story. Mary's statement in reply to Elizabeth has the qualities of one of the psalms of the Old Testament. It also offers several similarities to the exaltation expressed by Hannah after she had dedicated her son Samuel to the Lord (1 Samuel 2:1-10).

A. REJOICING IN THE LORD (vv. 46, 47)

46, 47. And Mary said:

"My soul glorifies the Lord and my spirit rejoices in God my Savior,

Just before Mary's expression of praise, Elizabeth blessed her through the inspiration of the Holy Spirit. Mary's own personal piety undoubtedly assists her in drawing upon phrases and other songs from the Old Testament, especially the song by Hannah. Her spontaneous comments in reply to Elizabeth give evidence of a genuine and sincere faith.

Mary states two emotions from the depths of her soul, and they seem to be expansions of previously held concepts. First is her exaltation of the Lord; second is the joy that she is experiencing in God, her *Savior.*

B. RECOGNITION BY THE LORD (v. 48a)

48a. " . . . for he has been mindful
    of the humble state of his servant.

One aspect of Jesus' life that goes unesteemed is his modest origin (to earthly eyes) in the family of Mary and Joseph. This is confirmed by the offering of two birds in the purification rites (Luke 2:21-24). The usual sacrifices are a lamb plus a pigeon or dove. But two birds are permitted if a family is too poor to afford a lamb (Leviticus 12:6-8). This is part of being in a *humble state.*

Mary often is portrayed as being rather young, but the concepts in the statements she makes reflect a maturity beyond her age. She is fully aware of her origins and of the blessing of being selected by God to be the mother of the Savior.

C. RECOGNITION BY OTHERS (v. 48b)

48b. "From now on all generations will call me blessed,

Two beatitudes about Mary have been stated already by Elizabeth, one in verse 42 and the other in verse 45. Mary's words show that she understands her distinctive part in bringing the Messiah into the world. It is thus appropriate to honor Mary for the responsible task that she has. Some have elevated her to a status beyond what the Bible suggests, however. Others, in a reaction to this extreme, almost ignore her importance in the plan of God.

D. REGARDING THE LORD (v. 49)

49. " . . . for the Mighty One has done great things for me—
    holy is his name.

Mary is filled with reverence for *the Mighty One.* He is the one choosing her for the *great things* being done. She is also fully aware of the importance of God's holiness. The Lord confronted the nation of Israel about being holy (Leviticus 11:44, 45; see also 1 Peter 1:15, 16).

When Mary says *holy is his name,* she may have in mind Isaiah 57:15. That passage says that God's "name is holy." Mary knows something about God!

E. RELATING TO THE LORD (v. 50)

50. "His mercy extends to those who fear him,
    from generation to generation.

The Ten Commandments prohibit making any graven image. The seriousness of this is seen in the promise of judgment to the third and fourth generations for those who bow down to such idols (Exodus 20:4, 5). Yet mercy is promised for thousands—for generations who love and keep God's commandments (Exodus 20:6). Many things are happening in Mary's life. These include her message from

WHAT DO YOU THINK?

Elizabeth provided a safe haven for Mary that included a listening ear. As we approach the end of the year, we can reflect on the ways in which we have served and can serve others. How can we do better in this regard?

[Matthew 25:40 can frame your answer.]

Gabriel, the dream to Joseph, and Elizabeth's situation. These cause her to realize that God is still keeping his promises *from generation to generation* after centuries.

In Mary's statement a condition for receiving mercy is *fear* of the Lord, whereas in the Ten Commandments it is obedience. These are not in conflict. Micah 6:8 enriches both ideas when it tells us of the Lord's desire for his people "to act justly and to love mercy and to walk humbly with your God."

F. REPERCUSSIONS FROM THE LORD (vv. 51-53)

51. He has performed mighty deeds with his arm;
    he has scattered those who are proud in their inmost thoughts.

The *arm* as a source of power is a frequent figure of speech for the ancient Hebrews (examples: Exodus 6:6; Deuteronomy 5:15). Except for the labor performed by livestock, the human arm is the most visible means of power in ancient domestic and military achievements.

The deliverance of Israel from Egypt was one of the great events in the history of that nation. God used his mighty arm to bring about the plagues, the crossing of the sea, and the provision of water and food to sustain the nation for its 40 years of wandering in the wilderness. A nation that was suffering under slavery was able to experience hope in its distress.

Sadly, there were episodes of rebellion. But hope eventually won the battles: Israel crossed the Jordan under Joshua's leadership; the walled city of Jericho collapsed according to God's plan; the nations of Canaan were conquered; and the people of Israel took over cities that they had not built. In each instance of victory, the Lord was scattering the proud who were opposing the people of God.

52. He has brought down rulers from their thrones
    but has lifted up the humble.

Mary's mental catalog of great victories over Israel's enemies is similar to portions of Hebrews 11, the Faith Chapter. Some of the incidents of the book of Judges may also be in her mind. In those instances, the people of Israel had been suffering, and God provided judges who gave them new hope. After the period of the judges, David delivered his people from oppression when he defeated Goliath. God had truly brought low the powerful and elevated the people who had been subdued.

The language employed here seems to be more than just a poetic expression. It is based on Mary's comprehension of the greatness of God.

53. He has filled the hungry with good things
    but has sent the rich away empty.

The emphasis changes from the events of war to meeting the basic need of hunger. The expressions of praise here are more likely to be poetic and general rather than referring to actual events.

There are specific occasions in the Old Testament, however, that involve miraculous multiplications of food for *the hungry.* One example involves the widow of Zarephath, who fed Elijah the prophet for quite some time (1 Kings 17:14-16). Another example is the feeding of 100 men with 20 loaves of bread in the time of Elisha (2 Kings 4:42-44). We should not overlook the possibility that spiritual hunger may be an issue (or even the issue) for Mary (compare Psalm 107:9).

A HEALTHY DIET

Go to the Web site www.bread.org. Then click on the "hunger basics" link. There you will see startling statistics. Hunger and malnutrition are problems that need to be addressed in our world today.

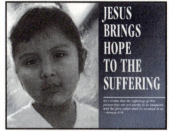

Visual for Lesson 3. *Point to this visual as you ask "How is the hope that Jesus brings different from the hope that many people actually have?"*

HOW TO SAY IT

Bethlehem. BETH-lih-hem.

Deuteronomy. Due-ter-AHN-uh-me.

Ecclesiastes. Ik-LEEZ-ee-AS-teez).

Elijah. Ee-LYE-juh.

Elisha. E-LYE-shuh.

Hannah. HAN-uh.

Hebrews. HEE-brews.

Isaiah. Eye-ZAY-uh.

Leviticus. Leh-VIT-ih-kus.

Magnificat. Mag-NIF-ih-cot.

Messiah. Meh-SIGH-uh.

Micah. MY-kuh.

Zarephath. ZAIR-uh-fath.

PRAYER

Our Father in Heaven, we read daily of suffering in the world, and that Christians are often the targets for persecution. We pray for them and for us that we may be steadfast because of the hope that we have in Christ, the hope of the world. In Jesus' name, amen.

THOUGHT TO REMEMBER

"May the God of hope fill you with all joy and peace as you trust in him" (Romans 15:13).

Even so, there is a more serious type of hunger all around us: it is spiritual hunger and malnutrition. In one sense, hunger can be a good thing because it pushes us to seek nutrition. In the Sermon on the Mount, Jesus said, "Blessed are those who hunger and thirst for righteousness, for they will be filled" (Matthew 5:6). Beyond the miraculous provisions of food God made for people in various times and places, spiritual food also is provided at the Lord's banquet table. In John 6:27 Jesus cautions his followers with these words: "Do not work for food that spoils, but for food that endures to eternal life, which the Son of Man will give you."

Sadly, opportunities for a solid spiritual diet are often neglected by God's people. Instead of finding the food that Jesus serves, many Christians gorge themselves on spiritual junk food. Some devotional books and Christian fiction are little more than pop culture with a spiritual spin. A world that is spiritually hungry is often treated to a version of the Word of God that bears little resemblance to the nutritional "meat" of the original.

Does your church monitor its programs to be sure a steady and healthy spiritual diet is offered? Do you as an individual take care to be sure that your spiritual diet is one that provides the essential ingredients for healthy, godly living?   —A. E. A.

G. REMEDY FROM THE LORD (vv. 54, 55)

54. *"He has helped his servant Israel,*
*   remembering to be merciful*

It is very obvious to Mary that the nation of Israel is truly blessed. Some conjecture that Mary's recollections include some of the great promises of a coming one who would be the Savior. In the book of Isaiah, the word *servant* does apply several times to the nation of *Israel*, but the ultimate purpose of that nation was to be the channel through which the Messiah would come into the world. It was essential that there be a righteous remnant, including godly people such as Mary, so that at the appointed time there would be a birth of the Son of God in Bethlehem. All of these things would work together to show both the patience and the grace of God.

55. *"... to Abraham and his descendants forever,*
*   even as he said to our fathers."*

The final words of Mary's song show that the promises made *to Abraham* are a part of her understanding of God's redemptive plan. God has been faithful. He has kept his word from generation to generation, and now the grand climax is ready to begin its fulfillment through the Son she will deliver.

It has often been said that Mary herself may have suffered because of the comments others probably made about her out-of-wedlock pregnancy. That is speculation, but one thing that is sure is that Mary has a tremendous faith that enables her to express her hope. She experiences this hope even in the midst of any such suffering that her situation may produce.

CONCLUSION

Some have a different hope at Christmas: they simply hope to be able to have a meal for the day. Some groups sponsor such meals for the needy in their communities. Churches often have benevolent programs that include delivering baskets of food to the underprivileged. Yes, there are some who take advantage of such kind acts, but there are others who express their sincere appreciation for these labors of love in the name of Christ. Such experiences in helping others to have their physical hopes fulfilled make the efforts worthwhile.

God has done so much for us. What will you do to provide hope for those who suffer physically and spiritually at this time of year?

Discovery Learning

*This page contains an alternative lesson plan emphasizing learning activities. Classes
desiring such student involvement will find these suggestions helpful. The next page
is a reproducible activity page to further enhance discovery learning.*

LEARNING GOALS

After this lesson, each student will be able to:

1. Compare and contrast the predictions of Isaiah 53:1-3 with Mary's song.

2. Explain why the suffering-servant concept is important to understanding the significance and joy of Christ's birth.

3. Express Mary's joy in a personal way.

INTO THE LESSON

Say, "Suffering contorts and disfigures. Look at these 'contorted' words and identify things that accompany suffering." Have each of the following scrambled words on a separate card or sheet: *ainp* (pain), *aegnr* (anger), *efgir* (grief), *aceeiimnpt* (impatience), *adensss* (sadness), *deeinoprss* (depression), *acdeegimnorstu* (discouragement). Show one word at a time, starting with the shorter ones. As words are unscrambled, write them for group display. Once all seven words are identified, ask, "What are other things that accompany suffering?"

As an alternate introduction, use the following activity that is included in the student books. Display this fill-in statement, "Christmas _____ hope," and ask the class for verbs they believe accurately complete the thought. If a suggested answer seems unclear, ask for an explanation. (Sample responses are *is, satisfies, gives, delivers, promises, completes, fulfills.*)

As another alternative, distribute the hope-focused activities on the reproducible page as students arrive. These will help set a tone for the lesson from the outset.

INTO THE WORD

Invite someone with music skills to bring a keyboard to class and play a few measures of some hymns and choruses. Give the musician your list of songs (see below) a week ahead of time for preparation.

First, ask the class to identify the song being played. Then ask students to identify Bible verses from today's text (in Isaiah 53 and Luke 1) that relate to that particular song. Suggested Bible verses are given in parentheses by each song, but accept student's suggestions for other Bible verses they may see relating to a particular song. Songs: "Hallelujah, What a Savior!" (Isaiah 53:3); "Magnify, O Magnify" (Luke 1:46); "What a Mighty God We Serve" (Luke 1:49); "Come, Desire of Nations, Come"

(Isaiah 53:2); "O Sacred Head Now Wounded" (Isaiah 53:3); "Holy, Holy, Holy" (Luke 1:49); "Leaning on the Everlasting Arms" (Luke 1:51); "Bread of Heaven, on Thee We Feed" (Luke 1:53); "God of Our Fathers" (Luke 1:55); "Man of Sorrows" (Isaiah 53:3). Add other hymns and choruses that your class knows. As Bible verses are identified, you will have opportunity for explanations about the text that you wish to add.

Also, recruit two women to present the following dialogue between Hannah (see 1 Samuel 2:1-10) and Mary. Introduce the activity to your class by saying, "Hannah and Mary had similar experiences with God. They sang similar songs of praise. Imagine what it would be like if they stood face to face." Have your actresses ready to stand at those words and begin the dialogue.

Hannah (H): Mary, you are indeed blessed of God, even more so than I was.

Mary (M): O Hannah, God has heard the prayers of his people. He answered with a Savior.

H: From my place of disgrace and shame, he has exalted me in the eyes of all.

M: Yes, praise his name. From my humble home of poverty, he has made me rich indeed.

H: God's people for all time will call our names in joy. Hannah . . . Mary . . . chosen!

M: With his strong hand he has touched me in holiness and power. He does great things.

H: In the midst of my pain, he showed me his mercy. His loving kindness endures forever.

M: He has brought down the pride of queens and noble women, but he has lifted me up.

H: His promise of seed to Abraham continues in my son Samuel and in your son, the Messiah.

M: Blessed be our God, dear Hannah; he keeps his word in love. You and I have seen it.

Next, have half the class turn to 1 Samuel 2:1-10. Have students compare and contrast the dialogue with both Hannah and Mary's songs.

INTO LIFE

Print the Thought to Remember on address labels. (If your home computer cannot do this, check with your church's office about the possibility.) Give each class member two or more copies to add to a card or letter to be sent during this holy season.

What Is Hope?

Which definition of hope do you like best? Write the reason for your choice after your preference.

1. *Hope is a glad anticipation of a positive future event.*

2. *Hope is the life preserver of a drowning person.*

3. *Hope is a mental assurance of a reality yet unseen.*

4. *Hope is a willful decision to step into the future.*

☞ What needs to be added to give each of these definitions a Christian perspective?

Why Hope?

Each of the following Scriptures is an affirmation of a reason for, or an object of, our hope. Look up each reference, and then complete the sentence.

John 14:1, 2—We hope because _____.

Romans 8:24, 25—We hope because _____.

1 Corinthians 15:19, 20—We hope because _____.

Colossians 1:26, 27—We hope because _____.

1 Thessalonians 5:8—We hope because _____.

Titus 1:1, 2—We hope because _____.

Hebrews 6:18, 19—We hope because _____.

My Hope

Peter admonishes both first-century and twenty-first-century Christians to "always be prepared to give an answer to everyone who asks you to give the reason for the hope that you have" (1 Peter 3:15). What is your ready answer? Write it here:

GOOD NEWS FOR THE WORLD

LESSON 4

DEVOTIONAL READING:
ISAIAH 52:7-12

BACKGROUND SCRIPTURE:
ISAIAH 61:1-3; LUKE 2:8-20

PRINTED TEXT:
ISAIAH 61:1, 2; LUKE 2:8-20

Dec 25

WHY TEACH THIS LESSON?

On a recent Sunday the preacher glanced at the clock and said, "I'm out of time; I have to close." A woman who was given to spontaneous responses uttered a loud "Hallelujah!" Minister and congregation alike burst out laughing. A good sermon had run a bit long and the dear woman's unintentionally humorous expression pointed out the "good news/bad news" nature of the situation.

Christians appropriately emphasize the good-news aspect of the Christmas story. Today's lesson will help your class see that just as the shepherds had to decide what to do with the good news they heard, we also have choices to make. Our decisions will determine whether his return will be good news or bad news!

INTRODUCTION

A. JESUS IS COMING—AGAIN!

What would life be like if Christ had not come? Sermons, books, and poems have presented their speculation on the subject. The influence of Christ cannot be discounted. His followers have had a profound impact in the areas of benevolence, education, the fine arts, and the histories of civilizations and nations. We shudder to think of a world without Christ and the forgiveness of sin he brought.

But Jesus was indeed born into the world. That fact causes us to remember that he is coming again! Jesus came the first time as the suffering servant, giving his life as an atonement for sin. He also warned that his return will be a time of condemnation for those who have lived in rebellion to him and his Word. The urgency is set one's life in order and be ready for the return of the Lord at any time. Jesus said that he will return—and he will!

B. LESSON BACKGROUND

The theme for the month of December has been "God's Redeeming Love." The Scriptures selected have included Old Testament passages that set forth God's plan to demonstrate his love for the world by sending a special servant. Each lesson has included passages from the book of Isaiah, and the final two Sundays of December also use portions from the book of Luke.

Isaiah sometimes has been designated as "the gospel prophet" or "the fifth evangelist" (adding Isaiah to Matthew, Mark, Luke, and John). Much of Jesus' life is given in predictive prophecy by Isaiah. The first few verses of Isaiah 61, the passage for today, will confirm the mission of Jesus.

The event from Luke in today's text takes place immediately after Jesus' birth. It is the announcement to shepherds that the Savior, the Christ, is in nearby Bethlehem as a baby in a manger. This part of God's plan for the ages had come to pass, just as it had been predicted for centuries.

LESSON AIMS

After participating in this lesson, each student will be able to:

1. Retell the events in the lives of the shepherds on the night Jesus was born.

2. Explain how Isaiah 61: 1, 2 applies to the lives of the shepherds.

3. Glorify and praise God for Jesus as the shepherds did.

KEY VERSE

"Today in the town of David a Savior has been born to you; he is Christ the Lord." —Luke 2:11

LESSON 4 NOTES

WHAT DO YOU THINK?

People initially thought well of Jesus when he quoted Isaiah 61:1, 2. But the mood turned ugly when he drew a comparison with the time of Elijah (Luke 4:24-29). What was the flaw in their attitudes that made them resistant to the good news Jesus was sharing? How are we susceptible to this flaw today?

I. ANOINTED ONE SPEAKS (ISAIAH 61:1, 2)

A. HIS CLAIMS (v. 1a)

1a. The Spirit of the Sovereign LORD is on me,
    because the Lord has anointed me
    to preach good news to the poor.

All of the previous selections from Isaiah this month have been from what are called the servant poems or servant songs. The word *servant* is not found in Isaiah 61, but that chapter is sometimes included as one of the poems because of its content and form.

Three interesting facts pertain to this verse and those that follow. First, this verse is quoted almost word for word by Jesus while in his hometown of Nazareth. That occasion is at the beginning of his ministry (Luke 4:16-19). When Jesus reads the opening verses of Isaiah 61, he will say that this Scripture is fulfilled that very day! After an initial gracious reception, Jesus' words will anger the assembled people. They will usher Jesus out of the city to throw him down a precipice. But Jesus, manifesting a portion of his divinity, will walk back through the hostile crowd without suffering any harm (Luke 4:28-30).

Second, the opening words of the verse at hand are fascinating in that all three personalities of the Godhead are mentioned: *the Spirit,* the *Lord,* and the *anointed* one speaking (the Christ or Messiah). The word *anointed* gives a different perspective to the role of the servant who had been introduced earlier. Anointing is a setting aside to a special office. In the Old Testament it is often reserved for prophets (example: Elisha's anointing by Elijah in 1 Kings 19:16b); kings (example: David's anointing by Samuel in 1 Samuel 16:1, 12, 13; 2 Samuel 2:7); and priests (examples: Exodus 28:41; 29:7; Leviticus 8:12, 30). A study of the person and work of Jesus in the New Testament shows that he fulfills all three functions: prophet, priest, and king.

Third, the foremost duty for the anointed one is *to preach.* The message of this preacher is the *good news* of the gospel. The specified audience consists of those who are not arrogant in their attitudes; they are those who are the downtrodden (compare Matthew 5:3-5). Such people understand the burden of sin, and they are receptive. (Some have attempted to say that the speaker in this passage is Isaiah. But Jesus applies it to himself in Luke 4:18.)

B. HIS COMMISSION (vv. 1b, 2)

1b. He has sent me to bind up the brokenhearted,
    to proclaim freedom for the captives
    and release from darkness for the prisoners,

To bind up the brokenhearted is a figure of speech, as if a bandage is to be applied to the heart that is broken because of sin. Several things can cause a broken heart, but the spiritual is foremost here.

The commission of the Savior includes proclamations for those who are in confinement. This does not mean that becoming a Christian removes the shackles of physical confinement, whatever that consists of. Rather, there is a spiritual liberation that enables a person to experience a *freedom* that does not depend on physical circumstances.

BREAKING FREE

Johnny had dropped out of church. He was disenchanted with the people of God, so he disassociated himself from them. He considered a relationship with the church to be unnecessary.

Then one day a fire destroyed his home and all family possessions. Churches and individual Christians responded with an outpouring of financial gifts, clothing, toys for the children, and prayers. Johnny was touched by the love of God's people. He and his family renewed their walk with God through a local church. Shortly after this, the best friend of Johnny's 7-year-old son was killed in a car accident. Johnny, motivated by the outpouring of love he had received, helped this family in their time of need.

Jesus came to bind up the broken, to liberate those captured by sin. He provided this relief while on earth in a physical body. He continues to provide this same help today through his spiritual body, the church. To be the people of Christ is to take on the work of Christ. Churches are often good at demonstrating this gift of love in the Christmas season. But it is a gift that needs to be a daily part of the church of Christ. The gift of love exhibited by the people of God is a gift that keeps on giving. Just ask Johnny.   —A. E. A.

2. . . . to proclaim the year of the LORD's favor
     and the day of vengeance of our God,
      to comfort all who mourn.

Several things are of special interest in this verse. One is the contrast in the designated periods of time: *year* vs. *day*. These terms are figures of speech in the ancient culture, and they are meant to express periods without concern for a precise number of hours or minutes.

The first phrase of the verse reminds us of the concepts associated with the Year of Jubilee, which was to occur every 50 years (Leviticus 25:8-17). In that year debts were to be canceled, servants were freed, and land went back to the original families. (So far no one is complaining that a phrase, found in Leviticus 25:10 and associated with the Year of Jubilee, is on the Liberty Bell in Philadelphia!)

We also note that justice in God's sight demands the *vengeance of our God.* There are many precious promises in the message of "good news," but there are also powerful warnings to those who do not listen to this preacher. Interestingly, when Jesus quotes Isaiah 61:1, 2 in Luke 4:18, 19, he stops with the phrase "to proclaim the year of the Lord's favor." It's as if Jesus is saying that his ministry ushers in the positive message of hope right then and there, while the dire reality of judgment will be delayed somewhat.

The final phrase of the verse at hand moves back to the message of comfort. What a great word at Christmas! The phrase is similar to one of Jesus' statements in the Sermon on the Mount in Matthew 5:4.

II. ANNOUNCEMENTS TO THE SHEPHERDS (LUKE 2:8-14)
A. SAVIOR FOR ALL (vv. 8-11)

8, 9. And there were shepherds living out in the fields nearby, keeping watch over their flocks at night. An angel of the Lord appeared to them, and the glory of the Lord shone around them, and they were terrified.

The message of Jesus' birth is not given to an emperor in Rome or to a high priest in Jerusalem. Rather, it is to humble *shepherds* that the heavenly angel appears.

The shepherds will remember this night for the rest of their lives, telling about it over and over. Perhaps these shepherds, like Simeon in Luke 2:25, are looking for the consolation of Israel. Perhaps some, like Joseph and Mary, are also descendants of David. Perhaps they know the prophecy about Bethlehem in Micah

WHAT DO YOU THINK?

The phrase "and the day of vengeance of our God" in Isaiah 61:2 may seem to be out of place in not being part of the "good news." What relationship do you see between that phrase and the other prophecies of that passage?

5:2, and therefore speak of such spiritual matters during the long hours of the *night* watches.

One of our favorite Christmas songs says that it was a "silent night," but we do not know that to be a fact. The shepherds are guarding their flocks from predatory animals, and they are alert to the sounds of the night. The sudden appearance of *an angel of the Lord* is startling in the darkness, and the added factor of *the glory of the Lord* combines to produce fright. That is the usual reaction whenever a person receives a heavenly visitor (examples: Luke 1:12; Acts 10:4).
10. But the angel said to them, "Do not be afraid. I bring you good news of great joy that will be for all the people.

The words of *the angel* provide assurance to the frightened shepherds. The impact of the angel's words builds to a positive climax that gives even more confidence.

Some students restrict the word *people* in this context to mean only the Jews. The reason for this is that other accounts mention salvation of "his people" (Matthew 1:21) as Jesus reigns over "the house of Jacob" (Luke 1:33). It is true that the church was primarily Jewish in background for the first few years of its existence. The prophecies of Isaiah, Amos, and others, however, support the view that the pronouncements include Gentiles—that they mean the same as the title for this lesson: "*good news* for the world." God intends salvation to be for Jew and non-Jew alike (Acts 10:34, 35; 11:18).
11. "Today in the town of David a Savior has been born to you; he is Christ the Lord.

The *Savior* does not come as a mature warrior. Instead, he arrives as a newborn baby. The terms continue to build in their significance, words such as *David, Savior, Christ,* and *Lord.* The shepherds undoubtedly have confirming thoughts with each word. We may safely conjecture that the shepherds are aware of the ancient connection between David and the city of Bethlehem.

B. SIGN OF A BABY (v. 12)
12. "This will be a sign to you: You will find a baby wrapped in cloths and lying in a manger."

The extraordinary happenings would seem unbelievable, even to those experiencing them. When it's all over, they may just think it was a hallucination. But to be given *a sign* will promote acceptance and belief. It's real! The sign is that of a *baby . . . lying in a manger.*

The birthing place for the Savior is not a sterilized room in a hospital, but place that includes a feed box for animals! The traditional pictures of this event show animals nearby, and that may be a valid assumption.

C. HEAVENLY HOST (vv. 13, 14)
13, 14. Suddenly a great company of the heavenly host appeared with the angel, praising God and saying,
> **"Glory to God in the highest,**
>   **and on earth peace to men on whom his favor rests."**

The appearance and announcement of one angel is dramatically emphasized with the sudden manifestation of a *heavenly host.* This angelic army has the joy and privilege of being a part of this special event.

A careful reading of the text indicates that the angels come *praising God and saying* something. There is no reference to singing as such. Yet over the years, composers have set the angelic words to music, with marvelous effect. The messages of the angels are bidirectional: *to God* and toward *men*. This birth will be more reason than ever before to give glory to God.

The second part of the statement refers to the genuine *peace* that can now be on earth. Rome had brought a military peace that would later permit the early Christians to spread the gospel. The peace mentioned here, however, is a peace between God and people. One of the greatest peace pronouncements of the New Testament is Romans 5:1: "Therefore, since we have been justified through faith, we have peace with God through our Lord Jesus Christ."

It is also fitting to note that Jesus said that he brought not only peace but also a sword (Matthew 10:34). Even today the very mention of the name *Jesus* in various parts of the world can produce tension and hostility that may turn violent.

Visual for Lesson 4. *Red and gold are important colors in this visual. Ask how each can remind us of Christ at Christmas.*

III. JOURNEY TO BETHLEHEM (LUKE 2:15-20)

A. DECISION (v. 15)

15. When the angels had left them and gone into heaven, the shepherds said to one another, "Let's go to Bethlehem and see this thing that has happened, which the Lord has told us about."

The angels deliver their praises and their message to humanity and then depart *into heaven*. This raises some intriguing questions. Do they simply disappear? Is there a visible departure until eventually they no longer can be seen? We are left to conjecture. What is not in doubt, however, is the shepherds' response. Stunned, they collect their thoughts and take the only reasonable actions that their experiences lead them to do.

First, *the shepherds* speak *to one another.* It is almost as if they need to have further confirmation among themselves that they had really seen and heard the heavenly messengers. Except for their own voices, only the sounds of night now are heard. But their conclusion is that they must leave in order to confirm what the angel had announced. They want to see this thing that has occurred in their own little town of *Bethlehem.*

B. DISCOVERY (v. 16)

16. So they hurried off and found Mary and Joseph, and the baby, who was lying in the manger.

It is just as the angel had said: shepherds find the infant Jesus *lying in* a *manger,* with *Mary and Joseph* in attendance. Without doubt, this is a privileged group that meets together this night.

As the shepherds come with all good speed to Bethlehem, does the excitement cause them to leave the flocks unguarded? Does someone volunteer to stay behind? Do they bring their flocks along? How long do they stay? The story may be familiar, but there is still much that arouses our curiosity!

C. DECLARATIONS (v. 17)

17. When they had seen him, they spread the word concerning what had been told them about this child,

An evangelist is someone who tells good news. These shepherds thus become the very first evangelists to testify about Jesus Christ, who has come in the flesh. What an amazing way that God works!

CAN YOU BELIEVE IT?

A man who worked on the streets near the World Trade Center in New York City was thought to be dead following the September 11, 2001 attacks. But almost a year later, his family received word that he was alive. The family of George V. Sims, 46, said they learned of his whereabouts in August 2002 when a hospital called and said that they believed Sims was a patient there.

How would you have responded to such good news? Stunned silence? Disbelief? Jump for joy? Maybe your response would be to grab the nearest person for a big hug. Many times good news is something we just have to share with others. One thing is certain though: when we hear *really* good news, something is bound to happen.

The response of the shepherds to the news of the birth of Jesus presented by the angels was one of desire. They wanted to check this out for themselves. And when they went to Bethlehem and saw that the good news was really true, they rejoiced and spread the message.

On this Christmas Day we reaffirm our belief that the coming of Jesus into the world actually happened. A proper response to this is rejoicing and sharing this good news with others.   —A. E. A.

D. DIFFERENT RESPONSES (vv. 18-20)

18. . . . and all who heard it were amazed at what the shepherds said to them.

The people who hear the accounts of *the shepherds* can do only what is stated here. The angels do not appear to these people to provide additional confirmation. Thus they can only wonder and think about what they are told. The rest of the story is still to unfold in the years ahead. That will provide their confirmation!

19. But Mary treasured up all these things and pondered them in her heart.

Mary's list of *things* associated with the birth of Jesus continues to grow. In the near future she will experience the visit by the wise men (Matthew 2:11), and then there will be the unexpected sojourn to Egypt (Matthew 2:13-15). Will she hear of the slaughter of the male infants in the vicinity of Bethlehem (Matthew 2:16)?

And then there are her thoughts when she finally finds her lost son in the temple, reasoning with scholars about the Law (Luke 2:41-51). What will she think as she sees him dying on a cross (John 19:25-27)? Mary will have much to ponder throughout her life.

20. The shepherds returned, glorifying and praising God for all the things they had heard and seen, which were just as they had been told.

We turn our attention once again to *the shepherds.* They must wonder why they are chosen to be a part of this special event. But then they do the right thing: they glorify and praise God for all the things they had been privileged to hear and see.

CONCLUSION

The prophecies and the birth of Jesus combine to make an unusual story. The prophecies that had accumulated through the centuries were fulfilled when Jesus became God incarnate—God in the flesh. As a new year dawns, will these things be just another telling of a familiar account, or will they make a difference in the lives of each one who has considered them again? As a new year dawns, will we resolve to make differences for Christ in the lives of others—differences that can determine where they spend eternity?

The events associated with Jesus' birth were not ordinary! They are a part of the message of Christ, and they are to be preached and taught by his followers to those who have never heard. It bears repeating: The purpose is to make a difference in the eternal destinies of those who hear.

Discovery Learning

This page contains an alternative lesson plan emphasizing learning activities. Classes desiring such student involvement will find these suggestions helpful. The next page is a reproducible activity page to further enhance discovery learning.

LEARNING GOALS

After participating in this lesson, each student will be able to:

1. Retell the events in the lives of the shepherds on the night Jesus was born.

2. Explain how Isaiah 61:1, 2 applies to the lives of the shepherds.

3. Glorify and praise God for Jesus as the shepherds did.

INTO THE LESSON

As class begins, have one of your better oral readers stand and read Luke 4:14-21. At the end of the reading say, "The text Jesus quoted from Isaiah would have sounded familiar to Jews of the first century. The rabbis had long taught that it was messianic. When Isaiah wrote it, it certainly brought hope to his first readers. It was good news then. It is good news now."

Then ask, "But what if Christ had not been born?" Write on the board "If Christ had not been born, then _____." Ask class members to think of different ways to complete this sentence. For example, "If Christ had not been born, then the church would not exist."

Let students offer completions for two or three minutes. Then lead into the lesson by saying, "That is all very bad news indeed. But we have, as the lesson title affirms, 'Good News for the World.'"

Another way to get the class in a Christmas frame of mind from the very outset is to have a copy of one or both of the activities on the reproducible page placed in each student's chair in advance. Naturally, many will begin to work on these right away as they arrive.

INTO THE WORD

Prepare copies of the following to be read antiphonally. It is today's text from Isaiah 61:1, 2 with a response added to each truth. Either read the leader's part yourself or have another do so. L=leader; G=group.

L: The Spirit of the Sovereign Lord is on me.

   G: God's Spirit has come to dwell in us.

L: Because the Lord has anointed me to preach good tidings to the poor.

   G: God wants the good news told to all.

L: He has sent me to bind up the brokenhearted.

   G: God cares when our hearts are broken.

L: To proclaim freedom for the captives.

   G: There is an escape from the bondage of sin.

L: And release from darkness for the prisoners.

   G: God offers freedom in Christ for the asking.

L: To proclaim the year of the Lord's favor.

   G: Now is the acceptable time.

L: And the day of vengeance of our God.

   G: God will see justice done.

L: To comfort all who mourn.

   G: God has given his Holy Spirit to be our comforter.

Next, ask learners to look at the text in Luke 2:8-20 and describe what the front of a Christmas card could look like that featured each verse (or a segment thereof). Suggest that students come up with some cards not typically found. For example, for "and they were terrified" (the last clause in verse 9) the card may show a close-up of shepherd faces with looks of terror. As a second example, "that will be for all the people" (the last phrase of verse 10) may be depicted on a Christmas card as a collage of photos of twenty-first-century ethnic groups. (A similar activity is included the student book.)

INTO LIFE

Prepare and distribute copies of a document containing the heading, "Resolutions!" with the following five statements printed beneath.

1. Mary actively meditated on the grand truths of the incarnation as well as her part in it. *Resolved: I will incorporate into my meditative life _____.*

2. The shepherds set the example of telling everyone they saw about the Messiah's birth. *Resolved: I will tell _____.*

3. Isaiah's description of the Messiah (Isaiah 61:1, 2) includes a variety of graces to those who are hurting. *Resolved: I will show grace by _____.*

4. The angels fulfilled their ministry of praise to God at Jesus' birth. *Resolved: I will enlarge my ministry of praise by _____.*

5. God loves me so much that he has given his Son. *Resolved: I will love him so much I will _____.*

Say to your class, "Take this resolution sheet home with you. This coming week is the traditional time when many people write resolutions for life changes. Use these stimulus statements to give consideration to some new commitments for the year ahead."

The Shepherds and the Shepherd

The following lines from a poem about the shepherds and Jesus, the Good Shepherd, have been "jumbled in transit." Only the first line is in the correct position. Number the lines in the correct order. When the three stanzas are in proper line order, the rhyme pattern for each five-line stanza will be AABBA. (The correct line sequence is revealed by looking at the poem's rhyming words that are listed in order and inverted at the bottom of the page.)

1. The shepherds have come to see one of their own;
___ He lies in a manger, no robe to adorn;
___ They know that their sheep are depending on them;
___ The babe will soon come to be Shepherd full grown;
___ So shepherds, greet Shepherd: O marvelous morn!

___ So shepherds return to their sheepfold in joy;
___ He knows that no bed for his rest will be found;
___ They've seen the Good Shepherd in small baby boy;
___ They know the discomfort of sleeping on ground;
___ So shepherds, greet Shepherd: Just call him God's joy!

___ He knows that lost sheep will be lost without him;
___ They know the cold nights keeping sheep in the fold;
___ The angels have told them the Christ is now born;
___ He knows of lost sheep from the Israel of old;
___ So shepherds, greet Shepherd: his glory is known!

Who Is It?

Messiah, shepherds, angels—all play a role in today's Bible texts from Isaiah 61:1, 2 and Luke 2:8-20. Read each action and indicate "Who did it?" by writing *M* for Messiah, *S* for shepherds, or *A* for angels on the line to the left. Each action may include one or more answers—or even no answer at all. To the right of each action, justify each of your answers with a Bible verse(s) reference.

____ scares someone by being present (v. ____)
____ creates a sense of wonder in listeners (v. ____)
____ receives revelation directly from God (v. ____)
____ glorifies and praises God (v. ____)
____ gets to tell others of God's plan and gift (v. ____)
____ serves God by serving others (v. ____)
____ speaks on the basis of God's will (v. ____)
____ acts as a go-between (v. ____)

own, grown, fold, old, known; born, adorn, ground, found, mom; in joy, boy, them, him, God's joy

Unit 2: *God's Gifts of Leadership*
(Lessons 5–9)

RELY ON GOD'S STRENGTH

LESSON 5

WHY TEACH THIS LESSON?

How can a church possibly stay healthy and grow in the midst of the current culture war? That war intimidates some, and they are unwilling to become engaged in it. Others feel pressured to compromise sound doctrine. As a result a church can drift into apostasy. The solution is wise leaders and leadership.

The type of leaders a church needs takes time to develop. That's where mentoring enters the picture. Without Paul's encouragement and example, Timothy may not have had the courage to fulfill the charge entrusted to him. It is a daunting task for a young preacher to confront both a hostile culture without and false teachers within. The encouragement, wise counsel, and prayerful support of godly elders can set such a man on a path of fruitful service in spite of such obstacles. In today's lesson, the apostle Paul—master mentor—shows the way.

INTRODUCTION

A. CHURCH LEADERSHIP AND CHURCH PURITY

There is an old story of a young man who entered a bank and asked to see the president. He stated that for a modest fee he would show him how to recognize all counterfeits. The president, upon hearing the proposition, saw the possibility of saving himself and the bank thousands of dollars. So he had the young man ushered in.

Expecting the young man to open his briefcase and spread out before him many counterfeits, the bank president was surprised when he simply removed a dollar bill from his billfold. The young man said, "Sir, if I can teach you to recognize all the marks of the genuine, then you will automatically recognize all that is counterfeit." Even in a modern era when currency contains watermarks, multicolored ink, and security threads, this is good advice!

An important part of today's lesson is the charge of "holding on to faith" (1 Timothy 1:19). Not everyone does this, as the rest of that verse and 1:6 make clear. "Holding on to faith" comes about through study. The psalmist said, "Your word is a lamp to my feet and a light for my path" (Psalm 119:105). When leadership accepts the charge to study the Word of God, their familiarity with it will enable them to protect the church from false doctrine. What a New Year's resolution this can be for 2006!

B. LESSON BACKGROUND

In the previous four lessons, we have studied God's marvelous plan for meeting humanity's desperate need. God met that need by sending his Son. The radical change Jesus makes in a person's life prepares him or her for service. Jesus becomes the great change agent. His presence in a person's life decisively alters one's eternal destiny. And the more a person walks by faith, the more the Lord is able to use him or her. This was the apostle Paul's experience. Paul wrote letters to his son in the faith, Timothy, to encourage him to walk the same path.

DEVOTIONAL READING:
ROMANS 16:17-27
BACKGROUND SCRIPTURE:
1 TIMOTHY 1
PRINTED TEXT:
1 TIMOTHY 1:12-20

Jan
1

LESSON AIMS

After participating in this lesson, each student will be able to:

1. Compare and contrast Paul's life before and after his transformation in Christ.

2. Tell how the power of the gospel can effect similar transformations today.

3. Write a letter to a young person in the church, encouraging progress in his or her faith.

KEY VERSE

I thank Christ Jesus our Lord, who has given me strength, that he considered me faithful, appointing me to his service.
—1 Timothy 1:12

Some suggest that Timothy was converted during Paul's first missionary trip to Asia Minor (modern Turkey). This trip included a visit to Timothy's hometown of Lystra (see Acts 14:8-20). The examples of Paul's life and preaching undoubtedly made an indelible impression on Timothy. These examples, coupled with the godly role models of Timothy's mother and grandmother (2 Timothy 1:5; 3:15), most likely are what led to his conversion to Christ. Timothy then became a coworker in Paul's evangelistic enterprise.

When Paul revisited the churches he had established, he recruited Timothy as a traveling companion. As Acts 16:1-4 tells us, Timothy's father was Greek but his mother was a Jewish believer. Paul circumcised Timothy because of his Greek background so that his influence among Jews would not be diminished.

The letter of 1 Timothy was written sometime after Paul's first imprisonment. The date was likely between A.D. 62 and 65, and Paul was probably somewhere in Macedonia as he composed it. The letter was written to reinforce certain instructions that Paul had given to Timothy after leaving him in Ephesus.

I. PAUL RECEIVED MERCY (1 TIMOTHY 1:12-14)

In the section preceding today's text, Paul reminded Timothy to repudiate false teachers and their erroneous doctrines. Paul began by citing the hostile culture into which he and Timothy had been called to minister. It was a culture that included reliance on "myths" and "endless genealogies" (1 Timothy 1:4).

A. HUMBLE GRATITUDE (vv. 12, 13)

12. *I thank Christ Jesus our Lord, who has given me strength, that he considered me faithful, appointing me to his service.*

Humility acknowledges that effective *service* is not accomplished by one's own efforts. Rather, effective service is through God's enablement (Acts 26:22; Philippians 4:13). A leadership role does not leave place for one to boast, but gives the glory to God. Paul had been specially called (Acts 9:15; 22:14-21; 26:16-20). *Christ* knew the character of Paul and knew he could be counted on. Paul, in turn, acknowledges the source of power in his ministry. Notice the terms Paul uses. The very nature of the one who put Paul into ministry signifies his enabling power: Christ, God's anointed one, is *Jesus our Lord*, which denotes his sovereignty. Paul is humbled by the fact that the Lord has seen fit to use him. This is the spirit of anyone involved in a church leadership role.

God has a work that each of us can do. If we don't do it, then it may not be done. It is awe inspiring to realize that God sees fit to use us in his work. It should humble us to think that we are privileged to labor in areas that have eternal consequences. Anything we do in his name is as unto the Lord (Matthew 25:34-40).

Paul's calling into ministry was spectacular, to say the least! How are Christians called to Christian leadership and ministry roles today? How can we tell the difference between a true call and a false call?

COUNTED FAITHFUL

Joshua Chamberlain was a college professor in Maine in 1862 when he volunteered his services to the governor for the American Civil War. Subsequently, he was appointed to be a senior officer in a regiment designated the Twentieth Maine. Wounded at the Battle of Fredericksburg, he commanded that regiment at Gettysburg when it had its appointment with destiny.

The Twentieth Maine was placed on a piece of ground known as Little Round Top at the extreme left flank of the Union Army. Chamberlain had to hold that position at all costs. If the Confederates turned his flank, they could roll up the entire Union Army. When his men were attacked by a much higher number of Confederates, they fought back until their ammunition was gone.

Then in an audacious move, Chamberlain led his troops in a bayonet attack that pushed the stalled Confederates off the hill and saved the left flank. Wounded again, he would later receive the Congressional Medal of Honor for his actions on Little Round Top. He received four more wounds in the war, was promoted to major general, and was given the honor of commanding the troops that received the surrender of Robert E. Lee's army at Appomattox.

Chamberlain had a weighty responsibility at Gettysburg. But he was faithful to his assigned duties, then and afterward. His wounds did not deter him from further service. Paul also was one who was "wounded in action" many times (see 2 Corinthians 6:3-10). But he stood firm. He could still be thankful that the Lord considered him faithful. He encourages Timothy—and us—to stand firm as well.

—J. B. N.

13. Even though I was once a blasphemer and a persecutor and a violent man, I was shown mercy because I acted in ignorance and unbelief.

Paul now cites the reason for his gratitude and sense of unworthiness: he once had been a violent opponent of Christianity. Jesus, appearing on the Damascus road, confirmed what Paul now affirms for himself: "Saul, Saul, why do you persecute me?" (Acts 9:4). Saul (before being renamed Paul) had sanctioned the death of Stephen (Acts 7:58–8:1). Further, Saul had intended to take into custody any Christians to be found in Damascus (Acts 9:1, 2).

Paul earlier affirmed that he had acted "in all good conscience" (Acts 23:1). From this we may conclude that conscience is not always a reliable guide. Conscience can operate only on the information it receives. Paul sincerely thought he was serving God while persecuting Christians. Paul thought he was preserving the Law of Moses. But he was sincerely wrong. Sinning in *ignorance* is still sin. As a judge will tell you, "Ignorance of the law is no excuse." Paul obtained *mercy* because he repented of his error.

This is also illustrated in the 3,000 who were saved on the Day of Pentecost. According to Peter's charge in his sermon, those present had been party to Jesus' crucifixion (Acts 2:36). When confronted by Peter's sermon, the people became convinced that this Jesus, whom they had crucified, was Lord and Christ. Similar to what Saul said on the Damascus road (Acts 22:10), they had cried out, "What shall we do?" (Acts 2:37). And like Saul (Acts 22:16), they submitted to the gracious conditions of pardon and were saved (Acts 2:38, 41).

What a lesson for all of us! Psalm 103:12 says, "As far as the east is from the west, so far has he removed our transgressions from us." The life and witness of Saul (Paul) illustrates the dramatic change that can take place through the power of God.

B. AMAZING GRACE (v. 14)

14. The grace of our Lord was poured out on me abundantly, along with the faith and love that are in Christ Jesus.

Given all that has happened to him, it is no wonder that Paul writes so much about *the grace of our Lord*. Arrogance and pride because of accomplishments have no place in God's service. That was the downfall of the Pharisees who loved to boast (Luke 18:11, 12). We owe to the riches of God's grace all that we are and hope to be.

II. CHRIST CAME TO SAVE (1 TIMOTHY 1:15-17)

The greatest love story of all time is now retold. It affirms what Jesus told Nicodemus (John 3:16) and Zacchaeus (Luke 19:10).

WHAT DO YOU THINK?

Why do you think that God chooses to use human agents to accomplish his purposes when we are so prone to be weak and wrong?

WHAT DO YOU THINK?

How can we describe God's love and grace in terms that unbelievers will understand?

[Use Acts 17:16-34; 22:1-21 to start your thinking.]

HOW TO SAY IT

Abraham. AY-bruh-ham.
Damascus. Duh-MASS-kus.
Ephesus. EF-uh-sus.
Hebrews. HEE-brews.
Hymenaeus. Hi-meh-NEE-us.
Lystra. LISS-truh.
Macedonia. Mass-eh-DOE-nee-uh.
Nicodemus. NICK-uh-DEE-mus.
Pentecost. PENT-ih-kost.
Zacchaeus. Zack-KEY-us.

A. CHRIST'S MISSION (v. 15)

15. Here is a trustworthy saying that deserves full acceptance: Christ Jesus came into the world to save sinners—of whom I am the worst.

A trustworthy saying means that what Paul is about to relay is true and can be believed by everyone. That goes for us too!

Paul is overwhelmed by the realization that God's love embraces someone such as himself—whom he considers to be *the worst* of *sinners.* Think about it: God incarnate *came into the world* for the express purpose of saving people as evil as Saul had been! We all need to believe this. A hopeless world needs to be told this good news over and over. We are the only vehicles through whom it will hear this message.

Earlier, Paul exclaimed "Woe to me if I do not preach the gospel!" (1 Corinthians 9:16). Our challenge is to see non-Christians as those needing salvation rather than as our enemies. We need to let them know that Jesus is the answer to the sinner's problem (John 3:17).

B. PAUL'S NEED (v. 16)

16. But for that very reason I was shown mercy so that in me, the worst of sinners, Christ Jesus might display his unlimited patience as an example for those who would believe on him and receive eternal life.

The conversion of a man like Paul should be an encouragement. "Therefore he is able to save completely those who come to God through him" (Hebrews 7:25). No person is hopeless.

If you think about it, Paul had been a most unlikely prospect. His conversion reminds us of the old cliché that the darkest hour is just before dawn. When a person is fighting the hardest may be when he or she is closest to surrendering to Christ, as in Paul's case. Jesus had chided Saul, "It is hard for you to kick against the goads" (Acts 26:14). How many times during revivals have I left someone's home thinking it was a hopeless case, only to see that individual respond to the gospel on that very night. So don't give up easily! Don't underestimate the work of the Holy Spirit and the power of the gospel.

Christians may be reluctant to share their faith because of the fear of failure in dealing with people like Paul. Remember, God has not called us to be successful, but to be obedient. We are simply seed sowers. It is God who does the harvesting. Only he can convert (see 1 Corinthians 3:6, 7). So don't be afraid of failure. When you share your faith in love, inevitably there will be a harvest.

Paul was saved by grace, not only for his own sake but for the sake of others. He is an example of God's love, grace, power, and *patience* (2 Peter 3:15). Where would we be were it not for God's great patience? God doesn't give up on us easily. Nor should we give up easily when working to win people to Christ. What Paul is saying is, "If Christ can save a sinner such as me, he can save anyone. My example gives hope to all."

C. PAUL'S DOXOLOGY (v. 17)

17. Now to the King eternal, immortal, invisible, the only God, be honor and glory for ever and ever. Amen.

Such an expression of praise is inevitable from one who realizes that he or she is a sinner saved by grace. It is uttered in admiration and awe.

The God whom Paul describes is *the only God* there is! He was willing to become incarnate in his Son. Although *invisible,* we catch a glimpse of God through Jesus: "Anyone who has seen me has seen the Father" (John 14:9). There is nothing hidden from God (Matthew 10:26). This one alone is the God able to fulfill his promise to aged Abraham for a son (Romans 4:18, 19), to deliver three Israelites from the fiery furnace (Daniel 3), to raise Jesus from the dead (Galatians 1:1), and to save to the uttermost all "those who come to God through him" (again, Hebrews 7:25).

Pagan deities—who are really no deities at all—have none of the attributes ascribed to God. Since these so-called gods originate in the minds of finite people, there is found in them only the attributes commonly found in humanity. But we serve the living God. He is transcendent, above all things. Yes, God is able. God alone is praiseworthy. He alone can do for us what we cannot do for ourselves.

God's name is thrown around very casually in postmodern culture. Even many Christians use it thoughtlessly in expressions of surprise or dismay. Have we lost our sense of reverence? (See Exodus 20:7.) He is our creator, our redeemer; we are the objects of his grace. He and he alone deserves the worship of our lips and hearts (Psalms 95:3-6; 96:1-9).

Visual for Lesson 5. *Keep this map posted for the final nine lessons of the quarter to help your students keep a geographical perspective.*

III. TIMOTHY HAS A CHARGE (1 TIMOTHY 1:18-20)

Paul's first charge to Timothy reveals the purpose for writing (1 Timothy 1:3-10). Now the charge is expanded, taking on an increased urgency.

A. FAITH AND INSTRUCTION (vv. 18, 19a)

18. Timothy, my son, I give you this instruction in keeping with the prophecies once made about you, so that by following them you may fight the good fight,

Paul encourages *Timothy* to proceed in the task entrusted to him. That encouragement comes from the fact that there have been prophecies made concerning him and his call to ministry and service in the kingdom.

The charge includes Timothy's participation in *the good fight*. It is not warfare against flesh and blood (see Ephesians 6:12). It is a good fight because it is against sin and Satan and because Timothy is in the Lord's army. So he is to stand up against false teachers and not be intimidated by their arrogance and rebellious spirit. We twenty-first-century Christians are engaged in this same kind of spiritual warfare. We dare not be pacifists in this regard.

19a. . . . holding on to faith and a good conscience.

Paul depends on Timothy not to abandon either his *faith* or his *good conscience*. There is no hint that Paul thinks it is OK for Timothy to tolerate, in the name of "diversity," the attitudes of those who do. The next verse shows why.

B. APOSTASY AND DISCIPLINE (vv. 19b, 20)

19b. Some have rejected these and so have shipwrecked their faith.

When *some* forsook *faith*, their consciences were left without any guidelines. As a result, their faith was wrecked like a ship that runs up on rocks because it has no rudder. We do well to heed Paul's admonition to Timothy: We must hold on to the Christian faith, because in so doing we will have an enlightened conscience. Then we won't blaspheme or contradict God and end up in apostasy (Hebrews 11:6). That is the danger these false teachers are in.

20. Among them are Hymenaeus and Alexander, whom I have handed over to Satan to be taught not to blaspheme.

Two men by the names of *Hymenaeus and Alexander* are examples of those who have defected from faith. Their consciences are seared (1 Timothy 4:2). They have sold out *to Satan*. Perhaps Paul had tried to teach these two men personally, so the sting of their apostasy hits him hard.

WHAT DO YOU THINK?

How would you respond to someone who said, "Christian discipleship involves primarily a life of peace"?

[Passages such as Isaiah 9:6; Matthew 10:34; Luke 14:26; Romans 5:1; Ephesians 4:15; 6:11, 12, 17; and 1 Timothy 4:1-3 will inform your discussion.]

WHAT DO YOU THINK?

How can the postmodern emphasis on tolerance shipwreck faith and disarm the church? What do we do to avoid this?

[Use 1 Corinthians 5:1-5 and Revelation 2:14-16, 20-23 as backdrops to your discussion.]

We learn of the necessity of church discipline in this verse. The New Testament sets forth three instances that call for church discipline: doctrinal defection (see Romans 16:17, 18; 1 Timothy 6:3, 4; and Titus 1:10-16); moral defection (see 1 Corinthians 5); and divisiveness (again, Romans 16:17, 28; plus Titus 3:10). This is consistent with Jesus' teaching in Matthew 18:15-17. A bad apple tolerated can destroy a whole bushel. This is true in the church.

These two propagators of false teaching needed to be dealt with. How many times has a church's witness in a community been nullified because it tolerated sin? Even so, the motivation for biblical discipline is to restore the errant person (2 Corinthians 2:5-11). It also is only a last resort (notice the sequence in Matthew 18:15-17). A diseased member of the body is removed only if the welfare of the body is in jeopardy.

When done properly, many times the object of discipline is brought to repentance and restored. Restoration may be in view here as Paul expresses his desire that Hymenaeus and Alexander learn *not to blaspheme.*

SHIPWRECKED FAITH

Many factors can be involved in a shipwreck. At 11:10 P.M. on July 25, 1956, in a heavy fog off Nantucket Island, the reinforced icebreaking bow of the Swedish-American liner *Stockholm* sliced into the starboard side of the Italian luxury liner *Andrea Doria.* Other ships quickly responded to the SOS, and within seven hours all survivors of the 1,662 passengers and crew were safely removed from the doomed ship. But 52 lives were lost. At 10:09 A.M., only 11 hours after impact, the *Andrea Doria* sank.

Later investigation indicated that the *Andrea Doria's* radar was not used properly. And at the last moment, the ship turned left into the *Stockholm's* path, rather than turning to the right, which was standard procedure for a head-on crossing at sea. Carelessness caused the loss of a $30 million ship, as well as the 52 lives.

Paul already had survived a shipwreck on the coast of Malta (Acts 27, 28). And he knew that bad judgment could bring on such a disaster. But even more tragically, he knew what could happen with spiritual carelessness. He mentions two men who had made spiritual shipwreck of their lives because they had not paid attention to faith and conscience. Neglect of either can lead to stormy times, malfunctioning relationships, too-late warnings, and an ignorance-is-bliss attitude that leads straight to disaster, spiritual and otherwise. Take heed: the ruins of shipwrecked lives litter the fields of history just as much as the ruins of ships litter the ocean's floors. —J. B. N.

CONCLUSION

Today's lesson should make each of us grateful for the grace of God that forgave us our sins. Our challenge is to translate that gratitude into a life of useful service. Paul's example and our own experience should teach us that we can trust God for he "is able to do immeasurably more than all we ask or imagine" (Ephesians 3:20).

Sadly, many would be willing to serve in leadership roles if such roles entailed no responsibility. But then that would not be leadership! The implementation of God's plan depends on leaders remembering that God never asks us to do anything that he will not enable us to do. Paul recognized his personal inability to carry out the task God had set before him. But he also recognized, as should we, that God uses the weak things of the world to demonstrate his power so that we have no basis to glory. As a result, it is God who is glorified (1 Corinthians 1:26-31).

Discovery Learning

This page contains an alternative lesson plan emphasizing learning activities. Classes desiring such student involvement will find these suggestions helpful. The next page is a reproducible activity page to further enhance discovery learning.

LEARNING GOALS

After this lesson, each student will be able to:

1. Compare and contrast Paul's life before and after his transformation in Christ.

2. Tell how the power of the gospel can effect similar transformations today.

3. Write a letter to a young person in the church, encouraging progress in his or her faith.

INTO THE LESSON

Testimonial: Recruit a young Christian, whose conversion to Christ brought a dramatic turnabout in his or her life, to give a short, life-change testimonial. The main focus should be on how his or her life has changed since accepting Christ, rather than on the specific conversion experience itself. (Caution your recruit about making too graphic a description of an earlier sinful lifestyle.)

INTO THE WORD

Photocopy the following word-find puzzle (it is included in the student books). Make a transition from the testimonial to this activity by saying, "Christ has been changing people for 2,000 years. Paul, when he was Saul, approved of the murder of Christians. But Christ changed him. This word-find puzzle draws attention to the characteristics of Christian leadership that the Christ-changed Paul could commend to Timothy in today's text of 1 Timothy 1:12-20."

```
H  L  R  O  I  R  R  A  W  E
A  U  D  R  E  R  D  L  T  E
C  A  M  D  E  E  E  N  R  F
H  L  E  B  L  N  E  E  A  A
A  A  X  B  L  D  N  V  D  I
N  E  A  R  N  E  L  I  E  T
G  N  M  E  D  L  N  G  S  H
E  A  P  E  R  L  L  R  E  F
D  E  L  A  E  A  D  O  E  U
D  R  E  R  L  C  E  F  A  L
```

The following words can be found in the puzzle, with the Bible verse references in parentheses: *called* (12), *changed* (13), *dependent*, *enabled* (12), *example* (16), *faithful* (12), *forgiven* (16), *humble* (15), *sinner* (15), *warrior* (18). Be sure to include all 10 words at the bottom of the puzzle as hints (but don't include the verse refer-

ences). Also say, "We're not looking for the exact words from the Bible text. Instead, we're looking for words that tell us of the concepts that we find in our text."

When all 10 words have been identified, ask students to identify which verses from today's text match each of the characteristics found in the puzzle. Finally, challenge students to create one remaining word using only the letters that served as filler spaces. (The word is *leader*.)

As an alternative or additional activity, write *blasphemer* and *persecutor* on the board. Tell the class, "Paul's change in Christ was sudden and complete." Have a student read Acts 9:1-6, 17-22.

Then say, "Select a letter in one of these two words, and I'll change it to a letter of another word that characterizes Paul's new lifestyle in the Spirit." As learners select letters, replace them as follows: **Word 1:** *b* to *e*; *l* to *v*; *a* to *a*; *s* to *n*; *p* to *g*; *h* to *e*; *e* to *l*; *m* to *I*; *e* to *s*; *r* to *t*—from *blasphemer* to *evangelist*; **Word 2:** *p* to *e*; *e* to *n*; *r* to *c*; *s* to *o*; *e* to *u*; *c* to *r*; *u* to *a*; *t* to *g*; *e* to *e*; *r* to *r*—from *persecutor* to *encourager.*

As each word is deciphered, complete the conversion of the letters. When both are identified, say, "Paul went from saying bad things to saying the best things; he went from treating enemies harshly to loving brothers kindly; he went from attacking others' well-being to building up others' health and strength. Those are changes each of us needs to make in Christ."

Time allowing, follow with the activities on the reproducible page. "Unlikely Prospects?" will help students see the unsaved from God's viewpoint. "Reasons for Church Discipline" will alert students to the problem of what could be called "reverse transformations."

INTO LIFE

Obtain a list of teenagers who participate in your church's youth ministry. Write each teen's name and address on a slip of paper and put the slips into a bag.

Say, "In this bag I have the names and addresses of several of our church's teenagers. We need volunteers to write short encouragement notes to them during this next week. Our study has been that of an 'encouragement letter' Paul sent to the younger Timothy. That biblical letter of 1 Timothy may offer ideas for your own note." Set the bag near the classroom's exit and recommend that each student take a name as they leave.

Unlikely Prospects?

The lesson writer, commenting on 1 Timothy 1:16, calls Paul a "most unlikely prospect" for the gospel. What are some things, to earthly eyes, that make it seem that way? On the other hand, what are some things, to God's eyes, that can make that same person a very likely prospect for the gospel? Luke 7:36-50; 19:1-9; and Acts 10:1-8 provide ideas for both questions!

What (to us) makes people unlikely prospects

_____

_____

_____

_____

What (to God) makes people very likely prospects

_____

_____

_____

_____

Reasons for Church Discipline

First Timothy 1:20 names two who proved themselves to be unfaithful—so much so that the apostle Paul had to disfellowship them. As we consider the entire witness of the New Testament, we see three issues that call for church discipline leading to disfellowshiping. These three issues are *doctrinal defection*, *moral defection*, and *divisiveness*. Use connecting lines to match the Scripture on the left with the correct issue to the right. (Any given Scripture may apply to more than one issue.)

Scripture	Issue	How well?	How important?
Matthew 18:15-17			
Romans 16:17, 18	Doctrinal Defection	_____	_____
1 Corinthians 5			
1 Timothy 6:3-5	Moral Defection	_____	_____
Titus 1:10-16			
Titus 3:10	Divisiveness	_____	_____

Using a scale from 0 (very poorly) to 5 (very well), rate today's church by how well it implements church discipline in each of the three areas. Write your response on the lines in the third column.

Finally, use a scale from 0 (not important at all) to 5 (critically important) to rate the importance of each of the three issues to a church's effectiveness. Write your response on the lines in the fourth column. Be prepared to defend your answers!

PRAY FOR EVERYONE

LESSON 6

WHY TEACH THIS LESSON?

Prayer is perhaps one of the most neglected areas of spiritual discipline. This may be due to the fact that many Christians were never taught to pray or how to pray. Perhaps they have not known for what to pray. Or perhaps they have never prayed in faith. They may have felt their prayers were never answered and just gave up praying. That may have been because they did not understand how, or in what ways, God answers prayer. They may not have been willing to accept his timetable. They may ask with wrong motives, praying for the wrong things and for the wrong reasons (see James 4:3).

Today's lesson gives a sense of direction to our prayer life. It moves us from uttering vague generalities to addressing specifics purposefully. Today's lesson will have an impact not only in our own lives but also in the lives of those for whom we pray.

INTRODUCTION

A. WHAT MAKES THE DIFFERENCE?

For years our church has had a prayer chain. This is an organized network of people who believe in the power of prayer. They have volunteered to spend time praying for others who may be in a crisis situation or who have emotional, financial, physical, relational, or spiritual problems. Our prayer chain is also the vehicle to communicate praises for answered prayers.

What a blessing this has been! The blessings are not only for the participants and the objects of prayer, but for the entire church. Our prayer chain has gained such a reputation that people outside of our church frequently will request to be put on our prayer chain. The inspiring testimonies many give with regard to answered prayers serve as towers of strength, encouragement, and rejoicing among fellow Christians.

Our prayer chain helps take the focus off self and place it on others. This in itself has curative value. Even the medical profession increasingly acknowledges the beneficial influence that prayer has on people.

If your church does not have a prayer chain or prayer ministry of some type, I would recommend it highly. Such a ministry recognizes the priority of prayer in the life of the church. It heightens church members' awareness of concerns that need attention. It focuses on God, who is able to meet those needs. It alters attitudes from being critical or judgmental to that of sympathetic concern.

Remember: "Pray for each other so that you may be healed. The prayer of a righteous man is powerful and effective" (James 5:16). Paul knew this too. That's why he stresses prayer to Timothy, who is ministering to a troubled church.

B. LESSON BACKGROUND

Paul had left his "true son in the faith" Timothy in Ephesus sometime during the interim between his own imprisonments in Rome. It was a daunting task that

DEVOTIONAL READING:
COLOSSIANS 4:2-6

BACKGROUND SCRIPTURE:
1 TIMOTHY 2

PRINTED TEXT:
1 TIMOTHY 2:1-8

LESSON AIMS

After participating in this lesson, each student will be able to:

1. List some methods and reasons Paul says believers should pray.

2. Identify some specific people for whom we should pray, based on Paul's general description.

3. Adjust his or her prayer life to match the pattern Paul sets forth.

Jan
8

KEY VERSE

I urge, then, first of all, that requests, prayers, intercession and thanksgiving be made for everyone.   —1 Timothy 2:1

LESSON 6 NOTES

he had assigned this young preacher. The great Ephesian church had some doctrinal problems that needed to be addressed. Timothy also had to cope with some strong personalities who were espousing false teaching. This situation is what brought forth Paul's letter of instruction and encouragement.

In last week's lesson, Paul reminded Timothy of his charge. Paul accompanied this reminder with further instruction. Paul also encouraged Timothy by citing himself as an example of the sufficiency of God's grace and his enabling power. With this as background, we make a transition into today's text.

I. OUR PRAYERS (1 TIMOTHY 2:1-3)

Remember that in the original manuscript, written in Greek, there were no chapter headings or breaks. Those were not put in until hundreds of years later. So Paul shows a movement in thought by connecting his preceding and following thoughts with a transitional form. His thought now stresses the role of prayer and its priority.

A. TYPES OF PRAYERS (v. 1)

1. I urge, then, first of all, that requests, prayers, intercession and thanksgiving be made for everyone—

The transitional word *then* connects what Paul is about to say with his foregoing statements. On the basis of the charge, encouragement, and instruction he has given to Timothy already (see last week's lesson), Paul now proceeds to cite the place and types of *prayers* in the church.

In addition to the general idea of prayers, Paul mentions *requests, . . . intercession, and thanksgiving* as specific ways of coming before God's throne. Requests may address our deep personal needs—strength for resisting temptation, the asking of forgiveness.

Intercession involves petitions that we offer up to God on behalf of others. Christ was a model of intercessory prayer (John 17:6-26) even as he prepared to make the ultimate intercession in his death (see Romans 8:34). The Holy Spirit also has a vital ministry of intercession for us before our heavenly Father (Romans 8:26). In 2 Thessalonians 3:1, Paul is specific in his request that others make intercession for him. Just because he is an apostle doesn't mean that he doesn't need prayer support too! Modern Christians are to offer intercessory prayer on a regular basis.

Thanksgiving is the outpouring of our hearts for God's beneficence, for the blessings he bestows upon us in so many ways. We thank God for the provision he makes for all our needs, both physical and spiritual. We do well to remember that "every good and perfect gift is from above, coming down from the Father of the heavenly lights, who does not change like shifting shadows" (James 1:17).

Notice that Paul does not prescribe a certain form or ritual to these prayers. There is no instruction for liturgical form. Rather, Paul cites the types of communication with God that have different meanings and applications.

Christians not only major in prayer for themselves but also in prayers *for everyone*. What Paul has in mind by that word *everyone* is the subject of the next verse.

B. SPECIAL OBJECTS OF PRAYER (v. 2a)

2a. . . . for kings and all those in authority,

Concerning the *everyone* in verse 1, Paul now makes clear that he is thinking of civil leaders. We are more prone to criticize them than to pray for them, aren't we? Government officials in Paul's day are pagans, of course. Such leaders in-

HOW TO SAY IT

Corinthians. Ko-RIN-thee-unz.

Deuteronomy. Due-ter-AHN-uh-me.

Ephesians. Ee-FEE-zhunz.

Ephesus. EF-uh-sus.

Gentiles. JEN-tiles.

Lamentations. Lam-en-TAY-shunz.

Malachi. MAL-uh-kye.

Thessalonians. THESS-uh-LO-nee-unz.

clude the infamous Nero, who eventually would have Paul beheaded. In another letter, Paul says "Bless those who persecute you; bless and do not curse" (Romans 12:14). Prayer, with the strength that comes from the Lord, is the only way we can do this.

Before we pray it will help to remember that civil government is ordained of God (Romans 13:1). For this reason we pray for those who are entrusted with the oversight of civil life. People *in authority* need our prayers because they are confronted daily with difficult decisions that affect the peace and safety of society as a whole. They have to deal with pressures exerted by all types of special interest groups whose offer of monetary support is very tempting.

A study of history makes clear that God rules in the affairs of humanity. *Kings* and kingdoms come and go, but God is still sovereign in his universe. Prayer can lead to a change in the attitudes and decisions of authorities.

God may answer your prayers for governing authorities by using you as an influence through your respectful e-mails, letters, and phone calls to those in government. As you voice your concerns, remember also to express gratitude for their support of what is right and good. Tell them that you are praying for them. This is a much-neglected ministry on the part of Christians.

C. RESULTS OF PRAYER (vv. 2b, 3)
2b, 3. . . . that we may live peaceful and quiet lives in all godliness and holiness. This is good, and pleases God our Savior,

Paul cites something that every Christian should long for: *peaceful and quiet lives in all godliness and holiness.* Paul does not say to pray for government leaders so that we will have all of our physical needs supplied by a "nanny" state. Rather, our prayers are for an environment in which we can function best as godly and holy people. In other words, we pray for the government to protect our safety as opposed to giving us what we think are our "entitlements." This matches Paul's thoughts in Romans 13:1-5 (see also 1 Peter 2:13-17).

When we pray like that and the result is a peaceful and quiet life, our gratitude is to be expressed in godly and holy living. But a peaceful and quiet life will not be our lot if we are not godly and holy. The trait of godliness is found in our right relationship with God. The Greek word that is translated *holiness* in this verse is also translated *respect* in 1 Timothy 3:4 and *seriousness* in Titus 2:7; these have to do with our dealings with others. Godliness and holiness in the senses used here are inseparable. One cannot truly exist without the other (compare 1 Peter 3:8-12). This is a vital part of discovering what *is good* and pleasing to *God our Savior.*

II. GOD'S PLANS (1 TIMOTHY 2:4-6)
When we Christians try to see the world through the eyes of God, it alters our prayer lives in profound ways. True, our world is sinful and rebellious. But that fact does not diminish God's love for all people. This is a love so great that he sent his one and only Son to save them (John 3:16; Romans 5:8). It is a love we must share!

A. SALVATION, KNOWLEDGE, TRUTH (v. 4)
4. . . . who wants all men to be saved and to come to a knowledge of the truth.

Here Paul asserts God's will for *all* humanity. Some may ask, "If it is God's will that everyone be saved, then why doesn't he save everyone?" The answer is that God created us to be free moral agents, with free will, with the ability to make opposite choices. When a person reads or hears the Word of truth, it causes his

WHAT DO YOU THINK?

Is it possible to make a prayer list too long? Why, or why not?

WHAT DO YOU THINK?

Do godliness and holiness produce a peaceful and quiet life, or is it the other way around? Explain.

or her life to arrive at a fork in the road. Standing at the crossroads of accepting or rejecting Christ, that individual makes a freewill choice. It is a decision that will determine his or her eternal destiny (Matthew 7:13, 14).

God created all people in his own image. He wants us to enjoy eternal fellowship with him. Our choice to disobey God alienates us from him. But God's love for his creation has made provision for the problem of sin so that anyone can be saved (Romans 10:13; 2 Peter 3:9).

We should not think that Paul is teaching a doctrine of universalism—that everyone will indeed be saved. Being saved requires that we comply with the gracious conditions of pardon that God has revealed to us. Having *a knowledge of the truth* is part of this. Jesus is the embodiment of truth (John 14:6). He said, "You will know the truth, and the truth will set you free. . . . If the Son sets you free, you will be free indeed" (John 8:32, 36). We study the Word of God because there we learn not only of truths but also of the one who was and is truth (2 Timothy 2:15; 3:14-17).

The fact that God wants *all men to be saved* has obvious evangelistic implications. Our role as Christians is to implement God's desire for the salvation of all. Jesus' Great Commission is the marching order of the church (Matthew 28:19, 20). Paul is very conscious of this (Romans 10:14-17).

B. GOD, MAN, CHRIST (v. 5)

5. For there is one God and one mediator between God and men, the man Christ Jesus,

Contrary to the pagan world all around him, Paul affirms that *there is one God*. The Bible affirms that fact time and again in both Old and New Testaments (examples: Malachi 2:10; 1 Corinthians 8:6). The pagan world, by contrast, has many "gods." That world worships created things rather than the creator (Romans 1:23, 25). The one true God is the God who has revealed himself; it is he alone who is to be worshiped and served (Exodus 20:3-5).

In his infinite love and mercy, the one true God has provided the means by which all can be reconciled to him. And that is through the *one mediator . . . the man Christ Jesus*. The fact that Jesus is the one mediator is a truth that a person must accept to be saved (see Acts 4:12). This eliminates a popular notion that there are many roads to God. It also disavows the idea that others can mediate. For example, we cannot (and need not) invoke "the saints" or the virgin Mary to intercede for us. No human can take the place of Jesus. It is because of what he has done for us on the cross that enables him to be our only mediator, intercessor, advocate (1 John 1:7–2:2).

ONE MEDIATOR

On numerous occasions I have been asked to pray at various functions other than church services. Sometimes these are meetings of service clubs (Lions, Kiwanis, Rotarians, etc.), or community memorial services, or giving the blessing for the meal at some civic occasion. Many times I have been asked politely to refrain from closing "in Jesus' name." Many of their members were Jews, my host would explain. Some were Muslims, or some had no religious inclination at all. To end my prayer in the traditional way would therefore be offensive to them.

In every instance, I have refused. That was probably not the time or place to go into a theology lesson, but I have tried to point out, briefly and just as politely as they asked, that the only way I can approach God is through Jesus. If I can't pray in Jesus' name, then I can't pray to God at all. "Oh," they would say, somewhat puzzled. And the conversation usually ended there, on a very awkward note.

WHAT DO YOU THINK?

How can we become more intentional about praying for the unsaved?

WHAT DO YOU THINK?

Without immediately quoting Scripture, how would you respond to someone who asks, "Aren't all religious people headed for Heaven?"

In these days of political correctness, non-Christian people are often bewildered by the Christian's insistence that Jesus is the only way to God and eternal life. This stance seems so bigoted to flexible and "tolerant" societies. In John 14:6, Jesus said, "No one comes to the Father except through me." Paul rightly states there is only one mediator. It may be politically incorrect, but it is certainly theologically correct.   —J. B. N.

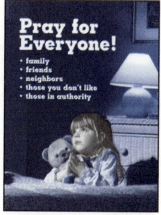

Visual for Lesson 6. *Point to these prayer categories as you ask "Who do you know that most needs your prayers?"*

C. RANSOM, TESTIMONY, TIME (v. 6)

6. . . . who gave himself as a ransom for all men—the testimony given in its proper time.

The reason that Jesus is the one mediator between God and humanity is that he alone is the one who paid the *ransom* for our deliverance from God's wrath. The price that Jesus paid was his blood that he shed when he died on the cross for sin (Romans 3:21-27; 1 Peter 1:18, 19). In his death Jesus canceled the effects of Adam's sin that have been passed on to all (Romans 5:12-21). He also paid the penalty for our own personal sins.

Being our mediator required that Jesus give himself to be a ransom (Mark 10:45; Hebrews 9:15). Jesus' death is the basis that made his mediation possible. He was the only one worthy (God-man) to perform such a deed. That's the reason no "saint" can qualify as a mediator.

That which was *the testimony given in its proper time* was Jesus' redemptive work on the cross. That's the reason Paul said, "We preach Christ crucified" (1 Corinthians 1:23). And now this testimony is to be preached everywhere.

D. PREACHER, APOSTLE, TEACHER (v. 7)

7. And for this purpose I was appointed a herald and an apostle—am telling the truth, I am not lying—and a teacher of the true faith to the Gentiles.

Here Paul expands a bit on his opening assertion in 1 Timothy 1:1. Paul's actions are consistent with the commission the Lord had given him (Acts 9:15; 22:15; 26:16-18). So Paul affirms again his apostleship, his special call of the Lord, as one sent to Gentiles (see also Acts 13:46-48; 18:6; Romans 11:13; Galatians 1:16). As such, he was to preach good news to non-Jews, even as Peter was to preach primarily to the Jews.

Paul's integrity and credibility in this regard are obviously quite important to him. This isn't the first time that he has felt obligated to defend his integrity and authority (see 1 Corinthians 9). A vital part of this integrity is preaching *the true faith*. He trusts the Holy Spirit of God to do his work through the Word of truth that he (Paul) faithfully preaches and teaches (Romans 1:15; 15:20; 1 Corinthians 1:17; Ephesians 3:8).

Our challenge is to share our faith with the same confidence. And we can if we teach the Word of God in love and leave the results to him. He just asks us to be faithful and go.

E. HOLINESS, PRAYER, ATTITUDE (v. 8)

8. I want men everywhere to lift up holy hands in prayer, without anger or disputing.

We know, of course, that God gives us wide latitude concerning time and place of prayer. We can pray in solitude at home (Matthew 6:6), with others at mealtime (Acts 27:35), and in public settings (Acts 20:36). That is part of what it means to "pray continually" (1 Thessalonians 5:17). But what about our posture during those times with God? In the verse before us, is Paul telling us that raising our *hands* is a requirement for prayer?

DAILY BIBLE READINGS

Monday, Jan. 2—Paul Prays for the Philippians (Philippians 1:3-11)

Tuesday, Jan. 3—Pray Without Ceasing (1 Thessalonians 5:16-22)

Wednesday, Jan. 4—God Hears Our Prayers (1 Peter 3:8-12a)

Thursday, Jan. 5—A Parable About Praying (Luke 18:1-8)

Friday, Jan. 6—Pray for Your Enemies (Matthew 5:43-48)

Saturday, Jan. 7—Pray for Everyone (1 Timothy 2:1-7)

Sunday, Jan. 8—Prayer Is Powerful and Effective (James 5:13-18)

In the Scriptures we find that some kneel to pray (Luke 22:41; Acts 20:36; 21:5), some stand (Luke 18:13), and some prostrate themselves (Deuteronomy 9:18; Mark 14:35). There also are occasions when people raise their hands as they address God (Exodus 9:29; 1 Kings 8:22, 54; Psalm 141:2; Lamentations 3:41). The thing that is stressed is that they be *holy* hands. To use one's hands in an unholy way one minute only to lift those same hands in prayer the next minute would be an abomination to the holy God.

Hands lifted up in prayer should be expressions of sincere faith and pure motives, not for show or as a prescribed form. To offer prayers *without anger or disputing* is an important part of this. Our motives and mind-set are important while praying. The Lord's own prayer can teach us even more in this regard (Matthew 6:9-15).

HOLY HANDS

In Lincoln, Illinois, there is a replica of the original Postville Courthouse where Abraham Lincoln once practiced law as a circuit-riding lawyer. Just a block away is Postville Park. One day Lincoln had taken the case of a farmer who was suing a man who had bought a pig but had never paid for it. The other man protested that he had paid for it and refused to pay again. As the case developed during the court proceedings, Lincoln came to the conclusion that his client indeed had been paid and was trying to collect twice.

During the noon recess, Lincoln went down to Postville Park to pitch horseshoes. When it was time for court to reconvene, Lincoln did not show up. The judge sent a clerk down to call Lincoln back to the courtroom. Lincoln sent the answer: "I can't. My hands are dirty." The judge, who had come to the same conclusion as Lincoln during the testimony, knew exactly what Lincoln meant. He dismissed the case.

By presenting the case of a man who was trying to extort extra money from a purchaser, Lincoln knew he had dirtied his own hands. Thus he refused to proceed with the case. How different it would be for most modern lawyers! They would say that they are only presenting the case for a client; it is not their place to determine the morality involved. Paul calls us to a different and higher standard. We are to lift up holy hands—not hands that have been soiled by defending immorality.—J. B. N.

CONCLUSION

Even as Paul charged Timothy, it is incumbent upon church leaders to teach the necessity and the powerful role of prayer in the lives of Christians. Church leaders do this, in part, by setting examples in their own worship lives.

Isn't it easy to fall into a rut and pray the same trite prayers, using the same phrases, year after year? We do well to give thought to praying for *specific* people and *specific* needs. Prayer at specific occasions ought to reflect those occasions. Invocations, for example, ought to be what the word implies—asking God's presence and blessing as we lift up pleasing worship to him. Communion prayers should focus on the event it commemorates and not wander over every other subject. The same kind of focus should be true of prayers during the time of offering. Such prayers acknowledge God as the giver of every good gift, express gratitude, and dedicate our gifts. We offer such prayers with an acknowledgment of our stewardship.

Prayer is God's powerhouse in the life of a Christian and the church. As we learn to pray, we will pray not only for our own needs, but also for the needs of others, for our civil and church leadership, and especially for the salvation of those still outside of Christ.

WHAT DO YOU THINK?

What posture do you prefer for praying? Why?

PRAYER

Father, help us to pray more intentionally, keeping in mind the things you have taught us in our lesson today. Help us to be more sensitive to the needs of others, both physical and spiritual. We trust you to create circumstances that will help bring about the answers to our prayers that are according to your will and for your glory. In Jesus' name we pray, amen.

THOUGHT TO REMEMBER

Prayer comes first.

Discovery Learning

This page contains an alternative lesson plan emphasizing learning activities. Classes desiring such student involvement will find these suggestions helpful. The next page is a reproducible activity page to further enhance discovery learning.

LEARNING GOALS

After participating in this lesson, each student will be able to:

1. List some methods and reasons Paul says believers should pray.

2. Identify some specific people for whom we should pray, based on Paul's general description.

3. Adjust his or her prayer life to match the pattern Paul sets forth.

INTO THE LESSON

Have this question on display as students arrive: "Why Pray?" As class begins, solicit students' responses. Expect such answers as the following: "because we are commanded to pray," "because Jesus set us an example," "because some matters are simply beyond our abilities," and "we need help." Ask students to cite relevant Scriptures. (Suggest they use Bible concordances, if necessary.) If you like to offer your students something to engage their thinking as they arrive, put copies of the "Truth" activity from the reproducible page in the chairs.

INTO THE WORD

Give each learner eight strips of paper, 5-1/2 inches long and 1-1/2 inches wide (cut from sheets of 8-1/2 by 11 inches). Ask students to write on each of their slips of paper a prayer request derived from Bible verses in today's text of 1 Timothy 2:1-8. Share these examples: "Give thanks for public workers who serve you, such as garbage collectors" (v. 4) and "Pray for those in difficult cultures who are trying to help people come to the knowledge of God's truth" (v. 4).

After allowing time for students to work, collect the completed slips, saying, "It is OK if you have fewer than eight." To make sure you have prayer thoughts related to all eight verses, you may want to add the following slips for any verses your students did not complete: "Pray for individuals whom you never have prayed for" (v. 1); "Pray that God's Spirit will enable a peaceful, quiet life for you" (v. 2); "Pray that you will please God with your prayers" (v. 3); "Pray for the convicting work of the Spirit in the life of someone whom you—and God—want to be saved" (v. 4); "Thank God that in his wisdom he provided a mediator for us in Jesus Christ" (v. 5); "Praise God that the Lord Jesus offered himself for our sins" (v. 6); "Thank God for the apostle Paul and for his ministry to us in the Word" (v. 7); "Pray for the personal holiness that makes your prayers effective before God" (v. 8).

Once the slips are collected, mix them up and then pull out one at a time. Read each one aloud and ask the class, "To which of the eight verses does this prayer request relate?" Some may be identified in ways other than the writer intended, but that will increase the group's examination of the text and possibly create more discussion.

Return to the question you displayed at the beginning, and ask the class, "What answers to our original question do you see Paul giving in these admonitions to Timothy?" Let the class respond freely, but if the following ideas are not suggested, do so yourself: "Paul says to pray because there is one God and one mediator between us and him" (v. 5); "Paul says to pray because all people need our intercession" (v. 1); "Paul says to pray that all will know the truth of the gospel" (vv. 4, 7).

INTO LIFE

Before class, make up some slips of paper that contain the identity of people with whom we often interact but for whom we are unlikely to pray. Some ideas include the checkout clerk at the grocery store, the cashier at a gas station, the garbage collector, the mayor, the receptionist at the doctor's office, construction workers, a neighbor whose property joins my own, the letter carrier, the hair stylist, the principal and teachers of a nearby school, police officers, airline pilots, etc. Have each student draw a slip of paper from a bag or box. (Use the "For Kings" activity on the reproducible page as an alternative.)

Ask the class members to post and use the slips they drew as a prayer stimulus for the coming week. Suggest that the prayers will be more focused if they know some specifics to add to their prayer. These specifics include the name of a person holding the occupation on the paper and the exact need that that person has. Challenge them to offer prayers of thanks for this person and to petition God for his or her spiritual well-being.

Bring the class to a close by asking your students to join you in unison in repeating as a prayer this petition offered by one of Jesus' disciple: "Lord, teach us to pray" (Luke 11:1). The "Time to Pray" activity from the reproducible page offers an alternate way to close.

For Kings and All in Authority

Paul admonishes Timothy (in 1 Timothy 2:1, 2) to pray for those in governmental authority over him. Identify each of the following government leaders in your own life and place of residence. As you write in the names, pray a short prayer for each.

President or prime minister _____

Leading judge or magistrate _____

National legislator _____

Governor of the state _____

Mayor or county commissioner _____

Police chief or sheriff _____

Other official under attack or stress _____

Truth

Scripture reveals God and his will. In every Bible study, we discover more of who God is, what he has done, what he is doing, and what he will do. In what verse(s) of today's text in 1 Timothy 2:1-8 do we find these truths about God?

_____ God wants us to live godly and holy lives.

_____ God is pleased when we live lives honoring him.

_____ God wants everyone to live eternally with him.

_____ God wills his Son to be the go-between for flesh and spirit.

_____ God provided a ransom.

_____ God designed a "delivery system" for the truth.

_____ God wants his people to pray.

Truth TRUTH Truth Truth Truth truth Truth

Time to Pray

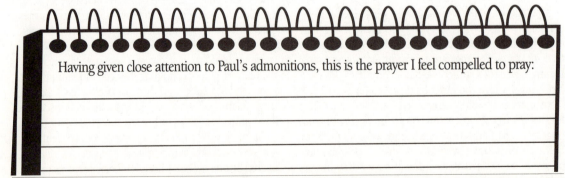

Having given close attention to Paul's admonitions, this is the prayer I feel compelled to pray:

God's Commitment—Our Response

Unit 2: God's Gifts of Leadership
(Lessons 5–9)

CALL GODLY LEADERS

WHY TEACH THIS LESSON

When men are confused about their roles in church leadership, an identity crisis results. Sadly, there are some who do not understand the nature of the office they occupy. Some do not understand the relationship of one church office to another. Some are in positions for which, unknowingly, they are not yet qualified.

These types of situations lead to a disruptive spirit. Love, harmony, and unity are displaced by suspicion, a critical spirit, and the impugning of motives. Such a situation renders the witness of the church impotent.

This lesson examines what God desires for church leadership. When his desires are implemented, the church can function effectively. The result is a unity that attracts the unbeliever. This fulfills God' purpose for his church.

INTRODUCTION

A. The Stories We Know So Well

"Let me tell you a story about a church elder I once knew." After hearing that statement, is there any one of us who doesn't have a sad story that involved a church leader who besmirched the integrity of his office? On the one hand, such stories can serve as valuable case studies to help future leaders not make the same mistakes. But on the other hand, such stories can cause us to have a jaded outlook toward all church leaders.

Having a kingdom perspective makes the difference in one's attitude toward positions of leadership and toward the people in those positions. If one perceives power, control, and "calling the shots" to be the main issues of church leadership positions, then skepticism and cynicism will result. Such attitudes inhibit a willing and joyful support of church leadership.

Negative attitudes can be turned around by those who serve in leadership positions. The turnaround occurs when service comes from a love of Christ, of the church, and an opportunity for service. When that happens, the members of the church respond with a like attitude. Self or kingdom: that choice is what makes the difference in the spirit and life of a church.

B. Lesson Background

The apostle Paul was concerned about the care of the churches. The first-century churches needed wise oversight because of a diversity of ethnic, cultural, and economic backgrounds. The needs were complex (compare Acts 6:1; 1 Corinthians 11:20-22; James 2:2-4). What was required was church leadership that would give proper direction, make wise decisions, and be a role model that inspired confidence and compliance on the part of its members.

So Paul set forth characteristics that were to be found in the lives of those who assume leadership responsibility in the church. Generally speaking, these characteristics should be found in every Christian's life. Those who have become mature in the ways that Paul speaks about are the ones to be considered as leaders.

DEVOTIONAL READING:
MARK 9:33-37

BACKGROUND SCRIPTURE:
1 TIMOTHY 3

PRINTED TEXT:
1 TIMOTHY 3:1-15

LESSON AIMS

After participating in this lesson, each student will be able to:

1. Compare and contrast the "must be" characteristics of elders (overseers) with that of deacons.

Jan 15

2. Cite some contemporary situations that especially call for, or especially challenge, the qualities Paul describes as essential to leadership.

3. Write a proposal for his or her church on how to cultivate leaders.

KEY VERSE

They must keep hold of the deep truths of the faith with a clear conscience.—1 Timothy 3:9

LESSON 7 NOTES

As such, they become examples for the entire body of believers (1 Timothy 4:12; Titus 2:7, 8).

The term *qualifications* is most frequently associated with the listing that Paul provides in today's text. (See, for example, the title of the visual on page 177 and headings in the daily Bible readings on page 179.) This terminology can lend itself to a legalistic approach to the selection process if it means a harsh, severe demand for perfection. Perhaps a better term would be *qualities*. This does not imply a casual or indifferent approach to Paul's instructions. Nor does it compromise the traits desired for biblical leadership. Rather, the term *qualities* speaks of a type of a man whose life is exemplary and commands respect; he is one who has demonstrated ability and a Christian spirit.

I. WHO CAN BE AN ELDER? (1 TIMOTHY 3:1-7)

So who can be called to church leadership? Does a man's past prohibit serving? In a letter to the Corinthian Christians, Paul gives a litany of sins and indicates that these had been the lifestyle of some of them prior to their conversion (1 Corinthians 6:9-11). If a man's past constitutes a prohibition, who could serve?

The principle we shall see Paul establish is that a man must prove himself. His commitment over time warrants his consideration for leadership. He must have a track record. The guidelines within which a man proves himself are set forth in Paul's instructions to Timothy.

A. WILLINGNESS TO SERVE (v. 1)

1. Here is a trustworthy saying: If anyone sets his heart on being an overseer, he desires a noble task.

The New Testament uses three distinct Greek words to denote the office that Paul is talking about. These three words come across in English as *overseer* (or *bishop*), *pastor* (or *shepherd*), and *elder*. These three are used interchangeably in the New Testament. It is a mistake to make them mean different things (compare Acts 20:17, 28; Titus 1:5, 7; 1 Peter 5:1, 2).

In discussing this office, Paul deals first with motivation or desire. A man who has to be coerced into serving will not serve well. Grudging service blesses no one. Men need to realize that the office of elder is the highest that God has ordained in the local church. It is a single honor and privilege to serve God and the church in this capacity.

However, a man is not to be motivated to serve by the honor of the office, to satisfy ego, or to occupy a position of authority. The emphasis here is not on the office but on the work. A love of Christ and the church, gratitude for his amazing grace, and a desire to see the work of the kingdom prosper are what lead a man to commit himself willingly to this position of leadership. How sad to see those who desire the office but not the work!

B. ELIGIBILITY TO SERVE (vv. 2-7)

2a. Now the overseer must be above reproach,

To be *above reproach* need not imply perfection. If it did, no one could be an elder! A better interpretation is that a man should have no moral flaw that would be an occasion to bring him into disrepute and thus nullify his witness.

2b. . . . the husband of but one wife,

This particular issue has resulted in much controversy—perhaps more so than any other issue in Paul's list! Does *husband of but one wife* exclude a man (1) who was divorced before he became a Christian? (2) who divorced his wife after he

WHAT DO YOU THINK?

How do we go about finding men who truly are willing to serve as elders, rather than those who are merely interested in title and position?

WHAT DO YOU THINK?

Can or should a church's pulpit minister also be an elder? Why, or why not?

became a Christian? (3) whose wife died and he remarried? or (4) whose wife died and he does not remarry? Discussion of all these would require more space than is allowed here. Certainly the issue must include demonstrated faithfulness of a man to his wife over time.

2c. . . . temperate, self-controlled, respectable,

These three go together. One must be careful about lifestyle (Ephesians 5:15-18; 1 Peter 5:8). This is true not only for the sake of the elder himself but also for the sake of those over whom he is exercising oversight.

2d. . . . hospitable, able to teach,

Being *hospitable* and being *able to teach* can go hand in glove. Informally sharing spiritual nourishment around the dinner table is one of the most effective ways of building bridges. This kind of hospitality can open doors.

Being apt to teach also means that a mature elder knows what he believes and why. He is a man of conviction who has a desire to share his faith. He can recognize false doctrine (1 Timothy 4:16; Titus 1:9; 2:1). A church that has shepherds (elders) who cannot recognize false viewpoints that are masquerading as "diversity of expression" is a church that is headed for trouble.

A MODEL OF HOSPITALITY

Alexander Campbell came to the United States from Ireland (via Scotland) in 1809 with little more than the clothes on his back. Yet by hard work and the fortunate occurrence of acquiring his wife's family farm, he ended his life in 1866 a considerably wealthy man. He realized that God had granted him comfortable resources, and he did not withhold those resources from others. He was a man given to hospitality.

Although his own family was large (14 children), the dining table was often set for 30—and sometimes 60. Selina Campbell, Alexander's second wife, reported that no needy person was ever turned from the door. Travelers, both foreign and American, were welcome. Even strangers caught by nightfall were taken in. Guests came to spend a week, a month, and some even a year, but all were made to feel at home. Campbell eventually added a wing to his house, which the local inhabitants began to call *Strangers Hall* because of the number of people who stayed for a while.

Hospitality can take many forms and may be governed by the limits of financial ability. But all Christian leaders are expected to demonstrate this virtue.   —J. B. N.

3. . . . not given to drunkenness, not violent but gentle, not quarrelsome, not a lover of money.

These characteristics speak much about social conduct and relationships. They describe a self-controlled man. These characteristics can influence one another. For instance, an alcoholic (someone *given to drunkenness*) is often violent as a result of intoxication (compare Proverbs 20:1).

4, 5. He must manage his own family well and see that his children obey him with proper respect. (If anyone does not know how to manage his own family, how can he take care of God's church?)

How one conducts his own household can indicate fitness to serve as elder. How does he treat family members? Do they honor and *respect* him? A man who cannot make responsible decisions at home probably will not be able to *take care of God's church.*

6. He must not be a recent convert, or he may become conceited and fall under the same judgment as the devil.

Spiritual immaturity mixed with pride is a disastrous combination for anyone but especially for a church leader (compare Proverbs 16:18). Pride was the

Visual for Lesson 7. *Point to the word* qualifications *as you open a discussion on the difference between that word and the word* qualities.

HOW TO SAY IT

Corinthians. Ko-RIN-thee-unz.
Ephesians. Ee-FEE-zhunz.
Ephesus. EF-uh-sus.
Hezekiah. Hez-ih-KYE-uh.
Jerusalem. Juh-ROO-suh-lem.
Judas Iscariot. JOO-dus Iss-
   CARE-ee-ut.
Uzziah. Uh-ZYE-uh.

downfall of Satan, *the devil*, and it led to his punishment or condemnation. Pride could place a novice Christian in great danger as an elder if a sense of authority goes to his head (compare the cases of Kings Uzziah and Hezekiah in 2 Chronicles 26:16; 32:25, 26).

There are other dangers. For instance, a novice Christian who becomes an elder can be too vulnerable to criticism. He also would lack the mature spiritual discernment to handle difficulties regarding doctrine or personal relationships. If this happens, a man can become discouraged, disillusioned, and ruined for future leadership opportunities (compare 1 Timothy 5:22).

7. He must also have a good reputation with outsiders, so that he will not fall into disgrace and into the devil's trap.

A man's *reputation* outside the church is important. Does he exhibit integrity to non-Christians? Is he considered moral, ethical, and honest by unbelievers? If his lifestyle becomes the occasion of ridicule, it may lead non-Christians to become skeptical and cynical.

The devil is an expert at setting traps. Hypocrisy is one of the devil's most deadly snares. When a leader falls into this *trap*, his credibility and witness are destroyed. A man needs to walk circumspectly lest he stumble into this danger.

II. WHO CAN BE A DEACON? (1 TIMOTHY 3:8-13)

Deacon is actually a Greek word. Translated it means "one who serves," "servant," and sometimes "minister" (2 Corinthians 3:6). Every Christian serves or ministers, but not in the technical sense of deacon as used in today's lesson. A Christian who serves the church in a general sense is not a deacon any more than an older man is automatically an elder.

Bible students generally assume that the seven men selected in Acts 6:1-6 to serve the church were the first deacons, even though that term is not actually used there. The role of deacon exists to meet certain needs. It was not created because the apostles thought they were too good to wait on tables (Acts 6:2), but because it was taking them away from their primary function as ordained by the Lord: prayer and teaching of the Word (Acts 6:4).

To show that this service was not considered menial, note the caliber of men Peter had the church in Jerusalem select: "known to be full of the Spirit and wisdom" (Acts 6:3). Paul sets before Timothy a similar high standard for those who would serve as deacons in Ephesus. High standards of moral character, practical qualities, and doctrinal soundness are expected for deacons as well as for elders.

A. ELIGIBILITY TO SERVE, PART 1 (vv. 8-10)

8. Deacons, likewise, are to be men worthy of respect, sincere, not indulging in much wine, and not pursuing dishonest gain.

Deacons have a great trust. The service they render is very public. Moral character is a prerequisite. Their service is as much a serious matter as is the service by elders.

In moving among people as they serve, deacons can fall into the trap of saying different things to different people to keep everyone happy. Hence the quality of sincerity is essential. Deacons, as all Christians, need to be truthful consistently. This honors God.

The potential danger in the use of alcoholic beverages is revealed both in Scriptures (Proverbs 21:17; 23:20, 21, 29-32) and in modern society. One who is trying to exemplify the Christian life may need to abstain completely in certain cultural settings. This will help avoid the appearance of evil. It will help avoid be-

WHAT DO YOU THINK?

How much weight should be given to reputation (whether deserved or undeserved) when discerning a man's suitability for church leadership? Are "minor" things like speeding tickets important in this regard? Why, or why not?

WHAT DO YOU THINK?

In recent years some congregations have opted for "ministry teams" in place of deacons. Is this a good idea? Why, or why not?

coming a stumbling block to others. This is the same standard that elders must meet (see v. 3, above).

The warning against *pursuing dishonest gain* speaks to a deacon's attitude toward money. This warning is especially important since many deacons have oversight of the church's material resources. Judas Iscariot's fascination with money led him to be a thief and a betrayer (Matthew 26:15; John 12:6).

FORKED TONGUE?

On the American frontier, a common saying among the Indians was "White man speaks with forked tongue." This was because so many times the Indians were told one thing, and then later they were told something entirely different. Sometimes this had to do with treaties when Indians ceded land to the U.S. government. Often Indians were told, "If you cede this land, we will guarantee that no settlers will cross over and interfere with your land west of this line."

The Indians trustingly accepted the treaty only to discover that the government was either unable or unwilling to stop westward settlement. Sometimes the government did indeed deal in subterfuge, realizing that the treaty was only a stopgap in the constant migration of settlers. Sometimes the government acted in good faith, fully intending to keep the settlers out, only to have things get out of control. One way or another, the Indians learned they could not trust the government promises.

Paul insists that the leaders in the church must not be known to speak with "forked tongue." As Jesus said, "Simply let your 'Yes' be 'Yes,' and your 'No,' 'No'" (Matthew 5:37; compare James 5:12). Anything else invites a mockery of truth and the integrity of the church.   —J. B. N.

9. They must keep hold of the deep truths of the faith with a clear conscience.

The deep truths of the faith refer to what had been concealed, meaning God's eternal purposes as prophesied in the Old Testament. This truth has now been revealed through apostles (see Romans 16:25, 26; Ephesians 1:9; 3:2-5, 9). Deacons are to live lives consistent with the Word. Many such conscientious men eventually are considered for the ministry of the eldership. Even so, some men may remain deacons for the remainder of their earthly service. The office of elder and the office of deacon each have a purpose. Both are important.

10. They must first be tested; and then if there is nothing against them, let them serve as deacons.

A man is *tested* for the office of a deacon over time. People should see in a potential leader faith and involvement in the life of the church. Only then will a church give a man prayerful consideration for this responsible position. It is a big mistake to place a man in this office in the hope that this will "get him involved."

B. CHARACTER OF WIVES (v. 11)

11. In the same way, their wives are to be women worthy of respect, not malicious talkers but temperate and trustworthy in everything.

The character of a man's wife can commend him or disqualify him for this type of service. A deacon whose wife has serious shortcomings in the areas mentioned may indicate a chaotic home life.

C. ELIGIBILITY TO SERVE, PART 2 (v. 12)

12. A deacon must be the husband of but one wife and must manage his children and his household well.

We refer back to what was said of the elders in verses 2, 4, and 5, above. Respected leaders model what God desires for the home.

DAILY BIBLE READINGS

Monday, Jan. 9—Moses Appoints Israel's Tribal Judges (Deuteronomy 1:9-18)

Tuesday, Jan. 10—Paul Is Welcomed as a Leader (Galatians 2:1-10)

Wednesday, Jan. 11—Respect Those Who Labor Among You (1 Thessalonians 5:6-15)

Thursday, Jan. 12—Qualities of a Leader (Titus 1:5-9)

Friday, Jan. 13—The Greatest Is Servant of All (Mark 9:33-37)

Saturday, Jan. 14—Qualifications of Overseers (1 Timothy 3:1-7)

Sunday, Jan. 15—Qualifications of Helpers (1 Timothy 3:8-13)

WHAT DO YOU THINK?

How do the wives of church leaders affect the work of their husbands, for good or for ill? How can an elder or deacon affect his wife's attitude in this regard?

D. RESULT OF FAITHFUL SERVICE (v. 13)

13. Those who have served well gain an excellent standing and great assurance in their faith in Christ Jesus.

A man who shows his passion for the Lord's work soon gets the attention of a congregation. When that happens, he comes under consideration for greater responsibility. With increased experience, deacons become stronger and more confident in their faith. They grow both in the grace as well as the knowledge of *Christ Jesus*.

Would that there could be raised up a host of deacons like this in our churches! What a blessing that would be. No wonder Paul speaks so well of those who serve faithfully. And someday there will be the divine benediction "well done, good and faithful servant" (Matthew 25:21). This is more than adequate compensation for the time and energy expended in serving the Lord and his church faithfully.

III. WHY THESE INSTRUCTIONS? (1 TIMOTHY 3:14, 15)

Paul has just told us "what's so." Now he answers the question "so what?"

14. Although I hope to come to you soon, I am writing you these instructions so that,

You can sense Paul's yearning to be with Timothy! Paul's presence would provide tremendous moral support. Face-to-face teaching would offer an opportunity to give further instruction.

15 . . . if I am delayed, you will know how people ought to conduct themselves in God's household, which is the church of the living God, the pillar and foundation of the truth.

There are no double standards of conduct in the kingdom of God. But it is incumbent upon leaders to set an example of Christian behavior. Paul is not talking about how Timothy is to *conduct* himself inside a church building. Rather, *God's household* refers to the body of Christ. It refers to Christians, to that great assembly of the called ones wherever they may be.

And note the emphasis that Paul places on God as *living*. He is not as the lifeless gods and idols of the pagan world. Only the living God can be the source of all *truth*. Apart from God, truth is suppressed (Romans 1:18). When that happens, humans become a law unto themselves. We are in a culture of increasing relativism and pluralism, where absolutes are denied (compare Judges 21:25). The church has a divinely given mandate to proclaim and defend truth. The church is both *pillar* (supporter) and preserver of God's truth as revealed in Christ (John 14:6) and in his Word (John 17:17).

CONCLUSION

A biblical eldership does not have to rule by mandate. Better is to lead by example in Bible study, prayer, generosity, and godliness. This type of leadership inspires trust and a willingness to follow. The biblical concept of leadership is not that of a business corporation where orders are given. Church leaders are out in front leading the flock, not driving it. On a tour of the Holy Land, we observed this to be true of the Bedouin shepherds. At the start of the day they would lead their flocks to pasture. That's the way the psalmist described it in Psalm 23:2, 3.

Such leadership is all the more urgent given the doctrinal and moral laxity of our age. Young Timothy labored in a very secular culture, and so do we. At no time in history is today's passage any more relevant than now. A prayerful commitment to a restoration of the biblical practice of church government is a priority. God always honors a people committed to doing his will.

Discovery Learning

This page contains an alternative lesson plan emphasizing learning activities. Classes desiring such student involvement will find these suggestions helpful. The next page is a reproducible activity page to further enhance discovery learning.

LEARNING GOALS

After this lesson, each student will be able to:

1. Compare and contrast the "must be" characteristics of elders (overseers) with those of deacons.

2. Cite some contemporary situations that especially call for, or especially challenge, the qualities Paul describes as essential to leadership.

3. Write a proposal for his or her church on how to cultivate leaders.

INTO THE LESSON

Say to the class, "I'm going to read 10 statements about church leadership. Decide whether you agree or disagree—no qualifiers. Do not answer aloud." Then read to the class the following:

1. Most church leaders are honorable and godly.

2. Church leaders are to be elected by vote.

3. Church leaders are to be followed.

4. All church leaders need a thorough knowledge of the Scriptures.

5. There are various church leadership ministries according to the New Testament.

6. All ages of adults can be selected as church leaders.

7. Others suffer when church leaders make mistakes.

8. In his ministry Jesus set the example for all spiritual leaders.

9. Church leaders should serve a preset, limited term and then be replaced.

10. Only God knows the heart well enough to appoint people to leadership.

Return to the statements one at a time and let learners express their views. Don't prolong the discussion. At the end say, "We may have differing views on church leaders in general, but we must agree on the attributes for church leaders that the Spirit reveals. Let's look at 1 Timothy 3:1-15."

INTO THE WORD

Use this "Another Word" activity to explore today's Bible text. Ask class members each to number a sheet of paper from 1 to 25. Tell them to write another word for each of the following words you will say aloud. Also tell students to skip any words about which they are unsure.

Words: 1. desire (verb); 2. overseer; 3. task; 4. irreproachable; 5. one; 6. temperate; 7. self-controlled; 8. hospitable; 9. able; 10. violent; 11. greedy; 12. money; 13. quarrelsome; 14. manage; 15. newcomer; 16. judgment; 17. disgrace; 18. trap (noun); 19. mystery; 20. clear; 21. deacon; 22. respectable; 23. malicious; 24. gain (verb); 25. pillar.

Now read 1 Timothy 3:1-15 aloud, pausing after each verse to ask for the "another word" students have on their lists. If an answer seems unclear, ask for an explanation. Be alert to substitutions that alter the meaning of the Spirit's intent.

If your class uses the student books, fill in the chart as a class under the "Who Needs It?" activity. The "God's Leader" activity from the reproducible page will allow you to extend this discussion of leader attributes.

INTO LIFE

Verse 9 gives a core characteristic of those who would be leaders in God's church: the ability to "keep hold of the deep truths of the faith with a clear conscience." Put the 13 words of the Bible verse on 13 half sheets of paper (8-1/2 by 5-1/2 inches). On a 14th half sheet of paper, put the reference "1 Timothy 3:9."

Shuffle those sheets of paper and put them on the wall or bulletin board in four rows of three and one row of two. Put them far enough apart so you can cover each of the 14 half sheets with a full sheet of 8-1/2 by 11 inch opaque paper. Tape those full sheets of paper over the half sheets as liftable flaps. Number the flaps 1 through 14. Very quickly lift each of the flaps, in numerical order, to let your class see the words underneath. Students are to take turns trying to say the Bible verse by calling out the correct flap numbers in the proper order for each of the hidden words of the verse.

Let a person continue as long as he or she is correct. After an error, let another student start at the beginning. (From time to time, as needed, you may want to lift the flaps one at a time for another look.) Continue until someone gets all the words in proper order. Use that moment to emphasize the high standards we must hold for our spiritual leaders. (An easier word-based activity is "Knowledge and Character" from the reproducible page.)

Finish by asking, "Does our church have a 'successor strategy' in place to develop new leaders?" Ask for volunteers to write a proposal (as homework) for cultivating leaders in your church.

God's Leader

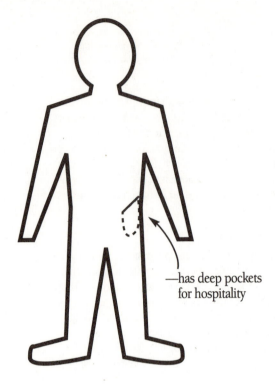

—has deep pockets for hospitality

Knowledge and Character

One verse in today's text is a good summary statement of what godly leaders know and what characterizes their moral and ethical choices. The 15 words of this verse are given below alphabetically. To the right of each word is a number. From left to right, find the blanks that correspond to the numbers and write the words in those blanks. When you have finished, you will have deciphered the verse.

Words: A-13, CLEAR-14, CONSCIENCE-15, DEEP-7, FAITH-11, HOLD-4, KEEP-3, MUST-2, OF-5, OF-9, THE-6, THE-10, THEY-1, TRUTHS-8, WITH-12.

_____ _____ _____ _____ _____

_____ _____ _____ _____ _____

_____ _____ _____ _____ _____

Find this Bible verse in today's text and write the Bible reference here: _____

Unit 2: *God's Gifts of Leadership*
(Lessons 5–9)

TEACH FOR GODLINESS

LESSON 8

WHY TEACH THIS LESSON?

"Being forewarned is being forearmed." This is what Paul is saying to Timothy and us. Many strange teachings today are paraded in the name of Christianity. These become the occasion of ridicule for the skeptics and a cause of confusion among many believers. Some in both circles are swayed by these religious fads. Although they may have different names, they still reflect the age-old rebellion against God and rejection of his Word.

Paul, through Timothy, throws light on the nature of apostasy. There will always be some who fall away from the faith and endeavor to enlist a following. So we should not be surprised at the presence of false teachers. And rather than objecting when godly people warn us, we are to be grateful. Their adherence to sound doctrine helps us to identify and reject the false teachers.

Your students may be new believers who need to learn how to recognize truth, or they may be mature Christians who should model and teach truth, or they may be a little of both. Today's lesson will empower both.

INTRODUCTION

A. WHAT DECEIVERS DO

Semantics. These are the word games that deceivers employ in leading people astray. They use good words with which everyone is familiar but give them different meanings.

In a sermon one Sunday, I cited a preacher who denied the deity of Christ and the inspiration of Scripture. Afterward a lady confronted me and vehemently denied that this was true of the man who had been her preacher for many years. The next week she confronted me again and said she had talked to her former preacher. Upon her inquiry, he responded that he believed Jesus was the Son of God and that the Bible was inspired.

I then suggested that she had asked the wrong questions. She should ask him if he believed Jesus was the Holy Spirit–conceived, virgin-born Son of God. I also suggested that she ask him if he believed the Bible to be the Holy Spirit–inspired, infallible, authoritative Word of God. The following week she approached me crestfallen. He had scoffed at her questions and said he only believed Jesus was "a" son of God, only to a greater degree than we are all sons of God. He also believed that the Bible was inspired only in the sense that the poet Tennyson was inspired when he wrote. False teachers are still with us!

B. LESSON BACKGROUND

Last week we saw the apostle Paul give instruction to Timothy with regard to leadership in the local church. Paul specifically wrote with regard to the selection of elders and deacons. He cited the qualities that should be found in men upon whom would be laid the responsibility of overseeing the affairs of the church and ministering to the material needs of its members.

DEVOTIONAL READING:
1 TIMOTHY 6:2b-10

BACKGROUND SCRIPTURE:
1 TIMOTHY 4

PRINTED TEXT:
1 TIMOTHY 4

LESSON AIMS

After participating in this lesson, each student will be able to:

1. Summarize Paul's warning about false teaching and the need for Timothy to pursue godliness.

2. Suggest some specific blessings that come to the one who pursues godliness.

3. Tell of one way that he or she will set an example of godliness in the coming week.

Jan
22

KEY VERSE

Watch your life and doctrine closely. Persevere in them, because if you do, you will save both yourself and your hearers.

—1 Timothy 4:16

Now Paul turns his attention to Timothy's responsibilities as an evangelist (see this description in 2 Timothy 4:5). These would relate to Timothy's duties in teaching and preaching as well as in his personal life. This retraces the charge Paul had given him earlier in this letter (see 1 Timothy 1:3, 18).

I. WARNING ABOUT FALSE TEACHERS (1 TIMOTHY 4:1-5)
A. APOSTASY PREDICTED (vv. 1-3)
1. The Spirit clearly says that in later times some will abandon the faith and follow deceiving spirits and things taught by demons.

False teaching infiltrated the church even as early as the first century. Timothy has to come to grips with this issue for his own sake as well as for the sake of the church at Ephesus. To *abandon the faith and follow deceiving spirits and things taught by demons* is summed up in our single word *apostasy*.

This prediction of apostasy comes about by direct revelation to the apostle Paul by the Holy *Spirit*. The *later times* refers to the Christian era—the church age, from Pentecost to the Lord's return (compare Acts 2:17; 2 Timothy 3:1; 4:3; Hebrews 1:1, 2) rather than only to the time of the second coming of Christ. The spread of false doctrine should come as no surprise to us. Paul notes its demonic origin.

It is a terrible thing to abandon the faith after once having accepted Jesus as Lord and Savior. Scripture offers several warnings in this regard (Galatians 5:4; Hebrews 6:4-6; 10:26-31; 2 Peter 2:20-22). Those who depart from the faith in Paul's day are those who allow their ambition and pride to control them (compare 2 Timothy 3:1-9). This makes them vulnerable to the seductive influence of demons. Such false teachers secure a following within the church through their pretensions (Titus 1:11). Church history reveals a dismal record of departures from biblical doctrine and apostolic practice.

2. Such teachings come through hypocritical liars, whose consciences have been seared as with a hot iron.

The Holy Spirit is the Spirit of truth. Truth is eternal. God is the source of all truth. False teachers tell lies because, as Jesus affirmed, they are of their father the devil (John 8:44).

False teachers are deceivers. In their hypocrisy they pose as one thing but are really something else entirely. They are masters at producing counterfeit religion. It has the appearance of the real thing but is flawed. Unfortunately, many people have a hard time recognizing truth and are easily fooled.

Those who go against the truth have to sear their *consciences* (compare Titus 1:15). Their hearts become scarred, tough, and hardened—dead. Truth no longer fazes them. Perhaps they lose the ability to distinguish truth from falsehood. Such folks often go instead with "whatever works" and see truth as relative (compare Judges 21:25). How sad—and dangerous—when one becomes an apostate.

A SEARED CONSCIENCE RENEWED
John Newton (1725–1807) grew up fully aware of the teachings of Christianity, but they had made little impression upon him. He entered into naval service as a young man and became involved in the slave trade. He saw the suffering of black slaves as they were separated from family and homeland. He saw them held in pens awaiting shipment to America, and he himself transported several shiploads to the New World. He saw young black women helplessly used to satisfy sailors' lust. He saw all this, but his conscience was seared, and it gave him no remorse at the time.

HOW TO SAY IT
Corinthians. Ko-RIN-thee-unz.
Cornelius. Cor-NEEL-yus.
Ephesians. Ee-FEE-zhunz.
Ephesus. EF-uh-sus.
Galatians. Guh-LAY-shunz.
Gentile. JEN-tile.
Gnostics. NAHSS-ticks.
Hebrews. HEE-brews.
Lystra. LISS-truh.
Titus. TY-tus.

Later Newton experienced conversion, became an Anglican minister, supported the evangelical revival in the church, and labored to stop the evils of slavery in the British Empire. He is perhaps best known today as the author of the hymn "Amazing Grace." The line that says, "that saved a wretch like me"—Newton knew what that meant.

When Newton's conscience was seared, he was totally insensitive to the evils and horror of slavery in which he participated. It took a conversion experience to remove the hard crust of his conscience and open him up to Christian virtue. Christ is working this way in lives right now!   —J. B. N.

3. They forbid people to marry and order them to abstain from certain foods, which God created to be received with thanksgiving by those who believe and who know the truth.

Paul likely is striking at the Gnostics. This movement teaches that the flesh and the material world are evil by their very nature. Thus the joining of husband and wife in marriage would be evil as well. The Gnostics carry their philosophy to the point where they even deny that Jesus had come in the flesh. The apostle John deals with this issue extensively in his letters (compare 2 John 7).

Yet there is nothing wrong with marriage and food. These are not evil in and of themselves (see Mark 7:17-19; Hebrews 13:4). There is nothing so refreshingly liberating as truth!

B. THANKSGIVING PRACTICED (vv. 4, 5)

4. For everything God created is good, and nothing is to be rejected if it is received with thanksgiving,

Paul repudiates outright what the false teachers promote. Those who know God's Word acknowledge that *everything God created is good* (Genesis 1:31).

To abuse the things that God gives us is wrong. But a proper regard and *thanksgiving* for all that God has created honors him. God used this truth in an illustration to the apostle Peter in preparation for his visit to Cornelius, a Gentile (Acts 10:15).

GOD'S GOODNESS

James Alfred Wight (1916–1995), better known under his pen name of James Herriot, was a country veterinarian in Yorkshire, England. In 1966 he began to write a series of books about his experiences with animals. His books became bestsellers. In winsome stories, he talks about dogs, cats, horses, sheep, and other livestock that he encountered in 50 years as a vet. He evokes a nostalgic love of animals and a slower country living that has given his books an appealing quality. In all, he wrote 15 books, which have sold 50 million copies in 20 countries.

Probably, his four best-known books are titles borrowed from the refrain of a hymn written by Cecil Frances Alexander, wife of an Anglican bishop in the nineteenth century. She wrote over 400 hymns, but "All Things Bright and Beautiful" is probably her best known.

> All things bright and beautiful,
>   All creatures great and small,
> All things wise and wonderful:
>   The Lord God made them all.

These words, together with the appeal of Herriot's stories, sum up what Paul is referring to. Genesis tells us that when God created, he saw that it was good. Paul reminds us that the creation is still good, and the bounty God has provided is to be enjoyed with thanksgiving.   —J. B. N.

DAILY BIBLE READINGS

Monday, Jan. 16—Moses Teaches Israel to Obey (Deuteronomy 4:1-8)

Tuesday, Jan. 17—Give Ear to My Teaching (Psalm 78:1-8)

Wednesday, Jan. 18—Rules for the New Life (Ephesians 4:25–5:2)

Thursday, Jan. 19—The Teacher's Gift Is Teaching (Romans 12:3-8)

Friday, Jan. 20—A Warning Against False Teaching (1 Timothy 4:1-5)

Saturday, Jan. 21—Exercise Yourself in Godliness (1 Timothy 4:6-10)

Sunday, Jan. 22—Put All These Things into Practice (1 Timothy 4:11-16)

WHAT DO YOU THINK?

How does mealtime prayer sanctify God's provisions and honor his name? How can we improve those prayers?

5. . . . because it is consecrated by the word of God and prayer.

To be *consecrated* means to be set apart, usually for a holy purpose as ordained by God. And what was the purpose for which God created all things? The answer is recorded as early as Genesis 9:3: they are for humanity's use. That is why offering grace before eating is appropriate.

II. DUTIES OF A FAITHFUL MINISTER (1 TIMOTHY 4:6-11)

A. THINGS TO COMMUNICATE (v. 6)

6. If you point these things out to the brothers, you will be a good minister of Christ Jesus, brought up in the truths of the faith and of the good teaching that you have followed.

The mark of *a good minister of Christ Jesus* is keeping the people informed about what is going on around them—about the things that jeopardize their faith. If a person is not *brought up* in *faith* and sound doctrine, he or she will not be equipped to recognize false doctrine when it comes.

Timothy had been spiritually equipped earlier by a godly grandmother and mother (2 Timothy 1:5; 3:14, 15). Now the apostle Paul continues that practice. This type of teaching in Christian homes and churches is an imperative. It is the best antidote for the high doctrinal and spiritual mortality rate that we are experiencing in our churches, especially among our young people.

B. THINGS TO AVOID (v. 7)

7. Have nothing to do with godless myths and old wives' tales; rather, train yourself to be godly.

Paul is blunt: Timothy doesn't have the time to listen to nonsense. It is easy to get caught up in theological fads, hand-me-down traditions, and various *myths* (compare Titus 1:14). Some people exploit every crisis by forcing interpretations on Scripture to fit the occasion. These interpretations often have their origin in legends and myths. Paul says to ignore them, whatever they are, and to expend energy on cultivating godliness instead.

The term *exercise* indicates that godliness takes effort. It doesn't just happen. It requires the discipline to study the Word in order to determine God's will and live it out (Psalm 119:11, 105; 2 Timothy 3:15, 16).

C. THINGS OF VALUE (vv. 8-10)

8. For physical training is of some value, but godliness has value for all things, holding promise for both the present life and the life to come.

Physical fitness is a booming industry today. The malls are favorite walking places. Hiking trails are popular. When one feels good physically, he or she functions better. Paul is not belittling *physical training*. Paraphrased, what he is saying is, "What good is it to gain a benefit from a physical fitness program if at the same time we are out of shape morally and spiritually for *the life* that is *to come*?"

9. This is a trustworthy saying that deserves full acceptance

There is a bit of doubt as to whether *this . . . trustworthy saying* refers to what Paul has just said in verse 8 or what comes next in verse 10. In either case we can be sure that everything Paul writes is under the inspiration of the Holy Spirit.

10. . . . (and for this we labor and strive), that we have put our hope in the living God, who is the Savior of all men, and especially of those who believe.

Paul affirms why he is willing to *labor* so hard. To appreciate his struggles, read in 2 Corinthians 11:23-28 what Paul suffered for the cause of Christ. And what was Paul's view of all this? His sufferings "are not worth comparing with the

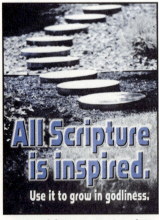

Visual for Lessons 8 and 12. *This visual may cause your learners to ask themselves "What am I really doing with my Bible?"*

glory that will be revealed in us" (Romans 8:18). Yes, God calls people to labor diligently, no matter the cost. This labor can result in suffering. The apostle Peter says that if we suffer as Christians, we are not to be ashamed but to glorify God in this (1 Peter 4:16).

God *is the Savior of all men* in the sense that he offers salvation to everyone. Jesus died for all and thereby draws everyone to him (John 12:32). But Jesus' drawing can be resisted, as the pages of Scripture and experience tell us. Thus Paul is not teaching universal salvation. He simply means that anyone and everyone can be saved. But there are conditions to meet (Acts 2:38; Romans 10:13; James 2:24; etc.).

D. THINGS TO DO (v. 11)

11. Command and teach these things.

The phrase *these things* refers to what Paul said in verses 6-10. Paul's charge to Timothy is very clear! As a result, those in the church at Ephesus are to be impressed with the necessity of Timothy's message regarding false teachers and godly living. The duty of every Christian leader is to impress upon all whom they teach the imperative nature of this kind of life. The result should be that the world may see the glory of God reflected in us (Matthew 5:14-16).

III. COUNSEL ON PERSONAL CONDUCT (1 TIMOTHY 4:12-16)

A. YOUTH, EXAMPLE, DEVOTION (vv. 12, 13)

12. Don't let anyone look down on you because you are young, but set an example for the believers in speech, in life, in love, in faith and in purity.

The Christian life is proactive. It is not enough to refrain from doing evil. No, the Christian must do good as well. So Paul encourages Timothy to continue living an exemplary life as the best way to silence any critics (compare Titus 2:8).

Although Timothy is to "command and teach" (v. 11), this may cause a problem because of his youth. There even may be godly people in Ephesus who believe that youth disqualifies one to be a leader. The way to overcome this is for Timothy to live a life that will lead people to respect him. The reality is that the preacher lives a "goldfish bowl existence." He needs to be sensitive to the fact that people are watching. The very nature of his calling makes him a role model.

Paul expands on the importance of being a role model when he says, "Follow my example, as I follow the example of Christ" (1 Corinthians 11:1). One teaches by *life* as well as by doctrine. One's lifestyle is to be above reproach.

13. Until I come, devote yourself to the public reading of Scripture, to preaching and to teaching.

Paul's intends to join Timothy at an unspecified date. Until then he provides Timothy certain instructions. We can see that when Timothy focuses on *reading of Scripture*, his *preaching* and *teaching* will have the best foundation. As such, he will be fulfilling Jesus' last directive as recorded in Matthew's gospel: "Teaching them to obey everything I have commanded you" (Matthew 28:20). This is a good agenda for every preacher and Christian leader. We must never stop learning! The Word of God is inexhaustible.

Sadly, however, there is very little attention given to doctrinally sound preaching in many pulpits today. In place of doctrine are feel-good sermons in many cases. There is an important place in sermons for meeting felt needs. But sound doctrine must serve as the basis. Feel-good sermons without that sound doctrinal basis may appeal to the emotions, but will not strengthen one against assaults on his or her faith (compare Ephesians 4:11-15).

WHAT DO YOU THINK?

Is there a problem of age discrimination in selecting church leaders today? If so, is such discrimination different from the problem of Timothy's youthfulness in Paul's day? Explain.

WHAT DO YOU THINK?

The challenges in this verse are vital! How can a preacher make these a priority?

PRAYER

Father, may our homes and churches be so wholly committed to you in word, spirit, and deed that our children will be inspired to lives of faithful service. May you find among them those who will be your Timothys in the church of tomorrow. We pray this in Jesus' name, amen.

This is not an either-or issue. God's Word appeals to both the intellect and the emotions (Acts 2:37; Hebrews 4:12). But these two must come in that order. That is the way the conscience is educated. Truth leads to right feelings and conduct. Emotions without intellect lead a person to being "zealous for God," but with a zeal that "is not based on knowledge" (Romans 10:2).

B. GIFT, PROPHECY, ELDERS (v. 14)

14. Do not neglect your gift, which was given you through a prophetic message when the body of elders laid their hands on you.

These instructions given to Timothy are not to be construed as rebukes. Rather, they are encouragements to "hang in there," to keep doing what he is already doing. There is the old saying: "If you don't use it, you will lose it."

To be able to "do the work of an evangelist" (2 Timothy 4:5) may be the *gift* alluded to (see also Ephesians 4:11). If so, this was bestowed by God through the laying on of the *hands* by *the body of elders*.

This action may have occurred when Paul recruited Timothy on the second missionary tour at the time when Paul stopped to confirm the church at Lystra (Acts 16:1-3). That was a church that Paul had established on his first journey (Acts 14:8-20). All of this had been revealed through Paul concerning the way Timothy was going to be used (1 Timothy 1:18).

C. DILIGENCE, PROGRESS, SALVATION (vv. 15, 16)

15. Be diligent in these matters; give yourself wholly to them, so that everyone may see your progress.

The matters of which Paul speaks are not frivolous. Timothy is to reflect not only upon the blessings and privileges that accrue to leadership but also on the corresponding responsibilities of the stewardship that have been given him. Such personal reflection takes time! If Timothy gets to be "too busy" doing his various daily tasks, he won't be able to meditate on *these matters*. This should be a facet of Timothy's leadership role. It is a facet that should not be overlooked by leaders in the church today.

WHAT DO YOU THINK?

Does your minister's contract or job description make provision for time to think and reflect? How much or how little is this emphasized?

One happy result will be that Timothy will be more able to *give* himself *wholly* to his God-given role. When that happens, everyone will take note of his commitment to ministry. What a witness!

16. Watch your life and doctrine closely. Persevere in them, because if you do, you will save both yourself and your hearers.

Paul sums up his instructions by telling Timothy to pay close attention to his own heart, beliefs, and conduct. A little indiscretion can jeopardize Timothy's influence and role as a leader. It is heartbreaking to see those who are disillusioned by the moral downfall of a leader they had trusted.

Timothy is to be careful also in what he teaches. How sad to see people espousing false *doctrine* because they themselves were taught wrongly. A life of faithfulness in ministry adds to the assurance of Timothy's own salvation. The crown of life is his (Revelation 2:10). A life of faithfulness also influences the eternal destinies of all those he is responsible for leading.

CONCLUSION

A host of leaders like Timothy would shake the church! They would be willing to let God use them in building up his kingdom. They would be leaders who are well trained in the Scriptures, are willing to take a stand for truth, and will back it up with a godly life. What is our church doing to train its Timothys to come?

THOUGHT TO REMEMBER

"The things you have heard me say in the presence of many witnesses entrust to reliable men who will also be qualified to teach others" (2 Timothy 2:2).

Discovery Learning

This page contains an alternative lesson plan emphasizing learning activities. Classes desiring such student involvement will find these suggestions helpful. The next page is a reproducible activity page to further enhance discovery learning.

LEARNING GOALS

After participating in this lesson, each student will be able to:

1. Summarize Paul's warning about false teaching and the need for Timothy to pursue godliness.

2. Suggest some specific blessings that come to one who pursues godliness.

3. Tell of one way that he or she will set an example of godliness in the coming week.

INTO THE LESSON

Bring to class a clear example of false doctrine from a religious group that considers its members to be following Christ. Your example could be in the form of a video clip, a newspaper clipping, magazine article, etc.

Discuss this problem, but don't get bogged down in details. Use this to stress that false doctrine is still with us today. To prepare for the Into the Word segment, say, "Recognizing false doctrine is just one issue among many for the church. I have several more issues for us to consider today." (If you like to give your students something to think about as they enter class, put copies of the "Picture of a False Teacher" activity from the reproducible page in their chairs ahead of time.)

INTO THE WORD

Prepare in advance the following statements (or others of your making) on 10 slips of paper, one statement per copy.

1. There is nothing more practical than sound doctrine.
2. Hardening of the arteries is not nearly as serious as hardening of the conscience.
3. All false doctrine originates in the mind of the devil.
4. A young person's folly is more forgivable than that of an older person.
5. Physical fitness is at the base of godly stewardship.
6. A minister's most important attribute is his gracious and friendly personality.
7. An effective evangelist/minister must be a reader.
8. Meditation speaks of Eastern mysticism and has no place in the Christian lifestyle.
9. A cauterized conscience has no value in terms of morality.
10. Recognizing that "the Spirit clearly says" is the basis for sound doctrine.

Have the class divide into groups of two or three. Give each group one of the statements. Say, "Read 1 Timothy 4 and then identify a verse or verses related to your statement. Discuss as a group whether you agree or disagree with your assigned statement. Did the Bible verses you identified change your initial opinion about the statement you received?" After a few minutes, have groups present their conclusions.

For an added activity, confer with several class members in advance and ask each to deliver in class a short defense for one of the following false doctrines:

1. "Truly spiritual Christians do not marry."
2. "Sometimes a lie is the kindest thing one can say to a friend."
3. "Every Christian should be a vegetarian."
4. "God is the Savior of all, as Paul declares, so missionary evangelism is unnecessary."
5. "One's lifestyle has nothing to do with eternal destiny, for salvation is purely by God's grace."

Allow time for responses. "False Teaching," on the reproducible page, is an alternative small-group activity.

INTO LIFE

Prepare a priority paper for each student using the heading, "More or Less" at the top. List the following seven priorities:

___Give more thanks to God for food and other daily provisions.

___Spend less time in idle talk about insignificant matters.

___Spend more time reading the Scriptures than I currently do.

___Read, watch, and listen to less false doctrine in the religious media.

___Share more of my understanding of God's truth with others.

___Use less of my time in sports and other physical pursuits.

___Deepen my trust in the living God and my Savior.

Distribute papers and say, "Number the items on this list from one to seven in the order that you think each item should be a priority for yourself as a Christian." Ask for volunteers to share the reasons for one or two of their answers.

False Teaching

The Spirit made it clear to Paul, as did Paul's personal experience among the churches, that false doctrine would exist throughout the church era. What do you consider to be the three most prevalent false doctrines in the church in 2006?

FALSEHOOD

1.

2.

3.

What Bible texts refute each of these false teachings? Use your Bible study tools and your classmates to help you answer.

TRUTH!

1.

2.

3.

Picture of a False Teacher

How would you characterize a false teacher? Draw and label descriptive characteristics of such a deceiver on the figure to the right. One example is given to get you started; other ideas are inverted at the bottom of the page, if you need them.

wears a mask of pretense

Ideas: Wears a mortarboard to revel in his superior education. Dresses conservatively (wears a tie) to imply his conservatism in all matters. Has one extra long arm from patting others on the back. Faces one way, but goes the other. Has one long index finger from pointing the way to so many others. Has patches on his clothes to show his personal self-denial. Has a mouth that lends itself to talking out both sides. Wears earmuffs to avoid hearing the truth. Has one cupped hand held out for constant solicitation of funds. Has holes in his body because he lacks integrity (that is, he lacks "wholeness").

God's Commitment—Our Response

Unit 2: *God's Gifts of Leadership*
(Lessons 5–9)

PRACTICE
JUSTICE AND MERCY

LESSON 9

WHY TEACH THIS LESSON

The first half of the twentieth century saw the battle of "liberals" vs. "conservatives" in the church. Those in the first group laid emphasis upon what was called *the social gospel*—concerns about poverty and the reform of society. Those in the second group occupied themselves primarily with a defense of the gospel of Jesus Christ and the salvation of people from sin and Hell; concern over social issues lagged behind. In the latter half of the century, however, the conservatives increased their attention to the needs of the elderly, the handicapped, etc. There has been great progress in these areas.

Even so, we still see a laxity with regard to personal responsibility on the part of believers concerning care of certain family members. Today's lesson is timely for those who live in a materialistic, self-centered culture. Paul offers a sobering reminder of those godly traits that should be inherent in family relationships, especially among believers.

INTRODUCTION

A. TOO BUSY?

Some of us can recall depressing images of the old county homes where the aged and orphans were left—forgotten, lonely, and despondent. And even with our modern, upscale, and highly regulated senior citizen facilities, the sense of loneliness often is no less. After being placed in a comfortable setting, many of the elderly are abandoned and forgotten by family and friends.

Many fine benevolent facilities try to compensate for this state of affairs by providing a broad program of activities and services. This helps alleviate the tendency of residents to lapse into self-pity and depression. Even with emotional well-being, however, advancing years are accompanied by breakdowns in health. That's the very nature of our humanity (see Psalm 90:10). The problems of the aging process are heightened with the loss of friends and the neglect of family members. Here is where the family and the church must come into the picture.

B. LESSON BACKGROUND

Last week we studied Paul's counsel to Timothy with regard to false teachers, their doctrines, and the necessity of exposing them. The lesson concluded with admonitions to Timothy concerning those things to which he needed to give continual attention in his personal life. Paul now makes a transition and calls attention to meeting needs among certain members of the church.

God's solutions to meeting needs are not always the same as human solutions. For example, the courts have made it legal to eliminate unwanted preborn children by way of abortion. In certain places and circumstances, the aged can be

DEVOTIONAL READING:
MATTHEW 23:23-28

BACKGROUND SCRIPTURE:
1 TIMOTHY 5

PRINTED TEXT:
1 TIMOTHY 5:1-8, 17-25

LESSON AIMS

After participating in this lesson, each student will be able to:

1. Describe some ways that Christians are to treat one another.

2. Give an example of how his or her church has honored its older (and perhaps needier) members and how it has recognized its leaders.

3. State one way he or she will honor an elderly Christian or dedicated leader this week.

Jan
29

KEY VERSE

Do not rebuke an older man harshly, but exhort him as if he were your father. Treat younger men as brothers, older women as mothers, and younger women as sisters, with absolute purity.
—1 Timothy 5:1, 2

LESSON 9 NOTES

removed through a murderous process referred to as euthanasia. Some would eliminate all who, in their eyes, no longer contribute to society. But God created us in his own image and likeness (Genesis 1:26, 27). Every person is to be regarded with dignity and respect at all stages and situations of life.

I. BEHAVIOR TOWARD OTHERS (1 TIMOTHY 5:1, 2)

A. TOWARD MEN (v. 1)

1. Do not rebuke an older man harshly, but exhort him as if he were your father. Treat younger men as brothers,

With both *older* and *younger men,* the attitude of one who rebukes or reproves has everything to do with how the admonition is received. If one is harsh, vindictive, or impugns motives, then defensiveness and resentment may be the result.

Offering correction to those in error is not easy. In the first case, Paul probably is referring to an aged man as opposed to someone who holds the office of elder since there is an older/younger contrast in both verses 1 and 2.

Youth are prone to be impatient with older men, who tend to be more deliberate in their actions. Of course, one does not tolerate indolence or incompetence. But the corrective approach should be that of encouraging industry and ability. The purpose is to build up, not to tear down. So the approach to those who are older is to be done with respect and dignity that their years deserve. This is the import of the word *exhort* in contrast to the word *rebuke.*

Treatment of younger men as *brothers* or equals is self-explanatory. Reproving those that need reproving calls for humility rather than haughtiness.

B. TOWARD WOMEN (v. 2)

2. . . . older women as mothers, and younger women as sisters, with absolute purity.

Paul continues to outline the type of treatment Timothy is to accord to those in his congregation. He is not to overlook faults or flaws that truly are detrimental. But he should not be motivated in correction by a mean spirit or by an attitude of super piety. That is the spirit that leads to noticing a speck in someone else's eye while having a plank hanging out of one's own (Matthew 7:1-5). Yes, judgments are required, but they are not to be hypocritical judgments (Matthew 7:15-20). This is part of treating one another with respect. This attitude allows Timothy to treat *older women as mothers.*

The Bible has much to say about *purity,* both of the sexual and non-sexual kinds. When men think of the *younger women* of the church *as sisters,* then purity will be easier to maintain. A man should not be guilty of any indiscretions. His conversations should not carry innuendos or double meanings.

II. CARE OF WIDOWS (1 TIMOTHY 5:3-8)

A. CATEGORIES (vv. 3, 4)

3. Give proper recognition to those widows who are really in need.

In the culture of Paul's time, a woman without a husband or family is in dire straits. It can be a heartless environment for those who have no means of support. Government-funded social insurance plans, heath care, and retirement centers do not exist. Paul's first instruction regarding the church's responsibility in this matter is that those who are *widows* in real *need* are to receive *proper recognition.*

The type of widows that Paul has in mind is those who are destitute and have no family members to take care of them. The early church in Jerusalem set a good example of benevolence when it came to the care of widows (Acts 6:1-7). Attention to such widows is certainly "pure and faultless" (James 1:27).

4. But if a widow has children or grandchildren, these should learn first of all to put their religion into practice by caring for their own family and so repaying their parents and grandparents, for this is pleasing to God.

The church as a whole is not responsible to provide for those widows who have family members who can support them (also 1 Timothy 5:16). The care given by *children* should be an expression of gratitude for the years *their parents* invested in them. It is also a duty imposed by the fifth of the Ten Commandments (Exodus 20:12). Jesus reiterated this in Matthew 19:19 and Mark 7:10-12.

Modern long-term care of the elderly is very expensive, however, and help from various agencies may be needed. Even so, we dare not dishonor elderly parents with a "let the government handle it" mentality. Fulfillment of this duty pleases and honors God. It is a vital part of showing piety at home.

PIETY AT HOME

Martin Luther (1483–1546) was the major leader of the Protestant Reformation. It was a time of significant change in the European church as well as European society. One of the challenges Luther faced was to reestablish the sanctity of marriage and family life for church leaders. When he married a former nun, Katherine von Bora, in 1525, it changed his life. It also changed Lutheran ministry for centuries to come.

This couple had six children and reared four orphaned children from his relatives as well. Luther saw the home as the school for character. Children were to learn to obey parents and also learn to fear God. Children learned daily Bible lessons, and in turn Luther learned of God's goodness by enjoying the presence of wife and family. The family shared the workload, with Luther doing the preaching, teaching, and writing, and Katie overseeing the home chores, the gardening, and the livestock. Under Luther's guidance, the home became the school for piety, manners, responsibility, and morality. Piety is responsible behavior as well as attitudes of devotion.

Paul's comment is that children should learn at home that part of their piety is supporting their parents in time of need. When that happens, more church resources become available to support those aged members who have no other means of support.   —J. B. N.

B. LIFESTYLES (vv. 5-7)
5. The widow who is really in need and left all alone puts her hope in God and continues night and day to pray and to ask God for help.

Paul describes a type of *widow* who is worthy of the church's help. Though without a visible means of support, she trusts God. She believes her prayers for her own needs as well as her prayers on behalf of others will be honored. She is keenly aware of God's presence (compare Luke 2:36, 37). Through his church, God provides for members of his family who are in genuine *need*.

6. But the widow who lives for pleasure is dead even while she lives.

In pagan Ephesus (the city where Timothy serves), there are strong temptations for a *widow* to resort to unholy means of livelihood. If she succumbs, she will become spiritually *dead*. The pleasures of sin are for a season (Hebrews 11:25). A widow who makes such a choice is not to be supported. Younger widows are not to be supported either (1 Timothy 5:9-15).

7. Give the people these instructions, too, so that no one may be open to blame.

Christians are to recognize the need for justice that is tempered by mercy. The world watches the church critically. How we treat and care for one another is a commentary on the genuineness of our profession.

WHAT DO YOU THINK?

How can the church be selective with benevolence without creating offense?

HOW TO SAY IT

Corinthians. Ko-RIN-thee-unz.
Deuteronomy. Due-ter-AHN-uh-me.
Ephesus. EF-uh-sus.
euthanasia. you-thuh-NAY-zhuh.
Hebrews. HEE-brews.
Leviticus. Leh-VIT-ih-kus.
Micah. MY-kuh.

C. OBLIGATION (v. 8)

8. If anyone does not provide for his relatives, and especially for his immediate family, he has denied the faith and is worse than an unbeliever.

Jesus affirmed the obligation to support one's parents, as we saw earlier. Therefore, to refuse one's duty is to deny *the faith*. Any conduct that is inconsistent with these instructions is equivalent to a repudiation of Christianity. And because such people sin against what they know, they are *worse than an unbeliever.*

The modern availability of pensions, insurance, social security, welfare, and retirement centers (mentioned with v. 3 earlier) causes us some challenges in applying this passage. These systems of support allow many seniors to maintain independent living. As much as possible, this should be honored.

The time may come, however, when hard decisions have to be made. When possible, elderly or indigent *relatives* can be taken into a family member's home. But there are circumstances where this is not possible or advisable. Assisted living and nursing care sometimes can be administered only through proper facilities. Placing loved ones in a care center or seeing their needs supplemented by government agencies does not relieve family members of responsibility of demonstrating financial and emotional support. Churches demonstrate their appreciation for the lives of faithful servants by including Christian retirement homes in their budgets.

III. HONOR FOR ELDERS (1 TIMOTHY 5:17-20)

A. WORTHY OF SUPPORT (vv. 17, 18)

17. The elders who direct the affairs of the church well are worthy of double honor, especially those whose work is preaching and teaching.

Paul now specifies the regard in which elders that do their work *well* are to be held. We know, of course, that *elders* serve as they are able and as time permits. A few elders are able to labor extensively in the word and doctrine, and they do a great job. Praise God for both part-time and full-time elders!

Some elders may no longer be in the workplace. They may have retired from occupations or livelihoods in order to serve full time in visitation, *teaching,* and *preaching.* Thoughtful churches can offer to subsidize the retirement income of such elders. Paul justifies such compensation by citing two biblical illustrations, as we see next.

18. For the Scripture says, "Do not muzzle the ox while it is treading out the grain," and "The worker deserves his wages."

The first quote is from Deuteronomy 25:4. Paul also cites this same passage in 1 Corinthians 9:9 to justify his own right to receive support. Oxen are allowed to feed while they work. Thus they participate in the fruit of their labor.

The second citation is from Jesus. It concerns support for his disciples as they labor (Luke 10:7). Elders who rule well should be honored in this way.

DOUBLE HONOR

Numerous individuals have been honored throughout history, and we celebrate their achievements. But most have been honored for only one specific area of expertise. Perhaps this area has been in athletics, politics, business success, or military leadership. Even more impressive, however, are the individuals who have achieved success in two or more fields. They are worthy of double honor.

Eddie Rickenbacker was a racecar driver who became a famous ace pilot in World War I and then the president of Eastern Air Lines. Benjamin Franklin was an inventor, a businessman, and a successful diplomat. Michelangelo was outstanding

WHAT DO YOU THINK?

Considering the availability of government assistance and megachurch resources today, how does a Christian know when it's time to ask for help in caring for an elderly parent?

WHAT DO YOU THINK?

Greater numbers of paid staff and paid elders in a church mean less money available for missions, building programs, benevolence, etc. Or does it? What's the balance here?

as both a painter and a sculptor. George Washington Carver was an outstanding college professor whose work also resulted in hundreds of uses for the peanut. John Glenn was an astronaut who served four terms in the U.S. Senate. George Washington was an outstanding military leader who became the greatest of American presidents. The list could go on and on.

Paul's comment, however, applies particularly to elders. Serving well as an elder is a significant achievement in itself and is certainly worthy of honor. But those who also serve in a more focused ministry in "preaching and teaching" are worthy of double honor. Does your church follow this pattern? —J. B. N.

B. ACCUSATIONS AGAINST ELDERS (vv. 19, 20)

19. Do not entertain an accusation against an elder unless it is brought by two or three witnesses.

Men who have the responsibility of oversight frequently become targets of criticism. A man's reputation can be destroyed so easily. So any accusation must be proven to be true by *two or three* credible *witnesses*. This helps avoid a miscarriage of justice (Deuteronomy 19:15; Matthew 18:16).

20. Those who sin are to be rebuked publicly, so that the others may take warning.

If the charges are proven to be true, action must be taken. The church's credibility is at stake. Since an elder is elected by the congregation (in most cases), it has a right to hear the charges, the proof, and to take appropriate action. In modern terminology, due process is to be followed.

Any church discipline procedure, whether or not the accused is an elder, presupposes that every effort has been made first to bring the person to repentance (see Matthew 18:15; 2 Corinthians 2:5-8). When a part of our body is diseased, we don't amputate that part immediately. First we do a diagnosis. We do everything within our power to restore or salvage it. But if the diseased part defies healing, and if its continuing existence threatens the survival of the body, then we amputate as a last resort. The scriptural procedure is outlined by Jesus in Matthew 18:15-17 and by Paul in 1 Corinthians 5. If the sin is public, the rebuke must be public for the church to maintain credibility. The example is a warning to others.

IV. NOTES TO TIMOTHY (1 TIMOTHY 5:21-25)

A. PARTIALITY FORBIDDEN (v. 21)

21. I charge you, in the sight of God and Christ Jesus and the elect angels, to keep these instructions without partiality, and to do nothing out of favoritism.

Administering justice is a serious matter. Of necessity it must be done impartially. *God and Christ Jesus and the elect angels* watch our actions. We will be held accountable. God does not like dishonest scales (see Leviticus 19:36; Proverbs 11:1; Micah 6:11). This especially applies to the scales of justice (compare Deuteronomy 1:17; 16:19; Proverbs 24:23).

Favoritism can destroy a church family the same as it can our earthly families (examples: Genesis 25:28; 37:3, 4). A leadership's judgments and actions are not to be based upon friendships, personality, position, or wealth, but on the basis of what is right and wrong.

B. LAYING ON OF HANDS RESTRICTED (v. 22a)

22a. Do not be hasty in the laying on of hands,

The laying on of hands is an issue of setting someone apart for an office or certain duties of the church (compare Acts 6:6; 13:3). This is not to be done hastily

WHAT DO YOU THINK?

How should you respond to someone who criticizes a church elder? What are the different reactions you can expect to your response? What do those reactions say about the critic?

Do nothing by partiality
—See 1 Timothy 5:21

Visual for Lesson 9. Post this visual as you ask "Whom do you hesitate to shake hands with out of favoritism? Why?"

or suddenly, as ordination is based on a person's demonstrated spiritual growth (compare 1 Timothy 3:6; also see pages 177, 178).

C. PURITY MANDATED (v. 22b)
22b. . . . and do not share in the sins of others. Keep yourself pure.

Timothy also is told not to participate in anyone's unworthy conduct. A leader is to be *pure* or circumspect in all behavior.

D. ADVICE OFFERED (v. 23)
23. Stop drinking only water, and use a little wine because of your stomach and your frequent illnesses.

We can only speculate about this parenthetical statement regarding Timothy's health. It may be connected to the admonition "keep yourself pure" in verse 22. Timothy should keep himself physically fit so he can serve effectively.

This passage has been used as a proof text to justify moderate consumption of alcoholic beverages. However, insistence on exercising our "rights" in this area may disregard the important principle of foregoing "rights" for the sake of another person who may be watching our example. For in-depth study of this vital principle, read Romans 14 and 1 Corinthians 8, 9.

The most that can be assumed here is that Paul's recommendation is for medicinal purposes only (*because of your stomach*). There is also the question as to whether the *little wine* Paul recommends could intoxicate. Today we have other medications for gastrointestinal problems.

E. ACTIONS RECOGNIZED (vv. 24, 25)
24. The sins of some men are obvious, reaching the place of judgment ahead of them; the sins of others trail behind them.

The sins of some are very obvious, aren't they? A flagrantly sinful lifestyle obviously disqualifies a person for consideration to be a church leader.

In others, the sins are not so obvious. They may even be cleverly concealed. A modern example would be surfing the Internet in private to lust after pornographic images. Yet the Scripture says "be sure that your sin will find you out" (Numbers 32:23). When Timothy refrains from laying on hands too soon to ordain elders (1 Timothy 5:22), he is allowing time for secret sins to surface.

25. In the same way, good deeds are obvious, and even those that are not cannot be hidden.

The *same* principle is true for the *good deeds* of some. Good deeds commend a person. Christian attitudes and conduct stand out. Even good deeds done in secret commend the person doing them; God will make sure of that (Matthew 6:3, 4). People respect integrity and credibility.

CONCLUSION
In sports, a person or team can be penalized for "delay of game." By contrast, Paul's instruction is to allow enough time to pass to observe attitude, character, lifestyle, and commitment to the Lord's work before setting a person apart for the responsibility of leadership. "Thus, by their fruit you will recognize them" (Matthew 7:20; compare Galatians 5:22, 23).

A church ignores God's instruction in the selection of leadership at its peril. No church will rise higher than its leadership. A congregation with godly leadership has a God-given gift; it should respect, encourage, support, and follow that leading.

Discovery Learning

This page contains an alternative lesson plan emphasizing learning activities. Classes desiring such student involvement will find these suggestions helpful. The next page is a reproducible activity page to further enhance discovery learning.

LEARNING GOALS

After this lesson, each student will be able to:

1. Describe ways Christians are to treat one another.

2. Give an example of how his or her church has honored its older (and perhaps needier) members and how it has recognized its leaders.

3. State one way he or she will honor an elderly Christian or dedicated leader this week.

INTO THE LESSON

Purchase candies wrapped with Christian sayings or Bible verses. Distribute one to each class member as he or she arrives. Instruct students not to eat their candies.

Once everyone is seated, say, "I want you to give your candy to another class member." After they have done so, say, "How Christians treat other Christians is the theme of today's study. Of course, our text is about more than just giving treats to one another. It is about how Christians treat one another in every aspect of life. Let's look at our text in 1 Timothy 5:1-8, 17-25."

INTO THE WORD

Recruit two class members to represent the concepts of justice and mercy as they present the two monologues below. Prepare a label for each volunteer to wear. One label should have the word *JUSTICE* and the other *MERCY*. Give your recruits their parts early enough that each can read through it before presenting.

JUSTICE: "I am an elusive ideal. Though many peoples and nations avow allegiance to me, I am all too seldom seen. Many sins attack me: envy, greed, prejudice, lying, and self-centeredness. I am often pictured as a blind-folded lady, carrying scales of balance above my head.

"Fair and equal treatment is my intent. But when flawed humans step into my presence, they seek to warp the balance in my weights. The laws of God established me; the laws of humanity either protect me or annul me. Ultimately, only God has the knowledge of humanity's affairs and an individual's heart clearly enough to make certain that I am properly administered. And he will. I am Justice. I am an elusive ideal."

MERCY: "I am a most desired and a desirable presence. The sins of which my associate, Justice, speaks make me absolutely essential. Justice may make things fair, but I make life bearable and delightful.

"Those who sense my presence are those who sense the weaknesses of us all. Those who understand me know that I am from the heart of a loving God. Those who deny me deny that God exists or deny that he is anything but an indifferent, or even fiendish, creator. Ultimately, only those who love as God loves can show me in their words and behaviors. I am Mercy. I am a most desired and most desirable presence."

After the monologues, relate the ideas to the admonitions that Paul makes in 1 Timothy 5:1-8, 17-25. Have the text read aloud and use the following questions in your discussion.

1. How do verses 1 and 2 tell us to treat people? *Note that neither age nor gender should negate justice.*

2. How do Paul's words regarding widows in verses 3-6 maintain a concept of justice? *Note that personal responsibility is a component of justice.*

3. How does providing for one's own family (verse 8) relate to justice? *Note that justice involves moral decisions as well as legal ones.*

4. In verses 17 and 18, how is justice shown?

5. In verse 20, what role does justice play in church discipline?

6. How do the sins mentioned in the justice monologue interfere with justice in relationships? How do the principles of justice and mercy relate to verses 22, 24?

Add other questions that you see as important for discussing the text and the dual concepts of justice and mercy. (The "Which Way to Look" activity on the reproducible page can be used as a small-group exercise. It will lead naturally to further discussion of the concept of mercy.)

INTO LIFE

Distribute small slips of paper. Ask students to write the name of a widow they believe deserves congregational support. On the other side, ask the students to write the name of an elder they believe merits a financial gift for special services to the local body of Christ. Say that you will tally the recommendations and address a letter to the church leadership noting the class's recommendations. Collect and make the recommendations as confidentially as the setting allows. You may wish to use the "A Tip of the C.A.P." activity on the reproducible page in addition (or as an alternative) to this activity.

A Tip of the C.A.P.

Look at today's text in 1 Timothy 5:1-8, 17-25 and come up with what you would consider to be the ideal "Church Assistance Program" (C.A.P.) for widows. Write your program ideas to the right. When finished, ask yourself these questions: What parts of my program is my church already doing? What is the most urgent part of my program that is not currently being done but should be? Who are the church leaders to whom I can make my recommendations? What will be my part in making it happen?

Which Way to Look

The writer says that this lesson "is timely for those who live in a materialistic, self-centered culture." How do you look at the world? By putting the following letters appropriately into the two-line grid below, you will identify the two choices each of us has for looking at the world. See the clues below for help.

E E E E F H H I I I L O R S S S S S T Y

							*			

					*				

Clues
Vowels go into shaded spaces.
The boxes with asterisks are for spaces.
The first line ends with letters with a "double meaning."
The first word in the bottom line begins with a round letter.
Boxes with a bar on the left side are to be filled with the letter that occurs most often.

Once you have both lines deciphered, fill in this prayer.

"Lord, forgive me when I look at the world with _____ _____."

"God, give me _____ _____, so I can see the world as you do."

BE TRUE TO YOUR CHRISTIAN HERITAGE

LESSON 10

WHY TEACH THIS LESSON?

One of the most significant passages in the Old Testament is Deuteronomy 6:4-9. There Moses stresses the importance of passing God's Word to succeeding generations. Tragedy befell the Jewish people because they did not remember those words.

It is often said that the church is never more than a generation away from extinction—or at least from irrelevance. Today's lesson impresses us with the supreme importance of faithfully teaching the gospel message to each succeeding generation. Young people do not automatically become Christians just because their parents were Christians. They must be taught to follow Christ. God has no grandchildren!

INTRODUCTION

A. THE TEACHER WHO MADE A DIFFERENCE

Do you remember a teacher who had a huge, positive impact on your life? Recently I ran across the name of my junior high school principal. I don't remember much that I learned in junior high or even many of my teachers, but I remembered this man instantly. I remember sitting in his office, having been sent there as a consequence of some stupid action. I remember that he dealt with me firmly but patiently. He talked frankly about my future goals. He took a special interest in me, a scrawny 13-year-old, and he challenged me to be a better person, to dream big, to work hard. What he was doing was investing a bit of himself in me. He was more teacher than principal in these encounters.

This man was not satisfied with being the principal of a small-town junior high school. He eventually became the superintendent of the school district and then the State Superintendent for Public Instruction. After a successful tenure in this office, he "retired" and was elected to be a state senator, an office he still holds. I took the time to write him a note and tell him that his pupil had turned out OK. I thanked him for his patience and interest in me so many years ago. As we grow older, are we able to identify those whom we have influenced in positive ways?

B. LESSON BACKGROUND

As far as we know, the apostle Paul had no children and was never married. We do know that Paul had a sister and nephew, so he did play the role of uncle (Acts 23:16). We also know little about Paul's relationship to his father. We know that his father provided him with an excellent education, with a trade (tent-making), and with Roman citizenship.

Paul noted that he had grown up in Jerusalem under the tutelage of a great rabbi, Gamaliel (Acts 22:3). It is likely that Gamaliel had served as a substitute

DEVOTIONAL READING:
2 THESSALONIANS 2:13-17
BACKGROUND SCRIPTURE:
2 TIMOTHY 1
PRINTED TEXT:
2 TIMOTHY 1:3-14

LESSON AIMS

After participating in this lesson, each student will be able to:

1. Identify some ways that Paul, Lois, and Eunice influenced Timothy's faith.

2. Explain how Paul's mentoring of Timothy can be a pattern for his or her church today.

3. Develop a plan for the week ahead to guard sound doctrine in his or her life.

Feb
5

KEY VERSE

I have been reminded of your sincere faith, which first lived in your grandmother Lois and in your mother Eunice and, I am persuaded, now lives in you also.
—2 Timothy 1:5

father for young Paul, if indeed Paul's formative years were spent in the temple city far from his family's home in Tarsus. Thus Paul well knew that the teacher-student bond could be more than a professional relationship. Teachers produce disciple-children. Teachers bear both joy and responsibility for the careers of these "offspring."

While Paul saw himself as the "father" of his converts (compare 1 Corinthians 4:15 and Titus 1:4), he considered Timothy to be his "son" is a unique way. He had taken a personal, paternal responsibility for Timothy's circumcision, because Timothy's natural father was not a Jew. Paul's role of substitute father seemed so appropriate that Paul convinced Timothy's mother to let the boy travel with him, even though Timothy probably was no more than a teenager at the time (Acts 16:1-3).

In this week's lesson we see Paul reflecting on this relationship from the vantage point of many years of fruitful association with Timothy. The book of 2 Timothy was written while Paul was in prison in Rome (2 Timothy 1:8, 16, 17), probably awaiting his execution (2 Timothy 4:6). Soon there would be no teacher to guide the student. Yet Paul was confident that Timothy was ready to assume full responsibility; Timothy was his prized pupil, his son in the faith, his joy and hope for the future.

I. JOY OF A TEACHER (2 TIMOTHY 1:3, 4)

A. PROUD TO PRAY FOR YOU (v. 3)

3. I thank God, whom I serve, as my forefathers did, with a clear conscience, as night and day I constantly remember you in my prayers.

Paul begins by reminding Timothy of his own rich heritage of faith. Paul's service to God is derived from his spiritual ancestors or *forefathers*.

We learn two important things from Paul by analyzing this expression. First, he sees no conflict between his service to God as a preacher of the gospel and the service to God given by ancestral Jews before Christ came. In other words there is no necessary conflict between past service to God under the Old Testament and current service to God under the New Testament. In both cases true service to God is motivated by faith and love.

Second, we learn the importance of faith that is passed on from one generation to the next. Paul did not discover service to God by chance or accident. He was taught it and saw it modeled by his teachers.

B. THRILLED TO SEE YOU (v. 4)

4. Recalling your tears, I long to see you, so that I may be filled with joy.

Isn't it amazing that in our world of instant communication, cell phones, and e-mail, we still *long to see* our loved ones in person? There is no substitute for face-to-face smiling, laughing, and hugging of ones whom we cherish! We will endure long plane flights or hours of driving just to spend a few days with friends or relatives.

Paul is no different. The trip from Rome to Ephesus would be a short plane hop today, but it is a journey of many weeks in the first century. Furthermore, the only hope Paul has for seeing Timothy is if the young man comes to Rome. Paul is in prison and travel is impossible for him. Paul desperately wants Timothy to come to Rome so he can *see* him one last time (2 Timothy 4:9).

Today, we who are able to get out and about should not forget the *joy* that a visit to a housebound friend can bring. A note or card is fine as far as it goes, but dropping in may bring great joy to a lonely person.

WHAT DO YOU THINK?

The best Christian teachers and mentors excel in prayer, teaching ability, knowledge of the Scripture, "practicing what they preach," and simply being available. Is any attribute more important than any other? Explain.

II. FAITH OF GENERATIONS (2 TIMOTHY 1:5-12)

A. FOREMOTHERS OF FAITH (v. 5)

5. I have been reminded of your sincere faith, which first lived in your grandmother Lois and in your mother Eunice and, I am persuaded, now lives in you also.

Acts 16:1 tells us that Timothy's *mother* was a Jewish woman who had become a Christian believer. They lived in Lystra, a city evangelized by Paul and Barnabas on the first missionary journey (see Acts 14:6-21). When Paul returned (now with Silas, perhaps three or four years later), he was impressed with Timothy. Luke, the author of Acts, describes Timothy as a disciple (Acts 16:1).

The verse before us fills in more details about Timothy's mother and *grandmother*. Acts 16:3 tells us that Timothy's father was not a Jew. How had *Lois* allowed daughter *Eunice* to marry a pagan Gentile? We do not know. We do know that the worship of the Greek gods was strong in Timothy's hometown of Lystra, as it supported a temple and a priest for Zeus (Acts 14:13).

Timothy, then, did not grow up with the benefit of a father to care for his proper religious development. These two godly women were the ones who had insisted that he know the Jewish Scriptures, our Old Testament (2 Timothy 3:15). They were concerned about more than his physical food and clothing!

Many preachers and missionaries today readily confess that the influence of a mother or grandmother was a key to their faith and commitment to ministry. These are the mothers who made sure their sons went to Sunday school, learned how to pray, memorized Bible verses, and lived by faith daily. Too often these women received little or no support from their husbands in this regard. Where would the church be without these grand foremothers in the faith!

MAKING A DIFFERENCE

The names of John and Charles Wesley are familiar to many Christians. Charles was a prolific writer of hymns, including such standards as "Christ the Lord Is Risen Today," "Hark! the Herald Angels Sing," and "Love Divine, All Loves Excelling." John was a great eighteenth-century gospel preacher whose influence is felt yet today. Their father, though a minister of the gospel, was not the dominant influence in their lives. Instead, it was their mother, Susanna, who molded their character.

Susanna bore 19 children in the span of 19 years. Nine died in infancy. In spite of difficult circumstances, she was committed to caring for her family. She started a school for her children, though resources were limited. She said her purpose was "the saving of their souls," so academics never took priority over instruction in God's Word. Because Susanna wanted to develop a personal relationship with each child, she scheduled a private appointment with each once a week for encouragement. These bonds of faith and love helped them survive continual hardships.

Many celebrities from the popular culture are having a profound influence upon the children of today. When a mother abandons her role as modeled by Susanna Wesley, Eunice, and Lois, these wrong influences can win the day. What can your church do to encourage Christian mothers in their role of spiritual formation of children?   —A. E. A.

B. GIFT OF GOD (vv. 6, 7)

6, 7. For this reason I remind you to fan into flame the gift of God, which is in you through the laying on of my hands. For God did not give us a spirit of timidity, but a spirit of power, of love and of self-discipline.

What is this *gift of God* that Paul gave Timothy by *laying* his *hands* on him? We should confess that we do not completely understand the nature of the

WHAT DO YOU THINK?

How can we honor our teachers and mentors? Or should we focus strictly on honoring God? Explain.

DAILY BIBLE READINGS

Monday, Jan. 30—God Gives the Heritage (Psalm 111)

Tuesday, Jan. 31—We Can Lose Our Heritage (Jeremiah 17:1-8)

Wednesday, Feb. 1—Stand Fast, Hold Traditions (2 Thessalonians 2:13-17)

Thursday, Feb. 2—Timothy's Mother Was a Believer (Acts 16: 1-5)

Friday, Feb. 3—Lois and Eunice Passed On Faith (2 Timothy 1:1-5)

Saturday, Feb. 4—Be Not Ashamed of Your Testimony (2 Timothy 1:6-10)

Sunday, Feb. 5—Hold Fast the Good Treasure Given You (2 Timothy 1:11-18)

specific gift or the significance of the laying on of hands. However, we do understand some of it.

Laying on of hands refers to the physical touching that accompanies a ceremony of commissioning a person for a task of ministry on behalf of the church (compare Acts 6:6; 13:3; Hebrews 6:2). This ceremony signifies the granting of authority necessary for accomplishing the task.

Today, this is usually part of an ordination service in which the elders of a congregation formally charge a person for ministry. That ordination may be to a full-time vocation such as preaching, or it may be to a volunteer position such as deacon. There is nothing magical about this ceremony. The elders have no supernatural power that zaps from their hands to the person's shoulders. Supernatural power comes only from God and is not controlled by human beings.

We know also that this gift to Timothy is a type of empowerment (compare 1 Timothy 4:14). Timothy does not have a gift that causes him to fear. We do not need cowards in ministry! The authority given to Timothy is characterized by *power* and *love* and *self-discipline*. Sloth and neglect will make us weak, selfish, undisciplined, and ineffective in ministry. Like Timothy, all disciples occasionally need to be called to accountability, to stir up our commitment. The power of the Holy Spirit is always available to us. We are the ones who quench this fire (1 Thessalonians 5:19).

WHAT DO YOU THINK?

How can we stir up our God-given gifts for Christian service?

C. POWER OF GOD (vv. 8-10)

8-10. So do not be ashamed to testify about our Lord, or ashamed of me his prisoner. But join with me in suffering for the gospel, by the power of God, who has saved us and called us to a holy life—not because of anything we have done but because of his own purpose and grace. This grace was given us in Christ Jesus before the beginning of time, but it has now been revealed through the appearing of our Savior, Christ Jesus, who has destroyed death and has brought life and immortality to light through the gospel.

Rather than operate from a position of fear or cowardice, Paul admonishes Timothy to *not be ashamed.* Jesus had prophesied that some disciples would be ashamed of him (Mark 8:38). This is a lack of courage to take a bold stand for their *Savior.* To be ashamed of the gospel, then, is to deny one's faith in Christ and his power to save (see Romans 1:16).

Paul mentions two areas that Timothy must address fearlessly: his testimony of *our Lord* and the fact that Paul, his mentor and spiritual father, is a jailbird. While Timothy's life probably was not threatened because of his preaching, Paul's was. Paul could have denied Jesus, begged for the intervention of the non-Christian Jewish leaders of Rome, and had his life spared. But he didn't. The time for faithful preaching is not determined by political climate or personal safety.

Paul goes on to give several essential elements to this fearlessly proclaimed message. First, the entire plan of salvation has been designed intentionally by God. We are not part of some make-it-up-as-you-go endeavor on God's part. God knows what he is doing.

Second, God has called us to be a part of this plan. This is a holy and noble calling, the summons to God's mighty service. God does not need us to accomplish his purposes, but God will use us powerfully if we commit to his service.

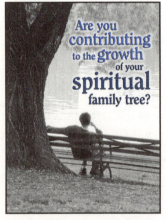

Visual for Lesson 10. *Start a discussion by repeating the question on this visual. Follow by asking "How?"*

Third, the power of God's plan has been demonstrated in the life and resurrection of Jesus. His resurrection *destroyed death* and shows us the way to salvation. This is precisely what Jesus saves us from: the terror and hopelessness of inevitable death (1 Corinthians 15:55).

D. MINISTRY WITHOUT SHAME (vv. 11, 12)

11, 12. And of this gospel I was appointed a herald and an apostle and a teacher. That is why I am suffering as I am. Yet I am not ashamed, because I know whom I have believed, and am convinced that he is able to guard what I have entrusted to him for that day.

Paul continues his theme of freedom from shame, from cowardice. He is beyond embarrassment and timidity.

A church in my area has the motto, "The Fellowship of the Unashamed." This does not mean there are no shameful things in their lives. It means they are committed to never being ashamed of being Christians. Christians in Western democracies do not live under the threat of death (unlike some countries). But many such Christians live with constant ridicule and pressure to compromise faith. It feels like it would be easier to keep our faith very private and personal.

Paul knows, however, that a hidden faith is an ashamed faith. This is why a good Jew like Paul—a Pharisee, a Hebrew of the Hebrews (Philippians 3:5), a former student of Rabbi Gamaliel—could accept shamelessly his call to be an evangelizer, *apostle*, and *teacher* of the Gentiles.

To guard what I have entrusted to him is literally "to safeguard my deposit." This is Paul's investment of biblical training in Timothy. Paul is confident that this "deposit" will be a credit on his account on *that day,* the day of reckoning or judgment. He is confident not only in Jesus but also in Timothy.

III. PATTERN TO FOLLOW (2 TIMOTHY 1:13, 14)

A. STANDARD BEARER (v. 13)

13. What you heard from me, keep as the pattern of sound teaching, with faith and love in Christ Jesus.

Timothy's job is not to tinker with Paul's gospel message. Rather, Timothy's job is to pass along that message faithfully. He will be able to do this only if he holds fast to that message himself. That's our job too!

NO IMPROVEMENT NEEDED

Tim Taylor, the character in the long-running TV series *Home Improvement,* was always trying to tweak things to make them better. Whether it be putting a lawnmower engine on a garbage disposal or turbo charging the engine of a garden tractor, his goal was to improve everything. Tim's recurring theme was to give "more power" to whatever he was working on. But more power usually resulted in hilarious problems!

The world is filled with people who want to practice "Scripture Improvement," but there's nothing funny about this. Many of these folks are well-meaning, sincere Christians. Others want to use Christianity to further a certain agenda. In either case, to change Scripture to make it say what it does not say is to pave a road to ruin, not relevancy. One thinks, for example, of attempts to reinterpret the Bible in order to give homosexuality a stamp of approval. When truth is undermined, collapse is not far away (Daniel 8:12).

Paul's words of warning to Timothy about maintaining soundness of doctrine ring as true today as they did in the first century. It is the task of Christians to hold on to this truth and spread this truth. It is only the truth of Jesus Christ that provides us anything solid upon which to stand for eternal life.　　　　—A. E. A.

B. TREASURE GUARDIAN (v. 14)

14. Guard the good deposit that was entrusted to you—guard it with the help of the Holy Spirit who lives in us.

WHAT DO YOU THINK?

What is the difference between fear and reserve? How do we take into account this difference among our fellow Christians?

HOW TO SAY IT

Barnabas. BAR-nuh-bus.
Ephesus. EF-uh-sus.
Eunice. U-NYE-see or U-nis.
Gamaliel. Guh-MAY-lih-ul or
　　Guh-MAY-lee-al.
Gentiles. JEN-tiles.
Jerusalem. Juh-ROO-suh-lem.
Lystra. LISS-truh.
Pharisees. FAIR-ih-seez.
rabbi. RAB-eye.
Silas. SIGH-luss.
Tarsus. TAR-sus.
Zeus. Zoose.

PRAYER

God of truth, as you used Paul to pass on the heritage of Christian faith to Timothy, use us to train and encourage the Timothys and Timothyettes you send our way. May we never hoard the gospel, but share it freely. We pray in the name of our Savior, Jesus Christ, amen.

WHAT DO YOU THINK?

What are some ways that you have found to "keep the faith"? How have you been able to "give it away" at the same time?

Should we use or hoard? Several years ago, I ran across a beautiful plush lamb that had been given to me as a baby. It was so fine that my wonderful, conscientious mother had hidden it to save it from baby drool and dirt. But bugs had gotten into the box and destroyed the once beautiful lamb. Her noble intention to safeguard something of beauty had resulted in losing the item without its ever being used.

When it comes to the grand doctrines of the gospel, should they be safeguarded or used? Can we trust new Christians with our truths? Won't they be distorted, misused, and lost?

The answer is that we must do both. On the one hand, we always must contend for the faith (Jude 3) and measure what we teach by the apostles' teaching as found in the New Testament. This body of teaching was committed to Timothy by Paul. It has now been entrusted to us.

On the other hand, we must encourage new converts to begin learning and using Christian doctrine immediately. As Alexander Campbell (1788–1866) said, "Doctrine is what you live." It is in the use of the Bible that it lives and breathes.

CONCLUSION

A. TRAINING OUR SUCCESSORS

Veterans' organizations that are built around World War II service members have fallen on very hard times in America. Their few remaining members are old and ill. Their ranks are dwindling rapidly as more than 1,000 veterans of that era die every day. They all will be gone in a few years. The church too is always one generation removed from extinction. Without constant replenishment of its members, it will die.

Research by the Barna Group tells us that the average person's moral foundation is in place by age 9. Most people have come to lifelong faith conclusions by age 13, and most adult leaders in churches were heavily involved in training and ministry when children. Yet many church programs today are designed to serve adults. Aging "Baby Boomers" (those born between 1946 and 1964) clamor for worship according to their tastes. The "Gen Xers" (who are in their thirties) want churches that are responsive to their needs.

We cannot ignore these voices, but the leaders of tomorrow's church are found among our pre-teens of today. Are we investing funds, time, and our very best people in training children? That "deposit on account" today will have a rich yield of Timothys and Timothyettes for the future.

B. OVERCOMING FAMILY UNFAITHFULNESS

Where would Timothy have been without the apostle Paul as his mentor? He probably would not have any books with his name in the New Testament, but I suspect he would have turned out all right. I think he would have become a strong leader in the little church in Lystra, perhaps even its preacher. Why? Because of the faith of his mother and his grandmother. When Paul came to town, it was their training that allowed Timothy to leave on his first missionary trip to Macedonia!

Modern families are often incomplete in some way. But inadequate families can be wholly adequate for raising godly adults if training in the Scriptures is prized and modeled. Sometimes this task falls upon the mother because there is no one else. In some cases this responsibility falls upon grandparents because the parents are absent. If you are in this situation, don't despair. God will strengthen, support, and honor you.

THOUGHT TO REMEMBER

You never know which of the teens of today will grow up to be the preachers of tomorrow, so invest your life in as many as possible.

Discovery Learning

This page contains an alternative lesson plan emphasizing learning activities. Classes
desiring such student involvement will find these suggestions helpful. The next page
is a reproducible activity page to further enhance discovery learning.

LEARNING GOALS

After in this lesson, each student will be able to:

1. Identify some ways that Paul, Lois, and Eunice influenced Timothy's faith.

2. Explain how Paul's mentoring of Timothy can be a pattern for his or her church today.

3. Develop a plan for the week ahead to guard sound doctrine in his or her life.

INTO THE LESSON

If your class does not use the student book, prepare a handout as follows. At the top of the page, write the heading "My Faith Family Tree." Under it draw a large tree with several branches. Do not include leaves. Also prepare a handout described in the Into Life portion of the lesson, below.

Open by asking class members to write the names of people who have been significant in the development of their faith and their service to Jesus. They may write these names on branches or at the ends of the branches.

Next, encourage class members to select and circle one name they would like to share with the class (or a small group). They should tell how that person influenced or encouraged his or her faith or service to Christ.

Make the transition to Bible study by telling the class, "There is a young man in the Bible who would include the names Lois, Eunice, and Paul on his faith family tree. Who is he?" (*Timothy*). Say, "From Timothy's experience we will learn principles for passing our faith along to others."

INTO THE WORD

Say, "God has blessed us with two wonderful institutions that are charged with passing along the faith: the family and the church. Either one may do the job. However, there is a special strength in being blessed with both institutions working toward that goal."

Divide the class into three or four groups of two to five people each. More groups may be added, duplicating the activities. Give each group some poster board, markers, and printed instructions as follows:

Group #1: "Your charge is to read today's printed text and list every word or phrase that teaches something about passing along the faith. Make notes beside these words or phrases about lessons learned."

Group #2: "Read the text to discover a few clues about how families may accomplish the task of passing on the faith. List these on the poster board. From your experiences and knowledge, list additional tips or principles in bringing up children to know and serve the Lord."

Group #3: [If there are grandparents present in the class, you may wish to create a special group with this challenge.] "Read the text and discover clues about how grandparents may be important in passing along the faith to grandchildren. List these. From your experiences and observations, list additional ideas or tips in helping grandchildren discover the Lord."

Group #4: "Make two columns on your poster board with the headings 'Encouraging Children/Youth' and 'Encouraging Young Adults.' Read the text and write clues about how the church may encourage its younger people, whom we may call Timothys and Timothyettes. Drawing on your experiences and observations, add additional ideas about how the church may accomplish this goal."

Allow several minutes for discussion. Then ask the groups to report their discoveries and suggestions. Write their ideas to the board as appropriate. (The "Interview with Paul" activity on the reproducible page can be an alternative or addition to this exercise.)

INTO LIFE

Thank the class for the abundance of ideas shared today. Explain that you would like to give an opportunity for each person to encourage faith or leadership in one young person or young adult. Distribute a piece of stationery you have designed with the following headings at appropriate intervals on the page.

Dear _____,
I wanted to send you this note because . . .
I especially have noticed and appreciate this particular quality in you: . . .
I would encourage you to . . .
　　　　　　　　　　　Yours in Christ, _____.

Ask class members to use this format or one of their own making. (This activity is also in the student book.) The "Life Decisions" activity on the reproducible page can be used instead of this exercise.

An Interview with Paul

After reading 2 Timothy 1:3-14, how do you think Paul might answer these questions? Pretend you are Paul and let answers to these questions pour from your heart.

1. "Paul, after hearing you praise Timothy's mom and grandmother, I know you appreciate the value of parental faith. What suggestions would you leave with young moms and dads today about raising children to know the Lord? What practical tips would you offer?"

2. "Paul, you didn't mention Timothy's dad or grandfather. I don't know why you omitted them, but it does raise this question. What special encouragement would you give to single parents . . . or to a mother or father who is married to an unbeliever?"

To single parents:

To a parent whose spouse is an unbeliever:

Life Decisions

It is time to let the lessons from this text become personal. Select *one* of the following three great potential influences in a young believer's life. Under the one you have selected, write the name of a young Christian whom you would like to contact and encourage this week. Jot notes about how you may accomplish the goal you have selected. Example: You may encourage a young person to share in a summer mission trip and volunteer to pay part of his or her way.

Ways I might influence a young believer:

1. Talking about faith and life.

2. Involvement in a service or mission project.

3. Developing spiritual disciplines such as prayer, selecting good friends, etc.

DEVELOP
CHRISTIAN CHARACTER

LESSON 11

WHY TEACH THIS LESSON?

Character development was once a primary goal of education. In ancient Greece both Aristotle and Socrates gave attention to how moral excellence might be transmitted to the young. In the seventeenth century John Locke, the English philosopher, saw character development as the goal of education. John Stuart Mill, a nineteenth century English philosopher, said "Development of character is a solution to social problems and a worthy educational ideal."

However, Western society lost its way in the twentieth century. As culture shifted toward secularism, education began to focus on pragmatics—the knowledge and skills needed to obtain and hold a job. Today's lesson shows what can happen, even in the church, when there is a failure to focus on godly character based on Scripture. It also offers solid encouragement for developing those traits of character that are distinctively Christian.

INTRODUCTION

A. THE SURVEILLANCE SOCIETY

Privacy. It has been cherished by most people, even touted as a constitutional right in America and other countries. Yet technological advances and the pressure to thwart terrorists and criminals have eroded personal privacy enormously. We use the Internet, scarcely aware that every move we make is being tracked, often for commercial purposes. We send personal e-mails, usually forgetting that they all are preserved on a network server somewhere. We drive around town, oblivious to the intersection cameras that are capable of reading our license plates and tracking our movements.

We use our credit cards, disregarding the fact that this use provides a permanent record of our purchases. We talk on cell phones, failing to remember that these are open lines on the public airways, and anyone with the right equipment can listen. We make withdrawals at cash machines, unmindful that cameras are taping us during the transaction. We deposit our trash after eating at the fast food restaurant, unaware that the napkin bearing a trace of our saliva could be used to pinpoint us via DNA testing.

Our smallest actions seem to be noticed and recorded. Even so, we certainly are not to the extreme of George Orwell's book *1984*, which depicted government cameras in citizens' houses to track them 24 hours per day. On the other hand, the Bible consistently presents God as one who is aware of everything we think, say, and do. Nothing is hidden from him. As the psalmist wrote, "You perceive my thoughts from afar. . . . you are familiar with all my ways" (Psalm 139:2, 3).

So often we behave contrary to this reality, don't we? We do things that we know displease God and somehow believe that he doesn't notice or care. Today's

DEVOTIONAL READING:
COLOSSIANS 3:5-11
BACKGROUND SCRIPTURE:
2 TIMOTHY 2
PRINTED TEXT:
2 TIMOTHY 2:14-26

LESSON AIMS

After participating in this lesson, each student will be able to:

1. Summarize Paul's advice to Timothy about the development of Christian character.

2. Identify an example of ungodly behavior that is just as prevalent today as it was in the first century.

3. Identify one ungodly behavior in his or her life to modify or eliminate.

Feb
12

KEY VERSE

Flee the evil desires of youth, and pursue righteousness, faith, love and peace, along with those who call on the Lord out of a pure heart. —2 Timothy 2:22

lesson teaches us that there is no room for hidden evil in the life of a Christian disciple. While God is gracious to forgive our sins, he also expects our best efforts in the pursuit of godliness. God is not the only observer of our behavior. Particularly if we are teachers, our actions will teach as much as our words.

B. LESSON BACKGROUND

This week we get a disturbing look at the troubles of the Ephesian church where Timothy ministered. It is disturbing because it seems too much like churches we have known. Teachers were leading believers astray with ridiculous, speculative doctrines. Most disturbing of these, for Paul, was a denial of future resurrection. Paul identifies the main perpetrators of this error by name: Hymenaeus and Philetus. Hymenaeus is known to us from 1 Timothy 1:19, 20, where he is described as having shipwrecked his faith, requiring that he be "handed over to Satan" (that is, cut off from the church and its fellowship).

The church at Ephesus had its choice of many flavors of false doctrine (as do Christians today). First Timothy 1:3-7 does give us some of the elements of the particular false teaching at Ephesus. Paul indicated that it contained a Greek, pagan element because of its concern for mythology (v. 4). It also had Jewish elements because of its concern for genealogies and the Law (vv. 4, 7). The part that is repeated in today's Scripture, however, was its characteristic of speculation that led to endless, meaningless discussion (compare 1 Timothy 1:4, 6).

I. WORD WRANGLING (2 TIMOTHY 2:14-18)

A. RUINING LISTENERS (v. 14)

14. Keep reminding them of these things. Warn them before God against quarreling about words; it is of no value, and only ruins those who listen.

The power of public speech is startling. In A.D. 1095, Pope Urban II gave a single, fiery speech that mobilized the gentry of Europe for the first crusade and radically changed the course of history. During World War II, the speeches of Adolf Hitler enflamed the patriotic passions of the German people for war, while the addresses of Winston Churchill gave the British people hope in their darkest days.

Paul well knows the power of speech. It can mobilize the masses for great good. It may also result in ruining *those who listen*. There is nothing more disillusioning to new converts than to see their leaders embroiled in public bickering. If Christianity is about love and forgiveness, about fellowship and charity, why do mature Christians quarrel *about words*, since *it is of no value*? Paul is not talking about shying away from confronting false doctrine. He is talking about the damage that quarreling causes. Paul also had to warn the Corinthians about quarreling (1 Corinthians 1:11; 3:3; 2 Corinthians 12:20).

B. RATIFIED EXPLAINER (v. 15)

15. Do your best to present yourself to God as one approved, a workman who does not need to be ashamed and who correctly handles the word of truth.

Timothy needs to show himself *as one approved* by God above all else. God is the intended audience. Timothy is not to seek Paul's approval, but God's. Paul gives Timothy three ways to reach the status of a Christian who has God's approval. First, Timothy is to study. The idea is that of diligent, persistent learning.

I have a motto that I have long used with my college students: "Whining is no substitute for hard work." Books are not understood unless carefully read. Classroom lectures are not comprehended unless the student listens and takes good notes. Written assignments are not profitable unless the student takes time to think and write clearly. Timothy will be studying mainly on his own, but it will still take hard work.

Second, Paul recommends that Timothy strive to be *a workman* who has nothing to fear from having his work scrutinized. This does not mean that Timothy is to reach a level where he knows everything and does everything right. Rather, it means he should be working to the extent that his effort is above criticism, and his performance is constantly improving. He is never to fake it.

Third, Paul defines for Timothy the primary object of his studies: he is to *correctly* handle *the word of truth*. This refers to the interpretation of Scripture.

Another saying that I drill into my students is this: "Biblical interpretation is hard work." Truly grasping the meaning of Scripture involves wrestling with the text: reading, rereading, pondering, meditating, praying. Too many Christians have an unnecessarily shallow knowledge of the Bible simply because they have not invested themselves in learning its truths. They expect to be spoon-fed by the preacher every week. Paul calls us to work hard and enrich ourselves through ever expanding knowledge of God's word.

C. ROTTEN TALK (vv. 16-18)

16-18. Avoid godless chatter, because those who indulge in it will become more and more ungodly. Their teaching will spread like gangrene. Among them are Hymenaeus and Philetus, who have wandered away from the truth. They say that the resurrection has already taken place, and they destroy the faith of some.

Perhaps Paul knows that Timothy's keen mind is drawn to debate theological issues. In the realm of debate, truth is not always the prize. Winning is! Paul uses some very descriptive words at this point. *Godless chatter* can be thought of as "irreverent and empty babbling." If we were forced to read a transcript of every word we uttered at the end of the day, what percentage would be classified "profane" and what percentage would be "pointless babble"?

Paul warns Timothy that this careless, worthless talk is a bad influence on others. He calls it *gangrene.* It is like rotten flesh that endangers the entire body. The only solution for gangrene is to cut it off. Irreverent and empty babbling, especially concerning doctrinal matters, can lead to spiritual decay and rottenness.

Paul then gives Timothy an example to show just how serious this issue is. He names two false teachers in Ephesus, *Hymenaeus and Philetus,* and identifies their main doctrinal error: *the resurrection has already taken place*. This doctrine is so important that Paul elsewhere spends a great deal of time discussing it (see 1 Corinthians 15).

THE POWER OF WORDS

A *malaprop* is an absurd misuse of words. Baseball legend Casey Stengel used this malaprop: "I want you all to line up in alphabetical order according to your size." Movie mogul Sam Goldwyn is quoted as saying, "A verbal contract isn't worth the paper it's written on" and "Don't pay any attention to the critics—don't even ignore them."

At one extreme, misuse of words can be downright humorous! But at the other extreme, misused words can wound and destroy. The old adage "Sticks and stones may break my bones, but words can never hurt me" is simply not true. Abusive words destroy families, subvert friendships, and ruin business partnerships.

When it comes to communicating the Word of God, our challenge is to take utmost care in using proper words in proper contexts. To fail in this can have negative eternal consequences for those who hear. Also it can have bearing upon the one speaking the words. James 3:1 cautions that teachers "will be judged more strictly"

WHAT DO YOU THINK?

When learning and applying Christian truth, how can we distinguish matters of doctrine from matters of expediency? Why is it important to do so?

[Be sure to include Romans 14; 1 Corinthians 8; Hebrews 6:1, 2; and Revelation 2:14, 15, 20 in the discussion.]

WHAT DO YOU THINK?

Can all doctrines and issues be debated with love, or should we simply avoid certain controversial subjects? Explain.

HOW TO SAY IT

Corinthians. Ko-RIN-thee-unz
Ephesian. Ee-FEE-zhun.
Ephesus. EF-uh-sus.
Hymenaeus. Hi-meh-NEE-us.
Philetus. Fuh-LEE-tus.

because of what they may wrongly teach. Choosing the best and right words is vital in Christian communication. How are you doing in this regard?　　　　—A. E. A.

II. FIRM FOUNDATION (2 TIMOTHY 2:19-21)

A. GOD'S INSCRIPTIONS (v. 19)

19. Nevertheless, God's solid foundation stands firm, sealed with this inscription: "The Lord knows those who are his," and, "Everyone who confesses the name of the Lord must turn away from wickedness."

Paul gives a word picture for the *foundation* of pursuit of biblical truth. The picture is that of a huge substructure of a building. Paul pictures this immovable foundation as being *sealed* with two inscriptions. The seal would be understood as God's mark of ownership. The inscriptions or messages are public statements of the building's purpose. The first *inscription* is *The Lord knows those who are his.* This indicates that we cannot fool God with religious activities. Some seek truth because they want to know God better, and God knows who they are.

The second inscription, which reads *Everyone who confesses the name of the Lord must turn away from wickedness,* is for us. If teachers of doctrine are to be taken seriously, they must live lives of righteousness and integrity. There is no place for one who professes Christ with lips or in writings, but denies Christ daily in action. We have every right to judge teachers by their lifestyle and activities (Matthew 7:15-20). This is why public moral failure among Christian leaders is so devastating. Even the truths that these fallen leaders proclaim become suspect when they stumble.

B. OUR PREPARATION (vv. 20, 21)

20, 21. In a large house there are articles not only of gold and silver, but also of wood and clay; some are for noble purposes and some for ignoble. If a man cleanses himself from the latter, he will be an instrument for noble purposes, made holy, useful to the Master and prepared to do any good work.

We are familiar with the ideas of "everyday dishes" and "good china." Some families even have a special set of holiday dishes that is unpacked but once a year. Paul points out that we use *some* household items *for noble* (honorable) *purposes and some for ignoble* (less than honorable). There is an interesting play on words here in the Greek, for the word translated *noble* is part of Timothy's name (which means "one who honors God"). Honor is Timothy's first name, not dishonor!

Paul's point is that in order for dishes to be used, whether for special occasions or every day, they must be clean. We may use flimsy paper plates for a cookout, but we don't mind as long as they're clean. We wash the Christmas plates after unpacking them because no one wants to eat from dusty, dirty dishes. Likewise, those teachers who will be most useful to God must care for more than perfecting their lectures and sermons. They must strive for godliness.

CLEAN AND READY

Contrary to what some may think, the phrase *cleanliness is next to godliness* is not in the Bible! Even so, we still place a high premium on cleanliness. We would not dream of allowing a doctor who had not properly scrubbed to operate on us. We expect that those who wait on us in restaurants will maintain proper personal hygiene. Moms send their children back to the sink before a meal if their hands are not properly washed.

Jesus stressed the importance of internal cleanliness when he pronounced a series of "woes" in Matthew 23. The objects of his criticism were people more inter-

Allow God to Shape You

Visual for Lesson 11. *Ask "What part of your life is in most need of chiseling away?" as you point to this visual.*

ested in looks than life, more concerned about legalistic rules than living right-eously. He tells them: "Woe to you, teachers of the law and Pharisees, you hyp-ocrites! You clean the outside of the cup and dish, but inside they are full of greed and self-indulgence. Blind Pharisee! First clean the inside of the cup and dish, and then the outside also will be clean" (Matthew 23:25, 26).

This kind of cleanliness is vital for those who would be effective servants of God. Outward behavior starts with inward attitude. Our lives need to reflect the holiness of God in both areas. The psalmist reminds us of this need for purity before God: "Who may ascend the hill of the Lord? Why may stand in his holy place? He who has clean hands and a pure heart, who does not lift up his soul to an idol or swear by what is false" (Psalm 24:3, 4).   —A. E. A.

III. SATAN'S SNARE (2 TIMOTHY 2:22-26)

A. FLEEING AND PURSUING (v. 22)

22. Flee the evil desires of youth, and pursue righteousness, faith, love and peace, along with those who call on the Lord out of a pure heart.

We are made spiritually righteous and holy by the blood of Jesus (1 John 1:7). It is a gracious, supernatural act of God. But a righteous, holy lifestyle is not auto-matic. The Christian lifestyle must be pursued. We must study Scripture to know how God expects us to live. Then we must go for it!

Paul gives a quartet of virtues that we are to run after: *righteousness* (doing the right thing), *faith* (daily trusting God to provide for us), *love* (caring for others), and *peace* (respecting others and not fighting with them). Furthermore, Paul ad-vises that this pursuit is much easier if we have some running companions: those who also follow God *out of a pure heart.*

B. ARGUMENTS AND INSTRUCTION (vv. 23-25a)

23-25a. Don't have anything to do with foolish and stupid arguments, because you know they produce quarrels. And the Lord's servant must not quarrel; instead, he must be kind to everyone, able to teach, not resentful. Those who oppose him he must gently instruct,

Why are some churches always in turmoil? And why are some Christians so downright quarrelsome? These are not new questions. The *quarrels* in Ephesus seem to have gotten so out of control that Paul heard about them in Rome. Tim-othy may be overwhelmed by these.

Paul's advice to Timothy is that in the final analysis he can control only his own behavior. He cannot change the behavior of every church member and im-mediately stop the fighting. Timothy's own behavior, however, will speak for itself if he follows five simple guidelines. First, quit arguing. Don't even worry about defending yourself. When things escalate into a quarrel, quit arguing. Second, *be kind to everyone.* Respect all people, even those with whom you disagree.

Third, be ready *to teach* anyone who will listen. Don't let doctrinal quarreling dictate what you teach. Always be ready to teach the core doctrines of the faith. Fourth, do not be *resentful.* Quick anger and harsh words never defuse an explo-sive situation. Fifth, demonstrate gentleness in all of this. Defend truth because it is the truth, not because it is your preference. Show some humility and you are more likely to gain a hearing.

C. TRUTH AND ESCAPE (vv. 25b, 26)

25b, 26. . . . in the hope that God will grant them repentance leading them to a knowledge of the truth, and that they will come to their senses and escape from the trap of the devil, who has taken them captive to do his will.

WHAT DO YOU THINK?

As we grow older can we ex-pect to be less tempted to sin? Defend your answer.

WHAT DO YOU THINK?

How can we, in meekness and humility, let potential quarrelers know that their questions are foolish?

PRAYER

God of truth, may you guide us in our pursuit of truth and righteousness. May we avoid quarreling and quarrelsome people. If we have been guilty of quarreling, forgive us and give us a new heart for truth. We pray in the name of Jesus, who has freed us by the truth, amen.

THOUGHT TO REMEMBER

Christian teachers communicate the truth by words and by actions.

WHAT DO YOU THINK?

When have you seen incidents in which church strife could have been defused by eliminating pride and selfishness? Explain.

[Use this question carefully if your church has suffered this problem recently. Make sure to consider Proverbs 6:19; Matthew 5:5; Romans 16:17, 18; Philippians 2:3; and 1 Peter 5:5.]

If we behave as Paul instructs Timothy, we may achieve our goal. This goal is the salvation of the wayward Christians. Seeking to crush and demolish their false teaching may destroy their faith altogether if we're not careful. God is concerned for their souls and for their salvation, and we must be as well.

Paul notes the spiritual realities that are at work here. False doctrines arise from more than idle human speculation. Quarrels and disputes come from more than human pride and egotism. They come ultimately from Satan, the hater of *the truth* and the father of lies (see John 8:44). His falsehoods are not excluded from our churches today.

The one thing that Satan cannot stand is the truth. The foundational truths of the gospel are that God loves us, he sent his Son to die for our sins, and he promises reconciliation and eternal life to those who trust and follow him. These truths of the gospel serve as our lifeline from the sea of sin and death. The truth of Jesus sets us free (John 8:32).

CONCLUSION

A. GODLY LIVING FOR THE LONG HAUL

Church leadership demands a consistent Christian lifestyle. Teachers must do more than teach the truth. They must also live the truth. This is a lifelong commitment. They must be committed to teaching the truth about God and living lives according to God's will.

Take time to examine your own life. Are you daily striving to do the right things, to respect all people, to teach patiently those who will listen, to act humbly without arrogance? Or do you have other lifestyle issues that you are hiding from the church? Ask God to forgive you and to help you overcome these burdens. Remember, you won't shock God when you own up to these sins. He already knows.

God also will give you spiritual resources to assist your quest for holiness. You do not have to run this race alone. He will give you godly companions. Most of all, he will guide and protect you with his Holy Spirit. The hymn writer Cyrus Nusbaum (1861–1937) put it this way: "Would you live for Jesus, and be always pure and good? . . . Let him have his way with thee. His power can make you what you ought to be."

B. CONTROVERSIES IN THE CHURCH

The list of controversies that has caused church quarrels is endless: One cup for Communion or separate cups? Immerse once for baptism or three times? Sing praise choruses or hymns? Red carpet or blue? One church I served actually had a major tiff over whether they should buy a Kirby® vacuum cleaner or a Hoover®!

But every church quarrel has casualties. Young people in particular are often spiritually scarred when church leaders quarrel. Fighting churches are not growing churches. They are not involved in evangelism. How could they be? They are too busy bickering.

We must remember that fighting in the church is a manifestation of Satan's power, not God's grace. We must strive to live in peace (Romans 12:18) and to follow truth (3 John 3, 4). Sometimes people have to be disfellowshiped because of divisiveness (Titus 3:10). More often we must have patience with those with whom we disagree. Part of our patience is based on the realization that we are all fallible. As such, we are open to correction from God's Word. Even in our own lives, let us pray that "truth will rise above falsehood as oil above water" (Miguel de Cervantes, 1547–1616).

Discovery Learning

This page contains an alternative lesson plan emphasizing learning activities. Classes desiring such student involvement will find these suggestions helpful. The next page is a reproducible activity page to further enhance discovery learning.

LEARNING GOALS

After participating in this lesson, each student will be able to:

1. Summarize Paul's advice to Timothy about the development of Christian character.

2. Identify an example of ungodly behavior that is just as prevalent today as it was in the first century.

3. Identify one ungodly behavior in his or her life to modify or eliminate.

INTO THE LESSON

Brainstorming! Say, "God expects certain spiritual and behavioral qualities in people who serve in Christian leadership roles. Help me create a list of desired characteristics of a Christian leader." Ask a "scribe" to jot these qualities or characteristics on the board as they are given.

Make the transition to Bible study by saying, "Our list, of course, is not complete. Paul also offers a list of characteristics and behavior traits of Christian leaders. Based on what Paul says elsewhere, we know that the list in 2 Timothy 2:14-26 is not a complete list. But it is a list that was appropriate for his audience."

INTO THE WORD

Prepare a very brief lecture from the lesson Background and the commentary on verse 14 of today's printed text. This will help the class understand a key reason why Paul wrote the letter we call 2 Timothy. As you lecture, have six letter-size pieces of card stock with the following (one word or phrase on each): *Ephesian Church; Wrong Teachings; Resurrection; Greek Mythology; Jewish Elements;* and *Endless Discussions.* Affix the one- or two-word phrases to the wall as you speak.

After introducing today's text this way, proceed to Activity #1. Use Activity #2 and/or Activity #3 as time permits. Decide in advance which activity or activities will be for the class as a whole and which you will do in small-group discussions.

Activity #1. Prepare a poster board with a heading "Approved by God." Under the heading make two columns with the headings "To Do" and "To Avoid." Explain that there are traits and practices that God expects of his leaders. Read through the text and ask the class to help you make a list of the things a Christian leader is to do or to avoid. Write the answers on the poster board in the appropriate column. As each is mentioned, you can ask what would be the result of failure concerning the particular trait under discussion.

Activity #2. Tell the class or the small groups that verses 17 and 20 contain some word pictures Ask the class as a whole (or give the small groups written copies) these two questions:

a. Verse 17 says *"Their teaching will spread like gangrene."* What was the problem? What lesson do we learn from this word picture?

b. In verse 20, what do you discover from the colorful language about articles of gold and silver, wood and clay? What does this word picture teach Christian leaders?

Allow time for discussion.

Activity #3. Before class prepare a poster board titled "Handling Troublesome Churches and People." Underneath, put the following phrases (but not the words in parentheses):

a. Avoid foolish and stupid _____ *(arguments)*
b. Do not _____ *(quarrel)*
c. Be _____ *(kind)*
d. Be able to _____ *(teach)*
e. Do not be _____ *(resentful)* and "Instruct others _____ " *(gently)*

Make a transition to this activity by asking "Have you noticed that some churches always seem to be in turmoil and that some Christians are so quarrelsome? How should Christian leaders handle those problems?" Ask for help in completing the phrases using verses 23-25a in the printed text. Comment on how these principles help diffuse problems.

INTO LIFE

Distribute one index card to each student. Say, "Write 'Approved Status' at the top of your card, then look at the 'to do' and 'to avoid' poster lists we compiled earlier. From those lists, identify one characteristic, trait, or practice that you would like to eliminate, modify, or develop during the coming weeks. Write it on the card."

Encourage students to carry their cards with them or to put them in a conspicuous place at home to serve as reminders. Close with prayer. You can also distribute the "Approval Status" activity from the reproducible page as an additional take-home exercise.

Approval Status

Paul encourages believers to "Do your best to present yourself to God as one approved" (2 Timothy 2:15). As you read through verses 14-26, you will discover several lessons on how to accomplish that goal in your life. Read these wonderful teachings from Paul noted by each exclamation bubble and jot the lessons or principles you learn about how to present yourself as one approved.

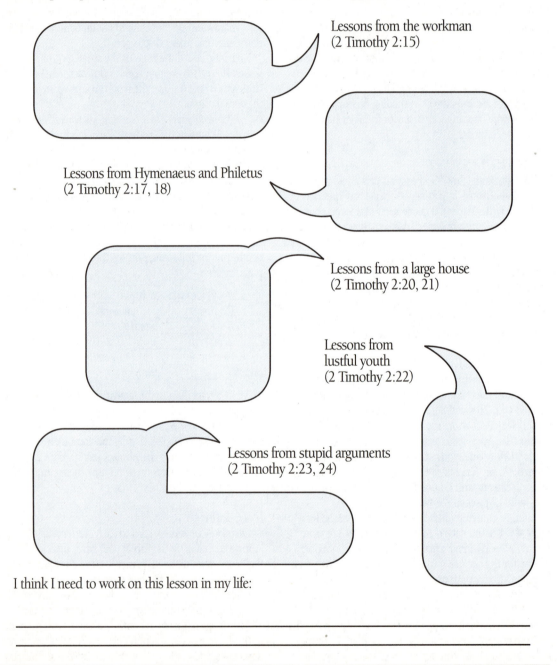

Lessons from the workman
(2 Timothy 2:15)

Lessons from Hymenaeus and Philetus
(2 Timothy 2:17, 18)

Lessons from a large house
(2 Timothy 2:20, 21)

Lessons from
lustful youth
(2 Timothy 2:22)

Lessons from stupid arguments
(2 Timothy 2:23, 24)

I think I need to work on this lesson in my life:

_____

_____

God's Commitment—Our Response

Unit 3: Faithful Followers, Faithful Leaders
(Lessons 10–13)

FOLLOW A GOOD MENTOR

LESSON 12

WHY TEACH THIS LESSON

In Greek mythology Odysseus was the king of Ithaca and a hero of the Trojan War. While he was absent from home fighting the war, he entrusted the care of his household and his son, Telemachus, to his faithful friend Mentor. Ever since, the name of Odysseus's friend has been synonymous for a wise and trustworthy counselor.

The apostle Paul was such a counselor—a mentor—for Timothy. In this lesson we glimpse just a small portion of the trustworthy advice Paul gave to his son-in-the-faith Timothy. Paul's words should resonate with your class. What church today is not also plagued with some of these same problems Paul writes about? As teachers, the extent to which we follow Paul's lead will determine our success in mentoring our students. This lesson is for class and teacher alike!

INTRODUCTION

A. THE PERILS OF MINISTRY

From where will the ministers of the future come? Will there be any full-time ministers left in 10 years? Recent research has shown some alarming trends in this regard. One publication recently estimated that 1,000 people were leaving full-time ministry in the United States every week among evangelical churches. A survey of ministers taken by the Institute for Church Growth revealed that 70 percent of ministers did not believe they had a close friend, 80 percent thought that ministry affected their families in a negative way, and 90 percent felt they had inadequate training to cope with the demands of ministry.

The corps of full-time ministers is in an ongoing state of crisis. One survey found that the average length of time spent in career ministry has dropped from 20 years to 14 years. Some believe it is now less than 10 years. Can these trends be reversed? Some ministers self-destruct as a result of immoral or unethical behavior. Others burn out from financial pressures, constant criticism, and lack of guidance and support. Can we do anything to help?

Some answers are found in today's lesson. As we consider Paul's advice to Timothy, we may realize that things haven't really changed that much. Ministry was in crisis in their day too! Young Timothy was facing pressures that threatened to overwhelm him and destroy his ministry. Paul, as his father in the faith and mentor in ministry, understood the danger. In today's text Paul speaks frankly and boldly about what it takes to succeed in ministry in the long term.

B. LESSON BACKGROUND

While 2 Timothy is difficult to date exactly, we usually understand it to have been written by Paul while he was imprisoned in Rome. This was his second Roman imprisonment, not where we find him at the end of the book of Acts. Tradition tells us that Paul was released from that first imprisonment, perhaps because his accusers from Judea never arrived to present their case.

DEVOTIONAL READING:
PSALM 119:9-16

BACKGROUND SCRIPTURE:
2 TIMOTHY 3, 4

PRINTED TEXT:
2 TIMOTHY 3:10–4:8

LESSON AIMS

After participating in this lesson, each student will be able to:

1. List some examples that Paul set as Timothy's mentor.

2. Explain how godly mentoring works and why it's important.

3. Take specific steps to have a mentor or be a mentor to someone.

WHAT DO YOU THINK?

How can we reverse the present vocational ministry crisis? Be specific!

KEY VERSE

But as for you, continue in what you have learned and have become convinced of, because you know those from whom you learned it.
—2 Timothy 3:14

Feb
19

Paul probably returned to Rome in about A.D. 65 or 66. He apparently was caught up in the persecutions by Emperor Nero while there. This second imprisonment would have been relatively brief, ending with Paul's execution in A.D. 66 or 67. This was when he wrote to Timothy a second time. Paul now had given up all hope of release and expected to be put to death (2 Timothy 4:6). His only hope of seeing Timothy again was dependent upon Timothy's coming to Rome (2 Timothy 4:9). We don't know if Timothy made the trip or not. But we do have Paul's letter to him.

I. PAUL'S GRIT IN MINISTRY (2 TIMOTHY 3:10-13)

A. HIS CORE VALUES (v. 10)

10. You, however, know all about my teaching, my way of life, my purpose, faith, patience, love, endurance,

In laying out his ministry before Timothy, Paul gives a list of characteristics. Some today would identify these characteristics as Paul's core values—the guiding principles by which he is identified. While the items in this list are well known to Timothy, the terms are significant and merit our attention.

By *my teaching* Paul means all the teaching that he has presented consistently throughout his ministry. For Paul this teaching is always in harmony with Scripture (see 1 Corinthians 15:3, 4). This teaching is always consistent with what Jesus taught (Acts 20:35). Paul's teachings could tackle heady theological issues (see Philippians 2:5-11) or be very practical (see 2 Thessalonians 3:10). Paul's *way of life* is his public and private behavior, which is in harmony with what he teaches. Paul never implies, "Do what I say, not as I do." He always demands, "Judge my teaching by my actions."

Paul's *purpose* is his fundamental goal in life. It implies a persistent plan that guides one's actions as used in God's design (see Romans 8:28). That goal for Paul is to be used by God to preach the gospel.

The *faith* of which Paul speaks is more than the sum total of his doctrine. It is Paul's ongoing drive to answer the call of God, despite many reasons to abandon this calling. This is coupled with Paul's *patience*. Paul strives faithfully and doggedly toward the goal that is not visible to his earthly eyes. He does so without losing heart or giving up (see 2 Corinthians 4:1; Galatians 6:9). His patience has lasted a lifetime.

All of Paul's actions are characterized by *love*. This is unselfishness. He always has wanted the best for his children in the faith with little regard for himself. Finally, Timothy is advised to remember Paul's *endurance*. Paul runs the race until the end. He never retires from ministry (2 Timothy 4:7).

B. HIS PERSECUTIONS (vv. 11, 12)

11, 12. . . . persecutions, sufferings—what kinds of things happened to me in Antioch, Iconium and Lystra, the persecutions I endured. Yet the Lord rescued me from all of them. In fact, everyone who wants to live a godly life in Christ Jesus will be persecuted,

Paul also reminds Timothy of some things that were not Paul's choice: the constant physical traumas he suffered in ministry. He was beaten up. In Timothy's hometown of *Lystra*, Paul's Jewish opponents stoned him and left him for dead (Acts 14:19). It is likely that this caused permanent damage to his body that left him somewhat disabled even after healing. Yet Paul does not regret this. From it he draws out a simple truism for ministry: In our world, you *will be persecuted* for godly living.

WHAT DO YOU THINK?

Some propose greater use of accountability partners as a way of solving the present vocational ministry crisis. Others say greater use of mentors would be better. What's the difference and why is it important?

HOW TO SAY IT

Antioch. AN-tee-ock.
Corinthians. Ko-RIN-thee-unz.
Galatians. Guh-LAY-shunz.
Iconium. Eye-KO-nee-um.
Lystra. LISS-truh.
Philippians. Fih-LIP-ee-unz.

Without doubt, godly living is at best an unnoticed lifestyle. At worst, it is ridiculed and punished. Why is this? The reason is that those of the world do not submit to the lordship of Jesus, and naturally they feel threatened by those who do. We should note that by *live a godly life in Christ Jesus,* Paul is not speaking of the belligerent, defiant "standing up for what's right" attitude that some Christians seem to take so much pleasure in today. He is talking about the quiet, simple life that is patterned after Jesus (compare 1 Thessalonians 4:11).

C. HIS OPPONENTS (v. 13)

13. . . . while evil men and impostors will go from bad to worse, deceiving and being deceived.

Paul's observations here could be drawn from any century of human history. *Evil* and sin rarely diminish in our world. They seem to grow in intensity on a daily basis. The word *imposters* refers to those who are like false miracle workers, driving their duped followers to new depths of evil.

Paul gives the underlying cause of all of this: those who are *deceiving* are themselves *deceived.* One day there will be no more possibility of deception, for all spiritual fraud will be exposed. Everyone will bow in reverence to the lordship of Jesus (Philippians 2:10, 11). That doesn't mean that everyone will accept Jesus as Savior. Rather, it means that people will have no choice but to acknowledge the truth about Jesus.

II. TIMOTHY'S EXPERIENCE IN LEARNING (2 TIMOTHY 3:14-17)

A. LEARNING FROM MENTORS (vv. 14, 15)

14, 15. But as for you, continue in what you have learned and have become convinced of, because you know those from whom you learned it, and how from infancy you have known the holy Scriptures, which are able to make you wise for salvation through faith in Christ Jesus.

As time moves on, Timothy probably will outlive his older teachers. Without their presence, what will sustain him then? Paul offers him two pillars of faith strength: the credibility of the lives of his teachers and the foundation of *the holy Scriptures.*

Many parents seek to give their children future advantages through specialized education. This may be music lessons, computer classes, foreign language instruction, or private schools. Yet true success in life will never depend upon such knowledge. There is no more important source of learning than the Bible. A parent who helps his or her children hide God's Word in their hearts (Psalm 119:11) has given them sustaining, life-giving values that never will go out of date.

Paul gives a theological reason for this: Scripture can make us *wise for salvation.* But this does not happen automatically or accidentally. People find salvation in the Bible only through faith in Jesus. Outside of that faith, the Bible will seem as myths, religious stories, and optional moral teachings. With faith, we meet Jesus and recognize him as Lord and Savior. With faith, we understand God's plan to save us from the eternal death that our sin has earned.

B. LEARNING FROM SCRIPTURE (vv. 16, 17)

16, 17. All Scripture is God-breathed and is useful for teaching, rebuking, correcting and training in righteousness, so that the man of God may be thoroughly equipped for every good work.

This is the most important text in the Bible concerning the nature of the Bible itself. It should be admitted that Paul has our Old Testament in mind as he

Visual for Lessons 8 and 12.
Point to this visual as you discuss how the Bible is our pathway to greater godliness.

speaks of *all Scripture*. This is because the New Testament is not yet compiled and some of its books are not even in existence as Paul writes. Even so, the principles hold for our entire Bible today.

Paul outlines three major reasons why Scripture must be held in high esteem by any Christian. First, it *is God-breathed*. When God breathes into something, he gives it life (see Genesis 2:7). When God inspires Scripture, he makes it alive. It becomes a living, active, powerful Word (see Hebrews 4:12).

Second, Scripture is *useful*. Think of its uses! It may be used for *teaching, rebuking* (pointing out wrong behavior), *correcting* (showing the way to right behavior), and *training in righteousness* (training to be godly).

Third, Scripture is a complete resource to bring believers to proficiency for ministry and life. We don't need to explore the writings of Buddhists or Muslims in order to learn how to live. Books on how to be successful in business do not tell Christians how to be Christian. The Bible has everything we need for that; we can (and do) spend our entire lifetimes just living up to its standards.

READ THE OWNER'S MANUAL!

Very rarely do I buy a new car. The high price and the deep depreciation after driving the car off the lot make it seem like a waste of good money. So I buy used cars. But one thing that always bothers me about doing that is that, more times than not, the owner's manual is missing.

It's hard to understand why someone would remove the manual from the car. What good is an owner's manual sitting on a coffee table or in a closet at home? You need the manual with the car to answer questions as they arise. But for some reason, people don't return them to their rightful place in the car's glove box.

Unfortunately for many Christians, the owner's manual—the Bible—is often missing. It is missing from both their hands and hearts. Some churches regularly put Scripture texts on an overhead projection system or print them in a program. This can add to the problem of people neglecting their own time in the Word.

Use of preprinted texts on PowerPoint® slides or in programs is not all wrong, of course. But preachers and teachers can encourage the people to turn to a passage of Scripture and read along during the course of a sermon or lesson. Biblical illiteracy is rampant. This is a starting point for curing this problem.   —A. E. A.

III. TIMOTHY'S CHARGE FROM PAUL (2 TIMOTHY 4:1-8)

A. ULTIMATE EVALUATION OF AN EVANGELIST (v. 1)

1. In the presence of God and of Christ Jesus, who will judge the living and the dead, and in view of his appearing and his kingdom, I give you this charge:

Elsewhere Paul teaches that Jesus is not only Savior but also judge (Acts 17:31). Jesus' first coming was to bring salvation, not judgment (John 12:47). But his second coming will be to render verdicts on all, both *the living and the dead*. Christians should never fear for the loss of their salvation. Instead, all Christians must remember that there is an ongoing, eternal evaluation being made of their ministries.

B. TIRELESS TASK OF AN EVANGELIST (vv. 2-4)

2-4. . . . Preach the Word; be prepared in season and out of season; correct, rebuke and encourage —with great patience and careful instruction. For the time will come when men will not put up with sound doctrine. Instead, to suit their own desires, they will gather around them a great number of teachers to say what their itching ears want to hear. They will turn their ears away from the truth and turn aside to myths.

WHAT DO YOU THINK?

Someone says, "Since only the Bible is inspired by God, we don't need commentaries to muddy the water and bring in people's opinions." How do you respond?

DAILY BIBLE READINGS

Monday, Feb. 13—Treasure God's Word in Your Heart (Psalm 119:9-16)

Tuesday, Feb. 14—Turn Your Heart to God's Statutes (Psalm 119:33-40)

Wednesday, Feb. 15—An Example to Imitate (2 Thessalonians 3:6-13)

Thursday, Feb. 16—Avoid Godless People (2 Timothy 3:1-9)

Friday, Feb. 17—Continue in the Things You Have Learned (2 Timothy 3:10-17)

Saturday, Feb. 18—Carry Out Your Ministry Fully (2 Timothy 4:1-8)

Sunday, Feb. 19—Final Instructions (2 Timothy 4:9-22)

The number one task of the preacher is the ministry of *the Word.* It must be preached faithfully whether it is popular or unpopular, whether it is received gladly or soundly rejected. Notice that there is a great deal of overlap between what Timothy is to do and the list of the Bible's uses in 2 Timothy 3:16, above.

Alas, much preaching today has little to do with the Bible. We hear sermons on social causes, self-help issues, or theological speculations. While entertaining, such preaching has little value in the long run. If preachers wrestle with Scripture deeply, their preaching will be of lasting consequence to their hearers. The Bible text must first be read carefully, then understood fully, then believed deeply, then proclaimed boldly. Preaching the great doctrines of the Bible will never go out of style and never needs an apology.

C. HARD WORK OF AN EVANGELIST (v. 5)

5. But you, keep your head in all situations, endure hardship, do the work of an evangelist, discharge all the duties of your ministry.

Being a minister is hard work! God does not reward laziness in *ministry,* although there are lazy ministers. God does not bless slothfulness in ministry, although there are sloppy, disorganized ministers. God wants ministers who are attentive, who will put up with discomfort, all for the opportunity to *do the work of an evangelist.*

There is some disagreement as to whether or not *evangelist* is a church office parallel to elder or deacon (compare Acts 21:8). The term means "gospel preacher," therefore the work of an evangelist is preaching the gospel (see 2 Timothy 4:2, "preach the Word"). The word *evangelist* does not carry the idea of having authority over elders. It makes no sense to say, "I preach the gospel, therefore I get to boss the elders around."

Preaching the gospel always must come first in the many tasks of ministry. Without it, Timothy has no hope of fulfilling his calling.

IT'S NOT A PRETTY PICTURE

In a practical ministry course in Bible college, the professor warned the students that things did not always go just right in the work of the ministry. Heartaches, frustrations, and conflicts would arise. Sometimes these would come in droves.

These students had spent much time complaining about the pressures of school and how time seemed so fleeting. They were looking forward to getting out of school so their time would be their own time without those pressures. Then the professor shared notes from recent graduates who were working in full-time ministry. Note after note spoke of the time pressures. One who had complained loudly during school said that time pressures at school did not even come close to equaling those in the ministry.

Some would say that these warnings should not be shared with young people who are excited about going into ministry. Yet as Paul sought to prepare Timothy for the continual work of ministry, he reminded him that those who live for God would suffer. Jesus, in training his disciples for their work, warned them that they would go forth as sheep among wolves (Matthew 10:16).

Care should be taken to help people understand what a call to commitment in Christ involves. The caution is in general for all who would make their initial commitment to Christ and in particular for those thinking of entering full-time ministry. There are eternal benefits, but with these come the trials. Being open about this up front can prepare new Christians—and new preachers—for what lies ahead. But we also stand with Paul in affirming that "it's worth it!" (See Romans 8:18.)

—A. E. A.

WHAT DO YOU THINK?

Which style of preaching is best? Which is the worst? Why?

WHAT DO YOU THINK?

Should specific *expectations be included in ministerial job descriptions? Or do the general expectations of 2 Timothy 4:2-5 give us all the job description that ministers need? Defend your answer.*

D. FINAL REWARD OF AN EVANGELIST (vv. 6-8)

6-8. For I am already being poured out like a drink offering, and the time has come for my departure. I have fought the good fight, I have finished the race, I have kept the faith. Now there is in store for me the crown of righteousness, which the Lord, the righteous Judge, will award to me on that day—and not only to me, but also to all who have longed for his appearing.

Paul does not write these things to give himself a pat on the back. He writes them to encourage Timothy in his discouraging times of ministry. Paul can die with no regrets. He knows the *fight* is nearly over; the *race* is nearing the finish line. He will be judged by Jesus, but he can face this judgment without fear. His prize will not be punishment but reward: *the crown of righteousness*, which is the reward of eternal life (see James 1:12; Revelation 2:10).

Paul is not speaking of crown in the sense of a headpiece that signifies royalty. In the ancient Greek world, the type of crown at issue here is given to the victor in athletic competitions (like the Olympic games). Such a crown is symbolic, but it carries great prestige and honor. It is something that athletes train their entire lives to win. Paul hopes that his influence on Timothy, even as death approaches, will encourage the young evangelist to strive for this crown of righteousness as he has.

CONCLUSION

There is a church in my area that has a reputation for chewing up ministers. What surprises me most is not that this church does this, but that it is able to find anyone to come and be its preacher! Churches earn reputations (as do ministers), and these are often very difficult to overcome. Maybe you know a church like this—a church with sharp-tongued evaluators and unrelenting criticism. Maybe your church is like this. Maybe you have experienced a parade of ministers, all of them run off because of perceived laziness, stubbornness, or inadequate preaching.

There is another church in my area that has a reputation for nurturing young people into full-time ministry. This church has produced dozens of ministers from within its own ranks. It has patiently trained other ministerial greenhorns and then released them to serve. It is not a big church, but its impact is felt around the world.

Some churches are consumers of ministers, and others are producers. Which kind of church is yours?

One thing that separates these churches is an attitude of gentle mentoring. At the first church, ministers are expected to fail and their critics wait eagerly. At the second church, ministers are allowed to fail, and leaders are there to pick them up and help them learn from their mistakes. The hapless ministers of the first church have no one within the congregation whom they feel they can trust or talk to. The fortunate ministers of the second church have leaders who befriend and encourage them from day one.

Now think of your minister (or one of them). Is this individual (as seen through human eyes) a pathetic, hopeless kind of person who seemingly does not belong in ministry? Maybe. Are you willing to risk yourself to speak sincere words of encouragement, to look out for his welfare, to pay loving attention to his family? Are you willing to allow for blunders and push him for excellence and faithfulness? Are you willing to give him opportunities for further education in the richness of God's Word? Do you pray for him daily? If so, you have begun to catch the vision that Paul has presented in today's lesson.

Discovery Learning

This page contains an alternative lesson plan emphasizing learning activities. Classes desiring such student involvement will find these suggestions helpful. The next page is a reproducible activity page to further enhance discovery learning.

LEARNING GOALS

After participating in this lesson, each student will be able to:

1. List some examples that Paul set as Timothy's mentor.

2. Explain how godly mentoring works and why it's important.

3. Take specific steps to have a mentor or be a mentor to someone.

INTO THE LESSON

Before the lesson, make a brief video of one or more of your church ministers speaking. The purpose of the video is to provide examples of how mentoring may be helpful to a minister or to any believer in Jesus. Ask the minister to open the video by completing the statement below. Then the minister is to share an example of someone who was (or is) an encourager or mentor.

The minister will begin with this statement: "Ministry is filled with joy. It is also packed with frustration and hurt. I am so thankful for people who have provided encouragement to me and who have been examples as I serve the Lord. One of those people was (or is) . . ."

Before playing the video, open the class by mentioning the alarming statistics about evangelical ministers as cited in today's lesson Introduction. Then play the video you have recorded. Make the transition to Bible study by explaining that mentoring is guidance of a less experienced person by someone with more wisdom. Say, "Mentoring has been a wonderful blessing to some in our churches. Today's text not only encourages mature believers to become mentors for younger believers but also gives clues to ways we can do this effectively."

INTO THE WORD

Say, "We will be looking at today's printed text with two sets of eyes. One set of eyes will focus on lessons about mentoring ministers. The other set will seek to discover how to mentor any believer."

The following activity may be done in small groups or by the entire class. Print the following instructions and questions to be distributed to the entire class or to small-group leaders.

Focus #1: Mentoring Ministers. Read 2 Timothy 3:10–4:8 and answer the following:

a. What does this text imply the primary task of a minister or senior minister to be? *(4:1, 2)*

b. What are a few other tasks given to these church leaders?

c. What are some personal traits or qualities the minister should cultivate?

d. Paul and Timothy faced problems in ministry. What were a few of those challenges?

Focus #2: Mentoring Other Believers. Read 2 Timothy 3:10–4:8 and answer the following questions. We are looking for principles or tips on how to mentor other believers effectively.

a. What clues do you find in this text about when or in what circumstances mentoring or encouragement would be helpful?

b. What are the goals for mentoring believers?

c. What clues are there about how to be a mentor? Add to that list other methods you think may work in today's church.

d. When should you seek out someone to be a mentor to you?

Allow groups (if used) to present their findings. Make the transition to application by reminding everyone that there are two lessons to apply in this passage: helping young ministers in addition to mentoring young believers.

INTO LIFE

Next, do both of the activities below.

Activity #1. Display a poster board with the heading "I commit myself to becoming a mentor to another believer." Then say, "This is an opportunity to commit to following Paul's model as a mentor. But who should take the initiative in forming a mentoring relationship, the mentor or the one being mentored? Why?"

After discussion, offer the chance to sign the poster after class. Leave the poster up for a few weeks to allow others to sign up after having a chance to think it over.

Activity #2. Write a note to a minister. The notes may express thanks, promise continuing prayer support, etc. Distribute inexpensive note cards and envelopes for this task. Play soft music while people write. If there is not enough time, ask students to take the cards home for completion. Encourage use of pen and paper rather than e-mail. (You can substitute the "Joys and Challenge" exercise on the reproducible page for this activity.)

Joys and Challenges

Read Paul's note to Timothy in 2 Timothy 3:10–4:8. This text is packed with Paul's joys and challenges in ministry as he encourages young Timothy. In these verses we find clues to understanding our ministerial staff in today's church.

Preacher's Perks

Ministry is packed with joy. Whether you serve adults, youth, or children, there are blessings unique to ministry. List some of those blessings as implied in today's text.

Now add other blessings you would consider a joy to today's minister.

Ministerial Madness

Ministry also has many frustrations and burdens. List some of those burdens or challenges as implied in today's text.

Now add other issues you think would be especially challenging or burdensome for today's minister.

Encouragement Needed!

List at least three creative ways you could encourage one or more of the ministers on your staff. Then circle at least one of these ideas that you will do for that person(s).

1.

2.

3.

LIVE AND TEACH THE TRUTH

LESSON 13

WHY TEACH THIS LESSON

High school or college teachers in your class today will be familiar with what is sometimes called "senior syndrome" or "senioritis." This is a malaise that afflicts many students who are in the final months of their last year in school. The primary symptoms are an inability to concentrate on studies, a failure to complete assignments, and wishing that graduation day would arrive more quickly. A certain weariness with classroom study, or even an "I've already learned enough" mind-set, may be part of the syndrome.

Church members, for their part, sometimes reach a point where they feel they biblically "know it all"—or at least know enough to get by spiritually. But like those high school or college seniors, after we "graduate" to our heavenly home we will realize that there was *much* more to learn! That's where our responsibility as teachers comes in. If we teach today's lesson with enthusiasm, if we make its truths winsome and the application to students' lives clear, we will have helped them avoid the Christian version of "senior syndrome." In certain cases, we may even snatch some "from the fire and save them" (Jude 23). What a privilege we have to teach this lesson!

INTRODUCTION

A. BIBLE LITERACY TODAY

On a recent late-night talk show, the host moved through the audience asking basic questions about the Bible. "Name one of the Ten Commandments," he requested. One brave soul answered, "God helps those who help themselves." The host then asked, "Name one of the 12 apostles." No one could. Finally, the audience was asked, "Name the Beatles." Quickly, the crowd responded, "John, Paul, George, and Ringo."

Knowledge of the Bible in historically "Christian nations" seems to be at an all-time low. A national survey published in 1989 revealed that less than half of those who identified themselves as Christians could name the original preacher of the Sermon on the Mount. In the 17 years that have passed since that survey, things certainly haven't gotten any better!

Those who teach in Bible colleges often swap stories about astounding Bible ignorance among incoming students. The most extreme example I can cite is the student who didn't understand the difference between the Old and New Testaments. Not only did this student not understand the difference, he didn't even know that such a division existed! And this was a young man whose family attended church regularly!

Yet the church has long taught that knowing Bible content and Bible principles is essential for godly living. Today's lesson reminds us that this is an ongoing, lifelong process. We never fully arrive at perfect knowledge of the Bible. Applying the Bible to our lives in an absolute manner is a goal that no one seems able reach. Education in godliness is crucial for young people, but older

DEVOTIONAL READING:
EPHESIANS 4:11-16
BACKGROUND SCRIPTURE:
TITUS 2
PRINTED TEXT:
TITUS 2

LESSON AIMS

After participating in this lesson, each student will be able to:

1. List the behaviors that must be taught to various age groups.

2. Explain why sound doctrine is necessary as a background to right behavior.

3. Participate in the teaching ministry of the church as both a learner and a teacher.

KEY VERSES

In everything set them an example by doing what is good. In your teaching show integrity, seriousness and soundness of speech that cannot be condemned, so that those who oppose you may be ashamed because they have nothing bad to say about us. —Titus 2:7, 8

Feb
26

people can gain from it too. Christians are called to be both teachers and learners of the Word.

B. LESSON BACKGROUND

The book of Titus involves events after the close of the book of Acts, but we have no exact knowledge of the sequence. Paul apparently was released from his imprisonment in Rome (where we leave him at the end of Acts), and he did more traveling. One place he visited was the island of Crete, where he evangelized successfully and started churches. It is likely, however, that the gospel already had reached Crete many years earlier through unnamed believers (see Acts 2:11).

Paul was accompanied on Crete by one of his most trusted associates, Titus. Titus was a Gentile believer (Galatians 2:3). Titus is not mentioned in the book of Acts, but he figures prominently in the letters of Paul. In 2 Corinthians he is named (in Greek) nine times (example: 2 Corinthians 8:23). Paul wrote his letter, in about A.D. 65, to Titus after departing from the island. Paul had left Titus behind to correct a chaotic situation in the Cretan churches. Titus especially needed to get an eldership in place in each congregation (Titus 1:5).

Crete was famous in antiquity as a source of culture and religion. The Cretan people, however, were not highly esteemed in the Roman world. In Titus 1:12, Paul quotes a native Cretan "prophet" who describes his own people as "always liars, evil brutes, lazy gluttons." While Paul does not name this person, he can be identified as Epimenides, a famous Cretan author who lived about 600 B.C. This statement has been called the Cretan Paradox, because if all Cretans are liars, and Epimenides was a Cretan, then was he lying when he made the statement?

Yet assuming some truth to that statement (as Paul himself claims in Titus 1:13), can you imagine trying to bring order to a church made up of lying, brutal, pleasure-seekers? You couldn't trust their word. You would be afraid they might turn on you. You would feel pressure to entertain and feed them. This sounds surprisingly contemporary!

Part of Paul's solution to this difficult situation is to institute an ongoing educational program within the congregation to train the believers in godliness (see Titus 1:1). Today's lesson, Titus 2, is the heart of this instructional program. This is the nitty-gritty of helping believers mature into godly men and women.

I. TEACHING SOUND DOCTRINE (TITUS 2:1)

1. *You must teach what is in accord with sound doctrine.*

The word translated *sound* is a medical term from which we get our English word *hygiene.* We could say that Paul wants healthy *doctrine.* Such teaching helps us maintain spiritual health.

There are many in churches today who suffer from general spiritual malaise, from a sickness of the soul. They live as victims of church conflicts, in fear that personal problems will be made public, or with serious doubts about the validity of their faith. Spiritual healing ultimately comes from God (Romans 8:26). Spiritual health may be achieved by serious, rigorous training in the ways of godliness.

II. TEACHING SENIOR MEMBERS (TITUS 2:2, 3)

A. TEACHING OLDER MEN (v. 2)

2. *Teach the older men to be temperate, worthy of respect, self-controlled, and sound in faith, in love and in endurance.*

Paul begins to speak about the groups that make up the Cretan churches. Everyone is included, but he begins with *the older men.* Then he works his way

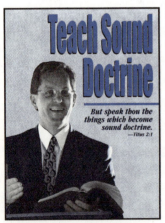

Teach Sound Doctrine

But speak thou the things which become sound doctrine.
—Titus 2:1

Visual for Lesson 13. *Post this visual and ask "What could happen to the church if this imperative is ignored?"*

down the social pecking order of the ancient world. Older men and women generally are those whose children (if they have any) are grown.

Paul asks Titus to give attention to four specific areas for the older men. First, they are reminded to be *temperate*. This implies that some of the older men, who should be church leaders, have drinking problems. Alcoholism among seniors is a hidden problem today. We may think that would never happen in my church, but it can and does. The men are expected to lead with clear and sober minds, not through an alcoholic haze.

Second, Paul demands that the older men be *worthy of respect*. While it is good for older people to remain "young at heart," it is important that they present an example that brings respect, not derision.

Third, Paul points out that older men need to be *self-controlled*. Our world today seems to encourage impulsiveness. It lionizes those who are the most conspicuous consumers. Self-control, however, is essential in church leaders, who are called to make decisions with far-reaching implications.

Fourth, Paul wants older men to be *sound* (or "healthy") in three areas: *faith, love,* and *endurance*. Churches need leaders who have a tested, deep faith, and who abound in patient, enduring love for those less mature than they. Yet in many churches the older leaders are crabby, sharp tongued, and in a state of constant complaining. Paul's guidelines still speak today.

B. TEACHING OLDER WOMEN (v. 3)

3. Likewise, teach the older women to be reverent in the way they live, not to be slanderers or addicted to much wine, but to teach what is good.

Likewise, *the older women* are to lead by example *in the way they live*. They are to act their age, a lifestyle one would expect from mature believers. Paul will give a specific rationale for this in verse 4: the older women are to be teachers of the younger women. The young are always looking for examples. Isn't it better if the younger women find examples of strong, confident women in their churches and thereby avoid the horrid examples of our celebrity-worshiping media world?

For Paul, two things characterize mature behavior: what you say and how much you drink. The older women are to be leaders in the way they talk about others. They should not be *slanderers,* fabricating or perpetuating rumors that damage reputations. A war of words often leaves no winners, only casualties.

As with the older men, the women must not give in to heavy drinking. Ancient society was comfortable with drinking diluted wine at meals in small amounts. This often amounted to little more than a flavored beverage and did not cause drunkenness. Young women hardly would be attracted to the life example of an older woman who spent most of her day intoxicated! It is a life of good behavior that allows a platform for the older women *to teach what is good*, especially to the younger women.

III. TEACHING YOUNGER MEMBERS (TITUS 2:4-10)

A. TEACHING YOUNGER WOMEN (vv. 4, 5)

4, 5. Then they can train the younger women to love their husbands and children, to be self-controlled and pure, to be busy at home, to be kind, and to be subject to their husbands, so that no one will malign the word of God.

Paul knows that the most effective teachers of *young women* are older women. He does not expect Titus to be their primary teacher in one-on-one situations. A young minister who spends much time with the young women of the church is asking for disaster. Paul's way is the better way.

The model for a young wife and mother that Paul presents may not fit our modern lifestyles exactly. But the foundational principles are sound. The young mother has the huge responsibility of ensuring that the home is a happy, secure place. She does this by loving her children and husband dearly, and by staying chaste or sexually pure at all times. The pressures of life bombard us outside the home. At home we need a refuge.

IT'S TIME TO GROW UP

Proverbs 16:31 says, "Gray hair is a crown of splendor." With the graying of hair comes growth and maturity, or at least that's the ideal. In that sense, gray hair is something to be honored. But you would not think that to be the case given all the hair-care products to counteract the graying process! The illusion is that taking away the gray counteracts aging. Do it and stay young!

Trying to be what one is not can create problems. Young men want to have the perks that go with increased age. Older men buy sports cars and have illicit affairs with younger women in order to create the illusion of being "young again." Such is the pattern of the world.

The church, however, must be different. Younger people don't need the older people as "pals" who try to be youthful in clothing, musical tastes, etc. The younger people need examples and mentors! The challenge is for those who are older to bring the young toward spiritual maturity. But when older people don't realize this responsibility, the result is immature churches.

Faith is passed on to succeeding generations by those who are older and, hopefully, more spiritually wise. The church needs those whose spiritual maturity matches or outpaces their maturity in years. Set a goal to be one of those.—A. E. A.

B. TEACHING YOUNGER MEN (vv. 6-8)

6-8. Similarly, encourage the young men to be self-controlled. In everything set them an example by doing what is good. In your teaching show integrity, seriousness and soundness of speech that cannot be condemned, so that those who oppose you may be ashamed because they have nothing bad to say about us.

Titus has an obligation to instruct the older men and women in godliness. The older women are to be the teachers of the younger women. *The young men,* though, are to be taught by Titus. They will be observing, of course, the example of his life. Paul describes this under the broad category of *doing what is good.*

People are looking for consistency in leaders, aren't they? They expect teachers to measure up to what they teach. If we teach others to live by faith, our lives should have evidence of living confidently for Jesus. If we teach the necessity of sacrificial giving, we should be leaders in contributing our time and money. If we teach the importance of godly speech, we should guard our words and not be found using questionable language or slander. Sin of church leaders made public has a huge impact on those who are new believers (and old).

It has been said that the greatest stumbling block for young people in the church is perceived hypocrisy of the leaders. Jesus said that if our hypocrisy causes the children of the flock to sin and fall away, it would be better to have a great stone tied to our necks and be drowned in the depths of the ocean (Mark 9:42). Paul then lays a great responsibility at the door of Titus. He is to live in such a way that his observers cannot doubt his commitment to godliness.

C. TEACHING SLAVES (vv. 9, 10)

9, 10. Teach slaves to be subject to their masters in everything, to try to please them, not to talk back to them, and not to steal from them, but to show that they can be fully trusted, so that in every way they will make the teaching about God our Savior attractive.

It is dangerous to apply this passage to anything in our modern situation, because we who live in Western democracies no longer have the institution of slavery that was widespread in the Roman world. Yet those of us who are employees and work for a living can find some principles here. We should be good employees so that our work habits show that we are serving a higher master. We should work diligently, not talking back or stealing from our employer. We are respectful. Again, there is the possibility that our actions are being monitored carefully by someone who reaches conclusions about Jesus by viewing us.

IV. TRAINING A DISTINCT PEOPLE (TITUS 2:11-15)

A. LIVING OUR SALVATION (vv. 11, 12)

11, 12. For the grace of God that brings salvation has appeared to all men. It teaches us to say "No" to ungodliness and worldly passions, and to live self-controlled, upright and godly lives in this present age,

Paul sums up all of this teaching by saying that we should live as saved people. God did not save us to continue to wallow in the filth of sin. God saves us *from* sin.

Forgiveness is also deliverance. Paul knows all too well that in his day godly living goes against the grain. Nothing is really different in that regard today. We are called to live in contrast to the values of *this present age,* which are controlled by *worldly passions*—namely, self-interest, self-gratification, and general selfishness.

WHERE ARE YOU NOW, REALLY?

The United States Army adopted a slogan a few years ago that tempted potential recruits to sign up and become "An Army of One." The statement is a contradiction in terms if you think about it. An army, by definition, is a large, organized body of soldiers. The recruiting idea thus seems to be something like, "Leave the civilian world behind as you come and join our team where individuality is more important than teamwork." Whew!

A somewhat similar mix-up of concepts is also found in the pages of Christian history. Centuries ago, some Christians sought to separate themselves from "the world" by joining together with others who wanted to do the same. These individuals were known as monks; this comes from the Greek *monos,* meaning "alone" or "solitary." These monks lived together in monasteries, which has the meaning of "to live alone"!

Yet Christians never were called to live alone, separated from the culture, whether individually or as a group. Christians live in this present world as active participants in culture and society (compare 1 Corinthians 5:10). Jesus, as he prayed for his followers, said to the Father, "My prayer is not that you take them out of the world but that you protect them from the evil one" (John 17:15).

Churches, along with individual Christians, constantly must find ways in which to engage this present world in order to be an influence of godliness. In this way we live in this world but not of this world until Christ returns. —A. E. A.

B. WAITING FOR JESUS (vv. 13, 14)

13, 14. . . . while we wait for the blessed hope—the glorious appearing of our great God and Savior, Jesus Christ, who gave himself for us to redeem us from all wickedness and to purify for himself a people that are his very own, eager to do what is good.

HOW TO SAY IT

Cretan. CREE-tun.
Crete. Creet.
Ephesians. Ee-FEE-zhunz.
Epimenides. Ep-ih-MEN-ih-deez.
Titus. TY-tus.

PRAYER

Holy God our Father, renew our love for your mighty Bible. May we dedicate ourselves more fully to learning your Word and to teaching it faithfully to others. Help us set our priorities to include digging deeply into the Word of life. Please, we ask, continue to bless us as we let your Word transform us. We pray in the name of the living Word, your Son, Jesus Christ, amen.

Christ has saved us and purified us, or made us holy. Paul is confident that Jesus has not forgotten us. He will return and claim his possession, his bride, the church (Revelation 19:7, 8).

C. BEING ABOVE REPROACH (v. 15)

15. These, then, are the things you should teach. Encourage and rebuke with all authority. Do not let anyone despise you.

This concluding verse underlines the urgency of what Paul commands Titus to do. Titus must gain a hearing for what he is to say. Titus must exercise the *authority* he has from Paul and from the moral imperative that teaching godly behavior requires. Paul demands that Titus *not let anyone despise* him in this effort. Teaching how to live the godly life is an essential task of church leadership.

CONCLUSION

A. IS THE SUNDAY SCHOOL DEAD?

Many churches today have abandoned the traditional Sunday morning Bible school hour. In some cases, all efforts are concentrated on the worship service, which often has been expanded. An emphasis is put on fellowship groups that meet in homes for prayer and support. Is there any place for Sunday school today? Is there a place for regular, systematic instruction in godly living?

If you are using this lesson series, you have answered *yes* to at least the second question. While "delivery systems" may change over the years, there will always be a place for godly, dedicated teachers instructing children, young people, and older people in the ways of our Lord.

Such instruction should lift up the timeless principles found throughout Scripture. It should also study the lives of the godly men and women in the Bible who practiced these principles. It always should include a modeling of this lifestyle by the teacher. We cannot lead where we have not been or are unwilling to go. In this regard, not all are fit to be teachers (James 3:1).

I have never ministered with a church that had a surplus of teachers. Has God called you to this ministry? Are you willing to study his Word carefully, prepare lessons, and live up to the principles you teach? The responsibility is great, but the rewards are eternal.

B. LIFETIME LEARNERS

Do we ever progress to the point where the Bible has nothing left to teach us? Do we ever get to the place where we think we've heard it all before? The truth is that some people have spent decades in weekly Bible study, and the material may seem repetitive at times. However, some of the greatest scholars in the history of the church have never tired of studying the Bible.

John Locke (1632–1704) was one of the greatest thinkers of his day. He is credited with being the primary influence in the British Enlightenment, of finally overcoming the antiquated thinking of the medieval period. Locke's writings still influence people today. Some of his essays on government helped begin the era of democracy and end the era of kings and queens. Yet at the end of his life, Locke had some regrets. His was one of the most powerful minds in the history of the world, but he was not content. He once stated that if he had it all to do over again, he would spend more time studying the Bible and learning its truths.

The Bible as the Word of God is an inexhaustible source of wisdom, inspiration, and knowledge. These things are available for everyone who is willing to study it.

Discovery Learning

This page contains an alternative lesson plan emphasizing learning activities. Classes desiring such student involvement will find these suggestions helpful. The next page is a reproducible activity page to further enhance discovery learning.

LEARNING GOALS

After participating in this lesson, each student will be able to:

1. List some behaviors that must be taught to various age groups.

2. Explain why sound doctrine is necessary as a background to right behavior.

3. Participate in the teaching ministry of the church as both a learner and a teacher.

INTO THE LESSON

Display a banner that reads, "We Learn from Our (and Others') Misteaks!" (The irony of the misspelling should provoke laughter.) Begin by asking students to share incidents from their childhood years when an admired adult disappointed them by inappropriate conduct or words. This may be done in small groups.

Make the transition to Bible study by saying, "We may learn lessons from such experiences. We learn about disappointment, human imperfections, and the power of a model in behavior. Today's study teaches how believers in Christ are to behave in a world that watches."

INTO THE WORD

Use the Lesson Background to prepare and deliver a brief lecture on the problems and culture on Crete. Emphasize the challenges facing Titus.

Prior to class, prepare the following four signs and affix them in the corners of the room:

1. Senior Members (Titus 2:2-4)
2. Younger Members (Titus 2:4-8)
3. Lessons from Servanthood (Titus 2:9, 10)
4. His Very Own People (Titus 2:11-15)

Also prepare a task sheet with the following instructions for the study teams:

Team #1: Paul suggests some "behavior biggies" for older members of the church. List these on the poster board and discuss why these are so important in Christianity. Then list a few practical ways today's church can encourage these traits in its older adults.

Team #2: Paul suggests some "behavior biggies" for younger members of the church. List these on the poster board and discuss why these are so important in Christianity. Then list a few practical ways today's church can encourage these traits in its younger adults.

Team #3: While those who live in Western democracies no longer experience slavery in church or culture, we do learn lessons from this passage that can be applied to Christian employees. List the lessons you learn from this passage about Christian behavior in that regard. Why are these traits so important for believers?

Team #4: Verses 11-15 cite some "behavior biggies" for Christians living in a watching world. List these traits or qualities on the poster board. Discuss why these behaviors or traits are so important to us and to the kingdom of God.

Say, "We are going to discover behavioral traits and challenges that face Christians. Paul teaches us about older adults, younger adults, the church in general, and even lessons from slavery." Ask students to take chairs and move to one of the signs you've posted. In order to keep the groups somewhat balanced, you may place a limit on the number of people allowed for each task. Give each group a copy of the task sheet, a piece of poster board, and a marker.

After the groups reach conclusions, allow time for them to report their discoveries to the class as a whole. Then make the transition to application by saying, "These lists of behaviors or values are not complete. We could add many other values or characteristics that are important as people watch us living out our faith."

INTO LIFE

Ask the teams to turn their poster boards over and write the word *Christlike* vertically. The teams are to compose a prayer expressing the traits or behaviors suggested in today's text. Post the following example:

I am thankful, Lord, that

You · **C**all me to

Hear and obey the

t**R**uths of your Word.

I know my

Speech and

ac**T**ions will bring either

g**L**ory or dishonor to you.

I, therefore,

Know I must commit myself to be an

Example for your glory. Amen.

Follow this with the "Values into Life" exercise on the reproducible page as a take-home activity.

Values into Life

Paul emphasizes behaviors and values that Timothy should teach to the people on Crete. Read Titus 2 and find the behaviors and values listed. Then locate the underlined words in the word search puzzle.

Verse 2:
T_____
Self-C_____
Sound in _____
L_____
E_____

Verse 3:
R_____
Not S_____
G_____

Verse 4:
Love your H_____

Verse 5:
P_____
K_____

Verse 7:
E_____

Verses 7, 8:
I_____
S_____
S_____ of speech

Verse 10:
Not S_____
T_____

Verse 12:
Say "N___"
U_____
G_____ lives

Word List: controlled; endurance; example; faith; godly; good; husbands; integrity; kind; love; no; pure; reverent; seriousness; slanderers; soundness; steal; temperate; trusted; upright

R	F	A	I	T	H	G	O	D	L	Y	Z	W
I	C	O	N	T	R	O	L	L	E	D	L	T
T	M	V	T	A	L	O	V	E	R	U	P	V
A	H	H	E	E	N	D	U	R	A	N	C	E
Y	U	N	G	O	U	P	R	I	G	H	T	S
O	S	E	R	I	O	U	S	N	E	S	S	O
J	B	X	I	T	X	K	Q	F	E	D	I	U
D	A	A	T	R	E	V	E	R	E	N	T	N
I	N	M	Y	U	L	V	R	L	B	I	K	D
F	D	P	P	S	T	E	A	L	K	K	X	N
T	S	L	R	T	E	M	P	E	R	A	T	E
S	R	E	R	E	D	N	A	L	S	O	V	S
K	B	S	O	D	S	U	L	W	L	S	Q	S

Spring Quarter 2006

Living in and as God's Creation

Special Features

Lessons

About These Lessons

Those who live in technologically advanced countries are always on the lookout for "the next big thing" as yesterday's gadgets become boring. In the spiritual life, however, the next big thing comes to us ever new from a source in the ancient past: the wisdom in God's unchanging Word. This wisdom is priceless. It serves us into eternity. It is our subject this quarter.

Mar 5

Mar 12

Mar 19

Mar 26

Apr 2

Apr 9

Apr 16

Apr 23

Apr 30

May 7

May 14

May 21

May 28

Repair and Prepare

by J. Michael Shannon

The late Steve Allen told of a lady named Liz who had been hurt in an automobile accident. A lawyer came to visit her and said, "I've come to assist you in getting damages." Liz replied, "I got all the damages I want. What I need is repairs." This is true of many hurting people we come in contact with every day. The church in general and we in particular are to assist people in making repairs to their lives. The world we live in is imperfect. It is a mixture of great beauty and ugliness, of triumphs and tragedies. The lessons this quarter will help us deal with the damages and make the repairs.

Yet at the same time let us not overlook the repairs that we ourselves are in need of. These repairs begin when we remember that we are part of the fabric of God's creation even as we live within that creation. Even though we recognize that God is the author of all creation, we often still live at odds with creation. Part of God's repair for our lives is to learn how to live in this world that God has created. This quarter's lessons will help.

Our studies primarily examine parts of what is called the wisdom literature of the Old Testament. Such literature very often is poetic. Some of our selected passages from Job, Psalms, Proverbs, and Ecclesiastes are widely read, while others often are avoided. We will see why as we allow those texts to assist us in understanding and living in this world even as we prepare ourselves for the next.

MARCH

THE GLORY OF GOD'S CREATION

The first unit offers us selections from the psalms. This is one of the books most precious to us because of its poetic beauty and frequent frankness. The book of Psalms is the Hebrew hymn book. The chapters are separate songs that speak to a variety of situations. These songs sing of God's power, creativity, and mighty acts. When we reach the end of this unit, we will be puzzled that people could look at the world around them and not believe in God.

Lesson 1: God Made Us Special. This lesson from Psalm 8 emphasizes how human beings are a glorious act of God's creation. This has profound implications concerning how we view ourselves and how we view God.

Lesson 2: God Created Wonderful Things. This lesson from Psalm 104 examines the more traditional elements of God's created order. It helps us express a sense of awe concerning the one who could make such beauty.

Lesson 3: God Created and Knows Us. This Sunday features an examination of Psalm 139 as our attention turns to the character of the creator himself. How completely he knows us and is ever present in our lives! We may look at ourselves a bit differently at the end of this lesson, even with regard to our physical forms. We are God's crowning act of creation.

Lesson 4: Sing Praise to the Creator. The final session in this unit, taken from Psalm 145, celebrates the God of creation. As such, it leads us into acts of worship. We will learn that praise has inner and outer aspects: our feelings and our actions.

APRIL

LIVING WITH CREATION'S UNCERTAINTY

The lessons for April deal with material that is more difficult. How do we respond when the entire created order, even the creator himself, seems to be against us? Sometimes there appear to be no answers. Here we will deal with a problem that is age old, yet as current as this morning's newspaper: the problem of tragedy. For these lessons we will examine primarily Job and Ecclesiastes. Both books are rather dark. Both seem to yearn for answers. We will find answers by looking at selected New Testament passages from the Gospels of Mark and John.

The book of Job begins with a scene in Heaven. There Satan charges that Job loves God only because that man has had life so easy. Life then becomes anything *but* easy for Job! Much of the book then features an ongoing discussion between Job and his friends concerning why all Job's tragedies have happened. In the end Job does not get complete answers, but he does get an audience with God.

Ecclesiastes, for its part, is a book of musings about the meaning of life. Most of the book sets a despairing and rather hopeless tone. Nevertheless, by the end of the book we are drawn inevitably back to God.

Lesson 5: Responding to Tragedy. The first lesson in this unit, taken from chapters 1 through 3 of Job, show us why Job's testing happened in the first place. It also examines Job's feelings of grief.

Lesson 6: Searching for Hope. For Palm Sunday, we will look at selected verses from Job 14, 32, 34, and 37. These passages follow some of Job's discussions with his friends. Those friends accuse Job of not being as good as he says. Yet Job maintains his innocence. This lesson deals specifically with the longing for eternal life.

Lesson 7: God Gives Life. The Easter lesson begins in Job 38 and 42. But we finish by visiting the Gospel of Mark to see how the resurrection of Jesus comes to bear on the questions raised in Job. Job believed he had a redeemer. We now know him as Jesus of Nazareth.

Lesson 8: Finding Life's Meaning. This lesson has its foundation in Ecclesiastes 1. Since this Sunday takes us to the afterglow of Easter, our lesson also finds us in the Gospel of John and one of the postresurrection appearances of Jesus. The writer of Ecclesiastes wonders about a sense of purpose. This lesson shows how Jesus provides just what we need in that regard.

Lesson 9: Living in God's Time. The last lesson in this unit takes us back to Ecclesiastes. This time we're in chapter 3. There we will ponder the meaning of time and history in one of the most well-known, yet hard to decipher, passages in the Bible.

When we come to the end of this unit, we may breathe a bit of a sigh, because we have dealt with many of the most perplexing and difficult issues of life. Yet we hope to come out with a new perspective!

Think about the issue of perspective. When you look at a field of dandelions, you probably see just weeds. When Peter A. Gail looks at it, he sees lunch! Dr. Gail, an ethno-botanist who is called "the wizard of weeds," eats many dandelions every day. He claims that the dandelion is both healthy and flavorful. Much of our enthusiasm in life is related to our perspective, isn't it?

LESSONS IN LIVING

Our final unit of the quarter teaches us how to conduct our lives in this fallen world. For these lessons we draw from the book of Proverbs. Most of this book consists of a collection of wise sayings written by, collected by, and in honor of King Solomon.

Certain themes are discussed repeatedly in Proverbs. Specifically, wisdom, industry, self-control, honesty, and humility are encouraged. While the book of

Proverbs is part of the Old Testament's wisdom literature, it cannot magically provide wisdom. We must study these passages thoroughly, ask God's help earnestly, and apply them diligently. Wisdom is developed with God's blessing. Without that blessing all we have is the world's "whatever works" wisdom.

Lesson 10: Seek Wisdom. The first lesson in this unit focuses on selected verses from Proverbs 2 and 3. There wisdom and its acquisition are praised. The distinction between secular and spiritual wisdom is vital to know.

Lesson 11: Accept Wisdom's Invitation. This lesson from Proverbs 8 portrays wisdom as a person calling out for those who desire her. The fact that wisdom really is attainable is a great encouragement of this study.

Lesson 12: Follow the Path of Integrity. This session from Proverbs 11 explores the matter of integrity in work and personal life. Integrity carries spiritual rewards. Since integrity is important to God, it should be important to us as well.

Lesson 13: Living Out Wisdom. The final lesson in this quarter, taken from Proverbs 31, provides a profile of the honorable wife and mother. She is no shrinking violet! The ancient challenges are quite relevant to today. Men will gain wisdom as well as they explore ways to honor the godly and diligent women in their lives.

WISDOM CALLS!

Wisdom does indeed call, but not everyone answers. How sad to see so many settle for worldly "street smarts"! In his book *A Wee Bit of Irish Wisdom,* Jim Gallery records this old Irish blessing: "May you have the hindsight to know where you have been, the foresight to know where you are going, and the insight to know when you are going too far." May God grant you this blessing as well through this quarter's lessons.

Solomon **and** Jesus

Solomon	Jesus
Wisest on Earth	**Wiser than Solomon**
1 Kings 4:29-34	Luke 11:31
Life of Splendor and Self-Indulgence	**Life of Sorrow and Self-Denial**
1 Kings 11:3; Ecclesiastes 2:3-10	Isaiah 53:2-5
Built Earthly Temple	**Rebuilt Bodily Temple**
1 Kings 6	John 2:19-22
Accepted as King	**Hailed then Rejected as King**
1 Chronicles 29:22	John 12:13; 19:15
Embraced a Kingship	**Refused a Kingship**
1 Kings 1:30	John 6:15
Had Wisdom from God	**Was Wisdom from God**
1 Kings 4:29	1 Corinthians 1:30
Lost Focus; Sinned	**Stayed Focused; Never Sinned**
1 Kings 11	Hebrews 4:15; 1 Peter 2:22

Living in and as God's Creation

The Glory of God's Creation	Living with Creation's Uncertainty	Lessons in Living
God Made Us Special: Crowned with Honor *Psalm 8*	Responding to Tragedy: Loss and Grief *Job 1, 3*	Seek Wisdom: Path of Happiness *Proverbs 2, 3*
God Created Wonderful Things: Heaven and Earth *Psalm 104*	Searching for Hope: Change is Coming *Job 14, 32, 34, 37*	Accept Wisdom's Invitation: God's Delight *Proverbs 8*
God Created and Knows Us: Marvelous Works *Psalm 139*	God Gives Life: Resurrection *Job 38, 42* *Mark 16*	Follow the Path of Integrity: God's Right Way *Proverbs 11*
Sing Praise to the Creator: Worship *Psalm 145*	Finding Life's Meaning: Peace in God *Ecclesiastes 1* *John 20*	Living Out Wisdom: A Noble Woman *Proverbs 31*
	Living in God's Time: A Season for Everything *Ecclesiastes 3*	

Living in and as God's Creation
Unit 1: The Glory of God's Creation
(Lessons 1-4)

GOD MADE US SPECIAL

LESSON 1

WHY TEACH THIS LESSON?

The self-worth movement in modern American education had worthy motive. That motive was that each child is worth equal opportunity to learn all that he or she is capable of learning. What sensible person would gainsay that?

Unfortunately, abuses in the movement led some children to think of themselves as worthy of praise, worthy of promotion, worthy of privilege simply because of existence. "I am; therefore, praise me!" Effort? Doesn't matter. Achievement? Who cares? A similar scenario worked itself out in the Garden of Eden. When tempted with the possibility of becoming godlike, the first humans said *yes!* Satan knew the power of human vanity.

Yet if self-ism and me-ism are wrong, then where exactly do we fit into God's scheme? The psalmist of Psalm 8 asked that question, as every person must. What gives me worth? What am I worth to God? Today's study will encourage the humility of self-understanding, but it will also encourage the knowledge of being the crown of God's creation. Everyone needs to learn both.

INTRODUCTION

A. OUR BIG ROCKS

There is a standard object lesson for children that requires two jars of the same size, several large rocks, some gravel, and some sand. Into the first jar the teacher pours several cups of sand. Then the gravel is dumped in. Finally, the teacher asks the children, "Can we fit the rocks into this jar?" By then, there is no way that the rocks can possibly get into the jar.

In the second jar, the teacher begins with the rocks. Gravel is then gradually added, with care taken to distribute it throughout the jar. Finally, the sand is poured in. If done correctly, the jar easily contains all of the material, even though the same number of objects did not come close to fitting into the other jar.

The point of that object lesson for children is *prioritization*: take care of the big things first and the smaller things will fit into place. That is a lesson that many of us adults need to relearn as well!

Today we see that this is a vital part of Psalm 8's message for us. When our priorities are correct, everything fits together. Those universal priorities are quite straightforward, though that does not make them easy to accept. Most Christians understand intellectually that God is first. It is living out that reality, truly putting him in first place, that we struggle with. Saying that *God is Number 1* is easy. Most of us, though, can relate with the lament of the orchestra conductor who noted that the hardest position to fill in any symphony was the position of second fiddle.

B. LESSON BACKGROUND

King David, who lived about a thousand years before Christ, wrote Psalm 8. We are not entirely sure of its historical context; its address to "the director of music" is tantalizingly brief.

DEVOTIONAL READING:
GENESIS 1:26-31
BACKGROUND SCRIPTURE:
PSALM 8
PRINTED TEXT:
PSALM 8

LESSON AIMS

After participating in this lesson, each student will be able to:

1. Describe the position of human beings in creation.

2. Explain how knowledge of humanity's place in creation enhances his or her self-worth and gives life meaning.

3. Sing a song praising God as creator or complete a self-worth chart based on truths from the lesson.

KEY VERSE

What is man that you are mindful of him, the son of man that you care for him? You made him a little lower than the heavenly beings and crowned him with glory and honor.

—Psalm 8:4, 5

I. CREATOR PRAISE, PART 1 (PSALM 8:1, 2)

A. MAJESTIC NAME, REVEALED GLORY (v. 1)

1. *O LORD, our Lord,*
>   *how majestic is your name in all the earth!*
>   *You have set your glory*
>   *above the heavens.*

The psalms are the music of faith. Many are intended to be sung as part of worship. When sung they can express the heart of the individual worshiper and the collective heart of the community of believers. The psalms accomplish this by pointing in each of the directions we face while worshiping. The main direction is upward (toward God). But we also face inward (personal reflection), sideways (toward other worshipers), and outward (toward unbelievers and nonworshipers).

The opening of Psalm 8 is decisively upward toward God. One Christian writer has noted that even though God is your Father, he is not your "old man." We may want so much to have a personal relationship with God that we may lose sight of God's transcendence (that is, his "otherness"). God the redeemer is also God the creator. That means we are accountable to him, and not he to us. God is love—but that love in no way diminishes the fact that God is God and we are not.

Even so, when David writes *O Lord . . . how majestic,* he is not writing to appease an unknowable, distant tyrant. David is writing in delight of a knowable, personal God. David is in awe of the God whom he knows, the God who can be known, the God who wants to be known. His *name* is majestic *in all the earth* not only because of its power but also because of its "knowability." God is worth knowing because it is his presence that gives value to everything and everyone. God's excellent name makes the earth a better place because of the association. How could it be otherwise?

Even so, this close association should not cause us to ignore or minimize the power and majesty of God. We've all heard the old saying "familiarity breeds contempt," and there is a certain danger here. Our association with God does not mean that we are to see him as a pal or a buddy. It is his *glory* that is *above the heavens,* and not our own.

God has set his glory above the heavens because it is natural for him to do so. My son likes to jump and touch the ceiling simply because he can—it shows he is growing and is able to do something he couldn't before. By contrast, God places his glory in the highest place not merely because he is able to do so, but because there is nowhere else that is more appropriate. The fact that a seven-foot-tall basketball player can reach the top shelf surprises no one. That is an expression of the person's height—a natural by-product of his physical nature. The fact that God's glory is above the heavens is an expected result of his transcendence.

As awe-inspiring as that is, what is even more remarkable is the fact that Jesus "who, being in very nature God, did not consider equality with God something to be grasped, but made himself nothing, taking the very nature of a servant, being made in human likeness, and being found in appearance as a man, he humbled himself and became obedient to death—even death on a cross" (Philippians 2:6-8). The transcendent God not only has a name that is majestic in all the earth, he actually walked upon the earth—and more.

B. ORDAINED STRENGTH, STILLED ENEMY (v. 2)

2. *From the lips of children and infants*
>   *you have ordained praise*

WHAT DO YOU THINK?

Comparing our lives with the majesty of our heavenly Father could give us an inferiority complex! What are some events from your life that have encouraged you to consider (or reconsider) your worth in God's eyes? How can you stay focused on your worth to him?

VISUALS FOR THESE LESSONS

The visual pictured in each lesson (for example, page 239) is a small reproduction of a large, full-color poster included in the Adult Resources packet for the Spring Quarter. The packet is available from your supplier. Order No. 392.

because of your enemies,
   to silence the foe and the avenger.

Despite the power and greatness of God, his name can be enjoyed and celebrated by the youngest. No one can ever fully know how great God is. However, even a child can have some level of appreciation of God.

No tyrant can ever remove our awareness of God from the creation. As part of the creation, we also have a fundamental appreciation for the creator. We may strive to ignore that appreciation, deny its source, flaunt its implications, reject its conclusions, or pretend to be unaware of it altogether. However, we cannot escape ultimate accountability (see Romans 1:18-20). Echoes of the creator are heard in the creation; his fingerprints are all over the firmament (compare Psalm 19).

We will see David explore more of the conclusions posed by this reality as Psalm 8 continues. Before moving on to consider that, we should not forget that Jesus quoted part of this psalm to his enemies in response to their complaint that children were praising him (Matthew 21:15, 16).

Visual for Lesson 1. *Refer to this visual as you ask, "How will you lift the glory of God's name in your own corner of the earth this coming week?"*

AN EXCELLENT REPUTATION

A woman living in southern California was looking for a home with a view of the Pacific Ocean. She spent $1.2 million on a home with the view she wanted, but it needed a larger kitchen and two more bedrooms to meet her ideal of what the home should be. So she hired a friend to remodel the house. He assured her of his professional qualifications and promised her that he could do the architectural plans as well as the construction work.

Six months and more than $100,000 later, her La Jolla house had been reduced to a concrete slab. The owner was forced to hire another builder and construct a new house from the ground up. A state investigator said the site was the worst case she had ever seen. The owner discovered to her chagrin that the "friend" had no architect's license, his professional reputation was seriously clouded by a string of lawsuits that he had lost, and he had avoided paying the judgments against him in those suits.

What a contrast to God's reputation! The glories of the creation speak of God's power, but there is more: the power of God eventually will silence the foes of goodness and righteousness. That process began on the cross and will be completed in God's time when the Lord returns for those who trust him.   —C. R. B.

II. CREATION PRIORITIES (PSALM 8:3-8)

A. HEAVENS AND HUMANITY (vv. 3, 4)

3, 4. When I consider your heavens,
   the work of your fingers,
the moon and the stars,
   which you have set in place,
what is man that you are mindful of him,
   the son of man that you care for him?

At this point David celebrates the faith of the child who looks upward and asks, "Daddy, who made the stars?" Lost in the modern conflict between faith and science is the fact that all exploration of the universe is driven by a common wonder. Each of us shares a desire to know more about our origin. Where did we come from? The same question drives both the astronomer and the theologian. Physics and faith are both vehicles for the curious and the intellectually adventurous. We should not be surprised that many of the greatest scientific minds belonged—and even today yet belong—to people of profound faith.

HOW TO SAY IT

Corinthians. Ko-RIN-thee-unz.
Hebrews. HEE-brews.
Isaiah. Eye-ZAY-uh.

WHAT DO YOU THINK?

How can we use the realities of special and general revelation to confront and defeat the post-modern idea that the only truth that exists is truth that is personal to each individual?

DAILY BIBLE READINGS

Monday, Feb. 27—God Creates Humankind (Genesis 1:26-31)

Tuesday, Feb. 28—God Creates Man and Woman (Genesis 2:7, 15-25)

Wednesday, Mar. 1—God Establishes a Covenant with Noah (Genesis 9:8-17)

Thursday, Mar. 2—God Is Our Help and Strength (Psalm 63:1-8)

Friday, Mar. 3—God Is Our Guide and Refuge (Psalm 73: 21-28)

Saturday, Mar. 4—God Leaves Nothing Outside Our Jurisdiction (Hebrews 2:5-10)

Sunday, Mar. 5—Created a Little Lower Than the Angels (Psalm 8)

Theologians describe two ways that God communicates with us. *Special revelation* occurs when God speaks through prophecy, miracles, etc. (compare Hebrews 1:1, 2). *General revelation* is much less precise, though vitally important in reflecting the character and nature of God. Creation itself is general revelation: principles evident in nature reflect the handiwork of the creator. Romans 1:19, 20 expresses it this way: "since what may be known about God is plain to them, because God has made it plain to them. For since the creation of the world God's invisible qualities—his eternal power and divine nature—have been clearly seen, being understood from what has been made, so that men are without excuse."

As David considers the power and care evident in the creation, his thoughts turn to the vast differences between created objects. Traveling through space, governed by physical laws that we are only beginning to understand, the moon and the stars reveal the awe-inspiring power of God's creative hand. Even with modern technology we cannot begin to approach the power that spoke the worlds into being. Speaking into the darkness, "God said, 'Let there be light,' and there was light" (Genesis 1:3). Many of us cannot get our own children to listen well enough to flip a light switch on or off!

The parallels between humans and celestial objects go back to Genesis. In Genesis 1, God created the sun and *moon* to govern day and night, whereas humans were granted authority to rule the earth (Genesis 1:14-18, 28). Given the similarity between these verses of Psalm 8 and selected parts of Genesis 1, this parallelism is almost certainly intentional on David's part.

As David considers the grandeur of the heavens, the apparent insignificance of humanity stands out. Rather than being awe-inspiring physical objects, having an observable presence and noticeable influence through the eons and across the light years, we are frail creatures of dust. Our lives are short. At first glance, nothing about us seems to compare favorably with those other parts of creation.

Yet one thing about us stands out to David: God's special care for us. Unique among creation, humanity is in the image of God (Genesis 1:26, 27). Alone among all the physical creations, humans communicate with God, provoke emotions in God, influence God's decisions and actions, exist in relationship with God, even reject God and engage in rebellion against him. No other physical creation of God rejects him (John 1:11) and denies his very existence (again, Romans 1). (Only the nonphysical angels—the next beings considered in verse 5, below—are at all like us in these ways.) Yet God continues to love us passionately and to remain deeply involved in our lives.

Before we move on, we should note that many students believe that this verse has two layers of interpretation: David, in speaking of *man* in the strictly human sense, may at the same time be speaking prophetically of the Messiah to come. Note the phrase *son of man*, which Jesus will later use to describe himself. Hebrews 2:6-8 quotes from Psalm 8 in a context that many commentators and translators believe applies to Jesus. Others think, however, that Psalm 8:4-6 as used in Hebrews 2 applies to us mortals instead—so we see the two potential layers of interpretation in the New Testament as well.

B. ANGELS AND HUMANITY (v. 5)

5. You made him a little lower than the heavenly beings
and crowned him with glory and honor.

David continues his meditations on the amazing priorities within the creation by commenting on the relationship between humans and *the heavenly beings* (angels). A first-glance view of the relative differences between humans and angels reflects very poorly on us. We humans seem to be bound by time and space. Our bodies present more limitations than they do opportunities. None of these physical limitations affects angels. Thus David's conclusion that we are *a little lower than the heavenly beings.*

But let's look deeper. True, we may not have some of the abilities or natural empowerments of angels, stars, or animals. But value does not come from comparisons such as these. Our value comes because we have been crowned with *glory and honor.* This is tied in with being created in God's image—something that is not said of angels. Our status of being *a little lower than the heavenly beings* is temporary. Ultimately, we will sit in judgment on angels (1 Corinthians 6:3).

C. OTHER WORKS AND HUMANITY (vv. 6-8)

6. You made him ruler over the works of your hands;
    you put everything under his feet:

David's words reflect the priorities of creation. They show the hierarchy of God's attention and intention. Certainly, God gave humans dominion over the earth, and we exercise that rule (both wisely and not so wisely) every day. That is not to say that we rule over every aspect of existence on earth. No one can predict the exact course of a hurricane or the time of the next earthquake, let alone control them. Being the dominant species on earth has not resulted in the defeat of AIDS or even the common cold. Our rule or dominion has limitations.

Having dominion also has implications for ecology. Although the environmental movement often errs on the side of fanaticism, we still have a responsibility for stewardship. That responsibility is a clear reflection of our mandate to rule *over the works of your hands.* Rulers bear responsibility in the eyes of God for that which they rule. We will answer to God for our deeds (or lack of deeds) in that role.

Acknowledging that God values humans more than other elements of creation does not negate the value of the rest of creation. Our concern for the creation is driven by our love for the creator. We look forward to the day when the ideal of Psalm 8 and Genesis 1:26 will be realized fully (compare Revelation 21:4, 5).

7, 8. . . . all flocks and herds,
    and the beasts of the field,
  the birds of the air,
    and the fish of the sea,
    all that swim the paths of the seas.

David now describes the extent of human rule. Obviously, domestic animals (*flocks and herds*) are ruled by people. There is no question about that. But what about the other creatures listed?

Birds, fish, and sea creatures in David's time are not particularly subject to humans in any practical sense. Apart from limited hunting and fishing techniques, ancient people have little impact upon such creatures. Perhaps David's confidence is a kind of prophetic hint—a God-given awareness that our future reach would extend to the depths of the ocean and beyond the heights of the atmosphere. Thus David's faith allows him to affirm that God has given us dominion over those creatures. Adding specifics to the general statement about rule in verse 6 makes the psalm more beautiful and more memorable. We can almost hear the Hebrew children pleading, "Sing the one about the birds and fish again!"

When we think of the idea of rule, we should remember that David is well acquainted with the reach and limitations of human power. Years before he became king himself, he was a regular in King Saul's presence. David knows that kings may rule countries, but their personal impact on the day-to-day lives of

WHAT DO YOU THINK?

David seemed amazed that God would entrust us to rule over his creation. How can we take this responsibility seriously today? What are some extremist positions to avoid, and why?

PRAYER

Father, your name is indeed majestic. May our lives be dedicated to glorifying and praising your majestic name. As we consider your works, may we always be mindful of the hand behind them. Guide us in fulfilling our role within your creative plan. In Jesus' name we pray, amen.

WHAT DO YOU THINK?

The visual for this lesson (page 239) offers the word excellent as another translation for majestic. With the excellence of the Lord's name as our own banner, what are some qualities of excellence for which we should strive? What would be the result if we neglect these?

WHAT DO YOU THINK?

How will you use Psalm 8 this week to deepen your appreciation of God?

THOUGHT TO REMEMBER

Acknowledge your place and role in creation.

their subjects is often quite limited. Many of a king's subjects will live their lives without ever seeing the king. Yet a king's influence can be felt profoundly through taxation, conscription into military service, etc. The king's rule is extensive, but also has certain limits.

We may draw a similar parallel concerning our rule over the earth and her creatures. We do not influence directly the daily lives of every bottle-nosed porpoise, sparrow hawk, or giant anteater. Yet human ability that is exercised improperly can result in eventual extinction of various species. As those with dominion over creation, we need to use extra care.

CARE FOR THE CREATION

The story of "Dr. Dolittle" has captured the fancy of children for nearly a century. The story began somewhere in France during the First World War. Captain Hugh Lofting (1886–1947) was writing home to his wife and children. Knowing that censorship of soldiers' letters was strict, he decided to tell his children a story.

Lofting had been thinking about the many horses in military use that were injured in combat. He wished they could be given medical treatment such as the soldiers received. But, Lofting reasoned, that would require learning "horse language." Thus was born the legend of Dr. Dolittle, a kindly, eccentric veterinarian who could talk to the animals. Lofting's wife suggested he write more stories. Eventually they were collected into a series of about a dozen books and several movies.

Who cannot relate to such compassion, even if it is fictional? However, concern for animals late in the twentieth century expanded into thinking of them as the equal of human beings. Reforms in the way animals were used for research certainly were needed. But some activists for "animal rights" ignored the significant scriptural difference that exists between humans and animals. However, the rule that God gave us over the lower creatures implies that we are to exercise care and discretion in how we treat his creation. —C. R. B.

III. CREATOR PRAISE, PART 2 (PSALM 8:9)

9. O LORD, our Lord,
    how majestic is your name in all the earth!

David returns to the main thrust of Psalm 8. It is the *Lord our Lord* whose *name* is *majestic*. Our value comes from him. Our authority comes from him. Our unique place in all creation comes from him. Our very being results from the creator's decision, and only the creator deserves praise as a result. The Bible reminds us of this often (compare Isaiah 42:8).

CONCLUSION

The ideal order of creation can be set forth this way: God (who is uncreated) is first, humanity is second, and everything else is third. Humans got themselves into big trouble when they tried to move up a notch (see Genesis 3:4-6). As a result, we often have to struggle against creation in trying to exercise our rule over it (Genesis 3:17-19). Never again should we confuse our intended role within creation with God's unique role as creator! Again, it is his name that is majestic, not ours.

If you ever need a reminder of God's majestic name, just look skyward on a starry night! When Job challenged God, God pointed him back to his creation to show just how much he cared and was in control. Job responded with humility and awe. The special revelation (God's conversation with Job) in that case was a bonus—Job really just needed to look around! Our relationship with God will be strengthened if we do the same.

Discovery Learning

This page contains an alternative lesson plan emphasizing learning activities. Classes desiring such student involvement will find these suggestions helpful. The next page is a reproducible activity page to further enhance discovery learning.

LEARNING GOALS

After this lesson, each student will be able to:

1. Describe the position of human beings in creation.

2. Explain how knowledge of humanity's place in creation enhances his or her self-worth and gives life meaning.

3. Sing a song praising God as creator or complete a self-worth chart based on truths from the lesson.

INTO THE LESSON

Distribute copies of the following agree/disagree exercise. (This is also printed in the student book.) Allow two minutes to complete the exercise, then discuss responses. Information to help in the discussion is in parentheses.

1. Humans and apes are basically the same animals because they have nearly identical genes. Agree/Disagree? (*Human DNA is 95 percent to 98.5 percent identical to chimpanzee DNA. However, even a difference of only 1.5 percent means a difference of millions of DNA base pairs.*)

2. Humans and apes have similar brains. Agree/Disagree? (*A human brain is much larger than an ape's.*)

3. Until about age 2, humans and apes develop at the same rate. Agree/Disagree? (*An ape's brain is half its adult weight at birth. A human's is only one-third its mature weight. Apes are more developed at birth, but by age 1 humans are quickly surpassing apes.*)

4. If apes could talk, they could learn to speak human languages as well as humans do. Agree/Disagree? (*Many scientists believe that language is unique to humans because only humans have the inborn intellectual capacity for something so difficult. Even the most primitive human tribes speak very complex languages! Yet children learn these languages very easily compared with efforts to teach apes rudimentary sign language.*)

After discussing students' responses to the survey, say, "Today's lesson deals with our unique place in God's creation."

INTO THE WORD

Divide your class into small groups of three or four. Assign half of the groups *Exercise #1* and the other half *Exercise #2* (also in the student books).

Exercise #1—Position: Use Psalm 8 and Genesis 1:26, 27 to answer these questions and determine our position in God's creation order: (1) How do you understand David's statement that we were made "a little lower than the heavenly beings"? (2) How are we "crowned" with "glory and honor"? (3) What does it mean to be made in God's image? (4) What is significant about the fact that humans were the last of God's earthly creations?

Exercise #2—Purpose: Use Psalm 8 and Genesis 1:28-31; 2:15 to answer these questions and determine what our purpose is in God's creation: (1) What commands did God give to the first humans after he created them? (2) How are we to exercise our rule over nature? (3) What was/is involved in subduing the earth? (4) What function did humans serve in the Garden of Eden?

Using your lesson commentary as a guide, discuss each group's answers.

INTO LIFE

Make a transition by saying, "As you know, not everyone agrees with these conclusions about our position and purpose. Let's take a look at some of their arguments." Then distribute copies of the statements below, omitting the material in parentheses. Ask your class to provide a biblical response to the key doctrines of the secular view of nature.

The Secular View of Nature vs.
The Biblical View of Creation

1. Nature is all that exists. (*God exists and has created the entire natural realm; Psalm 8:3.*)

2. Humans are just highly evolved animals, produced by natural selection. (*Humans are made by God; Psalm 8:5.*)

3. Because humans are the product of nature, we have no right to claim dominion over nature. (*God created us to rule over nature, to be stewards of nature for God's glory; Psalm 8:6.*)

4. Ethical values evolved in order to preserve the human species. (*Ethical values stem from the very nature of God and are unchangeable. Obeying them glorifies God.*)

Discuss responses and then ask volunteers to summarize how the Bible views the worth of each person. What effect should that have on the way we view and treat each other? (See James 3:9.)

Note: alternative or supplemental activities for evaluating human worth may be found on page 244.

What Is Man?

Test your knowledge of the human body! (Answers are at the bottom.)

1. Your body produces how many red blood cells every hour?
   a. 1,000   b. 100,000   c. 1,000,000   d. 10,000,000

2. The heart pumps how many times per day?
   a. 1,000   b. 10,000   c. 100,000   d. 1,000,000

3. Approximately how many gallons of blood does the heart pump daily?
   a. 1,000   b. 2,000   c. 3,000   d. 4,000

4. How many pounds of blood are purified by the kidneys each day?
   a. 100   b. 500   c. 1,000   d. 2,000

5. The human brain contains how many cells?
   a. 1,000,000   b. 100,000,000   c. 1,000,000,000   d. 100,000,000,000

6. The brain can store information equivalent to how many sets of encyclopedias?
   a. 500,000   b. 50,000   c. 5000   d. 500

7. How long does it take for the body to replace all of its cells?
   a. 7 days   b. 7 months   c. 7 years   d. 70 years

8. Which of these things can a human cell do?
   a. Build itself   b. Repair itself   c. Replicate itself   d. All of the above

9. How many color-sensing cone cells are in the human eye?
   a. 300,000,000   b. 100,000,000   c. 50,000,000   d. 1,000,000

10. How many miles of blood vessels are in an average adult human?
   a. 600   b. 6,000   c. 60,000   d. 600,000

Is That All I Am?

The human body is a marvel of design! But we're so much more than collections of cells. Jot down below some other reasons that contribute to your self-worth. Use today's text (and, perhaps, Romans 12:3) as a guide.

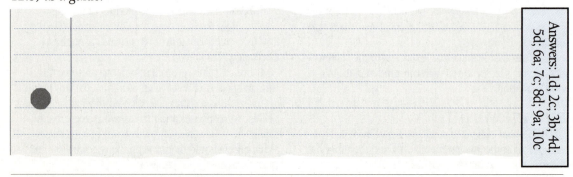

Answers: 1d; 2c; 3b; 4d; 5d; 6a; 7c; 8d; 9a; 10c

Living in and as God's Creation
Unit 1: The Glory of God's Creation
(Lessons 1-4)

GOD CREATED WONDERFUL THINGS

LESSON 2

WHY TEACH THIS LESSON?

The Bible rightly begins with God at work, at work using his wisdom, power, and love. Creation reveals all three. For the one who ponders all that is—such as the writer of Psalm 104—to praise God is a natural response.

Yet, most adults begin to take it all for granted. "Yes, the sky is blue, but it always is. Yes, the oceans are impressive, but they are always there. Yes, birds are fascinating, but they are dumb!" We see what is but have lost the wonder of the small child who can watch at length an ant in its seemingly meaningless meanderings. Everyone needs to recapture that excitement, that awe. Everyone needs to reconsider the creator of all things. For the one who does, praise will be as automatic as the sunrise. Let this study of Psalm 104 be a new beginning of wonder, awe, and praise.

INTRODUCTION

A. WORSHIP PRIVILEGE, WORSHIP STYLE

Worship is a marvelous privilege, isn't it? Participating in various styles of worship can enrich our Christian experience. Sadly, however, Christians have been known to quarrel over worship styles. Someone may go so far as to label a certain worship style as "worldly."

Too often lost in the bickering is the realization that God's people frequently have borrowed stylistically from the culture. For example, your church's youth may go to Christian summer camp and sing Christian lyrics that are set to the music of familiar secular compositions. The songs of the church frequently echo the songs of the marketplace. We fool ourselves if we think otherwise.

We also fool ourselves if we think the form and style of our own worship should transplant easily into faraway cultures. Most of us realize that the music of organ and piano translates poorly into the rhythm instruments and reed pipes of African jungle. It is admittedly difficult for many of us to accept the similar task of remolding a worship style of the 1950s into the multimedia experience of Western pop culture. Perhaps some biblical perspective would help a little!

B. LESSON BACKGROUND

Our text for today is Psalm 104, a beautiful recapitulation of the creation. Although we cannot consider the entire psalm today, take some time this week to read it through while keeping your finger in Genesis 1. The parallels are obvious, and the writer's intent may be to set Genesis 1 to music. If so, then Psalm 104 is an interpretative celebration of Genesis 1.

The original concept for the psalm, though, apparently came from a pagan source. Within Egyptian mythology of the fourteenth century B.C. is found

DEVOTIONAL READING:
PSALM 104:31-35

BACKGROUND SCRIPTURE:
PSALM 104

PRINTED TEXT:
PSALM 104:1-13

LESSON AIMS

After participating in this lesson, each student will be able to:

1. Describe some ways that God controls the forces of nature.

2. Contrast our attempts to control the forces of nature with God's ability.

3. Dramatize Psalm 104.

KEY VERSE

Praise the LORD, O my soul. O LORD my God, you are very great; you are clothed with splendor and majesty. —Psalm 104:1

Pharaoh Akhenaton's Great Hymn to the Sun, a hymn to a fictitious sun god. The fact that the pagan sun hymn came first means that the writer of Psalm 104 would be the borrower. Yet the two are not identical! Their conclusions, the focus of their tribute, and Psalm 104's dependence on Genesis 1 assured the ancient Hebrew that there would be no confusion between the two compositions.

Obviously, the writer of Psalm 104 wanted to communicate something. So perhaps he decided to borrow from the Egyptian sun hymn because his culture was already familiar with it. In the process the psalmist changed that hymn's glorification of the sun (a part of the creation) into a glorification of the true God (the creator). We should not find this procedure surprising. The apostle Paul, for his part, was able to use pagan thoughts and philosophy in his sermons and letters to uphold Christ (see Acts 17:28; 1 Corinthians 15:33; and Titus 1:12).

I. GREATNESS OF GOD (PSALM 104:1-4)
A. GOD HIMSELF (vv. 1, 2a)
1. Praise the LORD, O my soul.
   O LORD my God, you are very great;
      you are clothed with splendor and majesty.

The phrases "bless the Lord" and *praise the Lord* appear dozens of times in the Bible. The majority of these occurrences are in the psalms. The idea is to give God the honor and respect that is due him. Occasionally, the same Hebrew verb is used to show God's blessing or favor on people (as in Genesis 24:1; 39:5; 2 Samuel 6:11; Job 42:12, etc.). God has come to our level to bless us so many times! In the Garden of Eden, God came to walk with us. In the manger of Bethlehem, the Son of God came to live with us. And on the cross of Calvary, the Son came to die for us. God's goal always has been for us to walk with him and live with him, never to die.

The psalmist, of course, does not know of the accomplishments of the manger and the cross. Even so, we feel his exuberance as the words leap off the page! The God before whom we kneel today, the God who clothes himself *with splendor and majesty,* is also the psalmist's God—*O Lord my God.*

The *very great* God is also the God who wants a close relationship with us. It's easy to forget one or the other of these two aspects. If we focus on how God is personal to us, we may forget that he is also awe-inspiring. If we focus on God's transcendence, we may forget that he is available to us personally. Both facets are essential to a proper relationship with God.

WHAT DO YOU THINK?

David is probably kneeling as he acknowledges the Lord (compare 1 Kings 8:54; Psalm 95:6). Customs showing respect vary with time and culture. What ways do we show our respect for God? Why may it be difficult to teach some of these to our children or grandchildren?

IDENTITY CRISIS
Ransom E. Olds produced the first Oldsmobile in 1897. It would become a well-regarded brand, its sales boosted by popular culture, innovative engineering, and the advance of science. "In My Merry Oldsmobile," a song written in 1905, may well have been the most popular song ever written about a car.

Oldsmobiles were distinctive, with chrome plating in 1926 and the first fully automatic transmission in 1939. After World War II, Oldsmobile's *Eighty Eight* model with "Futuramic" styling appealed to buyers' interest in a bold new world of science. Other cutting-edge advances included turbo-charged fuel-injected engines in 1962, front-wheel drive in 1966, and air bags in 1974.

However, Oldsmobile eventually had trouble coping with changes in consumer tastes. The company tried to appeal to younger buyers with slogans such as "Not your father's Oldsmobile," but young adults bought neither the slogan nor the cars. At the end of the 2004 model run, Oldsmobile ceased production; America's oldest automotive brand name was unable to maintain an identity.

Identity is important, isn't it? We establish our identity when we understand our proper relationship to God. As the psalmist says, God is God. In that light we need to be cautious of thinking of God as just our big, friendly, cosmic buddy. He is our loving Father, but he is also the great and glorious creator, as the psalmist reminds us. God has no identity crisis. Do we?

      —C. R. B.

2a. He wraps himself in light as with a garment;

In sharp contrast to the pagan Great Hymn to the Sun, Psalm 104 distinguishes the creator from his creation. The sun as the source of light was god for Pharaoh Akhenaton. For the psalmist, on the other hand, God uses *light* as *a garment.* What a majestic, poetic expression!

B. GOD'S CREATION (vv. 2b-4)

2b. . . . he stretches out the heavens like a tent

Although today's text does not include the entire psalm, it is worth noting again the parallelism between Psalm 104 and Genesis 1. Day one of creation brought forth the light evoked by verse 2a, above. Day two divided *the heavens* and the earth. The second half of verse 2 makes oblique reference to this same creative act. The psalmist develops this reference more fully in the verse that follows.

3. . . . and lays the beams of his upper chambers on their waters.

   He makes the clouds his chariot

      and rides on the wings of the wind.

The psalmist obviously takes tremendous joy in his creator. God's power is something in which to take great delight. Of course we should not push the imagery too far since God has no need of a *chariot* of any sort. The figure of speech is one of majesty. The writer invites us to share his delight in the power of the creator, as exhibited in the greatness of the creation. God made the heavens and the earth, including the seas, the skies, *the clouds,* and *the wind.* All of that power belongs to "O Lord my God," the intimate and personal sovereign.

4. He makes winds his messengers,

   flames of fire his servants.

This verse is difficult to translate because some of the Hebrew words can be understood in different ways. The Hebrew word for *messengers* can also be translated "angels" (examples: it is translated "angels" in Genesis 19:1 and "messengers" in Ezekiel 23:16). The Hebrew word for *winds,* for its part, can also be translated as "spirits" (examples: it is "spirits" in Numbers 16:22 and "winds" in Ezekiel 5:10). In any case, verse 4 continues the song of praise for the creator's power. Hebrews 1:7 quotes this passage to examine the superiority of Jesus to the angels.

II. GRANDNESS OF THE EARTH (PSALM 104:5-9)

A. GOD'S HANDIWORK (vv. 5, 6)

5, 6. He set the earth on its foundations;

   it can never be moved.

You covered it with the deep as with a garment;

   the waters stood above the mountains.

The writer continues his poetic retelling of Genesis 1. The description now includes *the earth* being *covered* by *the deep* (probably the oceans) *as with a garment.* The psalmist sees the creative artistry of God at work. How often do we pause to think of God by means of the marvel of his creation?

At the conclusion of today's lesson, we will turn our attention to the occasional conflicts between faith and science. It is worth noting here, though, that

DAILY BIBLE READINGS

Monday, Mar. 6—*The Heavens Proclaim God's Handiwork (Psalm 19:1-6)*

Tuesday, Mar. 7—*Shout with Joy to God (Psalm 66:1-9)*

Wednesday, Mar. 8—*God's Steadfast Love Endures Forever (Psalm 136:1-9)*

Thursday, Mar. 9—*God, the Great Creator (Psalm 104:1-13)*

Friday, Mar. 10—*God's Creation Is Balanced and Orderly (Psalm 104:14-23)*

Saturday, Mar. 11—*Many Are God's Works (Psalm 104: 24-30)*

Sunday, Mar. 12—*Rejoice in the Lord (Psalm 104:31-35)*

WHAT DO YOU THINK?

Psalm 104:5 alludes to the permanence of the earth. How is this significant to our understanding of God's intentions toward us?

the entire premise of this psalm rests upon the reality of the creation. Every point the psalmist makes about creation depends upon God being the one who made the heavens and the earth. Any worldview that tries to explain the universe's existence apart from God as creator is inadequate. Without that foundational understanding, life has no ultimate meaning.

B. GOD'S CONTROL (vv. 7-9)

7-9. But at your rebuke the waters fled,
at the sound of your thunder they took to flight;
they flowed over the mountains,
they went down into the valleys,
to the place you assigned for them.
You set a boundary they cannot cross;
never again will they cover the earth.

The psalmist's thoughts offer a direct contrast to pagan religious beliefs. There is no possibility that a god of the sea exists to battle against a god of the land or some such (compare 1 Kings 20:23, 28). There is one God, and he is able to command his creation in any way he so chooses. God simply gives his command: *At the sound of your thunder they* [the waters] *took to flight.*

The psalmist may be reminding us of another truth as well. The Lord had chosen to devastate the earth with water in the days of Noah. At the conclusion of that flood, God sent the waters back to their places and promised never to destroy the earth again through a flood (Genesis 9:15). The psalmist perhaps echoes that promise in verse 9: *never again will they cover the earth.* This reminds us both of God's promise and of God's power to keep that promise. We note again the psalmist's genuine delight in the marvel of God's hand in creation.

III. GRANTING OF HABITAT (PSALM 104:10-13)

A. SPECIFIC EXAMPLES (vv. 10-12)

10. He makes springs pour water into the ravines;
it flows between the mountains.

The psalmist now partially explores the water cycle. Modern science gives us much more precise knowledge of how this cycle works. Does this mean that we have a greater appreciation of the creator who stands behind it?

"WATER, WATER EVERYWHERE . . . "

Chemicals at one time so polluted the Cuyahoga River in Ohio that it actually caught fire! That was in June 1969. Until then, Americans had given little thought to the long-term effects of the way they used (or abused) the water supply. After all, how could we ever run out of a resource that covers more than 70 percent of the earth's surface? Yet only 1 percent of that resource is readily available fresh water. One estimate predicts that two-thirds of the world's population may lack adequate, clean water by the year 2025 if current trends continue.

Nations around the globe are already beginning to feel the pinch. For example, the water levels in Lakes Powell and Mead in North America have declined sharply in recent years. Manufacturing and agriculture requirements along with expansive lawns in desert environments compete with health and hygiene needs to stretch this vital resource to the limit. The lament of Samuel Coleridge's mythical ancient mariner is coming true for landlubbers:

Water, water, everywhere,
Nor any drop to drink.

Our God is the Lord of the deep and has created the earth's cycle of weather and water. How we use or abuse this grand system will determine the quality of human life in the near future. We are learning that there is a price to be paid for violating the principles of God's creation in both the physical and spiritual realms!   —C. R. B.

11. They give water to all the beasts of the field;
   the wild donkeys quench their thirst.

The psalmist now makes a transition from water itself to the creatures that rely upon that water. The psalmist's thoughts never stray from the creator, however. It is God who sends the springs into the valleys (v. 10), thus providing for the creatures nearby.

Although Psalm 104 celebrates each day of creation, it does not follow the exact pattern of Genesis 1. Rather than directly moving from day three (formation of dry ground) to day four (creation of celestial objects), the psalmist spends some time foreshadowing the creation of the animals (day six) and of the birds (day five) as well as provisions for them (Genesis 1:30).

12. The birds of the air nest by the waters;
   they sing among the branches.

Birds have entered the poetry, but again the focus is on the creator. Because he gives them the ability to create their nests in a variety of places, birds can flourish in the wild places of the earth. One can almost hear the psalmist inviting the birds to *sing* with him the praises of their creator.

My children love to watch nature shows on TV. One of my sons fervently dreams of being another "Crocodile Hunter." His goal is to study exotic species. I love that dream, and part of me hopes to see him pursue it someday.

Part of me is quite concerned, though. The education required to attain a position like that almost requires one to disengage faith from science. Secular evolutionary theory allows no room for a creator. What a shame that in our eagerness to explore the world around us we have drifted away from the one truth that puts everything into context.

B. EARTH AS A WHOLE (v. 13)

13. He waters the mountains from his upper chambers;
   the earth is satisfied by the fruit of his work.

Rather than allow our study of the earth to pull us away from God, our response should be the same as the psalmist's. Examination of the earth leads that writer to conclude two things. First, the fact that the creator *waters the mountains from his upper chambers* means that he is personally involved in the inner workings of his creation. Second, the fact that *the earth is satisfied by the fruit of his work* means that creation depends upon that involvement.

Examination of the natural world should be a profoundly spiritual act. "The heavens declare the glory of God; the skies proclaim the work of his hands" (Psalm 19:1). As this lesson is being finalized, the Cassini-Huygens spacecraft is sending back close-up pictures of Saturn's rings. The ancient psalmist could not have dreamed of seeing such glorious images! Rather than be arrogant at scientific accomplishment, these images should cause us to stand in even greater awe of the creator.

TADPOLES, FLAMINGOS, AND OTHER CREATURES

How are tadpoles, basking sharks, flamingos, mallards, and blue whales alike? Think about that for a moment, but first note how we humans enjoy the water the psalmist speaks about. Along the various seashores of the world, a trip to the beach

Visual for Lesson 2. *Tell your students that this montage is just a start. Ask them to bring in additional pictures to place around the edge.*

WHAT DO YOU THINK?

The existence of Saturn's rings shows us God's command of the dynamics of science as well as his flair for the beautiful. What are some other examples? How do you use these to draw closer to God?

Lord, forgive us for those times when we have let the "wisdom of the wise" pull us away from the wisdom of the ages. Forgive us for those times when we have let the credentials of universities distract us from the creator of the universe. As we consider the earth, the seas, and all contained within them, remind us again of your hand behind the scenes. Thank you for leaving your fingerprints all over creation. May the psalmist's joy be ours. In Jesus' name, amen.

is a popular holiday event, whether for swimming, wading, surfing, or just sitting and staring out to sea. Farther inland, a day at the lake or on the river or beside a thundering waterfall can provide a restoration of the human spirit.

Perhaps our psalm today says so much about water in order to remind us of the glory of the creation. The psalmist mentions the beasts and birds on the land, but the sea creatures show God's creative genius as well.

Now, back to that question about tadpoles, flamingos, whales, etc. What they and other creatures have in common is that God has designed them to feed on small organisms suspended in the water. For example, each day a 30-foot basking shark will eat 140 gallons of zooplankton—tiny creatures only one millimeter long—filtering them out of thousands of gallons of water per hour.

The glory of God's creatures is amazing in its own right, but the important message from this is that it speaks more specifically to the glory of God. Here is the question for us: Since God's other creatures testify to his glory, do our lives speak that way as well?   —C. R. B.

CONCLUSION

Science and faith should not be at loggerheads. Both are means of exploring God's relationship with his creation, especially his relationship with us. Unfortunately, they do conflict at times. When that conflict occurs, both Christians and non-Christians can make the same mistake in deferring to ever-changing science over never-changing Scripture.

Certainly, committed Christians can and do disagree over the specifics of the creation. What cannot be avoided, though, is the clear foundation laid by those simple words from Genesis 1:1. Any explanation of origins that omits the presence of the creator is fatally flawed at the outset; it has no value.

As our text today makes clear, the implications of removing God from creation are far-reaching. The very God praised by the psalmist is the creator who laid the foundations of the earth. If God is not creator of the heavens and the earth, then very real questions about who he is—and indeed *if* he is—must be asked. Also, we note that the Bible does not recognize a god who is part of creation; rather, any god that is part of creation is an idol that has its origins in human thought.

But what about those disagreements between science and Scripture? When such conflict arises, wise students will step back and ask themselves some questions. First, is this truly a disagreement, or is it merely two perspectives of the same issue? The Bible is not a scientific textbook. We can affirm its accuracy while at the same time acknowledging that occasionally the Bible uses figures of speech and poetic imagery to make a point.

Second, is the issue at hand a matter of fact or one of speculation on the part of science? The nuclear "cold fusion" claims of the year 1989 is an example of a scientific mistake. That is not to say that all scientists, or even those particular scientists, deliberately mislead or misinform people. They are human, though, and as well as occasionally being wrong, they suffer from the very human desire to prove themselves. That can lead to excesses, mistakes, and overreaching. (To be fair we should also ask whether an issue at hand is a matter of fact or speculation on the part of the person who is reading Scripture.)

Scripture and science should be understood together. When they disagree, though, the biblical worldview takes precedence. Science, after all, is our attempt to understand creation—created beings analyzing creation. Scripture, however, is God's perspective. It is the creator speaking directly to us. Given our limited perspective, we should kneel before the one who made Heaven and earth! Only with his guidance can we understand the creation and our role within it.

"The fear of the Lord is the beginning of knowledge" (Proverbs 1:7).

Discovery Learning

This page contains an alternative lesson plan emphasizing learning activities. Classes desiring such student involvement will find these suggestions helpful. The next page is a reproducible activity page to further enhance discovery learning.

LEARNING GOALS

After this lesson, each student will be able to:

1. Describe some ways that God controls the forces of nature.

2. Contrast our attempts to control the forces of nature with God's ability.

3. Dramatize Psalm 104.

INTO THE LESSON

Distribute the following quiz concerning the earth's environment. (The quiz is also in the student book.) You also can put these in your students' chairs to give them something to work on and talk about as they arrive.

From answers *a–d* select the correct answers for questions 1–4. (1) If the earth were closer to the sun, which of the following would be true of the earth's atmosphere? (2) If the earth were farther from the sun, which would be true? (3) If the earth's gravity were stronger, which would be true? (4) If the earth's gravity were weaker, which would be true? *(a) It would be full of lethal ammonia and methane. (b) It would be too cool to maintain a stable water cycle (water evaporates from the oceans, forms rain clouds, falls as rain, flows back to the oceans). (c) It would be too warm to maintain a stable water cycle. (d) It would lose too much water into space.* (Bonus: Name planets in the solar system as examples.)

From *e–h* below, select the correct answers for questions 5–8. (5) It the earth took longer than 24 hours to rotate, which of the following would be true? (6) If the earth were not tilted on its axis, which would be true? (7) If the ozone level in the upper atmosphere were lower, which would be true? (8) If the ozone level in the upper atmosphere were higher, which would be true? *(e) There would be no seasons of the year. (f) Temperatures would be warmer in the day and cooler at night. (g) Both daytime and nighttime temperatures would be much higher. (h) Both daytime and nighttime temperatures would be much lower.* [Answers: 1c; 2b; 3a; 4d; 5f; 6e; 7g; 8h.]

After students complete the quiz and you have graded it together, ask what conclusions they can draw from their answers. The key answer you should look for is that this world is just the way it ought to be to maintain life as we know it. Make a transition to the lesson by saying, "Today's lesson will explore the greatness of God, who created and controls this amazing world."

INTO THE WORD

To explore today's text, students will work in pairs to complete two activities based on Psalm 104. Allow pairs several minutes to complete the first activity, then discuss their conclusions as a class. Follow the same procedure for the second activity (both printed in the student books).

Activity #1: Read Psalm 104:1-4, answer the following questions, and discuss with your partner what *the psalmist* tells us about God. (1) What does the statement "Praise the Lord, O my soul" suggest about worship? (2) How is God "clothed with splendor and majesty"? (3) What do the various imageries of God suggest about his control of nature? (4) Why did God create certain messengers?

Activity #2: Read Psalm 104:5-13, answer the following questions, and discuss with your partner what *nature* tells us about God. (1) What does the imagery of the "earth on its foundations" suggest about God? (2) How does setting boundaries illustrate his power? (3) How does God provide for animals? (4) What is the result of God's care of the earth?

INTO LIFE

Say, "Our lesson writer suggests several principles that will help us to better understand God's relationship to his creation." Then offer these statements for consideration: (1) Any explanation of the origins of the universe that omits its creator is fatally flawed. (2) We must distinguish between matters of fact and matters of opinion in our interpretation of Scripture. (3) In science also we must distinguish between matters of fact and testable theories on the one hand and unsupported speculation on the other.

Using these principles, discuss possible solutions to the following hypothetical situations:

1. Dave is a college biology major whose faith is being challenged by his study of Darwinism. How can you help him resolve this spiritual crisis?

2. Rachel believes that all scientists are agents of Satan. She wants to homeschool her children so they won't be exposed to that "brainwashing." How would you counsel her?

Close the class with the antiphonal reading on the reproducible page.

Praise the Lord!

Use the printed text below as the basis for an antiphonal reading of today's lesson text. One individual or group should read the lines marked *A* and another individual or group replies with the lines marked *B*. Lines marked *All* should be read in unison by both individuals or groups.

A: Praise the Lord, O my soul.
    B: O Lord my God, you are very great;
All: You are clothed with splendor and majesty.

A: He wraps himself in light as with a garment;
    B: He stretches out the heavens like a tent
A: And lays the beams of his upper chambers on their waters.
    B: He makes the clouds his chariot
All: And rides on the wings of the wind.

A: He makes winds his messengers,
    B: Flames of fire his servants.

A: He set the earth on its foundations;
    B: It can never be moved.

A: You covered it with the deep as with a garment;
    B: The waters stood above the mountains.

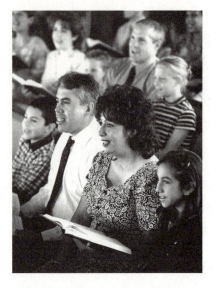

A: But at your rebuke the waters fled,
        B: At the sound of your thunder they took to flight;
A: They flowed over the mountains,
        B: They went down into the valleys,
All: To the place you assigned for them.

A: You set a boundary they cannot cross;
        B: Never again will they cover the earth.

A: He makes springs pour water into the ravines;
        B: It flows between the mountains.

A: They give water to all the beasts of the field;
        B: The wild donkeys quench their thirst.

A: The birds of the air nest by the waters;
        B: They sing among the branches.

A: He waters the mountains from his upper chambers;
        B: The earth is satisfied by the fruit of his work.

Living in and as God's Creation
Unit 1: *The Glory of God's Creation*
(Lessons 1-4)

GOD CREATED AND KNOWS US

WHY TEACH THIS LESSON?

"Camera here, camera there; big brother's got a camera everywhere!" This is an unhappy chant in the modern world. Cameras for weather, traffic, and high-crime areas; cameras on school buses; cameras at ATMs—one cannot escape being seen. Even the innocent resent the intrusions on personal privacy.

Yet, God's own eye is everywhere. Sinners are oblivious. Saints are thankful. Today's lesson will provide the needed reminder that God knows and cares what befalls his children. For any Christian there should be great comfort in the knowledge that God is familiar with all his or her ways, that God is ready to lead in the way everlasting. Who does not need the strength that that awareness provides?

Rather than resentment and fear, the godly response must be that simple prayer of the psalmist: "Search me . . . test me . . . lead me." In today's study your job—your joy—as teacher is to direct your learners toward such a response.

INTRODUCTION

A. As If He Owned the Place

Some years ago, two people entered a home and surprised a man taking a shower. The man in the shower was not nearly as surprised, though, as were the "intruders"—a father and son—who were the residents of the house!

When the father and son arrived home, they heard the sound of running water. Checking out the noise, they found a stranger in their bathroom. They confronted the man, who then began to unscrew the showerhead, claiming that he was a plumber who had come to fix the shower. When the father and son withdrew to call the police, the man fled—leaving his clothes behind! Police found him in a neighboring yard, knocking on the back door of another house. They took him into custody for a psychological evaluation. It seems safe to assume that he had some kind of confusion that affected his behavior.

I wonder if we are sometimes as confused as this man was. We wander around God's creation acting as though we own the place. We behave as though no one is watching us, as though no one cares about what we are doing. Then, when we realize that God is indeed watching us, we quickly try to cover up or justify our actions (compare 1 Samuel 15:19-21). We may even flee, hoping somehow to escape his attention.

B. Lesson Background

True wisdom requires that we acknowledge God's ability to know everything. We cannot hide from him. Psalm 139 captures the futility of hiding from God.

More than being unable to hide from God, though, David—who was the author of Psalm 139—affirms the positive aspect of this truth: we never can be lost

DEVOTIONAL READING:
PSALM 100
BACKGROUND SCRIPTURE:
PSALM 139
PRINTED TEXT:
PSALM 139:1-3, 7-14, 23, 24

LESSON AIMS

After participating in this lesson, each student will be able to:

1. Cite various ways that God knows and watches over him or her.

2. Give reasons why God's continuous presence should provide comfort, not concern.

3. Write a sentence or brief paragraph that will remind him or her daily of God's presence.

KEY VERSE

I praise you because I am fearfully and wonderfully made; your works are wonderful, I know that full well. —Psalm 139:14

from his sight. David was one who knew both truths! (See Psalm 69:5.) Ecclesiastes 12:14 reveals that his son Solomon knew it as well. We may be uncomfortable with God's total knowledge during times when we are disobedient. Even so, there is incredible comfort in the awareness that we are always under the watchful eye of our loving heavenly Father (Psalms 33:18; 34:15; Proverbs 15:3).

I. GOD KNOWS ME (PSALM 139:1-3, 7-14)

A. MY NOW IS KNOWN (vv. 1-3)

1. *O LORD, you have searched me*
   and you know me.

David, the author, begins with a simple declaration. We could rephrase it by saying, "God, you know all about me." This knowledge includes David's faults and his strengths, his sin and his nobility. God knows all about David—and about each of us. No part of our psyche, no piece of our personal history, no secret longing, hidden sin, or private behavior escapes the awareness of God. His knowledge is total, complete, and comprehensive.

This truth is explored more fully later in the psalm, but it is implicit in the personal address David uses: *O Lord, you.* David is not lamenting God's knowledge or fearing God's involvement. David is simply recognizing a fact and addressing the God of all knowledge. "You," David says, "know me."

Does that fact sink into our thoughts as well? Many people fear that if God really knew what they were like, he would not want anything to do with them. These people recognize their sin and understand that God hates sin. What they fail to understand, however, is that God already knows all about their sin. He knows everything about us. We are not a mystery to him. Nothing we do surprises him. Certainly, he often is disappointed, even angry, about our behavior. But never is he surprised.

The morning before I wrote this lesson, I was getting my sons ready for school. As I finished a few tasks, two of them disappeared. They were supposed to be in the car, buckling up and preparing for the ride. When I went to the car, though, they were not there. Now I know my sons. I knew exactly where they were. They had gone downstairs and turned on the TV. We have strict rules in our house about the TV. Among those rules is this one: no TV before school in the morning. They know this rule. They understand the consequences of being caught watching TV against the rules. Yet they were downstairs watching *Animal Planet.*

Although I was disappointed, I was not surprised. Children will do things they should not do. Part of my job as a loving father is to teach them right from wrong; part of that lesson is meting out appropriate consequences for wrong behavior. Never, though, do those consequences involve any less love from me. I love my children deeply, and nothing they do will make me love them any less.

Far more than I am capable of loving my children, God loves us. "God is love" (1 John 4:16). God knows us. God knows all of our secrets and all of our sins. It is "he who searches our hearts" (Romans 8:27). With all of that knowledge, God never abandons us, rejects us, or gives up on us. Rather, God loves us just as deeply and intimately as he knows us. In his knowledge he disciplines us for our good (Deuteronomy 8:5; Job 5:17; Proverbs 3:12; Hebrews 12:5-11).

2. *You know when I sit and when I rise;*
   you perceive my thoughts from afar.

David expands upon his initial statement that God knows us. Even in the ordinary business of living, God is aware and involved. Sitting and standing are hardly worth noting. Yet no movement we make can escape the attention of God.

Similarly, our thoughts do not escape his awareness. We may try to hide our feelings and fail to express our emotions. We may lock our mouths shut, keeping our thoughts to ourselves. But God knows what we feel and think. He is more aware of our motives and passions than even we ourselves are aware of.

The ancient Israelites sometimes bowed down to physical, visible idols, and sometimes they bowed down to idols in their hearts (Ezekiel 14:1-8). God knew about their idols, and he knows about ours!

3. You discern my going out and my lying down;
    you are familiar with all my ways.

The word *discern* translates an intriguing word. The idea is "to measure." In other contexts the Hebrew verb being translated refers to the threshing process (example: Ruth 3:2). Here, though, the concept focuses more on God's knowledge than on God's actions. He knows it all: *my going out, my lying down,* and *all my ways.* In other words, nothing I do is too insignificant for God's attention.

Even after nearly 20 years of marriage, I must admit that the light in the room seems to brighten when my wife enters. In a room full of people, she still captures my attention simply by smiling. Her voice, though soft, is the one I hear above all other voices. When she laughs, my heart leaps. I cannot say I am the most observant person in the world—I have no idea how long she has owned any dress in her closet!—but I am much more aware of her than I am of anyone else. She captures my attention because I love her. Far more than the attention I give to my wife is the attention God gives to me and to every other person. His attention is limitless, his awareness is total, and his love is comprehensive. We capture his attention because he loves us.

HE KNOWS HIS CHILDREN

A 6-year-old girl vanished in 1986 while playing hide-and-seek in the yard of her home. Seventeen years later, a woman called the little girl's parents, saying that she was the long-lost daughter. Of course, the parents' hopes for a joyful reunion skyrocketed. Over the next few days the "lost daughter" talked to the police and news media, sometimes pretending that she was yet another person corroborating the story.

Then the story fell apart, shattering the parents' hopes. The perpetrator of the hoax admitted her guilt, but pleaded mental illness and was sentenced to 18 months in prison. During the trial, her mental condition was described as predisposing her to a compulsion to perpetrate "grand hoaxes" for the attention these would gain her. It turned out that her list of previous illegal activities in several states included crank calls, false fire alarms, bad checks, bomb threats, and stolen credit cards.

In this tragic case evil people (not the daughter herself) inflicted the pain of loss not once but twice. In our case it is we who inflict the pain of loss on God each time we accept the enemy's enticements and run away from him. But God knows his children. If they wander, he still knows who they are, why they are gone, and where they are. If we try to return to him in pretense, he is not fooled. But neither is his love for us dimmed when we return in complete repentance. What a steadfast love!
          —C. R. B.

B. MY FLIGHT IS FUTILE (vv. 7-12)

7. Where can I go from your Spirit?
    Where can I flee from your presence?

David's questions here are rhetorical. The answers are obvious: there is no place to hide from the scrutiny of God. David understands that space and time

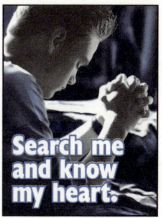

Visual for Lesson 3. *Point to this visual as you ask, "Who among us is willing to invite God to do this today?"*

HOW TO SAY IT

Elihu. Ih-LYE-hew.
Ezekiel. Ee-ZEEK-ee-ul or Ee-ZEEK-yul.
Hebrews. HEE-brews.
Immanuel. Ih-MAN-you-el.
Jonah. JO-nuh.
Onesimus. O-NESS-ih-muss.
Philemon. Fih-LEE-mun or Fye-LEE-mun.

do not constrict God. His presence is not limited to one area, nor must his actions follow linear time as we know it. God is not following us around like a private investigator. Rather, he already has arrived anywhere we may wish to go long before we get there.

When my children were babies, we would play a certain game. They would begin crawling away from me, possibly even into another room. I would tiptoe around and over them, out of their line of sight. Then I would stand directly in front of them. From their perspective, I suddenly appeared from nowhere. They were trying to escape from me, but there I was ahead of them! I would giggle, they would squeal, and then we would do it again.

In our childishness, foolishness, or ignorance, we may believe that we can crawl out of our Father's sight. We cannot. Never does his attention waver; never does his stamina wane. We may attempt to flee from him only to realize that he has moved in front of us. Jonah discovered that the hard way!

8. If I go up to the heavens, you are there;
*   if I make my bed in the depths, you are there.*

We could paraphrase by saying "from the highest mountain to the deepest part of the ocean" or "from the clouds to the caves." We are probably not stretching David's meaning of the word *heavens* too far to view it "as reaching to the stars."

9, 10. If I rise on the wings of the dawn,
*   if I settle on the far side of the sea,*
* even there your hand will guide me,*
*   your right hand will hold me fast.*

The poetry again focuses on the physical realm. The phrase *wings of the dawn* is a reference to the east, which is the direction of the sunrise. The phrase *far side of the sea* refers to the west, which is the direction of the Mediterranean Sea from Israel. Poetically, David is saying "from the east to the west you are with me." So once again David is emphasizing how comprehensive God's presence is. Go as far to the east or to the west as you wish. Regardless of how far you travel, God is there.

This presence, though, is not one of concern and fright to David. Rather, it is one of comfort. Even after traveling as far as possible, God's hand is there to *guide* and to *hold*. We cannot elude his attention, which means we cannot escape from his protection. Nor should we wish to escape from his protection. His presence is there because he is God, but the fact that he is there results in benefit to those who love him.

Make no mistake: God is not there because of us. He is there because of who he is. Part of God's nature is his ability to be present everywhere. God is not every*thing* in the sense that some false viewpoints hold. Nevertheless, God is every*where*. And the fact that he is present everywhere is good for us.

11, 12. If I say, "Surely the darkness will hide me
*   and the light become night around me,"*
* even the darkness will not be dark to you;*
*   the night will shine like the day,*
*   for darkness is as light to you.*

Shadows obscure our vision. Darkness hides what light reveals to us. This is especially true in an ancient culture that does not have streetlights or night-vision goggles.

God, however, is not limited by human senses. Presence and absence of light mean nothing to him who looks at the heart. Compare the words of these two

WHAT DO YOU THINK?

Many of us have been irritated by the persistent salesman who follows us around the store. When have you felt the same way about God? In what ways are you both concerned and thankful for his ever-present, watchful eyes?

verses with the words of Elihu in Job 34:22: "There is no dark place, no deep shadow, where evildoers can hide."

No Darkness Dark Enough . . .

H. G. Wells (1866–1946) wrote a famous story entitled *The Invisible Man*. It's about the temptation we would face if we could hide our identities (in effect, becoming invisible). The story is fantasy; the premise behind it is not. From time immemorial people have gone to "the big city" to become lost in the crowd—invisible to those who knew them before and unknown to people in their new surroundings. That may be the reason Onesimus (see Paul's letter to Philemon) went to Rome, where he was "found" by Paul and converted to Christ.

The 1997 movie *Face/Off* also toys with the idea of hidden identity. An FBI agent fighting a terrorist puts the criminal into a coma. Surgery results in having their faces switched. The agent, with his true identity and motives hidden, then can go into the prison where the terrorist's brother is in order to discover the details of a terrorist plot. When the terrorist comes out of his coma, he escapes to pose as the agent.

Fantastic? *Yes!* But no more in the realm of fantasy than the attempts many people make to escape the view of God so they can sin with impunity. We may be able to hide our sins from others, but we cannot hide from God (see Isaiah 29:15). As our text today says, we cannot find a darkness so dark that the light of God's purity cannot penetrate.   —C. R. B.

C. My Creation Is Key (vv. 13, 14)

13. For you created my inmost being;
    you knit me together in my mother's womb.

The phrase *my inmost being* refers figuratively to the heart, which we consider to be the seat of our emotions. It is God who has created that place. The psalmist (David) has no doubt of this fact. David also knows that God's ownership of our lives begins from the moment of conception. That's what David means when he says *you knit me together in my mother's womb.*

14. I praise you because I am fearfully and wonderfully made;
    your works are wonderful,
    I know that full well.

Staying focused on David's main point, we celebrate with him the fact that God's presence in our lives blesses us tremendously. God is present with us because he is God—it is his nature. That presence, though, cannot help but benefit those who love him.

The phrase *fearfully and wonderfully made* affirms the value of human life. God's handiwork in our lives extends back to the point of conception, as noted above. Unfortunately, many assume that life and individuality begin at some undefined, subjective point after conception. This viewpoint is what allows abortion, embryonic stem-cell research, and a host of other dehumanizing procedures. This dehumanization is also seen at the other end of human life. One politician spoke of a "duty to die" for elderly and terminally ill people. A nursing home attendant convicted of murdering elderly patients said that they were "useless eaters."

Interestingly, those whose lives often are defined as having little or no value—preborn children, those with mental disabilities, those with terminal illnesses, etc.—also have little or no political power. Could it be that we define the value of someone's life in terms of that which is useful to me or to society rather than to God?

WHAT DO YOU THINK?
David notes differences between how light and darkness affect us vs. how they affect God. Why are these two perspectives so different? How does this matter in your daily life?

WHAT DO YOU THINK?
Some may resist Christianity because they are afraid of being controlled. How would you respond to someone who expressed such a reservation?

WHAT DO YOU THINK?

Scientists are now able to clone life or at least control certain characteristics by tinkering with the DNA structure. Does this mean that the declaration that we are the products of God's design is losing its value? Why, or why not?

WHAT DO YOU THINK?

We are sometimes reluctant to share our secrets with others because of potentially damaging results. David, however, invited God to do a thorough search of his innermost thoughts and actions. How can we do the same while maintaining right motives?

PRAYER

Father, when Elijah felt alone, you sent him a storm, an earthquake, and a fire. But you were not present in these. Instead, you came to Elijah in a whisper. Help us to recognize your presence in the silences, in the quietness, when we are alone. In the name of Jesus, who came into our presence in the softness of a baby's cry, we pray, amen.

THOUGHT TO REMEMBER

"Reputation is what others think about you. Character is what God knows about you."

When someone's life becomes a burden or an inconvenience, that's when many see life as ceasing to be valuable. Some wonder how long God will delay his judgment on cultures that travel this path. Perhaps God also will judge the silence of his church in these matters.

God is the God of the living and the dead; he is the God of the widow and the orphan; he is the God of the preborn, the disabled, and the aged. Regardless of our physical health or social status, we are indeed *fearfully and wonderfully made.* We must remain fully aware of that truth.

II. GOD SAVES ME (PSALM 139:23, 24)

23, 24. Search me, O God, and know my heart;
    test me and know my anxious thoughts.
See if there is any offensive way in me,
    and lead me in the way everlasting.

Psalm 139 invites God to do within us that which he wishes. He searches us anyway. That is part of his nature. He knows our thoughts and our intentions. Our sins do not escape his notice (see Hebrews 4:13). How could it possibly be otherwise?

But it is only by invitation that he comes in and cleanses us. God will not impose himself on anyone in this regard. If we desire his direction, though, he will lead us into *the way everlasting.* When that happens, we can rejoice with David, "For as high as the heavens are above the earth, so great is his love for those who fear him" (Psalm 103:11).

"THE GENOCIDAL KILLER IN THE MIRROR"

With startling frequency we hear of the systematic killing of masses of people. They become victims due to race, ethnicity, religion, or nationality. The 1940s saw the Nazis try to destroy the Jews; in the 1970s it was the infamous Cambodian killing fields; in the 1990s Rwandan Hutus slaughtered the Tutsis. In the twenty-first century, religious extremists attempt to gain access to weapons of mass destruction daily.

Perhaps it is not so much *governments* that commit these atrocities as it is *individuals* who get caught up in their own passions when they are inflamed by demagogic leaders. Some students of psychology see several factors at work: (1) blind deference to authority, (2) response to social consensus, (3) stereotyping people in groups, and (4) willingness to make moral compromises to protect the security of one's own group. As one social commentator has said, there is a "genocidal killer in the mirror" if we look closely.

Given the right circumstances (and except for the grace of God), each of us is capable of sinful acts that horrify us when we see others committing them. This is why the psalmist's prayer in these verses is so significant and why it ought to be the daily prayer of every Christian. —C. R. B.

CONCLUSION

What David knew in part, Jesus revealed in full. "The way everlasting" is the "new and living way" (Hebrews 10:20) created for us by Jesus' birth, life, death, and resurrection. He is the one who bridged the chasm between us and God—the chasm of sin. The total presence that David celebrated became Immanuel, "God with us."

The promise of God's presence continues today with the indwelling of the Holy Spirit (Acts 2:38; Ephesians 1:13). May we allow him to continue to lead us in that everlasting path!

Discovery Learning

This page contains an alternative lesson plan emphasizing learning activities. Classes desiring such student involvement will find these suggestions helpful. The next page is a reproducible activity page to further enhance discovery learning.

LEARNING GOALS

After participating in this lesson, each student will be able to:

1. Cite the various ways that God knows and watches over him or her.

2. Give reasons why God's continuous presence should provide comfort, not concern.

3. Write a sentence or brief paragraph that will remind him or her daily of God's presence.

INTO THE LESSON

To begin the class, reproduce and distribute these questions to no more than three couples (married or dating) or to pairs of good friends. You may wish to ask for volunteers in order to preserve the good-natured aspect of this exercise. (The questionnaire is also printed in the student books.)

Be sure that both parties are present to fill out the questionnaire and that they do not collaborate on their answers. Say, "So that those not filling out questionnaires won't get bored, your time limit is two minutes."

How Well Do You Know Him/Her?

Working independently, answer the following questions about yourself and your spouse or friend:

1. What is his/her favorite color?
2. What is his/her favorite dessert?
3. What is his/her favorite TV program?
4. What is the last book he/she read for enjoyment?
5. When is his/her birthday?
6. What is his/her dream vacation?
7. What is your favorite color?
8. What is your favorite dessert?
9. What is your favorite TV program?
10. What is the last book you read for enjoyment?
11. When is your birthday?
12. What is your dream vacation?

When all the pairs have completed the questionnaires, ask volunteers to reveal their answers to see how well they really know their spouses or friends. The results can be humorous, but do not allow this exercise to drag out. Make a transition by saying, "Today's lesson deals with God's intimate knowledge of our deepest secrets." (An alternate way to begin class is to distribute copies of the reproducible page's crossword puzzle for students to work on as they arrive.)

INTO THE WORD

Divide your class into small groups of two or three. Half of the groups will do *Study #1* regarding God's ability to know everything. The other half will do *Study #2* regarding God's ability to be everywhere. (If your class uses the student books, space is provided there for this activity; otherwise, copy the activities below and provide one for each group.)

After the groups finish, discuss findings with the class as a whole. Use the lesson commentary to guide your discussion.

Study #1—God's Ability to Know Everything: Read Psalm 139:1-4, 13, 14, 23, 24. Together with your group members, write a paraphrase of these verses in the space provided, restating the verses in your own words. Next, write a brief paragraph to explain why these verses should bring comfort to the believer who reads them.

Paraphrase of verses 1-4, 13, 14, 23, 24:

[Provide several blank lines for writing.]

These verses give us comfort because:

[Provide several blank lines for writing.]

Study #2—God's Ability to Be Everywhere: Read Psalm 139:7-12. Together with your group members, write a paraphrase of these verses in the space provided, restating the verses in your own words. Next, write a brief paragraph to explain why these verses should bring comfort to the believer who reads them.

Paraphrase of verses 7-12:

[Provide several blank lines for writing.]

These verses give us comfort because:

[Provide several blank lines for writing.]

INTO LIFE

Make a transition by saying, "One way to draw closer to God is to write our own psalms. Although we should not pretend that we are writing Scripture, God will be pleased when we pour out our hearts to him."

Then ask students each to create a brief psalm. It is to remind themselves daily that God is ever-present in their lives. Provide paper for this exercise or refer your class to the student books, where space is provided. Ask volunteers to share their work and then close with prayer, thanking God for knowing our hearts. If time is too limited, suggest this activity as homework. Those who wish can read their psalms to the class next week.

God Knows Me: Psalm 139:1-3, 7-14

Across

1. Married to father.
3. God has made us this way.
6. Something I recognize is _____.
8. God is this (v. 7)
9. "Where can I flee from your _____?"
11. Made by God.

Down

2. The things I think.
3. Babies grow inside this.
4. Something God can do without needles.
5. Opposite of light.
6. God has made me this way (v. 14).
7. Opposite of darkness.
8. Means "looked for."
10. A time when a light is useful.

Living in and as God's Creation
Unit 1: The Glory of God's Creation
(Lessons 1-4)

SING PRAISE TO THE CREATOR

WHY TEACH THIS LESSON?

Which is more common: (1) to ask God to meet a need or (2) to praise him for what he is doing and who he is? The truth is, most of us spend a lot more time *asking* than *praising*. Yet our praise should be continuous and loud, private and public! That is the lesson of Psalm 145, the study of the day. The wise teacher will use this lesson to guide those who need to learn how to praise God to the fullest.

INTRODUCTION

A. PREFERENCES AND PASSIONS

One can gain an appreciation for the differences in people by watching a youth soccer game. Parents approach the games with very different mind-sets. Some of them are totally focused on the experience, shouting out "Good job, sweetie" as their daughter falls in the mud for the sixth time. Others emphasize the team skills more, cheering on every good pass or other quality team play while paying little attention to individual efforts. Still others are just the opposite: "Pass it to my son!" "That's my boy!" etc.

Some parents shout until they are hoarse. Others will call out a couple of times to let their child know they are present but will not get too enthusiastic or passionate. Some go all out, wearing the team's colors and chasing their team up and down the field to show their support. And, sadly, a few do not understand the goals of youth sports and focus solely on winning or on negativity. Styles!

We can see similar differences in stylistic approaches to worship, from very expressive to very subdued and reverent. The different ways that people cheer at youth soccer games reflect cultural background, social mores, emotional temperament, and personal values. This is true in worship as well. Yet God is the same God, whether we worship him in exuberant celebration or in stately reflection. We are the ones who differ.

Too often people let those superficial differences divide them. I may not paint my face blue or wear the latest fad in team apparel at sporting events. That does not mean that I am any less committed to my team than those who are more expressive. In worship I may lift my hands or sit serenely. I may worship with guitars or with pipe organs or with voices only. I may pray in English or Swahili, but if I am worshiping the one true God, then it does not matter. Differences in worship style do not change the fact that God is the same yesterday, today, and forever.

B. LESSON BACKGROUND

King David was a man who knew all about the ups and downs of life. His victory over Goliath, being chased by Saul, selection to be king, adultery with

Mar 26

DEVOTIONAL READING:
PSALM 150

BACKGROUND SCRIPTURE:
PSALM 145

PRINTED TEXT:
PSALM 145:1-13

LESSON AIMS

After participating in this lesson, each student will be able to:

1. Review the reasons the psalmist gives for praising God.

2. Describe various ways to praise God.

3. Create a plan for one generation to express God's praise to a different generation.

KEY VERSE

The LORD is gracious and compassionate, slow to anger and rich in love.   —Psalm 145:8

LESSON 4 NOTES

Bathsheba—so many experiences on both the spiritual mountaintop and in the spiritual valley! Probably it was both types of experiences that drove David to greater praise and worship.

I. MY PRAISE OF GOD (PSALM 145:1-3)

A. HIS NAME (vv. 1, 2)

1. I will exalt you, my God the King;
    I will praise your name for ever and ever.

Notice the words *exalt, praise,* and *extol* in the first two verses of Psalm 145. Each word has the same essential meaning: to lift high, to give honor publicly and openly, and to promote. David makes very clear from the outset what this psalm is about. He intends to promote God publicly and vigorously.

Although David addresses God directly, the intended action is for others to notice. David wants to make sure that the fame of God is spread everywhere. No one should fail to know or understand how great God is, and David will make sure that God's greatness is unmistakable and undeniable.

2. Every day I will praise you
    and extol your name for ever and ever.

David intends to promote God over two time periods. The first is daily. The promise *Every day I will praise you* is a promise to be consistent in doing so.

Sometimes we fool ourselves into thinking that we will do great things for God "someday." That usually is neither necessary nor valuable. Daily consistency in small things will win out in the long run. Daily prayer is a start. Following that, we may make it our goal to speak to one person today about Jesus Christ. This could be very low key—perhaps a comment like, "I am grateful to God for my family." Such conversation starters may not seem like much, but God can use them to do great things. Do not let another day go by without publicly praising and blessing the name of God.

The second time period that David refers to is *for ever and ever.* Eternity will not be too long a "time" to sing the praises of God. Indeed, that will be our main task (compare Revelation 19:1-8). Those who know God will find new things about his deeds, creativity, character, etc., for which to praise him constantly.

B. HIS GREATNESS (v. 3)

3. Great is the LORD and most worthy of praise;
    his greatness no one can fathom.

The *greatness* of God is inexhaustible. The more we know him, the more we want to praise him. The idea of praise is so important that it is repeated in Psalms 48:1 and 96:4, among others.

I spent four years in Bible college. During that time, I met some of the best people in the world. I learned some of the most dynamic concepts that I will ever encounter. I could go on and on describing the value of my alma mater. If Bible college can give me such rich material with which to sing praises, imagine what a lifetime spent knowing God will provide! We will begin entirely new symphonies of praise after our time on earth is finished.

PINK MARGARINE AND THE WORSHIP OF GOD

In some places in America a half-century ago, one could not buy yellow margarine. The dairy industry was protecting its butter production. Margarine was sold in an unappetizing white form with a pouch of yellow food coloring. Thus yellow margarine was a do-it-yourself project.

WHAT DO YOU THINK?

Sunday worship is important, but how we live each weekday is really a better overall measure of our relationship with our Lord. What are some ways that you continue to worship God throughout the week?

Actually, the story starts much earlier. In the late 1890s, New Hampshire law required that margarine be colored *pink!* The theory was that pink is not a color most people are attracted to in food—except, perhaps, for strawberry ice cream. In 1898 the New Hampshire Supreme Court struck down the law. Eventually margarine became accepted as a substitute for butter.

How silly! Yet don't we see some Christians going to curious lengths to protect their favorite style of worship? They act as if all other forms of worship are to be rigorously rejected, resented, and prevented. They try to protect their only-true-butter by seeing all else to be pink margarine.

Many who resist changes in worship would loudly reject the worship of medieval times with its very different styles of music and preaching. But God is not locked into any one culture, time, or place. As time passes, culture changes and people need culturally acceptable, yet still *scriptural*, ways to worship God. We should praise God when each new generation of Christians finds meaningful ways to worship, even if those ways are not particularly helpful to us!   —C. R. B.

Visual for Lesson 4. *Have your students repeat these verses together. Then ask for examples of how one generation witnesses to the next.*

II. OTHERS' PRAISE OF GOD (PSALM 145:4-7)

A. HIS DEEDS AND MAJESTY (vv. 4-6)

4. One generation will commend your works to another;
     they will tell of your mighty acts.

Communication of God's greatness must cross from *generation* to generation. Moses recognized how important this task was in his own day (see Deuteronomy 4:7-9; 11:18-21).

5. They will speak of the glorious splendor of your majesty,
     and I will meditate on your wonderful works.

There is a bit of uncertainty about some of the Hebrew words in this verse regarding who is to *speak.* Is it "I" or "they"? Verses 1 and 2 stress "I" (meaning David), while verses 4, 6, and 7 have "one generation" and "they" offering praise. Surely it is everyone who is to tell *of the glorious splendor of your majesty!* Not only must we teach about God to each succeeding generation, we also must model our awe of God to our children and grandchildren. Knowing God's Word without knowing God's *works* is incomplete: the works lend power and credence to the words.

Obviously, we are responsible for sharing the gospel with others of our own generation. The reality, though, is that most evangelism occurs from parent to child. Thus we exert every effort to bridge the gap between generations. One of the challenges is to prevent personal feelings and stylistic choices from interfering.

I visited a very contemporary church one weekend where a smiling couple, who appeared to be in their 70s, greeted me at the door. As we took our seats, I asked them about their church. "Actually," the wife said, "I hate the music! Oh, they play it very well but it is not to my taste. But I will never go to another church. This church brought my grandchildren to Christ. If they can do that, they can play any kind of music they want to!"

6. They will tell of the power of your awesome works,
     and I will proclaim your great deeds.

The *awesome works* of which David speaks should be thought of as "things that cause fear" or "things that inspire awe." Such acts witness to a power of God that is far beyond our comprehension. David's son Solomon rightly tells us "the fear of the Lord is the beginning of knowledge" (Proverbs 1:7; also see Job 28:28; Psalm 111:10; Proverbs 9:10).

Declaring the *great deeds* of God is parallel to speaking of his acts that inspire awe or cause fear. On the night the angel appeared to the shepherds, they were

WHAT DO YOU THINK?

What have you found that improves communication when teaching teens about their need for God?

WHAT DO YOU THINK?

There are many Old Testament passages where God's vengeance is mentioned. Yet David's own life events could allow him to stress God's greatness and kindness. How can you add David's life events to your own to allow you to see God's greatness and kindness today?

DAILY BIBLE READINGS

Monday, Mar. 20—*Glory in God's Holy Name (Psalm 105: 1-11)*

Tuesday, Mar. 21—*I Sing Your Praise (Psalm 138)*

Wednesday, Mar. 22—*Sing to God a New Song (Psalm 149)*

Thursday, Mar. 23—*Praise the Lord! (Psalm 150)*

Friday, Mar. 24—*I Will Extol You, O God (Psalm 145: 1-7)*

Saturday, Mar. 25—*Your Kingdom Is an Everlasting Kingdom (Psalm 145:8-13a)*

Sunday, Mar. 26—*God Is Faithful (Psalm 145:13b-21)*

quite afraid (Luke 2:9). After recovering from their fear and seeing the baby Jesus, they spread the good news and praised God (Luke 2:17, 20). That's one example of what it means to stand in awe of God's deeds and *proclaim* his greatness.

THE OBJECT OF OUR PRAISE

"Pastor's acquittal praised, scorned" read a headline of the *San Diego Union-Tribune* on March 22, 2004. At issue was the ordination of a "self-avowed, practicing" lesbian. A church court had determined that she had done nothing wrong according to the denomination's *Book of Discipline,* even though one section reads that "the practice of homosexuality is incompatible with Christian teaching, [thus] self-avowed practicing homosexuals are not to be accepted as candidates, ordained as ministers, or appointed to serve."

Many praised the decision as being compassionate, forward-looking, and in touch with the times. Those who objected to the church court's verdict found it to be hypocritical, heretical, and out of touch with Scripture.

We live in a time when much that is sinful is praised in the media and advocated by the noisy opinion makers of Western culture. In recent years laws have been proposed in Canada, Sweden, and other nations that would make churches guilty of "hate speech" if they quoted biblical prohibitions against the homosexual lifestyle. On this and many other issues the church today thus is faced with the question "Who or what is to be the object of our praise?" Will it be God? Or will it be the sinful customs of an irreligious and increasingly pagan culture?   —C. R. B.

B. HIS GOODNESS AND RIGHTEOUSNESS (v. 7)

7. They will *celebrate your abundant goodness*
    and joyfully sing of your righteousness.

The Bible speaks of God's *goodness* and *righteousness* in dozens of passages. But this is a rare case in which these two exact words stand side by side. God extends his goodness especially to those whose hearts are clean and pure (Psalm 73:1). Even so, he offers some of his goodness to the unrighteous people as well (Matthew 5:45).

The concept of righteousness, for its part, is the same as justice when applied to God. It means that God always does the right thing. This is the very foundation of God's throne (Psalms 89:14; 97:2). What kind of heart is it that never can ponder the goodness or righteousness of God?

III. WORTHINESS OF GOD (PSALM 145:8-10)

A. LORD'S ATTRIBUTES (vv. 8, 9)

8. The LORD is *gracious and compassionate,*
    slow to anger and rich in love.

David makes a transition from praise to God for what he has done to a more general praise to God for his character. Some commentators have tried to argue that the God we see in the Old Testament is very different from the God revealed in the New Testament. According to this line of thinking, the God of the Old Testament is an angry, vengeful God while the God of the New Testament is one of love and grace. This distinction is far from the truth!

Although David knows the wrath of God from firsthand experience, David also knows God as *gracious and compassionate.* This is the same God that Moses knew hundreds of years before: "The Lord, the Lord, the compassionate and gracious God, slow to anger, abounding in love and faithfulness" (Exodus 34:6).

God does indeed administer corrective punishment from time to time. He may do this in calling us to repentance, to restoration of the covenant relationship that we break. God has done this even when people have rejected and despised him repeatedly. (See also Numbers 14:18; Nehemiah 9:17; Psalms 86:15; 103:8; Joel 2:13; and Jonah 4:2.)

9. The LORD is good to all;

    he has compassion on all he has made.

We may refer back to our comments on verse 7 that God's goodness extends to both just and unjust. He is truly *good to all!* One example of this that we see in Scripture is the prayer of Elijah that restored rain to Israel. God used drought to punish the country for sin, especially for the sin of King Ahab. For years Ahab and the people sinned grievously. But Elijah prayed, and God restored the rain. The number of righteous people in Israel seemed to be very small, with only 7,000 who had not worshiped Baal. But God blessed everyone with rain nonetheless (1 Kings 17:1; 16:29-33; 18:41-45; 19:18).

Earlier in Israel's history, Aaron led the people to create an idol of gold and worship it. God's initial response was to destroy the people and begin afresh with Moses as the father of a new nation. Through Moses' prayer, however, God granted mercy on the people even though their own sin made them worthy of death (Exodus 32). God is good!

B. DOUBLE PRAISE (v. 10)

10. All you have made will praise you, O LORD;

    your saints will extol you.

Jesus said that people could be evaluated by their works or fruit (Matthew 7:15-20). God's own works speak volumes about his nature (Psalm 19:1; Romans 1:20). The truest praise we can give to God is to discover his character and his will, then align our own character and will with them. Thus we as his *saints* honor and *extol* him.

In one sense the rest of the creation is better equipped to give praise to God than we are since the rest of creation is less affected by the fall. All creation suffered from humanity's sin (see Romans 8:20-22), but no part of creation suffered as much as humanity—though certainly that suffering is self-inflicted. For our own part we are both ill-equipped and well-equipped to praise God. The quagmire of sin mutes our praise; sin weakens our ability and desire to glorify him. We have gone further from God than any other part of creation, except perhaps Satan and the fallen angels.

Because of the grace of Christ, though, we are also the best equipped to praise him. No other part of creation has been so singularly blessed, nothing else has been made in God's image and likeness. Our voices should sound the loudest symphony of praise in all creation!

IV. KINGDOM OF GOD (PSALM 145:11-13)

A. GLORIOUS MAJESTY (vv. 11, 12)

11, 12. They will tell of the glory of your kingdom

    and speak of your might,

so that all men may know of your mighty acts

    and the glorious splendor of your kingdom.

Praise to God is valuable for its own sake. Praise also benefits the one doing the praising. But a third reason to praise has a testimonial purpose: praising God is part of sharing his good news with others.

Churches that ignore this aspect of worship fail to take full advantage of one of the best tools for witness and outreach. When we truly worship, praise, and exalt

HOW TO SAY IT

Ahab. AY-hab.

Bathsheba. Bath-SHE-buh.

Elijah. Ee-LYE-juh.

Goliath. Go-LYE-uth.

Nebuchadnezzar. NEB-yuh-kud-NEZ-er.

Nehemiah. NEE-huh-MY-uh.

WHAT DO YOU THINK?

While all creation may praise God, we humans have very distinct reasons for doing so. What could be some reasons why our praise would be different from the songs of the angels? How will your praise be different from theirs this week?

WHAT DO YOU THINK?

You may or may not have the poetic flair of a David. Still, we all are called to praise God. If you were called upon to declare your personal testimony in the worship of God, where would you begin and what would you say?

PRAYER

Father, we lift your name on high. We exalt your name. May those in our families, in our neighborhoods, at our jobs, at our schools, and in our communities see you lifted high. May they be attracted to your presence by our worship. In Christ's name we pray, amen.

THOUGHT TO REMEMBER

God—and only God—is worthy of worship.

the God who is living and active and involved in our lives, the church is at its most inviting. Many people are drawn to true worship. Worship is an attractive, beautiful activity. When that worship declares the glory of God and his kingdom, seekers may catch a glimpse of whom and what they have been seeking all along.

B. ENDURING DOMINION (v. 13)

13. *Your kingdom is an everlasting kingdom,*
    and your dominion endures through all generations.
   The LORD is faithful to all his promises
    and loving toward all he has made.

King Nebuchadnezzar was another who acknowledged the fact of God's enduring *kingdom* (Daniel 4:3, 34). The simple truth is that God is going to do his will. We will be happiest and most fulfilled when we align ourselves with that will. This is essentially what David is saying here in speaking of an *everlasting kingdom* and God's enduring *dominion*. God does not need our cooperation. God invites us to choose to be part of his movement, part of his kingdom. Operating on our own is self-destructive.

CONCLUSION

For several months I worked in retail sales while my wife attended graduate school. One of my job requirements was to sell extended warranties on products. I learned very quickly that this area of sales was not a strength of mine. Sometimes I would stumble over the words. Other times I would rush through the pitch too quickly. Communicating the features and benefits of the products came quite easily to me, but I struggled throughout my brief sales career with the more speculative features and benefits of this form of product insurance.

Similarly, selling credit cards never came easily to me. I am a firm believer in the principle that less debt is better than more debt. Since I do not like credit cards, I had a hard time investing myself in offering them. Although my employer used a carrot-and-stick approach—the carrot being commissions and financial incentives—I struggled for months to achieve even rudimentary results in promoting these things.

My personal desires and giftedness, though, were irrelevant to my employer. Part of my job was to sell those products! For as long as I worked in that company, selling those products was required. My evaluations were based in large measure on my success in those areas. Although I was not skilled in those areas, they were part of the job. Eventually, I mastered the skill enough to attain a measure of success, yet without compromising my integrity.

There are certain tasks in the Christian life that we sometimes try to assign only to those who are spiritually gifted in those areas. "Evangelism is the preacher's job," we may say, or, "The worship leader takes care of the praise in worship." Such excuses may comfort us for a while. But Bible study will convince us that all Christians are called by God to share the good news. All of us are called by God to praise his name. Whether we are skilled or gifted or equipped, we are responsible to do our part.

The challenge is to recognize that these are God's expectations. We also need to recognize, though, that the benefits to us are staggering. There is no feeling in the world like that of leading someone to know Christ. Baptizing someone is a great privilege! Worship and praise do much more for me than they do for God—although I am praising his name, he graciously blesses me more than I am capable of blessing him.

Discovery Learning

This page contains an alternative lesson plan emphasizing learning activities. Classes desiring such student involvement will find these suggestions helpful. The next page is a reproducible activity page to further enhance discovery learning.

LEARNING GOALS

After participating in this lesson, each student will be able to:

1. Review the reasons the psalmist gives for praising God.

2. Describe various ways to praise God.

3. Create a plan for one generation to express God's praise to a different generation.

INTO THE LESSON

Write these open-ended statements on the board:

> I like to praise God by . . .
> I praise God because . . .

Ask students to write down as many responses to each statement as they can generate in a minute or two, and then call on volunteers to share their answers with the class. Say, "Today's lesson deals with the *hows* and *whys* of worshiping God in the twenty-first century."

INTO THE WORD

Divide your class in half. One half will study Psalm 145:1-7 to identify the different *methods* that David used to praise God. The other half will study Psalm 145:8-13 to look for *reasons* why David praised God.

Instruct each group to use the questions below (also printed in the student books) to help them complete their studies. Within the two large groups, you may have your students work independently, in pairs, or in small groups depending on class size, seating arrangements, and available space.

Encourage students to refer to the additional Scriptures listed below for background information. You will want to study them yourself in advance to see how they illustrate David's teaching in Psalm 145.

Methods Group (Psalm 145:1-7):
How did David praise God?

1. How often did David praise God (v. 2)?

2. How is it possible to praise God "for ever" (vv. 1, 2)?

3. How is recognizing God's greatness a specific type of praise (v. 3)?

4. How can one generation praise God's works to another (v. 4)? What techniques did the Jews use to do this? (See Deuteronomy 11:18-21.)

5. What is involved in declaring the "mighty acts" of God (v. 4)? (See Exodus 15.)

6. In what ways could David and other Jews have spoken of God's greatness, majesty, and works (vv. 4-6)? (See 2 Samuel 6.)

7. How would the ancient Jews have sung of God's righteousness (v. 7)? (See Psalm 33:1-3.)

Reasons Group (Psalm 145:8-13):
Why did David praise God?

1. What do the terms *gracious, compassionate, slow to anger,* and *rich in love* suggest about God's nature (v. 8)?

2. How did God show his mercy and compassion to David? (See 1 Samuel 16; 2 Samuel 22.)

3. How does God demonstrate his goodness to all people? (See Matthew 5:45.)

4. How do God's works praise him (v. 10)?

5. What are some examples from the Old Testament of how the ancient Jews testified of God's glory, kingdom, and mighty acts (vv. 10, 11)? (See 1 Kings 10:1-13; Isaiah 52.)

6. Why would the eternal nature of God's kingdom be a reason to praise God (v. 13)? In our present age, what would be involved in testifying to the world about God's kingdom?

Allow 10 to 15 minutes, then have groups discuss their findings with the entire class. Use the lesson commentary to guide the discussion. Emphasize, in particular, the relationship between *how* we praise God and *why.* Ask students to suggest ways to praise God specifically for one of his traits (for example, the trait of mercy).

INTO LIFE

Make a transition by saying, "Now let's think about applying our hows to various groups within the church." Divide your class into small groups of three or four. Provide each group with a paper that is blank except for these three headings: *Adults, Teens, Children.* (Space for this exercise is also in the student books.)

Ask each group to take one of God's traits as discussed in the previous activity and spend several minutes brainstorming ways for each of the generational groups to praise God for that attribute. Remind your students that adults, teens, and children may not prefer the same styles of music, sermons, or other worship activities. Discuss each group's answers.

You can also use the "Praise Service Plan" on the reproducible page to achieve lesson aim #3.

Praise Service Plan

Use the form below to plan a worship service designed to praise God based on today's lesson. (You might decide to use or to not use all the "features" listed below, and you may decide to add others.)

Theme:

Key Scripture:

Target Audience (Adults, Teens, Children, Blended):

Praise Leader:

Praise Team Members/Musicians:

Hymns, Songs, and/or Praise Choruses:

Communion Hymn:

Communion Servers:

Scripture/Responsive Readings:

Other Praise Activities/Special Music:

Preacher/Devotional Leader:

Sermon/Devotional Text:

Invitation Hymn/Chorus:

Closing Hymn/Chorus:

Living in and as God's Creation
Unit 2: Living with Creation's Uncertainty
(Lessons 5-9)

RESPONDING TO TRAGEDY

WHY TEACH THIS LESSON?

C. S. Lewis pictured spiritual warfare by using a variety of literary types. Written for children—but also for their parents—are *The Chronicles of Narnia*, resembling the legends of Arthur. For adults he wrote, in a similar fantasy style, the futuristic trilogy *Out of the Silent Planet, Perelandra*, and *That Hideous Strength*. But perhaps most effective of all, he wrote a series of hypothetical letters from one demon (Screwtape) to another (Wormwood). The letters characterize the devious and persistent attacks the devil makes against the child of God.

The biblical book of Job paints a similar picture. Because this book is from the hand of the Spirit, all Christians should read it. The devil's use of catastrophe, physical distress, family grief, impoverishment, and the pseudowisdom of trusted friends—all are part of his "normal" warfare tactics.

Every child of God comes under attacks that are both vicious and subtle. This is why the timeless book of Job must be taught again and again. When Job's struggles become our own, we cast ourselves more fully on God's strength.

INTRODUCTION

A. AGE-OLD PROBLEM

The tragic element of life is painfully obvious. We need look no further than this morning's newspaper or our own experience to know that tragedy is everywhere. This is not just a concern of the modern world. The book of Job, which is the basis for our next three lessons, is an ancient book. There the author explores the meaning of suffering, particularly unjustified suffering. Admittedly, some suffering comes from our own poor decisions. At other times we suffer because of the poor decisions of other people. Some suffering, however, is inexplicable, and we must turn to God for answers.

Some believe that the issue of suffering is Christianity's greatest problem. They ask, "Why would a good God allow the suffering of innocent people?" But it is not just a problem for Christianity. Every religion and philosophy must address the problem of suffering. The author of Job takes these themes quite seriously.

B. LESSON BACKGROUND

The book of Job is the subject of countless opinions. Scholars disagree about the author. Some say Job himself wrote it. Others try to make a case for Moses or even Elihu, a friend of Job who appears near the end of the book. Since no author is given, we cannot know for sure. Its value comes from the fact that the book is inspired by God; the value is not dependent on knowing the identity of the human author.

Scholars also differ as to the date. Their estimates range from Job's being one of the earliest Old Testament books to one of the last. Even the language is hard to translate. That would be an indication of its being a very old book. A good guess is that Job himself lived sometime in the age of the patriarchs, between

DEVOTIONAL READING:
PSALM 22:1-11
BACKGROUND SCRIPTURE:
JOB 1–3
PRINTED TEXT:
JOB 1:14-22; 3:1-3, 11

Apr
2

LESSON AIMS

After participating in this lesson, each student will be able to:

1. Recite the fundamental facts about the person and book of Job.

2. Discuss the nature of grief and right ways to respond to it.

3. Make a plan to worship God when personal grief comes.

KEY VERSE

"Shall we accept good from God, and not trouble?" In all this, Job did not sin in what he said.   —Job 2:10

2000 and 1500 B.C. It is possible that the time period of Job himself and the time of the writing of the book are not the same.

Scholars also differ about the man Job. Was he an Israelite or not? We don't know. We are certain, however, that Job was not a fictitious character (see Ezekiel 14:14, 20; James 5:11). He is described as being from Uz (Job 1:1). This is in the territory of the Edomites, south of Palestine (Lamentations 4:21).

The book of Job depicts Job as a righteous man. He feared God. He turned from evil. He was good to his neighbors. He worshiped God and offered sacrifices. God himself declared Job to be "blameless and upright, a man who fears God and shuns evil" (Job 1:8). That will be important to remember as we explore this book. The book of Job is more than just the story of a man with patience. It forces us to wrestle with our understanding of, and our response to, suffering.

After chapter 1 introduces us to Job, we move quickly to an assembly in Heaven. God is there, and standing in His presence are *the angels* (Job 1:6).

Among the angels is one called Satan, which means "adversary" or "accuser." (It is more of a title than a name.) God brags about Job, but Satan accuses God of taking it easy on that man. Satan tells God that Job's faithfulness is understandable considering all the material blessings God has given him. Satan then proclaims that Job will curse God to His face if God makes Job's life difficult (Job 1:11). Consequently, the Lord grants Satan permission to oppress Job. "Very well, then, everything he has is in your hands, but on the man himself do not lay a finger" (Job 1:12).

I. JOB'S LOSSES (JOB 1:14-19)

Our text begins in the middle of chapter 1 as we see Satan beginning his assault on Job.

A. BY THE SABEANS (vv. 14, 15)

14. A messenger came to Job and said, "The oxen were plowing and the donkeys were grazing nearby,

The first attack is on Job's possessions. As our text unfolds, we see a pattern as each disaster is followed by one surviving messenger bringing the bad news to Job. The first disaster falls upon the domesticated farm animals, the *oxen* and *donkeys*. Job has "seven thousand sheep, three thousand camels, five hundred yoke of oxen and five hundred donkeys, and had a large number of servants" (Job 1:3), so a lot is at stake here!

15. . . . and the Sabeans attacked and carried them off. They put the servants to the sword, and I am the only one who has escaped to tell you!"

The first attack involves human villains, namely *the Sabeans*. They engage in brazen theft and murder. The Sabeans can be found in several areas in the ancient world. Some are associated with an area in southern Arabia we know as Sheba (Isaiah 60:6; Jeremiah 6:20). The queen of Sheba will visit Solomon (1 Kings 10:1-13).

Some think that these particular Sabeans are associated with Tema in northern Arabia (Job 6:19). In any case the amount of loss to Job is incredible, even at this early stage.

B. BY THE FIRE OF GOD (v. 16)

16. While he was still speaking, another messenger came and said, "The fire of God fell from the sky and burned up the sheep and the servants, and I am the only one who has escaped to tell you!"

WHAT DO YOU THINK?

Where do most people seem to put the blame for evil? How would you respond to them?

[Make sure that you consider 1 Thessalonians 3:5 and James 1:13.]

WHAT DO YOU THINK?

How important are your earthly possessions to your faith in God?

The tragic drama is underscored by the appearance of *another messenger* while Job is still talking with the first. This second calamity appears to be a kind of natural disaster. *The fire of God* is most likely a lightning strike, although it also may refer to something like a volcanic eruption (compare 2 Kings 1:10, 12, 14). The amount of sheep lost is 7,000, since Job 1:3 says that that's what Job owns. Immeasurably more tragic is the loss of human life.

C. BY THE CHALDEANS (v. 17)

17. While he was still speaking, another messenger came and said, "The Chaldeans formed three raiding parties and swept down on your camels and carried them off. They put the servants to the sword, and I am the only one who has escaped to tell you!"

The sad pattern repeats. Yet *another messenger* arrives on the heels of the others to report a third disaster. This one is at the hands of *the Chaldeans*. Again we see theft and murder.

We don't know exactly how many servants are slain. Job's 3,000 *camels,* for their part, are now the property of bandits. Camels are of great value to nomads in the ancient world. Their ability to carry loads and adapt to the desert heat is prized even today.

D. BY A GREAT WIND (vv. 18, 19)

18, 19. While he was still speaking, yet another messenger came and said, "Your sons and daughters were feasting and drinking wine at the oldest brother's house, when suddenly a mighty wind swept in from the desert and struck the four corners of the house. It collapsed on them and they are dead, and I am the only one who has escaped to tell you!"

Job has 7 *sons* and 3 *daughters* (Job 1:2). He has lost animals and servants to this point, but now the tragedies strike much more personally. The problem occurs at the home of Job's son. This feast he is hosting may be a birthday celebration, or the 10 children simply may socialize together from time to time. Each of the 7 sons takes a turn hosting the periodic gathering (Job 1:4). It is Job's custom to offer sacrifices for his children afterward (1:5).

Job 1:13 says much of what 1:18 says. This reinforces the fact that all these disasters happen on the same day. This fourth disaster happens when a great wind topples the house on those gathered for the meal. These winds, called sirocco winds, are common problems for nomadic peoples (compare Jeremiah 4:11).

II. JOB'S REACTION, PART 1 (JOB 1:20-22)

None of these tragic circumstances is necessarily rare in the desert. But the accumulation of all in such a short time means they can't be happening by chance.

A. GRIEF AND WORSHIP (v. 20)

20. At this, Job got up and tore his robe and shaved his head. Then he fell to the ground in worship

The fact that Job gets up means that he has been sitting to this point. He expresses his grief in a way that is normal for his time and place as he tears his outer garment and shaves *his head.* The tearing of garments can been seen in numerous passages, including Genesis 37:34; Joshua 7:6; Ezra 9:3, 5; and Acts 14:14. The tearing and the shaving indicate profound grief of the heart. We also see a connection of shaved heads with mourning in Jeremiah 16:5-7; 47:5; and 48:36-38, to name just a few.

DAILY BIBLE READINGS

Monday, Mar. 27—Job, a Blameless and Upright Man (Job 1:1-5)

Tuesday, Mar. 28—Satan Determines to Strike Job (Job 1:6-12)

Wednesday, Mar. 29—Job Loses All, but Remains Faithful (Job 1:13-22)

Thursday, Mar. 30—Job Falls Ill, but Praises God (Job 2:1-10)

Friday, Mar. 31—Job Curses His Day of Birth (Job 3:1-10)

Saturday, Apr. 1—Job Wishes for Death (Job 3:11-19)

Sunday, Apr. 2—Job Questions God's Benevolence (Job 3:20-26)

WHAT DO YOU THINK?

Cultures around the world have varying traditions regarding expressions of grief and sorrow. What are some examples? In what ways are these helpful or harmful spiritually?

"The Lord gave, and the Lord hath taken away; blessed be the name of the Lord" (Job 1:21).

Visual for Lesson 5. *Use this poster as a discussion starter as you ask, "In what other ways does the Lord give and take away?"*

In spite of his grief, Job still worships God. Sometimes people are prone to stop attending church and to stop their personal devotions when grief comes. A newlywed couple had just started coming to church, but stopped when they found out that the wife had contracted AIDS from a previous, immoral situation. They lost faith. What a great mistake to close ourselves off from the one who can help us in our pain!

B. PRAISE AND INTEGRITY (vv. 21, 22)

21. . . . *and said:*
  "Naked I came from my mother's womb,
    and naked I will depart.
  The LORD gave and the Lord has taken away;
    may the name of the Lord be praised."

In the midst of grief, Job makes a rather philosophical statement. He points out—correctly—that he came into the world with nothing and will leave with nothing anyway (compare Ecclesiastes 5:15). Job sees all his possessions, as well as his family, as a blessing from God. Ultimately they all belong to *the Lord*.

What may be troublesome to us is that God is named as being responsible for taking away the lives of Job's family. In what sense is that true? Since God has given each of us the breath of life, ultimately he can take us back to himself whenever and wherever he wishes. That is his right. But what is going on in this case? Job is not aware of what is happening behind the scenes. It is Satan who has taken away Job's children. This does not completely solve our problem, because the Lord gave Satan permission to do it.

In technical language we say that while it was not God's *prescriptive* will, it was definitely his *permissive* will. That means that while God did not prescribe for the tragedies to happen, he definitely permitted them. Such a distinction undoubtedly is of little use to Job in the midst of his profound distress. To Job, it is all from God. Job may not even be aware of the existence of Satan.

22. *In all this, Job did not sin by charging God with wrongdoing.*

Looking at the situation from a worldly viewpoint, we may say that Job has every reason to curse God. Job's wife even suggested it (Job 2:9). But he never does. The book of Job tells us that Job does not sin throughout this ordeal. He never charges God with any sin.

It's not that Job does not question God. Job will ask some tough questions of the Lord. Some of these questions will irritate God (see Job 38:2; 40:2). Even so, in the final analysis it is Job and not his friends who speaks what is right of God (Job 42:7). Some people assume that a faith that questions is a weak faith. To the contrary, it is through respectful questioning that we learn and our faith deepens.

IN THE FACE OF DEATH

Daniel Pearl was beheaded in Pakistan in 2002—the first of a grisly string of murders by Islamic militants that would continue for years. Most victims were civilians from the nations in the coalition of forces trying to break up al-Qaeda, the Islamic terrorist group. Pearl was a news reporter; others were business people helping Iraq rebuild after the war. In many cases Islamic television and Web sites showed pictures of the extremists committing their atrocities.

The poignancy of these murders was due partly to the fact that we saw the victims' family members pleading for the lives of the hostages. The scenes we saw on television moved us to empathize with their feelings of helplessness. Job, for his part, didn't get any advance warning. The fact that all of his children died in a natural disaster rather than by human barbarity scarcely made it easier to take.

WHAT DO YOU THINK?

What was an occasion when you felt confused or disappointed with God? What hard questions did you desperately want God to answer? How did such times affect you spiritually?

Death is heart-wrenching. We all hope that the lives of our loved ones will run their full courses. When life is cut short, we fall back on our spiritual resources. In this Job set the example: he did not blame God for his loss, but instead found his strength in God. Like Job we realize that God is our only source of hope when we are faced with our own death or of those we love.   —C. R. B.

III. JOB'S REACTION, PART 2 (JOB 3:1-3, 11)

Several things happen in the intervening verses that are not in today's text. For one, Satan makes another visit to Heaven to argue with God. Satan admits that Job has done well, but points out that Job himself has not been stricken. Thus Satan proposes to harm Job physically. Job then is afflicted with painful boils all over his body. Satan believes this will cause Job to curse God.

Some have supposed that Satan has overplayed his hand. He already has done his worst with Job's family. It is quite probable that Job cares more about his family than about his own health. Thus the additional problems in Job 2:7 are less important to Job than the losses he has already suffered. Nevertheless, the pain is great.

Interestingly, Satan does not appear after chapter 2. He is defeated, so there is no reason for him to reappear. The focus shifts to discussions between Job and his friends. They make some attempt to comfort Job. They offer their most valuable comfort in Job 2:13 as they sit with him without saying a word. Simply being there is so important. But then things go downhill after they open their mouths to speak. Their attempts to help come after Job speaks first.

A. DESIRE TO TURN BACK TIME (vv. 1-3)

1. After this, Job opened his mouth and cursed the day of his birth.

Job does not curse God, but he does express his great grief. Job is sorry he was ever born! As fruitless as it is to try to change the past, many spend much time and energy reliving the past or wishing things had been different. While Job's curse is understandable in the midst of his pain, the wish not to be born is fruitless. We are here, and we have to deal with the hard realities. At this point Job cannot see any beauty or good in his life.

2, 3. He said:

> **"May the day of my birth perish,**
> **and the night it was said, 'A boy is born!'"**

Verse 1 announced Job's curse. Now verses 2 and 3 tell us the words of the curse as we see Job cursing even his birth announcement! Yet Job does not curse God. The closest he comes is in cursing the *day of* his *birth*. This is very similar to something the prophet Jeremiah said in Jeremiah 20:14, 15.

In Job's day male children are particularly celebrated. They will be the ones to take leadership of the family in a patriarchal society. There now appears to be nothing left for Job to live for in this regard.

B. DESIRE TO TURN BACK LIFE (v. 11)

11. "Why did I not perish at birth,
> **and die as I came from the womb?"**

Verses 4-10 (not in our text for today) continue Job's curse against the day of his birth. Now in verse 11 Job even begins to wish that he had not survived birth. He wishes he had been stillborn. If not that, then he wishes he had died as a newborn infant. This indicates severe emotional trauma. The curse against the very beginning of his life continues in verses 12 and following.

HOW TO SAY IT

Al-Qaeda. Al KAI-duh.
Arabia. Uh-RAY-bee-uh.
Edomites. EE-dum-ites.
Elihu. Ih-LYE-hew.
Ezekiel. Ee-ZEEK-ee-ul or Ee-ZEEK-yul.
Isaiah. Eye-ZAY-uh.
Jeremiah. Jair-uh-MY-uh.
Sabeans. Suh-BE-unz.
Satan. SAY-tun.
Sheba. SHE-buh.
Solomon. SOL-o-mun.

WHAT DO YOU THINK?

What would you do if you heard someone say, "I wish I had never been born"?

PRAYER

Dear Lord, like your servant Job we often do not understand. Like Job we struggle with the whys of life. When tragedy comes, may it draw us near to you that we may overcome. In the name of Jesus, who also suffered unjustly, amen.

ANXIOUS, TROUBLED, DEPRESSED?

"When the Lord sends tribulations, I think he expects me to 'tribulate.'" Those are the sentiments attributed to a (probably) imaginary Christian. Most of us know the feeling, don't we? When troubles come to us, even if not to the extent that they did to Job, we feel troubled!

Scientists have discovered that the human brain is "hardwired" for fear; it helps us respond quickly to danger so that we can take the necessary steps to avoid serious harm. When the driver in the lane next to us is using the cell phone with one hand, is eating a hamburger with the other, and then suddenly crosses over into our lane, it is our fear that makes us able to take the necessary evasive action. Along with fear, the emotions of stress, apprehension, and depression are common (and normal) reactions to a world that sometimes seems to be spinning out of control.

As we examine how we react to the unsettling circumstances of our world—even when they don't affect us directly—we can hardly blame Job for the thoughts he expresses in our text today. Who wouldn't be depressed after experiencing all the bad things that happened to Job? Take heart: next week we will see what we can learn from Job's response to his troubles.   —C. R. B.

CONCLUSION

A. ONE OF CHRISTIANITY'S GREATEST CHALLENGES

Job brings us face-to-face with one of Christianity's greatest challenges: If God is good, then why does he allow the innocent to suffer? It was not God who brought the problems into Job's life—but neither did God interfere with Satan as he oppressed Job.

Sometimes suffering comes about as a direct consequence of the personal choices that people make (example: contracting a sexually transmitted infection through immoral behavior). Sometimes God himself inflicts suffering because of sin (example: Ezekiel 32:1-15). But at other times, as with Job, the suffering is unexplainable from an earthly point of view. God may have a bigger plan in mind that we can't see. (In Job's case we can see it but he can't.) In such instances we continue to trust God above all else (Job 13:15; 19:25). Job thought the solution to his problem was more knowledge (see Job 13:23; 23:5). But that was not God's viewpoint.

We should notice in passing that Satan is limited. He cannot do anything that God will not allow him to do. In the end even the devil must honor God's sovereignty. Satan has tried to put God down through Job. But ultimately it is Satan who is proven wrong.

B. WHEN LIFE TUMBLES IN

Even though Job eventually passes his tests, this lesson does not end on a high note. We will have to wait for the next two lessons to have a more satisfactory conclusion. Still, our lesson displays the great faith of Job. Even in despair he does not make foolish statements nor does he take foolish actions.

Many do not follow Job's example, but some do. Arthur John Gossip was a preacher in Aberdeen, Scotland. In 1927 he lost his wife quite suddenly. On his first day back in the pulpit, his sermon title was "When Life Tumbles In—What Then?" That sermon has become a classic because it deals with fresh grief.

Arthur John Gossip communicated that when all is lost, we must turn to God. Gossip said, "I do not understand this life of ours. But still less can I comprehend how people in trouble and loss and bereavement can fling away peevishly from the Christian faith. In God's name, fling to what? Have we not lost enough without losing that too?"

THOUGHT TO REMEMBER

The ultimate loss is to reject God.

Discovery Learning

This page contains an alternative lesson plan emphasizing learning activities. Classes desiring such student involvement will find these suggestions helpful. The next page is a reproducible activity page to further enhance discovery learning.

LEARNING GOALS

After this lesson, each student will be able to:

1. Recite the fundamental facts about the person and book of Job.

2. Discuss the nature of grief and right ways to respond to it.

3. Make a plan to worship God when personal grief comes.

INTO THE LESSON

Give each student a sheet of paper and pen. Direct everyone to draw a 12-block chart—three columns and four rows. Tell students to write J, O, B in the top row of three boxes.

Next, say, "We are going to play a game of Job by the Numbers. I am going to say both a category related to the book of Job and give the answer that goes with that category. All the answers will be numbers. You are to choose 9 of the 12 categories that I read. Write them down in your chart—1 category per box. Do not write down the answers/numbers, only the category."

Use the following categories or others of your own composition. Remember to state the answers/numbers, but remind the class not to write down the answers/numbers: (A) number of chapters in the book of Job—42; (B) number of friends who came to comfort and console Job—4; (C) number of Job's family members referred to in the book—21 (10 children killed, 10 children born later, plus his wife); (D) number of the chapter in which God finally confronts Job—38; (E) number of chapters that are predominantly in poetic format—39; (F) number of occasions Satan speaks to God about Job—2; (G) number of messengers who brought Job news of disaster—4; (H) number of times Job spoke with a monologue of affirmation or defense—10; (I) number of enemy nations said to have taken Job's livestock—2; (J) the number of animals Job lost—11,500; (K) number of chapters containing God's challenge to Job—3; (L) number of people mentioned by name in the book—5.

Before class, write all answers/numbers on slips of paper and put these in a bag or box. After reading the categories and the answers/numbers, say, "Next I'm going to pull out the slips one at a time and read them. Write the answer/number down in the matching category on your charts. When you have three in a row, call out 'Job!' and we will declare you the winner."

Pull out numbers and read them until someone wins. Verify the winner's responses.

INTO THE WORD

Say, "Most of us know something of the book of Job, but perhaps we need some familiarization with the various elements of that story." Assign the following roles for the reading of the text by distributing to students slips of paper with the following words (one word per slip): messenger, oxen, Sabeans, servants, sheep, Chaldeans, camels, sons, daughters, Job. Repeat any of the words (except Job) as necessary to give a role to each student.

An alternate use of these assigned roles involves selecting one person to stand, identify his or her role, and call for any others to stand with him or her if the roles are somehow related in the text. For example if a "sheep" stands, other related roles would be "servants" and "messenger," for the servants would have been keeping the sheep, and one servant would have been the messenger who ran to Job regarding the sheep's being stolen. Continue until each student has stood and joined a group at least once. Save the word *Job* until last, and all can stand.

INTO LIFE

Make a transition by saying, "We've had a bit of fun so far, but the book of Job is serious business. When we examine the life of Job, we must ask, 'How would my faith hold up in similar circumstances?'"

Then give your students a copy of the following list (also found in the student book). Ask each to respond honestly and personally to the following circumstances using this rating scale: 1 (=doubt would overwhelm) to 5 (=faith would grow). Discuss as time permits.

"How would you fare if …"

1. A flood destroys your property?
2. An adversary profits from an idea you had?
3. Criminals steal your family's valuables?
4. Your spouse gives up on God?

(Note: the Meeting Life's Tragedies activity on the reproducible page is a fuller version of this list. Box It Up is an alternative or additional activity to follow with.)

Meeting Life's Tragedies

How do you believe you would respond in each of the following life circumstances? Rate yourself on a five-point scale: 5 = full of faith, 3 = wavering, 1 = losing faith.

___ Loss of a spouse to an "early" death
___ Bankruptcy because of a partner's illegal activity
___ Death of a young child to illness
___ Destruction of home by fire or flood
___ Murder of a family member
___ Wrecked car not fully covered by insurance
___ Incarceration of child's spouse for a felony
___ Loss of long-time job due to company downsizing
___ Adversary profits from one of your ideas
___ Your spouse gives up on God and says you should too

What prayer do you feel compelled to pray as a response to your answers? Write it here.

How do you continue to worship God in any of the above cases? Put your plan here.

Box It Up

Job's possessions were taken from him by Satan's devious attack. Some things matter; some things, ultimately, do not. Sort your "possessions" into the two boxes shown here. The one is labeled "TOSS," the other, "KEEP." For example, what about your dress shoes? What about your Bible? What about your personal dignity?

Which box needs to be bigger? Which box is "fireproof"?

Living in and as God's Creation
Unit 2: *Living with Creation's Uncertainty*
(Lessons 5-9)

SEARCHING FOR HOPE

WHY TEACH THIS LESSON?

The silly TV sitcom *Hope and Faith* manages a few truths about family relationships. But the truth it best communicates is in its title. We Christians know that hope and faith are intrinsically interwoven. Without faith in God's revelation of himself and his plans, what is there to hope for? When Job's faith in God's essential goodness and fairness wavers, his hope also fades. Thus is the universal experience. For where there is no faith, there can be no hope.

The book of Job is, as every biblical book, designed to reveal God and his will. Job's response to his circumstances causes him to teeter on the brink of doubt. To see him resist his wife, his friends, and the devil himself, and then to see him wilt humbly and submissively in the face of God, has potential for helping every person of God. Today's lesson shows the way to meet discouragement and distress through deeper faith.

INTRODUCTION

A. UNWELCOME SUBJECT

Death is an unwelcome visitor. We don't even like to read about it, much less experience it. We don't want to see it happen to our family and friends, and we sometimes (or often) fear the day we must face it ourselves.

Death is an unwelcome subject. It's not talked about in polite society. Sometimes the only opportunity to deal with the subject of death is when it has happened, while the hurt is still fresh and the mind still confused.

There is a sense in which we are touched by death every day. We see stories about it in the newspaper or on TV. Or we hear about a friend of a friend who has died. There also come those tragic moments when death hits home to us. Death indeed is a subject we need to talk about. Since God's Word meets our deepest needs, it certainly will have much to say to us on the subject of death. So let's force ourselves to look at death. It is not so bad to speak of this subject at this particular season of the year. In the next seven days we will deal with both death and life. We already know that life will win out. But for now let us put ourselves in the shoes of people who have no hope, or at least people like Job who struggle.

In some ways you would think that we would get used to death. After all, everything that lives a physical existence dies. Even the tiniest plant that is given the privilege of life must die. The small microorganisms die. The animals die. The most difficult concept of all, of course, is to realize that we are going to die.

Death comes at various times. Sometimes the newborn is subject to death. Other times death waits until the summertime of life when someone is in his or her teens. We all are touched by the tragedy when death takes one away in middle age, often when there is still family to take care of. Even when death waits until old age, we are never quite ready for it.

Death comes in various ways. We are certain we don't want to experience any of them. Death may come through accident, sickness, or old age.

DEVOTIONAL READING:
JOB 36:24-33
BACKGROUND SCRIPTURE:
JOB 14; 32:1-8; 34:10-15; 37:14-24
PRINTED TEXT:
JOB 14:1, 2, 11-17; 32:6, 8; 34:12; 37:14, 22

Apr
9

LESSON AIMS

After participating in this lesson, each student will be able to:

1. Articulate the reasons why Job felt his life situation was so hopeless.

2. Identify those beliefs that can give a person both earthly and eternal hope.

3. Write a prayer that expresses hope for the current life and the life to come.

KEY VERSE

If a man dies, will he live again? All the days of my hard service I will wait for my renewal to come. —Job 14:14

WHAT DO YOU THINK?

What are the different ways that people view the idea of death? Which are most and least biblical? Why is it important to sort this out?

[Important Scriptures to consider are Genesis 2:17; 3:3; Ezekiel 18:20; Romans 6:23; 1 Corinthians 15:26; 2 Corinthians 5:1, 2; Philippians 1:21; James 1:15; Revelation 1:18; 14:13; 20:14.]

WHAT DO YOU THINK?

Why do you think that it is difficult for many people to express despair while at church? What can be done about this?

[Psalms 42:3-6; 69:1-3 can inform your discussion.]

Though it comes in various ways at various times, the inescapable fact is that death comes to all. No one can bargain his or her way out of it. There will be no escape. It happens to the good and the bad, the successful and unsuccessful, the attractive and the plain. It happens to the religious and irreligious, young and old, intelligent and ignorant.

Even though we know death will happen to us, we still try to avoid the ramifications in our emotional life. Indeed, it probably would be quite unsettling if we had to think of death every day. Still, we know that death will come. We see it as the common experience of all, yet there is something within us that says this should not be so.

B. LESSON BACKGROUND

Last week we looked at Job's initial response to tragedy. This week we examine Job's musings on life and death. To Job, this is not idle chit-chat. He is discussing these issues in depth with his friends, with grief still in his heart and scabs still on his body.

Throughout this book Job goes back and forth in his thinking. This polar swing is normal for grieving people. Chapter 14 seems to return to the despair of Job expressed earlier in the book. Our lesson picks up at the end of the first cycle of dialogues with Eliphaz, Bildad, and Zophar. Some evaluate Job's responses to these three men as being almost totally negative and fatalistic. Others see in his words hints of hope.

It is important for us to take the ride with Job. What he says in this section is not to be taken as the last word. He is not sharing final conclusions or convictions. He is engaged in a give-and-take where he answers some questions but raises others. We must engage in the discussion with Job and his friends.

I. REALITY OF DEATH (JOB 14:1, 2, 11, 12)

A. ARE OUR LIVES BRIEF AND TROUBLED? (v. 1)
1. *"Man born of woman*
     is of few days and full of trouble.

Job ponders the length and quality of life. To a young person, time seems like it lasts forever. To those in middle years, time seems short as they begin to note that there are more years behind them than ahead. The elderly ponder how it all happened so fast. No matter how much time we have, it is in some sense short.

Not only are our days brief, in Job's view, they are also *full of trouble*. Jacob also was one who noted the brevity and difficulty of life when he said, "My years have been few and difficult" (Genesis 47:9)—and he was age 130 when he said it! We should recall that Job was a wealthy and blessed man most of his life. No doubt Job had experienced many good days. But grief often colors one's perceptions.

B. ARE WE LIKE FLOWERS AND SHADOWS? (v. 2)
2. *"He springs up like a flower and withers away;*
     like a fleeting shadow, he does not endure.

In beautiful but sad words, Job compares human life first to *a flower*. How short is a flower's beautiful life! Flowers bring great joy due to their radiance and fragrance. But soon their petals are dropping, they lose their color, and they smell like dirt itself. The Bible writers often compare the brevity of life to that of flowers (see Psalm 103:15, 16; Isaiah 28:1, 4; James 1:10, 11; 1 Peter 1:24).

Job also compares human life to a *shadow*. Is there anything more transitory than that? Shadows come and go with the sun and clouds as well as our movement. They appear for a moment and then are gone (compare 1 Chronicles 29:15; Job 8:9; Psalms 102:11; 109:23; 144:4; Ecclesiastes 6:12).

Job's thoughts on the brevity of life in verses 1 and 2 here lead up to his question in verse 3 (which is not in today's text). Paraphrased, that question is something like "Lord, why do you even bother paying attention to creatures like us whose lives are so fleeting?" This is part of Job's agony: the Lord has (in Job's view) singled out one of his creatures—a creature with a vanishingly short life span—to punish. That creature is Job himself.

C. ARE WE LIKE RIVERS? (vv. 11, 12)

11, 12. "As water disappears from the sea
or a riverbed becomes parched and dry,
so man lies down and does not rise;
till the heavens are no more, men will not awake
or be roused from their sleep.

In the intervening verses Job contrasts humans with a dried up tree stump and tree root that may still hope to spring forth with new life (vv. 7-9). Unlike that tree, "man dies and is laid low" (v. 10). A stump may bring new life—that's hope. But is there any hope for humanity?

Job's words come from strong emotion. His mood seems to swing a bit in comparing humans to *water* that evaporates. A similar use of water evaporation also is found in Isaiah 19:5. There we see a prediction of Egypt's downfall. Water evaporates. So do people and nations. But is that evaporation permanent? A lake may dry up, but with time the drought ends and the waters may return. By saying that we do *not rise; till the heavens are no more,* there is the possibility that Job may be thinking that humans can have life again after the heavens undergo some kind of turmoil. After the prediction of disaster on Egypt in Isaiah 19:5, that prophet predicts restoration of that country (Isaiah 19:19-25). The thoughts of Job and Isaiah on evaporation and restoration are interesting to compare!

We should pause to remember that Job does not have a full revelation about life after death. He does not have the revealed promises of Christ or the New Testament testimony of resurrection. Still, Job longs and dreams for something more that his current earthly life.

Some have argued that the Old Testament saints do not believe in an afterlife. Others convincingly argue that life after death is indeed affirmed in the ancient texts (see Daniel 12:2). Today we still don't understand everything about life after death, but the New Testament does bring this idea into sharper focus.

In both Old and New Testament eras, God gives his people all they need to know on this subject. Probing further than what God has revealed is dangerous (see Revelation 22:18). Even so, we note that Jesus declared that his return would be connected with the disruption of the heavens (Matthew 24:29-31; Mark 13:24-27; Luke 21:25-27; Revelation 6:12-14).

II. DESIRE FOR LIFE (JOB 14:13-17)

A. WILL GOD REMEMBER US? (v. 13)

13. "If only you would hide me in the grave
and conceal me till your anger has passed!
If only you would set me a time
and then remember me!

A faint hint of life after death is noted in this verse. Job wants to have a final word with God. Job has assumed all along that his troubles are happening be-

"If a man die, shall he live again?"
—Job 14:14

Visual for Lessons 6 & 7.
Use this visual to illustrate how Jesus provides the answer to Job's question.

cause God is angry with him. He wants a restored relationship. Above all else, he wants God to *remember* him. When God does remember him, he wants it to be when God's *anger has passed.*

B. WILL WE LIVE AGAIN? (vv. 14, 15)

14. "If a man dies, will he live again?
    All the days of my hard service
    I will wait for my renewal to come.

If a man dies, will he live again? is a question often asked yet today. Job has no proof of life after death, only a hunch. As one preacher pondered, "Would God go to all the trouble of creating great personalities only to see them utterly destroyed? That would be like a crazy artist who paints paintings, only to tear them up."

There are several theories about what Job is talking about when he speaks of his *renewal to come.* One theory is that Job is speaking of a renewal in his relationship with God—that God will pardon him and be angry with him no more. Others think that Job is speaking of a mortal or terminal illness; his renewal would then refer to his healing from that illness. Some other theories rest on the idea that *renewal* should actually be translated *change.* Under this idea, some think that that Job is merely saying that he will have to wait to find out what happens when his life changes—that is, when he dies. Finally there is the theory that Job is holding out hope for life after death. The change or renewal would refer to his transition from death to new life beyond the grave.

All of these explanations have some credence. But in light of the question the verse begins with, we should favor the last theory. Even though Job has no detailed revelation about life after death, he still hopes for it. See the next verse.

15. You will call and I will answer you;
    you will long for the creature your hands have made.

Job believes, quite logically, that the creator will long for what he has *made*—that he will call him forth from the grave. What kind of god would create, but then take no interest in his creation? That doesn't make sense! Job believes that God will indeed take interest in what he has taken so much care to create. In Job's case that will happen when God *will call* and Job *will answer.* To Job it doesn't work the other way around.

MUMMIES, PYRAMIDS, AND OTHER STRANGE IDEAS

For "only" $74,000 you can become a mummy! Sitting in the pyramid in the front yard of his Salt Lake City home, Corky Ra, a former Mormon missionary, is promoting a patented system for preserving the dead. To sell his system he uses the image of a moth wrapping itself in silk. He guarantees that "You will stay like this for eternity. There will be no decomposition" (*Los Angeles Times,* June 21, 2003).

This is all a part of the beliefs of the church that Ra founded, based on ancient Egyptian religious ideas (as you probably already have guessed). Oh, that $74,000 fee? Easily covered by life insurance policies taken out by the customers in favor of Ra's company. So far Ra has convinced more than 1,400 people to take advantage of his mummification services. (One may wonder, of course, who it is being taken advantage of!)

Isn't it interesting how anxious people are to preserve these mortal bodies? This is true even of people who believe there is no life beyond this one. (But perhaps it makes more sense for them, since the decaying body would be all that remained of them if their beliefs were true.) However, Job's faith—even without the validation of Christ's resurrection—is solid: God will keep Job safe in the grave. At the appointed time God will call him forth from the dead. Christ *proved* it! —C. R. B.

HOW TO SAY IT

Barakel. BAR-uh-kel.
Bildad. BILL-dad.
Buzite. BEW-zyet.
Elihu. Ih-LYE-hew.
Eliphaz. EL-ih-faz.
Zophar. ZO-far.

C. WILL GOD FORGIVE US? (vv. 16, 17)

16. "Surely then you will count my steps
    but not keep track of my sin.

By using the word *then,* Job refers to his hoped-for situation of verse 15. This strengthens the idea that Job believes in (or at least yearns for) life after death.

God knows what is going on in Job's life—and Job knows that God knows. God counts Job's *steps* (compare Job 31:4, 37). He also knows all about Job's *sin* (Job 7:20; 10:14). The type of relationship that Job wants with God is one in which Job will not be fearful of God analyzing Job's steps and sins. That idea is extended in the next verse.

17. "My offenses will be sealed up in a bag;
    you will cover over my sin."

The picture here is that God will collect Job's sins *in a bag* and then seal the bag so that the sin is never seen again. Thus Job expresses a confidence in God's grace, an idea that will find fuller treatment in the New Testament.

III. RELIABILITY OF GOD (JOB 32:6, 8; 34:12; 37:14, 22)

A. GOD GIVES WISDOM (32:6, 8)

6. So Elihu son of Barakel the Buzite said:
    "I am young in years,
        and you are old;
    that is why I was fearful,
        not daring to tell you what I know.

Elihu is a fourth friend of Job who speaks up after all the others have had their say. Interestingly, Elihu's name means "He is my God."

Elihu sums up and counters the arguments of the others. His analysis is closest to the truth, but it comes with an attitude. Not all students appreciate the contributions of Elihu. One commentator describes him as a man who is confident that he has a message but is in fact a "pompous bore." Readers are free to draw their own conclusions. Just remember that Elihu begins his remarks with customary deference to his elders. Also, his words may sound harsher to modern ears than they do to ancient ones.

8. "But it is the spirit in a man,
    the breath of the Almighty, that gives him understanding."

Elihu makes his case for entering the debate. Although he admits to being relatively young, he reminds the others that wisdom does not always come from those who are older. He contends that it is *the breath* or inspiration *of the Almighty* that grants *understanding.*

B. GOD DOES WHAT IS RIGHT (34:12)

12. "It is unthinkable that God would do wrong,
    that the Almighty would pervert justice."

One thing that Elihu is steadfast about is his belief that *God* cannot *do wrong.* Whatever question we may ask, we must assume that God will always do right.

C. GOD DOES MARVELOUS THINGS (37:14, 22)

14. "Listen to this, Job;
    stop and consider God's wonders.

In the verse before us, Elihu confronts and questions *Job* directly. Elihu's questions are similar to those that God will ask of Job in chapter 38. This verse appears in the middle of a discussion of God's rule over nature. Elihu speaks of the

WHAT DO YOU THINK?

Is Elihu right? If so, does his attitude get in the way? Or is he just the young well-intentioned friend who gets it wrong? Defend your answer.

WHAT DO YOU THINK?

Someone asks, "If your God is so good and powerful, how can there be suffering and evil in the world?" How do you answer?

WHAT DO YOU THINK?

A popular Christian song, drawing on Matthew 8:26, claims that God may indeed calm the storms of life, but at other times he calms his child while the storms continue to rage. What other options does God have? How has God dealt with you during your own storms?

PRAYER

Dear Father of life, your servant Paul described death as an enemy, but a defeated enemy. Help us to have that same perspective. Help us neither to welcome death as a friend nor to fear it as an enemy. Thanks to your Son, death becomes a doorway not a dead-end street. Through Christ who gives us eternal hope, amen.

THOUGHT TO REMEMBER

"One short sleep past,
* we wake eternally,*
And death shall be no more;
* death, thou shalt die."*
*   —John Donne (1572–1631)*

chill of winter and the fierceness of storms. However problematic these storms may be, they have their place in the rhythms of nature.

22. *"Out of the north he comes in golden splendor;*
    God comes in awesome majesty."

This verse is Elihu's conclusion of his poetic tribute to God's work in nature, and he simply is talking of the awe-inspiring nature of God. Perhaps Elihu also is suggesting that God will reveal himself in *majesty* to Job. Despite the storms of Job's life, God is still there.

GOD'S AMAZING WORKS

Racetrack Playa is a dry lake bed in Death Valley National Park. It is so flat that the north end is only two inches higher in elevation than its south end, nearly three miles away! Dozens of rocks—ranging in size up to several hundreds of pounds—are on the clay surface, having tumbled there from the nearby mountains. But the amazing thing about them is that they move on this perfectly flat surface!

The trails that the rocks make vary from perfectly straight to angular to circular. Geologists have been trying for more than 50 years to come up with the reason for this strange phenomenon. But so far all they have are theories, none of them proven. Some scientists theorize that wind is behind the movement. Others believe winter rains that freeze at night may "float" the rocks enough to be blown by the wind. But no one has ever seen the rocks move.

The phenomenon of the erratically moving rocks of Death Valley is just one of many strange and wonderful facets of God's marvelous creation. In chapters 36 and 37 of the book of Job, Elihu calls Job's attention to many of God's wonders. This is good for us to consider as well. We all have found that life can bring some violent storms, but Elihu advises us to remember that after the storm—and sometimes even in the midst of it—God shows his grace by sending evidence of the sunshine of his love.   —C. R. B.

CONCLUSION

What should our attitude be as we ride out the storms of life? Should we cozy up to death as just a natural part of living? Everyone dies, after all. On the other hand, should we cower in fear over this universal experience?

When an official of the Episcopal Church spoke at a certain historic church, he noted that some thought he desired to be buried in that church's graveyard. "That's nonsense," he responded as he expressed his desire not to be buried *anywhere!* None of us particularly wants to face death. Even if we are at peace with God and totally prepared, it is still a new experience, and there is always some anxiety associated with mystery. Death is God's penalty for sin (Genesis 2:17), and it is not to be embraced as a "friend."

We also must admit that it is not so easy to think of eternity when our feet are still planted firmly on the surface of the earth. We can scarcely do better than to have the attitude of the apostle Paul: "I am torn between the two: I desire to depart and be with Christ, which is better by far; but it is more necessary for you that I remain in the body" (Philippians 1:23, 24).

We should not waste any of our moments fearing the time of death. Every moment spent on fear robs us of a moment to dwell on our hope in Christ. The brevity of life should motivate us to devote it to something important. Indeed, the fact that death is coming ought to drive us to Jesus Christ. He is the one who forgives, renews, and has gone to prepare a place for us. In the meantime let us remember the words of James S. Stewart, the Scottish preacher: "Let us live as people preparing to die so that we might die as people preparing to live."

Discovery Learning

This page contains an alternative lesson plan emphasizing learning activities. Classes desiring such student involvement will find these suggestions helpful. The next page is a reproducible activity page to further enhance discovery learning.

LEARNING GOALS

After participating in this lesson, each student will be able to:

1. Articulate the reasons why Job felt his life situation was so hopeless.

2. Identify those beliefs that can give a person both earthly and eternal hope.

3. Write a prayer that expresses hope for the current life and the life to come.

INTO THE LESSON

Divide the class into small groups of three or four. Give each group one or more "similes on life" from the list that follows (or those of your own creation). The number of similes you give each group will determine how much time is spent on this activity.

You may decide also to give groups the same similes or not. Without explanation, simply say, "Please finish these thoughts." (If you like to give your students something to work on individually as they arrive, place copies of similes in each chair ahead of time.)

1. Life is like a river because . . .
2. Life is like a rubber band because . . .
3. Life is like a bowl of cherries because . . .
4. Life is like a round-trip flight because . . .
5. Life is like a candle because . . .
6. Life is like a jack-in-the-box because . . .
7. Life is like a birthday present because . . .
8. Life is like a box of chocolates because . . .

After 10 minutes have groups share their answers with the class. Secretly keep count of how often the concept *hope* comes up. At the conclusion of the discussion, say, "I noticed that *hope* was mentioned _____ times. What does this say about our outlook?"

For an alternate introductory activity emphasizing the title of the lesson, hand each person a card bearing one of these letters: *H, O, P, E.* Give the following directions: "Circulate and find three people with letters that you do not have. With your four letters, a key word can be made. When the four of you have formed your group, bring your cards to me and be seated. Do not talk during this exercise."

If the total number of students in your class is an exact multiple of four (not including yourself), give yourself a letter to ensure that there will be one or more "leftover" students at the end. Once all the groups have been formed, say, "Well, [fill in name(s) of those who were unable to form the word *hope*], I guess there's no hope for you!"

After either activity, introduce today's texts and lesson title. Say, "To discuss hope, we have two distinguished guests with us today. They are Job and Elihu."

INTO THE WORD

Prior to today's lesson, invite two class members to deliver monologues on behalf of Job and Elihu, using the verses of today's text. Give your two orators a copy of relevant verses and suggest that the monologues be memorized and delivered emphatically. (If necessary, reading the texts will suffice.)

"Job" will deliver Job 14:1, 2, 11-17 (about 175 words); "Elihu" will give Job 32:6b, 8; 34:12; 37:14, 22 (about 75 words). Have the two actors wear large name tags labeled *JOB* and *ELIHU.*

If time permits after the monologues, use the Job's God exercise on the reproducible page to show the nature of God as our basis of hope. Afterward make a transition to the Into Life segment by saying, "People of all eras search for hope and meaning. This was as true of Job and Elihu as it is of us."

INTO LIFE

Ask your class to identify Bible verses that reveal the hope that Christians share. Give as examples biblical truths such as found in Psalm 23:1 and John 14:2.

Write their examples on the board. Then distribute blank-inside note cards to each student. (Such cards often can be found in multiple packs at dollar stores.) Suggest that each person "send a little hope" this week to someone they know who is tired and discouraged. Have them write the following on the inside: "Searching for hope? Remember what the Spirit says"; then add one of the verses and references from the list that is on the board or another of their choice.

This exercise will be most effective if the cards don't sound preachy and/or don't pretend to give pat answers. Cards delivered personally will have the most positive effect. Discourage use of e-mail. (The Voice of the Youth activity on the reproducible page is an alternative.)

Job's God

Job occasionally expresses ideas about God that are questionable. But his concept of God is generally accurate, based on what God himself says in Job 42:7, 8. Look at Job 14:13-17 in today's text. For any of the correct views of the nature of God given in the following list, write a verse number that reflects Job's outlook.

___ 1. God is a God of wrath.

___ 2. God will provide life after death.

___ 3. God will call each person.

___ 4. God has righteous expectations for each person.

___ 5. God knows all people.

___ 6. God decides the fate of all.

___ 7. God is not aloof.

___ 8. God is capable of forgiveness and grace.

Voice of the Youth

Elihu says that because of his young age, he hesitated to speak his views to Job and Job's other friends. Elihu, however, did have truth to offer. Contact one of the younger Christians in your congregation and ask his or her views on the questions that follow and other questions of your own interest.

1. What is the church doing right in its confrontation with culture? What is it doing wrong?

2. What do you consider the most significant attribute of God? Why?

3. How can the Christian approach those of other religious beliefs and expect any success?

4. How do you see yourself as a Christian leader in the church of the future?

5. Why is there sometimes a rift between older Christians and younger ones? What can we do to begin breaking any barriers down?

After your dialogue, send your younger sister or brother a thank-you note, including this verse of encouragement: "Don't let anyone look down on you because you are young, but set an example for the believers in speech, in life, in love, in faith and in purity" (1 Timothy 4:12).

Living in and as God's Creation
Unit 2: Living with Creation's Uncertainty
(Lessons 5-9)

GOD GIVES LIFE

LESSON 7

WHY TEACH THIS LESSON?

Job desperately wanted a face-to-face with God. Just one. He thought he could convince God of the error of his ways! He quickly learned something altogether different, when God appeared in power and holiness.

Many people still want to challenge God in a face-to-face. "What kind of God would . . . ?" is about as far as their question will get. His whirlwind presence will leave them dizzy in humility.

He has already given every person a face-to-face in Jesus' incarnation and resurrection. Only the stubborn hearted person has not seen him. As John would testify, "The Word became flesh and made his dwelling among us. We have seen his glory, the glory of the One and Only, who came from the Father, full of grace and truth" (John 1:14). Job experienced that grace. Jesus' disciples—filled with Job's doubt and fears—also received his grace in resurrection appearances.

God's grace in the face of our feeble faith—that is the lesson we all can learn from today's study.

INTRODUCTION

A. "I WANT ANSWERS!"

Those who want definitive answers will find the passages we discuss today virtually unsatisfactory. Those who are willing to trust will find that when human understanding fails, God is still there. In biblical research there is an area of study called apologetics. Apologetics seeks to defend the truth of Christianity by finding answers to perplexing questions. Many have found it comforting to know that Christianity is intellectually respectable. You don't have to check your brain at the door when you go to church. Many are heartened when they find out there are explanations for the things they have been told were contradictions.

Still, there are elements of faith that depend on trust. Our understanding may well be built on what we can reason through and be convinced of, but we cannot comprehend all that God knows. Parents often discover that their children ask questions that the parents cannot answer satisfactorily. The parents may indeed know the answer. But the reason that the parents can't fully respond to the questions is that their children do not yet have the intellectual ability to grasp the answers. So parents try to answer as simply and as honestly as they can—hoping that the children will trust them when the answers seem incomprehensible.

In today's lesson we will see that Job is satisfied with God's response, even though he does not get answers to all his questions. Hundreds of years later Jesus' disciples will preach the gospel with incomplete knowledge of God's future plans (see Acts 1:7). But they will have enough knowledge to trust God.

B. LESSON BACKGROUND

This lesson sets two passages of Scripture in counterpoint: one from Job and the other from Mark. The passage in the book of Job offers a personal encounter

DEVOTIONAL READING:
LUKE 24:1-9

BACKGROUND SCRIPTURE:
JOB 38:1-4, 16-17; 42:1-6;
MARK 16

PRINTED TEXT:
JOB 38:1, 4, 16, 17; 42:1, 2, 5;
MARK 16:1-14, 20

LESSON AIMS

After participating in this lesson, each student will be able to:

Apr 16

1. Tell how the texts from Job and Mark affirm God's power over life and death.

2. Explain how Job's hope is realized in the resurrection of Christ.

3. Express confidence that he or she can deal with all circumstances in life without anxiety because of the resurrection.

KEY VERSE

"You are looking for Jesus the Nazarene, who was crucified. He has risen! He is not here. See the place where they laid him.
—Mark 16:6

between God and Job. The section from Mark deals with a personal encounter between the risen Christ and his disciples. Both passages deal with difficult issues. They both deal with the need to trust. Both passages provide tangible reasons to trust. In the first passage God appears to Job and honors his request for a personal meeting. Many of Job's questions go unanswered. But Job is content in fellowship with God. Job is content to trust in the God who gives life.

Some of Job's unanswered questions are dealt with in the passage from Mark and elsewhere in the New Testament. Job wondered about life after death. Jesus' crucifixion and resurrection settle the issue. Job wondered why the good suffer. Jesus was perfect, yet he faced horrific suffering. The disciples had something in common with Job: personal encounter with God caused them to trust God for what was not clear.

I. GOD UNDERSTANDS LIFE (JOB 38:1, 4, 16, 17; 42:1, 2, 5)

Back in Job 13:3, Job asked for an audience with God (see also 9:14-19; 31:35). God now answers that bold request. There is an old cliché: "Be careful what you ask for, because you just may get it!" Job is about to "get it."

A. GOD SPEAKS TO JOB (38:1, 4, 16, 17)

1. Then the LORD answered Job out of the storm. He said:

Isn't it interesting that God speaks through a *storm*? It would seem that Job has had enough storms. After all, it was a windstorm that killed his children (Job 1:19). His friends had accused him of uttering words that amounted to nothing more than strong wind (Job 8:2; 15:2).

This storm is different however. This storm announces the presence of God. God's presence occasionally is associated with storms elsewhere in the Old Testament (compare Jeremiah 23:19; 30:23; Ezekiel 1:4; Nahum 1:3; Zechariah 9:14; contrast 1 Kings 19:11, 12). But none of those associations is quite like this one!

4. "Where were you when I laid the earth's foundation?
*   Tell me, if you understand.*

Using a particular teaching method, God answers Job's questions with questions of his own. The questions are rhetorical—they don't really need an audible answer from Job because both God and Job know what the point of the questions is.

Through his questions God reminds Job that he was not there when the earth was planned. God was the one there at creation, not Job. This passage also reinforces the idea that the world is not here by accident. God designed it.

16. "Have you journeyed to the springs of the sea
*   or walked in the recesses of the deep?*

Modern underwater explorers such as Jack Ballard can take us to the depths of *the sea*. But Job has not been there. He does not understand its secrets. The sea is a fearful and mysterious place to ancient Middle Eastern peoples. Job's people and those around him probably are not seafarers.

Even those today who know the ocean well are stunned by its mystery. In some ways it still remains a great mystery, having been called the earth's last frontier. Our increased knowledge of the sea today should cause us to walk in even greater humility before the creator of that sea.

17. "Have the gates of death been shown to you?
*   Have you seen the gates of the shadow of death?"*

As Job has not been to the depths of the sea, neither has he seen beyond *the gates of death*. He has not seen beyond this life. None of us will be able to have a practice or trial run *death*. No movie or book can prepare us for what will happen. Medical science cannot answer all unknowns. *Death* is still in the hands of God.

WHAT IS THE SHAPE OF PIE?

You may have heard about the backwoods fellow who sent his son off to college to get some "book l'arnin'." When the son came home at Christmas break, the father said, "Son, tell us somethin' in 'rithmetic." The son thought back to his course in geometry and replied "Pi r²." (Pronounced "pie are squared," this is the formula for calculating the area of a circle.) Embarrassed, the father rebuked the young man: "Son, everyone knows pie are round; corn bread are square."

Despite his bad grammar, that backwoods father was correct in his conclusions. The problem was that the limits of his knowledge didn't allow him to see what his son was really talking about. And when we compare our knowledge and perspective with that of God, this can be our problem too. To help Job see his place in the overall scheme of things, God asks dozens of questions. No matter how smart we are, compared with God we are like the backwoods father. We have ample reason to be humble about our ignorance.

We also do well to remember that more knowledge doesn't always lead to greater wisdom. Think again on the issue of pi. Most of us learned its mathematical value to be 3.14, or perhaps we learned it to a few more decimal places. Not satisfied with this, a certain college professor used a computer to calculate pi out to 1.24 trillion places! This is definitely greater knowledge, but is it greater wisdom?

Job's response to God, which we will see next, shows us spiritual wisdom. If it ever comes down to having to choose between greater knowledge or greater wisdom, the path is clear.   —C. R. B.

B. JOB RESPONDS TO GOD (42:1, 2, 5)

1, 2. Then Job replied to the LORD:
   "I know that you can do all things;
      no plan of yours can be thwarted.

We now reach the climax of the book. Job admits his limitations and testifies to God's absolute power.

5. *"My ears had heard of you*
      but now my eyes have seen you."

How is it that Job has *heard of* God? At the time there may not be much (if any) of the Old Testament even written! Even so, Job says that he has heard of God. All of us depend to some extent on what others tell us of their spiritual pilgrimages. Job's faith is no longer a hearsay faith. Now, his eye sees. He does not mean to say that he literally has *seen* God (compare Exodus 33:20). Rather, he means that his faith is now personal and experiential. The hope of Job 19:27 is realized. The presence of God is better than intellectual answers. Grieving people often state that the most helpful thing another person can do is just to be there.

II. GOD BESTOWS LIFE (MARK 16:1-14, 20)

We come now to the New Testament part of our lesson. Here in the Gospel of Mark we can find more complete answers to the dilemma that Job faced. As we begin we find ourselves with the women who struggled with the unfair and seemingly meaningless death of Christ.

A. RISEN CHRIST APPEARS (vv. 1-7)

1. When the Sabbath was over, Mary Magdalene, Mary the mother of James, and Salome bought spices so that they might go to anoint Jesus' body.

HOW TO SAY IT

Capernaum. Kuh-PER-nay-um.
Cleopas. CLEE-uh-pass.
Emmaus. Em-MAY-us.
Galilee. GAL-uh-lee.
Joses. JO-sez.
Magdalene. MAG-duh-leen or
   Mag-duh-LEE-nee.
Nazareth. NAZ-uh-reth.
Salome. Suh-LO-me.
Zebedee. ZEB-eh-dee.

WHAT DO YOU THINK?

How would you react if God responded to you as he did to Job? In the end would you, like Job, be satisfied with God's response? Why, or why not?

WHAT DO YOU THINK?

How does just "being there" help someone who is suffering? What was a time when someone helped you just by being present?

WHAT DO YOU THINK?

Are there times when being first in line to serve means you end up being first in line to be blessed? How can we guard our motives in this regard?

Jesus' body had been taken down from the cross in a hurry because a special Sabbath approached (John 19:31). Some of the women now come to finish the burial preparation. *Mary Magdalene* is part of the delegation. Jesus had delivered her from great spiritual oppression (Mark 16:9; Luke 8:2). The second *Mary*, who is *the mother of James* (and Joses; see Mark 15:40), is unknown to us. *Salome* is the mother of James and John (combine Matthew 4:21 with 27:56).

The first to witness the resurrection are not priests, the Romans, or even Jesus' closest 11 disciples. Rather, he reveals himself to a group of women who had supported his ministry and had been blessed by him (Mark 15:40, 41).

2. Very early on the first day of the week, just after sunrise, they were on their way to the tomb

The first day of the week is, of course, Sunday. The Jews worship on Saturday according to Sabbath regulations (Exodus 20:8). Before Christ's resurrection there is no particular significance to the first day of the week. This is a normal workday to these women.

They arrive at *the tomb* at about dawn. This is just a simple historical detail, but it also has some poetic meaning for us. It is surely the dawn of a new era when Jesus rises from the dead.

3. . . . and they asked each other, "Who will roll the stone away from the entrance of the tomb?"

Burial places often are carved into the sides of hills in ancient Palestine. There may be several burial spots grouped together in one room. The entrance would be covered by a large *stone*. The concern of the women is the removal of that stone. No doubt such an effort will take several strong hands. The women apparently are in such a rush that they don't remember this important fact until they are almost there.

4. But when they looked up, they saw that the stone, which was very large, had been rolled away.

To their surprise the stone is *rolled away* already. This means that they now have full access to Jesus' body inside. At least two of these women had seen the tomb and its stone previously (Mark 15:46, 47). They know where to go and what to look for.

THE MEANING OF THE STONES

"How did they get there?" The question is a common reaction from people upon first seeing the circle of monoliths at Stonehenge in England. The upright stones weigh up to 40 tons! How the prehistoric builders could raise the stones, and how they could put the horizontal "caps" in place, is still a source of speculation.

An equally relevant question is "why did they get there?" Stonehenge is just one of several similar arrangements of stones spread across the Salisbury Plain of England. It was once theorized that the monuments were prehistoric astronomical observatories. More recently, researchers have found evidence that the complexes were ancient burial grounds and crude temples for the worship of Druidic deities. People flock to the sites yet today to conduct pagan worship.

Compare those stones with the one that blocked the entrance to Jesus' tomb. That stone may still exist—somewhere. Or it may have been broken down into smaller rocks centuries ago and scattered. We don't care! That stone existed to be cast aside by the power of God so Jesus' followers could see that the tomb was empty.

The continued presence of Stonehenge serves as mute testimony to the futility of idolatry. The absence of the stone that sealed Jesus' tomb serves as evidence for the truth of the Christian faith. That stone is missing for our benefit.　　—C. R. B.

5. As they entered the tomb, they saw a young man dressed in a white robe sitting on the right side, and they were alarmed.

Inside the tomb the women see what Mark describes as *a young man*. He appears seated beside the shelf that had contained the body of Jesus. We are not meant to understand this man as a normal human being. Putting all the Gospel accounts together, it is clear this is an angel (Matthew 28:2-5). The women understandably are gripped with fear.

6. "Don't be alarmed," he said. "You are looking for Jesus the Nazarene, who was crucified. He has risen! He is not here. See the place where they laid him.

Without even asking, the angel knows whom they seek. He informs them that they will not find *Jesus* in the tomb, but that he is *risen*. As partial proof the angel even allows them to look at *the place* where Jesus' body had been. Full proof will come when they see their risen Lord.

7. "But go, tell his disciples and Peter, 'He is going ahead of you into Galilee. There you will see him, just as he told you.'"

The women are given a mission: remind the *disciples* that Jesus had promised to meet them in *Galilee*. That area, particularly its city of Capernaum, had been Jesus' base of operations. Most of his disciples are from Galilee. The Gospel of John relates Jesus meeting his disciples by the Sea of Galilee, having breakfast with them, and teaching them after his resurrection (John 21).

B. STARTLED FOLLOWERS RESPOND (vv. 8-14, 20)

8. Trembling and bewildered, the women went out and fled from the tomb. They said nothing to anyone, because they were afraid.

The scene at the tomb prompts several actions on the part of the women. First, they leave quickly. The angel had told the women in verse 7 to "tell his disciples," but at least for a while the women seem to be too frightened to say any thing *to anyone*. Their fear is coupled understandably with amazement. After calming down the women speak freely (Mark 16:10; Luke 24:9).

9. When Jesus rose early on the first day of the week, he appeared first to Mary Magdalene, out of whom he had driven seven demons.

Even though Jesus appears to these women briefly (Matthew 28:9, 10), he has a specific meeting with *Mary Magdalene*. See John 20:11-17. It was Mary Magdalene who was last at the cross and first at the tomb.

10, 11. She went and told those who had been with him and who were mourning and weeping. When they heard that Jesus was alive and that she had seen him, they did not believe it.

Mary's dramatic announcement comes as Jesus' followers express grief over the death of Jesus. It must be quite frustrating for Mary when, at first, they do not *believe* her (Luke 24:11). Others will soon have the same experience that Mary had.

An important part of the Christian message is that the first reports of Jesus' resurrection are met with skepticism by his closest followers. They aren't expecting it. They are not out preaching confidently, "Just wait a few days—you'll see!" They aren't planning a celebration. Rather, they are cowering behind locked doors (John 20:19).

12. Afterward Jesus appeared in a different form to two of them while they were walking in the country.

This refers to the encounter that Jesus has with the two disciples on the road to Emmaus. This story is told more fully in Luke 24:13-35. Two disciples—one named Cleopas, the other not named—travel with Jesus as they journey away

"If a man die, shall he live again?"
—Job 14:14

Visual for Lessons 6 & 7. *Use this visual to continue last week's discussion on how Jesus' resurrection answers Job's question.*

WHAT DO YOU THINK?

Often we should remain in dialogue with people who don't believe what we have to say about Christ. There are other times, however, when it's better to back off for a while. How do we know when to do which?

PRAYER

Dear Lord, I thank you that our redeemer does live and that we shall live again. Help us to be ready to experience new life as well as to live well in this one. Through the risen Christ, amen.

THOUGHT TO REMEMBER

The presence of the Lord is better than answers.

WHAT DO YOU THINK?

Someone says to you, "I believe in Jesus, but belief in a literal resurrection is not essential for a person to be a Christian." Why would a person think this way? How do you respond?

[Make sure that 1 Corinthians 15:12-19 is part of your response!]

from Jerusalem. They have conversations about the Messiah and the death of Christ, but they do not recognize Jesus.

As night approaches, they invite Jesus to stay with them. Eventually they recognize him. We know there were many appearances of Jesus after his resurrection; this one is particularly sweet.

13. These returned and reported it to the rest; but they did not believe them either.

Like Mary, the disciples on the road also face skepticism. This counters the claim of some critics that the story of Jesus' resurrection was the product of some psychological wish-fulfillment. It is claimed that the disciples' overwhelming desire to see him alive ends up "producing" the belief that he indeed is alive. The Bible, however, portrays the disciples as quite slow to accept the news that Jesus is risen.

14. Later Jesus appeared to the Eleven as they were eating; he rebuked them for their lack of faith and their stubborn refusal to believe those who had seen him after he had risen.

The appearances of Jesus in the body are very mysterious to us. He does not have to obey the laws of nature—laws that he created. But he is no mere phantom or disembodied spirit either (see Luke 24:36-42; John 20:19-29). He can eat food and does so.

On the occasion mentioned here, Jesus has to speak sternly to *the Eleven* because of their *lack of faith* and discernment. This is hardness of heart (also Mark 3:5; 6:52; 8:17). The phrase *stubborn refusal to believe those who had seen him after he had risen* means that Jesus expects us to believe credible testimony about him. Very few people have had the privilege of seeing the risen Jesus personally. But Jesus still expects belief.

20. Then the disciples went out and preached everywhere, and the Lord worked with them and confirmed his word by the signs that accompanied it.

This is a summary statement of all that happens in the earliest church. Above all, the word is preached. It is obvious that *the Lord* blesses the efforts as the disciples are able to do the things that Jesus himself did.

CONCLUSION

God did not explain the meaning of suffering in the book of Job. But Job was satisfied with God's presence. After Jesus' ascension the disciples were satisfied too because they knew they eventually would be in Jesus' presence for eternity.

Do you eagerly await the personal presence of God? Like Job who stood humbly before the Father, we stand humbly before Mark's account and admit that there is much we don't understand. Like Job, we may think that more knowledge is what we really need. Yet the Gospel accounts of the resurrection, as brief as they are, are what the Father has decided we should have. They are enough to assure us of God's presence both now and in the age to come.

A Sunday school teacher once asked, "What does Easter mean to you?" One boy answered honestly, "Egg salad sandwiches for the next three weeks." We all know that Easter is more than eggs, bunnies, and flowers. Still, many do not contemplate the absolute changes it signifies. If Jesus is risen, then he is who he claimed to be. If he is risen, then the truth-claims of the Bible are validated. If he is risen, then there is life after death that is only hinted at in Job 14:14; 19:25.

The death and resurrection of Jesus change everything. Because he died, our sin penalty is paid and we can come into the presence of God. Because Jesus rose again he defeated death. This allows us to be in God's presence for all eternity (Revelation 1:18).

Discovery Learning

This page contains an alternative lesson plan emphasizing learning activities. Classes desiring such student involvement will find these suggestions helpful. The next page is a reproducible activity page to further enhance discovery learning.

LEARNING GOALS

After this lesson, each student will be able to:

1. Tell how the texts from Job and Mark affirm God's power over life and death.

2. Explain how Job's hope is realized in the resurrection of Christ.

3. Express confidence that he or she can deal with all circumstances in life without anxiety because of the resurrection.

INTO THE LESSON

As students arrive hand each a piece of paper (about 4" x 6") that has a large question mark printed on one side. When class begins, say, "This is a lesson of hard questions. What would you say are some of life's hardest questions?" Pause for responses and discussion. When you're ready for a transition, say, "Life is full of hard questions. We may begin to answer some of these in today's study."

As an alternative activity say, "Our texts today are records of people meeting God in different settings. See if you can identify the people who met God as represented by the following short monologues." At this point give the following monologues to volunteers to read. (Make sure that the volunteers don't accidentally read the answers!)

1. "God spoke to me in the strangest place. I even had to take off my shoes! I suppose if one can stand in God's presence, one can stand before the most powerful man on earth." (Moses)

2. "I was certainly in no mood to meet God like I did. Even though I thought I was doing his work, I discovered otherwise. You may say that I 'saw the light.'" (Saul/Paul)

3. "I came into God's eternal presence when I was very old. Though my island home was very beautiful, God was more so." (the apostle John)

Make a transition by saying, "Given a choice, we all would prefer to meet God as the apostle John did, right? But that is not necessarily God's plan in all cases, as we shall see."

Move into a study of today's Old and New Testament texts, using the commentary as an aid. Make sure to compare and contrast the two sets of texts. Do not study either without observing how it relates with the other.

INTO THE WORD

After you have familiarized your students with the Old and New Testament texts for today, use the following Hard Questions activity. You can read the questions to the class for discussion as a whole or make copies of the questions for small-group study. Ask students to decide which verses of today's texts give insight to the question at hand. (Verses are given in parentheses after each question. Do not print these on the handout.)

1. What knowledge do we still lack regarding the origins of the universe? Why is it important to realize what we don't know? (Job 38:4)

2. If God would grant you a question and answer session with him just for the asking, would you accept it? What would you ask? (Job 38:4)

3. In what way(s) is it possible to "see" God today? How have people gone astray with their imaginations in this regard? (Job 42:5)

4. What kind of evidence do you need to believe that Jesus died and rose again? (Mark 16:6)

5. Why is it possible to hear the gospel account from credible witnesses and still reject it? (Mark 16:10, 11)

(The More Hard Questions exercise on the reproducible page is an alternative activity.)

INTO LIFE

Make a transition by saying, "A key line of thought in today's lesson has been that of life, death, and rebirth. Let's do some further thinking about that." Buy a package of large seeds ahead of time. Place seeds in small, unsealed envelopes, one seed each. Ask one of your students who enjoys crafts to stamp the following words on each envelope: "Dead or Alive?"

Distribute one envelope to each student and ask all to look inside. Some questions to ask as they look are "Is it dead or alive?" "In what sense does God give it life?" "What is its potential?" "What is its destiny?" "In what ways do you resemble the seed?"

At some point, be sure to mention (if a student does not point it out first) 1 Corinthians 15:37 and the surrounding verses. Allow time for discussion. Then suggest that students carry their envelopes in a pocket or purse for a time to recall the great truth of future resurrection. (The Empty Tomb activity on the reproducible page can follow as a good take-home exercise.)

More Hard Questions

Today's text begins with questions God asked Job in order to challenge Job's confidence in his own understanding and righteousness. What hard questions do you ponder that only God can answer? Write one question in the upper portion of each question mark below. If the Scriptures have an answer to a question—even an incomplete one—write the reference in the circle at the bottom of the question mark. One example is given for you.

What is it like to die?

Job 38:17

An Empty Tomb That Fills—and Empties

Jesus' empty tomb fills the believer with a variety of gifts. Jesus' empty tomb also empties the believer of many of his or her negatives. In the tomb below, write some of that which is blessedly emptied because of the empty tomb. On the stone below, write some of the positive things with which the empty tomb fills you. Two examples will get you started.

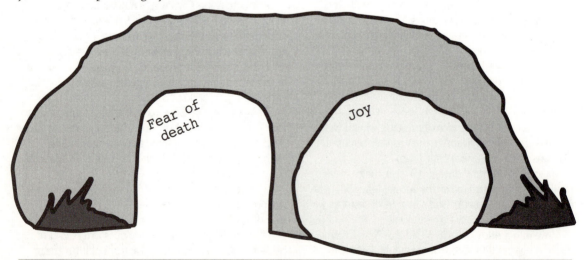

Fear of death

Joy

Living in and as God's Creation
Unit 2: Living with Creation's Uncertainty
(Lessons 5-9)

FINDING LIFE'S MEANING

WHY TEACH THIS LESSON?

Jerry Seinfeld and his costars got million-dollar laughs as self-centered pessimists who could end any discussion with a simple "Whatever!" Perhaps that show was funny because it was so close to reality: sometimes it seems that the whole world cries "Emptiness!" followed by the immediate echo "Whatever!"

Sadness, depression, and suicidal futility indeed fill the earth. Only the resurrected Christ can give all the earth's peoples meaning and purpose, joy and hope. He lived a life of steadfast purpose: his face was set—like granite—toward Jerusalem and sacrificial, atoning death. There he could cry, "It is finished!" His was a completed purpose, announced fully in resurrection. God's church echoes back, "Amen. Come, Lord Jesus." Use today's study to establish the importance of a Christ-centered life, a life with God-determined meaning and purpose.

INTRODUCTION

A. ANY DESPAIR OUT THERE?

During the past week have you met someone who is in despair? Chances are you have. Such folks keep hospitals, police, bookstores, counselors, and churches very busy. Maybe you need look no further than your own home or heart to find someone in despair. Like Solomon of old, people look to relieve their despair in a variety of unproductive and even destructive ways. People try to make their lives more enjoyable by giving in to various excesses.

Some finally sit down and, with the ultimate shrug of the shoulders, declare "There is no meaning." Are they right? The author of our first text today might well have felt at home with them. But at the end of his book, he judges that to fear God and keep his commandments form enough purpose for anyone. If we take Solomon's words out of context, we may feel better *before* we read his words than *after*!

As ancient as the book of Ecclesiastes is, it is in a sense contemporary. People still try to discover the meaning of life. They still experiment with power, possessions, and pleasure. And they still find such things as fruitless as Solomon did. People today have an advantage here. Not only can we learn from Solomon's mistakes, we also have Jesus and the New Testament to give us redemptive insights.

B. LESSON BACKGROUND

Today's lesson comes from the unusual Old Testament book of Ecclesiastes and the New Testament Gospel of John. The name *Ecclesiastes* means something like "assemblyman" (see comment on Ecclesiastes 1:1, below). This fact does not really tell us what Ecclesiastes is about. We have to read the book to discover that. When we do we see that it is a book of musings on the nature of life "under the sun." The author uses that expression more than two dozen times, and it appears nowhere else in the Bible. This expression refers to a life focused on this present world and its values. This helps us make more sense of this book, since it

DEVOTIONAL READING:
LUKE 24:36-48

BACKGROUND SCRIPTURE:
ECCLESIASTES 1:1-11; JOHN 20:19-23

PRINTED TEXT:
ECCLESIASTES 1:1-9; JOHN 20:19-23

LESSON AIMS

After participating in this lesson, each student will be able to:

1. Articulate the basic features and purpose of the book of Ecclesiastes.

2. Explain how Solomon's quest for meaning finds fulfillment in the resurrected Christ.

3. Write a vision statement for his or her life that is based in Jesus' concept of peace.

Apr
23

KEY VERSE

Again Jesus said, "Peace be with you! As the Father has sent me, I am sending you."
—John 20:21

can be depressing in many ways. It is particularly depressing if we do not read all the way through to the end.

The other book we find ourselves exploring today is the Gospel of John. This Gospel account is different from the other three Gospels (Matthew, Mark, and Luke) in paying greater attention to Jesus' ministry south of Galilee—in Judea and Samaria. It features much of Jesus' personal teachings to the disciples.

Today we are looking at a postresurrection appearance of Jesus. All four Gospels give great attention to the last week of Jesus' life, including the crucifixion and the resurrection. The most complete account of Jesus' life presents itself when we compare all four Gospels. Today's passages will let Solomon pose some problems then let Jesus propose some solutions. Our teachers will be the wisest man on the face of the earth (1 Kings 4:29-34) and God's own Son, whose wisdom surpasses even that of Solomon (Luke 11:31).

I. PROBLEM OF HOPELESSNESS (ECCLESIASTES 1:1-9)

A. DECLARED BY THE TEACHER (vv. 1, 2)

1. *The words of the Teacher, son of David, king in Jerusalem:*

Students debate the identity of the author of this book. But the opening words surely make Solomon the most obvious choice, even though he is not mentioned by name. In fact we would be hard pressed to make the words point to anyone other than Solomon. He is attributed also as the author, or primary author, of Proverbs and Song of Solomon (also called Song of Songs).

You will recall Solomon's role as the third *king* of Israel. He was a *son of David* and Bathsheba. Many students believe that the book of Ecclesiastes represents Solomon's musings in old age. These are the words of a man who has tried it all and is weary of his attempts to understand any meaning in life.

When Solomon is described as *the Teacher,* the idea expressed is an "assembly-man" or "one who addresses an assembly." Solomon is one who had great opportunity to try all the various roads to happiness. He was known also as a man of great wisdom. We yet can learn much from both his successes and his failures.

2. *"Meaningless! Meaningless!"*
     says the Teacher.
    "Utterly meaningless!
     Everything is meaningless."

We are hit by the writer's dark mood at the outset in a sense of hopelessness or at least resignation. By using the expression *utterly meaningless,* he underlines just how hopeless he thinks it all is. He has tried everything. Instead of bringing happiness, his attempts have brought the opposite. Remember: the Teacher (Solomon) has had more money, lovers, wisdom, and fame than we can imagine (1 Kings 3:1-15; 4:20-34; 11:1-3, etc.). But he declares *everything is meaningless.*

B. ILLUSTRATED IN NATURE (vv. 3-7)

3. *What does man gain from all his labor*
     at which he toils under the sun?

The Teacher (Solomon) is someone who can see the results of *labor.* Over the course of 20 years, he had built two magnificent structures: the temple and his own palace (1 Kings 9:10). Essentially, Solomon built whatever he wanted to build (examples: 1 Kings 9:17-19, 26).

Even after all this, however, Solomon can wonder what it all really amounts to. We may be prone to assume that his answer would be "nothing" by the way he asks the question. But Solomon takes a leisurely journey to his conclusion.

4. Generations come and generations go,
*   but the earth remains forever.*

The Teacher (Solomon) begins to recite a list of things that he has noticed are repetitive. *Generations* of people *come* and *go.* That pattern never changes. *The earth,* for its part, doesn't come and go but seems to abide *forever.* The earth certainly is more stable than the people on it. But that stability also is as predictable as the succession of generations.

We know now from the New Testament that the *earth,* as we are familiar with it, will not remain forever (Luke 21:25; Revelation 21:1). In Solomon's day, the *earth* is a symbol of permanence. He says more about the earth in Proverbs 8:29.

5. The sun rises and the sun sets,
*   and hurries back to where it rises.*

The Teacher (Solomon) begins to speak of the various cycles of nature. The *sun* is repetitive and predictable in moving in its order day after day. Some have tried to criticize the Bible because it says that the sun *rises* and *sets,* when the scientific truth is that the earth goes around the sun. This criticism doesn't take into account the fact that the Bible uses phenomenological language. That is, it speaks from the standpoint of how we experience life. We do not think it unusual when the evening news report tells us what times the sun will rise and set tomorrow. From our perspective it does rise and set. That's how we view the phenomena of dawn and dusk.

Solomon may also be describing the brevity of life in noting that the sun *hurries back to where it rises.* In other words, a day happens quickly—how true!

6. The wind blows to the south
*   and turns to the north;*
* round and round it goes,*
*   ever returning on its course.*

The wind may seem to be aimless, but it is not. The wind goes *round and round* according to natural laws. It has its *course,* which seems to be repetitive.

7. All streams flow into the sea,
*   yet the sea is never full.*
* To the place the streams come from,*
*   there they return again.*

This is an illustration from the water cycle. *Streams flow into the sea,* yet the sea level remains relatively constant. Water continues to go back into the sky, fall to the ground again, and run into the sea. Again, the process seems repetitive.

THE CYCLE OF NATURE

Almanacs have a long history. Benjamin Franklin's *Poor Richard's Almanac* is one of the best-known examples. It is famed for its proverbs, such as "Would you live with ease, do what you ought, and not what you please." That one from the 1734 edition sounds almost biblical, doesn't it? Another almanac—this one still in publication—is the *Old Farmer's Almanac.* Since we live in the Information Age, you can of course access it on the Internet. Do you want a planting guide to help you in your gardening? long-range weather forecasts? consumer trends? recipes? interesting facts? It's there!

But that's not all. Phases of the moon, times for the rising and setting of sun and moon, tide tables, etc., also are covered by these books. Many generations past considered them to be essential in the same way we think of The Weather Channel® today.

In our text the Teacher (Solomon) takes a look at the same cycles of nature, but from a philosophical perspective. We may not be used to such an approach. And

WHAT DO YOU THINK?

How often do you think about your own mortality? Do you think about it too much or too little? What value is there in thinking about this subject?

HOW TO SAY IT

Bathsheba. Bath-SHE-buh.
Jerusalem. Juh-ROO-suh-lem.
Sanhedrin. SAN-huh-drun or
    San-HEED-run.
shalom (Hebrew). shah-LOME.
Solomon. SOL-o-mun.

although we may find his (apparent) fatalism to be uncomfortable, we must agree with him that humans always have been at the mercy of the weather and the seasons. This is all the more reason to be on good speaking terms with God, who created and controls them!   —C. R. B.

C. Illustrated by Human Endeavor (vv. 8, 9)

8. All things are wearisome,
    more than one can say.
  The eye never has enough of seeing,
    nor the ear its fill of hearing.

By saying *All things are wearisome,* the Teacher (Solomon) is proposing that we cannot explain the meaning of our labor. Also, humans cannot see or hear enough to satisfy themselves. As people in Solomon's day experience the "latest and greatest" things, they want even more new experiences of *seeing* and *hearing.* Sound familiar?

9. What has been will be again,
    what has been done will be done again;
    there is nothing new under the sun.

Solomon looks for something *new,* but everything finds reference in the past. He despairs of finding anything novel. The past just keeps repeating itself. As we move from the book of Ecclesiastes to the book of John, we will see God take action to reverse that problem. Jesus will give us something to live for.

Perhaps what Solomon is experiencing is the problem of sin that subjects creation "to frustration" and "its bondage to decay" (Romans 8:20, 21). While nature has its cycles, it does not mean that they are meaningless cycles. History is going somewhere, moving toward a goal. Satan tried to derail that goal in the Garden of Eden. But Jesus is the one who corrected the problem, as we shall see.

II. PROVIDER OF HOPE (JOHN 20:19-23)

A. Peace Given (v. 19)

19. On the evening of that first day of the week, when the disciples were together, with the doors locked for fear of the Jews, Jesus came and stood among them and said, "Peace be with you!"

We now shift forward in time more than nine centuries. The incident at hand happens the same day as Jesus' resurrection, being *the first day of the week,* which is Sunday. *The disciples* are *together* in secret because they are understandably afraid of the ruling authorities. John uses the phrase *the Jews* to refer to the chief priests and their associates on the Sanhedrin, which is the Jewish ruling council.

We may safely assume that these disciples are of the original 12 apostles. But only 10 are present since Judas is dead (Matthew 27:1-5) and Thomas is absent (John 20:24). Somehow, moving past or through the *doors,* the resurrected Jesus appears to them. Jesus' resurrection body does not appear to have the same limitations as our normal human bodies. Jesus can appear without having to open the door. Remember that even before the resurrection, Jesus could defy the laws of nature. Walking on water is a good example of this (Matthew 14:25).

Still, Jesus is no ghost or phantom. He can be touched and he can eat (Luke 24:36-43). As we will see in the next verse, there is a certain continuity between his preresurrection body and his postresurrection body.

The first word Jesus utters is *peace.* That is what he offers a group of discouraged disciples not once but three times (here and vv. 21, 26). In some ways we may see this as a simple greeting. (Modern Jews still greet each other with the

What Do You Think?

In what sense is it still true that there is nothing new under the sun? How does this fact help you serve Christ better?

Visual for Lesson 8. *Refer to this visual as you ask, "In what ways can we experience the peace of Jesus in the twenty-first century?"*

word *shalom,* the Hebrew word for *peace*.) Yet after the resurrection we surely can see this as stronger than a mere greeting! Before the crucifixion Jesus had promised to bestow peace (John 14:27; 16:33). Jesus' payment of sin's penalty on the cross has now brought true peace—it is a peace with God.

B. PROOF GIVEN (v. 20)

20. After he said this, he showed them his hands and side. The disciples were overjoyed when they saw the Lord.

It is important to prove that the one who died on the cross is the same one who rose from the dead. That is why Jesus' resurrected body still bears the marks of the crucifixion. The scars prove he is the same person. Christianity always has claimed to be a historical religion with verifiable truth claims. Jesus has kept his promise to turn their grief into joy (John 16:20). He does this by showing *them his hands and side.*

C. PURPOSE GIVEN (v. 21)

21. Again Jesus said, "Peace be with you! As the Father has sent me, I am sending you."

See the commentary on verse 19 concerning Jesus' *peace*. Along with this peace Jesus gives them a directive: *I am sending you.* This is a foretaste of the Great Commission, which he will give before his ascension (Matthew 28:19, 20). Jesus was sent to earth with the gospel. In his absence the apostles must carry on the task (John 17:18). The task seems daunting to us who read about it today; it may have seemed impossible to those who first heard it.

We can only wonder what the disciples would have done if they had not witnessed the risen Lord. They are not meeting in the secret room to plot church growth strategies! Rather, they are there to figure out how to save their own skins. The proof of Jesus' resurrection changes the whole course of their lives—and the direction of history.

PEACE WITH A PURPOSE

Jet Propulsion Laboratory is a corporate success story—a company that has played a leading role in the exploration of space over the last half-century. But one of its founders—John Whiteside Parsons—is an example of how even successful people may find no peace in life.

In spite of having dropped out of college, Parsons became a highly respected scientist. His private life was something else, however, as he entered into pursuits that would eventually destroy him. He got involved in Satanism and the occult, calling himself antichrist. Hallucinogenic drugs became part of his unfulfilled quest for peace. In his own words, he had a "madness that burns at the heart." Parsons died in 1952 at the young age of 38 in an explosion that was either suicide, murder, or a drug-related accident.

How greatly Parson's life contrasts with those of the apostles! Jesus offered them a peace with God that would empower them for a great mission. Although they faced extreme hardships, this peace gave meaning to their lives. Those who commit themselves to Christ and his mission can know that same peace today.

—C. R. B.

D. POWER GIVEN (vv. 22, 23)

22. And with that he breathed on them and said, "Receive the Holy Spirit.

By breathing *on* the disciples, Jesus seems to convey *the Holy Spirit* to them. This verse causes us to wonder what the link is to Acts 1:4-8. There Jesus asks

WHAT DO YOU THINK?

In what ways is the mission of Jesus one that believers share? In what ways was his mission unique to him? How do you make sure you keep these two questions separate?

PRAYER

Dear God, we are eternally grateful that you came into this world and brought us meaning. We sometimes fail to recognize it, but thanks to Jesus we always have meaning. We thank you for our mission and your indwelling Spirit whom you gave us to complete it. It is in Jesus' name we pray, amen.

them to remain in Jerusalem until they receive the Holy Spirit. Since that is indeed what happens on Pentecost (Acts 2), then what do they experience here?

There are several theories. One idea is that the first granting of the Spirit here in John 20:22 is a "sprinkling" while the second granting of the Spirit in Acts 2 is a "saturation." Another theory is that the first bestowal of the Spirit grants power for new life to the disciples while the second bestowal grants them power for ministry.

These are just two possible answers among many proposals! The best answer is that when Jesus breathes, it is symbolic of what happens when the Holy Spirit later descends dramatically on the Day of Pentecost. What is crucial to recognize is that Jesus does not give them their mission without also promising them the power to succeed.

23. *"If you forgive anyone his sins, they are forgiven; if you do not forgive them, they are not forgiven."*

This verse has troubled some people, but it need not be a problem. Jesus is speaking to his chosen apostles. They will become his personal representatives in this world. As Jesus came to deal with the problem of sin, the apostles will also continue this ministry of liberation.

As the apostles share the message of the gospel, they can, under Christ's authority, assure those who listen and accept the message that they are forgiven. The use of the passive voice *they are forgiven* points to God as being the one who does the forgiving. It does not mean that if the apostles forgive someone, then God is obligated to forgive them. It means that the apostles are to announce the forgiveness that God already offers—that's the preaching of the gospel. When people hear the gospel, they either accept it or reject it. Accepting the gospel means forgiveness of sin. Rejecting the gospel means the opposite. This is God's plan.

We should not forget that the assurance that God forgives us is the greatest truth we shall ever know. There is freedom in the knowledge that God will not count our sins against us. He let Jesus take care of them on the cross. That is a message to embrace and to share.

CONCLUSION

We frequently speak of the empty tomb as being a sign of the resurrection of Jesus. That is true enough, but there is much more. Also highly significant are the postresurrection appearances of Jesus. The disciples had more than a month to interact with the risen Lord (Acts 1:3). It was his very presence that convinced them that the resurrection was real. If he had risen from the dead only to return to Heaven immediately and secretly, then they would always doubt. Jesus made postresurrection appearances not only to convince the disciples that he was alive but also to give them their marching orders.

In the end we see quite a contrast between the lives of Solomon and Jesus. Jesus proclaimed of himself that one greater than Solomon had arrived (Luke 11:31). Jesus did not live the kind of royal lifestyle Solomon did. Jesus did not engage in all the experimentation. In his dark moments, Solomon wondered if life "under the sun" had any meaning. We may sympathize with Solomon as we echo Paul's words "what have I gained? If the dead are not raised, 'Let us eat and drink, for tomorrow we die.'" (1 Corinthians 15:32).

But Christ has indeed been raised! And it is "life under the Son" that gives "life under the sun" ultimate meaning. This is meaning that Solomon could only long for and catch a glimpse of (see Ecclesiastes 12:13).

WHAT DO YOU THINK?

How does the Holy Spirit help us in ways that are both similar to and different from the way the Spirit helped the apostles in the first century? Why is this question important?

WHAT DO YOU THINK?

Jesus included both the idea of forgiveness given and forgiveness withheld in his promise to the apostles. In what ways should your church reflect both ideas? What improvements can your church make?

THOUGHT TO REMEMBER

History, in Jesus, is going somewhere.

Discovery Learning

This page contains an alternative lesson plan emphasizing learning activities. Classes desiring such student involvement will find these suggestions helpful. The next page is a reproducible activity page to further enhance discovery learning.

LEARNING GOALS

After this lesson, each student will be able to:

1. Articulate the basic features and purpose of the book of Ecclesiastes.

2. Explain how Solomon's quest for meaning finds fulfillment in the resurrected Christ.

3. Write a vision statement for his or her life that is based in Jesus' concept of peace.

INTO THE LESSON

If you like to give students something to work on just as they are arriving, put copies of the For Better or Worse activity from the reproducible page in their chairs. Otherwise, prepare two copies of the word bank and puzzle that follow. *Word Bank:* here, now, Queen, Solomon, south, wisdom. *Puzzle:* "The ___ of the ___ . . . came . . . to listen to Solomon's ___, and ___ one greater than ___ is ___ " (Matthew 12:42).

Divide the class into two teams. Give one copy of the word bank and puzzle to each team. Say, "At my signal, fill in the blanks of this Scripture quotation about the wisdom of Solomon and Jesus as quickly as you can."

Have the team that finishes first read the completed quote to the rest of the class. Make a transition to Bible study by saying, "Solomon's wisdom is famous. But the wisdom of Jesus far exceeds that of Solomon. In the words of the Father about his Son, 'Listen to him.' We will discuss both Solomon and Jesus today."

INTO THE WORD

Pass out paper and pencils. Say, "Solomon's musings on life and reality paint a black-and-white, universal-truth existence. Everything is . . . or nothing is. Number from 1 to 10 on the paper. Then, based on your knowledge of the New Testament, answer *agree* or *disagree,* for the following 10 statements Solomon makes." Read:

1. Everything is meaningless.
2. Work gains one nothing.
3. One generation lives, then another.
4. The earth lasts forever.
5. The sun rises and sets predictably.
6. Wind follows relatively predictable paths.
7. Rivers run to the sea, but the sea does not overflow.
8. As long as the eye can see, it sees; as long as the ear hears, it hears.
9. The same things occur over and over.
10. There is nothing new under the sun.

After reading all the statements and allowing time for responses, go back through the list and ask for class decisions. Ask for explanations where appropriate. Make a transition by saying, "Solomon saw things as cut-and-dried, black-and-white. When Jesus was killed, however, the disciples may not have viewed the world that way in the midst of their pain."

Next, divide the class into small "huddle" groups. Students are to sit as closely together as comfortably possible. Say, "After Jesus was crucified and buried, the disciples fearfully huddled in a small room. For this activity we will assume the role of the disciples. Each group will be given an assignment, and then you are to huddle up and respond!"

Hand out the following assignments:

Group #1: You are afraid. What are some of the fears you are sensing?

Group #2: Someone says, "If only Jesus were here . . ." How would your group be different if Jesus were there?

Group #3: Someone says, "I remember what our Lord said." What specific sayings of Jesus would be recalled in this setting?

Group #4: Now that Jesus has died, what is your group planning to do? When are you planning to do it?

Group #5: As you gathered in fear, Jesus appeared and offered you peace. What did he mean? (If you have more than five groups, give duplicate assignments. If you have fewer than five groups, select the assignments you believe will elicit the most responses.)

Give the huddle groups time to work, then ask for reports. For a more dramatic effect, ask the group reporters to use a stage whisper appropriate to their hiding-place atmosphere.

INTO LIFE

Focus on Group 5's response. Say, "Each of us is now going to write a vision statement for life that is based on Jesus' concept of peace." Stress that vision statements should be short and easy to remember. A sample would be, "I will demonstrate godliness—anytime, any place." Ask for volunteers to share their vision statements. Close by distributing the two Meaning exercises on the reproducible page as take-home assignments.

For Worse or Better

Solomon in Ecclesiastes and Jesus in the Gospels sometimes express ideas about life from different viewpoints. To the right, write what Jesus said that serves as an answer to Solomon's observation. Use today's lesson texts as a help.

Nothing has any true meaning   _____

Better if I had never been born   _____

Only the earth itself lasts   _____

Life is just the same old same old   _____

Life never satisfies   _____

Meaning and Explanations

Humanity has devised a variety of philosophies and religious systems that attempt to explain the meaning of life. Use your reference sources to write a brief statement of how each of the following explains life and its value.

Confucianism   _____

Existentialism   _____

Hinduism   _____

Nihilism   _____

Pantheism   _____

Meaning and Me

Finish the following statement:

My life has meaning

because . . .

when . . .

Living in and as God's Creation
Unit 2: Living with Creation's Uncertainty
(Lessons 5-9)

LIVING IN GOD'S TIME

WHY TEACH THIS LESSON?

Slow-witted Forrest Gump often reiterated his momma's clear teaching: "Stupid is as stupid does." Unfortunately, stupidity is rampant both in fiction and reality. Often it is government policies that lead the way in this regard. Stupidity and its consequences seem to curse the earth, second only to the way sin does.

By God's design, however, there is a godly wisdom that allows the one who finds and adopts it to rise above the common existence. Though the book of Ecclesiastes often reflects cynicism, the writer knows God and knows that there is more to life than what exists "under the sun." Every adult stricken with the "malaise of sameness" needs the whole message of Ecclesiastes. Every adult swayed by the discouragement of foolishness needs the truth of Ecclesiastes. Today's study will allow you to encourage your learners in that truth.

INTRODUCTION

A. TIME MANAGEMENT?

Take a trip to your local bookstore and discover how many best-sellers have been produced that deal with the subject of time management. Whole industries have been built around helping people to manage time. Executives keep buying each new book, hoping it will contain an insight that will forever enable them to make the best use of time. We are interested in time, but we don't really manage it. We can only manage ourselves. Time continues at a regular pace for everyone; the only difference is how we fill up those years, months, weeks, days, hours, minutes, and seconds.

As interested as we are in time, its definition is slippery and elusive. Think of the many ways we use the word *time*. We say "I don't have time to go" or "It's time for a new car." We may say "Time to get up" or "Time's up." There are other uses such as "What time is our meeting?" or "I think it's time for me to reevaluate my life." There are so many uses of the word *time*!

These various uses demonstrate that there are different kinds of time. There is clock time, which focuses on minutes and hours. There is also seasonal time, which means the right or appointed time for something. For example, there is a time for snow and a time for sun. The seasons of the year reflect the design of the creator. It is this kind of time Solomon is interested in when he says that for everything there is a season.

B. LESSON BACKGROUND

Last week we considered Solomon's musing on the apparent emptiness of life "under the sun." We must admit that little if any meaning can be constructed out of life without God.

Today's text is a section containing a poem that describes the many seasons or cycles we will face in life. These seasons are ordained and controlled by God. This passage contains a list of 14 pairs of opposites that describe our lives. One

DEVOTIONAL READING:
PSALM 34:1-8
BACKGROUND SCRIPTURE:
ECCLESIASTES 3
PRINTED TEXT:
ECCLESIASTES 3:1-8, 14, 15

LESSON AIMS

After participating in this lesson, each student will be able to:

1. Recite the rhythms of life as Solomon understood them.

2. Illustrate Solomon's rhythms of life with modern examples.

3. Explain to an unbeliever or new Christian how history is "going somewhere" even as the rhythms of life continue.

Apr
30

KEY VERSE

There is a time for everything, and a season for every activity under heaven. —Ecclesiastes 3:1

of the big questions scholars discuss is whether this passage is to be taken positively or negatively. Is it praising the divine order of nature and God's control over it, or is it bemoaning the circular, unrelenting regularity of life?

It is possible that we may take it as neither positive nor negative. There is a middle position: Solomon simply may be stating facts. We can either accept those facts or rebel against them. That these comments should not be taken as completely negative is seen in the Teacher's (Solomon's) statement that God makes "everything beautiful in its time" (Ecclesiastes 3:11). In that same verse, Solomon says that God has "set eternity in the hearts of men." Thus we see that in spite of frustration concerning the unending cycles of life, God still directs us to look to the future, to eternity.

The pairs of contrasts have a fairly consistent pattern. Interestingly, we see the positive activity mentioned first about half the time with the negative coming first the other half. These items are polar opposites. As such they seem to be mutually exclusive. That is, one side of a pair cannot happen at the same time as the other side.

This passage defies an attempt to determine a definitive outline. You don't just outline a poem! That would be like dissecting a flower and then complaining that it had lost its beauty. For the purpose of teaching, however, we can isolate some very general categories for the seasons and times. These categories involve physical life, emotional life, business life, and social life.

I. SEASONS OF PHYSICAL LIFE (ECCLESIASTES 3:1-3)
A. TIME AND PURPOSE (v. 1)
1. There is a time for everything,
and a season for every activity under heaven:

This verse opens what is probably the most familiar passage in the book of Ecclesiastes. This passage even inspired a famous rock song in the 1960s. The next few lines list a wide range of human activity. They do not cover every single activity *under Heaven*, but they do cover the landscape of human endeavor in a big-picture kind of way.

B. LIVING AND DYING (v. 2a)
2a. . . . a time to be born and a time to die,

The Teacher (Solomon) begins with the most basic cycle of life—two seasons that mark the beginning and the end of earthly existence. *A time to be born and a time to die* are the two bookends of life. Birth and death—each is a great mystery, even today. Scientists and ethicists still ponder the meaning and proper responses to these two milestones. Under normal circumstances, neither is under our control. Ultimately only God can (and should) control the conditions for life and death.

C. PLANTING AND HARVESTING (v. 2b)
2b. . . . a time to plant and a time to uproot,

Solomon also uses the figure of speech of seedtime and harvest, a vital concept in an agricultural society. This makes the point that God has ordained various activities for various times.

It is true, literally, that there would be no fruit, vegetables, and grain if we did not have *a time to plant* and a time to pluck up that which is planted. But the law of the farm may be applied to many other human activities. When it comes to the most important things of life, we sow in one season and reap in another. Ed-

WHAT DO YOU THINK?

Since many deaths are caused by people doing sinful things such as drunk driving, how does that fact fit with the claim that "ultimately only God can (and should) control the conditions for life and death"? Why is it important for you to sort through this issue personally?

ucation, health, spiritual growth, church growth, and countless other things operate by this law of sowing and reaping. See Jeremiah 1:10; 4:3 and Matthew 13:24-30 for sowing and reaping in a nonagricultural sense.

D. KILLING AND HEALING (v. 3a)
3a. . . . a time to kill and a time to heal,

When the Teacher (Solomon) says that there is a time to kill, he does not mean murder. Instead, Solomon may be describing self-defense, war, or capital punishment. Ethicists and theologians debate the circumstances when the taking of life may be appropriate (compare Genesis 9:6; Exodus 19:13; Acts 25:11).

We have often found time for killing. We must take time to heal—a much more difficult job. A life may be taken with ease in a moment, but healing can take much skill and patience.

E. BREAKING AND BUILDING (v. 3b)
3b. . . . a time to tear down and a time to build,

The words *tear down* and *build* are quite general but probably refer to constructing a house or tearing one down. Think how much emotion is associated with those acts. With the destruction of a house comes the strong emotion associated with the many memories that are attached to it. There is also the excitement of moving into a newer and bigger house.

II. SEASONS OF EMOTIONAL LIFE (ECCLESIASTES 3:4, 5)
A. LAUGHING AND CRYING (v. 4a)
4a. . . . a time to weep and a time to laugh,

People often apologize when they cry, but there is indeed *a time to weep* in sorrow (compare James 4:9). Crying can be a very cleansing experience for the soul. Tears may have been created to lubricate the eyes, but how quickly they are used to express deep emotion and grief.

Our faith should inform us that there is also *a time to laugh*. We don't prove we are Christians by continual gloomy expressions. Have you ever noticed how close together weeping and laughing are? We may hear a person tell an emotional story and sum up "I didn't know whether to laugh or cry." (Compare Ezra 3:11-13.) A Christian needs to do both. If we do one but not the other (or do neither), we may be bottling up our emotions to our detriment.

B. MOURNING AND CELEBRATING (v. 4b)
4b. . . . a time to mourn and a time to dance,

Mourning (here) and weeping (in v. 4a) seem very much the same thing, don't they? The distinction may come down to private emotions (v. 4a) vs. public emotions (v. 4b). Sharing the emotions of others is important. "Rejoice with those who rejoice; mourn with those who mourn" (Romans 12:15). The Teacher (Solomon) undoubtedly had heard of the time when his father David danced publicly (2 Samuel 6:14). Mourning over a death could include professional, public mourners (Matthew 9:23, 24).

C. SCATTERING AND GATHERING (v. 5a)
5a. . . . a time to scatter stones and a time to gather them,

Students disagree as to the meaning of this couplet. What may be in mind is *to scatter stones* into an enemy's field to make it unusable for harvest (2 Kings 3:19, 25). The scattering of stones in this respect would be done in anger.

Visual for Lesson 9. *This image is a reminder of the seasons of life. Use it to introduce the Discovery Learning activities.*

WHAT DO YOU THINK?

In what ways does (or should) the life of your church reflect the cycles of life and death, laughter and tears, up and downs—of life here "under the sun"?

To gather stones may refer to the opposite: to restore a field to usefulness. This could be an act of civic kindness. Not only does gathering stones make a field useful, the stones themselves can be used to build something—perhaps a fence. Neighbors helping one another do such things from that sense of kindness. Thus we see that this discussion of stones does have to do with the emotional seasons of life, but it is not obvious at first glance.

D. EMBRACING AND REFRAINING (v. 5b)

5b. . . . a time to embrace and a time to refrain,

Some scholars believe that this has to do with romantic love. Others say that it is more general and can refer to any kind of love. It is certainly true that there are limits and boundaries to all human intimacy, especially sexual intimacy. Sex is not evil, but it is so powerful that it must be regulated. What is holy and healthy in marriage can be quite destructive outside of it.

A DELICATE BALANCE

A man we'll call Mr. B was changed by the power of the gospel from a fighting, drinking, angry man to one who raised his children in the peaceable way of Christ. The church fellowship in which he found the Lord had a strongly rationalistic approach to interpreting the Bible; this fact reinforced the rational side of Mr. B's own personality.

There was another side to Mr. B: a deep undercurrent of emotion that probably was repressed in the way his faith was expressed. This emotional side would show, for example, when family members who lived at a distance would come for a visit. Later, as they were preparing to leave, Mr. B would disappear until after they had gone. In a time when men were not supposed to show their feelings, this was a way for Mr. B to weep without getting caught. (Perhaps some of us can relate to that!) And yet he reared a family that greatly enjoyed laughing; family get-togethers were filled with hilarity. In short there was a marvelous balance to their emotional lives that mirrored the sentiments of this part of today's text.

Many church fellowships fail to find a proper balance in expressing the faith, with traditionalism, emotionalism, and rationalism all vying for supremacy. What dangers do you see in overemphasizing any of these?   —C. R. B.

III. SEASONS OF BUSINESS LIFE (ECCLESIASTES 3:6, 7a)

A. GAINING AND LOSING (v. 6a)

6a. . . . a time to search and a time to give up,

There is an appropriate manner and time in which one may acquire wealth. The half-verse before us seems to apply to many situations beyond one's control. Success often requires hard work, but we know that outside factors can intervene.

B. SAVING AND DISCARDING (v. 6b)

6b. . . . a time to keep and a time to throw away,

This second half of verse 6 may apply to conditions under which one consciously makes decisions. Some possessions should be kept; others can safely be cast away. Isn't this often a difficult decision? We have a hard time deciding which mementos *to keep*. We wonder if things in our basement really could be useful in the future. Wisdom tells us that some things need to be saved, while others need to be discarded.

C. TEARING AND SEWING (v. 7a)

7a. . . . a time to tear and a time to mend,

WHAT DO YOU THINK?

How do you decide when it is time to save and when it is time to discard?

Some say that this verse refers to tearing one's garment during a period of mourning (as in Esther 4:1). It more likely refers to household practices: sometimes we *tear* clothing into rags; at other times we sew and repair our clothing. Tearing has applications beyond mere clothing (compare Joel 2:13).

IV. SEASONS OF SOCIAL LIFE (ECCLESIASTES 3:7b, 8)

A. KEEPING SILENT AND SPEAKING (v. 7b)

7b. . . . *a time to be silent and a time to speak,*

Many have learned this truth by hard experience. Have you ever spoken up and later realized that you should have kept your silence? (Compare Job 13:5; Psalm 4:4; Amos 5:13.) Have you ever kept *silent* and later realized that you should have taken advantage of *the time to speak?* (Compare Esther 4:12-14; Isaiah 62:1; Matthew 28:19, 20.) When we are prone to speak out of anger, malice, or selfish interest, then perhaps we should keep quiet. If an injustice is at issue and our motives are good, then maybe we should speak up.

FAMILY TIME

A certain family court judge in Las Vegas is a good man and highly respected—a good judge who tries to help families whose children are in trouble. But he has a major problem in his own family.

Once his home was a place of pleasant conversation; now it often knows only a sullen silence. There was a time when his home was a place of love between the man and his daughter; now it knows, if not hate, at least feelings of extreme ambivalence. At one time his home was a place of peace; now it is, if not a battleground, at least a place where lines are drawn in the sand. Father and daughter are each firmly entrenched on opposite sides of a deep emotional divide.

The judge and his family are not unique. The scenario is replicated tens of thousands of times across the continent. Like the judge, many parents find their own children have fallen into sin and a pattern of self-destruction. The parents may have contributed to the problems by not knowing when to speak and when to keep silence. As a sad result, parents and children—Christian or not—often find cold silence an easier choice than hot words. How can our church help them find reconciliation with each other and with God?   —C. R. B.

B. LOVING AND HATING (v. 8a)

8a. . . . *a time to love and a time to hate,*

It may bother some that the Teacher (Solomon) says that there is a time to hate. But are we not to hate evil? (See Psalm 97:10; Romans 12:9; Revelation 2:6.) A good rule of thumb is that we should hate what God hates; we find possibilities in this regard in Proverbs 6:16-19; Isaiah 61:8; Malachi 2:16. Jesus offers us an important caution in Matthew 5:43, 44.

C. WARRING AND PEACEMAKING (v. 8b)

8b. . . . *a time for war and a time for peace.*

War should always be a last resort. To a certain extent, we all would like to be pacifists, wouldn't we? Yet there are occasions when a just war is needed to correct an unjust peace (Romans 13:4).

V. SEASONS IN PERSPECTIVE (ECCLESIASTES 3:14, 15)

A. GOD DOES GOOD WORK (v. 14)

14. *I know that everything God does will endure forever; nothing can be added to it and nothing taken from it. God does it so that men will revere him.*

HOW TO SAY IT

Corinthians. Ko-RIN-thee-unz.
Isaiah. Eye-ZAY-uh.
Malachi. MAL-uh-kye.
Solomon. SOL-o-mun.

WHAT DO YOU THINK?

What are some circumstances where reasons for conducting a just war would outweigh the reasons for enduring an unjust peace?

PRAYER

Dear Father, just as you have a design for your creation, I believe you have designed me with a sense of purpose. I thank you for the miracle of life and pray that you would help me respond properly to the seasons of life. Through Christ the Lord, amen.

WHAT DO YOU THINK?

What kinds of things can (or should) be learned from history? What kinds of things cannot (or should not) be learned? Why is it important to know the difference?

Verses 11-13 (not in today's text) show us the optimistic side of the Teacher (Solomon). He describes God's timing as "beautiful." He also counsels that we should learn to enjoy life, particularly simple pleasures.

Solomon then says in the verse before us that God's works are permanent, for whatever God does, it shall be *forever.* By this Solomon does not mean that all God's works must last eternally. We know of God's promise of "a new heaven and a new earth" (Revelation 21:1). Solomon means that compared with those things that inhabit it, the earth appears to last forever. We remember that Genesis 8:22 says, "As long as the earth endures, seedtime and harvest, cold and heat, summer and winter, day and night will never cease."

Further, Solomon says that the earth is just fine the way it is. *Nothing can be added to it,* nor anything *taken from it.* Therefore, we human beings must stand in fear before him.

B. GOD RULES PAST, PRESENT, AND FUTURE (v. 15)
15. *Whatever is has already been,*
   and what will be has been before;
   and God will call the past to account

This verse reminds us of one of Solomon's themes: there is nothing really new (Ecclesiastes 1:9, 10). This is vitally true in terms of human nature. People keep making the same mistakes. We keep seeing the same old sins over and over. Admittedly there are new technologies, but people (and what motivates them) stay pretty much the same. When Solomon states that *God will call the past to account,* he simply may be saying that nothing escapes the rule of God. God is the one who is in a position to judge what happened in the past. God is the one who calls all of history to account.

CONCLUSION

We accept the fact that the seasons of life are only partially within our control. We cannot stop the progression of time. We can, however, control our attitude as we face each season. Every season has some kind of lesson to teach us if we are willing to learn. Time marches on, and we must decide how we fill our days.

There is the story of an army private who was loafing when he should have been working. When his sergeant asked what he was doing, he decided that since he had been caught red-handed he may as well just be honest. "I'm procrastinating, Sergeant," he said. "All right," said the sergeant after carefully considering the response, "as long as you're busy." Many people are "busy procrastinating" while time hurries along!

Most of the seasons mentioned in today's lesson have some seed of joy in them. This does not mean that every event is joyous or positive in and of itself. But since each cycle has a purpose in God's cosmic design, we can be happy we are part of a universe on purpose.

Our priority can be to make the most out of the seasons of life. We can compare this a bit with the rhythms of the individual calendar week. The first day of the week, Sunday, brings us together for worship. This is a time of spiritual reflection. Monday takes us back to the reality of the workaday world. Wednesday has a feeling, for many, of being "over the hump" toward the weekend. Friday night and Saturday offer opportunities to unwind.

Each day can bring its joys and challenges. This depends on the rhythm of the week and our own mind-sets. Keeping an eternal perspective through it all is our challenge.

THOUGHT TO REMEMBER

The cycles and seasons of life have lessons to teach us.

Discovery Learning

This page contains an alternative lesson plan emphasizing learning activities. Classes desiring such student involvement will find these suggestions helpful. The next page is a reproducible activity page to further enhance discovery learning.

LEARNING GOALS

After participating in this lesson, each student will be able to:

1. Recite the rhythms of life as Solomon understood them.

2. Illustrate Solomon's rhythms of life with modern examples.

3. Explain to an unbeliever or new Christian how history is "going somewhere" even as the rhythms of life continue.

INTO THE LESSON

Divide your class into four brainstorming groups. Give each group one category based on the lesson writer's outline of today's text: Seasons of Physical Life, Seasons of Emotional Life, Seasons of Business Life, or Seasons of Social Life. Ask each group to write other "a time for . . . " statements based on their assigned season.

Provide groups with the following examples. For the Seasons of Physical Life group: "a time to rue aging and its consequences and a time to rejoice in the wisdom of age." For the Seasons of Emotional Life group: "a time to share your great disappointments and a time to keep quiet." For the Seasons of Business Life group: "a time to raise prices and a time to mark prices down." For the Seasons of Social Life group: "a time to forgive and a time to demand justice."

After 10 or 12 minutes, let groups share their work with the class. Ask them to comment on the godly wisdom and truthfulness of each statement. Say, "Now let's compare your ideas with Solomon's."

INTO THE WORD

Assign each of the contrasts from Ecclesiastes 3:1-8 to a pair of volunteers to pantomime. (If you have two class members who are good at drama, they could do all the pantomimes.) Have the pantomimes performed in a random order. As each pantomime is completed, ask other class members to identify the contrast and the verse number that pantomime represents. Before class, print up the pantomime directions that follow, but tell your volunteers to feel free to improvise.

1. One actor shows the motions of cradling and carrying a baby; the other lies down, closes eyes, and folds arms across the chest (v. 2a).

2. One actor walks like a sower scattering seed from a pouch at his or her waist; the other follows behind as if picking ears of corn, pulling husks back, and gnawing across the ear (v. 2b).

3. One actor marches, as if a sentry carrying a gun—suddenly ducking and looking afraid; then he stands, aims his gun, fires, and then nods approvingly. The other examines the first actor's shoulder, wipes it, and applies a bandage (v. 3a).

4. One actor, as if wearing goggles and a hard hat, wields a sledgehammer against a brick wall; the other mimes putting mortar into place and setting bricks one on top of another (v. 3b).

5. One actor pulls out, as it were, a large handkerchief and puts it to his or her eyes, occasionally putting it down to show a sad, sobbing face; the other looks, points, and then doubles over all to simulate a large laugh (v. 4a).

6. One actor, with a sad but otherwise expressionless face, leans as if over a casket, shakes his head, and turns away in tears; the other simply does a jig of joy (v. 4b).

7. One actor bends over as if picking up a rock, straightens, throws the object, and repeats; the other moves around, showing the effort of picking up something heavy, and makes an invisible pile (v. 5a).

8. The two actors walk toward each other, hug each other with smiles, and then pass on by. They reverse directions, frown as they approach, fold their arms, and deliberately pass each other by (v. 5b).

Create additional pantomimes for the remaining contrasts, to use as time allows.

INTO LIFE

Say to your class, "Ephesians 5:16 speaks about the importance of 'making the most of every opportunity, because the days are evil.' What are you doing in obedience to this instruction?" Suggest that students memorize this brief phrase as a defense against the devil's challenge to waste time in worthless or less significant activities.

If time allows, use the Putting Your Hands on Time activity from the reproducible page as a follow-on exercise. This activity can also serve as useful homework in requiring each student to evaluate privately how he or she invests (or wastes) time.

Putting Your Hands on Time

For this activity you will need colored pencils. The clock face below is divided into 24 half-hour segments. Color in spaces for each of the "uses of your hands" during a typical 12-hour waking portion of your day. In the small circle at the end of each "uses of hands," fill the circle with the color you are using to mark the clock. What improvements can you see that you need to make?

lifting your hands in prayer or worship ○

turning pages as you read Scripture ○

driving someone in your car as a deed of service ○

writing a note of encouragement or thanks ○

preparing food for others ○

cleaning or repairing a home for those unable to do so ○

working for an income to support self and family ○

working for an income to support God's work ○

using the phone in a listening or counseling ministry ○

SEEK WISDOM

WHY TEACH THIS LESSON?

The Bible uses the word *seek* dozens and dozens of times. But is that really necessary? Don't people automatically seek things that are in their best interest?

Rare indeed is the person who seeks nothing! Everybody, it seems, seeks something: money, fame, education, food, family, home, health, job—the list goes on and on. But how many dedicate themselves to seeking God's wisdom? Very few, if common behavior is any indication!

Your students need to have more of God's wisdom. In the New Testament era, that wisdom points to Jesus Christ. When we accept him and honor his expectations, we will have more wisdom than even Solomon was privileged to have.

INTRODUCTION

A. POOR CHOICES, WISE CHOICES

Today the headlines are filled with stories of people who have made incredibly poor choices. A soldier at a nearby Army base recently was arrested for participating in Internet chat rooms in which he offered to help Islamic terrorist groups. What was he thinking? On another front the media reported the bankruptcy of a famous athlete, despite enormous cash flow. This former heavyweight champion is estimated to have earned $300 million in his boxing career, but is now broke. Where did those mega-millions go? Some of this may be explained by reckless spending such as a $410,000 bill for his birthday party a few years ago. What was he thinking when he made such poor choices? Proverbs 17:16 says, "Of what use is money in the hand of a fool, since he has no desire to get wisdom?"

Life is a series of choices. As adults we are required to make dozens of choices every day. Some are mundane: What clothes should I wear today? What should I eat for lunch? What TV shows will I watch this week? But other, far more important choices confront us on a regular basis: Should I quit my lousy job and look for another? Should I honor my marriage commitment when someone else entices me? Should I tell the truth when I find myself in a tight spot?

Parents are expected to help their children learn how to make good choices. Young adults need to know how to handle money, how to decide which friends are safe and good influences, and to understand the benefits of being a hard-working, dependable employee.

In an increasingly chaotic society, however, what standards do we use to make our decisions? Do we follow the hedonistic advice, "If it feels good, do it"? Do we fall back on the cult of irresponsibility's quick answer to everything, "It's not my fault; I didn't do anything wrong." Or should we use the survivalist approach of making it up as we go, rolling with the punches in order to adapt, survive, and find out "what works" in the various situations in which we may find ourselves?

The book of Proverbs has a better way. It lays out many guidelines for our lives. These guidelines have served the people of God well for 3,000 years. It is to this book that we now turn for the next four lessons.

DEVOTIONAL READING:
PROVERBS 2:6-15
BACKGROUND SCRIPTURE:
PROVERBS 2, 3
PRINTED TEXT:
PROVERBS 2:1-5; 3:1-6, 13-18

LESSON AIMS

After participating in this lesson, each student will be able to:

1. List the blessings that can come from acquiring godly wisdom.

2. Suggest ways that obedience to God can result from having wisdom.

3. Make a plan to change one thing in his or her life in order to better reflect godly wisdom.

WHAT DO YOU THINK?

What was a time in your life when you had the godly wisdom necessary to make the right decision, but you voluntarily chose to make your decision based on ungodly "wisdom"? What was the outcome?

May 7

KEY VERSE

Blessed is the man who finds wisdom, the man who gains understanding.   —Proverbs 3:13

LESSON 10 NOTES

B. LESSON BACKGROUND

What is the difference between a wise person and a foolish person? In the book of Proverbs, this usually has nothing to do with education. Many of us can name someone with a college degree who acts the fool on a regular basis. We may be able also to point to a person who never graduated from high school, yet stands as a source of quiet, reliable wisdom.

In Proverbs wisdom is a matter of how one responds to the will of God. The wise person is the one who knows what is right and wrong from God's perspective and chooses to do the right thing. The foolish person is the one who knows what is right or wrong from God's perspective and chooses to do the wrong thing. Foolishness, then, is not a matter of ignorance. Conversely, wisdom is not a matter of education. Both the wise and the foolish are assumed to be educated in the ways of God, knowing what is right from wrong. The fools consistently disregard God's standards and freely do the wrong thing (sin).

Central to the message of Proverbs, however, is that foolish behavior is more than just displeasing to God. The life of the fool is also self-destructive. When we shun God's standards to follow our own desires, we will be frustrated, unhappy, and without hope. "The way of a fool seems right to him, but a wise man listens to advice" (Proverbs 12:15).

The book of Proverbs in general is attributed to King Solomon (see Proverbs 1:1). Solomon's wisdom was given to him by God (1 Kings 4:29). This wisdom was legendary even during Solomon's own lifetime (1 Kings 10:24). We know that some of the proverbs of Solomon were compiled several hundred years later by the advisers of King Hezekiah (Proverbs 25:1). Apparently, this compilation process included a few authors beyond Solomon. The book also contains proverbs that are attributed to Agur (Proverbs 30:1) and Lemuel (Proverbs 31:1), although we know nothing about these men.

I. LISTENING FOR WISDOM (PROVERBS 2:1-5)

A. WANTING TO BE WISE (vv. 1, 2)

1, 2. My son, if you accept my words
    and store up my commands within you,
  turning your ear to wisdom
    and applying your heart to understanding,

Proverbs often uses a form of Hebrew poetry called *parallelism*. This means that there are two or more lines of text that make the same basic point using different words. This is seen twice in these verses. In other words, *accept my words* is equal to *store up my commands* while *turning your ear to wisdom* is equal to *applying your heart to understanding*. In fact all four of these lines are similar in meaning—so much so that we can think of *my words* and *my commandments* and *wisdom* and *understanding* all as parallel concepts for Solomon.

Proverbs 9:10 teaches that wisdom begins with the "the fear of the Lord." Does this mean that the wisest person is the one who most cowers in terror before God? Not exactly. It means that the wise person is the one who fears or respects God to the point of obedience. We are on the path of wisdom when we listen for God's directions for our lives. This is the path that Solomon desperately wants his hearers to find and follow.

B. SEEKING WISDOM OBSESSIVELY (vv. 3, 4)

3, 4. . . . and if you call out for insight
    and cry aloud for understanding,

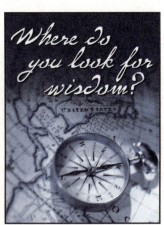

Visual for Lesson 10. *Use this provocative question to help your class examine both the sources and the types of wisdom.*

and if you look for it as for silver
    and search for it as for hidden treasure,

Again, Solomon uses a couple of vivid metaphors to describe the necessary quest *for understanding*. We holler for it, crying out and lifting our voices. We also go on a treasure hunt for it, seeking and searching. The point is that wisdom is available, but still must be sought. We are not born wise. Wisdom is not intuitive. In fact the wisdom of God is sometimes counter-intuitive because it goes against our impulses of self-preservation, self-importance, and greediness.

C. FINDING THE TREASURE OF WISDOM (v. 5)

5. . . . then you will understand the fear of the LORD
    and find the knowledge of God.

The quest for wisdom is not an impossible dream walk. It is very much within our grasp if we turn to God. Our search is governed by our respect for God and his ways. Our goal is to know God and his ways more fully so that we may better follow them. This is a happy, joyous journey, the lifelong pursuit of godliness.

AVOIDING SPIRITUAL ALTITUDE SICKNESS

Altitude sickness affects you when you exert yourself in such activities as climbing high mountains. It can make you violently ill even at a relatively low 8,000 to 10,000 feet if you have not conditioned your body for the climb. (Sitting in the pressurized environment of an airliner at 35,000 feet doesn't count as conditioning!)

The best way to avoid altitude sickness when mountain climbing is to train for the activity at intermediate altitudes. Spending a few days at those heights will help your body get adjusted before tackling the bigger peaks. Many amateur climbers get into trouble when they try to cram as much activity into their vacation time as possible and are not patient until their bodies adjust to the higher elevation.

Gaining wisdom is somewhat like mountain climbing. We all would like to "get to the top" as soon as possible without the struggle of conditioning and preparation that is required to do it correctly. Getting a bit of wisdom may come occasionally by what some would call blind luck. More frequently it will come, as our text says, because we actively listen, apply ourselves to understanding what is going on, call out (pray) for insight, and seek wisdom as if it were the greatest of treasures. If we try to attain life's heights by shortcuts, we may experience the spiritual sickness that lack of divine wisdom brings.   —C. R. B.

II. TRUSTING IN GOD (PROVERBS 3:1-6)

A. LIFELONG OBEDIENCE (vv. 1, 2)

1, 2. My son, do not forget my teaching,
    but keep my commands in your heart,
for they will prolong your life many years
    and bring you prosperity.

Here we see some of the rewards for the one who seeks to live wisely: long *life* and *prosperity*. We are confronted with a great paradox. If we seek God and shun the quest for material prosperity, God will cause us to be prosperous and satisfied. This pattern was seen in the life of Solomon himself, who asked God for wisdom and was given both wisdom and wealth (see 2 Chronicles 1:11, 12).

B. LIFELONG MERCY (vv. 3, 4)

3, 4. Let love and faithfulness never leave you;
    bind them around your neck,
    write them on the tablet of your heart.

WHAT DO YOU THINK?

Think of the differences between knowledge, understanding, and wisdom How do you relate each of these to your service for Christ?

[Proverbs 2:6; 9:10; Isaiah 11:2; 1 Corinthians 8; Colossians 1:9; and James 2:19 can help frame your answer.]

WHAT DO YOU THINK?

Where are you most likely to search for wisdom—in the Scriptures themselves, in the words of preachers and teachers (or perhaps their books you read), or in the counsel of godly friends and mentors? Why?

Then you will win favor and a good name
in the sight of God and man.

The ethical keys to godly behavior are given here: *love and faithfulness*. The person who lives a loving and faithful life will be honored by God and people. The word translated *love* is one of the key words in all the Old Testament. It is a rich word and can also be translated "kindness" (as it is in Jeremiah 9:24).

This concept of showing love to others is central to godly behavior. To behave like God is not to be mean-spirited, yet many Christians (even church leaders) have fallen into this sinful pattern. The Lord requires that his people are to "love mercy" (Micah 6:8). This is not a legalistic regulation as in "Aw, do I have to be merciful again?" Rather, it is a pattern that should come naturally and joyfully.

C. LIFELONG TRUST (vv. 5, 6)

5, 6. *Trust in the LORD with all your heart*
    and lean not on your own understanding;
  in all your ways acknowledge him,
    and he will make your paths straight.

One of the most famous pieces of advice in the history of the world is found here: *trust* your life to God and you will not be disappointed. It was true in Solomon's day, and it is still true today. God is our creator, and he has not abandoned us to find our own way. He has given us patterns for successful living. But living a flourishing life begins with our acknowledgement of God in the proper way. He is great and we are small. He is powerful and we are weak. He consistently loves and we are fickle. No matter how smart, educated, or experienced we are, we will fail repeatedly in life if we ignore God and try to make our own way.

Why don't we trust God more? Just as children must often learn life's lessons the hard way, we want to be independent. We want to be responsible for our own success and not share the credit. We are fiercely proud, and pride is the opposite of trust. Faith in God requires humility, and nothing in modern culture celebrates humility. But the promise is sure: if we humble ourselves and trust God, no matter how painful it may be, he will reward us with a richness of life beyond our dreams.

III. ENJOYING WISDOM'S REWARDS (PROVERBS 3:13-18)

A. WISDOM'S PROFITS (vv. 13, 14)

13, 14. *Blessed is the man who finds wisdom,*
    the man who gains understanding,
  for she is more profitable than silver
    and yields better returns than gold.

The story is told of a very wealthy man who lay sick and near death. His daughter asked him if he wanted anything. In a moment of lucid candor, the sick man replied, "Two things: a clear conscience and a good night's sleep." He had accumulated the riches of the world but died miserably.

Proverbs teaches us that *wisdom* and *understanding* will ultimately be more rewarding than wealth. This does not mean that wealth and wisdom are incompatible. We can be wise, wealthy, and happy. We can be wise, poor, and happy. But we cannot be foolish, wealthy, and happy.

B. WISDOM'S RICHES (vv. 15-17)

15-17. *She is more precious than rubies;*
    nothing you desire can compare with her.

Long life is in her right hand;
  in her left hand are riches and honor.
Her ways are pleasant ways,
  and all her paths are peace.

Wisdom can never be purchased because no one can fix a price for it. Its value is beyond any monetary standard. We must work to be wise, but we do not earn wisdom. Wisdom is gained by obeying God's instructions for our lives; God does not charge us anything but obedience.

Proverbs emphasizes that the ways of godliness are *pleasant ways*. This is not a tedious, joyless path. Truly godly people are both wise and happy, and yet the world does not understand this. People of faith often are portrayed as narrow bigots who are missing the best things in life. When the apostle Paul confronted the Roman governor Festus with the wisdom of the gospel of Christ, Festus concluded that Paul was insane (Acts 26:24). Yet Paul knew that he wasn't crazy. He was satisfied with his life of the pursuit of godliness and obedience to God's will. He faced death secure in the knowledge that he had chosen well and that God's rewards awaited him (2 Timothy 4:8).

C. WISDOM'S BLESSINGS (v. 18)

18. *She is a tree of life to those who embrace her;*
  those who lay hold of her will be blessed.

Solomon offers a striking description of wisdom as *a tree of life*. This image comes from the Genesis account of creation in which the tree of life is in the center of the Garden of Eden. Eating its fruit apparently could give Adam and Eve immortality.

The Bible mentions this tree in three places: Genesis (original paradise), Revelation (restored paradise), and four times in Proverbs. In the text before us, it is equivalent to personal happiness. It also is a product of righteousness (Proverbs 11:30), the hope a faithful person has (Proverbs 13:12), and wholesome speech (Proverbs 15:4). The version of the tree of life in Proverbs is not something in the future, but a present blessing in the life of the wise, godly person.

In the book of Genesis, Adam and Eve were barred from access to the tree of life after they sinned (Genesis 3:24). In the book of Revelation, access is regained. The Revelation version of the tree of life has 12 kinds of fruit, and its leaves produce a healing balm (Revelation 22:2). Why, then, does Proverbs see wisdom as a tree of life? It is because the wise life brings us back into a relationship of obedience with God, a relationship first broken by Adam and Eve. We will not have paradise restored completely until the end of time. But we can have our own personal paradise of peace and contentment in the present life if we trust and obey God.

A COLOSSAL HOAX

Have you seen the satellite pictures of North and South Korea taken at night? If you have, you have noticed that the Korean peninsula is as starkly divided visually at the 38th parallel as it is divided politically. The satellite picture shows the north almost totally dark, while the south blazes with the lights of prosperous cities.

The government of North Korea tries to hide its dismal performance. One of the ways it does so can be seen in the village of Kijongdong, on the border of the demilitarized zone between the two Koreas. From the south, one can see impressive apartment buildings designed to lure South Koreans northward to the supposed good life in the "people's paradise." But no one lives in the village; the apartments are façades like those built for Wild West movies. The whole thing is a colossal hoax.

WHAT DO YOU THINK?

Make a list of the advantages of wisdom—how it truly makes life better. Which items on this list do you crave most in your life right now? Why?

WHAT DO YOU THINK?

What kinds of things compete with a quest for wisdom? Why is it significant that items of high monetary value are mentioned several times in Proverbs 3:13-18? How does our pursuit of wealth frequently hinder gaining wisdom?

HOW TO SAY IT

Agur. AY-gur.

Dietrich Bonhoeffer. DEE-trick BON-huh-fur.

Hezekiah. Hez-ih-KYE-uh.

Lemuel. LEM-you-el.

Lucius Annaeus Seneca. LOO-shuss Uh-NEE-us SEN-uh-kuh.

Solomon. SOL-o-mun.

Søren Kierkegaard. SO-ren KIR-kuh-gard.

PRAYER

Great God, the wise and the true, grant to us the strength to find reward by trusting your Word in faith and obedience. May we not revert to trusting our own wisdom but always rely on your guidance for our lives. May we never look upon you as a strict taskmaster who deprives us of fun, but rather as a loving creator who has given life to us. We pray this in the name of our Savior, Jesus Christ, amen.

THOUGHT TO REMEMBER

A wise person trusts God and his Word to show the best way to live.

The message of Proverbs alerts us: the so-called "good life" the world promises, with all its baubles and beauty, is also a colossal hoax. It is worth nothing compared to the precious jewel of the wisdom that comes from God. Do we want something more substantial that the proverbial 15 minutes of fame that this life offers? We'll find that "something more" in the wisdom of God.   —C. R. B.

CONCLUSION

A. RISKY FAITH: TRUSTING AND DOUBTING

The Danish Christian writer Søren Kierkegaard (1813–1855) wrote "without risk, no faith." This outlook has many implications for the man or woman trying to live a godly life. Believers must trust that God, their creator and master, knows what is best for them. God's instructions for living are not designed to deprive us of enjoyment. The moral guidelines found in Scripture are not legalistic attempts to ruin everybody's fun. Instead, the Bible teaches us how we should live if we are to get the most out of life.

Often, though, we think we know better. The Bible teaches that there should be no sex outside of marriage. We think we know better. The Bible teaches that we always should tell the truth. We think we know better. The Bible teaches that we should not be greedy for luxury possessions. We think we know better. Ignoring the Bible's rules for living always invites disaster: children born without the support of fathers, a career destroyed for being caught in a lie, and overextended credit and financial ruin.

Trusting in God's ways is risky from a human perspective. Does God's advice always work? Aren't there loopholes and exceptions? Don't we need new moral guidelines for this century? Such questions of doubt are normal, given our human frailty and limitations. But one of the central promises of Scripture is that God's way is a better way, that we can trust him with our lives. As the German martyr Dietrich Bonhoeffer (1906–1945) wrote from his Nazi prison, we must "throw ourselves completely into the arms of God." That means trusting that his way is superior even if we don't understand it completely.

We are strange creatures in which faith and doubt reside side by side. May we allow the doubts to grow weaker as we live by faith, trusting God's Word as a pattern for our living.

B. TRAGEDY AND GODLINESS

Proverbs seems to be giving a blanket promise that the wise, godly life will be a long happy life. Why, then, do some of God's finest people tragically die early? Why would God allow a faithful, young Christian mother to die and leave her small children behind?

As I write this lesson, I am in prayer for one of my college's graduates who suddenly fell into a coma last week while alone at his church's office. Without a powerful miracle, he will soon die and leave behind his ministry and his young family. He is a fine, godly man who rejected worldly success for the call of God to preach. Why does it seem that he will die so young?

It is impossible to answer that question because we can never totally understand it from God's perspective. But I know that this young man recently had won a great victory. After many years of prayer and discussion, he finally had led his brother-in-law to the Lord. Maybe that was the most important thing he could ever do. Perhaps in God's eyes his faithful life already has been long and successful. And maybe part of wisdom is not fighting or resenting God when he calls a faithful servant home, but trusting that he knows best in everything.

Discovery Learning

This page contains an alternative lesson plan emphasizing learning activities. Classes desiring such student involvement will find these suggestions helpful. The next page is a reproducible activity page to further enhance discovery learning.

LEARNING GOALS

After participating in this lesson, each student will be able to:

1. List the blessings that can come from acquiring godly wisdom.

2. Suggest ways that obedience to God can result from having wisdom.

3. Make a plan to change one thing in his or her life in order to better reflect godly wisdom.

INTO THE LESSON

As your students arrive, distribute copies of the following quotes about wisdom (or direct their attention to the student books, where these quotations are printed). Ask students to read these quotations about wisdom, and then to write their own definition or description of wisdom.

Wisdom quotations: "It's so simple to be wise. Just think of something stupid to say and say the opposite" (Sam Levinson). "Wisdom consists of the anticipation of consequences" (Norman Cousins). "The perfection of wisdom and the end of true philosophy is to proportion our wants to our possessions, our ambitions to our capacities; we will then be a happy and a virtuous people" (Mark Twain). "Science is organized knowledge. Wisdom is organized life" (Immanuel Kant).

After students have had time to complete their definitions, ask several volunteers to share their conclusions. Then tell the class that today's lesson will deal with the nature of true wisdom as defined by the book of Proverbs.

INTO THE WORD

Before completing the following exercise, ask three volunteers to read aloud one of the three passages from today's text: Proverbs 2:1-5; 3:1-6; 13-18. Next, ask your students to study these three passages independently and complete a true/false quiz. (This quiz is reprinted in the student books.) Correct answers are in parentheses.

T F 1. Proverbs 2 makes wisdom and understanding parallel ideas. (*True*)

T F 2. To receive wisdom, one must search for it. (*True*)

T F 3. According to Proverbs 2, our fear of the Lord depends on our knowledge of God. (*False. Verse 5 has it the other way around: the fear of the Lord leads to the knowledge of God.*)

T F 4. Proverbs 3 says keeping God's commandments will contribute to prosperity and long life. (*True*)

T F 5. Proverbs 3 says we should inscribe the words *love* and *faithfulness* on our doorposts so that won't forget them. (*False. They are to be written on the heart.*)

T F 6. If we practice love and faithfulness, we will find favor with both God and people. (*True*)

T F 7. Proverbs 3 says that if we trust God rather than relying on our own wisdom, he will give us direction in life. (*True*)

T F 8. According to Proverbs 3, wisdom is better than diamonds. (*False. It says silver, gold, rubies.*)

T F 9. Proverbs 3 says that wisdom holds riches and honor in her right hand. (*False. In her right hand is long life. Riches and honor are in her left hand.*)

T F 10. Proverbs 3 compares wisdom to a tree of life. (*True*)

As you correct the quizzes together, use this time to discuss the meaning of the text with your class.

INTO LIFE

Lucius Annaeus Seneca, a Roman philosopher and playwright who was born about the time that Jesus was, said of wisdom, "If wisdom were offered me with this restriction, that I should keep it close and not communicate it, I would refuse the gift." Read this quote to your class. Next, ask students to brainstorm some ways that they could communicate godly wisdom to others, both Christians and non-Christians, without coming across as arrogant or as wise guys.

After you have discussed possible ways to share godly wisdom with others, ask students to return to the definitions they wrote for the Into the Lesson exercise. Incorporating what they have learned about wisdom from today's lesson, students should rewrite their first definitions. Ask volunteers to read both versions of their definitions. What changes did they make and why? Follow with the Cost/Benefit Analysis from the reproducible page as time allows.

Close with a prayer for your students that each would desire to live a wise and godly life pleasing to God. Pray that each would change one thing in his or her life in order to better reflect godly wisdom to others.

A Cost/Benefit Analysis of Wisdom

A cost/benefit analysis is a technique for deciding whether or not to change a way of "doing business." To do the analysis, one must add up the value of the benefits of a certain course of action and then subtract the costs associated with it. Focusing on Proverbs 3:13-18, do a cost/benefit analysis of the value of wisdom in a Christian's life. The chart below divides that life into various categories. If a Christian exercises godly wisdom in these areas, what costs and benefits will he or she likely experience? Record the costs in the left-hand column, the benefits in the right-hand column. Feel free to add other categories as needed. An example is given to get you started.

COSTS OF WISDOM   BENEFITS OF WISDOM

Marriage/Family

Foregoing a potential spouse who is wealthy but un-Christian   Joy of seeing godly children grow into adults

Friendships

Career

Recreation

Finances

Spiritual Development

ACCEPT WISDOM'S INVITATION

WHY TEACH THIS LESSON?

Adults deal with foolishness every day. Foolish drivers. Foolish employees. Foolish employers. Foolish media. Foolish politicians. Foolish educators. Foolish relatives. The clear affirmation of Proverbs, however, is that wisdom is available, even eagerly crying out her nearness. Why would anyone ignore her plea and power?

Today's study will allow your learners to hear again the cries and claims that wisdom makes. Once again they will have opportunity not only to grow in personal wisdom but also to grow in ability to deal with the foolishness of worldliness as they confront it in themselves and in others.

For those confused by the notion that wisdom comes by experience or education, today's text will allow them to see that wisdom is of God. Only experience with God builds wisdom. Only education in God's Word enhances wisdom. No adult is truly wise without God. Your students need today's reminder!

INTRODUCTION

A. THE UNACCEPTED INVITATION

Many years ago I was involved in a state math competition for high school students. Surprisingly I came in second and was awarded a scholarship to attend the local university. The scholarship, however, required that I be a math major. This was not my interest, so I turned the offer down and let it go to the third-place student.

I have wondered, though, how different my life would have been had I accepted this offer. Would I have made a contribution to the field of mathematics? Would I have become a high school or college math teacher? Would I have met people at that university who influenced my life and pointed me in other directions? There is no way to know these things. But whenever we reject an invitation, we make a choice that has an effect on our future.

Today's lesson invites us to join the people of God in the path of wisdom. It is an invitation that comes from God himself. He invites us to wisdom because he knows this is the best course for us to follow. The wise life is the life for which God created us.

B. NATION OF FOOLS

In the book of Proverbs, knowledge is a clear understanding of what is right and wrong from God's perspective. The wise person is the one who has this knowledge and chooses to do right. The fool is the one who knows what God has ordained as right and wrong, but chooses to do the wrong thing, the thing that is displeasing to God. Thus there is a direct correlation between wisdom and righteousness and between foolishness and sin (see Psalm 37:30; Proverbs 24:9).

DEVOTIONAL READING:
PROVERBS 8:10-21
BACKGROUND SCRIPTURE:
PROVERBS 8, 9
PRINTED TEXT:
PROVERBS 8:1-5, 22-32

LESSON AIMS

After participating in this lesson, each student will be able to:

1. Identify imagery the writer uses to give human qualities to wisdom.

2. Tell how godly wisdom is seen in a person's actions.

3. Use Scripture in a case study format to help someone make a wise decision.

May
14

KEY VERSE

Does not wisdom call out? Does not understanding raise her voice? —Proverbs 8:1

LESSON 11 NOTES

WHAT DO YOU THINK?

If foolishness and sin mean the same thing in Proverbs, then modern culture demonstrates a monumental lack of wisdom! What are some specific behavioral examples that show the foolishness of the world? Defend your choices.

HOW TO SAY IT

Corinthians. Ko-RIN-thee-unz.

Ecclesiastes. Ik-LEEZ-ee-AS-teez.

Ephesians. Ee-FEE-zhunz.

Hosea. Ho-ZAY-uh.

Machiavelli. MA-key-uh-VEH-lee.

Mao Tse-tung. Mau dzuh-DUNG.

Napoleon Bonaparte. Nuh-POL-yuhn BO-nuh-PART.

Solomon. SOL-o-mun.

Zechariah. ZEK-uh-RYE-uh.

Recently an American state court ruled that an abstinence-based sex education course could not be taught in public schools. The ruling stated that such a course promoted a particular type of morality, and the state must be morally neutral. This illustrates the confusion between religious neutrality and moral neutrality. It is ridiculous to expect a government to be morally neutral. This confusion has led courts to define acceptable morality as that which is not promoted by any religious group. Thus, governments often have promoted the views of a minority of citizens. National and local governments and court systems are on a course of losing any sense of morality, any sense of virtue.

The Bible teaches that the divine purpose for government is to reward good and punish wrong (1 Peter 2:14). Governments that cease to do this will not endure. If truth is excluded from public discussion, there will be no morality. If there can be no sense of absolute truth, there can be no guiding principles of morality. Increasingly we live in a culture that has little regard for God's standards of morality. It was recently revealed that the president of my state's largest university (40,000+ students) was having an extramarital affair with one of his staff members. This relationship was an "open secret" among many on the campus, but no one spoke up to condemn it. This issue of a powerful person's disregard for traditional standards of moral behavior was seen as a private matter, and no one else had the right to criticize this man.

Today's culture retains a basic understanding of God's standards for behavior because of the Bible's enormous influence on Western civilization across the centuries. But while the culture has this knowledge, it increasingly disregards these standards and chooses to accept and normalize immoral behavior. The verdict of Proverbs, then, is that while education levels may be at an all-time high, we live in a nation of fools. Our TV shows are written by fools. Our legal system is controlled by fools. Our educational system listens carefully to fools.

It does not have to be this way. In today's lesson, wisdom calls us, inviting us to join her in partnership with God. We don't have to join the stampede toward foolishness engulfing our culture. The ancient, timeless ways of righteousness and godliness will bring blessings to us and to our children and grandchildren.

C. LESSON BACKGROUND

Proverbs 8 uses an exciting literary technique called *personification* to portray wisdom. This means that wisdom is not presented as an abstract, doctrinal item that can be reduced to a list of dos and don'ts. Instead, wisdom takes a personality and becomes the companion of God in creating Heaven and earth. Wisdom is also the channel of God's blessing.

I. INVITATION TO WISDOM (PROVERBS 8:1-5)

A. WISDOM'S CALL TO US (vv. 1-3)

1-3. Does not wisdom call out?
> *Does not understanding raise her voice?*
> *On the heights along the way,*
> > *where the paths meet, she takes her stand;*
> *beside the gates leading into the city,*
> > *at the entrances, she cries aloud:*

A common cartoon situation depicts someone scaling a tall mountain to talk to a person on the top. This person is assumed to be a fount of wisdom, able to answer any and all human questions. The cartoon punch line is often based on the fact that such isolated hermits have little insight and give ridiculous advice.

The Bible does not portray *wisdom* this way. Wisdom calls to us. Wisdom is presented as making this invitation at the most public places of the ancient city: *on the heights,* at the most trafficked *paths,* at the city's entrance *gates,* at the *entrances* to all the homes. Wisdom does not play hide-and-seek with us. We can find wisdom and understanding in the pages of Scripture if we approach them with faith and willing obedience.

Last week in our study of Proverbs 2, we saw the use of a poetic technique called *parallelism.* Here it is again! *Wisdom* and *understanding* are parallel with one another; their meanings tend to overlap. The same is true of *call out* and *raise her voice.* We can note in passing that the Hebrew words for *wisdom* and *understanding* are both feminine. This is what leads the writer of Proverbs to use the feminine pronouns *she* and *her* in personifying wisdom.

B. WISDOM'S CHALLENGE TO US (vv. 4, 5)
4, 5. "To you, O men, I call out;
I raise my voice to all mankind.
You who are simple, gain prudence;
you who are foolish, gain understanding.

Wisdom submits a universal challenge: Get me! There is no elitism here. Wisdom is not restricted to highly intelligent or deeply spiritual people. The most foolish among us can reverse course and begin to incorporate godliness in his or her life. Likewise, the wisest, most godly people can be even wiser and more consistently righteous in their choices. No one is ever beyond hope for wisdom, nor is anyone above the need for becoming wiser still.

It is never too late or too early to begin to live wisely. I have crossed paths with many young people who are sold out to living for God and make careful, prayerful choices. I have also known people who have come to faith late in life and begin to make consistent, godly choices for the first time. This does not mean that the effects of all their bad choices instantly disappear, but error is no longer compounded by additional error. Things do get better, even in the most chaotic of lives.

II. ORIGINS AND PURPOSE OF WISDOM (PROVERBS 8:22-32)
A. WISDOM IS CREATED (v. 22)
22. "The LORD brought me forth as the first of his works,
before his deeds of old;

God is the creator of wisdom. See Genesis 4:1 where this same Hebrew verb is used in the sense of "giving birth to."

Proverbs does not present wisdom as something uncreated, then. Wisdom is the initial creation of God. In the Genesis account, the first thing created is light (Genesis 1:3). In some ways, wisdom is indeed light—the enlightenment of humans as to the ways of God. (See the parallel between wisdom and light in Ecclesiastes 2:13.)

In other ways wisdom is the foundation of creation. God does not create wisdom after designing the universe. The universe is not self-explanatory. God's wisdom is shown in every aspect of creation: material, spiritual, and ethical. "The heavens proclaim his righteousness" (Psalm 50:6).

B. WISDOM AT CREATION (vv. 23-29)
23-26. "I was appointed from eternity,
from the beginning, before the world began.

WHAT DO YOU THINK?
What would it mean for you to respond to wisdom's invitation today? How would your life be different in your schedule, family relationships, and finances?

WHAT DO YOU THINK?
Who is the wisest person you have ever known? What made him or her wise? What did that look like in practical terms of how he or she talked, spent time and money, and carried himself or herself publicly?

When there were no oceans, I was given birth,
* when there were no springs abounding with water;*
before the mountains were settled in place,
* before the hills, I was given birth,*
before he made the earth or its fields
* or any of the dust of the world.*

This text emphatically states that wisdom precedes any aspect of material creation. Even the most spectacular geographical features of our planet—the heights of *the mountains* and the depths of the *oceans*—came after the creation of wisdom. Wisdom takes second place to nothing in the created *world*.

Those who study the natural world are repeatedly amazed by the complexity they find. Single mountains comprise entire ecosystems of stunning interdependence. When fields such as cell biology and quantum mechanics cease to search for naturalistic explanations for life, their discoveries are breathtaking in their depth. It is estimated that human cells have 3.5 billion genetic bases, allowing for almost infinite genetic variety. Each human being is made up of billions of such cells. Each cell contains billions of lines of genetic code.

When these findings are put under the perspective of faith in a creator, we stand in awe. The raw intellectual power behind all of this is far beyond our comprehension (Jeremiah 10:12). Yet the Bible does not speak of God's intelligence, but of his wisdom. God's wisdom permeates every aspect of the created universe. We will never be able to comprehend that wisdom fully.

27, 28a. *"I was there when he set the heavens in place,*
* when he marked out the horizon on the face of the deep,*
* when he established the clouds above*

The author now describes wisdom's presence at the creation of *the heavens*. For those in the ancient world, the heavens are everything above the landmass of the earth. This would include both the sky (where birds fly) and the place of spiritual residence for God and the angels. The spiritual world was also created by God according to his pattern of wisdom. It is neither chaotic nor contradictory, but exists as a part of God's orderly creation.

Some people believe that spiritual principles are unscientific and illogical. Proverbs will not stand for this line of argument. Just as God created an orderly and brilliant material world, he created a spiritual world intended to conform to his patterns of wisdom. The fact that sin exists on the spiritual level is a testimony to the reality that created beings have been able to choose against God's mandates and thus play the spiritual fool.

WISDOM IN THE HEAVENS

Quick, now: what is the outermost planet in the solar system? You're right: it's Pluto—or maybe not! Since Pluto was discovered in 1930, astronomers have debated its status. All the other planets orbit in the same plane; Pluto's orbit is tilted 17 degrees. The four inner planets are rocky bodies while the next four are gas giants; Pluto, for its part, is a tiny ball of ice. One scientist says it is merely a comet; others say there are many other planets that are not counted.

First estimates of Pluto's size were that it was the size of the Earth. But now we know that its icy brilliance confused those who made those guesses. Next, we discovered the early estimates also were fooled by including the brightness of Pluto's large moon. In the 1990s the situation became even more complex when hundreds of icy planetary bodies similar to Pluto were discovered orbiting the sun beyond Neptune. To make matters more complicated, the innermost planet, Mercury, is not a planet by some definitions!

WHAT DO YOU THINK?

The apostle Paul notes in disparaging terms that "Greeks look for wisdom" (1 Corinthians 1:22). If he were to restate this for the twenty-first century by saying "secular scientists look for wisdom," what would he mean? Give some examples.

Perhaps the one thing we can be sure of in all of this is what Proverbs says: when God prepared the heavens, his wisdom was at work. Our own wisdom—or perhaps we should say our mere *knowledge*—regarding the universe is finite. We need to be reminded of that occasionally!   —C. R. B.

28b, 29. . . . and fixed securely the fountains of the deep,
* when he gave the sea its boundary*
*   so the waters would not overstep his command,*
* and when he marked out the foundations of the earth.*

The vast seas are very mysterious and majestic to people in both the ancient and modern worlds. While we know more about the oceans today, they still remain untamed. Yet as with the rest of creation, the oceans are subject to the laws of God. God has not created something that he cannot control. The mammoth might of the oceans is a part of the master plan of the wise creator.

C. WISDOM AS A DELIGHT TO GOD (vv. 30, 31)

30, 31. "Then I was the craftsman at his side.
* I was filled with delight day after day,*
*   rejoicing always in his presence,*
* rejoicing in his whole world*
*   and delighting in mankind.*

The personification of wisdom takes a new twist here. God has not only created wisdom and used it to design the rest of creation, he also takes special delight in wisdom. Likewise, wisdom rejoices at being with God. We see here echoes of God's judgment at the end of creation: "God saw all that he had made, and it was very good" (Genesis 1:31).

As we find elsewhere in the Bible, the crown of God's creation is humanity itself (Psalm 8:5). God created us in his image, to be in fellowship with him. This brings a *delight* to God that we cannot fully understand but only appreciate. This appreciation, however, helps us understand why God wants us to behave wisely. When we choose sin and act as fools, we take away God's delight and joy and cause him grief (Genesis 6:5, 6; 1 Samuel 15:11, 35; Ephesians 4:30).

WHY WE DON'T FIND (OR CAUSE) DELIGHT

Dave Barry has a weekly humor column that appears in many newspapers. In one column he describes what he calls Male Genetic Dirt Blindness, a factor at the heart of many husband-wife problems. There is scientific evidence that the male brain takes in less sensory detail than the female brain. This is one reason why many wives cannot take delight in their husbands as much as they both would like—men simply do not "see" dirt the way women do. As Barry quotes one household conversation, "What snow tires in the dining room? Oh, 'those' snow tires in the dining room."

We probably shouldn't risk the peace of the class today by pressing the matter any further! But the fact is that differences in people (of either gender) can create problems in relationships. Wisdom is the daily delight of God, and that's what he wants us to be to him as well. But part of bringing delight to God involves our use of wisdom in dealing with differences between people. Improper relationships between family members can result in relationship problems between us and God, as 1 Peter 3:7 establishes.

Our problem is that we often have neither sought wisdom nor invited her into our lives in this regard. The result is that we sometimes do not bring delight to the God who created us.   —C. R. B.

Visual for Lesson 11. *This question reminds your students that they will be listening to something this week—but exactly what is their choice.*

DAILY BIBLE READINGS

Monday, May 8—Learn Prudence and Acquire Wisdom (Proverbs 8:1-9)

Tuesday, May 9—Receive Advice, Wisdom, Insight, and Strength (Proverbs 8:10-21)

Wednesday, May 10—Wisdom Participated in Creation (Proverbs 8:22-31)

Thursday, May 11—Listen to Wisdom's Instruction (Proverbs 8:32-36)

Friday, May 12—Wisdom Extends an Invitation (Proverbs 9:1-6)

Saturday, May 13—Wisdom Multiplies Our Days (Proverbs 9:7-12)

Sunday, May 14—Folly Extends an Invitation (Proverbs 9:13-18)

PRAYER

God, our creator, you have formed the heavens and the earth according to your master plan. This plan is too marvelous for us ever to understand fully. You have given us access also to the knowledge of right and wrong. Help us understand this fully, knowing right from wrong according to your will.

Help us to make wise choices for the right and reject the foolish choices for the wrong. May we be granted the blessings of wisdom from your hand. We pray these things in the name of Jesus, your Son, amen.

THOUGHT TO REMEMBER

The life-changing invitation to wisdom is open to all, and its promises are sure.

WHAT DO YOU THINK?

What similarities and differences do you see between the invitation to get wisdom and the invitation to follow Jesus? How do you apply these similarities and differences in your own life?

D. WISDOM AS A BLESSING TO US (v. 32)

32. *"Now then, my sons, listen to me;*
    blessed are those who keep my ways."

The invitation to wisdom is repeated, now with the promise of a blessing to those who heed her. This invitation is a win-win situation. We win because we begin to make wise, moral choices that will be honored by God and will avoid the chaos and self-inflicted pain of the foolish life. God wins because his lost children have come home. His delight is restored. What a motivation to make wise choices, to live lives of godliness! May we not do this as a way of earning a reward. May we do this, rather, out of the realization that God, our creator, has shown us how to live, even in our culture of moral confusion and relativity.

CONCLUSION

A. CONFIDENT, GODLY LIVING

My great-grandfather, who spoke German much better than English, used to say, "Da proplem is dat we be too soon olt and too late schmaht." (Translation: The problem is that we are too soon old and too late smart.) That rings true for many of us. How we wish we knew then what we know now! Yet old age is no guarantee of wisdom. Adults who are mature in years often make incredibly foolish decisions. Both the old and young make unwise decisions with money, selfish decisions with relationships, and destructive decisions with spiritual matters.

If we depend on our own resources, wise decisions always will be a matter of chance. If we depend on God's instructions for living, we can confidently choose the right thing, knowing that God will never lie to us or mislead us. God created us to enjoy life and live it to the full as we glorify him. But this can happen only if we study his Word and model our lives after his patterns.

The greatest example of this is found in the life of Jesus, God's Son. Studying his teachings and actions is a reliable way to godly living. But Jesus is not available to us in the flesh as a life example to see with our own eyeballs. Paul understood this when he urged his readers to "follow my example, as I follow the example of Christ" (1 Corinthians 11:1). We all need godly examples to pattern our lives after, people we know and love. One of the central elements of wise living is to pattern our lives after truly godly people. When we find these people, we can learn from them as they have learned from God's Word and from other godly people. We can live the godly life with confidence.

B. JESUS CHRIST AS THE WISDOM OF GOD

Proverbs 8:22-32 personifies wisdom and finds her dwelling with God. This passage also pictures wisdom as the agent of God in creation (see also Proverbs 3:19). The Gospels, for their part, portray Jesus as being a manifestation of superior wisdom (Luke 2:40; see also v. 52). Jesus answered his critics by mentioning wisdom in an obvious reference to himself (Matthew 11:19). He claimed superiority over the wisdom of Solomon, the wisest person in history (Matthew 12:42). The great wisdom of Jesus was astounding to those he encountered (Mark 6:2). Jesus promised to impart wisdom to his followers in times of trials (Luke 21:15).

In Paul's great discussion of the inadequacy of human wisdom (1 Corinthians 1:18–2:5), he is not shy about identifying Jesus as "the wisdom of God" (1 Corinthians 1:24) and "who has become for us wisdom from God" (1 Corinthians 1:30). Thus, the Old Testament's invitation to wisdom is continued in the New Testament's invitation to Jesus. If wisdom is a matter of correct choices, we can make no wiser choice than choosing to believe in him.

Discovery Learning

This page contains an alternative lesson plan emphasizing learning activities. Classes desiring such student involvement will find these suggestions helpful. The next page is a reproducible activity page to further enhance discovery learning.

LEARNING GOALS

After this lesson, each student will be able to:

1. Identify imagery the writer uses to give human qualities to wisdom.

2. Tell how godly wisdom is seen in a person's actions.

3. Use Scripture in a case study format to help someone make a wise decision.

INTO THE LESSON

To begin today's lesson, ask your students to write down several examples of well-known sayings that reflect worldly wisdom. (Provide paper or direct your class to the student books, where this activity is printed). Such expressions could include common sense advice like "change your oil every 3,000 miles." Or they could reflect a worldly view of life, such as "it's a dog-eat-dog world." (Alternative: Have students complete the You Don't Say! exercise from the reproducible page instead.)

After several minutes call on volunteers to share their work. Ask them to decide which sayings are truly wise and which are actually foolish or flawed in some way. Then tell your class that today's lesson will help them recognize the difference between genuine, godly wisdom and the worldly imitation.

INTO THE WORD

A popular teaching technique used by ancient philosophers was the dialogue. For today's text, ask your class to pretend that wisdom is a person, as in Proverbs 8. Imagine that wisdom is having a dialogue with a seeker who is trying to uncover wisdom's true nature.

Below are the questions the seeker asks. Distribute copies of these questions (but not the answers in brackets). Then instruct students to supply the answers given by wisdom in Proverbs 8:1-5, 22-32. (This exercise is printed in the student books also.) After students complete the exercise, discuss their answers with the aid of the lesson commentary.

Seeker: Where can you be found? From where do you call to us?

Wisdom: *[Everywhere! On the heights, on the paths, at the gates, in the entrances of the city; vv. 1-3.]*

Seeker: What is your challenge to us?

Wisdom: *[Get me! Gain an understanding heart; vv. 4, 5.]*

Seeker: Where do you come from?

Wisdom: *[I am of the Lord, from eternity before he created the universe; vv. 22-26.]*

Seeker: How were you involved in creation?

Wisdom: *[God showed his wisdom in the creation of the heavens, the oceans, and the earth; vv. 27-29.]*

Seeker: What do you think of the world in general and people in particular?

Wisdom: *[I rejoice in the world and take great delight in humanity; vv. 30, 31.]*

Seeker: What is promised to those who follow you?

Wisdom: *[They will be blessed; v. 32.]*

INTO LIFE

Below are quotations that reflect a worldly point of view. Say, "Now let's look at wisdom from a different angle." Ask students to respond to each quote with an appropriate Scripture passage that indicates God's wisdom on the subject. Discuss responses in light of today's lesson. Suggested Scriptures follow each quotation. (The quotations are also printed in the student books. For an alternative approach, print the quotations down the left side of a page and Scripture references in biblical order down the right side; then have students match them.)

1. "Religion is the opium of the masses."—Karl Marx *[John 8:31-36; 1 Corinthians 1:18-25]*

2. "Political power grows out of the barrel of a gun." —Mao Tse-tung *[Romans 13:1-5]*

3. "If you wish to be a success in the world, promise everything, deliver nothing."—Napoleon Bonaparte *[Matthew 5:33-37; Zechariah 8:16, 17]*

4. "You can get much farther with a kind word and a gun than you can with a kind word alone."—Al Capone *[Matthew 5:38-47; Romans 12:17-21]*

5. "Christ died for our sins. Dare we make his martyrdom meaningless by not committing them?"—Jules Feiffer *[Romans 6:1-7]*

6. "I am free of all prejudices. I hate everyone equally."—W. C. Fields *[Matthew 5:43-46]*

7. "Under capitalism man exploits man; under socialism the reverse is true."—Polish proverb *[Philippians 2:1-4]*

8. "Success is the sole earthly judge of right and wrong."—Adolf Hitler *[Proverbs 21:2, 3; Hosea 14:9; Micah 6:6-8]*

You Don't Say!

Complete the following well-known bits of folk wisdom. Circle your evaluation to the right.

1. A stitch in time saves _____. Biblically wise? Foolish?

2. A penny saved is a penny _____. Biblically wise? Foolish?

3. Pretty is as pretty _____. Biblically wise? Foolish?

4. Brevity is the _____ of wit. Biblically wise? Foolish?

5. Absence makes the _____ grow fonder. Biblically wise? Foolish?

6. The way to a man's heart is through his _____. Biblically wise? Foolish?

7. The best things in life are _____. Biblically wise? Foolish?

8. You can't make a silk _____ out of a sow's ear. Biblically wise? Foolish?

9. Nothing is certain but _____ and taxes. Biblically wise? Foolish?

10. Virtue is its own _____. Biblically wise? Foolish?

11. A chain is no stronger than its weakest _____. Biblically wise? Foolish?

12. A man is known by the _____ he keeps. Biblically wise? Foolish?

13. A rolling _____ gathers no moss. Biblically wise? Foolish?

14. _____ speak louder than words. Biblically wise? Foolish?

15. All is fair in _____ and war. Biblically wise? Foolish?

16. All that glitters is not _____. Biblically wise? Foolish?

17. _____ is only skin deep. Biblically wise? Foolish?

18. Discretion is the better part of _____. Biblically wise? Foolish?

19. Experience is the mother of _____. Biblically wise? Foolish?

20. Familiarity breeds _____. Biblically wise? Foolish?

21. Fools rush in where _____ fear to tread. Biblically wise? Foolish?

22. Measure twice; cut _____. Biblically wise? Foolish?

23. Good fences make good _____. Biblically wise? Foolish?

24. Laughter is the best _____. Biblically wise? Foolish?

25. Necessity is the mother of _____. Biblically wise? Foolish?

Answers: 1. nine; 2. earned; 3. does; 4. soul; 5. heart; 6. stomach; 7. free; 8. purse; 9. death; 10. reward; 11. link; 12. company; 13. stone; 14. actions; 15. love; 16. gold; 17. beauty; 18. valor; 19. wisdom; 20. contempt; 21. angels; 22. once; 23. neighbors; 24. medicine; 25. invention

FOLLOW THE PATH OF INTEGRITY

WHY TEACH THIS LESSON?

Satan does not need to accomplish much to destroy integrity. Because integrity has to do with wholeness, even a small chink destroys it. Integrity is a true 24/7 concept. Consistently right choices create (or reveal) integrity. One evil choice creates a fault line of potential catastrophe.

Adults need to learn that they must "sweat the small things" in ethics and morality. Even a small thing like an unfair weight is hated by God. Hypocrisy, pride, love of wealth, bad words, loose tongue—all are chisels at the granite of integrity. And what adult in your class does not find himself or herself being tempted to sink into these behaviors? Today's study can make your adults more "biblically savvy" in their choices for integrity.

INTRODUCTION

A. "I ALWAYS TELL THE TRUTH, LOIS"

A great fantasy hero of the twentieth century was Superman, "the man of steel." The Superman story arose out of the hard times of the Great Depression and served as an inspiration during the years of World War II.

Superman was touted as fighting for "truth, justice, and the American way." Some would dismiss this motto today as being too simplistic and too focused on America. Yet this childhood hero of many was more than a superb athlete— strong, fast, and able to fly. Superman was always portrayed as a man of great moral strength, a man of integrity.

In the motion picture version of the Superman saga, there is a scene in which the man of steel meets with the skeptical Lois Lane for the first time. During this encounter in her rooftop garden, there comes a point where Lois questions whether or not Superman is lying to her. In perfect sincerity, without a trace of guile, Superman says, "I always tell the truth, Lois."

I always tell the truth. How wonderful it would be if we all could say this! We are confronted dozens of times every day with situations that demand that we be either truthful or deceitful. Truth is an absolute value. In matters of integrity, there is no gray area. We either tell the truth, or we don't. We all know that we are lied to constantly in our culture. We are lied to by advertisers. We are lied to by politicians. We are lied to by employers. We are lied to by employees. Tragically, we are sometimes lied to by church leaders, family members, and even spouses.

A basic definition of integrity is doing what you say you will do. For example, a person who refuses to help and, in fact, does not help has not violated integrity. But the person who promises to help and then refuses (or denies making the original promise) has compromised integrity. This week's lesson hits us where we live: the daily decisions of telling the truth and keeping our commitments.

DEVOTIONAL READING:
PROVERBS 10:27-32
BACKGROUND SCRIPTURE:
PROVERBS 11
PRINTED TEXT:
PROVERBS 11:1-14

LESSON AIMS

After participating in this lesson, each student will be able to:

1. Contrast the actions of a righteous person with those of one who is dishonest.

2. Explain how personal integrity can be destroyed by pride and dishonesty.

3. Perform an integrity checkup in his or her life.

WHAT DO YOU THINK?

What are some times that people think it is OK to lie? What are some methods or philosophies we should be on guard against that excuse lying?

KEY VERSE

The integrity of the upright guides them, but the unfaithful are destroyed by their duplicity.   —Proverbs 11:3

May
21

LESSON 12 NOTES

WHAT DO YOU THINK?

How has living a life of integrity benefited you? What was a time when the temptation to compromise integrity could have helped you in a way that the world considers profitable?

HOW TO SAY IT

caveat emptor (Latin). *KA-vee-at EMP-ter.*

Ecclesiastes. Ik-LEEZ-ee-AS-teez.

shekel. SHEH-kul.

B. LESSON BACKGROUND

It is helpful to review the concepts of knowledge and wisdom as presented in the book of Proverbs. Knowledge is knowing what God expects us to do, recognizing his standards of right and wrong. Wisdom is discerning these standards and choosing to obey God. Foolishness is knowing the expectations of God but choosing to do the wrong thing. The Bible teaches that our integrity is never for sale and never to be sacrificed. Wisdom, therefore, is keeping one's word, no matter what the consequences. The fool is the person who breaks his or her word for money or other selfish reasons that are within his or her control. A vivid illustration of the importance of integrity is found in Job 2:9, 10.

The Hebrew word translated *integrity* in Proverbs 11:3 (below) has several related words with various shades of meaning in the Old Testament. It can have the sense of *blameless* (Job 1:1). It can also mean *innocence* (2 Samuel 15:11). The "innocent" person (the person of integrity) may be a target of attack by the wicked (Psalm 64:4). Integrity can have a protective function (Psalm 25:21). Most importantly, God is a protective shield to those who are "blameless" (Proverbs 2:7).

I. INTEGRITY OF A PERSON (PROVERBS 11:1-9)

A. INTEGRITY IN BUSINESS (v. 1)

1. The LORD abhors dishonest scales,
    but accurate weights are his delight.

Nothing is prepackaged in the ancient world. Basic items are bought and sold based on weight, quantity, or volume. Merchants measure at the time of sale. This is done using a beam-balance scale with dishes on either end. Such *scales* are dependent upon standardized weights being used on one side.

Commodities such as spices or incense are weighed out on the merchant's scale using his set of stone *weights*. The basic unit of weight measurement in Old Testament times is the shekel (Ezekiel 4:10; 45:12). It weighs about four-tenths of an ounce (11.5 grams, or about the weight of two U.S. quarter dollars). Stone weights are sized in fractions and multiples of shekels.

If payment is being made in gold or silver, the customer's metal also will be weighed because there are no absolute standards. A dishonest merchant might keep two sets of weights. One would be lighter, thus favoring him when weighing his commodity. The other would be heavier, thus penalizing the customer when weighing the money. The Bible teaches that such dishonesty is more than bad business practice; it is offensive to God himself (see Deuteronomy 25:13-16; Proverbs 20:10; Amos 8:4, 5; Micah 6:11).

Consumers today are warned by the Latin phrase *caveat emptor*: "Let the buyer beware!" Although modern government standards require truth in packaging, such packaging often is misleading anyway. The people of God should have no part in this business philosophy. A business with integrity builds a loyal customer base because the merchant treats the customers fairly. Deception and lack of integrity may build short-term profits but will lead to collapse in the long run. Think of the Enron scandal.

KNOW ANY CHRISTIAN "MUSIC MEN"?

Not quite a century ago, a very entertaining (fictitious) con man—"Professor" Harold Hill by name—got off the train in River City, Iowa. Who doesn't remember that story from the stage play and film *The Music Man*? Although Hill had no musical talent, he was a mesmerizing salesman. He convinced the citizens of River City that the recent addition of a pool table to their community would lead to the degradation of their youth. His solution? A boys' marching band would "keep the young ones moral after school."

His plan to skip town after collecting the money for mail-order instruments and uniforms went awry when he fell in love with the town librarian. Of course it all ended well, with the uniforms magically fitting and the "76 trombones" miraculously hitting all the right notes in the hands of the untutored, juvenile musicians.

We all know that real life doesn't work out so nicely. Too often the dishonest salesman gets the money, and the victim realizes the deception too late. Technology has provided substitutes for dishonest scales in the form of Internet scams, telemarketing frauds, etc. Times change and the means of cheating may change, but the Lord still abhors dishonesty. Christians, of all people, are to be known for integrity in business dealings.   —C. R. B.

B. INTEGRITY AND HUMILITY (vv. 2, 3)

2. 3. When pride comes, then comes disgrace,
*   but with humility comes wisdom.*
* The integrity of the upright guides them,*
*   but the unfaithful are destroyed by their duplicity.*

There is a direct correlation between boastful *pride* and lack of *integrity*. When we inflate and tout our accomplishments and virtues, credibility and integrity evaporate. Sometimes it feels good to be able to say we are the smartest, the richest, or the cleverest in a given situation.

The wise person realizes that *pride* is fleeting, that false claims will be found out. It is better to live in humility and simplicity, not seeking the acclaim of others. While this kind of life may not seem as exciting, it will safeguard the wise person from the social embarrassment that inevitably comes to the boastful, exaggerating individual.

C. INTEGRITY AND GOD'S JUDGMENT (vv. 4-6)

4-6. Wealth is worthless in the day of wrath,
*   but righteousness delivers from death.*
* The righteousness of the blameless makes a straight way for them,*
*   but the wicked are brought down by their own wickedness.*
* The righteousness of the upright delivers them,*
*   but the unfaithful are trapped by evil desires.*

There are some things that money cannot buy (compare Proverbs 11:28). Money cannot buy a happy, stable home and family. Money cannot buy a happy marriage.

Neither can money buy the satisfaction that comes from a task well done. Money cannot buy friends who will stick with you when there is no money (the prodigal son in Jesus' parable found this out). Money cannot buy a fulfilling and satisfying relationship with God. Money cannot buy a faithful church. In fact, when we consider the most important things in life, money can buy none of them.

Greek mythology tells the story of King Midas, who was given the power to turn everything he touched into gold. His greed caused him to be delighted with this ability until mealtime came. Then Midas found that all food and drink became gold before he could eat or drink. He learned that great wealth is not life's greatest blessing.

In the book of Proverbs, wisdom is the realization that money is to be used, not worshiped. The wise use money for godly purposes. Foolishness, therefore, is to trust wealth for salvation or happiness. Money can never buy integrity.

Visual for Lesson 12. *Point to this visual as you ask, "What are some life-path choices that you will face this week?"*

D. INTEGRITY AND GOD'S DELIVERANCE (vv. 7-9)

7-9. *When a wicked man dies, his hope perishes;*
*   all he expected from his power comes to nothing.*
The righteous man is rescued from trouble,
*   and it comes on the wicked instead.*
With his mouth the godless destroys his neighbor,
*   but through knowledge the righteous escape.*

Is the life of integrity one in which we have no problems, trials, or *trouble*? God does not promise this. To the contrary, the Bible is full of stories of people who suffer because of their personal stand for integrity.

Proverbs teaches that *righteous* people, those who walk in integrity, have the blessing and the protection of God (see Proverbs 28:18). This does not mean that righteous people never suffer or that the way of integrity is easy. It means that God ultimately will vindicate us and reward our intentions to live lives of integrity and righteousness (compare Revelation 6:9-11). To some degree, righteousness is its own reward. But the Bible promises more than this. God notices our efforts. He smiles upon those who choose integrity.

II. INTEGRITY OF A COMMUNITY (PROVERBS 11:10-14)

A. CITY CELEBRATES (vv. 10, 11)

10, 11. *When the righteous prosper, the city rejoices;*
*   when the wicked perish, there are shouts of joy.*
Through the blessing of the upright a city is exalted,
*   but by the mouth of the wicked it is destroyed.*

Proverbs throws in an unexpected twist at this point and focuses on a community's integrity rather than an individual's. Communities take pride in the integrity of their leaders. There is reason to celebrate when a community achieves a reputation for integrity. On the other hand, a city that tolerates dishonesty and corruption among its officials will earn a bad reputation.

I once lived in a large city that was having an election for prosecuting attorney between two men of very questionable reputation. Both men were under indictment by federal grand juries for corruption. Remarkably, though, the political parties could find no better candidates. When the campaign mudslinging began, the message for each candidate was basically "my indictment is not as serious as my opponent's indictment." What an embarrassment to that city!

It is doubly embarrassing if Christians run for office, are elected, and then fall because of corruption and dishonesty. It is an embarrassment to *the city,* to the church, and to our Lord. We should encourage believers to be involved in civic affairs. But the battle for integrity will be ongoing and intense. How joyous it is when a person retires from office with a long and distinguished career marked by both accomplishment and integrity!

COMMUNAL INTEGRITY

Missionaries in third-world countries sometimes have to deal with corruption on the part of government officials. One missionary, for example, found himself frustrated time and again by officials looking for a "dash," as bribes were called. When mission business required a government permit, officials created numerous delays in hopes of eliciting a bribe. Policemen often expected a bribe as the price of overlooking an imaginary traffic offense.

After several such incidents, the missionary was reaching the proverbial boiling point. It was then that he recalled the many cities in his home country that had

WHAT DO YOU THINK?

What are some key words in Proverbs 11:7-9 that speak most strongly to your life situation right now? Explain your choices.

DAILY BIBLE READINGS

Monday, May 15—God's Way Is a Stronghold (Proverbs 10:27-32)

Tuesday, May 16—Wisdom, Not Pride (Proverbs 11:1-5)

Wednesday, May 17—Righteousness, Not Treachery (Proverbs 11:6-10)

Thursday, May 18—The Importance of Guidance and Counsel (Proverbs 11:11-15)

Friday, May 19—Blameless Ways, Not Wickedness (Proverbs 11:16-21)

Saturday, May 20—Generosity, Not Stinginess (Proverbs 11:22-26)

Sunday, May 21—Goodness, Not Evil (Proverbs 11:27-31)

similar problems. Back home the wheels of government often were greased with kickbacks, payoffs, and favors of various kinds.

Such failures of communal integrity (wherever they may take place) are an indication that the common people accept the situation as normal and nothing to be concerned about. Of course in some cases it may be impossible for "the little guy" to have any influence on entrenched governmental corruption. But in democracies, where the people have a voice, Christians ought to be in the front ranks of those who demand that their leaders conduct themselves with integrity. A community or nation will destroy itself if it lacks such godly counsel.   —C. R. B.

B. DAMAGE OF CARELESS ACCUSALS (vv. 12, 13)

12, 13. A man who lacks judgment derides his neighbor,
    but a man of understanding holds his tongue.
 A gossip betrays a confidence,
    but a trustworthy man keeps a secret.

In the movie *Bambi*, little Thumper the rabbit is taught by his father, "If you can't say something nice, don't say nothin' at all." There are times when we must stand up for righteousness and be vocal. But what about the times when our criticisms are little more than attempts at self-righteousness? The way of wisdom is often marked by holding our tongues (Ecclesiastes 3:7).

Holding our tongues naturally involves prudence in dealing with secrets. Those who have been leaders in the church for many years often know awkward things about many people. What do we do with this knowledge? First, we cannot and should not feel obligated to deny or alter the facts. But second, we also must trust that people grow and change.

When we see that a person has abandoned a sinful behavior, we serve no purpose by bringing up past problems. Instead, we rejoice that God has changed a person for the better. When we are entrusted with *a secret,* our integrity is being put to the test. Will we use this knowledge as power to hurt or destroy someone unnecessarily? Or will we keep our word by keeping the secret?

We all have done things in the past that we are not particularly proud of. Let's let those things die as we live for the future as servants of our gracious Lord. This does not mean, however, that we become silent facilitators for criminal behavior. It's always dangerous to give a blanket *yes* answer in advance to someone who says "I need to talk to you about something, but you have to promise not to tell anyone." The person may be about to divulge information that involves the safety of others. When in doubt about issues of confidentiality, consult someone who is spiritually mature in this area.

C. NATION ADRIFT (v. 14)

14. For lack of guidance a nation falls,
    but many advisers make victory sure.

The proposition in the first half of this verse is that lack of integrity among national leaders will have widespread implications. There is no such thing as a morally neutral society. We have every right to demand integrity and honesty from public officials. We should not stand for the conventional wisdom that says a campaign promise equals a lie to help get the candidate elected.

A nation that ignores foundational issues of truth and justice will not be blessed by God. Wisdom should extend into the civic arena. We should desire leaders who are wise by God's standards, not fools. A look at who is serving as a leader's *advisers* can be very revealing! (See 1 Kings 12:8-11.)

WHAT DO YOU THINK?

What was a time that someone revealed a secret that ended up hurting you? Have you ever done that to someone else? Why do you think people are so prone to gossip?

WHAT DO YOU THINK?

Some people easily and frequently seek the counsel of trusted individuals, while other people almost never do so. Why is that? What can we do to increase godly counsel in our lives?

PRAYER

God of truth, we ask that you help us follow your examples. You always tell the truth. You always keep your promises. You are the ultimate and perfect model of integrity. Make us people of truth and integrity. We pray this in the name of your Son Jesus, the full embodiment of truth, amen.

CONCLUSION

A. SATAN HATES INTEGRITY

The book of Job has a lot to say about integrity. In the conversation between God and Satan at the beginning, God points to Job as a shining example of this characteristic (Job 2:3). Satan thinks that Job's integrity will crack under pressure and proceeds to test him mightily. Satan is always looking to attack the people of God in the area of integrity.

There is a practical side of this for Christians. In the book of Titus, Paul instructs his apprentice to appoint church leaders who are "blameless" or men of integrity (Titus 1:6, 7). Titus himself is to be a model of integrity or incorruptness (Titus 2:7; see Lesson 13 from winter).

Why is this? The underlying principle is that church leaders need to be seen as people of integrity in the community so that unbelievers will not be offended. The church is open to all who believe, even those who struggle with matters of integrity. But leadership must be restricted to those who have proven themselves to be people of honesty and truth. Otherwise the reputation of the church will be damaged, and our Lord Jesus will suffer undue disgrace.

Satan would like nothing better than to besmirch the name of Jesus and his followers. May we have the strength to resist giving Satan that victory.

B. THE HARD CHOICE FOR INTEGRITY

Sir Thomas More (1478–1535) was a prominent statesman during the reign of Henry VIII, king of England. More was a man of great principle. Although he wanted to see young Henry succeed, More was unwilling to sacrifice his integrity. Eventually More was accused of treason and imprisoned because of his unwillingness to yield to the king's demand to be recognized as the lawful head of the Church of England.

While in prison More's daughter Margaret visited and implored him to take the oath that would save his life. She reasoned that he could say the oath but think otherwise in his heart. For More, though, this was a matter of integrity. He cupped his hands as if holding water and told her that when a man makes an oath, he is holding his own self in his hands. More then opened his fingers to show Margaret that when an oath is false, the man will lose himself like the water that would slip away. Then there would be nothing left.

More was executed for his refusal to take the oath. Today, however, he is celebrated and honored as one of the greatest examples of integrity in all of history. He was nicknamed by a friend as the "man for all seasons." For More, integrity was worth dying for!

For most of us, decisions of integrity are not matters of life and death. A little lie here, a little cheating there, who will ever know? Shouldn't people look out for themselves? Think of your own life. Do you have limits to your integrity? If a cashier incorrectly gives you back extra money, do you see this as good luck or as an opportunity to act with integrity? How much would you need to be paid to lie for your employer? Would you do it for $100,000? What value makes something worth stealing? Would you steal something worth $10,000 if there were little risk of being caught?

The Bible teaches that no monetary value can be assigned to our integrity. Honesty applies in things little or big. As Proverbs 28:6 says, "Better a poor man whose walk is blameless than a rich man whose ways are perverse." Faithfulness applies to things small and big (Luke 16:10). May we learn to live wisely and to walk with integrity in everything we do.

THOUGHT TO REMEMBER

Sacrificing integrity for temporary benefit is a long-term disaster.

Discovery Learning

This page contains an alternative lesson plan emphasizing learning activities. Classes desiring such student involvement will find these suggestions helpful. The next page is a reproducible activity page to further enhance discovery learning.

LEARNING GOALS

After this lesson, each student will be able to:

1. Contrast the actions of a righteous person with those of one who is dishonest.

2. Explain how personal integrity can be destroyed by pride and dishonesty.

3. Perform an integrity checkup in his or her life.

INTO THE LESSON

Place in chairs copies of the word search from the reproducible page for students to work on as they arrive. When the class comes to order, ask students to put their word searches aside in order to focus on the following three case studies. For each scenario below, your class should decide what advice to give the central character. The scenarios are also printed in the student books.

Scenario #1. Martha has joined with several other investors to purchase some real estate they hope to develop into a residential community. However, Martha has learned from a friend on the zoning commission that the property has drainage problems that will be very costly to correct. Unaware of the problems, another investor wants to buy Martha's share of the land. Should she tell him about the problems?

Scenario #2. Ken owned a thriving gas station and convenience mart. He invited his friends and employees to invest in his expanding business and many did. Now, however, new competition has hurt his business. Ken has enough money to sell out, take a loss, and start over elsewhere. But many others will lose their jobs and/or their investments. What should he do?

Scenario #3. Arthur is an accountant for a local cell phone provider. He knows the company is headed toward bankruptcy. But the owner has offered him a bonus to keep that information secret so the other employees and customers won't go elsewhere. What should Arthur do?

Discuss your students' responses to each scenario. Then tell your class that today's lesson concerns issues of personal and community integrity.

INTO THE WORD

Lead your class in a discussion of today's text, Proverbs 11:1-14, using the lesson commentary and the following discussion questions:

1. How should we apply the standard of an honest "balance" (v. 1) to our business practices today?

2. What is the relation between integrity and humility (vv. 2, 3)?

3. Why is integrity better than wealth in the Day of Judgment (vv. 4-9)?

4. What does integrity have to do with the well-being of a community (vv. 10, 11)?

5. What can happen to a community beset by dishonesty (vv. 12-14)?

Return to the three scenarios from the Into the Lesson activity. Say, "Based on today's study so far, what would you now say to Martha, Ken, and Arthur?"

INTO LIFE

To close today's lesson, make and distribute copies of the self-evaluation activity that follows. (This exercise also is printed in the student book.) Tell students that they will not be asked to share their responses.

Integrity Self-Check

How trustworthy are you? Grade your sense of integrity by circling your response to each question below.

A. Would you return a wallet full of money you found in a parking lot? *1. Never; 2. Maybe; 3. For a reward; 4. Probably; 5. Absolutely.*

B. Would you break the rules to win a game or improve your golf score? *1. Of course; 2. Probably; 3. If it were important; 4. Doubtful; 5. Never.*

C. Would you cheat on your taxes to save $500? *1. Sure; 2. Probably; 3. Only for $1,000 or more; 4. No, I'd fear an audit; 5. Never.*

D. Would you lie to get out of a difficult situation? *1. Why not? 2. Define lying; 3. Depends on the situation; 4. Rarely; 5. Never.*

E. Would you obey a stop sign on a deserted road? *1. What stop sign? 2. Not unless a cop is nearby; 3. Usually, unless I'm running late; 4. Normally, unless it's an emergency; 5. Of course.*

Figure your IQ ("Integrity Quotient") by adding the scores for all five responses. Here are possible results:

22–25	Habitually honorable
17–21	Generally trustworthy
13–16	Dubiously reliable
9–12	Ethically challenged
5–8	Morally bankrupt

Proverbs 11 Word Search

In the blanks below, write God's words concerning integrity found in Proverbs 11:1-14. Then locate the words in the word search below. Look across, up, down, and diagonally. (Answers at the bottom.)

"The Lord abhors dishonest _____, but accurate weights are his _____. When _____ comes, then comes disgrace, but with _____ comes _____. The _____ of the upright guides them, but the unfaithful are destroyed by their _____. Wealth is worthless in the day of wrath, but _____ delivers from death. The righteousness of the _____ makes a straight way for them, but the wicked are brought down by their own _____. The righteousness of the upright _____ them, but the unfaithful are trapped by evil _____. When a wicked man dies, his _____ perishes; all he expected from his _____ comes to nothing. The righteous man is _____ from _____, and it comes on the wicked instead. With his mouth the _____ destroys his _____, but through knowledge the righteous escape. When the righteous _____, the city rejoices; when the wicked perish, there are shouts of _____. Through the _____ of the upright a city is exalted, but by the mouth of the wicked it is _____. A man who lacks _____ derides his neighbor, but a man of _____ holds his tongue. A _____ betrays a confidence, but a trustworthy man keeps a _____. For lack of _____ a nation falls, but many _____ make victory sure."

```
T  N  E  M  G  D  U  J  N  E  I  G  H  B  O  R  D  R  C  J  S
K  R  S  S  E  N  D  E  K  C  I  W  S  L  H  T  R  X  R  S  Y
S  K  N  W  L  N  T  Z  R  X  Z  S  U  A  T  M  N  X  Y  K  K
K  R  S  H  B  T  R  N  M  Z  K  N  M  L  Y  R  R  N  G  Z
T  T  R  E  U  V  J  N  S  K  Y  X  D  E  W  C  C  B  N  V  D
S  P  L  P  O  K  R  S  T  N  V  D  E  L  I  G  H  T  Z  H  D
E  X  J  O  R  E  S  C  U  E  D  J  R  E  S  V  K  Z  R  U  E
R  I  G  H  T  E  O  U  S  N  E  S  S  S  D  G  G  J  V  M  S
I  N  N  R  E  W  O  P  R  I  D  E  T  S  O  Y  Z  L  S  I  T
S  E  L  A  C  S  R  E  S  I  V  D  A  R  M  N  J  S  Y  L  R
E  G  S  R  E  O  V  K  Y  B  C  K  N  D  N  P  E  P  J  I  O
D  B  D  C  S  S  R  E  V  I  L  E  D  U  P  L  I  C  I  T  Y
G  Z  R  P  Y  T  I  R  G  E  T  N  I  S  D  K  K  V  G  Y  E
N  E  E  M  B  L  E  S  S  I  N  G  N  O  K  Y  D  R  S  O  D
T  R  D  R  C  E  C  N  A  D  I  U  G  O  S  S  I  P  J  J  I
```

LIVING OUT WISDOM

LESSON 13

WHY TEACH THIS LESSON?

The role of women in society, family, and church often has been debated, sometimes hotly. Some cultures consider women to be nothing more than chattel or simple possessions. Women have, at times, been denied their God-given rights and value. Today's text in Proverbs 31 is one statement of God's view of a woman's potential. Blessed indeed is the family (and church and business) that has the woman of "noble character"!

The woman pictured here is but one person meeting God's grand plan for a life of righteousness and service. Every adult needs to be reinforced in his or her drive to be God's person of nobility and virtue.

INTRODUCTION

A. GODLY MOTHERS AND WIVES

Traditional motherhood is under attack as never before. One of the current complaints of Generation X (those born between 1965 and 1980) is that they often were reared in very unstable family situations. Their parents (members of the Baby-Boomer Generation, born between 1946 and 1964) had divorces, substance abuse problems, and financial catastrophes. It is not uncommon to hear stories of Gen Xers who, in effect, became the parent, the responsible adult, in their households during their teenage years. Some tell stories of mothers who dragged them from marriage to marriage, boyfriend to boyfriend, nightmare to nightmare. They tell tales of abusive or absent fathers.

The Bible teaches us that it does not have to be this way. While all parties in a successful family are important, the book of Proverbs lifts up the essential nature of a stable wife and mother, a woman who gives selflessly to her children and to her husband. Such a woman is acting in a godly manner. The children of this kind of godly woman will "arise and call her blessed" (Proverbs 31:28).

The Bible is full of accounts about godly mothers. Think of Jochebed (mother of Moses), Hannah (mother of Samuel), Ruth (great-grandmother of David), Eunice (mother of Timothy), Mary (mother of Jesus), and others. Not all had stable or ideal situations. Hannah had a rival who tormented her (1 Samuel 1:6, 7). Ruth's husband and brother-in-law died (Ruth 1:3-5). Eunice probably had no help from her husband in young Timothy's spiritual upbringing (Acts 16:1; 2 Timothy 1:5; 3:14, 15).

Yet one thing these mothers had in common was their devotion to family. They loved unselfishly and are still remembered because of it. William Ross Wallace (1819–1881) wrote "the hand that rocks the cradle is the hand that rules the world." Let us never undervalue the call of God for godly mothers.

B. LESSON BACKGROUND

There is no question but that the household and family life reflected in the book of Proverbs is quite different from what we see in the modern, industrial-

---

DEVOTIONAL READING:
PROVERBS 4:10-15
BACKGROUND SCRIPTURE:
PROVERBS 31
PRINTED TEXT:
PROVERBS 31:8-14, 25-30

LESSON AIMS

After participating in this lesson, each student will be able to:

1. Describe the Old Testament ideal for wives and mothers.

2. Explain why principles of justice and character are best learned first in the home.

3. Write a thank-you letter to a woman who has been a godly influence in his or her life.

WHAT DO YOU THINK?

If you were to submit your own mother as "mother of the year" (even if she is deceased), what would you say about her? What did she do that blessed your life?

KEY VERSE

Charm is deceptive, and beauty is fleeting; but a woman who fears the Lord is to be praised.
—Proverbs 31:30

May
28

LESSON 13 NOTES

ized world. Our world of machines has made many household tasks quicker and simpler. In the ancient household, meal preparation was ongoing, almost throughout the day. Such preparations could require a trip to the market for items such as oil or meat. The household garden, which provided produce and spices, had to be tended.

Preparations also required the frequent baking of bread, perhaps made from flour that had been ground at the village mill (or by hand). Cooking was done using an open fire, and this required constant procurement of adequate fuel. Water had to be toted from the well, whether for drinking or for washing. Other household tasks were repetitive and numerous. The idea of a woman having a job or career outside the home would have seemed impossible. There was no time! Stay-at-home wives were not women of leisure. They worked hard from dawn until dusk just keeping their households functioning.

Our modern world may have eliminated some of the work involved in managing a household. Yet this same world of conveniences has brought onto women new pressures that were undreamed of in the ancient world. Women in ancient times were not confronted with all the stresses of employment. Their children were less independent and less likely to be corrupted by bad influences outside the home. Divorce in the ancient world was uncommon. Even less common would have been the stresses of a blended household, where children from two families are brought together and expected to get along.

Few would want to go back to the grinding labor of the ancient household. Yet the modern home presents a complex series of challenges for wives and mothers. This week's lesson pictures the woman of Old Testament times, but we will find many principles that still apply today.

Proverbs 31 was not written by King Solomon, but rather by King Lemuel. In fact Proverbs 31:1 indicates that Lemuel's mother is the original source for this chapter. The name *Lemuel* means "one devoted to God." Outside of his name, we know nothing about this king. Some have suggested that Lemuel may be a nickname for Solomon himself, since he was characterized by his devotion to God early in life. If this is true, then the mother mentioned in Proverbs 31:1 was Bathsheba.

At any rate, it is amazing to see that the mother of the king knew the value of a woman who managed the household well. Even at the royal, wealthy level—where there are many servants—there was a need for a faithful wife and mother. Such a person was to be honored.

I. PLEADING FOR JUSTICE (PROVERBS 31:8, 9)

A. DEFENDING THE SILENT (v. 8)

8. *"Speak up for those who cannot speak for themselves,*
    for the rights of all who are destitute.

Our first section deals with general issues of social justice. A constant theme in the Old Testament is the call for a fair society, where all people can have their basic needs met and live life with dignity. This is part of "Living Out Wisdom," our lesson title. God loves justice (Proverbs 21:3).

Those who cannot speak for themselves refers to those who have no voice that matters. They have no political clout. They must suffer injustice without effective protest. They are further pictured as being *destitute.* The most vivid example of a person in this condition comes in Isaiah's prophecy of the Messiah. He will be a suffering servant (Isaiah 53:7). Jesus fulfills this prophecy as an innocent man unjustly accused and executed, one who will not speak in his own defense.

Jesus suffered silently for our sins, but this is no excuse for letting the powerless in our communities endure injustice quietly. In democratic societies the citizens have voices that are heard if they are used. We who are able must speak up for the homeless, the poor, the weak, the sick, and the disabled. Jesus loved these people, and so must we. See the next verse.

B. DEFENDING THE NEEDY (v. 9)
9. *"Speak up and judge fairly;*
*   defend the rights of the poor and needy."*

The phrase *judge fairly* reveals an outstanding concept in the Old Testament. The concept of impartial justice was a hallmark of Jewish law. This ideal stood opposed to the all-too-often practice of awarding judgment based on a bribe.

Justice should never be for sale. Consistent justice for all parties is very difficult, but both the *poor* and the rich are entitled to justice in the Hebrew courts (Leviticus 19:15). Similarly, both citizens and resident aliens were to be given equal justice (Deuteronomy 1:16). Kings were appointed by God in order to judge righteously among the people (2 Chronicles 9:8). Ultimate justice, however, is to come with the Messiah (Jeremiah 23:5).

One wonders, however, what this has to do with the picture of the virtuous woman, the focus of Lemuel's proverbs. This is not entirely clear, but it makes sense to assume that Lemuel thinks that justice begins in the home. We learn our lessons of right and wrong, of fairness and unfairness, from our mothers. Mothers are naturally inclined to love all their children and not favor one over another. This attitude serves anyone well who is called to render judgments.

II. RECOGNIZING A NOBLE WOMAN (PROVERBS 31:10-14)
A. WORTHY OF TRUST (vv. 10, 11)
10, 11. *A wife of noble character who can find?*
*   She is worth far more than rubies.*
* Her husband has full confidence in her*
*   and lacks nothing of value.*

Just as wisdom is better than rubies (Proverbs 3:15; 8:11), so is the *wife of noble character.* She cannot be bought. She is truly priceless (see Proverbs 12:4). The essential idea behind *noble* is that of strong moral character. The virtuous person is not necessarily blessed with great physical beauty or strength. She displays her beauty in her life (compare 1 Peter 3:3, 4).

Lemuel knows that such a person may be overlooked when young men are seeking wives. They will be attracted to women of beauty. The wise man, however, realizes that a woman of integrity and moral strength is a great treasure. If he can have such a woman for a wife, he has chosen most wisely. The result is that he *lacks nothing of value.*

B. BRINGS GOOD (v. 12)
12. *She brings him good, not harm,*
*   all the days of her life.*

Brings him good has the sense here of repayment. The man who wisely chooses a noble wife will reap the reward many times over. She will be faithful to him *all the days of her life.*

How sad when marriages fall apart because of mistrust and selfishness. Lifelong commitment has become so rare that it surprises us when we encounter it. Sometimes a marriage fails because one or both of the partners is not virtuous.

WHAT DO YOU THINK?

How is a noble woman like a treasure? What benefits can she bring to her husband or potential future husband? How can her husband show his gratitude for all she does?

She is unfaithful to her husband, or he is unfaithful to his wife. Other times, however, marriages crash and burn because the partners do not esteem the faithfulness of their spouses. They mistake loyalty for boringness and take fidelity for granted. The relationship is neglected and loses the key ingredient of mutual respect.

This is not the course of the wise; it is the path of fools. Much later the apostle Paul will advise, "Husbands, love your wives and do not be harsh with them" (Colossians 3:19).

C. WORKS HARD (vv. 13, 14)
*13, 14. She selects wool and flax
   and works with eager hands.
She is like the merchant ships,
   bringing her food from afar.*

The manager of the ancient household works hard to provide for her family. She procures *wool* and *flax*, raw materials of clothing, so that she can provide garments for her family. She shops in unusual places to bring a variety of tasty meals to the family table. None of these things are done to earn the adoration of her children and husband, to earn "mother of the year" honors. She simply does these things because she loves her family.

TRUE NOBILITY

Once upon a time (as the saying goes), nobility was a cherished virtue. *Nobility* conjures up the image of brave knights of old, rewarded by their king or queen with a title such as the fabled Sir Lancelot.

Yet it appears that nowadays the notion of nobility has been watered down considerably. Perhaps no society feels this more than the British. Just a few years ago, a committee of parliamentarians recommended doing away with the nobility system. Their report said that "Increasingly, titles appear to be an embarrassment rather than a cause for celebration."

The reason for this embarrassment is that the titles of nobility are given at the rate of some 3,000 per year, and not just to people who have made great contributions to British society. Recipients are more likely to include rock stars and lower-level bureaucrats who just happen to be good friends of members of parliament. As a result, some who really deserve recognition for their contributions refuse their titles in embarrassment.

But truly noble people aren't in it for the title anyway. The noble, virtuous woman of Proverbs 31 does her work because she treasures the blessings that come from God to those who exercise wisdom. She does not do it for the acclaim of some government bureau. Even so, she need not be embarrassed at any praise she receives, for it is a recognition of her godly virtue.   —C. R. B.

III. APPRECIATING A STRONG WOMAN (PROVERBS 31:25-30)
A. HONORABLE (v. 25)
*25. She is clothed with strength and dignity;
   she can laugh at the days to come.*

Again, the noble woman is pictured as a person of great moral character. She is so confident that *she can laugh at the days to come.* This is not cockiness or arrogance. It is because she does not fear the future. She knows that her children love her, her husband trusts and respects her, and that she is serving God by caring for her family. Of course she is confident! Why shouldn't she be? She is prepared for the days ahead.

"A woman that feareth the LORD, she shall be praised" —Proverbs 31:30

Visual for Lesson 13. *This visual can be a backdrop to your question "How can we encourage godly motherhood?"*

B. WISE (vv. 26, 27)

26, 27. She speaks with wisdom,
and faithful instruction is on her tongue.
She watches over the affairs of her household
and does not eat the bread of idleness.

The vast majority of women in the ancient world have little influence in community or national affairs. Yet Lemuel sees the noble woman as a source of *wisdom*. Her restricted sphere of influence does not limit her effectiveness.

This wisdom is characterized three ways. First, she uses *faithful instruction*. The Hebrew word being translated here is one of the great words of the Old Testament. This word is translated *kindness* in various other Old Testament passages (examples: Genesis 19:19; Joshua 2:12). It is an eternal, essential quality of God. The noble woman is godly because she embodies this.

Second, the noble woman has set her priorities so that the efficient and happy operation of her household is her number one job. She doesn't let outside interests intrude at the expense of her husband and children. This is what it means when she *watches over the affairs of her household*.

Third, she has no time for *idleness*. Ancient households may not have soap operas to watch, but there are temptations to idleness nonetheless (see 1 Timothy 5:13). She keeps herself busy. This is not for the sake of busyness or because she is a workaholic, but because she loves her family and takes great joy in serving them.

WHAT DO YOU THINK?

What do you think are the most important things a woman can communicate to her children and her husband? What are the benefits of such communication?

C. GRATEFUL CHILDREN (vv. 28, 29)

28, 29. Her children arise and call her blessed;
her husband also, and he praises her:
"Many women do noble things,
but you surpass them all."

Too often conflicts come between a mother and her children in late childhood. Her strong love is mistaken for overprotectiveness. Her diligence is misunderstood as prying. Her steadiness is seen as boring and restrictive. The promise of this text, though, is that wise children will grow in their appreciation for a godly mother. They will grow up and join with their father to bless and praise this woman.

Lemuel departs from generalities and moves to the praise of a noble woman who is well known to him—a real person. We do not know who this is. It may be his own mother (see Proverbs 31:1). It may be his wife. At any rate, some of us could disagree with him about the identity of the noble woman he describes throughout this chapter: we want to argue for our own mothers or wives as the most excellent of all noble women! If so, how blessed we are.

WHAT DO YOU THINK?

In the twenty-first century, what's the difference between rest and idleness? Why is it important to draw a distinction?

D. INNER BEAUTY (v. 30)

30. Charm is deceptive, and beauty is fleeting;
but a woman who fears the Lord is to be praised.

The central aspect of the noble woman's beauty is finally revealed: she *fears the Lord*. This is not terror but rather obedient respect. With this verse, Proverbs has come full circle. Fear of the Lord was the beginning of knowledge and wisdom (Proverbs 1:7). Fear of the Lord is also the end of wisdom and worthy of praise.

This connection between fear and praise is found elsewhere in the Bible. Praise for God is expected from all who fear him (Psalm 22:23; Revelation 19:5).

PRAYER

Holy and righteous Father, we thank you for providing us with mothers and the institution of motherhood. Help us to appreciate godly mothers and wives and to have the courage to express this appreciation to them. We pray for them to have a proper fear for you that leads them to a wise and satisfying life. In the name of your only Son, Jesus Christ, amen.

THOUGHT TO REMEMBER

"I regard no man as poor who has a godly mother."
—Abraham Lincoln

WHAT DO YOU THINK?

What can our church do to empower women to fulfill their giftedness to the glory of God? What do the women of our church need in order to become the godly women they were intended to be?

Yet in this verse it is the noble woman rather than God being praised. What is going on?

It's true that we never praise any human in the sense of worship. Worship is reserved only for God. But here we are called to praise this servant of God for her godly character. This is an honest expression of gratitude for someone who may not expect it but who richly deserves it.

I myself am the son of a truly noble woman who was tragically killed in an accident nearly 20 years ago. Fortunately I did tell her many times how much I appreciated her love for me and all she did to try and bring me up to be a man of God. I will always be in her debt, as will my children and grandchildren.

HIDDEN TREASURES

Through the years the Philadelphia public school system had been given more than a thousand works of art of the previous two centuries. These included paintings, sculptures, and murals. After being on display for a while, they were put away in basements, boiler rooms, and closets throughout the system's 264 school buildings.

In 2004 school officials discovered that they had a treasure on their hands worth millions of dollars! Art experts said that over 100 of the pieces were "very important" works of art. Then came the question "What shall we do with it all?" The school system was in financial peril, so some wanted to sell the art. But the school system's chief of staff declared that the works should be kept to teach students the value of the arts.

Secular voices have concluded that the only place for a woman of value is in the world of business. To those who hold this view, only a woman with no talent, skill, or drive to succeed would be content to stay at home with her children. But such a judgment mirrors the school system's ignorance of its hidden treasures. Women who spend full time rearing their children with godly wisdom are true "works of art." Women who use God's gifts in the public square deserve honor too, but we must not overlook those who spend full time training the next generation in the ways of God.   —C. R. B.

CONCLUSION

I recently read of a radio talk-show host who was running a contest to find the best all-around mother in his city. A young girl called in and spoke in such glowing terms about her mother that the host announced she was the prizewinner. Then the host asked, "What does she do?" Expecting to learn of some challenging career position, he was taken off guard when the little girl said, "She just stays at home to be my mom." The outraged host rudely withdrew the prize and hung up on the child.

Society has developed a certain contempt for the traditional role of devoted wife and mother. Economic pressures have forced many mothers into the labor force. Some women manage to juggle the demands of job and family very well, often by gaining the help of husband and children. Others realize that the growing-up years of their children are irreplaceable, so they sacrifice in other ways to stay at home with their families. Both models of motherhood can be successful, given the right motivations and circumstances.

The lesson of Proverbs, however, is that the woman who concentrates on household management should not be looked down upon or disrespected. A noble woman is identified by her devotion to godliness and to her family. This does not mean, by the way, that single women cannot be godly. If they are noble, they too will find ways to serve church and family.

Discovery Learning

This page contains an alternative lesson plan emphasizing learning activities. Classes desiring such student involvement will find these suggestions helpful. The next page is a reproducible activity page to further enhance discovery learning.

LEARNING GOALS

After this lesson, each student will be able to:

1. Describe the Old Testament ideal for wives and mothers.

2. Explain why principles of justice and character are best learned first in the home.

3. Write a thank-you letter to a woman who has been a godly influence in his or her life.

INTO THE LESSON

For this activity provide your class with colored pencils/markers and paper. (Space for this activity is also provided in the student books.) Ask students to draw a picture of an ideal wife or mother. The picture may be realistic, abstract, or even a stick figure, depending on the skill of the artist. The important thing is to show the qualities represented by their ideal wife or mother.

Allow several minutes for your class to finish their drawings. Then ask volunteers to share their work, indicating which features were most important to them. Make a list of those characteristics on the board. Then tell your class that this lesson will analyze the qualities of a godly woman as discussed in Proverbs 31.

INTO THE WORD

Begin this portion of the lesson by using the lesson commentary to explain the meaning of Proverbs 31:8, 9. Point out that King Lemuel was taught these principles of justice by his mother, as indicated by the first verse of the chapter. The rest of the chapter is a tribute to a wife of noble character or a virtuous woman.

After you finish your lecture, divide your class into several small groups. Half of the groups will do the three activities in *Exercise One*. The other half will complete the three activities in *Exercise Two*. If your class does not use the student books, you will need to provide copies of the exercise activities for each group. Allow 10 minutes for groups to complete the exercise activities. Then ask each group to report its findings to the entire class.

Exercise One

Activity A: Have a volunteer read aloud Proverbs 31:10-14. Identify what you think is the theme of this passage.

Activity B: Work as a group to paraphrase these verses. Since this passage was written in ancient times, you may need to modernize some of the tasks for which the virtuous woman is praised.

Activity C: Discuss the following questions regarding today's text:

1. How important to a healthy marriage is mutual trust between husband and wife?

2. Our society says marital fidelity is optional. How would King Lemuel respond to that?

3. In King Lemuel's day, most wives stayed home and managed the household. Today, many wives have to work outside the home to supplement the family income. How are verses 13 and 14 still relevant today?

Exercise Two

Activity A: Have a volunteer read aloud Proverbs 31:25-30. Identify what you think is the theme of this passage.

Activity B: Work as a group to paraphrase these verses. Since this passage was written in ancient times, you may need to modernize some of the tasks for which the virtuous woman is praised.

Activity C: Discuss the following questions regarding today's text:

1. How does strong moral character help a person to face the uncertainties of the future?

2. What is "faithful instruction"?

3. What kind of example does a noble woman set for her children that causes her husband and children to praise her?

4. What is the ultimate source of her wisdom?

INTO LIFE

To close today's lesson, provide paper and pens for students to write thank-you notes to godly women who have influenced their lives. Such women could include students' mothers, sisters, or Bible school teachers—any woman who has made a spiritual impact on them. The notes should explain briefly why these women have been positive influences and indicate some of their godly traits that most affected the note writers' lives.

After several minutes of writing, have volunteers read their thank-you notes to the class. Encourage students to mail their notes.

As an additional or alternative exercise, use the two activities from the reproducible page. Small-group discussions can be very powerful with these!

Wanted: an Ideal Woman!

Below is a list of characteristics that might be associated with an ideal woman (who may also be a mother or wife). Pick 10 qualities you think are most important and number them from 1-10, with 1 being the most essential. If you think of a "top ten" quality not listed, you may add it on one of the blank spaces.

____thrifty   ____honest   ____sincere   ____gracious   ____patient

____godly   ____diligent   ____attractive   ____cheerful   ____intelligent

____creative   ____wise   ____talented   ____organized   ____motherly

____loving   ____gregarious   ____humble   ____quiet   ____humorous

____zealous   ____generous   ____hospitable   ____athletic   ____artistic

____graceful   _____   _____   _____   _____

Needed: an Ideal Support System!

What can our church do to support mothers and wives in becoming more pleasing to God? Write your ideas on the weight lifter.

Summer Quarter 2006

Called to Be a Christian Community

(1 & 2 Corinthians)

Special Features

Lessons

About These Lessons

One definition of community is "a unified body of individuals who have a set of common interests." So far, so good! But what exactly are those common interests for Christians? This quarter's lessons provide answers.

Jun 4

Jun 11

Jun 18

Jun 25

Jul 2

Jul 9

Jul 16

Jul 23

Jul 30

Aug 6

Aug 13

Aug 20

Aug 27

The Old and the New

by Tom Thatcher

In 1864 U.S. President Abraham Lincoln was determined to end the American Civil War. The city of Atlanta was devastated as a result. Yet this short-term devastation did not reduce Atlanta's long-term status as a cultural and economic center. Today, Atlanta is a modern American city.

The ancient city of Corinth was much like Atlanta in this regard. Corinth was a center of Greek commerce and culture until Roman forces destroyed the city in 146 B.C. After lying in ruins for a century, Julius Caesar rebuilt Corinth in 44 B.C. The city quickly became large and wealthy. The Corinthian church that received Paul's letters was also new and developing. Paul's letters to that church reveal that the new believers were struggling to escape from their old way of life, being divided over a variety of issues.

Lesson 1 establishes the basis for Christian unity: Christ is undivided. A church focused on Christ can work together effectively to reach a lost world.

Lesson 2 highlights the unity of the gospel by emphasizing its source. True teachers will point people to this fact rather than cause division by pointing to themselves.

In **Lesson 3** Paul demonstrates that the church's growth depends on the diverse gifts of many people working together. Paul uses himself as an illustration of this principle in **Lesson 4**. Paul's humble position makes it ridiculous to think that the church would be divided between himself, Apollos, and other leaders.

Lesson 5 lays out the foundation for sexual purity. What a change in mind-set the Corinthians needed!

Lesson 6 addresses the serious problem of moral "gray areas." How our actions affect other people is a key.

In **Lesson 7** Paul calls us to lives of preparation and self-discipline. Temptations are inevitable, but failure is not.

Lesson 8 touches on one of our most significant challenges: pride. How easy it is to get caught up in the glamour of certain skills!

Lesson 9 explores one of the most beautiful, and most familiar, passages of the Bible. First Corinthians 13 provides a central thesis for this letter: love never fails.

Lesson 10 offers what may be the sequel to 1 Corinthians 5. Paul's earlier exhortations led unintentionally to an unforgiving attitude. While the church must remain pure, it must also remain generous in forgiveness upon repentance.

Lessons 11 and 12 urge us to be generous with our material resources as well. Sharing is an inherent aspect of Christian fellowship. God often answers the prayers of others through our helping hand. When we give we imitate the unspeakable gift that comes from God through Christ.

Lesson 13 closes the unit by emphasizing God's grace. Paul's own "thorn in the flesh" demonstrates that we are often strongest at our weakest moments, because at these times we are forced to rely solely on God.

A WORLD OF CHANGE

We are living in a world that changes constantly. New problems and temptations come our way daily, challenging us to abandon the ancient faith. Like the Corinthians, we must confront these challenges with a sharp awareness that we are to be different.

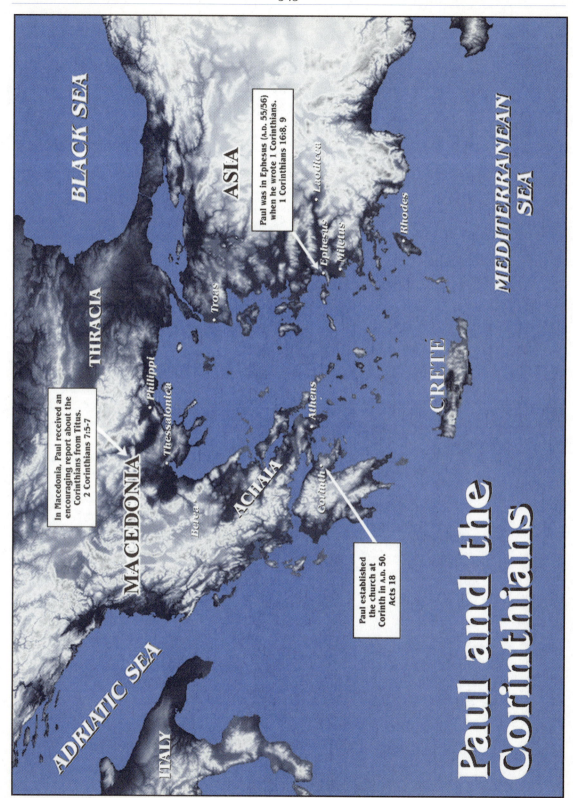

BLACK SEA

ASIA

Paul was in Ephesus (A.D. 55/56) when he wrote 1 Corinthians. 1 Corinthians 16:8, 9

Laodicea

Ephesus
Miletus

Rhodes

MEDITERRANEAN SEA

THRACIA

Troas

Philippi

Thessalonica

MACEDONIA

In Macedonia, Paul received an encouraging report about the Corinthians from Titus. 2 Corinthians 7:5-7

Berea

ACHAIA

Athens

Corinth

CRETE

Paul established the church at Corinth in A.D. 50. Acts 18

ADRIATIC SEA

ITALY

Paul and the Corinthians

Called to Be a Christian Community

Unit 1: Servants of God

Live in unity

Find wisdom

Build wisdom

Serve responsibly

Unit 2: Called to Obedience

Build relationships

Help others

Run the race

Commit to the common good

Love as God loves

Unit 3: The Spirit of Giving

Offers forgiveness

Gives generously

Witnesses to others

Rejoices in God's grace

SERVING IN UNITY

LESSON 1

WHY TEACH THIS LESSON?

Is the unity of the church still important? Previous generations spoke often of church unity, yet seemed to have little success in finding it. Today, many churches are so busy with their own programs that cooperation with other congregations is pushed down on the priority list. Church unity? "It's desirable, but too much work," our actions seem to say.

Such attitudes may be understandable but fall short of the biblical ideal for unity. The unity of the body of Christ is more than a desirable option; it is mandated and expected in the New Testament. To be the church divided falls short of being the church that Christ intended.

We often assume that church unity is to be sought on the "macro" level, that is, between churches or denominations. But the apostle Paul knew that unity began on the "micro" level, that is, among groups and individuals within local congregations. Today's lesson arises from Paul's desire to correct many serious problems in the Corinthian church. Significantly, the first problem he tackled was their lack of unity. Application of his principles is timeless and will serve every church struggling to be the united body of Christ today.

INTRODUCTION

A. DOES UNITY REALLY MATTER?

One of the ancient fables of Aesop (620–560 B.C.) was about a hungry lion and four oxen. The lion often tried to find a way to attack the four oxen as they stood together in a field. But the lion was no match for all four together.

Then one day the oxen had a quarrel and separated. When the lion came, he found them standing as far away from one another as they could get. Now it became an easy matter for the lion to pick them off one by one. Aesop's moral to the story was this: "United we stand, divided we fall."

As Paul's opening chapter to the church in Corinth shows, God's will is for his people to serve in unity. In the 2,000 years since Christ, the church has divided into so many different faith expressions that it is virtually impossible to list them all. These divisions have existed for so long that they seem to be almost normal, right, and unchangeable. In this light the question must be asked: Does unity really matter? The answer must be yes for three reasons.

First, unity matters because division denies Jesus' prayer. On the night before he died, Jesus prayed earnestly for the unity of his followers (see John 17:20-26). Sincere followers of Christ simply must not ignore that solemn prayer.

Second, unity matters because division exposes us as worldly. Division is a work of the flesh (see 1 Corinthians 3:3, 4; Galatians 5:20). When the church divides because of power struggles and personality conflicts, it thinks and acts like the world.

Third, unity matters because division destroys our witness. Jesus said the world would recognize his disciples by their sincere love for one another (John

DEVOTIONAL READING:
1 CORINTHIANS 1:2-9

BACKGROUND SCRIPTURE:
1 CORINTHIANS 1:10-17

PRINTED TEXT:
1 CORINTHIANS 1:10-17

LESSON AIMS

After participating in this lesson, each student will be able to:

1. Retell how the church at Corinth fractured.

2. Explain how interpersonal loyalties and insistence on personal preferences can cause division within the church.

3. Tell one way that he or she can give up a personal preference for the sake of church unity.

KEY VERSE

I appeal to you, brothers, in the name of our Lord Jesus Christ, that all of you agree with one another so that there may be no divisions among you and that you may be perfectly united in mind and thought.

—1 Corinthians 1:10

LESSON 1 NOTES

13:35). The reverse of this is also true. Many people are content to ignore Christ and the call of the gospel because they are repulsed by the confusion of so many different churches competing for their souls.

B. LESSON BACKGROUND

The church in Corinth was founded by Paul himself (Acts 18:1-21). Despite the wickedness that pervaded this city, many people came to Christ in response to Paul's preaching. Apollos and others stepped in to help lead after Paul left the city to continue on his missionary journeys (Acts 18:24–19:1).

However, serious problems developed in Paul's absence. When Paul heard what was happening some four or five years later (about A.D. 55/56), he found it necessary to write to the Corinthians to correct the situation. Foremost among the problems in Corinth was the way the church had divided itself into factions. As the lesson text will show, the Corinthian Christians were aligning themselves with various leaders. Paul would have none of it. Their duty was to serve God—together!

I. APPEAL FOR UNITY (1 CORINTHIANS 1:10)

A. AUTHORITY OF THE APPEAL (v. 10a)

10a. I appeal to you, brothers, in the name of our Lord Jesus Christ,

In his greeting that opened the letter (vv. 1-3), Paul reminded his readers of his position as an apostle. Now, as a spokesman for the Lord, he presents an authoritative exhortation. Paul's *appeal* is an impassioned plea; Paul's appeal is a call for action!

Paul addresses his readers as *brothers*, a reminder that he and they are part of God's family. Paul addresses them in this way numerous times. The Corinthians have many problems, but they are still Paul's brothers and sisters in Christ. Together they have been called into a great fellowship (v. 9).

It is important to notice that Paul's appeal for unity does not come merely as a recommendation. Neither is it just his take-it-or-leave-it opinion of the way things ought to be. The appeal is a strong exhortation that comes by *the name of our Lord Jesus Christ*. Any apostolic instruction that comes in his name must be followed!

B. AIM OF THE APPEAL (v. 10b)

10b. . . . that all of you agree with one another so that there may be no divisions among you and that you may be perfectly united in mind and thought.

To *agree with one another* does not mean that Christians must have identical opinions (compare Romans 14:5). Rather, it means that they must stand together in their core doctrinal beliefs. They must stand ready to give a united testimony to the watching world. In order to present this united testimony, there must be *no divisions* within the church. The body of Christ is not divided; it is one. Paul has more to say about divisions in Romans 16:17; 1 Corinthians 3:3; 11:18.

Furthermore, unity must be more than a matter of external appearances. It must arise from the inward harmony of people who believe in the same God, obey the same Lord, and share the same Spirit. Such people are perfectly joined together. They share the same *mind*, attitude, and way of thinking. They share the same judgment, ultimate conclusion, and intended purpose. The aim of Paul's appeal is that God's people live and serve in unity. See also Ephesians 4:3, 13; Philippians 2:2.

WHAT DO YOU THINK?

How does Paul's description of Christians as family (brothers) help us understand and live out Christian unity today?

WHAT DO YOU THINK?

A focus on Christ is understood by some believers to mean that doctrine should be deemphasized since, as they claim, "doctrine divides." How should we respond?

[Be sure to consider 1 Timothy 4:16; Titus 1:9; 2:1.]

A PERFECT FIT

My wife enjoys working on jigsaw puzzles. It seems at times the more pieces the better for her. One of the more original puzzles she has done was called "Hay in a Needle Stack." It was a 1,000-piece puzzle that featured a pile of sewing needles with a small piece of hay in the center. The color on most of the pieces is the same, to say the least! This meant that the puzzle could be completed only by matching the edges of the interlocking pieces. Finding those perfect fits was a time-consuming task.

In a way the church is like a jigsaw puzzle. There are many pieces that need to be joined together to complete the whole picture. As a jigsaw puzzle does not come already put together, so the church is not complete from its inception. It takes time, effort, and meticulous attention to detail to come up with the final "product."

One difference from the jigsaw puzzle, though, is that a puzzle consists of a preset number of pieces while the church does not. The numbers, types, and opinions of people in the church who must fit together are always changing. As a result, the puzzle is never finished but is a continual work in progress.

This extraordinary complexity means that no matter how hard we try to fit the puzzle of the church together, we are always at a loss to do it by our own knowledge and power. This is why we must allow the Spirit of God to work in and through us to move this task forward.   —A. E. A.

Visual for Lesson 1. *Use this outline of the quarter to remind your students of the multi-faceted nature of the Christian community (the church).*

II. LACK OF UNITY (1 CORINTHIANS 1:11, 12)

A. EXPOSED BY QUARRELS (v. 11)

11. My brothers, some from Chloe's household have informed me that there are quarrels among you.

Paul's strong appeal is necessary because of what has been declared or revealed to him about the *brothers* in the Corinthian church. Family members or servants of the house of a certain *Chloe* have either sent a letter to Paul or visited him in person, exposing the problem of disunity that has arisen. Their communication to Paul also may have included information about the other problems that Paul will address in 1 Corinthians. The number one problem, however, appears to be division.

The lack of unity among the Corinthian Christians is caused and exposed by the *quarrels* that exist among them. What Paul means by quarrels is the kind of strife that exists where people do not get along with one another for various reasons (compare 2 Corinthians 12:20; Galatians 5:20; 1 Timothy 6:4; Titus 3:9). When people quarrel and wrangle, they expose their failure to be the undivided body of Christ.

B. EVIDENCED IN DIVISIONS (v. 12)

12. What I mean is this: One of you says, "I follow Paul"; another, "I follow Apollos"; another, "I follow Cephas"; still another, "I follow Christ."

The specific problem that exists in Corinth is a childish act of choosing up sides. This problem apparently is not limited to just a few people! Their man-made divisions and cliques threaten to undo all of Paul's work in founding that church.

The divisions appear to be at least four in number. Some say, "We *follow Paul*." Such people probably think they are honoring the apostle in this way as the founder of their church (see Acts 18). Others say, "We *follow Apollos*." This group in some sense rejects Paul, with his weak public image (see 1 Corinthians 2:1-4); they prefer the powerful oratory of the leader who followed after him (Acts 18:24-28).

Still others say, "We *follow Cephas*," the Aramaic form of Simon Peter's name (John 1:42). This faction pledges allegiance to a man who was an apostle even before Paul and who has a focused ministry to those of Jewish heritage (Galatians 2:7-9). Each party is guilty of exalting a man, thus minimizing everyone who does not join them.

Members of a fourth group are reported to be saying, "We *follow Christ.* What they mean by this is open to question. Perhaps they sincerely want to be faithful to the Lord, so they correctly refuse to align themselves with any mere man. On the other hand they may think they have found a way to make their group superior to the others. ("You may follow Peter or Paul, but we follow Christ!") They may even be claiming that they are the only ones who are following Christ.

Significantly, Paul does not commend any of the groups, even the one claiming to be following Christ. By listing all four on the same basis, he makes them all guilty of dividing the body. Their petty cliques are tearing apart the fabric of unity. They should feel shame, not pride, for what they have achieved.

Follow the Leader

In many childhood team games, two children serve as captains and then take turns choosing teams. Each child has his or her favorite captain and will do all they can to get the attention of that captain in order to be chosen. In the world of politics, people line up behind certain leaders and question the motives of anyone who would follow any other. We choose our favorite ball team or player and feel that that team or person is always right.

Unfortunately, people in the church are guilty of the same. It began early in the life of the church with this lining up of the Christians behind their favorite leader. Yet the problem goes back even further. Old Testament Israel experienced problems on several occasions because of the exaltation of certain men and their ideas over the will of God.

Much of this problem in the church is based upon the principle of "what's in it for me." The leader who will provide what I want, agree with what I believe, hold to the traditions I want to hold to, or make the changes I want to see made is the one who is followed. Too often these decisions are not based on God's will. So before we criticize the speck of sawdust in the eye of the cult-hero worshipers in the realms of celebrities and politicians, we do well to see if there is a plank in our own eye in the way we follow church leaders (Matthew 7:3).   —A. E. A.

III. BASIS OF UNITY (1 CORINTHIANS 1:13-17)

A. Unity in Christ (v. 13)

13. Is Christ divided? Was Paul crucified for you? Were you baptized into the name of Paul?

The Corinthians need to learn what the nature of the church really is. Their divisions serve to cut themselves off from other believers; they have, in effect, expelled the others from membership in the body. To teach them the true basis of unity, Paul asks several questions—each with an obvious answer. These questions show that the basis of unity is Christ.

Paul first asks, *Is Christ divided?* The obvious answer is no. God does not divide him; "God is one" (Galatians 3:20). Neither does Jesus divide himself (compare Matthew 12:25). If the Corinthians in their day—or we in ours—try to divide Christ, then the intent of God is being opposed.

Second, when Paul asks, *Was Paul crucified for you?* he shows himself to be unworthy of a group's devotion. The question implies the same about Apollos and

Peter. Neither Paul nor Apollos nor Peter can give his life in atonement for anyone. Only Christ was worthy to carry our sins on that tree.

The third question, *Were you baptized into the name of Paul?* is significant in that baptism is to be done in the name of the Father and the Son and the Holy Spirit (Matthew 28:19) or, by abbreviation, in the name of Jesus (Acts 2:38; 8:16; 10:48; 19:5). Baptism is certainly not in the name of any mortal man.

B. UNITY IN BAPTISM (vv. 14-16)

14. I am thankful that I did not baptize any of you except Crispus and Gaius,

The Corinthians, as other Christians, have the baptismal experience in common. Their oneness or unity should find expression in "one body and one Spirit . . . one hope . . . one Lord, one faith, one baptism, one God and Father of all" (Ephesians 4:4-6). As Paul considers the situation, he is aware that some are placing false importance on the person who does the baptizing. When Paul says, *I am thankful that I did not baptize any of you,* his desire is to remove that false view of baptism that contributes to disunity. As such, this statement serves to deemphasize the importance of the person performing the baptism.

The focus instead is to be on Christ, into whose name we are baptized. Paul does not minimize the importance of being baptized—that's not the issue here. Rather, Paul wants to remove himself from the spotlight. By implication he is also removing from the spotlight anyone else who performs baptisms.

Almost as an afterthought, Paul adds, *except Crispus and Gaius.* Paul did baptize a few people personally. But he thinks that fact to be of little consequence as the next verse makes clear.

15. . . . so no one can say that you were baptized into my name.

Paul knows that people are quick to take pride in the wrong things. The very reason that he leaves the act of baptizing to others is lest any should say they *were baptized* in Paul's own *name.* They may think that to be baptized that way carries some kind of merit or special virtue. Certainly Paul never baptizes anyone into his own name! Neither does he ever take any credit for anyone's conversion as though he were hanging scalps from his belt or putting notches on his gun. As Paul elsewhere explains, baptism is "into Christ Jesus" (Romans 6:3). The focus of baptism must be on Christ, not on any mere man.

16. (Yes, I also baptized the household of Stephanas; beyond that, I don't remember if I baptized anyone else.)

As Paul reviews his work in Corinth, he also remembers that he *baptized the household of Stephanas.* Paul hastens to add these people to his very short list, apparently in order to be completely honest. Other than the people he now has named, Paul simply does not *remember* if he baptized any other. It is obviously not a matter of any importance to Paul whether new believers are baptized by him or by someone else.

We should note that the household of Stephanas constituted Paul's first converts in Achaia, the province that includes the city of Corinth (1 Corinthians 16:15). This group would include both members of the family and servants in the home. Following their conversion, they devoted themselves to "the service of the saints." Since they were the first converts in the area, who else would have baptized them except Paul or a traveling companion?

C. UNITY IN THE GOSPEL (v. 17)

17. For Christ did not send me to baptize, but to preach the gospel—not with words of human wisdom, lest the cross of Christ be emptied of its power.

VISUALS FOR THESE LESSONS

The visual pictured in each lesson (example: page 347) is a small reproduction of a large, full-color poster included in the Adult Resources *packet for the Summer Quarter. The packet is available from your supplier. Order No. 492.*

DAILY BIBLE READINGS

Monday, May 29—Jesus Is Lord of All (Romans 10:9-13)

Tuesday, May 30—We Are Reconciled in Christ (Colossians 1:15-20)

Wednesday, May 31—One Body and One Spirit (Ephesians 4:1-6)

Thursday, June 1—Called Together in Christ (1 Corinthians 1:1-9)

Friday, June 2—Be United in Christ (1 Corinthians 1:10-17)

Saturday, June 3—We Proclaim Christ Crucified to All (1 Corinthians 1:18-25)

Sunday, June 4—God Brings Us to Christ (1 Corinthians 1:26-31)

Father, forgive us for promoting divisive squabbles. Help us to find the ways to resolve them. Show us how to serve you in true and loving unity. In the name of Jesus, amen.

Paul's statement that Christ sent him not *to baptize, but to preach the gospel* can be easily misunderstood. Paul is not intending to exclude baptism, for the Great Commission given by Jesus specifically includes it (Matthew 28:18-20). Neither is Paul minimizing baptism, given the importance he places on it in his other letters (Romans 6:1-4; Galatians 3:27; Ephesians 4:5; Colossians 2:12).

Rather, Paul's point is that his primary job is to do the preaching that leads people to accept Christ and submit to baptism. If Paul preaches and someone else baptizes, all is well.

Paul certainly feels the weight of his commission to preach the gospel. That is the central purpose of his life. He knows that he has been sent by no less than Christ himself, so he must stay true to this mission. Furthermore, Paul knows that he will not fulfill his task by trying to do it with his own power and with his own clever *words of human wisdom.* (Perhaps he is thinking of Zechariah 4:6 as he writes this: "'Not by might nor by power, but by my Spirit,' says the Lord Almighty.") Paul's task is to tell the good news that Jesus has died for our sins. That is why Paul resolves "to know nothing . . . except Jesus Christ and him crucified" when he preached in Corinth (1 Corinthians 2:2; see next week's lesson).

Without "eloquence or superior wisdom" (1 Corinthians 2:1), Paul had preached the simple gospel facts to these people. The message of the cross of Christ has pierced their hearts (compare Acts 2:37) and has drawn them to accept Jesus as Lord. Had Paul chosen to rely on his own forcefulness or powers of persuasion rather than the facts of the gospel, then the death of Jesus on the cross would have been made of none effect. The power of the gospel lies in the historical facts of the cross and the empty tomb, not the force of the preacher.

Paul goes on in 1:19-22 (not in today's text) to warn further of mere human wisdom. Human wisdom divorced from God's Word will only divide. True unity in the gospel is found in the wisdom of God (1 Corinthians 1:24).

CONCLUSION

A. COST OF DISUNITY

Lack of unity in the church is a costly problem, one that lies at the root of many other problems. Lack of unity prevented the Corinthians from coming together to confront an immoral brother (1 Corinthians 5:1-5). Lack of unity led them to take each other to court before pagan judges (6:1-6). Lack of unity drove a wedge between those who ate certain foods and those who did not (8:1-12). Lack of unity even corrupted their observance of the Lord's Supper, which should have been central to their oneness (10:14-17; 11:18-22). Lack of unity produced the situation where members were in competition with each other to show off their spiritual gifts (chapters 12–14). None of these problems in Corinth could be resolved as long as disunity existed.

B. CURE FOR DISUNITY

Disunity can be cured! In the opening chapter of this letter, Paul noted how divided Christians can come together: we must set Christ, the Son of God, above any other loyalty. Loyalty that places anyone else above Christ for any reason can only result in defeat.

Unity will never happen as long as we insist that everyone else has to come and join our group. Unity will happen only when we come together at the foot of the cross. God's Spirit can make us one—but only if we are willing. The way we respond to Paul's plea will determine whether or not we will be found serving in unity.

Service for Christ begins with unity in Christ.

Discovery Learning

This page contains an alternative lesson plan emphasizing learning activities. Classes desiring such student involvement will find these suggestions helpful. The next page is a reproducible activity page to further enhance discovery learning.

LEARNING GOALS

After participating in this lesson, each student will be able to:

1. Retell how the church at Corinth fractured.

2. Explain how interpersonal loyalties and insistence on personal preferences can cause division within the church.

3. Tell one way that he or she can give up a personal preference for the sake of church unity.

INTO THE LESSON

Place two or three pieces of poster board on different walls of the classroom. Divide the class into the same number of groups as you have poster boards. (If you have a large class, create more groups and provide more poster board.) Appoint a "scribe" for each group. Groups are to stand by their assigned poster boards and list as many Christian faith groups that they can think of within three minutes.

When time is up, acknowledge the group with the longest list. Ask: "What are some of the reasons for so many groups?" List answers on the board. Then ask: "Does unity in the church really matter? Why is unity better than having so many divisions in the church?" (Alternative: Distribute the two activities on the reproducible page to students to work on as they arrive.)

Make the transition to the Bible study by saying (paraphrased from the Lesson Introduction), "The church has been divided into so many 'pieces' that it is virtually impossible to list them all. Such divisions have existed for so long that they seem almost normal and right. Unfortunately, these are not the only divisions experienced in Christianity. Local congregations themselves often experience division and disharmony. The apostle Paul addresses this problem when he writes to the church at Corinth."

INTO THE WORD

Prepare a brief lecture using the background information in the commentary. Illustrate the lecture with a map showing Corinth, if available.

Following the background lecture, read aloud today's printed text. Use the questions that follow to stimulate discussion. The questions may be asked of the whole class or may be assigned to small groups for discussion.

1. "What is the significance of the words 'in the name of our Lord Jesus Christ' in verse 10? Why does Paul include this phrase in his letter?" (*The authority for this teaching is in Jesus, not in Paul's own feelings. This plea is more than just a recommendation or opinion. It is an exhortation from our Lord.*)

2. "What is the source of division in the Corinthian church? See verses 11 and 12." (*Church members are quarreling as they form groups claiming allegiance to different leaders. The result is disunity and contentions.*)

3. "Some Corinthians claimed to follow Paul, some Apollos, some Cephas, and some said they were following Christ. What do you think the last group may have meant when they said they followed Christ? Do you think this was a good claim to make or was it just another way to divide the church?" (*Perhaps they were sincerely following Jesus alone as their master. Or they may have been trying to make themselves sound superior to the other groups. They may even be thinking they were the only real Christians in the church. We do not know their motivation.*)

4. "Paul speaks at length about baptism, using it as an illustration of division and unity. Baptism is to be a basis of unity in the Lord's body (Ephesians 4:5). Tragically, baptism in the contemporary church still divides but in different ways. What are some ways that different views of baptism divide the church today?" (*What it does and does not result in, when to perform it, how to perform it, etc.*)

INTO LIFE

Ask students to brainstorm issues that are not listed in today's text that cause division in the local church. Write these on the board. Have the class discuss the negative impact of disunity in the local church. Review the sources of disunity compiled by your class.

Ask each person to identify a potential problem in this regard in his or her life. An example would be insisting on a particular style of music in the worship service. Encourage each person to make a commitment during the prayer time to resist becoming divisive over his or her particular issue. After a time of prayer, close the lesson by having the class sing "Bind Us Together, Lord" or another familiar song that calls for unity and fellowship in the church.

The Fight Is On

 An old gospel song carries the title, "The Fight Is On." Unfortunately, that title could be the motto for some churches today. On the image below, list a few of the issues that may cause division in the local congregation.

Division And Dissension

 Now list some of the reasons that Christianity has divided itself into so many faith expressions. What are some of the issues that have caused these divisions

What are the benefits of these divisions, if any?

What are the consequences and damages to Christianity from these divisions?

What do you think God would like to see happen to today's fractured form of Christianity?

SERVING WITH SPIRITUAL WISDOM

LESSON 2

WHY TEACH THIS LESSON?

What is the message of the true and faithful church? How has is changed over the centuries? What modifications will be needed in the future? These questions seem reasonable to many who view the church as an ancient relic living in the past. Churches too often give mixed signals and a wide range of messages.

But there is a central, core word for the church. It is a message that was in the mind of God for ages, revealed directly to the apostles. It is a vital, unchanging message that the world desperately needs and will always need. Today's lesson presents Paul at his most foundational level: his timeless message of salvation and the source of that wisdom. Without a clear understanding of what this lesson teaches, all our efforts to share our faith will be misguided and ultimately futile.

INTRODUCTION

A. THE SOURCE OF TRUE WISDOM

Terrence was born in Carthage in about 195 B.C. As a young man he was brought to Rome as a slave. He lived only a short life, dying in his mid-thirties. Yet he still had time to become a famous writer. One of his observations is worth remembering: "What a difference there is between a wise person and a fool!"

Everyone would rather be known as wise than as foolish. No one enjoys being ridiculed or called stupid. But where can we find true wisdom? Is it from humans or from God? And what shall we do if following God's wisdom makes us look foolish in the eyes of the world? These were the issues that Paul faced in his counsel to the Corinthians, and they are the same issues that we must face today.

B. LESSON BACKGROUND

Before Paul reached Corinth on his second missionary journey, he suffered repeated rejection. He was beaten and jailed in Philippi, chased out of Thessalonica by a riot, forced to flee Berea, and laughed out of the Areopagus by the philosophers in Athens (see Acts 16, 17). When he came to Corinth (Acts 18), he probably was out of money and out of friends. Paul had left his various coworkers along the way to help lead the new churches (Acts 17:14). In Corinth Paul worked daily as a tentmaker (Acts 18:3) and tried to present the message of Christ in the synagogue every Sabbath (Acts 18:4). Eventually he had to leave that place as well (Acts 18:5-7).

Since Paul faced so much opposition, what should he do? Should he adjust his message to make it less offensive? Should he use more eloquent oratory? Should he try to impress people with his education or his wisdom? It was a crucial point in Paul's ministry. As Paul writes his first letter to the Corinthians, he carefully reminds them which choice he made.

DEVOTIONAL READING:
EPHESIANS 1:15-21
BACKGROUND SCRIPTURE:
1 CORINTHIANS 2
PRINTED TEXT:
1 CORINTHIANS 2:1-16

LESSON AIMS

After participating in this lesson, each student will be able to:

1. State what Paul said was the primary content of his preaching.

2. List some differences between human wisdom and spiritual wisdom.

3. Apply spiritual wisdom to one area of life.

KEY VERSE

This is what we speak, not in words taught us by human wisdom but in words taught by the Spirit, expressing spiritual truths in spiritual words.
—1 Corinthians 2:13

LESSON 2 NOTES

I. OUR WEAK WISDOM (1 CORINTHIANS 2:1-5)

A. PAUL'S ACTION, PART 1 (vv. 1, 2)

1. When I came to you, brothers, I did not come with eloquence or superior wisdom as I proclaimed to you the testimony about God.

Paul wants his *brothers* in the church in Corinth to think back a few years to the time when they first met him. He had come with a difficult task: to preach the gospel in a city that was notoriously wicked and worldly. They should well remember that Paul does not make a very impressive appearance (compare 2 Corinthians 10:10).

Apparently, Paul's lack of *eloquence* stands in contrast to that of Apollos, who ministered in Corinth after Paul left (Acts 18:24-28). Good speaking skills serve many preachers well. But ultimately the testimony of God requires neither eloquence nor *wisdom* to shine through. The wisdom that Paul refers to is human wisdom that is divorced from God's wisdom. Paul will make this distinction between the two wisdoms clearer in verses 5-7, 13 (below).

2. For I resolved to know nothing while I was with you except Jesus Christ and him crucified.

As Paul preached in Corinth, he was aware that the message of the cross was "a stumbling block to Jews and foolishness to Gentiles" (1 Corinthians 1:23). After all, the cross is an ugly, horrible means of execution. Yet Paul also knows that the cross represents the power and wisdom of God. Despite opposition everywhere, Paul refuses to abandon this core belief. Nothing and no one *except Jesus Christ* can save people. It is not Jesus' exemplary life or fascinating parables that can save, as valuable as those are; rather, it is the fact that he was crucified (Romans 3:25, 26). Thus, Paul refuses to be ashamed (Romans 1:16).

B. PAUL'S CONFESSION (v. 3)

3. I came to you in weakness and fear, and with much trembling.

Paul readily admits that his public oratory had not been impressive. In fact he had stood before them in noticeable *weakness*. This weakness may have been his own inadequacy, or it may have been a physical ailment such as he had in Galatia (Galatians 4:13). However, as Paul would later write to the Corinthians, God's strength is made perfect in weakness (2 Corinthians 12:9).

Paul's preaching in Corinth with *fear* and *much trembling* (compare 2 Corinthians 10:1) does not mean that Paul had been afraid of the people or the authorities. Rather, it was that Paul knew that the eternal destinies of his listeners hung in the balance (see also Philippians 2:12).

C. PAUL'S ACTION, PART 2 (vv. 4, 5)

4. My message and my preaching were not with wise and persuasive words, but with a demonstration of the Spirit's power,

Paul's *preaching* had been, above all, a proclamation of the gospel of Christ. Paul knows that the power is in the gospel message itself (again, Romans 1:16); therefore, he makes no effort to embellish or "contextualize" the gospel with *persuasive words* of man's wisdom. Worldly philosophical arguments may have wider appeal, but Paul rejects that approach. There is nothing wrong with philosophy as such. But one must always be on the alert to philosophy that is rooted in the human mind rather than God's mind (Colossians 2:8).

Paul's preaching in Corinth had been a demonstration of the Spirit and of God's *power*, not a display of human wisdom (see also 1 Thessalonians 1:5). The gospel message puts God's Spirit, not God's spokesman, on display. When the

---

WHAT DO YOU THINK?

What are some things that may cause sincere, committed congregations to slip accidentally into approaches that impress people with the packaging of the gospel rather than the message of the gospel? How do we avoid this trap?

WHAT DO YOU THINK?

What are some practical steps we can take to cultivate a mindset like that of Paul, who recognized the eternal stakes involved in proclaiming the gospel?

WHAT DO YOU THINK?

What is the appropriate role of personality and persuasion in preaching and teaching?

clear facts of the gospel had pierced the hearts of Paul's hearers, the Spirit moved to bring them under conviction (compare John 16:8). Thus was exhibited God's great power, not the feeble power of Paul.

5. . . . so that your faith might not rest on men's wisdom, but on God's power.

If Paul had impressed the Corinthians with his own communication skills, they could well have become "Paul-ites" instead of Christians. Perhaps it was the oratorical skills of Apollos that had led some to become "Apollos-ites" (1 Corinthians 1:12). But no person deserves our allegiance more than God does. When the Corinthians make sure that their *faith* does not stand in the *wisdom* of men, but in the *power* of God, they will make no mistake in this regard.

II. GOD'S CONCEALED WISDOM (1 CORINTHIANS 2:6-9)

A. HIDDEN SINCE THE BEGINNING (vv. 6, 7)

6. We do, however, speak a message of wisdom among the mature, but not the wisdom of this age or of the rulers of this age, who are coming to nothing.

When Paul said that he did not speak in words of *wisdom* (vv. 1, 4), he was referring to human wisdom. He now makes plain that he does indeed speak wisdom but with two qualifications. First, he speaks wisdom among the *mature* believers. Unbelievers do not understand it, and "baby believers" are ready only for the "milk" of the Word (1 Corinthians 3:2, next week's lesson). Only the mature can appreciate fully how wise God's *message* is (see Ephesians 4:13, 14).

Second, the wisdom that Paul speaks is not the wisdom of this world or of its *rulers*. The world and its leaders eventually will come to nothing; all earthly powers will pass away. But Paul speaks with a type of wisdom that does not originate within the world and is not recognized by the world.

7. No, we speak of God's secret wisdom, a wisdom that has been hidden and that God destined for our glory before time began.

Paul rejects human wisdom so that he may proclaim the *wisdom* of God. God has given this *hidden* wisdom as a kind of mystery. Paul's message from God is not a mystery because it is complicated or difficult to understand, but because it was kept *secret* until God was ready to reveal it.

In the distant past God was already preparing for our salvation. He ordained that salvation would not come by human merit but by the atoning death of his own Son. This great plan for salvation was for our benefit and unto *our glory.* How privileged we are to have this mystery revealed to us!

B. MISSED BY RULERS (v. 8)

8. None of the rulers of this age understood it, for if they had, they would not have crucified the Lord of glory.

The rulers of this age, such as the Roman officials and the Jewish chief priests, do not understand God's wisdom. Nothing about Jesus makes any sense to them. All the evidence was there, but they ignored it. Their self-inflicted blindness resulted in Jesus' death for our sin according to God's plan (see Acts 4:25-28). In one sense even Satan can be included in the reference to rulers of this age (see John 14:30). Just like the human rulers, Satan was unaware of God's real plan. If Satan had known that Jesus would defeat him at the cross, would he have moved the heart of Judas to betray *the Lord of glory*?

NO MULLIGAN FOR SATAN

"If I had known then what I know now, I would have done things a lot differently." People often would like to have an opportunity to do something over in the

WHAT DO YOU THINK?

The lesson contrasts God's wisdom with that of this world. What are some examples and sources of the latter? How do we guard against it?

Visual for Lesson 2. *Point to this visual as you ask, "How do we make sure that any wisdom we gain in this world has God as the ultimate source?"*

hope of getting it right the second time around. Some circumstances do allow a "do over." For example an actor may retape a scene until it's just right. In golf a "do over" is called a mulligan. Mulligans are used to make up for errant shots. There never seem to be enough mulligans in real life as we would like!

Although it's safe to say that we would all like more mulligans, we can rejoice that God did not allow Satan to have one at Calvary. Sometimes Christians wish that Satan had not temporarily "succeeded" in the way that he did. But if things had gone differently, then the sacrifice for our sins would not have been established.

We can thank God that Satan did not get a mulligan; we can also thank God that we do get one. And not just one, but many. Each new day, each new minute, we get a "do over" with Christ. If we confess our sins, God is faithful to forgive us (1 John 1:9). In this we have a perpetual clean slate. Praise God!   —A. E. A.

C. PREPARED FOR GOD'S PEOPLE (v. 9)

9. However, as it is written:
  "No eye has seen,
    no ear has heard,
 no mind has conceived
    what God has prepared for those who love him"—

Paul reminds his readers, in a general way, of Isaiah 64:4. In that context God, unlike false idols, actually steps into history to take action on behalf of those who wait on him. Yet even the prophet Isaiah himself did not know what the entire plan would be; he only knew that something wonderful was coming.

We who live on this side of the cross can marvel at the great sacrifice Jesus made, but even we have not yet seen the end of it. When we try to imagine the unseen joys of Heaven, or hear the distant praise, or conceive of the place that is *prepared* for us, our minds simply are too small.

III. SPIRIT'S REVEALED WISDOM (1 CORINTHIANS 2:10-16)

A. THE SPIRIT'S KNOWLEDGE (vv. 10, 11)

10. . . . but God has revealed it to us by his Spirit.
The Spirit searches all things, even the deep things of God.

The world and its rulers did not know God's secrets, but now he has *revealed* them to Paul and the other inspired writers of the New Testament. Paul does not want his readers to overlook the importance of sharing in this revealed wisdom. What God has revealed to his divinely appointed spokesmen is for the church. As with the holy men of old, who spoke and wrote "as they were carried along by the Holy Spirit" (2 Peter 1:21), the Spirit can reveal these things because of his intimate connection with the mind and will of God the Father. The Spirit continues to work in ways involving *the deep things of God* in the lives of Christians (Ephesians 1:17-19; 3:16-19).

11. For who among men knows the thoughts of a man except the man's spirit within him? In the same way no one knows the thoughts of God except the Spirit of God.

It is reasonable that only *the Spirit of God* can know the mind of God. After all, who can possibly know the inner *thoughts of a man* except the *spirit* that is in that man? A man can know his own mind, but no one else (other than the creator) can know it without that man revealing it. So if anyone wants to know what is on God's mind, he or she must turn to what God's Spirit has said. Only the Spirit— and those to whom the Spirit chooses to reveal things—can know the deep things of God.

B. THE SPIRIT'S TEACHING (vv. 12, 13)

12. We have not received the spirit of the world but the Spirit who is from God, that we may understand what God has freely given us.

In a unique way Paul and certain others have been prepared by *the Spirit* to be spokesmen of God's truth (John 14:26). They do not speak a human message, as though they have received merely a *spirit of the world.* Rather, they speak a revealed message that was *freely given* to them from God by means of the Spirit who is of God.

The New Testament writers, then, have conveyed to us the truth that was taught to them by God's Spirit. As a result, all believers can say, in a sense, that we have received divinely revealed truth. It is wrong, however, for later believers to put themselves on the same level with the first-century apostles in claiming to speak authoritatively for God.

13. This is what we speak, not in words taught us by human wisdom but in words taught by the Spirit, expressing spiritual truths in spiritual words.

Paul makes a bold claim: the very *words* that he and the other apostles speak have been *taught* to them *by the* Holy *Spirit.* This is in sharp contrast to the *words* which man's *wisdom* teaches.

Yet we should caution that Paul does not mean that the Holy Spirit has used him as a kind of computer keyboard, merely pushing words through Paul's mind and fingers and onto the parchment. Each author's own style and vocabulary show through in Scripture, but the message—every word of it—carries the divine stamp of ownership. In this way the divine message comes through with words approved by the Spirit.

C. THE SPIRIT'S HELP (vv. 14-16)

14. The man without the Spirit does not accept the things that come from the Spirit of God, for they are foolishness to him, and he cannot understand them, because they are spiritually discerned.

The natural man is one who acts on his own without God's guidance. As such, he cannot take in *the things* of the *Spirit.* Divine truths seem mere *foolishness* to him. He cannot know them; *he cannot understand them;* he probably doesn't even want to bother with them. The truths are *spiritually discerned* by those who have given their lives to God (compare John 8:47; 14:17).

It was much the same during the earthly ministry of Jesus. When he spoke in parables, he revealed deep truths about God. But the stories seemed to be foolish and pointless to people who refused to follow the Spirit's leading. Jesus said that those who chose to do God's will would know that his teaching is from God (John 7:17).

MISUNDERSTOOD RICHES

The quest for wealth has been a part of the human condition as long as anyone can remember. Seeking the riches of this world has led to theft, murder, divorce, and war. Sometimes we are astonished at how people are willing to risk life, limb, and reputation in the pursuit of things.

At other times, however, it is our personal ignorance that causes us to look on in astonishment at the price that someone is willing to pay for various items. For example a person may go to a flea market and see some glass products for sale. Having an eye for collectibles, she buys the whole batch.

The previous owner thinks he has done well to unload those old hand-me-downs. Unbeknownst to the seller, however, is the fact that the buyer has just ended up with many thousands of dollars worth of rare glassware. She knew what

PRAYER

Father, thank you for revealing your wisdom to us through your Spirit. Help us to hold to your truth and to serve you faithfully. In the name of Christ, amen.

she was doing all along! We see this kind of thing described all the time on *Antiques Roadshow.*

To people of the world, the things that Christians are willing to sacrifice for their faith seems foolish. But the Christian realizes that eternal life is worth any cost of ridicule, discrimination, or persecution that he or she may have to endure. The person of this world thinks the foolish Christian is being duped. But what is foolishness in the eyes of the world is the very wisdom of God.   —A. E. A.

15. The spiritual man makes judgments about all things, but he himself is not subject to any man's judgment:

In contrast to the natural person, the *spiritual* person is able to discern that which is spiritual, not just that which is earthly. The inspired apostles passed on to us the revealed truth of the Spirit, and it is by that light that we are able to discern spiritual things as well as earthly. To be *not subject to any man's judgment* means that faithful believers do not need to worry what the world thinks of them.

16. "For who has known the mind of the Lord
that he may instruct him?"
But we have the mind of Christ.

Paul already has said that only the Spirit of God can know the mind of God. Obviously, no mere human can know *the mind of the Lord.* How foolish for a mere human to think that he or she could *instruct* God or teach him anything he does not already know! (See Isaiah 40:13; Romans 11:34.)

Although no one has known the mind of the Lord in terms of being able to instruct him, it is also true that *we have the mind of Christ.* We see this truth in the fact that the writers of the New Testament have Christ as their source of wisdom. The early church is careful to continue faithfully in the apostles' doctrine (Acts 2:42). When we today hold faithfully to this same revealed truth, we also have the mind of Christ.

CONCLUSION

A. RECOGNIZING SPIRITUAL WISDOM

Our greatest goal is to receive eternal life. But recognizing and following true wisdom comes first. While the wisest philosophers disagree with each other and the greatest scientists are revised by each new generation, the wisdom from above never changes. If we are to reach the goal of true wisdom, we must not be impressed by eloquent oratory or clever intellectualism. We must recognize the power and permanence of spiritual wisdom.

The highlight of God's wisdom is the cross and empty tomb. God's plan was in his mind from the beginning, but what was revealed only partially to the Old Testament prophets becomes known more fully in the life of Jesus and the gospel proclaimed by the apostles. We must see Christ's great sacrifice not as a stumbling block or as foolishness but as a demonstration of divine wisdom and power.

B. SERVING WITH SPIRITUAL WISDOM

Paul and the other apostles revealed the truth that was given to them through the Spirit. The first-century church and its leaders accepted this truth and served God faithfully. Through the centuries the torch has been passed, and now it has come to us. Just as Paul exhorted the believers in Corinth, believers today must rely not on their own strength but on the power and wisdom of God. In that way the message—and not the messenger—will offer the bright beacon of light to a lost world.

THOUGHT TO REMEMBER

May we allow God's wisdom to be our own.

Discovery Learning

This page contains an alternative lesson plan emphasizing learning activities. Classes desiring such student involvement will find these suggestions helpful. The next page is a reproducible activity page to further enhance discovery learning.

LEARNING GOALS

After participating in this lesson, each student will be able to:

1. State what Paul said was the primary content of his preaching.

2. List some differences between human wisdom and spiritual wisdom.

3. Apply spiritual wisdom to one area of life.

INTO THE LESSON

Early in the week, ask a class member or guest to prepare a ten-minute introduction on New Age philosophy. This person will probably need time to visit the church library or Christian bookstore for resources. Material you can provide may be the best alternative.

Begin the class by putting up a poster that reads, "New Age Movement & Mysticism." Ask the class to cite illustrations or examples of New Age philosophy and mysticism from movies and television shows. After the exercise, explain that sometimes it's difficult to define New Age philosophy. Introduce the person who will make the presentation mentioned above.

After the presentation, ask: "Why do you think there is such an interest in New Age spirituality and other mystical concepts? What do these imply about our culture?" Make the transition to Bible study by saying, "Paul wrote to a culture much like ours in certain ways. The people were exploring all kinds of religions and were having trouble sorting out truth. Even many Christians, like some Christians today, were struggling with identifying true wisdom. We'll find wonderful lessons for believers today as we learn from this struggle in the Corinthian church and culture."

INTO THE WORD

Briefly set the stage for the Bible study by summarizing the thoughts from the Lesson Background. Then say, "As long as we are seeking wisdom, we are going to play school and take a test. We will do this in small groups [or pairs]." Distribute separate handouts as below. (Note: a similar activity is included in the student books.)

Group #1. Your portion of the test is to do some creative writing. Read 1 Corinthians 2:13-16. Then paraphrase the passage, making its wisdom speak clearly to our culture. Please note that verse 13 is often considered the key verse of this chapter.

Group #2. Your portion of the test is to write part of a test question. Read 1 Corinthians 2:1-5. Then give four possible answers to the multiple choice question below. Your possible answers should include an absolutely wrong answer, two answers that are partially correct, and an absolutely correct answer. The question: Why did Paul emphasize his weakness and fear in 1 Corinthians 2:1-5?

Group #3. Your portion of the test is to do some creative thinking. After reading 1 Corinthians 2, list your conclusions about the difference between human wisdom and God's wisdom.

Group #4. Your portion of the test is a brief essay that cites examples of how to apply the principles taught in 1 Corinthians 2:14.

Allow each group to share its test results. [Option: Use the reproducible page as a substitute or additional small-group activity.]

INTO LIFE

Begin the application segment with two brainstorming exercises. For the first exercise ask, "What are some examples of 'worldly wisdom'—wisdom that is untrue since it does not come from God? These may be huge philosophical positions such as the New Age philosophy or simple statements such as 'Nice guys finish last.'" List the answers on the board.

Make the transition to the second brainstorming exercise by explaining, "The world seeks wisdom, but from the wrong places. Believers also want true wisdom, something that is of eternal significance. Today's text tells us the Holy Spirit offers us that wisdom. In this exercise we want to create a list of tips for allowing the Holy Spirit to give us that precious wisdom. What are some ways we can encourage this?" List the answers on the board. Make sure to stress that the Holy Spirit offers wisdom through God's written Word.

Conclude by reading Solomon's prayer for wisdom in 1 Kings 3:5-14 and God's response. As you close with prayer, tell students you will allow them a quiet moment when they can ask for wisdom for any issue of life. Remind students to remember Solomon's selfless prayer as they make their requests.

Wisdom for Believers

Paul said he did not speak "the wisdom of this age or of the rulers of this age." Look up the Scriptures listed on the left; then use the words *Spirit of God* as an acrostic to list things you learn about true wisdom. One blank is filled in as an example

Paul's Power:
1 Corinthians 2:4, 5

Wisdom from the Spirit:
1 Corinthians 2:6-8

The Spirit of God:
1 Corinthians 2:10-16

S_____

P_____

It's from God's Spirit

R_____

I_____

T_____

Of

G _____

O _____

D _____

Wisdom from Believers

**"This is what we speak,
not in words taught us
by human wisdom
but in words taught
by the Spirit,
expressing spiritual
truths in spiritual words."**

—1 Corinthians 2:13

How will you share spiritual wisdom with an unbeliever this week? Write three possible ways below.

1.

2.

3.

Called to Be a Christian Community
Unit 1: Servants of God
(Lessons 1-4)

SERVING TOGETHER

LESSON 3

Jun
18

DEVOTIONAL READING:
MATTHEW 13:3-9

BACKGROUND SCRIPTURE:
1 CORINTHIANS 3:1-15

PRINTED TEXT:
1 CORINTHIANS 3:1-15

WHY TEACH THIS LESSON?

Diversity is celebrated by many elements of society. Some of this diversity, however, goes radically beyond the traditional standards of Christianity. When diversity and tolerance include acceptance of grossly sinful behavior, the church must say no. Is the church, then, an enemy of diversity?

Today's lesson is a celebration of diversity within the church, but not in the way that secular forces propose. The church is composed of many types of people having a diversity of gifts and abilities. A beautiful aspect of a properly functioning church is found in this variety, with all working toward a common goal. In today's lesson Paul shows a badly divided and fractious church how God intended different leaders to perform various functions, with all being vital to the growth of the church. Each member can find an avenue for service that becomes a part of the overall success of the church's ministry. Such unity-from-diversity was a winning combination for the Corinthians and can be for us today.

INTRODUCTION

A. POWER OF UNITY FROM DIVERSITY

The headline read, "Managers Err If They Limit Their Hiring To People Like Them." The story went on to quote a company's "chief people officer" as saying, "The power of any group of people is the power of the mix" (*The Wall Street Journal*, October 12, 2004). Some will read that conclusion as if it were something new. But the apostle Paul knew and taught this truth some 2,000 years ago. Like the human body itself, strength starts with diversity—with the specialization of body parts (see 1 Corinthians 12:12-31).

Diversity, however, isn't enough by itself. Those diverse parts must work together in unity. Nothing good can happen in the church (the body of Christ) without unity. Unity creates strength because it combines the separate spiritual gifts and abilities of each member. When people are united, their power is far greater than just the sum of their separate strengths.

B. LESSON BACKGROUND

Paul founded the church in Corinth on his second missionary journey. He continued to work in that city for at least a year and a half (Acts 18:11, 18). Soon after Paul left, Apollos came to Corinth and had a fruitful ministry working with the new church (Acts 18:24-27). As previously discussed in the first chapter of his letter, Paul warned his readers that they must not choose up sides. To align themselves with human leaders such as himself or Apollos or Cephas (Peter) was wrong because it divided the body of Christ (1 Corinthians 1:12, 13).

In today's lesson Paul expands his argument. While division is a mark of immaturity and worldliness, unity is a beautiful part of God's master plan. If the Corinthians will learn the lesson that Paul is teaching, they will heal the divisions in their church; they will become productive coworkers in the kingdom of God.

LESSON AIMS

After participating in this lesson, each student will be able to:

1. Paraphrase Paul's description of the immaturity of the Corinthian Christians.

2. Explain how a diversity of gifts can help the fulfillment of the church's mission.

3. Make a plan to work cooperatively in a specific area of church ministry.

KEY VERSE

We are God's fellow workers; you are God's field, God's building.   —1 Corinthians 3:9

Lesson 3 Notes

I. DIVISION IS BAD (1 CORINTHIANS 3:1-4)

A. Mere Infants (vv. 1, 2)

1, 2. Brothers, I could not address you as spiritual but as worldly—mere infants in Christ. I gave you milk, not solid food, for you were not yet ready for it. Indeed, you are still not ready.

Paul reveals his feeling of goodwill when he once again addresses the Corinthians as *brothers* (see previously 1 Corinthians 1:10; 2:1). However, this sense of fellowship moves quickly to words of rebuke. The believers in Corinth are indeed brothers—but they are still baby brothers.

When Paul first arrived in Corinth he spoke to audiences that were not *spiritual*, that is, they were not in tune with divine things. The ungodly people were *worldly;* they lived their lives in response to the desires of their flesh. As worldly people they were totally unprepared to receive the deep things of God—the *solid food* of the Word. Thus Paul had had to start teaching with the very basics, what he figuratively calls *milk.* (Hebrews 5:11– 6:2 gives us a list of some things that are considered "milk.")

Now Paul evaluates their lack of progress toward spiritual maturity. A wise teacher knows how much the students are able to tolerate at any given time (John 16:12). That's why Paul started with "milk." But yet now, some four or five years later, they are still unable to digest *solid food.* This is unacceptable! This refusal to grow to maturity is a root cause of the division in their church.

BEYOND BABY TALK

If you've ever been embarrassed when caught making nonsense sounds to an infant, take heart! You actually were doing a good thing. A new study shows that baby talk is ideal for the infant's developing neural system. A researcher noted that "the singsong, drawn-out, exaggerated form of speech has a melody to it. Inside the melody is a tutorial for the baby that contains exceptionally well-informed versions of the building blocks of language" (www.nwrel.org).

While this kind of speech may work in "conversations" with an infant, trying it with your boss could land you in the unemployment line! There is a time to move beyond baby talk. In the spiritual life all Christians should desire to move beyond being spoon-fed their spiritual diet. Teaching Bible stories through cute songs such as "Only a Boy Named David" is fine for youngsters. But to continue that into the Sunday morning worship service would be out of place.

Yet, sadly, many Christians never seem to move beyond the most elementary spiritual truths. We use the description *arrested development* when we notice people holding on to certain emotional patterns from early childhood as they grow physically toward adulthood. Unfortunately, arrested development on a spiritual level is too often considered normal and acceptable. —A. E. A.

B. Mere Men (vv. 3, 4)

3. You are still worldly. For since there is jealousy and quarreling among you, are you not worldly? Are you not acting like mere men?

The statement *you are still worldly* is a strong rebuke. *Worldly* is the word that described the Corinthians before they came to Christ (v. 1, above). It is a tragedy that it still describes them four or five years later. The existence of *jealousy and quarreling* are symptoms of spiritual failure. Unfortunately, Paul will have to address these same problems again (2 Corinthians 12:20). Paul also warns the churches of Galatia that "dissentions, factions and envy" are products of the flesh, not of the Spirit (Galatians 5:20, 21). The plain fact is that the members of the church at Corinth are not acting as Christians ought.

What Do You Think?

What are some things that you have allowed to hinder your own spiritual growth at times? How do you guard against these?

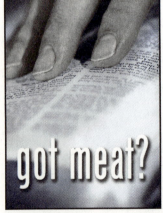

Visual for Lesson 3. *As you begin discussing verses 1, 2, ask if anyone recognizes the tie-in to a famous commercial.*

4. For when one says, "I follow Paul," and another, "I follow Apollos," are you not mere men?

If the Corinthians resist being called worldly and immature, Paul is quick to offer proof. When one member of the congregation says *I follow Paul* and another proclaims *I follow Apollos,* these very divisions expose their worldly state and immature mind-set. As *mere* humans they split up over the issue of who baptized them (1 Corinthians 1:13-16). As mere humans they turned the observance of the Lord's Supper into class warfare (11:18-22). As mere humans they have a problem with orderly worship (14:26-33). As mere humans they are destroying the body of Christ!

II. DIVERSITY IS GOOD (1 CORINTHIANS 3:5-9)

A. THE LORD ASSIGNS TASKS (v. 5)

5. What, after all, is Apollos? And what is Paul? Only servants, through whom you came to believe—as the Lord has assigned to each his task.

Paul challenges his readers to remember the nature of both his own ministry and that of *Apollos.* Paul, of course, came along first to found their church (Acts 18:1-21). Then Apollos came after Paul. He was "a learned man, with a thorough knowledge of the Scriptures" (Acts 18:24). When he came to Corinth he "was a great help" and "vigorously refuted the Jews . . . proving from the Scriptures that Jesus was the Christ" (Acts 18:27, 28).

So although Paul was the founder, Apollos apparently was more eloquent and in some ways more effective. Their relative merits, however, are not the point. Both are *servants* of the gospel. As the Lord's servants they carry out the tasks assigned to them. They present the message; the people believe. All of this happens *as the Lord* provides.

WHAT DO YOU THINK?

How should viewing ourselves as servants make a difference in the way we approach our ministries?

B. THE WORKERS DO THEIR JOBS (v. 6)

6. I planted the seed, Apollos watered it, but God made it grow.

At this point Paul uses familiar agricultural imagery. Neither man should be idolized; they are just workers doing their jobs. The most important role belongs to God. He is the one who empowers the church planter; he is the one who gives eloquence and ability to the church builder. All the credit for the growth and increase of that which is *planted,* therefore, belongs to God.

TEAMWORK

Employers recognize the need for good teamwork. But what about employees who let the team down in various ways? The following are some suggestions for letters of "recommendation" (with double meanings!) for such folks as they seek employment elsewhere. For the chronically absent employee, you could write: "A man like him is hard to find"; for an employee with no ambition: "You would indeed be fortunate to get this person to work for you"; for an employee who is so unproductive that the job is better left unfilled: "I can assure you that no person would be better for the job" (www.crosswalk.com).

The church also has its share of chronically absent, poorly motivated, and unproductive members who let the team down. At the same time there are those who do quite a bit of work but also want others to know how much they have done. This is a bit like the chest thumping and strutting that goes on in sports: the player seeks to draw attention to personal accomplishments while ignoring the contributions of teammates.

Paul calls instead for the church to recognize that ministry is a cooperative effort. It is teamwork. He models this in his own ministry. It is not a matter of who gets the glory, because all the glory belongs to God. The work of the church, the team, is simply to get the work done.   —A. E. A.

C. GOD BLESSES AND REWARDS (vv. 7-9)

7. So neither he who plants nor he who waters is anything, but only God, who makes things grow.

The lesson to be learned is reinforced. The Corinthians should not think that he *who plants* is anything special; neither should they give undue credit to the one *who waters.* No one can make a plant grow. All the praise and glory must go to God.

Even today, people should not be too quick to give people the credit—or the blame—for the way a church grows. When the workers do their assigned jobs, when every part is working effectively (Ephesians 4:16), and when Christ is honored as the head, then the body exhibits a growth that comes from God. This kind of growth is God's blessing.

8. The man who plants and the man who waters have one purpose, and each will be rewarded according to his own labor.

There are several truths included in the statement *The man who plants and the man who waters have one purpose.* In terms of necessity both workers are one and the same, because if either is left out no plant will grow. In terms of purpose both workers are *one,* because they are working to accomplish the same end. In terms of honor in the eyes of humanity, they are the same, for neither worker should be exalted above the other.

God will attend to whatever reward a person should receive for his or her work. Paul does not specify at this point what kind of reward that may be. Surely the highest reward any servant of God could ever receive will be to hear the master say, "Well done" (Matthew 25:21).

9. For we are God's fellow workers; you are God's field, God's building.

Paul and Apollos, as well as other leaders of the church, are *fellow workers.* They work together on the same team, striving to accomplish the same purpose. Even more importantly, in this endeavor they are also coworkers with God. What a vast thought: they are working side by side with their creator at his invitation! Their joy is seeing their work blessed by God and growing as he gives it increase.

The church is *God's* cultivated *field.* The growing church represents a harvest that belongs to God (compare Matthew 13:3-9). Using another type of imagery, Paul says the church is also God's building. Each of God's workmen helps to construct it, but the *building* itself belongs to God. Paul expands on this picture in the next several verses.

III. COOPERATION IS ESSENTIAL (1 CORINTHIANS 3:10-15)

A. LAYING THE FOUNDATION (vv. 10, 11)

10. By the grace God has given me, I laid a foundation as an expert builder, and someone else is building on it. But each one should be careful how he builds.

In the ancient world the *expert builder* has the responsibility of conceiving what a building should look like, setting out the *foundation,* and supervising the workmen. As the expert builder of the church in Corinth, Paul laid the spiritual foundation on which the new congregation was built. It was his faithful preaching that called the church there into existence.

Only by the grace of God is the man who had once persecuted the church now allowed to become one who lays the foundation of new congregations! Paul accepted his role as the wise expert builder of churches in Asia Minor and in

---

WHAT DO YOU THINK?

Does verse 7 mean that we should not evaluate periodically the effectiveness of our own ministries and those of others? If we do evaluate ministries, how do we balance personal responsibility with God's role in providing the increase?

WHAT DO YOU THINK?

Paul seems to indicate that God's reward functions as a motivating influence for Christians. How do we serve God without our motivation for service becoming selfish as a result?

Greece, but he never forgot that this role was given to him. He had done nothing to deserve it (compare 1 Corinthians 15:10).

Paul was not the kind of missionary to hang around in any one place too long with any one church. His task was to keep moving and planting new churches (Romans 15:20-24). When God led Paul to continue his missionary journeys, the task of building upon the work in Corinth necessarily fell into other hands. Those who followed Paul had to be aware of this caution: let *each one . . . be careful* in continuing the building project.

11. For no one can lay any foundation other than the one already laid, which is Jesus Christ.

The most important thing for Paul and for those who follow him is that the church must be built on the right *foundation*. The foundation chosen by God and recognized by Paul *is Jesus Christ*. It is the sovereign decree of God that *no one can lay* any *other* foundation (Isaiah 28:16; 1 Peter 2:4-6). Wherever and whenever we may try to establish churches, the foundation must always be Jesus Christ. The truth that he is the Messiah (Matthew 16:16), the reality that he is the Son of God (John 5:17-23), and the fact that he died on the cross and rose from the dead—this is the bedrock upon which Christianity stands.

B. CHOOSING THE MATERIALS (vv. 12, 13)
12. If any man builds on this foundation using gold, silver, costly stones, wood, hay or straw,

When a *foundation* has been laid, then each worker has the responsibility to build upon this foundation with certain material. The worker may be found adorning the structure with costly materials such as *gold, silver,* or *costly stones* in a given building project. Or perhaps the worker may decide to use ordinary *wood,* or even cheap materials such as *hay or straw.* In each instance the worker chooses the material and then is held responsible for the result.

As we join the ongoing project of building the church of God, we should be careful to use our very best. Our commitment to live in God's truth and our sacrifices for that cause should be as if they were gold, silver, and costly stones. Any lesser effort would be like the wood or even like the hay or straw. The way we approach our task does make a difference, as the next verse makes clear.

13. . . . his work will be shown for what it is, because the Day will bring it to light. It will be revealed with fire, and the fire will test the quality of each man's work.

Poor workmanship with inferior materials will not stand the test on Judgment *Day.* As one observer said, "Holy shoddy is still shoddy." The *test* of the *fire* will have different effects on works of gold and works of hay!

In the context of the leaders of the church in Corinth, this means that when they teach the pure truth of God, they make a lasting contribution. On the other hand if they focus on human doctrines or mere personal opinions, then their *work* will have no lasting value.

C. RECEIVING THE REWARD (vv. 14, 15)
14. If what he has built survives, he will receive his reward.

Godly people will be the ones who rejoice to see their work survive. They did not waste their time on trivial issues; they did not put major emphasis on things of minor importance. They *built* on the true foundation; they chose to use the most important building materials. Therefore their work will last into eternity.

God will reward such faithful workers. The exact nature of this *reward* is not stated. Part of the reward could be the satisfaction of seeing that their lives had

DAILY BIBLE READINGS

Monday, June 12—Spreading God's Word (Matthew 13: 3-9)

Tuesday, June 13—Let Both Grow Together (Matthew 13: 24-30)

Wednesday, June 14—The Need for Teachers (Hebrews 5: 7-14)

Thursday, June 15—Strengthened with Power Through the Spirit (Ephesians 3:14-21)

Friday, June 16—Servants Through Whom You Believe (1 Corinthians 3:1-9)

Saturday, June 17—Building on the Foundation of Christ (1 Corinthians 3:10-15)

Sunday, June 18—Do Not Boast About Human Leaders (1 Corinthians 3:18-23)

HOW TO SAY IT

Apollos. Uh-PAHL-us.
Barnabas. BAR-nuh-bus.
Cephas. SEE-fus.
Corinth. KOR-inth.
Corinthians. Ko-RIN-thee-unz.
Ephesians. Ee-FEE-zhunz.
Isaiah. Eye-ZAY-uh.
Thessalonians. THESS-uh-LO-nee-unz.

made an eternal difference. Perhaps an additional reward in Heaven is in mind. Paul only assures his readers that there is a reward to be gained. The Bible does teach that there are degrees of reward and punishment (Luke 12:47, 48; 19:11-27).

15. If it is burned up, he will suffer loss; he himself will be saved, but only as one escaping through the flames.

On the other hand the work of certain others will not last. A teacher who does not teach the sure truths of God but wastes time on insignificant trifles builds a house of straw. Such a person has not necessarily done evil things; rather, this kind of teacher simply has not done the best things. This person works to build something that will not matter in eternity.

Paul does not say that such a person will lose eternal salvation. We are not saved, after all, by how much we have contributed to the building of the kingdom. We are saved by the grace of God that is available through the atoning death of Christ that pays the penalty for sin. The kind of person in this context who shall suffer loss shall *be saved*, but the result will be like a person who has lost possessions in a fire.

CONCLUSION

A. WORKING TOGETHER

Sometimes spiritually mature Christians will "part ways" from one another because of thoughtful, sincere differences of opinion. The split between Paul and Barnabas in Acts 15:36-41 is an example. In that instance good things resulted as two missionary teams went out rather than one.

More often, however, division in the church is a terrible thing when the root is spiritual immaturity. But diversity in the church is a good thing. It happens when God gives each person spiritual gifts, talents, and abilities to be used in building the kingdom.

We should not feel threatened when other people serve God in ways that we ourselves cannot. Instead, we should thank God that he has designed the body of Christ to have such a variety of spiritual gifts. When we each do the work God has given us to do, we can accomplish great things for his glory. Paul was not jealous of Apollos's speaking skills, and Apollos was not jealous of Paul's church-planting skills.

Cooperation is key. We are coworkers with God and with one another. Like Paul and Apollos, we serve God in assigned roles. We cooperate with God by following his instructions; we cooperate with one another by lending mutual support. God does not just want us to serve him; he wants us to serve him together.

B. WINNING TOGETHER

The church that serves together wins together. Following the church's beginning on the Day of Pentecost in Jerusalem, it was no coincidence that victory and unity went hand in hand; believers were solidly united in victorious fashion (Acts 1:14; 2:1, 42-47). By their love for one another and their complete confidence in God, the whole city knew that they were disciples of Jesus Christ.

Winning together is more than just the result of "team spirit" or of "many hands making light work." It is the success that comes from doing what God wants in the way that he directs—and then receiving God's blessing. If we can learn to serve God together with the same spirit that Paul and Apollos had, planting and watering according to our own specific roles, then God will give the increase.

Discovery Learning

*This page contains an alternative lesson plan emphasizing learning activities. Classes
desiring such student involvement will find these suggestions helpful. The next page
is a reproducible activity page to further enhance discovery learning.*

LEARNING GOALS

After this lesson, each student will be able to:

1. Paraphrase Paul's description of the immaturity of the Corinthian Christians.

2. Explain how a diversity of gifts can help the fulfillment of the church's mission.

3. Make a plan to work cooperatively in a specific area of church ministry.

INTO THE LESSON

Display a poster with the old saying, *United We Stand, Divided We Fall.* Say, "This truth illustrates national strength. It is a saying that is also true for the local church." Ask class members to discuss strife that they witnessed in other congregations. (Make sure to stress that the question is about other congregations, which should not be named.) What were the issues? How did the contentions surface in church life?

Make the transition to Bible study by reminding the class that divisions and contentions are not new. We have illustrations of contention in the Bible—and advice on how to overcome them.

INTO THE WORD

Ask a volunteer to read aloud today's printed text. Ask students to watch for causes of the divisions and quarrels in the Corinthian church during the reading.

Next, distribute handouts printed with the title and questions that follow; you can display them on the board instead if you wish, or use the first activity on the reproducible page. (The words in parenthesis are suggested answers to help the teacher; they should not be printed for the students.)

What About Division and Teamwork?

1. What is the evidence of problems in the Corinthian church? (*v. 3: worldliness, jealousy, strife, division; vv. 4, 5: allegiances to different leaders*)

2. What does Paul see as the source of the divisions and quarrels? (*vv. 1, 2: spiritual immaturity, a failure to grow up as Christians*)

3. How does Paul illustrate the importance of teamwork in the church? (*vv. 6-8: an illustration of how leaders have different roles and gifts*)

4. What is Paul saying about the relationship of church leaders and members in verse 9? (*Leaders have different roles to play yet work together for the same purpose. Leaders and members must also work together in building the church.*)

5. What is one of the principles implied in verses 10-15 that we must remember in building a strong church? (*Build the church on a strong foundation.*)

6. What do you think Paul implies in verse 15? (*God doesn't view all work done for him to be of equal quality.*)

Divide the class into groups of two or three students. Groups are to review the Bible passage and try to discover the truths about unity and division that Paul teaches. After several minutes, call for answers and responses to each question.

INTO LIFE

Divide the class into four groups. Give each group a piece of poster board, marker, and one of the tasks that follow. After several minutes, allow each group to share its conclusions.

Group #1: *Sources of Quarrels and Division!* Brainstorm potential sources of quarrels and divisions in churches. The list will be long and will highlight our need to be diligent.

Group #2: *How Diversity Works!* Use your imagination and list the many different gifts and passions that people bring to the church. Remember: today's Scripture makes it clear that the church is to enjoy and use these to labor together for the glory of Christ.

Group #3: *Diversity in Our Class!* List the many different spiritual gifts, skills, and passions of members in our class. Feel free to mention class members' names as you make this list. However, if you do list names, be sure to use everyone's name who is present today.

Group #4: *Working Together!* Your task is to brainstorm several projects that we as a class could do for our church. Then select one of these projects to propose to the class as a whole. Explain how the project would use the different skills and gifts of class members. [*Option:* the second activity on the reproducible page can be an additional or substitute group topic.]

Be sure to make plans to complete Group 4's proposal. It may be necessary to appoint two or three people to complete the planning. Conclude the class with a prayer time of thanks to God for the diversity of gifts he has given to the church leadership and members.

Learning About Church Quarrels

Read 1 Corinthians 3:1-15. What lessons do we learn about church disharmony? By answering the questions below, you will discover truths that will provide help for the church in today's world.

1. What are some evidences of divisions and quarrels in the Corinthian church?

   Verse 3 _____

   Verses 4, 5 _____

2. What was the source of the divisions or reason for the quarrels in the Corinthian church?

   Verses 1, 2 _____

3. How does Paul illustrate the importance of teamwork and cooperation in the church?

   Verses 6-8 _____

4. What is the relationship between church leaders and church members?

   Verse 9 _____

5. What is a key principle that must be remembered for building a strong church?

   Verses 10-15 _____

6. What do you think Paul is implying in verse 15? _____

Demonstrate Harmony!

Complete this thought: Knowing that I am also a part of the team at my church, I see one (or more) of my roles or contributions to the congregation as . . .

Called to Be a Christian Community

Unit 1: Servants of God
(Lessons 1-4)

SERVING FAITHFULLY

LESSON 4

WHY TEACH THIS LESSON?

When the church talks of stewardship, many think automatically of money. Our stewardship campaigns are usually designed to teach church members how to be obedient to biblical principles of giving money for the work of the Lord. But stewardship is much larger than principles of giving money.

This week's lesson helps us understand the concept that service should be considered from the perspective of stewardship. In this perspective we are not judged by salary, acclaim, or even by effectiveness. Rather, we are judged as wise stewards if we are faithful and committed to our ministries. Our rewards will not be measured by standards from the business world. If we serve God, we look to him for reward.

The church with many willing servants will find itself with ministries that make a difference. This lesson will challenge every student to commit himself or herself to a useful ministry and to remain faithful to this task.

INTRODUCTION

A. HARD LESSON TO LEARN

The lesson of humble servanthood is hard to learn. It is a lesson that goes against human nature, against our inner drive to climb to the top of the ladder. That's why the apostles still had not mastered it even after three years with Jesus. They were still competing with each other for the chief seats in the kingdom (see Mark 10:35-41). Even the beauty of the Last Supper was marred by their arguing over who should be regarded as the greatest (see Luke 22:24).

Fortunately, the apostles finally did learn the lesson of humble servanthood. They learned to honor Christ as the head of the church and to see themselves as his servants. As a result, they worked hard in those early years to spread the gospel and to plant churches. They did not waste time worrying over the roles assigned to anyone else. They understood that serving Christ faithfully was the most important thing.

B. LESSON BACKGROUND

Paul had to teach the Corinthians the same lesson. The believers in Corinth were still jockeying for positions, even four or five years after their church had come into existence. They looked for ways to set themselves apart as superior to others in the church. Part of the way they tried to gain importance was by lining up behind favorite leaders. When they did this, they exposed their lack of understanding of who those leaders really were.

Paul addressed this problem across four chapters in 1 Corinthians. As he moves to a conclusion, he shows how the Corinthians should regard Apollos and himself. More importantly, he insists that they adopt a new way of regarding themselves. Their pride and divisions had to be set aside before the church could go forward. They had to learn the lesson of serving faithfully as God's stewards.

DEVOTIONAL READING:
MATTHEW 23:8-12

BACKGROUND SCRIPTURE:
1 CORINTHIANS 4:1-13

PRINTED TEXT:
1 CORINTHIANS 4:1-13

Jun 25

LESSON AIMS

After participating in this lesson, each student will be able to:

1. List the word pictures that Paul uses to describe the ministry of the apostles.

2. Give examples of the demands, costs, and sacrifices often required of faithful stewards.

3. Make a commitment to be a faithful steward in a specific ministry.

KEY VERSE

So then, men ought to regard us as servants of Christ and as those entrusted with the secret things of God.
—1 Corinthians 4:1

I. FAITHFUL STEWARDS (1 CORINTHIANS 4:1-5)

A. POSITION OF A STEWARD (v. 1)

1. So then, men ought to regard us as servants of Christ and as those entrusted with the secret things of God.

Paul insists that a person must regard Apollos and himself as nothing more than what they really are. These thoughts follow the stern "no more boasting about men" admonition of 1 Corinthians 3:21. It is no compliment to Paul for any of his supporters to try to put him on a pedestal. It is important for the Corinthians to recognize that men such as Paul and Apollos are *servants of Christ*.

Another word for *those entrusted* is "steward." In ancient times a steward has the responsibility of taking care of something. For instance, it is typical for a trusted slave to be put in charge of running a household. (See Genesis 39:2-19, where Joseph was given this role in Potiphar's household.) Paul and Apollos, as stewards, have been entrusted with the task of proclaiming *the secret things of God* to the church at Corinth. These secret things include the divine plan for salvation, a plan that previously had been disclosed only partially (see Luke 10:21, 22). In addition to this function, Paul has something to say about his role as apostle in verse 9, below.

B. REQUIREMENT OF A STEWARD (v. 2)

2. Now it is required that those who have been given a trust must prove faithful.

To be *given a trust* by God does not mean that Paul and Apollos are men of unusual importance. Instead, it means that they have been given a job to do. As God's stewards with a responsibility in the household of God, they answer to him for how they carry out their tasks. God requires above all that his servants be found *faithful*. This is an important point because to focus on being faithful is a bit different from a focus on being successful.

Since it is God who gives the increase (see 1 Corinthians 3:6), God's servant must not assume credit or blame for success. The Lord warned the prophet Jeremiah that he would not be successful (Jeremiah 7:27). But the Lord expected him to be faithful nonetheless.

The servant who makes success the primary goal may rationalize that the end justifies the means. The faithful steward, however, obeys the instructions of the Lord. Unlike King Saul in the Old Testament (see 1 Samuel 15), the faithful steward does not yield to the temptation of thinking that he or she has a better idea than the master. See also Jesus' extended remarks in Luke 12:42-48.

WHAT MEASURE OF SUCCESS?

Dr. Clarence Jordan began Koinonia Farms in Sumter County, Georgia in 1942. The Greek word *koinonia* means "fellowship," and this venture was an attempt to provide an opportunity for the poor, both black and white, to better themselves through farming. By the 1950s, however, "the locals" began to boycott this effort. Businesses would not trade with Koinonia Farms. Koinonia's roadside market was attacked. Shots were fired into Koinonia homes. The Ku Klux Klan held rallies.

On one occasion following a massive attack and destruction by opponents of Koinonia Farms, a local reporter came to interview Jordan. He asked Jordan how successful he felt now that the crops as well as many buildings on Koinonia Farms were destroyed. Jordan's response was, "As successful as the cross."

Think about it: Jesus' crucifixion did not seem like a success at the time. Yet it was the faithfulness of Jesus in going to the cross that paved the way for the ultimate success. So it was faithfulness that kept Koinonia Farms going, even to today (www.koinoniapartners.org).

Will the next generation find us faithful?

Visual for Lesson 4. Point to this visual as you ask for specific examples of how one generation demonstrates its faithfulness to the next.

God's desire for his people is that they remain faithful. Human definitions of success, however, are often bound up in numbers or "metrics." That can be a trap! Numbers of Scripture verses memorized, services attended, Sunday school pins earned, etc., are things that, at their best, result from faithfulness. At their worst, they become a basis for salvation by works (Luke 18:9-12).   —A. E. A.

C. EVALUATION OF A STEWARD (vv. 3-5)

3. I care very little if I am judged by you or by any human court; indeed, I do not even judge myself.

It is a very small thing to Paul whether the Corinthians praise him or condemn him. Paul has no interest in winning a popularity contest. It is God's judgment that matters (v. 5, below).

In a sense not even Paul's own judgment matters. Think about how important that is! If Paul were to *judge* himself highly, he could become arrogant (Romans 12:3). On the other hand, to judge himself too low may lead to despair; it may lead him to forget about the Spirit as his source of strength.

Thus it is irrelevant whether Paul holds himself in high esteem or in low. The only evaluation of Paul and his ministry that really counts will not come from any human. It will not even come from Paul himself.

4. My conscience is clear, but that does not make me innocent. It is the Lord who judges me.

Paul goes on to strengthen the argument of verse 3. His statement that his *conscience is clear* is the same kind of statement he made to the Sanhedrin in Acts 23:1. Paul thinks that a good conscience is important (see Acts 24:16; Romans 9:1; 2 Corinthians 1:12; etc.). However, a good conscience alone will not make him innocent or proved right. Paul's self-assessment is not the evaluation that counts. The one to evaluate Paul is *the Lord*. Paul is a servant of God; therefore God must be the judge who rules on Paul's case. God will do this through Jesus Christ, to whom he has assigned all judgment (see John 5:22).

5. Therefore judge nothing before the appointed time; wait till the Lord comes. He will bring to light what is hidden in darkness and will expose the motives of men's hearts. At that time each will receive his praise from God.

The issue of human judgments is somewhat complicated in the New Testament. In the verse before us, Paul tells the Corinthians to *judge nothing*. But then in chapter 5 he will stress the importance of judging the immoral behavior of a church member. How shall we sort this out?

The solution is the context. Notice that the word *therefore* ties *judge nothing* to what was said in verses 1-3. Thus the Corinthians are not to try to evaluate anything about the ministries of Paul and Apollos before *the time* of the Lord's return. At the proper time all servants will present their accounts. It is *the Lord* who *will bring to light* even the *hidden* things of *darkness*, the things that people think that no one else even knows about. The Lord, who knows the *hearts* of all, is the one who will make manifest their secret thoughts and counsels.

For the faithful servant this future time of judgment need not be feared. Everyone who has faithfully done his or her duty will have the praise of God. The faithful servant will be rewarded by the master.

II. UNWORTHY JUDGES (1 CORINTHIANS 4:6-8)

A. UNWARRANTED PRIDE (v. 6)

6. Now, brothers, I have applied these things to myself and Apollos for your benefit, so that you may learn from us the meaning of the saying, "Do not go beyond what is written." Then you will not take pride in one man over against another.

HOW TO SAY IT

Apollos. Uh-PAHL-us.
Corinth. KOR-inth.
Corinthians. Ko-RIN-thee-unz.
Jeremiah. Jair-uh-MY-uh.
koinonia (Greek). koy-no-NEE-uh.
Lamentations. Lam-en-TAY-shunz.
Potiphar. POT-ih-far.
Sanhedrin. SAN-huh-drun or San-HEED-run.
Thessalonians. THESS-uh-LO-nee-unz.

WHAT DO YOU THINK?

What was a time when learning by example helped you develop selflessness in a way that a sermon or lesson may not have?

DAILY BIBLE READINGS

Monday, June 19—Good Stewards of God's Grace (1 Peter 4:1-11)

Tuesday, June 20—Jesus Washes Peter's Feet (John 13:2-9)

Wednesday, June 21—Serve One Another (John 13:12-17)

Thursday, June 22—Become a Servant (Mark 10:41-45)

Friday, June 23—Stewards of God's Mysteries (1 Corinthians 4:1-7)

Saturday, June 24—We Are Fools for Christ (1 Corinthians 4:8-13)

Sunday, June 25—A Fatherly Admonition on Responsibility (1 Corinthians 4:14-21)

This verse cements the idea of "judge nothing" in verse 5. Up to this point the Corinthians have been taking *pride in one man over against another.* This means that when the Corinthians started choosing sides—lining up behind Paul, Apollos, etc.—they naturally began to think "our group is more in the right than your group." This kind of arrogance must come to an end.

By seeing that Paul does not desire to be glorified, the Corinthians will learn that no one among their number should seek such glory either. Their thinking should be controlled by what Scripture says *(what is written).* When that happens, they will refrain from giving mere men their allegiance. Thus there are two parts to the issue: mature leaders who wisely know not to accept undue praise and church members who learn not to give it.

B. UNDESERVED GLORY (vv. 7, 8)

7. For who makes you different from anyone else? What do you have that you did not receive? And if you did receive it, why do you boast as though you did not?

Next, Paul challenges his readers to give honest answers to three questions. First, who is it that makes any one of them any *different from anyone else?* The necessary answer is "God"; thus unless the Corinthians get out of the judging business they will find themselves judging God's choices! The Corinthians must stop trying to set up a "pecking order" to assign the relative worth of each person (see also 2 Corinthians 10:12).

Second, what does anyone have that was not received as a gift from God? Paul has much more to say about spiritual gifts in Romans 12; 1 Corinthians 12; and Ephesians 4. The bottom line is that every person's position is a stewardship that he or she has received from God.

Third, since it must be admitted that no one has anything that was not a gift from God, why should anyone *boast?* How can anyone try to pretend that he or she has any good thing that was not a gift? It is a dangerous thing to receive glory from other people, as Herod learned at his death (see Acts 12:23).

8. Already you have all you want! Already you have become rich! You have become kings—and that without us! How I wish that you really had become kings so that we might be kings with you!

Up to this point the Corinthians apparently have responded incorrectly to the issues of verse 7. So Paul uses irony to rebuke his readers. In their spiritual immaturity they see themselves as satisfied and *rich;* since they reign as *kings* in their own minds, they think they do not need Paul and the apostles.

Generously, Paul says he wishes that the Corinthians actually were kings. If they really did hold positions of power and authority, then they could share the benefits with the church. Paul and the other apostles would then *be kings with them.* But surely the Corinthian Christians see that the lofty positions of their imaginations are false!

III. SUFFERING APOSTLES (1 CORINTHIANS 4:9-13)

A. SPECTACLE TO THE WORLD (v. 9)

9. For it seems to me that God has put us apostles on display at the end of the procession, like men condemned to die in the arena. We have been made a spectacle to the whole universe, to angels as well as to men.

As an antidote to the sickness of the Corinthians' pride, Paul shows them what God has done with the *apostles* themselves. God has not put them on "church thrones" with special glory and privileges. Rather, he has set forth the apostles as men appointed to death. In contrast to the self-importance of the

Corinthians, Christ's own apostles are treated as though they are *condemned criminals*. The world gawks at them in derision. The apostles suffer and are put on display while *angels* above and *men* below look on. (See also Romans 8:36; Hebrews 10:32-34.)

B. FOOLS FOR CHRIST (v. 10)
10. We are fools for Christ, but you are so wise in Christ! We are weak, but you are strong! You are honored, we are dishonored!

The irony continues. Paul and the apostles are regarded by the world as *fools*, and they willingly accept that role for Christ's sake. By contrast, the proud Corinthians see themselves as *wise in Christ*. Although they are really just babies in their spiritual understanding, they proudly exalt themselves above their teachers. If they are really wise, they would not need this harsh lesson!

Pushing the irony yet further, Paul shows how the apostles are willing to be *weak*, but the Corinthians see themselves as strong. The Corinthians claim to be honorable, even though their original leaders are despised. They do not understand the principle of a steward caring only for the approval of the master and disregarding human judgments.

WISE FOOLS
Students in the second year of college or high school are called sophomores. This label actually is not very flattering! It's a combination of two Greek words: *sophos,* meaning "wise," and *moros,* meaning "foolish." Thus a sophomore is a wise fool, a seeming contradiction in terms. Perhaps the idea is that a little knowledge can be dangerous. Some Christians, wise in their own eyes, are rightly called fools by the world because of their immaturity and self-promotion.

Other Christians (like the apostle Paul) are indeed very wise in the knowledge of God, yet they too are called fools by the world. The reason for this is that the world, in its "wisdom," does not understand the things of God (Romans 1:22). True Christian wisdom appears to be foolishness to this world. Sometimes true Christian wisdom even appears to be foolishness to some spiritually immature Christians.

A mark of spiritual maturity is the willingness to be considered foolish by all others, knowing that you are wise toward God (see 1 Corinthians 1:18-31). We could say that the idea is to be a permanent sophomore—a permanent wise fool—in the kingdom of God. Any takers? —A. E. A.

C. MISTREATED BY ALL (vv. 11-13)
11. To this very hour we go hungry and thirsty, we are in rags, we are brutally treated, we are homeless.

When Paul lists these sufferings, he is not asking for pity. Rather, he is hoping that the Corinthians can see the folly of their pride. The apostles are not treated like princes of the church; instead, they hunger and thirst. See a more graphic list in 2 Corinthians 11:23-28.

Although bringing the message of salvation to all, the apostles are mistreated. They accept this as part of the role that God has assigned to them. Living as they do, they show what things are important and what things really are not. Jesus had warned the apostles that it would be like this. He had no place to lay his head (Luke 9:58); he was despised and rejected (Isaiah 53:3). The apostles are not surprised when they don't receive any better treatment than he did (see John 15:20).

WHAT DO YOU THINK?
Was there ever a time when the example of Paul's own experiences of suffering helped you through a time of hardship for Christ? Explain.

WHAT DO YOU THINK?
Paul's criticism contains a fair amount of what can be termed "sanctified sarcasm." What are some benefits and dangers of employing this same strategy ourselves?

12. We work hard with our own hands. When we are cursed, we bless; when we are persecuted, we endure it;

Rather than living off of the offerings of the people, Paul and the others often labor and *work with* their *own hands* (Acts 18:3; 20:34; 1 Corinthians 9:14, 15; 1 Thessalonians 2:9; 2 Thessalonians 3:8). This is not the pattern of traveling pagan teachers of the day. Do the Corinthians now look down on Paul for lowering himself to manual labor? (See 2 Corinthians 11:7.)

When the apostles are *cursed*, they *bless* and encourage in return. In so doing the apostles are only doing what Jesus himself taught (see Matthew 5:44). When the apostles are *persecuted*, they *endure it*. They ask for no special treatment.

13. . . . when we are slandered, we answer kindly. Up to this moment we have become the scum of the earth, the refuse of the world.

This sounds like Lamentations 3:45, which speaks of the condition of the Jews in exile. The apostles serve Christ in unique positions, yet they are treated like *refuse* and *the scum of the earth*. They have been made to be no better than the mud people scrape off their feet. But when the apostles are defamed, they respond with kindness.

If the apostles are willing to be treated like garbage, why should the Christians in Corinth try to climb ladders of self-importance? How can they wallow in their own pride while ignoring greater issues of stewardship and faithfulness to their master? Surely the vivid language of Paul will wake them up and make them see the truth.

CONCLUSION

A. Help Wanted: Inquire Above

God is hanging out the "Help Wanted" sign in every congregation. He is not looking for more people to serve as critics; there are already too many people who have taken that job. God does not need any self-inflated people who waste their time trying to establish the order of importance of all the members of his family.

The job openings that God has available are for servants. The people who apply for this position do not need to be highly skilled; neither do they have to have a history of great success. What they really need is a commitment to be faithful. God will place certain job responsibilities in the hands of his servants, with each job suited to the worker. God will work side by side with his servants. There always will be an opening for the person who is sincerely interested.

B. Anticipated Salary?

The reward for self-appointed critics is minimal. They are making no real contribution to the kingdom; they are not doing anything God has asked them to do. But the reward for servants is great, even more than they can imagine.

The reward may not be immediate. Like the apostles in the first century, faithful servants of God may face persecution and suffering. They may endure hunger and thirst; they may be dishonored and homeless. In the eyes of the world they may be as worthless as the garbage scraped from dirty pots and pans. The world may think they are fools.

If the steward is a fool to work for this kind of wage (in the eyes of the world), then he or she is a fool for Christ's sake. This steward is faithful to a heavenly calling, obedient to a worthy Lord. This kind of servant knows of those things that have lasting significance. Most of all, he or she puts all trust in God, believing that God will reward.

Discovery Learning

This page contains an alternative lesson plan emphasizing learning activities. Classes desiring such student involvement will find these suggestions helpful. The next page is a reproducible activity page to further enhance discovery learning.

LEARNING GOALS

After this lesson, each student will be able to:

1. List the word pictures that Paul uses to describe the ministry of the apostles.

2. Give examples of the demands, costs, and sacrifices often required of faithful stewards.

3. Make a commitment to be a faithful steward in a specific ministry.

INTO THE LESSON

Before class begins, display a sign that says, *Valuable Church Leadership Traits and Qualities.* On a nearby table have painter's tape (so walls and paint are not damaged), paper, and markers.

As class members enter the room, ask each to jot on a sheet of paper one characteristic that he or she values in a church leader. Have students tape their completed papers to the wall around the sign you prepared.

Begin the lesson by telling the class, "Today's study obviously has something to do with church leadership. We've already learned from each other what we value in church leaders." Review the characteristics that students posted on the wall. You may want to ask why some of these traits are significant in church leaders.

Tell the class, "Today we'll discover some unexpected traits and characteristics valued by the apostle Paul." Put up signs with the following words: *hungry and thirsty, rags for clothes, persecuted, slandered and cursed, scum of the earth,* and *servant.* Say, "This is how Paul described himself as an apostle of Christ. While Paul would not belittle the valuable traits in leadership we've already posted, he has something to teach us about church leadership in today's encounter with the Corinthian church."

INTO THE WORD

Activity #1: *A Brief Lecture.* Prepare your lecture from the notes in the lesson Introduction, using the following main points: 1. A Hard Lesson; 2. Lessons Learned; 3. A Lesson to Teach. List the outline on the board as you speak.

Make the transition to activity #2 by saying, "Today's Bible text could be confusing at first glance. We must realize that Paul, while sounding like he is filled with praise for the Corinthian church, occasionally writes with sarcasm and irony. In our last study Paul accused the church of failing to grow up. They were still merely babes feeding on milk. Today's text is not one of praise but is laced with irony."

Activity #2: *Listing and Lessons.* This activity can be done in small groups or completed as a whole class. (This activity can also be found in the student books.)

Prepare handouts (or a visual if the whole class is working together) that have three columns. The left column will have the verse references below. The middle column should have the heading "Paul's Description of Himself." The right column should have the heading "Lessons from Observing the Corinthians."

Students are to look up each verse, determine what the passage teaches about Christian leadership, then write what they learned under the two headings. Discussion ideas are listed below in parentheses. Before work begins, remind students that Paul uses irony and sarcasm in verses 8-12. Allow time for students to share their answers.

Verses for column 1: v. 1a (*servants of Christ*); v. 1b (*those entrusted with the secret things of God*); v. 2 (*faithful*); vv. 3, 4 (*God's judgment matters, not man's*); v. 5 (*be careful in judging leaders*); vv. 6, 7 (*Paul practices what he preaches*); v. 8 (*irony: teaching a false self-sufficiency*); v. 9 (*a spectacle to the world*); v. 10 (*irony: the apostles are fools and weak while the Corinthians are wise and strong*); v. 11 (*hungry, thirsty, naked, persecuted, homeless*); v. 12 (*hard labor, cursed yet blessing the cursers, persecuted*); v. 13 (*defamed, scum of the earth*).

[*Option:* Use one or both activities on the reproducible page as an alternative to Activity #2.]

INTO LIFE

Use one or more of the following as time allows:

Activity #1: Ask the class what additional characteristics of church leaders they would add to the signs created at the beginning of the lesson.

Activity #2: Ask the class for names of church leaders who demonstrate positive qualities listed in the previous activity.

Activity #3: Distribute inexpensive thank-you cards to each student. Ask class members to write an appreciation note to a church leader and mail it this week. Better yet, deliver the note with a homemade dessert!

Scripture Highlights

The Corinthians needed to grow up; they were acting like babies—still feeding on milk (1 Corinthians 3:1, 2). In 1 Corinthians 4 (below), we discover wonderful attributes of church leaders as Paul describes his own experiences. Underline words/phrases that imply a quality of leadership desirable in today's church.

¹So then, men ought to regard us as servants of Christ and as those entrusted with the secret things of God. ²Now it is required that those who have been given a trust must prove faithful. ³I care very little if I am judged by you or by any human court; indeed, I do not even judge myself. ⁴My conscience is clear, but that does not make me innocent. It is the Lord who judges me. ⁵Therefore judge nothing before the appointed time; wait till the Lord comes. He will bring to light what is hidden in darkness and will expose the motives of men's hearts. At that time each will receive his praise from God.

⁶Now, brothers, I have applied these things to myself and Apollos for your benefit, so that you may learn from us the meaning of the saying, "Do not go beyond what is written." Then you will not take pride in one man over against another. ⁷For who makes you different from anyone else? What do you have that you did not receive? And if you did receive it, why do you boast as though you did not?

⁸Already you have all you want! Already you have become rich! You have become kings—and that without us! How I wish that you really had become kings so that we might be kings with you! ⁹For it seems to me that God has put us apostles on display at the end of the procession, like men condemned to die in the arena. We have been made a spectacle to the whole universe, to angels as well as to men. ¹⁰We are fools for Christ, but you are so wise in Christ! We are weak, but you are strong! You are honored, we are dishonored! To this very hour we go hungry and thirsty, we are in rags, we are brutally treated, we are homeless. ¹²We work hard with our own hands. When we are cursed, we bless; when we are persecuted, we endure it; ¹³when we are slandered, we answer kindly. Up to this moment we have become the scum of the earth, the refuse of the world.

Irony and Sarcasm

Verses 8-10 are filled with irony and sarcasm. Paul rebukes the Corinthians for having wrong values and choices, and he contrasts these with the Christlike values and choices of his own life.

1. What values or choices to you think Paul was trying to teach in verse 8?

2. How would you apply verse 9 to leadership in today's church?

3. What is the sarcasm noted in verse 10, and what values does it teach for today's church leader?

CALLED TO RELATIONSHIPS

LESSON 5

WHY TEACH THIS LESSON?

Divorce. Marriage. Sexual activity. These sensitive issues often are avoided by church teachers. Should we talk about marriage when some in our church are single? Can we talk about divorce when people in our class are divorced? May we ever talk about sex without being embarrassed and uncomfortable?

This week's lesson offers the opportunity to address all of these important issues. But we are not being asked to trade opinions and strive for compromise in these areas. Our primary text, 1 Corinthians 7, is the most extensive passage from Paul about marriage, divorce, remarriage, and sexual relations. Paul knew such things needed to be talked about, because the Corinthian church was floundering in these areas. Careful attention to Paul's words will give us solid, biblical principles that help us understand God's will for our lives in these areas.

The timeliness of this lesson should not be ignored. The Corinthian church existed in a city widely known for immorality. Our churches also live within an immorality-exalting society and also need to hear Paul's words.

INTRODUCTION

A. WHAT WOULD YOU DO?

Ray was a godly man faced with a dilemma. He had been a faithful Christian for almost 30 years and was very active in his church. His wife, Susan, had been raised in a Christian home and was also involved in various types of service. Not surprisingly, Ray eventually was asked to consider serving as a deacon, but he was unsure whether to accept the nomination. When Ray accepted Christ, his first wife left him because she was not interested in religion.

Susan, for her part, had divorced her husband after suffering years of mental and physical abuse; he immediately remarried a nonbeliever. Ray and Susan eventually met through a mutual Christian friend, and they have been married for almost 20 years. Many in the church were not even aware that this was a second marriage for both. Yet Ray still was concerned that his divorce could threaten his credibility as an officer of the church.

Valerie also had a problem. She had lived with a man for 10 years, finally marrying him when she became pregnant. But before the child's first birthday, her husband announced that married life was not for him and dissolved the union. She then began to date a coworker who recently was widowed. Soon after their marriage they accepted Christ together. Valerie knew that her past sins were forgiven but remained plagued with doubt as to whether she should accept certain service opportunities in the church.

Situations such as these often are the norm rather than the exception. They bring with them doubt, guilt, and uncertainty. They were all too common in Corinth, a city known throughout the ancient world for sexual immorality. Paul attempted to address such problems by giving the Corinthians clear instructions for sexuality, marriage, divorce, and remarriage.

DEVOTIONAL READING:

1 JOHN 4:7-16

BACKGROUND SCRIPTURE:

1 CORINTHIANS 7

PRINTED TEXT:

1 CORINTHIANS 7:1-15

Jul
2

LESSON AIMS

After participating in this lesson, each student will be able to:

1. Summarize Paul's views on singleness, marriage, and divorce.

2. Give examples of how the secular world rejects Paul's views on marriage and divorce.

3. Use scriptural principles to recommend godly conduct on issues or cases of singleness, marriage, and divorce.

KEY VERSE

I wish that all men were as I am. But each man has his own gift from God; one has this gift, another has that.

—1 Corinthians 7:7

B. LESSON BACKGROUND

As we have seen thus far in our summer lessons, the Corinthian church was troubled with many problems. Paul had received reports of these issues from individuals who visited him (1 Corinthians 1:11). They apparently also had brought a letter from the church to request Paul's insights on certain issues (7:1).

At the time Paul wrote his letter, the church in Corinth was no more than five years old. Given the moral climate within that church (see 1 Corinthians 5:1-11) and in that city, Paul sees the need to discuss at some length godly values about sex and marriage.

I. SEXUAL PURITY (1 CORINTHIANS 7:1, 2)

A. WHAT IS GOOD, PART 1 (v. 1)

1. Now for the matters you wrote about: It is good for a man not to marry.

This statement is apparently a summary answer to a specific question that is not indicated in the text. The phrase *the matters you wrote about* indicates that the Corinthian believers had asked Paul whether Christians ought to be married in the first place. Some religions and philosophies of the time teach that the physical body is inherently evil. They therefore advocate strict abstinence from all physical pleasures, including sex. Or perhaps the Corinthians had asked whether Christians must be married in order to be faithful to Christ.

When Paul states, *It is good for a man not to marry,* is he saying that people who take a vow of chastity are somehow more spiritual? It is important to stress that the word *good* here could be paraphrased "fine" or "OK." Thus it is valid for a person to remain single if he or she wishes—provided, of course, that such a person is not sexually active. Marriage is the norm (Genesis 2:18), but Christians are not obligated to get married.

B. WHAT IS GOOD, PART 2 (v. 2)

2. But since there is so much immorality, each man should have his own wife, and each woman her own husband.

While it's fine to stay single, Paul realizes that most people will seek sexual intimacy. He therefore clarifies two things about God's design for sexuality. First, sex outside of marriage (*immorality*) is wrong. Sex between unwed people is a sin, and marriage is God's solution. Being single is fine as long as one can control sexual desires and avoid sexual temptation. Paul's second clarification is in the verse that follows.

II. SHARED OWNERSHIP (1 CORINTHIANS 7:3-5)

A. DUTY TO FULFILL (v. 3)

3. The husband should fulfill his marital duty to his wife, and likewise the wife to her husband.

Paul now describes the sexual responsibilities inherent in marriage. Sex between married partners is not simply for reproduction. The desire for sexual intimacy with a spouse is a natural and important aspect of marriage, even when it does not result in childbirth.

The idea of fulfilling one's *marital duty* is one of obligation or, some would say, responsibility. In cultures where sexual immorality is rampant, a Christian should protect his or her spouse from temptation by fulfilling the partner's reasonable desires and needs. It should go without saying that a Christian should be sensitive to his or her spouse's needs and should not use sexual intimacy as a bargaining chip or a reward. Such conduct can ruin the marriage.

WHAT DO YOU THINK?

What are some cultural factors that make it difficult for us to maintain and demonstrate sexual purity? How do we guard against these?

B. TEMPTATION TO AVOID (vv. 4, 5)

4. The wife's body does not belong to her alone but also to her husband. In the same way, the husband's body does not belong to him alone but also to his wife.

Verse 4 emphasizes the point in verse 3 by appealing to the principle of Genesis 2:24: husband and wife are united as one flesh in a bond. The mutual nature of Paul's remarks is encouraging, for in the ancient world women typically are viewed as the property of their husbands, with few rights.

The stress of mutual "ownership" in the marriage relationship should not be taken as a license to be insensitive or inconsiderate. The larger context of Paul's teachings simply won't allow that idea. That larger context speaks of the need to show respect to all, especially members of one's family. If one's spouse is ill or burdened temporarily with stress, it should be assumed that sexual expectations will be set aside for a time. Further, a spouse's legal rights are to be respected because we are bound to obey the laws of the land (Romans 13:1-7). A spouse is not to be forced into unwanted sexual contact.

5. Do not deprive each other except by mutual consent and for a time, so that you may devote yourselves to prayer. Then come together again so that Satan will not tempt you because of your lack of self-control.

In some cases, however, a couple may voluntarily choose to refrain from sexual contact. Such periods must be by mutual agreement and for spiritual purposes. Caution: one cannot use spiritual concerns as an excuse to withhold sexual intimacy, especially in cases where this would tempt the spouse to be unfaithful.

III. STAYING SINGLE (1 CORINTHIANS 7:6-9)

A. SINGLENESS AS A CHOICE (v. 6)

6. I say this as a concession, not as a command.

This verse presents us with a slight problem: does the word *this* refer to what Paul has just finished saying, or does it refer to what he's about to say next? The context of permission, and not of commandment makes us think that it's what Paul is about to say next regarding the choice to remain single. Sexual intimacy in marriage is expected. But whether or not one gets married in the first place is a matter of personal choice. Paul therefore offers the following comments as good advice, not as an absolute rule that every person must follow.

B. SINGLE LIKE PAUL (vv. 7, 8)

7a. I wish that all men were as I am.

Very little is known about Paul's pre-Christian life. We are not certain if Paul was ever married, but verses 7, 8 inform us that he is single at the time he writes this letter (see also 1 Corinthians 9:5). The fact that he is not responsible for a wife and children allows him greater freedom to pursue his ministry.

NO SIN IN SINGLE

Remember the old "Pairs and Spares" Sunday school class name? We should thank the Lord that the insensitive viewpoint expressed by such a designation is largely behind us! Scripture does not consider singleness to be a sin or something that must be "corrected." For those who can resist the sin of fornication, singleness is even praised in the New Testament.

Churches must find ways to minister effectively to singles. Churches should also open doors of opportunities for singles to be involved in the ministry of the church. Both imperatives require churches to be sensitive to the special circumstances in which singles sometimes find themselves. On the occasion of a Christmas dinner

Visual for Lesson 5. *Refer again to this quarter's outline to remind your students of the multi-faceted nature of the church.*

WHAT DO YOU THINK?

Paul makes it clear that single people are whole persons. What are some ways we can affirm unmarried adults in our churches?

in a nice restaurant, a married man sitting next to a single woman suggested that she was better off than others at this meal since she had to pay only for one. She quickly replied, "Yes, but I have only one income."

Does your church have a deliberate, intentional plan for singles? Or do your church's ministries to and by singles happen pretty much "by accident"? There is no sin in singleness, but there is sin in ignoring this group.   —A. E. A.

7b, 8. But each man has his own gift from God; one has this gift, another has that. Now to the unmarried and the widows I say: It is good for them to stay unmarried, as I am.

Later Paul will say that believers should serve Christ as well as they can in whatever situation they find themselves (1 Corinthians 7:17-24). Viewed from this perspective, singleness and marriage are both gifts of God, opportunities for service.

Those who are single therefore should not feel like second-class citizens. They should not rush into a marriage just because they think that that's what "normal" people do. Paul apparently does not feel compelled to find a wife, even though almost all Jewish men in his culture have families. If you can best serve God by remaining single and celibate, then don't get married.

C. SELF-CONTROL (v. 9)

9. But if they cannot control themselves, they should marry, for it is better to marry than to burn with passion.

This verse refers to controlling one's sexual desires. Some may wish, like Paul, to remain single. Paul advises them to try that lifestyle for a time and see if it suits them; if sexual desires become a distraction or threaten to lead one into sin, then get married.

Singleness may open distinct opportunities for service. But if sexual temptation is too much of a distraction, then singleness becomes counterproductive. This same philosophy underlies Paul's remarks in 1 Timothy 5:9-15.

IV. TILL DEATH DO US PART (1 CORINTHIANS 7:10-15)

A. GOD'S IDEAL (vv. 10, 11)

10. To the married I give this command (not I, but the Lord): A wife must not separate from her husband.

Paul now turns from the situation of the single believer to that of the married Christian. The Corinthians are apparently uncertain about godly standards for divorce and remarriage. As in our culture, divorce is common in the ancient world. Paul's general rule for divorce is simply this: don't do it.

Not I, but the Lord means that Paul is referring back to something that Jesus said about this issue, probably the teaching in Matthew 5:27-32 or 19:3-9 (or both). Jesus taught that husband and wife are joined together by God. As such, divorce must always be the very last option in marital difficulty. God hates divorce (Malachi 2:16).

Paul also undoubtedly supports Jesus' conclusion that divorce is permissible in cases where one's spouse is guilty of adultery (note: permissible, not required). But since the situation under consideration in these verses does not involve adultery, Paul states the general rule without mentioning Jesus' exception clause.

11. But if she does, she must remain unmarried or else be reconciled to her husband. And a husband must not divorce his wife.

WHAT DO YOU THINK?

What are some benefits and dangers of discussing sexual matters as openly as Paul does in this passage?

HOW TO SAY IT

Corinth. KOR-inth.
Corinthians. Ko-RIN-thee-unz.
Deuteronomy. Due-ter-AHN-uh-me.
fornication. for-neh-KAY-shun.
Malachi. MAL-uh-kye.
Mosaic. Mo-ZAY-ik.

Paul seems to be touching on a loophole in the Mosaic law about divorce that Jesus also anticipated. Jesus notes in Matthew 5:31 that someone theoretically could get divorced and remarried just to avoid adultery—simply *divorce* your current wife, following Deuteronomy 24:1-4, and then marry the other woman whom you now desire.

To avoid this problem both Jesus and Paul insist that the divorced person must not remarry. In other words, you cannot divorce your wife and then marry another just so that you can fulfill your sexual desires, even though this technically would avoid the sin of adultery (because you did not have sex with the other person before the divorce).

B. OUR RESPONSIBILITIES (vv. 12, 13)

12. To the rest I say this (I, not the Lord): If any brother has a wife who is not a believer and she is willing to live with him, he must not divorce her.

I, not the Lord means that Paul now is going to extend Jesus' principle about divorce to a situation where a believer is married to an unbeliever. In cities such as Corinth, people would often accept Christ whether their spouses did or not. This means that many Christians were married to people who continued in pagan beliefs and lifestyles.

One might point to Paul's teaching that believers should not be unequally yoked (2 Corinthians 6:14) in order to justify the divorce of an unbelieving spouse and getting remarried to a member of the church. While this would be a more reasonable grounds for divorce than mere lust, it still violates the basic integrity of marriage. Marriage is an institution that is ordained by God even when the marriage partners do not believe in him.

13. And if a woman has a husband who is not a believer and he is willing to live with her, she must not divorce him.

The fact that one's husband does not go to church is not sufficient grounds for divorce. In verse 16 (not in today's text), Paul urges Christians who are married to nonbelievers to view their situations as opportunities for evangelism. It is hard to imagine that a man would accept Christ after his wife had left him due to his lack of faith. Paul hopes that over time the witness of a godly wife will gradually win her husband.

C. SANCTIFIED HOMES (v. 14)

14. For the unbelieving husband has been sanctified through his wife, and the unbelieving wife has been sanctified through her believing husband. Otherwise your children would be unclean, but as it is, they are holy.

Paul's remarks about *the unbelieving husband* being *sanctified* by the *wife* reflect the purity language of the Old Testament. The Christian may feel that the unbelieving spouse's influence is unhealthy, leaving her unholy in God's sight. She may fear that her husband's evil influence will corrupt her and her *children*, providing just grounds for divorce.

But Paul argues that the presence of the believer will sanctify the household; the believer's influence should pervade the home (compare Romans 11:16). God will not judge the children by the father's unfaithfulness but will rather bless them through their mother's faith.

One may be concerned legitimately about the moral influence of an unbelieving spouse on the family. Yet the fact that an unbeliever presents a threat of moral corruption is not grounds for divorce. It simply means that the believer will have to work that much harder to create a Christian atmosphere in the home.

WHAT DO YOU THINK?

Many people, including some believers, think that Paul's teaching about divorce is outdated and irrelevant. How do you respond?

DAILY BIBLE READINGS

Monday, June 26—God Is Love (1 John 4:7-16)

Tuesday, June 27—Instructions for Husbands and Wives (1 Corinthians 7:1-5)

Wednesday, June 28—Advice to the Unmarried and Widows (1 Corinthians 7:6-11)

Thursday, June 29—An Unbelieving Spouse (1 Corinthians 7:12-16)

Friday, June 30—Live as God Called You (1 Corinthians 7:17-24)

Saturday, July 1—Remain as You Are (1 Corinthians 7:25-31)

Sunday, July 2—Unhindered Devotion to the Lord (1 Corinthians 7:32-40)

Lord, we live in a world full of temptations. It is a world where sexual sin and divorce are rampant. Please give us strength to resist sin with our bodies and our minds. Help us preserve our homes and our marriages as godly witnesses to your power and grace. In Jesus' name, amen.

WHAT DO YOU THINK?

What are some specific ways we can ease the burden on those in our congregations who are married to unbelieving spouses?

THOUGHT TO REMEMBER

Don't ruin your relationship with God by ignoring his rules on human relationships.

While Paul hopes that a believing spouse eventually can lead an unbelieving partner to faith, he clearly does not think that the believing partner's faith can save the nonbeliever. Such an interpretation would be entirely inconsistent with Paul's emphasis elsewhere on personal acceptance of God's grace.

MY MISSION, MY MATE

Leslie's wife became a Christian. She desired nothing more than to see her husband come to Christ as well. But Leslie was more involved in things he enjoyed, and church was not one of those things.

Leslie's wife sought to live out a life of faith before her husband. A small group would gather weekly with Leslie's wife to pray for his salvation. Over time Leslie's resistance to the gospel melted away. He became a Christian.

Mac and Jane, a married couple, were both seeking the Lord. They attended church where they heard many sermons and lessons. They participated in home Bible studies as well. Each waited for the other to make the first move.

One Sunday evening during a closing song of commitment, Mac decided it was time to go forward to proclaim to the congregation his desire to commit his life to Christ. Jane was looking at the words in the hymnal, so she did not see Mac go forward. When she looked up and saw Mac standing with the preacher at the front of the auditorium, she stepped out to join her husband. Together they committed their lives to Christ.

Do you have a mate who needs the master? If so, make it your mission to be that influence personally. If you are not in this situation but know someone who is, make a commitment to be a prayer warrior on his or her behalf.   —A. E. A.

D. NOT UNDER BONDAGE (v. 15)

15. But if the unbeliever leaves, let him do so. A believing man or woman is not bound in such circumstances; God has called us to live in peace.

Paul's reference to being not under bondage means that we are not responsible for another person's actions. Just as the unbelieving spouse cannot be saved by the faith of the believer, the believer is not responsible if the unbeliever seeks a divorce on his or her own initiative. In this instance, the believer is free to remarry a Christian if desired.

CONCLUSION

In considering divorce or remarriage, it is important to avoid two extremes. On the one hand, some act as though divorce were the unpardonable sin. There are, in fact, biblical provisions for divorce and remarriage. On the other hand, the fact that Jesus and Paul allow for divorce in some circumstances does not mean that the church can take a lax posture toward that practice. Solid marriages and families are the backbone of a stable society. The church always must protect the integrity and sanctity of marriage as an institution and must denounce every form of sexual sin.

It is also critically important to remember that God forgives through the grace that is available to us through the blood of Jesus. In today's society most people are sexually active before marriage—indeed, before they finish high school. Thus most members of any given congregation have been guilty at some point of sexual immorality. Further, many are divorced, some more than once. Yet sins are erased when we embrace Jesus as Savior. God is not concerned about what we used to do when we were sinners; he is concerned about how we use our bodies now.

Discovery Learning

This page contains an alternative lesson plan emphasizing learning activities. Classes desiring such student involvement will find these suggestions helpful. The next page is a reproducible activity page to further enhance discovery learning.

LEARNING GOALS

After participating in this lesson, each student will be able to:

1. Summarize Paul's views on singleness, marriage, and divorce.

2. Give examples of how the secular world rejects Paul's views on marriage and divorce.

3. Use scriptural principles to recommend godly conduct on issues or cases of singleness, marriage, and divorce.

INTO THE LESSON

Begin by relating this real-life situation: Rex is a 32-year-old single man. He has grown up in the church and has been active in many roles. He now plays drums for the worship band. However, Rex has been disappointed that he's never been asked to serve in any leadership roles. While his married friends are asked to serve on committees and as ministry leaders, Rex is never approached. He knows his singleness has somehow kept church leaders from viewing him as a mature individual.

Assuming that you are able to interact only with Rex and not his church's leadership, what counsel would you offer? Would "giving advice" be appropriate, or should you stick to being a sympathetic listener? Why?

After a bit of discussion, make the transition to the Bible study by saying, "Singleness is an important issue of today's church. In addition to issues of singleness and marriage, Christians wrestle with the ethics of sexuality, divorce, remarriage, and more. Paul speaks to these issues when writing to the Corinthian church."

INTO THE WORD

Introduce the Bible study by sharing information with your class from the Lesson Background. Be sure to stress the loose sexual standards of Corinth.

Read aloud the printed text. Then divide the class into groups of three to five. Provide each group a prepared copy of the work sheet below. (Alternative: use the "Issues" activity, which is worded somewhat differently, from the reproducible page instead.) Assign each group one of the issues on the work sheet. (Larger classes will have two or more groups working on the same issue.) After groups have finished working, allow each to report its conclusions.

Work sheet: Issues of Sexuality and Marriage

Read the text and jot down some notes about Paul's teaching on the following topics.

Group #1: *Singleness* (1 Corinthians 7:1, 2, 6-9)
  Paul's preferences:
  Sexual practices:
  The widowed:
  How the world rejects these views:

Group #2: *Divorce for Christians* (7:10-15)
  Paul's general rule for divorce:
  After divorce:
  Divorce and an unbelieving spouse:
  Explain verse 14:
  How the world rejects these views:

Group #3: *Marriage for Christians* (7:2, 3-5, 9)
  Some reasons to marry:
  Sexual responsibilities in marriage:
  How the world rejects these views:

INTO LIFE

With students still in their small groups, assign each group one of the scenarios below that you have written out ahead of time. Allow time at the end for groups to share their responses.

Bill and Bev have been married four years. Bill is a believer. Bev is not a Christian and has become increasingly hostile to Bill's faith. Bill has come to you for counsel. He says Bev has threatened to leave him if he continues in what she calls "religious nonsense." How do you respond? How would you know if you needed to refer Bill to someone with more spiritual insight?

Jim and Jean have been living together for two years. They've begun attending your church and want to get married. But the church policy states that couples cannot be living together if they want to have a church wedding. Jim and Jean have come to you wanting to talk about the church's policy and what the Bible says about all this. What would you tell them?

Sue is married to Fred. Both are Christians, but Fred has become sexually abusive. Sue suspects that Fred is involved with pornography. Another Christian tells her that needs to be submissive to her husband. Her counselor says that she needs to leave him. Sue wants your opinion. What do you say? (Follow with the "Letting God Speak" activity from the next page, time permitting.)

Issues in Sexuality and Marriage

Today's Christians wrestle with many of the same issues as those in the Corinthian church. Like Corinth, our society is one of loose sexual standards. In order to be faithful to God, we need to know his standards, live by those standards, and be ready to pass those standards on to others. Read 1 Corinthians 7:1-15 and jot down notes about Paul's teaching on the following topics.

Issue #1: Singleness (1 Corinthians 7:1, 2, 6-9)

Paul's preferences:

Cultural attitudes, then and now:

The widowed:

Singleness and church leadership:

Issue #2: Divorce for Christians (1 Corinthians 7:10-15)

Jesus' rule for divorce:

Paul's rule for divorce:

After divorce:

Explain verse 14:

Issue #3: Marriage for Christians (1 Corinthians 7:2, 3-5, 9)

Some reasons to marry:

Sexual responsibilities within marriage:

Letting God Speak to Me

What one thought about any of the above topics has grabbed your heart today? Why?

- _____
- _____
- _____
- _____

CALLED TO HELP THE WEAK

LESSON 6

WHY TEACH THIS LESSON?

"The church must hold firm on traditional moral values." "Legalism restricts the growth of the church." Extremes of these two statements are found in some churches. Controversies still abound over the permissibility of alcohol, tobacco, dancing, gambling, or watching movies—not to mention body piercing! Some demand the church teach clearly what is right and wrong in these areas. Others desire more leeway, citing the value of freedom in Christ. This is most difficult when considering practices unknown in the ancient world and therefore not specifically addressed in the Bible.

The Corinthian church also suffered from the tension between legalism and liberty. Their question of eating meat that had been sacrificed at a pagan temple is unlikely to be a raging issue in your church. But the principles Paul uses to guide his instructions are still valid. The bottom line is that *we are not free to make choices that might hurt another person's faith.* This lesson lays out foundational principles that will guide our decisions in this regard.

INTRODUCTION

A. TO EAT OR NOT TO EAT?

Not long ago I was talking to a friend in my office, and we decided to go out for lunch together. On the way to the restaurant, he told me about a movie he had seen recently. While I did not say anything to him, I was somewhat surprised by his taste in films and by the frankness of his discussion. I had not seen the movie he mentioned. But I knew from the advertisements and his description that it included scenes that I would consider sexually inappropriate.

As he spoke, I reflected on my own standards for evaluating such issues. I avoid movies with explicit sex scenes but have no difficulty watching films with graphic violence or profanity, because such things do not tempt me. I also generally do not see R-rated films in movie theaters but occasionally watch them on video or cable television at home.

As I thought about my own inconsistencies and my friend's taste in movies, we arrived at the restaurant. I was in the mood for Chinese food, but he hesitated. He explained that he had been involved deeply in Eastern religions before accepting Christ. The owner of this restaurant displayed statues of Asian gods in the front of the store. He even set out fruits as symbolic offerings to these deities for luck. My friend wondered if I would mind eating somewhere else. He suggested a place where he knew they had specials on draft beer at lunch.

Moral issues relating to drinking in moderation, smoking, dancing, movies, television programs, and styles of clothing are especially difficult simply because there is no precise, clear biblical teaching about the right thing to do in these specific areas. Each individual must therefore make a personal choice as to whether or not he or she may participate. A major "gray area" in Paul's time was eating food that had been sacrificed to idols.

DEVOTIONAL READING
MARK 9:42-48
BACKGROUND SCRIPTURE
1 CORINTHIANS 8:1-13
PRINTED TEXT
1 CORINTHIANS 8:1-13

LESSON AIMS

After participating in this lesson, each student will be able to:

1. Restate the reasons that Paul gives for eating or not eating meat sacrificed to idols.

2. Propose one modern parallel to the first-century issue of eating meat sacrificed to idols.

3. State how he or she has made a sacrifice of personal liberties for the sake of another, or state an area in which he or she will do so in the immediate future.

Jul
9

KEY VERSE

Food does not bring us near to God; we are no worse if we do not eat, and no better if we do. Be careful, however, that the exercise of your freedom does not become a stumbling block to the weak.
—1 Corinthians 8:8, 9

B. LESSON BACKGROUND

As in Judaism, animal sacrifices were a key feature of most pagan religions in the ancient world. Worshipers typically would bring goats, bulls, doves, or other animals to the pagan priest. These animals would be killed and offered to the deity to appease his anger or in thanksgiving for some blessing.

In most cases, however, only a portion of the animal actually was burned on the altar. For example, the Law of Moses prescribed that priests could keep the hides from burnt offerings and a portion of the ground meal from grain offerings (Leviticus 7:7-10). The pagan religions had similar stipulations that allowed their "priests" to eat or sell the leftover meat. In large cities such as Corinth, it was common for pagan temples to run butcher shops to sell excess meat.

This created an awkward situation for some newer Christians. Those who had come out of Judaism may view such meat as unholy because of its association with pagan religions; for those Christians who once had been pagans themselves, the food may bring back memories of the old way of life. On the other hand older, more mature Christians who were no longer committed to the Jewish kosher laws or who had not been involved in paganism for many years may have no scruples at all about eating this meat. In fact they might even bring a plate of such meat straight from the butcher shop at the temple of Isis to a church dinner, bragging about the bargain they got.

At least some of the Corinthians apparently were uncertain of how to handle this issue. Perhaps they were aware of the letter of the Jerusalem church to the church at Antioch that encouraged abstaining from eating food that had been sacrificed to idols (Acts 15:29). Whether or not they were aware of that letter, Paul used their concern to lay down principles for respect and sensitivity as befitting Christians.

I. PROBLEM: WRONG EMPHASIS (1 CORINTHIANS 8:1-3)

A. LOVE VS. ARROGANCE (v. 1)

1. Now about food sacrificed to idols: We know that we all possess knowledge. Knowledge puffs up, but love builds up.

Paul begins by establishing some common ground: *we know that we all possess knowledge.* Who could disagree with that? Part of this knowledge for believers is that there is only one God; thus idols are nothing (more on this below).

The real issue is in the attitude that Christians adopt toward one another. Some could justify their decision to eat *food sacrificed to idols* through elaborate theological arguments. "Being right" can thus become more important than being sensitive to another person's conscience. Knowledge, Paul says, tends to breed arrogance unless it is checked by a genuine *love* that seeks to build up and edify others.

B. KNOWLEDGE VS. IGNORANCE (v. 2)

2. The man who thinks he knows something does not yet know as he ought to know.

Obviously, Paul is not indifferent to sound doctrine. He does not mean that what one believes or thinks is of no importance. The issue here is not the content of someone's knowledge ("what they know"). Rather, the issue is what Christians do with that knowledge.

Some may use their intellect to justify personal actions or to disregard others. A person who travels this path may indeed know a great deal of abstract theology while not understanding a basic teaching of the Christian faith: the need to love one's neighbor as oneself (Leviticus 19:18; Matthew 22:39; 1 Corinthians

WHAT DO YOU THINK?

What are some "gray area" issues that currently create struggles for Christians? How are these similar to or different from those listed in the lesson Introduction?

WHAT DO YOU THINK?

How can we show respect and love for those whose opinions differ from ours in areas related to Christian behavior? How can we keep people from manipulating church policy through suspicious claims of having a weak conscience?

10:24). Truly wise people exercise humility, aware of all the things that they don't understand (compare Galatians 6:3).

C. LOVE AND KNOWLEDGE OF GOD (v. 3)
3. But the man who loves God is known by God.

We rightly emphasize knowing Bible facts, but knowing those facts should lead to a greater goal: to love God with every fiber of our being (Matthew 22:37). This is a proper response to God, who knows us and recognizes as his children (compare Galatians 4:7, 9). To love God is the most important commandment; the second most important commandment is love of neighbor (Matthew 22:38, 39). If the "knowledge" that the Corinthians have is not leading them in this path, then they need a change in course!

II. GROUNDWORK: TRUE GOD (1 CORINTHIANS 8:4-6)
A. MANY "GODS" AND "LORDS" (vv. 4, 5)
4, 5. So then, about eating food sacrificed to idols: We know that an idol is nothing at all in the world and that there is no God but one. For even if there are so-called gods, whether in heaven or on earth (as indeed there are many "gods" and many "lords"),

With the problem of "knowledge over love" clearly identified, Paul proceeds to lay a groundwork for a solution. He noted in verse 1 that there are certain things about which "we all have knowledge." One of those things is that *idols* do indeed exist as physical objects. Every house and street in Corinth is full of them, just as our world today is filled with material objects of misplaced devotion. In this sense the Corinthians are familiar with idols and shrines representing *many "gods" and many "lords"*—Apollo, Zeus, Dionysius, Isis, just to name a few.

Yet all worship of these amounts to nothing because these "gods" do not, in fact, have any existence beyond their representations in wood, stone, etc. (compare Isaiah 44:6-20). The basic fact that there is *no God but one* should be the starting point for any discussion about idolatry. Paul's acknowledgment reflects the truth of Deuteronomy 4:35, 39; 6:4.

B. ONE GOD AND LORD (v. 6)
6. . . . yet for us there is but one God, the Father, from whom all things came and for whom we live; and there is but one Lord, Jesus Christ, through whom all things came and through whom we live.

The *one God* truth of verse 4 now receives fuller expression. The verse before us is based on the formula, "one/all, we/him." While people may make many idols, in truth there is only one God; he is the creator of all things in the universe. While people may serve many false deities, there is only *one Lord,* the *Christ* who sustains all things in the universe. Because this is the case, we know that we exist and receive salvation only in him and by him.

While verses 4-6 expose the lie of idolatry, they also underline the very point under debate in the Corinthian church. Some believers, whom we can call *Group #1,* can appeal to such knowledge to argue that there can't be any harm in eating food from the altar of idols since pagan gods don't exist in the first place. But others, whom we can call *Group #2,* can point to Deuteronomy 4:35, 39; 6:4 to argue that any participation in or financial support of paganism (through food that is bought with money) represents support of idolatry. Therefore it should be avoided at all costs. This group may consist of the Corinthian Jews who became Christians (Acts 18:4, 8). Our next verse may reveal a third group.

WHAT DO YOU THINK?
How should increased knowledge of Scripture make us ever more humble?

WHAT DO YOU THINK?
What are some ways the spiritual climate of Corinth is paralleled in modern society? Why is it important to draw those parallels?

HOW TO SAY IT
Apollo. Uh-PAH-low.
Corinth. KOR-inth.
Corinthians. Ko-RIN-thee-unz.
Dionysius. Die-oh-NISH-ih-us.
Isaiah. Eye-ZAY-uh.
Leviticus. Leh-VIT-ih-kus.
Zeus. Zoose.

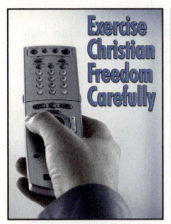

Visual for Lesson 6. *This image is a starting point for the question, "How can freedom get us into spiritual trouble?"*

WHAT DO YOU THINK?

What are some ways to train the conscience so that its prompting is in harmony with God's desires?

III. SOLUTION: TEMPERED FREEDOM (1 CORINTHIANS 8:7-13)

A. WEAKNESS OF CONSCIENCE (v. 7)

7. But not everyone knows this. Some people are still so accustomed to idols that when they eat such food they think of it as having been sacrificed to an idol, and since their conscience is weak, it is defiled.

We sketched two groups at Corinth in considering verse 6. Both groups realize that idols are nothing. But here in verse 7, the phrase *but not everyone knows this* may introduce us to *Group #3*. This group would consist of newer Gentile members of the church who are fresh out of paganism. (Note that Paul identifies at least four groups in 1 Corinthians 1:12.) This particular group would be on the verge of confusion when they see others eat this food. Those in Group #3 have learned the basics that there is one God and Lord. But their memories are still vivid regarding all the other "gods" and "lords" that they used to worship. In this way their *conscience is weak* and *defiled*.

Some students think, however, that Paul is still speaking about Group #2. Under this theory this group remains very conscious of the fact that this food was once the property of *an idol*, despite their understanding of Deuteronomy 4:35, 39; 6:4. Their knowledge of the truth of those verses has not yet penetrated into their conscience. For some reason they still feel bad about eating this *food*, even though they know that other gods don't really exist. If this theory is true, it means that their conscience is weak in the sense that their feelings of right and wrong have not yet come fully into line with their knowledge of God's truth. Thus they feel guilty even about something that they are free to do.

Whichever group Paul is thinking about, we must remember that our conscience does not carry an authority comparable to God's Word. Nevertheless, it is definitely not a good idea to get into the habit of doing things that we feel are wrong, even if we cannot explain logically what is wrong with them (see Romans 14:23). When a person feels bad about something that is not specifically forbidden in the Bible, his or her conscience is defiled in some way (Romans 14:14).

B. MATTERS OF OPINION (v. 8)

8. But food does not bring us near to God; we are no worse if we do not eat, and no better if we do.

Paul places the question of eating *food* sacrificed to idols in the category of "matters of opinion." What we *eat* or don't eat doesn't inherently affect our relationship *to God*. Jesus said that nothing that goes into our mouths can make us unclean, because purity is a matter of the heart (Mark 7:17-23).

Theoretically, then, the food makes no difference in and of itself. Some would see this as parallel to modern concerns about moderate consumption of alcoholic beverages, clothing styles, body piercing, etc. But it is important to stress both sides of Paul's argument: such activities don't necessarily hurt our faith, but they don't necessarily help it either. We therefore decide whether or not to participate on the basis of other factors. Those other factors include the long-term effects on us or other people.

C. EXERCISE OF CONSCIENCE (vv. 9-11)

9. Be careful, however, that the exercise of your freedom does not become a stumbling block to the weak.

This verse is a major thesis statement in this letter. Because eating food that has been offered to idols is not specifically sinful, Christians have *freedom* to decide whether they will eat it or not. We do not, however, have freedom to do things that may cause other people to go off track in their faith. If eating food cannot make my faith stronger (v. 8) but may make someone else's faith weaker, then it's best to choose not to do it.

The opening words *be careful* show us the consideration that a mature Christian should show in this regard. Our carefulness does not mean, however, that we are enslaved to another person's sensitivities. Later Paul will note that his own freedom should not be subject to the judgment of another person's conscience (1 Corinthians 10:29, 30).

This would be especially true of matters of conscience that have no real biblical basis. At some point the weaker brother or sister must simply grow up in the faith, bringing his or her conscience into line with the facts of Christian freedom. In fact the veteran Christian's example may save the rookie believer from legalism. The mature believer is not obligated to live by another person's sensitivities and may do as he or she pleases as long as personal actions do not harm another (see also Romans 14:13, 15, 21; Galatians 5:13).

FREEDOM ISN'T FREE

Those of us who grew up in Western democracies undoubtedly remember singing all those patriotic songs from childhood. Those songs often echoed a common theme: the value and cost of freedom. We know that free nations do not achieve their freedom easily. Wars were fought. Our spiritual, eternal freedom also came at a high cost: the death of the Son of God.

Most everyone also knows that the existence of democratic liberties does not mean we have absolute freedom to do just anything we wish. How many children cannot wait until that eighteenth birthday, graduation, or departure for college as they ponder the freedom they think they will have! Eventually, that young adult realizes that this freedom has continuing price tags attached. One of those tags is lawful behavior.

Spiritual liberty also has continuing price tags, as 1 Corinthians 8:9 demonstrates. Also vital is Galatians 5:13: "You . . . were called to be free. But do not use your freedom to indulge the sinful nature; rather, serve one another in love." Considering the price that Christ paid, is what he asks really so burdensome?—A. E. A.

10. For if anyone with a weak conscience sees you who have this knowledge eating in an idol's temple, won't he be emboldened to eat what has been sacrificed to idols?

Paul touches on the responsibility that the more mature believers have for setting a good example. While each person is responsible for his or her own actions, the newer Christian may not be in a position to make the best decision or to understand the implications of the decision.

Eating in an idol's temple probably refers to a banquet at a pagan shrine. This is a typical practice of the time, similar to an American business meeting at a local civic club. The mature Christian may freely accept an invitation to such a feast and may even see it as an occasion to evangelize. But the potential gain of such a choice is offset by a greater loss if it leads a weaker, less astute person to conclude that the other Christian is endorsing idolatry.

11. So this weak brother, for whom Christ died, is destroyed by your knowledge.

Paul returns to the theme introduced at the beginning. The mature Christian knows that idols represent fictitious gods. But can that Christian really say that he or she understands what is most important when doing something that does not show love for a *weak brother*? If *Christ* was willing to die for this person's salvation, is it too much of a sacrifice for you to choose not to eat a piece of meat to help that same person's faith?

WHAT DO YOU THINK?

How can we demonstrate a commitment to the spiritual health of others without becoming completely controlled by another person's weakness of conscience?

DAILY BIBLE READINGS

Monday, July 3—Called to Life and Light (John 1:1-5)

Tuesday, July 4—Do Not Tempt Others (Mark 9:42-48)

Wednesday, July 5—Love Your Neighbor As Yourself (Mark 12:28-34)

Thursday, July 6—Do Not Make Another Stumble (Romans 14:13-19)

Friday, July 7—We Have One God, One Lord (1 Corinthians 8:1-6)

Saturday, July 8—Do Not Create a Stumbling Block (1 Corinthians 8:7-13)

Sunday, July 9—Do All to God's Glory (1 Corinthians 10:23–11:1)

PRAYER

Lord, please give us compassionate hearts. Help us to be sensitive to the conscience of others, and help us to help them remain faithful to you. Please open our eyes to the truth of your Word, so that our conscience will reflect your perfect will for our lives. In Jesus' name, amen.

D. RESTRICTION OF FREEDOM (vv. 12, 13)

12. When you sin against your brothers in this way and wound their weak conscience, you sin against Christ.

This statement is the flip side of Matthew 25:40. There Jesus says that anything we do "for one of the least" of his followers is done for him. In a similar way, anything we do that hurts one of the *brothers* having a weak conscience is a sin against Christ. This error shows that we have violated Jesus' new commandment: "As I have loved you, so you must love one another" (John 13:34). When spiritual pride clouds our thinking about what is ultimately right and wrong, then we prove that we "[do] not yet know as [we] ought to know" (1 Corinthians 8:2, above).

13. Therefore, if what I eat causes my brother to fall into sin, I will never eat meat again, so that I will not cause him to fall.

Paul's conclusion is clear, both here and in Romans 14:21: If it's a matter of choice, choose to do what will help the other person. This may mean that I will abstain from eating meat or watching certain movies for as long as necessary. But isn't that a small price to pay to honor Christ?

OFFENDED, UNCOMFORTABLE, OR . . . ?

I do not care for tattoos. Yet my two adult daughters each have one. My son-in-law has more than one. Does that offend me? No. Do I have a weak conscience in this area that makes tattoos a stumbling block to me? No. They do not even make me as uncomfortable as they used to. A flower painted on a foot, a dolphin painted on the back, or a cross painted on the leg do not violate Leviticus 19:28. Those tattoos do nothing to undermine my faith in Christ or my love for my family members who choose to have them.

But you may be different. You may find tattoos, certain kinds of music, etc., to be offensive when I do not. But let's keep our terminology straight: what is "offensive" is not necessarily a "stumbling block" that is traced to a weak conscience. And your discomfort may be the price you pay when someone else is being ministered to by music you don't like.

There are doctrinal lines that should never be crossed. Then there are issues of preference that may be crossed freely as long as they don't lead to sin. It is important to learn the difference. As we do, we also remember to practice the grace of humility and kindness. The gospel will move forward in unexpected ways when we do.
—A. E. A.

CONCLUSION

In applying this passage to our lives, it is important to stress the type of situation that Paul has in mind. He is not thinking of differences of opinion over comparatively minor issues between two mature Christians. Paul's extreme statement "if what I eat causes my brother to fall into sin, I will never eat meat again" in verse 13 pertains to situations where a person's conscience is jeopardized by our actions, leading him or her to question personal faith and possibly abandon it in confusion.

Every person is responsible for his or her own actions before God, and we are responsible only to God, not to the consciences of other people. At the same time, however, we must remember that love for others and considering the results of our behavior are our responsibilities (compare Luke 17:1). The key issue is not whether we are "right" in questions of Christian liberty; the key issue, rather, is the attitude we exhibit toward others who do not share our views.

THOUGHT TO REMEMBER

My freedom takes a back seat to others' faith.

Discovery Learning

*This page contains an alternative lesson plan emphasizing learning activities. Classes
desiring such student involvement will find these suggestions helpful. The next page
is a reproducible activity page to further enhance discovery learning.*

LEARNING GOALS

After this lesson, each student will be able to:

1. Restate the reasons that Paul gives for eating or not eating meat sacrificed to idols.

2. Propose one modern parallel to the first-century issue of eating meat sacrificed to idols.

3. State how he or she has made a sacrifice of personal liberties for the sake of another, or state an area in which he or she will do so in the immediate future.

INTO THE LESSON

Open the class by reading the illustration "To Eat or Not to Eat?" given in the Introduction of the lesson commentary. Pass out paper and pens and say, "Let's take a sampling of the different views from within our own group. Write *agree* or *disagree* to each of the following statements:"

I will not allow alcohol to be served at events I host.

I have beer in my refrigerator.

I am offended if I see a Christian smoking.

I go to R-rated movies but hope my minister doesn't see me there.

Ask why there are different answers to the above statements. Then transition to Bible study by saying, "We are not the only believers in who have struggled with the 'gray areas' of Christian behavior. The Christians at Corinth also struggled. The gray area for them was whether or not to eat food that had been offered to idols."

Continue by saying, "Christians today might read today's passage and think, 'This doesn't apply to us because we don't struggle with eating food offered to idols.' Those who make such a statement will miss one of the greatest principles in the Bible about behavior and witness."

INTO THE WORD

Prior to class ask a student to prepare a brief presentation (no more than five minutes) summarizing the practice of eating food sacrificed to idols and the problem it presented for some of the Corinthian Christians. Provide your volunteer with a copy of the Lesson Background as the basis of his or her presentation.

After the presentation thank your presenter. Make the transition to the next activity by telling the class that Paul's teaching about food sacrificed to idols can serve as a model for some of the issues mentioned earlier.

Next, display one poster with the heading, *Arguments to Allow Believers to Eat Meat Offered to Idols* and another poster with the heading, *Why Believers Should Not Eat Meat Offered to Idols.* Read the printed text for the class. Then divide the class into two groups, assigning one poster to each group. Have groups fill in their posters using today's text for their answers.

Answers for the first poster can be found in verses 4-6 (idols are not gods; therefore, there is no harm in eating meat sacrificed to them) and in verse 8 (what food we eat doesn't matter). Answers for the second poster are found in verses 7 and 9 (we may become a stumbling block), verse 12 (we may sin against our brother or sister in Christ), and verse 13 (Paul's example).

INTO LIFE

Use the following two questions as a transition:

1. What principle does Paul teach in today's text that can be applied to the gray areas of Christian behavior? *(We should realize that our actions, even though not harmful to us spiritually, may be a stumbling block to a weaker Christian. To ignore this and act as we please is to sin.)*

2. Paul applies the above principle in the context of watching out for weaker Christians. How could this principle be applied in the context of showing concern for nonbelievers?

Next, ask the class to compile a list of gray areas of personal behavior that have potential for becoming gospel hindrances to non-Christians or stumbling blocks to weaker Christians. (A few ideas: using chewing tobacco, celebrating Halloween, buying lottery tickets, watching certain kinds of movies or TV programs, buying an expensive car, wearing certain styles of clothing, having body piercing or tattoos, missing worship while traveling.) [Option: Use the two activities on the reproducible page as an alternative or as homework.]

After discussion, stress that the key to Christ-honoring behavior is to be aware of those who watch our actions. As we do, we will not knowingly become a stumbling block to another person's faith or potential faith.

Conclude with prayer partners. One person should pray for this awareness. The other person should pray for wisdom to make right choices.

Looking Back . . . with Regret

It's time to "fess up"! Recall some times when you did or said things that were not sinful in and of themselves but that were potential or actual stumbling blocks to others. List at least one of those below next to the unsmiley face. (Caution: A stumbling block is not the same as an offense or an irritation.)

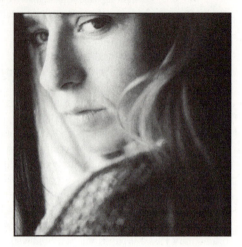

Looking Ahead . . . I Promise!

Now is the time to make your commitment to not willfully be a stumbling block again. Write your prayer of commitment next to the cross of Christ below.

"Be careful, however, that the exercise of your freedom
does not become a stumbling block to the weak."
1 Corinthians 8:9

CALLED TO WIN THE RACE

LESSON 7

WHY TEACH THIS LESSON?

Have you ever trained for anything? Some training, such as military basic training, is long and rigorous and includes expert trainers. Training for a marathon requires intense self-discipline and daily commitment. On-line training for the use of a software application may be self-directed and proceed at one's own pace. But all training involves preparation necessary for meeting future goals.

Perhaps you have not thought much about it, but we also must train to be able to avoid temptations. When we prepare to deal with temptations before they confront us, we are more likely to pass the test! In this week's lesson Paul exhorts the Corinthians to be ready to win the battle against sin. Being a Christian does not automatically give us victory over temptation. This lesson will teach us about the spiritual resources and principles that God has provided to keep us pure in an increasingly evil world.

INTRODUCTION

A. BE READY TO RUN

In auto racing races are often won by inches, with one car crossing the finish line only tenths of a second ahead of the closest competitor. Crossing the finish line of a race is not the time to read a *How to Race* manual! Similarly, the middle of Round 3 is not the time for a boxer to realize that he should have been hitting the punching bag instead of eating pizza and watching television. Common sense tells us that athletes must train and practice before the event so that they will be ready to compete well when the time comes.

In a similar way, we cannot be successful in our Christian lives if we do not prepare. The middle of a moral dilemma is not the time to realize that we aren't really sure about the right thing to do. Paul therefore insists that we train and discipline ourselves so that we will always be ready for anything that comes our way.

B. LESSON BACKGROUND

Today's passage falls in the middle of a lengthy discussion about whether or not Christians may eat food that has been offered to idols. In last week's lesson Paul warned mature believers to respect the sensitivities of weaker consciences. This discussion reminded Paul of the ancient Israelites, who were punished in the wilderness for their participation in idolatrous practices. He therefore takes a bit of a sidetrack to urge his readers to discipline themselves. Our weakness is not an excuse for sin but rather an opportunity for spiritual discipline and training so that we may receive God's full reward.

Paul likes to use illustrations from sports, and he opens the discussion here by comparing the Christian life with running a race. Corinth was the site of a major international athletic festival, the Isthmian Games, which drew participants and tourists from a wide area. The Corinthians would be familiar with many of the best athletes of that time and could relate easily to Paul's analogy.

DEVOTIONAL READING:
HEBREWS 12:1-12

BACKGROUND SCRIPTURE:
1 CORINTHIANS 9:24–10:13

PRINTED TEXT:
1 CORINTHIANS 9:24–10:13

LESSON AIMS

After participating in this lesson, each student will be able to:

1. Restate the positive and negative examples that Paul gives regarding following through to the end.

2. Draw one parallel between the ancient Israelites' experiences in the wilderness and the challenges of modern Christian life.

3. Plan to overcome a specific temptation.

Jul
16

KEY VERSE

Do you not know that in a race all the runners run, but only one gets the prize? Run in such a way as to get the prize.
—*1 Corinthians 9:24*

I. OUR EFFORTS (1 CORINTHIANS 9:24-27)

A. How to Run (v. 24)

24. Do you not know that in a race all the runners run, but only one gets the prize? Run in such a way as to get the prize.

Paul begins with the most basic rule of racing: everyone runs but *only one* person wins. This is not to suggest that the Christian life is a competition in which we get to Heaven by being better than everyone else (although we may often act that way). The emphasis lies in the second part of the verse: *run . . . to get the prize*. The participants in a race cannot control how fast their competitors will run. Each only can run as fast as possible. Christians should be prepared to run the race of faith as hard as they can so that nothing will hinder them (compare Philippians 3:14; 2 Timothy 4:7; Hebrews 12:1).

B. How to Train (vv. 25-27)

25. Everyone who competes in the games goes into strict training. They do it to get a crown that will not last; but we do it to get a crown that will last forever.

Winning athletes in the ancient Isthmian Games are awarded a *crown*, a wreath made of pine garlands that is worn on the head. We saw a throwback to this in the 2004 Olympic games in Athens, where the modern gold-medal winners received similar wreaths.

The actual value of these crowns is minimal but they symbolize victory. An ancient athlete would go *into strict training* for a year to compete *in the games* at Corinth, in hope of wearing one of these perishable, corruptible wreaths. How much more valuable is the imperishable, incorruptible eternal reward that God gives to those who strive to please him! There is simply no comparison.

That fact leads to an obvious conclusion: if an athlete is willing to expend every ounce of energy for a fleeting honor, then surely we should be willing to discipline ourselves so that we may win the crown of eternal life (2 Timothy 4:8; James 1:12; 1 Peter 5:4).

What Do You Think?

What are some examples of modern "prizes" that we are tempted to pursue that pale in comparison with what is available through Christ? How do we keep a proper focus?

The Masters

Augusta, Georgia, becomes the focus of the golf world each April. The Masters golf tournament that is held there is one of golf's most prestigious events. Phil Mickelson had this to say about his win there in 2004: "I think that winning this tournament, the reason it's so special, is that now I get to be a part of this great event for the rest of my life. I'll be back here every first week of April" (source: www.masters.org).

This is a tournament that demonstrates that you are among the great masters of this game, as Mickelson is. To reach this achievement demands countless hours of practice, strict training, and the denial of distracting interests. Poor eating, exercise, and sleeping habits do not produce a Masters' champion. In the Christian life it takes personal discipline in all areas to receive the Master's approval. We recall that we are saved by grace. Even so, poor Bible study habits, inconsistent church attendance, and wrong moral choices do not put a person in position to win the prize.

In addition to money the winner of the Masters golf tournament receives another prize: a green jacket. It is an award that these champions wear proudly—for this life. For those who prevail in the Christian life, there is a white robe to be gained—for eternity (Revelation 7:9-17).   —A. E. A.

26, 27. Therefore I do not run like a man running aimlessly; I do not fight like a man beating the air. No, I beat my body and make it my slave so that after I have preached to others, I myself will not be disqualified for the prize.

Victory requires focused training, not random effort. Olympic runners do not rely on leisurely jogs along the beach! A boxer in training does not use worthless training methods. Instead, he labors in the gym every day under a strict regimen of exercise, diet, and practice sparring.

Both running and boxing require the athlete to train intensively. Similarly, believers are to train to be ready at all times for any spiritual challenge that may arise. We keep our bodies under control so that bad habits and lusts don't weaken us. Such weakness would make us easy prey to the temptations that seem to come when we least expect them.

Here, as elsewhere, Paul uses himself as an example. He is not just a fat coach who walks the sidelines. He practices what he preaches! He can say from experience that a constant state of personal discipline is critical to one's spiritual life.

II. THEIR EXAMPLES (1 CORINTHIANS 10:1-6)

A. PARALLEL BLESSINGS (vv. 1-4)

1. For I do not want you to be ignorant of the fact, brothers, that our forefathers were all under the cloud and that they all passed through the sea.

Paul now applies the principle of a disciplined life to the problem immediately at hand. Some of the Corinthians are struggling with the temptation to participate in pagan religious practices and the immorality that surrounds them. Paul thus emphasizes the real danger by reminding the Corinthians of what happened to the Israelites.

The phrase *our forefathers* refers to the ancient Jews who came out of Egypt in the exodus under Moses over 14 centuries previously. This analogy sets the tone for the illustration to follow by indicating that Paul is speaking in spiritual terms. Many of the Corinthians are Gentiles by birth. Yet Moses and the Israelites are still their spiritual ancestors in common, godly faith. The ancient Jews' experiences of temptation are similar to those faced by modern Christians. We may see in them an example of the dangers of a careless approach to godly commitment.

Paul begins by describing the blessed state of divine protection and provision that the Israelites enjoyed. Under Moses' leadership, they *passed through the sea* and onto dry land (Exodus 14). God was constantly present, leading in the form of a *cloud* by day and a pillar of fire by night (Exodus 13:21, 22). Such obvious manifestations of God's loving presence should have led them to a deep and abiding appreciation of his salvation and ongoing provision. That appreciation should have expressed itself in loyalty and obedience.

2. They were all baptized into Moses in the cloud and in the sea.

Paul likens the Israelites' experience to that of Christians. We are baptized "into Christ Jesus" (Romans 6:3, 4), while the ancient Israelites were, in a sense, *baptized into Moses.* While Moses obviously was not divine as Christ is, Moses did serve as something of a mediator between God and the ancient Jew. The verses that follow draw further parallels. (See also comparisons between Jesus and Moses in Hebrews 3:1-6.)

3, 4. They all ate the same spiritual food and drank the same spiritual drink; for they drank from the spiritual rock that accompanied them, and that rock was Christ.

The exodus was not the end of God's care for his people; it was only the beginning. After crossing the sea, they entered a wasteland in which they found themselves homeless and without food or water. God, however, sustained them by miraculous provisions of food (Exodus 16). God also miraculously provided water from a *rock* when they were thirsty, through Moses' intervention (Exodus

WHAT DO YOU THINK?

What are some additional similarities between the Christian life and athletics that can help us live faithfully for God? Which similarity do you find to be most important? What hidden dangers are there?

WHAT DO YOU THINK?

What is the biggest difficulty you face in following Paul's example of setting a positive example? How have you tried to overcome this difficulty?

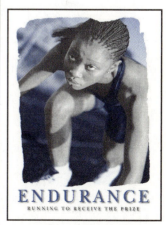

ENDURANCE
RUNNING TO RECEIVE THE PRIZE

Visual for Lesson 7. *Ask your students to examine this image closely before answering the first of the two questions directly above.*

17:1-7). In fact, God provided water in this way twice, in two different locations (see Numbers 20:1-11).

This double blessing led some of the ancient rabbis to suggest that God made the rock that yielded the miraculous water to travel with the Jews through the desert. Thus, as the story goes, they had refreshment whenever needed. Paul may be drawing upon this legend when he discusses the rock that followed them: *and that rock was Christ*. More important than the physical food and water that the Israelites enjoyed was God's *spiritual food* and *spiritual drink*.

Paul's point is that the believers at Corinth enjoy this blessing as well. Do we fail to appreciate how much such blessings are really worth?

B. LOST BLESSINGS (vv. 5, 6)

5. Nevertheless, God was not pleased with most of them; their bodies were scattered over the desert.

With all the blessings and advantages described in verses 1-4, it would seem that the Israelites couldn't lose! They had received God's Word directly through Moses, knew God's power when they shook the sand from the floor of the Red Sea off their sandals, felt God's love when they ate quail and drank fresh water in the desert. With all these obvious signs of his favor, how could they possibly fail to remain loyal to him?

But, as Paul points out, the facts of history show that even the most privileged life can end in tragedy when it is not guided by focused discipline. Of all the Jews who came out of Egypt, only two lived to see the promised land (Numbers 14:26-35). Even Moses faltered in a moment of weakness (Deuteronomy 32:48-52).

6. Now these things occurred as examples to keep us from setting our hearts on evil things as they did.

This verse shows that the fate of the Israelites is not just an interesting story from long ago. It reveals a very significant aspect of God's nature and serves as a warning for all time. God is quick to bless, but he also judges those who disregard his gifts and betray his trust. Despite their many advantages, the Israelites continued to sin and offend God, with dire consequences. Similarly, those Christians who lose focus and do not run the race with discipline are in great danger.

WARNING! WARNING!

Before leaving home this morning, I told my wife that I was going into the kitchen to get some pills that I needed to take at lunchtime. I remember walking up to the kitchen counter, but when lunchtime came I did not have the pills! In the span of just a few seconds, something else occupied my thoughts. So I had forgotten to get them.

We are a forgetful people, aren't we? On more than one occasion I have heard a young person say that he or she will never make the mistake of driving under the influence of alcohol after having lost a friend who did just that. The pain of the recent loss is vivid, a reminder of the fragility of life. But in the matter of a few weeks, those lessons are forgotten. Careless driving, even driving after drinking, returns as a pattern.

As we read through the Old Testament, we are often appalled at the number of times God's people turned their backs on him. They reform, promising to follow and honor him. Yet almost in the next breath they are again committing apostasy. We think we would never do such a thing. But it does not take too close of an examination of our lives to see that we are the same. God has left us the Old Testament as a warning and example of what happens when his way is forsaken. How well are we doing at heeding these warnings? —A. E. A.

WHAT DO YOU THINK?

What modern factors can cause us to take spiritual blessings for granted? How do you guard against these? What will be the result of failure?

III. OUR TASK (1 CORINTHIANS 10:7-13)

A. LEARN FROM EXAMPLES (vv. 7-12)

7, 8. Do not be idolaters, as some of them were; as it is written: "The people sat down to eat and drink and got up to indulge in pagan revelry." We should not commit sexual immorality, as some of them did—and in one day twenty-three thousand of them died.

The example of the Israelites shows what happens when focused discipline is lost. It is imperative for all believers to remain committed to God and ready to resist temptation.

To press home this point, Paul begins with one of the most flagrant acts of treason in history. The quotation in verse 7 comes from Exodus 32:6. The Israelites were worshiping a calf idol made from gold even while Moses was on the mountain receiving commandments from God. After eating and drinking, they indulged in unholy, *pagan* festivities.

Essentially, the Jews engaged in the idolatrous worship that they had known about in Egypt. They did this almost immediately after coming out of that country. Their lack of patience is remarkable, especially in view of their incredible experience at the Red Sea only a few weeks earlier. How quickly we forget God's past provision in moments of stress and temptation!

Many more sins followed, and Paul reminds his readers of another occasion when lack of focus led the Israelites into lust and idolatry. Numbers 25:1 records a situation where Jewish men "began to indulge in *sexual immorality* with Moabite women." Further, many Israelites began to worship the Baal of Peor. He punished them by sending a plague that killed 23,000 people.

We should note that Numbers 25:9 in our modern Bibles sets the death toll at 24,000. The difference is most likely due to what is called a textual variant. Paul probably is citing a manuscript that is no longer available to us. The severity of God's judgment remains clear nonetheless (compare Psalm 106:28, 29; Hosea 9:10).

9. We should not test the Lord, as some of them did—and were killed by snakes.

Of course, "God cannot be tempted by evil, nor does he tempt anyone" (James 1:13). But people often do things that *test the Lord* in the sense of challenging his authority over their lives. Like a young child who defies his mother's commands in order to see whether she is serious, believers sometimes flagrantly defy God's will. Paul's point is that God is prepared to punish those who act in this way.

One example may be taken from the famous story of the bronze serpent in Numbers 21:4-6. Just before this incident, God had given the Israelites a great military victory; they responded by complaining that they were tired of eating manna. This flagrant defiance resulted in God's defending his own honor by sending a plague of *snakes* into the camp. That punishment was lifted only after the people confessed their sin.

10. And do not grumble, as some of them did—and were killed by the destroying angel.

Some students think that Paul is referring to Korah's rebellion here (Numbers 16). But the verse before us is most likely a general summary statement, for the type of incidents described in verses 7-9 were by no means unique. The Jews' dissatisfaction with God's provision is a running theme in Exodus and Numbers (compare Hebrews 3:7-19).

11. These things happened to them as examples and were written down as warnings for us, on whom the fulfillment of the ages has come.

DAILY BIBLE READINGS

Monday, July 10—Run the Race with Perseverance (Hebrews 12:1-12)

Tuesday, July 11—Keep Alert and Always Persevere (Ephesians 6:10-20)

Wednesday, July 12—Be Doers, Not Just Hearers (James 1:19-27)

Thursday, July 13—Press On Toward the Goal (Philippians 3:12-16)

Friday, July 14—Run for the Gospel's Sake (1 Corinthians 9:22b-27)

Saturday, July 15—Do Not Follow Our Ancestors (1 Corinthians 10:1-7)

Sunday, July 16—God Will Help You Endure Testing (1 Corinthians 10:8-13)

WHAT DO YOU THINK?

Which do you find more useful in guarding yourself against falling into temptation: God's judgment or God's love? Why?

HOW TO SAY IT

Baal Peor. Bay-al PE-or.

Corinth. KOR-inth.

Corinthians. Ko-RIN-thee-unz

Deuteronomy. Due-ter-AHN-uh-me.

Hebrews. HEE-brews.

Hosea. Ho-ZAY-uh.

Isthmian. IS-me-unh.

Korah. KO-rah.

Moabite. MO-ub-ite.

Moses. MO-zes or MO-zez.

Pharaoh. FAIR-o or FAY-roe.

Philippians. Fih-LIP-ee-unz.

The experiences of the Israelites are *examples,* meaning that they function as *warnings* for future generations. Some may think that God no longer punishes sin because of the grace shown through Christ. But Paul dispels this notion. *The fulfillment of the ages* is the Christian era. The time of the fulfillment of God's plan for the Christ is here.

Even now, under the grace available through Christ's blood, we must remain focused and disciplined. Dare we risk losing the ultimate prize of eternal life? (Again, see 1 Corinthians 9:27.)

12. *So, if you think you are standing firm, be careful that you don't fall!*

Paul now returns to the theme that opened his discussion of food offered to idols (1 Corinthians 8:1, 2). Many people think they are wise. But their arrogance leads them to miss the obvious and *fall* into sin. Many people think that they are strong. But this complacency leads them to become careless and undisciplined, leaving them unprepared to resist temptation.

B. LOOK TO THE FUTURE (v. 13)

13. *No temptation has seized you except what is common to man. And God is faithful; he will not let you be tempted beyond what you can bear. But when you are tempted, he will also provide a way out so that you can stand up under it.*

The closing verse in this section provides both encouragement and warning. When we are *tempted,* we can rest assured that what we are facing is no worse than what other people have faced. And if other people have passed this test, so can we! God knows our strengths and weaknesses. He will not allow us to get into situations that cannot be overcome.

Every temptation has a built-in escape route. The most common is the fact that we can always simply say no. But at the same time, this assurance places all responsibility for sin on our own shoulders, not God's. God's faithfulness is a common Bible theme (Deuteronomy 7:9; 1 Corinthians 1:9; 1 Thessalonians 5:24). Unfortunately, human unfaithfulness is all too real.

CONCLUSION

Several years ago, NASCAR driver Steve Park was involved in a serious accident when his steering wheel came off. The doors on race cars do not open, so drivers must crawl in and out of the vehicle through a window. To make this easier the cars are equipped with removable steering wheels.

Park's accident occurred during a caution period in a race, when the cars move slowly around the track. While he cannot remember exactly what happened, it seems that Park turned his head momentarily as another vehicle approached on his left. In that split second, his steering wheel somehow detached. Park's car veered suddenly and was broadsided by the passing car. Someone at some point had not securely fastened the steering wheel. That momentary loss of focus could have cost Park his life!

When Paul compares the Christian life with a race, he does not mean to encourage a competitive spirit. He means to stress our need to be prepared and vigilant at all times. Unfortunately, we usually do not know when trials and temptations will crop up; they often seem to come when we least expect them or are least prepared to deal with them.

The danger may be greatest when we feel the strongest, because at these moments a false sense of security may lead us to drop our guard. We therefore are on the alert constantly. We discipline ourselves spiritually so that we will be ready for any challenge that comes our way.

PRAYER

God, please give us the discipline and focus to remain pure in an evil world. Help us to keep focused on the prize ahead, and help us to draw on your strength to endure temptations. Help us also to understand that you are a holy God and that you have called us to be a holy people for you. In Jesus' name, amen.

THOUGHT TO REMEMBER

Stay focused and disciplined to win life's race.

Discovery Learning

This page contains an alternative lesson plan emphasizing learning activities. Classes desiring such student involvement will find these suggestions helpful. The next page is a reproducible activity page to further enhance discovery learning.

LEARNING GOALS

After this lesson, each student will be able to:

1. Restate the positive and negative examples that Paul gives regarding following through to the end.

2. Draw one parallel between the ancient Israelites' experiences in the wilderness and the challenges of modern Christian life.

3. Plan to overcome a specific temptation.

INTO THE LESSON

Option #1: Have teams of students list the hurdles or obstacles that racers must overcome in order to win the following kinds of races: NASCAR, 26-mile marathon, Tour de France bicycle race, and hot-air balloon race. Have each team list their answers on poster board.

As teams report, ask what types of qualities racers must possess in order to successfully clear the hurdles and obstacles. When someone mentions endurance (or a similar word), tell the class that this quality is also a key to the discipline that Paul teaches about our spiritual lives.

Option #2: Display a list of the following competitions on a poster board: Olympics, bowling, NASCAR, Kentucky Derby, county fair pie-baking contest, ancient Olympic games. Ask the class what prizes are awarded for winning these games or events (Olympics: medals and wreaths; bowling: trophies; NASCAR: cup; Kentucky Derby: flowers and cup; county fair pie-baking contest: ribbon; ancient Olympic games: wreath crowns.) Write the answers on the poster board.

Make the transition to the Bible study by saying, "The actual value of many awards is minimal, like the ancient Olympic wreath crowns. The real value of awards is that they symbolize victory. Victory requires lots of discipline and sacrifice. Paul uses sports imagery to teach real lessons about spiritual victory. And the reward is worth more than we could ever imagine."

INTO THE WORD

For this portion of the lesson divide your class into teams of three to five. Give each team a copy of one of the following assignments.

Team #1: Your key word is *prize.* Read 1 Corinthians 9:24-26 and discuss its implications for the Christians in the church at Corinth and for today's believers.

Team #2: Your key word is *hurdles.* Read 1 Corinthians 10:1-11 and discuss the implications of obstacles and failure. How do we keep our focus? What parallel do you see between the experiences of the Corinthians and today's Christians?

Team #3: Your key word is *endurance.* Read 1 Corinthians 10:11-13 and summarize Paul's teaching about endurance and temptation. What assurance comes from these verses?

Allow each team's spokesperson to report. If you have more than one team working on the same task, ask one team to report and others to add to comments already made. Then say, "One thing should be clear: we need a road map to beat temptation!"

INTO LIFE

Prepare a work sheet with three columns. Column headings should read, *Temptations, Helpful Scriptures,* and *Ideas for a Plan.* List the following temptations in the first column: swearing, sexual temptations, worry, greed, not giving, poor worship habits. At the bottom of the chart, print the promise found in 1 Corinthians 10:13.

Divide the class into pairs. Give one work sheet to each pair. Ask pairs to select two of the temptations listed in the first column of the chart and jot down Scriptures and ideas that may be helpful in defeating these temptations. Be sure to have a few Bible concordances available. Allow a couple of pairs to report their findings for each of the temptations listed. (This activity can also be found in the student books.)

To close the session say, "All Christians face temptations. Overcoming these hurdles is a key to running a successful spiritual race." Give each student an index card and a shoestring. Ask them to write the following three words on their cards: *temptation, Scriptures,* and *plan.*

Students can use their cards as reminders to help them identify temptations and the resources to defeat them. The shoestrings can serve as reminder of the need for faithful endurance in the spiritual race. Encourage students to fill out their cards before the end of class. Suggest that they carry their cards and shoestrings in a pocket or a purse for at least one week.

[Option: Use the two exercises on the reproducible page as alternative Into Life activities.]

My Thoughts and Reflections . . .

Read 1 Corinthians 9:24–10:13. When we read and take time to think about God's Word, we can't help but make profound discoveries. Write a word or two in the thought bubbles, noting your reactions, thoughts, or discovery about the verses selected.

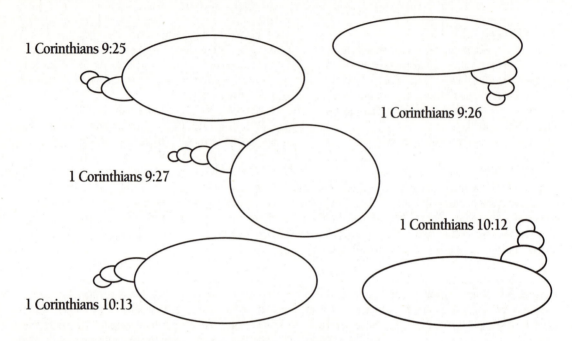

1 Corinthians 9:25

1 Corinthians 9:26

1 Corinthians 9:27

1 Corinthians 10:12

1 Corinthians 10:13

My Temptation and My Plan

All Christians face temptation in some form. It is important that we identify those temptations and make a plan to defeat them. Use the space below to tell God your plan to defeat a specific temptation and to ask for his help.

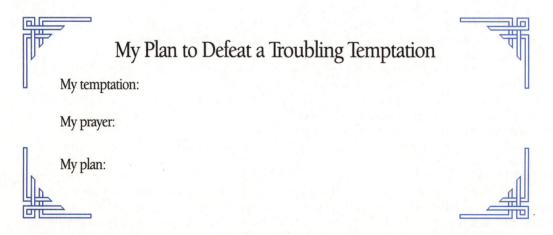

My Plan to Defeat a Troubling Temptation

My temptation:

My prayer:

My plan:

CALLED TO THE COMMON GOOD

LESSON 8

WHY TEACH THIS LESSON?

Many churches have split over the issue of spiritual gifts. What a controversial topic! Today's lesson reveals an ancient church's struggle over such gifts.

Above all, our understanding and use of spiritual gifts should be in line with a vital truth: these gifts are for the benefit of the church, not just the individual. Such gifts are for service, not for self-edification. Study and application of this lesson will be of great value for all who are confused about spiritual gifts but who sincerely wants to know what God's Word teaches on this important matter.

INTRODUCTION

A. THE MAKER'S MARK

Several years ago, the Hallmark® greeting card company ran a series of ads that encouraged viewers to look at the back of a card rather than the front. Typically, these commercials would show a young man purchasing a romantic card for his lady friend and presenting it before a date. After opening the envelope, the young woman would immediately turn the card over. If she saw the Hallmark® company logo, the gentlemen was in for a pleasant evening; if she saw another brand name, he could rest assured that she would want to end the evening early.

This ad campaign may or may not have brought grief to well-meaning people who dared to buy other brands of greeting cards. Yet it does illustrate the value that we attribute to a "maker's mark." Companies that take pride in their products generally attempt to display their names or logos prominently, whether it be on a card, an automobile, or a line of clothing. When we see these logos, we are reminded immediately of the quality and reputation of the item.

In today's passage Paul applies this same philosophy to the issue of spiritual gifts that God gives us for service in his church. Because they proceed from God, true spiritual gifts always bear two distinct labels: they always point to doctrinal truth, and they always work toward the common good of the church.

B. LESSON BACKGROUND

From the founding of the church on the Day of Pentecost (Acts 2), spiritual gifts have been a characteristic feature of Christianity. It is everywhere clear in the New Testament that these gifts represent the power of God working through individuals to benefit the whole church and to advance the gospel. But Paul's extended comments on the gifts in 1 Corinthians 12–14 indicate that they had actually become a source of pride and division in the Corinthian church.

This problem made it necessary for the apostle to lay down strict guidelines on how and for what purposes spiritual gifts should be used. Our lesson today covers the beginning of this discussion in 1 Corinthians 12.

DEVOTIONAL READING:
1 CORINTHIANS 12:27-31

BACKGROUND SCRIPTURE:
1 CORINTHIANS 12:1-13

PRINTED TEXT:
1 CORINTHIANS 12:1-13

LESSON AIMS

After participating in this lesson, each student will be able to:

1. Summarize what Paul says about the purpose and function of spiritual gifts.

2. Discuss ways that spiritual gifts can contribute to the common ministry of his or her church.

3. Conduct a spiritual self-examination to determine personal spiritual gifts and suggest a specific ministry in which they can be put to use.

Jul 23

KEY VERSE

Now to each one the manifestation of the Spirit is given for the common good.

—1 Corinthians 12:7

LESSON 8 NOTES

DAILY BIBLE READINGS

Monday, July 17—Excel in Gifts That Build Up (1 Corinthians 14:6-12)

Tuesday, July 18—Be Rich in Good Works (1 Timothy 6: 13-19)

Wednesday, July 19— Varieties of Gifts (1 Corinthians 12:1-6)

Thursday, July 20—All Gifts Activated by the Spirit (1 Corinthians 12:7-11)

Friday, July 21—The Body Consists of Many Members (1 Corinthians 12:12-20)

Saturday, July 22—If One Member Suffers, All Suffer (1 Corinthians 12:21-26)

Sunday, July 23—Strive for the Greater Gifts (1 Corinthians 12:27-31)

I. SPIRIT'S MARK (1 CORINTHIANS 12:1-3)

A. NEED TO KNOW (vv. 1, 2)

1. Now about spiritual gifts, brothers, I do not want you to be ignorant.

The first four chapters of 1 Corinthians reveal that this church is divided along certain lines. The discussion here suggests that a misunderstanding of *spiritual gifts* may be one aspect of that debate. The opening formula for this chapter indicates that the Corinthians had asked Paul to comment on the issue in their letter to him (see also 1 Corinthians 7:1 in Lesson 5).

2. You know that when you were pagans, somehow or other you were influenced and led astray to mute idols.

Many of the Corinthians believers are Gentiles rather than Jews. As such, this group has a strong connection to the pagan religious beliefs that they held to prior to becoming Christians (Acts 18:4-8). Before accepting Christ they had worshiped objects of wood, stone, silver, and gold that could say nothing and reveal nothing about God.

Now things are different for all the Corinthian Christians: the true God speaks to the church frequently and powerfully through the Holy Spirit in various ways (vv. 8-10, below). The Corinthians therefore need to be discerning in order to distinguish those who truly speak by the Spirit of God from those who do not. The truth that Paul is about to offer will help them from being *led astray* again into idolatry.

B. TEST OF THE SPIRIT (v. 3)

3. Therefore I tell you that no one who is speaking by the Spirit of God says, "Jesus be cursed," and no one can say, "Jesus is Lord," except by the Holy Spirit.

Sound doctrine is the most basic measure of the Spirit's presence. Like the apostle John, Paul insists that *the Spirit of God* will never inspire anyone to say anything false about *Jesus* (compare 1 John 4:1-6). Paul's comments echo Deuteronomy 18:20. There Moses indicates that no true prophet will ever speak in the name of other gods or attempt to lead people into idolatry. Similarly, *the Holy Spirit* will never lead a Christian away from the truth of Christ. Anyone who claims to speak on behalf of the Spirit while denying biblical doctrine is a liar.

Of course Paul's test *no one can say, "Jesus is Lord," except by the Holy Spirit* would apply only to those professing to be Christians. A nonbeliever obviously can utter the three words "Jesus is Lord" without conviction; this certainly would not prove that such a person possesses the Spirit. Paul means that those Corinthian believers who are prophesying, teaching, or speaking in a tongue under the Spirit's influence will always say what is true. Correct doctrine is therefore the first and most basic test of the Spirit's presence.

II. SPIRIT'S ONENESS (1 CORINTHIANS 12:4-7)

A. DIFFERENCES AND UNITY (vv. 4-6)

4-6. There are different kinds of gifts, but the same Spirit. There are different kinds of service, but the same Lord. There are different kinds of working, but the same God works all of them in all men.

Unfortunately, people who confess Jesus as Lord may still use their gifts in ways that glorify themselves rather than him. Paul, therefore, stresses that all gifts proceed from a common source. As such they should all work together in harmony for God's purposes.

Paul emphasizes harmony and unity here through a series of contrasts built on the formula, *"different* but *the same."* There are different *gifts,* but all come from the same *Spirit;* different kinds of *service,* but all from the same *Lord;* different kinds of *working,* but all through the power of the same *God.*

At a more subtle level, Paul is relating the diversity and unity of gifts in the church to the diversity and unity of God. These verses contain the most direct statement of the doctrine of the Trinity anywhere in the Bible. The three different personalities of the Trinity—Spirit, Lord (Christ), and God (the Father)—exist and work together in complete harmony. So also should Christians, in a sense, be unified in their use of differing spiritual gifts.

It is probably not useful to push for too much of a distinction between the words *gifts, service,* and *working.* Rather than focus on technical shades of meaning among these three, it's much more useful to see Paul's broader point: the Corinthian Christians have no reason to be arrogant. Their gifts, service, and work, whether miraculous or not, are from God. Their use of these should not lead to division.

THE SAME THING, ONLY DIFFERENT

Remarking on the statement, "It's the same thing, only different," one observer said, "It's commonly used by people who really have no idea what they're talking about. As a phrase, it represents either total ambivalence or total ignorance. Take your pick."

"It's the same thing, only different" does sound like a contradiction in terms, doesn't it? But in the realm of the work of the Holy Spirit, the statement has some validity. The same Holy Spirit works in the lives of all the people of God; yet the Spirit works in different ways. The purpose of the Spirit's work is to accomplish another thing that seems at first glance to be an impossibility: he is seeking to make many into one. Yet the coach of a basketball team has a similar task. So does the army drill sergeant.

Instead of being jealous of the gifts of another person or resentful of the accomplishments of another church, we are to rejoice. We will rejoice when we realize that what they are doing is what we are doing, as we are all one in Christ. We may do it in different ways, we may have different gifts, but in the end it is all the same thing, only different. —A. E. A.

B. COMMON GOOD (v. 7)

7. Now to each one the manifestation of the Spirit is given for the common good.

The implications of the phrase *each one* is somewhat controversial. Some argue that Paul means that each individual Christian receives a spiritual gift: every person has received a gift *for the common good.* This claim may be supported by appeal to Romans 12:6-8 and Ephesians 4:7-13. In those passages Paul includes among the gifts of the Spirit certain general abilities such as teaching, leadership, and generosity.

Others, however, interpret the phrase each one more narrowly as a reference to certain people who possess gifts, a limited number within the church. Thus the idea would be that every person who has received such a gift should use it *for the common good.* Those who think this interpretation is the correct one point to the word *manifestation.* They propose that this term suggests miraculous abilities (such as healing) that only certain people possess.

In either case, Paul's main point is clear: all spiritual gifts are given for the benefit of the church at large. These gifts are not for the private edification of the person who has been gifted. As Paul indicates in Ephesians 4, the gift is a gift to the church, not to the individual. The individual is simply the vessel through whom God administers the needed skill.

WHAT DO YOU THINK?

Paul emphasizes the unity of the Godhead. What are some ways that our worship services can avoid underemphasizing any member of the Trinity?

WHAT DO YOU THINK?

What steps can we take to determine how God has equipped us for service?

WHAT DO YOU THINK?

What are some practical ways we can inspire others to use their ministry gifts?

III. SPIRIT'S MANIFESTATIONS (1 CORINTHIANS 12:8-10)

A. WISDOM AND KNOWLEDGE (v. 8)

8. To one there is given through the Spirit the message of wisdom, to another the message of knowledge by means of the same Spirit,

In verses 8, 9 Paul lists ways in which *the Spirit* manifests himself in the church. All are tied together by the repetition of the phrase *the same Spirit*. The Spirit holds the church together and unites the efforts of individual Christians.

The first listed is *message of wisdom*. This is the ability to apply godly principles to problems of everyday life. The person with this gift is able to interpret situations from the perspective of the gospel of Christ. Such an ability is especially needed in the church in pagan Corinth, for the congregation is only about five years old at the time this letter is written. The leaders of this church, as newer Christians, need the Spirit's help to add maturity to their outlook. The fact that Paul lists wisdom first may indicate that he thinks this is the most important item in this list.

Some think that *message of knowledge* relates to information about spiritual and doctrinal issues and the ability to communicate these to others. Others, however, think *message of knowledge* means pretty much the same thing as *message of wisdom*. If this is the case, it means that Paul is using variety of expression as he does with gifts, service, and work in verses 4-6, above.

B. FAITH AND HEALING (v. 9)

9. . . . to another faith by the same Spirit, to another gifts of healing by that one Spirit,

Faith, in this context, does not mean "saving faith." Rather, it refers to a supernatural gift of especially effective faith, perhaps relating to prayer. Some students propose that the term should be translated *faithfulness*. This would mean that the person receives a special gift of patience and perseverance to endure hardship and perhaps even martyrdom as a witness to Christ.

The gifts of healing refer to the ability to cure people of illness miraculously but only as a testimony to God's power for purposes of evangelism. Paul had to leave his friend Trophimus behind sick on one occasion (2 Timothy 4:20), and Timothy was plagued by a persistent stomach problem (1 Timothy 5:23). Thus Paul did not always seem to have the gift of healing as he did in Acts 14:8-10; 28:7-9.

C. PROPHECY AND DISCERNMENT (v. 10a)

10a. . . . to another miraculous powers, to another prophecy, to another distinguishing between spirits,

In half-verses 10a and 10b, Paul ends his list with four types of gifts that seem to be connected with the most trouble in Corinth. These gifts involve claims about God revealing something through the individual. At the outset we should note that *miraculous powers* is a general term that includes other items on the list.

Prophecy is the first of the four. It refers to the ability to speak on behalf of God, perhaps including predictions of what will happen in the future (see Acts 11:27, 28; 21:10, 11). *Distinguishing between spirits* is the ability to determine whether someone's words and actions are motivated by genuine desire to please God or by selfish interests or perhaps even by demonic influences. First John 4:1 indicates that all Christians should be able to do this to at least some extent. But Paul seems to be using *distinguishing between spirits* in a narrower, deeper sense.

HOW TO SAY IT

Corinthians. Ko-RIN-thee-unz.
Deuteronomy. Due-ter-AHN-uh-me.
Moses. MO-zes or MO-zez.
Trophimus. TROFF-ih-muss.

D. TONGUES AND INTERPRETATION (v. 10b)

10b. . . . to another speaking in different kinds of tongues, and to still another the interpretation of tongues.

Tongues is the ability to speak in languages that one has not studied. The key example is what happened on the Day of Pentecost (Acts 2:1-11; compare 10:46; 11:15; 19:6). This gift apparently is intended to emphasize the universal nature of the gospel by illustrating God's rule over all people groups. Paul's remarks in 1 Corinthians 14 suggest that the content of such utterances is parallel to prophecy in some respects.

Just as in any situation where someone is speaking a language that we do not understand, *interpretation* is needed. The Spirit therefore enables some of the Corinthians to interpret and translate these tongues so that others can benefit from the message (see 1 Corinthians 14:27, 28).

Such gifts can lead to division easily. That division occurs when people lose track of the difference between their own opinions and divine revelations, or when they become more interested in their ability to deliver God's message than in the actual contents of that message. Paul therefore stresses that all these gifts, because they proceed from the same source, should proclaim a unified message that benefits all members of the church. See the next verse.

IV. SPIRIT'S BLESSINGS (1 CORINTHIANS 12:11-13)

A. MANY GIFTS, ONE SPIRIT (v. 11)

11. All these are the work of one and the same Spirit, and he gives them to each one, just as he determines.

From a human perspective, some gifts are more impressive than others. As such, it is easy for those who possess such gifts to feel more important than, say, the person who is blessed with a uniquely generous spirit or the ability to encourage others (Romans 12:8). Those who are tempted to rank people based on their gifts should keep in mind the source of all gifts. God chooses which gifts go to which people; they come to the receiver like inherited property—something the receiver had never earned and did nothing to deserve.

B. ONE SPIRIT, ONE CHURCH (vv. 12, 13)

12. The body is a unit, though it is made up of many parts; and though all its parts are many, they form one body. So it is with Christ.

Earlier, Paul compared the exercise of spiritual gifts with the workings of the Trinity. Now he turns to an analogy of the human *body* as he does in Romans 12:4-8. The parts of the human body are different from one another, with unique functions. Even so, the human body as a whole can function effectively only if each part works properly and in unison with the other *parts.* Even the simple act of walking across a room involves the coordinated efforts of dozens of bones and muscles.

By analogy, the church can function smoothly and fulfill its mission in the world only when each member uses his or her individual gifts in ways that benefit the common cause of the gospel. God is glorified when that happens.

13. For we were all baptized by one Spirit into one body—whether Jews or Greeks, slave or free—and we were all given the one Spirit to drink.

When we consider the membership of any given congregation, it is sometimes surprising that churches can be unified at all! People come to Christ from many different backgrounds, and Paul highlights two categories here. Before they entered the church, the Corinthian Christians came from different ethnic

WHAT DO YOU THINK?

What factors may cause Christians to value some ministry abilities over others? How do we guard against this danger?

Visual for Lesson 8. *Point out that the picture on the right is from the 1940s. Then ask, "How has the church improved in making 'many' into 'one'?"*

and religious environments (*Jews or Greeks*). They also came from different social classes (*slave or free*).

But the people that they once were took on a new identity in Christian baptism (Romans 6:1-4; Galatians 3:26-29). God brings us back to life as his child in faith. In this way we have a common heritage, a common family, and a common sense of purpose—at least, we should have a common sense of purpose that helps us overcome our differences.

The phrase *one Spirit to drink* may refer to Jesus' description of the Spirit as "living water" that flows to everyone who believes on Jesus (John 7:37-39). On the Day of Pentecost, the gift of the Spirit was associated with baptism (see Acts 2:38). We share a common rebirth as God's children (Galatians 4:1-7). As God's children we all enjoy the privileges of the Spirit's ministry. This being the case, it is an ironic abuse of the Spirit and of our spiritual birthright when we take pride in the gifts God has given us for the common good.

PRIDE AND EGO

Rap singer Queen Latifah was asked about the sin of pride. "Pride is a sin?" she asked. "I wasn't aware of that." Actress Kirstie Alley added, "I don't think pride is a sin. I think some idiot made that up." Rapper Ice-T echoed the same idea: "Pride is mandatory. That's one of the problems of the inner-city. Kids don't have enough pride" (source: "MTV," John MacArthur, Jr. via www.biblebb.com).

Our English word *ego* is from the Latin. It has to do with 'I,' the self. It is often used in a negative sense as someone who has "an inflated ego" or "is an egomaniac." When one's ego wins out, he or she becomes the center of his or her universe. It is seen in the strutting, chest-thumping athlete. It is seen in the politician who expects preferential treatment. It is seen in the preacher who leads his congregation with a "holier than thou" attitude. A good acrostic for the word ego is Easing God Out.

The remedy for human ego is submission to the Holy Spirit. Ego and misdirected pride disappear when we realize that "self" is bound up in the person of Christ and not in our own personhood. Our boasting, as Paul indicates, does not come in our accomplishments but in the cross of Christ (Galatians 6:14). Is pride a sin? It depends on what we are proud of. A good ego check never hurts.

—A. E. A.

CONCLUSION

Abraham Lincoln famously said, "A house divided against itself cannot stand." Yet that quote is not original to Lincoln. Jesus said it first (see Luke 11:17). The principle involved is timeless. It is true of every type of organization, from a marriage to a sports team to a large corporation. The whole group always benefits when everyone works together.

But the church differs from every other organization in one key respect, a fact that Paul underscores in verses 12, 13 in our passage today. When the Christ was in this world, he inhabited a physical body. In that body he prophesied, taught, gave wise counsel, and performed miracles. All this was done to draw attention to the presence of the kingdom of God and to call people to repentance. Now Christ has returned to Heaven, yet he continues his ministry in the world through a different kind of body: the church.

This fact makes unity and harmony in the exercise of gifts vital; it is through the church's message, supported by spiritual gifts, that Christ continues his work of calling the world to a relationship with God. A church divided cannot stand and accomplish this mission.

WHAT DO YOU THINK?

Beyond our use of spiritual gifts, how can viewing the church as "one body" practically affect the way we relate to other Christians?

PRAYER

Father, please help us to discover the special ways you have gifted us to help your church. As we use these gifts, give us the humility to be thankful for what you have done. Help us to appreciate others as we work together to fulfill your mission for our congregation. In Jesus' name, amen.

THOUGHT TO REMEMBER

Lift the body of Christ with your spiritual gifts.

Discovery Learning

This page contains an alternative lesson plan emphasizing learning activities. Classes desiring such student involvement will find these suggestions helpful. The next page is a reproducible activity page to further enhance discovery learning.

LEARNING GOALS

After participating in this lesson, each student will be able to:

1. Summarize what Paul says about the purpose and function of spiritual gifts.

2. Discuss ways that spiritual gifts can contribute to the ministry of his or her church.

3. Conduct a spiritual self-examination to determine personal spiritual gifts and suggest a specific ministry in which they can be put to use.

INTO THE LESSON

Begin the lesson with three mini-skits prepared by a team of four actors. The skits will illustrate the importance of teamwork. The setting for each skit is the construction site of a house. Each skit should last only about 15 seconds.

Skit #1: The actors should wear signs around their necks that read *Foreman*. Each actor, holding a clipboard and pencil, tries to tell the other "foremen" what to do and how to build the house. The result is confusion.

Skit #2: The actors flip their signs over to the other side that reads *Framer*. Actors lay down their clipboards, and each picks up a hammer. Actors try to work framing the house but lack direction. They ask each other for building plans and opinions on how to build the house. Again, the result is confusion.

Skit #3: One actor keeps his hammer and keeps his sign turned to *Framer*. Another actor grabs his clipboard and turns his sign back to *Foreman*. The other two actors put on new signs. One puts on a sign that reads *Plumber* and the other a sign that reads *Electrician*.

The plumber picks up a couple pieces of pipe and the electrician some electrical wire. The foreman gives brief instructions stating that work will be done on the master bathroom today. He then assigns appropriate tasks to each actor. As soon as the actors start pantomiming the building process, lead the class in applause.

Ask: "What is the obvious point of these skits?" Affirm students' answers and then make the transition to the Bible study by saying, "Teamwork in the church is equally important. One of the challenges, however, is discerning what each of our roles on the team is and how we each fit into the overall plan. Paul's letter to the Corinthian church can help us."

INTO THE WORD

Give each student a photocopy of today's printed text, two pencils of different colors, and a regular pencil. Read the entire text to the class and then ask them to do the tasks that follow.

Say, "Use your regular pencil to circle words or phrases in the Bible text that illustrate the diversity or differences in gifts within the church family." After reviewing the answers ask: (1) "What point is Paul trying to drive home to the church with these words and phrases?" (2) "Do you think that the categories of gifts that Paul lists is meant to be all-inclusive? If not, why did he focus on the gifts listed?"

Then say, "Use one of the colored pencils to circle words or phrases that illustrate the unity that we as believers should enjoy—even in our differences." After reviewing the answers ask: (1) "What lesson is Paul teaching in verses 4-6 by using the names Spirit, Lord, and God?" (2) "Why do you think it is important for us to recognize the various gifts within the church?"

Tell students, "Use the other colored pencil to underline what you think is the key verse in this passage." Students will likely underline either verse 7 or 12. Ask students why they chose their particular verse. [Option: Use the two exercises on the reproducible page as alternative, small group activities.]

INTO LIFE

Study in advance Paul's descriptions of spiritual gifts (and gifted offices) as found in Romans 12:6-8; 1 Corinthians 12:8-10; and Ephesians 4:11. Make a handout list of those gifts (and gifted offices) that are still in effect today. (Check with your church's leadership if in doubt.)

Write your list in a column down the left side of the handout. On the right side of the page, make a list of all your church's ministries. You may want to add some hypothetical ministries; these are ministries that don't yet exist at your church but are possibilities.

Distribute the handout during class. Ask each student to do a self-evaluation by circling his or her own spiritual gifts. Then say, "We are to use our gifts for the common good of the church. With that in mind, match your gifts on the left with ministries on the right." Remind your students of the blessings that a diversity of gifts brings. Close with a prayer to use the gifts wisely.

Working Together as Christ's Body

Today's text calls the church the "body." This analogy is a wonderful picture of the church's many members contributing gifts and talents that cause the church to function as it should.

On the picture to the right, identify parts of the human body that could represent spiritual gifts. For example, knees could represent prayer. Write your ideas next to the appropriate body parts.

Next, draw circles around the gifts or talents you can contribute to Christ's church.

← **Prayer**

Headline News

THE CORINTH TIMES-DISPATCH

Imagine yourself as a newspaper reporter assigned to write an article about Paul's teaching in 1 Corinthians 12:1-13. Write a headline for the article that will capture your readers' attention. Then add a subheading describing the main thought of the article.

Called to Be a Christian Community

Unit 2: Called to Obedience
(Lessons 5-9)

CALLED TO LOVE

LESSON 9

WHY TEACH THIS LESSON?

Popular songs abound in lyrics about *love*. Love is generally understood as a romantic emotion, something that makes us feel special about another person. But feelings may change daily, so we think we fall in or fall out of love all the time.

Paul understood love in a much deeper way. He based this understanding on the way God has shown his love to us. For Paul, love was not simply an emotion. It was a commitment of lifestyle. We love by doing, not by feeling. This lesson teaches the essential value of love in the Christian community. The thread that ties all actions together should be love. Great abilities or spiritual gifts are a destructive factor in the church unless they are used in love, in selfless service for others. In this view love is not temporary but eternal. Drawn from the famous Love Chapter (1 Corinthians 13), this lesson is a timely reminder of what constitutes love from God's perspective.

INTRODUCTION

A. ACTION LOVE

"I just don't know," Jane said, "whether we can learn to love each other again." She was speaking to a counselor while Craig, her husband, sat next to her in silence. Several months earlier, Jane had discovered that Craig was having an affair with a woman he had met on a business trip.

Jane responded by forcing Craig to leave their home until he made up his mind. After three weeks in a hotel, he renounced his sinful behavior and begged for forgiveness. She was willing to try but was skeptical about the future. "Could it really ever feel the same?" she asked. "We've been through so much together, but I just don't know if I even love him anymore."

In response the counselor pointed out that love is primarily a sense of commitment rather than an emotion, although we do often have loving feelings. Loving commitment to another manifests itself in a way of living. Love, in other words, is a set of behaviors, a way that we act toward others. Despite her anger, Jane was clearly acting in a loving way by attempting to forgive Craig. The counselor was, therefore, hopeful that the relationship could be healed.

Many of us live in a culture where the word *love* is used so often and so casually that it has become virtually meaningless. We say that we love God, but we also say that we love our family members, chocolate ice cream, and the sales at Wal-Mart®. Paul clarifies that love is not a feeling but rather a mode of living. He stresses that nothing we do can possibly bring glory to God if we do not exhibit a loving spirit.

B. LESSON BACKGROUND

First Corinthians 13 is a key part of Paul's solution to the problems of a divided church. Up to this point in the letter, he has discussed several serious

DEVOTIONAL READING:
JOHN 3:16-21
BACKGROUND SCRIPTURE:
1 CORINTHIANS 13
PRINTED TEXT:
1 CORINTHIANS 13

LESSON AIMS

After participating in this lesson, each student will be able to:

1. List the features that characterize Christian love.

2. Contrast the nature of Christian love with the worldly idea of love.

3. Identify a unique, personal way to demonstrate Christian love.

Jul
30

KEY VERSE

And now these three remain: faith, hope and love. But the greatest of these is love.
—1 Corinthians 13:13

issues that were points of conflict for the Corinthian church. These ranged from sectarianism, to sexual sin, to lawsuits among believers, to divorce, to Christian liberties, to propriety in worship.

Chapter 12 begins a long section on the pride and arrogance that had entered the church through, ironically, the use of spiritual gifts. That discussion continues into chapter 14, but Paul pauses to give the short answer to all the questions thus far: love. Love for one another, properly understood, will put everything into perspective. Love will unify the church and empower believers to glorify Christ together.

I. MATHEMATICS OF LOVE (1 CORINTHIANS 13:1-3)
A. Spiritual Gifts Minus Love (vv. 1, 2)
1. If I speak in the tongues of men and of angels, but have not love, I am only a resounding gong or a clanging cymbal.

The first three verses of today's text establish the importance of love as a guidepost for the exercise of spiritual gifts. Paul frames his argument with a series of statements based on a formula: "If I do X, even if I do X to the highest possible degree, but do *have not love*, then I am nothing." In mathematical terms, this formula may be restated as, "X minus love equals zero," where X is any one of the spiritual gifts under discussion. Without love, nothing we do makes any difference in God's sight.

Paul's first example is that of speaking in *tongues*. The miraculous, Spirit-given ability to speak foreign languages is a great thing to the Corinthians. But suppose someone could speak not only tongues that other human beings use but also could speak the language used by the *angels* in Heaven (whatever that language may be). This surely would represent the highest form of speaking in tongues!

Yet a person who spoke that angelic language out of selfish motives—to draw attention to self or to demonstrate personal spirituality—would be of no use to anyone. As far as God is concerned, without love even the most elegant speech is like *a resounding gong or a clanging cymbal*—in other words, just loud noise. Therefore, a tongue that is empowered by the Spirit must also be guided by genuine love.

2. If I have the gift of prophecy and can fathom all mysteries and all knowledge, and if I have a faith that can move mountains, but have not love, I am nothing.

Paul gives more examples. Suppose that someone has *the gift of prophecy,* the ability to speak on God's behalf and perhaps even to predict the future. Also imagine a person who is so endowed with prophetic insight as to have *all knowledge* and to understand *all mysteries,* with a profound awareness of the mind of God. Even such gifts, Paul says, are worthless if not exercised in *love.*

Faith here is not "saving faith." Rather, it refers to a supernatural gift of especially effective faith (see comment on 1 Corinthians 12:9 from last week's lesson). Jesus once spoke of a kind of faith that was great enough to move a mountain into the sea (Matthew 17:20). Such faith would indeed be impressive to other people! Yet God will be impressed only if the prayer is offered in a spirit of love.

B. Self-Sacrifice Minus Love (v. 3)
3. If I give all I possess to the poor and surrender my body to the flames, but have not love, I gain nothing.

Generosity is not listed as a manifestation of the Spirit in 1 Corinthians 12, but Paul does include it in the list of gifts in Romans 12:6-8. All Christians are obligated to give, but some are specially gifted to give more freely to those in need.

Ultimate giving is found in the phrase *surrender my body to the flames*. This probably refers to some act of Christian martyrdom. It's one thing to give your money to feed the poor but much more to sacrifice even your very life for the faith! But even the most extreme self-sacrifice is worth nothing in God's sight if it is done without *love*.

CHEAP TALK, ROTTEN WALK

The young man, trying to impress his girlfriend, told her, "I would climb the highest mountain to be with you. I'd walk through a snake-infested jungle to be with you. I would swim the widest river just to be able to be with you." Then, after he kissed her, he said, "I'll see you at church Sunday if it's not raining." There is no limit to the promises some people are willing to make! We call that cheap talk.

At other times there is indeed the fulfillment of a noble task but from wrong motives. At a hospital near a town where I once ministered, there was a man who would go into patients' rooms to pray with them. He seemed to be such a loving and kind individual. But it was discovered that he would slip rings from their fingers as he held their hands. On other occasions he would see jewelry or other articles on a surface and pocket them. Love was not the motivation by which he served. What a rotten walk!

It is the scoundrel who makes the headline news, but the compassionate ones make the heart new. They are the ones who have answered the call to minister to the poor and downcast through the years. No cheap talk, no rotten walk, just giving themselves day after day to caring for the needs of others. This pleases God.

—A. E. A.

II. CHARACTERISTICS OF LOVE (1 CORINTHIANS 13:4-7)

A. WHAT LOVE IS, PART 1 (v. 4a)

4a. Love is patient, love is kind.

After stating that no act of service is valuable in God's sight without love, Paul moves on to specify just what love is. Saying that *love is patient* means that love does not express itself through vengeance, retaliation, or by giving up on people quickly. Instead, love actively extends kindness to others, even those who do not "deserve" our grace.

WHAT LOVE DOES

A man visits his wife in a nursing home. She has Alzheimer's disease. Daily he stops by to see her. He reads to her from the Bible. He tells her how nice the weather is and how the children and grandchildren are doing. He holds her hand and sings some of her favorite hymns to her. After two or three hours he leaves, only to return the next day for the same routine. Only this is not a routine. This is love.

Another man has a wife in the same nursing facility. She too has Alzheimer's. For the first few weeks he visits daily. Then the visits become every other day, then weekly. Then he comes only at Christmas and on his wife's birthday. His thought is, "This is not fair. I've got a life to live."

Both couples had stood before the same minister years ago. They recited vows to each other that said they would love, honor, and cherish each other in sickness and in health. Those vows were to be in effect until death would separate them. One's man's love suffered long, the other refused to "suffer" for long. One man was self-seeking while the other man served his wife and his Lord. Which choice would you make?

—A. E. A.

WHAT DO YOU THINK?

What are some ways that expressions of giving come with an unloving attitude? How do we guard against this trap?

DAILY BIBLE READINGS

Monday, July 24—God So Loved the World (John 3:16-21)

Tuesday, July 25—Conquering Love (Romans 8:31-39)

Wednesday, July 26—Love One Another (John 13:31-35)

Thursday, July 27—Loving One Another Fulfills the Law (Romans 13:8-14)

Friday, July 28—Let Us Love (1 John 3: 11-18)

Saturday, July 29—Love Defined (1 Corinthians 13:1-7)

Sunday, July 30—The Greatest Gift Is Love (1 Corinthians 13:8-13)

HOW TO SAY IT

Apollo. Uh-PAH-low.
Athens. ATH-unz.
Corinthians. Ko-RIN-thee-unz.
Delphi. DEL-fi.
Moses. MO-zes or MO-zez.
Philippians. Fih-LIP-ee-unz.
Thessalonians. THESS-uh-LO-
*   nee-unz.*

B. WHAT LOVE ISN'T (vv. 4b, 5)

4b. It does not envy, it does not boast, it is not proud.

Paul now emphasizes some things that love is *not* or does not do. *Envy* is a desire to obtain what other people have, often accompanied by feelings of bitterness or hatred. Envy and covetousness are never motivated by genuine love.

At the same time, a person who loves does not try to make other people envious by making a display of the things that he or she has. Paul may be thinking here of the pride the Corinthians are taking in their spiritual gifts. All gifts are given by the same Spirit and are of equal importance in God's plan (1 Corinthians 12:4-7, 14-26). Thus it is senseless to boast about them or to envy what someone else has received.

5. It is not rude, it is not self-seeking, it is not easily angered, it keeps no record of wrongs.

Neither does love behave in a *rude* manner. That means that love does not lead us to do anything that we would be ashamed of later. In this context Paul probably is thinking especially of envious or prideful things that we may say. Pride and envy are eliminated categorically by the fact that love is not selfish: love always leads us to act in the best interests of the other person (compare Philippians 2:4).

Neither is love compatible with a quick temper. Of course we may be angry at the sins that people commit and we may be frustrated by their poor choices. But these feelings should be motivated by genuine concern that the person is doing something harmful to self, others, or the cause of Christ. Keeping *no record of wrongs* means that we should not continue to harbor ill feelings toward those who make us angry. Instead, we should forgive and forget.

C. WHAT LOVE IS, PART 2 (vv. 6, 7)

6. Love does not delight in evil but rejoices with the truth.

As we have seen, many of the Corinthian Christians seem to be prideful and arrogant about their spiritual gifts. Others may be angry and resentful toward those individuals. When they feel this way they may *delight* to see the arrogant ones fall into some sinful behavior. But the person who harbors such sentiments is no more loving than the person who constantly boasts about personal abilities. Love always *rejoices with the truth* in the sense that it makes us happy to see other people succeed and do the right thing.

7. It always protects, always trusts, always hopes, always perseveres.

These four qualities summarize the way that love responds to other people. The repetition of *always* emphasizes that we are to act this way despite anything that anyone may do to us.

These qualities do not suggest that love must be naïve but rather that love always remains positive towards others. As such, love does not break under pressure but instead always bears up. The Greek verb for *protects* can refer to the idea of something remaining watertight, so that no harm comes from the outside. Love always continues to expect and hope for the best from people even when we must wait a long time to see it.

III. GREATNESS OF LOVE (1 CORINTHIANS 13:8-13)

A. THINGS THAT WILL END (v. 8)

8. Love never fails. But where there are prophecies, they will cease; where there are tongues, they will be stilled; where there is knowledge, it will pass away.

The Corinthians apparently take great pride in certain spiritual gifts. But a time is coming when they won't need *prophecies*, *tongues*, and *knowledge*. Even when

WHAT DO YOU THINK?

How have you been able to develop a mind-set that sees the worth of people and anticipates their becoming more than they currently are? How can you improve in this area?

that time comes, however, love will continue to be the guide. We will always need *love*, both in this life and the next. For this very reason Paul opened the discussion in 1 Corinthians 12:31 by calling love "the most excellent way," which is superior to the selfish pursuit of spiritual gifts.

B. WHY THEY WILL END (vv. 9-12)

9. For we know in part and we prophesy in part,

Through a special gift of knowledge (v. 8), some of the Corinthians have supernatural insight into spiritual matters. This insight can guide their counsel and teachings. Other Corinthians are empowered to *prophesy*. But the Corinthians' knowledge and prophecies of God are only partial *(in part)*. Any person who takes pride in these gifts should realize that he or she doesn't know everything!

10. . . . but when perfection comes, the imperfect disappears.

This verse is not a prediction in the original Greek but rather is a proverb. Paul is, in other words, making a general statement about how things normally work. The word being translated *perfection* can also be understood to mean being "mature" or "complete," depending on context (compare Matthew 5:48; 19:21; 1 Corinthians 2:6).

As a rule, something that is partial or incomplete is discarded when the complete thing comes onto the scene. If someone gives me a photocopy of an article from a magazine, I do not need to keep those photocopied pages after I have gone out and bought my own copy of the whole edition. Why this principle is important is the subject of the next verse.

11. When I was a child, I talked like a child, I thought like a child, I reasoned like a child. When I became a man, I put childish ways behind me.

Paul now gives an example of the principle he stated in verse 10. A *child* thinks and talks about things according to his or her limited physical and mental capabilities. For this very reason, the things that children say and do often amuse us by their simplicity.

But as we grow older, these simplistic ways of thinking are replaced by a more mature perspective. The new perspective is based on a better, more adult understanding of the world around us.

12. Now we see but a poor reflection as in a mirror; then we shall see face to face. Now I know in part; then I shall know fully, even as I am fully known.

Paul now applies the principle of maturity to the use of spiritual gifts. As he noted in verse 9, the revelatory gifts of knowledge, prophecy, and the like are partial and incomplete. They reveal many important things about God and his will, but they don't reveal everything.

Paul compares the knowledge of God that the Corinthians receive through these gifts with a *reflection* in *a mirror*. Fine mirrors are manufactured in Corinth at the time, but ancient mirrors are not made of glass like ours today. Instead, they are made of polished metal and therefore cannot give a sharp image; the picture they offer is dark, a pale reflection of one's actual features. The gifts, similarly, give us a partial knowledge of God but not the complete picture. This is not due to any lack on the part of the Spirit but rather simply to our inability to comprehend him *fully*.

Yet the time will come, Paul says, when the Corinthians' partial knowledge is to be replaced. Scholars are divided on the specific experience to which this verse refers. Some say that Paul is thinking of the second coming of Jesus, a moment when the glorified Christ will reveal himself to the world and all will "see him as he is" (1 John 3:2). Others believe that Paul is referring more generally to

How would you respond to a believer who thinks that Bible study is not all that important since someday we will know God more fully anyway?

[Make sure to use Psalm 119:105 and 2 Timothy 3:16, 17 to frame your answer.]

Visual for Lesson 9. *Ask students to fill in this blank: "Love is greater than _____." Use this image to set the tone for the responses.*

Love lasts forever; implement it now!

our life in Heaven, where we will dwell in God's direct presence and behold his perfect glory.

Still others think that this refers to the more complete knowledge that comes to the church as a whole when the New Testament is finished by the end of the first century A.D. Those who hold this theory point to Exodus 33:11 where Moses' "face to face" conversations with God refer to clear communication (since literally seeing God's face meant death; Exodus 33:20).

Whichever theory is true, the point not to be missed is that of all the things that are temporary, love is not one of them! Paul brings this thought home in the next verse.

C. WHAT REMAINS (v. 13)

13. And now these three remain: faith, hope and love. But the greatest of these is love.

Above all, our thoughts are to be guided by *love.* Indeed, God is love, and anyone who truly knows anything about God will show godly love to others (1 John 4:7, 8). We have not seen God in this world, and we do not know everything about him. As such, we must exhibit *faith,* trusting that he knows best because we do not understand all his ways and plans. *Hope* is not wishful thinking but rather the confident assurance that we eventually will be in his eternal presence if we live a faithful life (compare 1 Thessalonians 1:3).

Both faith and hope are critical to our lives now. But both of these will, to some extent, become obsolete later on. In Heaven we will have what we now hope for; "hope that is seen is no hope at all" (Romans 8:24). Our faith will be replaced by complete confidence as we see the reality of God's eternal promises. But love will never be obsolete: it will continue to characterize our relationship with God and other redeemed saints forever.

Love is therefore the greatest of the three in the sense that it never ends. When we exercise our spiritual gifts with love, we are acting with eternity in view.

CONCLUSION

In Paul's day the great Oracle at Delphi was a major tourist attraction. Legend had it that Delphi, a little over 100 miles northwest of Athens, was the center of the earth. A famous temple to the god Apollo housed a sacred stone marking the spot. Worshipers of Apollo could come to this temple to ask the idol for advice, similar to modern fortune-telling.

Answers came cryptically through a prophetess, who went into a trance and spoke in nonsensical gibberish. These ravings were "interpreted" by priests at the temple to provide the answer to the supplicants' questions. Despite the obvious flaws of these practices, the oracle at Delphi remained a significant aspect of Greek religion for hundreds of years.

The best advice that pilgrims to Delphi received did not, however, come from a raving prophetess or priest of Apollo. Rather, the best advice came from the famous inscription over the doorway to the temple: *Know Thyself.* Worshipers were, in other words, to reflect on their own motives, weaknesses, and limitations before approaching.

The Corinthians were obsessed with spiritual gifts that offered special insights. As a result, they knew marvelous things about God and his ways, but they obviously did not know their own hearts. For this reason they failed to see that their actions were not truly driven by love or a desire to please God. Without love their greatest efforts could never truly glorify him.

Discovery Learning

This page contains an alternative lesson plan emphasizing learning activities. Classes desiring such student involvement will find these suggestions helpful. The next page is a reproducible activity page to further enhance discovery learning.

LEARNING GOALS

After participating in this lesson, each student will be able to:

1. List the features that characterize Christian love.

2. Contrast the nature of Christian love with the worldly idea of love.

3. Identify a unique, personal way to demonstrate Christian love.

INTO THE LESSON

Decorate the classroom with 20 to 24 large hearts affixed to the walls. Using several different colors of hearts will look attractive, but be sure they are light colored so that writing will show.

Open the lesson by dividing the class into small groups of four or five. Within groups students should relate demonstrations of great love that they have experienced. These examples could be from family experiences, church relationships, etc. To get the groups started, give a personal illustration from your life. [Option: Use one or more of the exercises on the reproducible page as an alternative.]

After a few minutes of sharing, make the transition to the Bible study by reminding the class that, "Love is manifested in many ways in our everyday lives. The need to be loved never ends. Today's study is a classic text that encourages the deepest love we can ever give or experience. While this passage is often read at weddings, its applications reach every relationship, especially relationships within the church."

INTO THE WORD

Tell the class that they will remain in their small groups throughout today's lesson. Begin the Bible study by reading 1 Corinthians 13 to the class. Then distribute the materials and four small-group assignments listed below.

Group #1: Materials needed: several dark crayons (don't use markers as they may bleed through the paper hearts). Handout narrative: "First Corinthians 13:4-8a is often read at weddings. As time goes on, we discover ways that the characteristics of love found in these verses can be applied to our marriage experiences. Write on the hearts taped to the wall the characteristics from these verses. Be prepared to share an illustration of how each of these characteristics can be demonstrated in a marriage."

Group #2: Materials needed: poster board and a marker. Handout narrative: "Your task is to list the characteristics of love mentioned in 1 Corinthians 13:4-8a. While these characteristics of love are often applied to marriage today, Paul is directing them to personal relationships within the Corinthian church. Beside each of the characteristics listed on your poster board, note a practical way this characteristic can be illustrated in church life today."

Group #3: Handout narrative: "Your task is to read 1 Corinthians 13:4-7 and select two of the characteristics of love to mime for the class. Class members will try to guess the characteristic. Have fun!"

Group #4: Handout narrative: "Read 1 Corinthians 13 and answer the following: (1) Given the quest for power and spiritual gifts in the Corinthian church, what is Paul's point in verses 1-3? What does this say to today's church? (2) In verses 8-12 Paul stresses to the Corinthians that a time would come when spiritual gifts would cease to be relevant but that love endures. Why is that important to know today? (3) Verse 13 is often quoted. Why is love greater than faith and hope?"

Allow Group #3 to present its mimes for the class, and then have the other groups report their findings.

INTO LIFE

Ask students to share, in their small groups, stories about people who embody the characteristics of love Paul mentioned in today's text. After a short time, ask a representative from each group to be prepared to share one of the more creative or unusual stories with the entire class.

Before allowing groups to share their stories, tell the class that you are going to extend a challenge for each person to find a unique way to demonstrate Christian love within the next week. The stories they hear may stimulate an idea.

Then ask each group's representative to share one story with the class. As the stories are being told, walk through the classroom quietly handing each student a piece of heart-shaped candy (or a heart-shaped trinket). Tell the class that the candy is a reminder to find one way to demonstrate Christian love this week.

Living Love!

The need to be loved never ends, and giving love is one of life's great adventures. First Corinthians 13 stimulates the imagination to think of ways to demonstrate deep and enduring love. Use the exercises below to make this love personal for you.

A Jewel in My Life!

Write about one of the great acts of love shown to you by someone else.

Love Demonstration of the Year!

The church member who deserves this trophy for demonstrating love so well is_____, because . . .

A Snapshot of God's Love!

Draw a simple picture representing God's love. Be sure to include yourself in the drawing.

Called to Be a Christian Community

Unit 3: The Spirit of Giving
(Lessons 10-13)

GIVING FORGIVENESS

WHY TEACH THIS LESSON?

Counselors say that unresolved guilt is one of the great destroyers of relationships. When we feel guilty, we have a spiritual malaise that can incapacitate us. Yet guilt is caused by recognition of sin, and we all have sin in our lives. How, then, do we escape the debilitating effects of guilt?

In this lesson Paul deals with the root cause of this matter: the need for repentance and forgiveness. Confrontation of sin in the lives of Christian brothers and sisters can be extremely painful, as Paul well knew. He confronted the Corinthian church in several areas that caused them (and him) deep grief. But Paul knew that if repentance were shown and forgiveness were given, a sour relationship could become even stronger than it was before the confrontation.

God desires that we be people of forgiveness. By looking at how Paul dealt with his beloved church in Corinth, we will learn how we can develop our own churches into communities where forgiveness is practiced in a loving, godly manner.

INTRODUCTION

A. JOSEPH'S ATTITUDE

The Old Testament character Joseph models the ability to maintain a gracious spirit in spite of suffering. His divine gifts of wisdom and insight made him Jacob's favorite son but also inspired the resentment of his brothers. In a fit of rage they mistreated him and sold him into slavery. He eventually wound up in prison in Egypt.

But God remained with him, and after a series of remarkable events, Joseph found himself to be second in command over all Egypt. From this exalted position, he could have exacted vengeance easily. A prime opportunity presented itself when his brothers came to purchase grain during a famine. But, incredibly, Joseph did not condemn them because, as he says in Genesis 45:8, "It was not you who sent me here, but God."

Joseph was able to maintain this attitude because he saw God's hand at work in the situation (see Genesis 45:4-7). Repairing relationships can be difficult, especially when we have suffered because of another person's actions. The key lies in understanding that God is ultimately in control and that he can work his will in every situation.

B. LESSON BACKGROUND

From an earlier lesson, we know that Paul founded the church at Corinth as noted in Acts 18:1-18. A few years later, Paul spent a significant amount of time in Ephesus. While there he received a letter from the Corinthians asking for guidance on several difficult issues (1 Corinthians 1:11; 7:1). He responded by sending the letter of 1 Corinthians and also by sending Timothy to assist the struggling church (4:17; 16:5-11).

DEVOTIONAL READING:
MATTHEW 18:21-35

BACKGROUND SCRIPTURE:
2 CORINTHIANS 2:5-11; 7:2-15

PRINTED TEXT:
2 CORINTHIANS 2:5-11; 7:2-15

LESSON AIMS

After participating in this lesson, each student will be able to:

1. Tell how Paul responded to the evidence of repentance in the Corinthian church and what he urged them to do.

2. Explain why full forgiveness is essential when repentance has taken place.

3. Identify one person to whom he or she needs to extend forgiveness or from whom forgiveness should be asked.

Aug
6

KEY VERSE

Godly sorrow brings repentance that leads to salvation and leaves no regret, but worldly sorrow brings death.
—2 Corinthians 7:10

But these remedies apparently were unsuccessful. After Timothy returned to Paul with the bad news, Paul paid them a "painful visit" (2 Corinthians 2:1). This was an unpleasant experience, as Paul apparently had to confront a number of individuals. Paul also suffered slanderous accusations (2 Corinthians 10, 11, 12:11).

After he returned to Ephesus, Paul sent Titus to supervise the situation. Upon hearing no report, he began to worry and decided to return to Corinth. On the way, however, he met Titus coming back to Ephesus over land through Macedonia (Acts 20:1, 2; 2 Corinthians 7:5-7).

Paul was generally pleased with Titus's report, but some issues still needed to be addressed. He therefore sent the letter of 2 Corinthians to prepare the church for his impending return (2 Corinthians 13:1).

I. MERCIFUL JUDGMENT (2 CORINTHIANS 2:5-11)

A. SUFFICIENT SUFFERING (vv. 5, 6)

5. If anyone has caused grief, he has not so much grieved me as he has grieved all of you, to some extent—not to put it too severely.

While in Ephesus, Paul received word that a member of the church in Corinth was having an affair with his stepmother. Paul recognized that the sin involved demanded that this man be barred from the fellowship until he repented (1 Corinthians 5). The Corinthians were tolerating something that should not be tolerated.

In the text before us, we see the opposite extreme. Apparently the Corinthians refuse to forgive a certain man even after he confesses his sin. (This may or may not be the same man in 1 Corinthians 5.) *"To some extent,"* Paul says, "what this individual said or did *grieved all* of us, not just me." This sets the tone for the remainder of Paul's remarks.

6. The punishment inflicted on him by the majority is sufficient for him.

Disciplinary actions sometimes are needed to underscore the seriousness of sin or false doctrine. By barring the wayward individual from Christian fellowship, the church unites to let him know that he cannot continue to enjoy the company of the redeemed while such behavior continues. The New Testament presents three reasons for disfellowshiping: *doctrinal defection* (Romans 16:17, 18; 1 Timothy 6:3, 4; Titus 1:10-16), *moral defection* (1 Corinthians 5), and *divisiveness* (Romans 16:17, 18; Titus 3:10).

In the case at hand, Paul's advice apparently was too effective! The Corinthians, roused from their complacency, apparently dismissed someone from the church for an appropriate reason. But *the punishment* the man received is now *sufficient*. The punishment has served its purpose in bringing him back to his senses.

B. CONFIRMING LOVE (vv. 7, 8)

7. Now instead, you ought to forgive and comfort him, so that he will not be overwhelmed by excessive sorrow.

There are two goals to the extreme action of disfellowshiping. One goal is to protect the church's doctrinal and moral purity. The other goal is to bring about the repentance of the wayward believer. The church is not empowered to punish those who are outside the church; God himself will hand out their punishments in the next life.

The church, instead, is to discipline the backslider who is within the church (1 Corinthians 5:12, 13). A person may be overwhelmed with *sorrow* and grief as

Visual for Lesson 10. *Paul's movements are complex. This map will help your students keep a perspective on a segment of one of his journeys.*

a consequence. But if the final result is the person's restoration to a relationship with Christ, then the best possible outcome has been achieved! Godly sorrow leads to repentance (see below).

8. I urge you, therefore, to reaffirm your love for him.

Even though this man has caused considerable grief, love must still be the guiding force, not anger and vindictiveness. Paul had reminded the Corinthians in his first letter that "love is patient, love is kind" (1 Corinthians 13:4). He now urges them to put this principle into action. Church discipline should have a re-demptive purpose (Luke 17:3, 4; 2 Thessalonians 3:14, 15; James 5:19, 20).

C. UNANIMOUS FORGIVENESS (vv. 9-11)

9. The reason I wrote you was to see if you would stand the test and be obedient in everything.

There is a subtle warning behind this verse. Paul says that he has written as a *test* of their loyalty to his teaching. Obviously, if they fail to recognize his author-ity in such matters, then their obedience will again be called into question. As he says in 2 Corinthians 13:1-3, they need to be ready to answer for their actions when he comes on a third visit.

10. If you forgive anyone, I also forgive him. And what I have forgiven—if there was anything to forgive—I have forgiven in the sight of Christ for your sake,

True repentance before *Christ* brings true forgiveness from Christ (1 John 1:9). The man in question probably has already received Christ's forgiveness based on what Paul has just said in verses 7, 8. Will the Corinthians have the mind of Christ by forgiving that man as well?

FAILURE ISN'T FINAL

It was a typical chapel session on the campus of a certain Bible college. The aca-demic dean was preaching on the ability of God to use even the most difficult mo-ments of life to bring glory to his name. Near the end of his message, he called to the platform—to everyone's surprise—a former professor who had been released from his teaching duties because of a moral failure.

The auditorium fell silent as the young man ascended to the podium. He had been much loved and greatly respected. All who knew his story had been hugely affected by the disclosure of the problems within his life.

The young man began by relating to the student body the nature of his strug-gles, errors in judgment, and behavior that had so affected his life and ministry. Then he spoke of God's amazing grace working through his own repentance and the loving care and forgiveness of his people.

When he finished there was a keen awareness that we were witnessing the amazing work of God in his ability to use a horrible mistake to bring glory and honor to his name. What an encouragement to realize that God can work even in the midst of our mistakes to bring us back to him—if we will let him.   —T. B.

11. . . . in order that Satan might not outwit us. For we are not unaware of his schemes.

Satan loves to see people fall away from Christ, and he is having a field day with the Corinthians! Their unforgiving spirit is sinful in and of itself. Satan is tak-ing advantage of the situation to keep the penitent backslider away from God for good. Paul hopes that they will see how counterproductive their actions are and that they will evaluate their own motives to be sure they aren't doing more harm than good.

WHAT DO YOU THINK?

When someone is to be re-stored to full fellowship in the church, what practical steps may be necessary for the offending in-dividual to feel welcome again? What is necessary for others to accept that person and feel com-fortable around him or her?

WHAT DO YOU THINK?

Paul had to "sweat it out" about what would happen as someone else took his instructions to the church at Corinth. What practical advice might we gain from looking closely at Paul's ap-proach throughout this process?

WHAT DO YOU THINK?

If one person of a group for-gives an individual, do all have to fall in line and also forgive? Why, or why not?

II. PAUL'S COMFORT (2 CORINTHIANS 7:2-7)

A. SELF-DEFENSE (vv. 2, 3)

2. Make room for us in your hearts. We have wronged no one, we have corrupted no one, we have exploited no one.

When Paul returned to Corinth earlier, he apparently had been accused of misleading and exploiting the church (see 2 Corinthians 10:1-11). Paul thus sets an example of forgiveness by implying that he harbors no hard feelings in this regard. His motives and actions are always pure. Specifically, Paul never treated anyone disrespectfully, never said anything to encourage moral corruption, and never told the Corinthians what they wanted to hear just to get money (see 1 Corinthians 9:1-12). His actions were always honorable, thus the church is responsible for any hard feelings that ever passed between them.

3. I do not say this to condemn you; I have said before that you have such a place in our hearts that we would live or die with you.

Although Paul is not responsible for the conflict, he does not lord it over the Corinthians. Even when he uses strong words, Paul's goal is not *to condemn*. Instead, he always acts in their best interests. He models the type of loving forgiveness that he now asks them to demonstrate.

B. ENCOURAGING REPORT (vv. 4-7)

4, 5. I have great confidence in you; I take great pride in you. I am greatly encouraged; in all our troubles my joy knows no bounds. For when we came into Macedonia, this body of ours had no rest, but we were harassed at every turn—conflicts on the outside, fears within.

Paul begins to review the recent situation. After his confrontational visit, Paul was forced to return quickly to Ephesus to attend to pressing concerns. He therefore sent his disciple Titus to manage the situation in Corinth (see v. 6, next).

The volatility of the situation left Paul plagued with doubts. At that point in time, Paul was making successful inroads in Troas (2 Corinthians 2:12, 13) but his concern for the Corinthians was such a distraction that he set out to visit them once more.

6. But God, who comforts the downcast, comforted us by the coming of Titus,

Paul's fears turned to joy, however, when he met *Titus* halfway, in Macedonia. God's comfort is a major theme in 2 Corinthians, and it is notable here that God's comfort came to Paul through the report of Titus. God gave Paul spiritual peace in a difficult situation. But the Corinthians gave him an even deeper peace by resolving the problem (next verse).

7. . . . and not only by his coming but also by the comfort you had given him. He told us about your longing for me, your deep sorrow, your ardent concern for me, so that my joy was greater than ever.

Paul wants to make clear that he wasn't just happy to see that Titus had survived (as in "Praise God that those people didn't kill you!"). What truly impressed him was Titus's report that the Corinthians had decided to follow his advice and that they had an earnest desire to do so.

III. GOOD GUILT (2 CORINTHIANS 7:8-15)

A. PAUL'S JOY (vv. 8, 9a)

8. Even if I caused you sorrow by my letter, I do not regret it. Though I did regret it—I see that my letter hurt you, but only for a little while—

Many of Paul's comments in 1 Corinthians were very strong and could easily cause distress (see 2 Corinthians 2:3, 4). But true love does not seek simply to placate people; it seeks to do what is ultimately best for them. The Corinthians' actions were displeasing to God, and Paul had to make them aware of this fact. Because they eventually responded in the proper way, Paul can look back on the situation and say that he does not really *regret* his actions. Any was temporary, and the result was well worth it.

9a. . . . yet now I am happy, not because you were made sorry, but because your sorrow led you to repentance.

Paul is not happy to have hurt anyone's feelings. He rejoices, rather, that strong words led the Corinthians to repent—to change their minds and take the correct course of action.

B. GODLY SORROW (vv. 9b-11)

9b, 10. For you became sorrowful as God intended and so were not harmed in any way by us. Godly sorrow brings repentance that leads to salvation and leaves no regret, but worldly sorrow brings death.

Guilt is a powerful force. In our spiritual lives, feelings of guilt can lead to conviction of heart (examples: Psalm 51; Acts 2:37). *Sorrow* of this type reflects what God desires. We should feel ashamed when we sin, but that feeling should lead us to repent. If our feelings of guilt lead to transformation, then it is truly *godly* in the sense that it helps us to grow in obedience.

WILLING TO CHANGE?

One quiet evening the smiling face of the youngest elder of our church appeared at my office door. I had been waiting because I knew he wanted to discuss something. We always had had an amiable relationship, so I was intrigued by what the nature of this conversation would be.

After exchanging pleasantries, he proceeded to share with me several of my faults. After 45 minutes he had outlined every minor character flaw I had ever possessed and even threw in a few I didn't believe existed! After the ordeal I thanked him for sharing these things with me, and we prayed. He left, no doubt thinking that he had done me a huge favor.

I must admit that my immediate reaction was anger. On the outside I remained calm, but on the inside I was fuming, "Where does he get off thinking he has the right to say these things to me?" I harbored bitterness. I imagined a retaliatory strike.

As the weeks rolled on, however, I began to think. Some of his observations were out of line, but several were right on. I realized I needed to address these areas of my life. Now, nearly 25 years later, I look back on that evening as a key moment in my life. God used it to help me become a more faithful servant.

How we receive discipline is a mark of Christian maturity. God is often waiting for our pride to expire so he can work his will in us. —T. B.

11. See what this godly sorrow has produced in you: what earnestness, what eagerness to clear yourselves, what indignation, what alarm, what longing, what concern, what readiness to see justice done. At every point you have proved yourselves to be innocent in this matter.

The Corinthians' follow-up actions have proved that their sorrow over Paul's rebuke was not simply embarrassment at getting caught. Once he brought the issue to their attention, they realized their error and did something about it.

In this context *indignation* means that they became angry with themselves for being lax. Thus Paul is commending the Corinthians for taking proper steps after realizing that they had been tolerant of sinful behavior.

HOW TO SAY IT

Corinth. KOR-inth.
Corinthians. Ko-RIN-thee-unz.
Egypt. EE-jipt.
Ephesus. EF-uh-sus.
Macedonia. Mass-eh-DOE-nee-uh.
Titus. TY-tus.
Troas. TRO-az.

WHAT DO YOU THINK?

In what practical ways do both the offending person and the church benefit if there is both forgiveness and reconciliation?

PRAYER

Father, we live in a world where people rejoice in the failure of others. Help us to be lights of forgiveness and love. Give us the grace to give others the benefit of the doubt, when called for. Help us to share the forgiveness we have received from you with people who do wrong but repent. In Jesus' name, amen.

C. MUTUAL COMFORT (vv. 12-15)

12. So even though I wrote to you, it was not on account of the one who did the wrong or of the injured party, but rather that before God you could see for yourselves how devoted to us you are.

The backslidden person's flagrant violation of Paul's teachings, combined with the church's subsequent failure to protect its own purity, was a serious situation. Paul's goal was to assist the church in doing the right thing. He achieved that goal, even though it was painful.

In the process the Corinthians saw how much they really did care for Paul. His disciplinary actions actually led to a deeper relationship between them. They, in turn, should take similar steps to restore their fallen brother to full fellowship.

13. By all this we are encouraged.

In addition to our own encouragement, we were especially delighted to see how happy Titus was, because his spirit has been refreshed by all of you.

Titus not only managed a difficult situation but actually left Corinth *refreshed*. This is a testimony to his pastoral skill. Titus is mentioned in the New Testament most often in the book of 2 Corinthians.

14. I had boasted to him about you, and you have not embarrassed me. But just as everything we said to you was true, so our boasting about you to Titus has proved to be true as well.

In the ancient world, to be *embarrassed* means to lose status in the eyes of another person. Even at their worst, Paul remained confident that the Corinthians would not put him to shame. His hopes were fulfilled by God's providence.

15. And his affection for you is all the greater when he remembers that you were all obedient, receiving him with fear and trembling.

Although the Corinthians had received Titus *with fear and trembling,* Paul does not mean that people should fear church leaders. The Corinthians had not been afraid of Titus himself but rather of the implications of his message. They suddenly realized how serious their situation was and how deeply they had offended Paul.

But Titus, like Paul, showed true love toward them. Could the Corinthians not extend the same love and forgiveness to a man who repented of a sin, admitting that he had done wrong?

WHAT DO YOU THINK?

Under what circumstances is it wise to send others to help with the "cleanup work" when a messy situation is not improving? What instructions should they receive?

CONCLUSION

Those of us who are parents recall many times when our children made us angry. We go into our son's room after telling him several times to get dressed, only to discover him sitting on the floor in his underwear playing with toys. Such offenses make us mad, and we often lash out in frustration. But stop and think for a moment: Are such actions intended truly to discipline the child or merely to punish him?

Discipline is an action we take to help another person develop and mature. Discipline may result from some crime but does not focus on the crime. Rather, it focuses on the right things the person should do in the future. Discipline encourages the errant one to do better. When in anger we merely punish our children for jumping on the bed, we are not helping them improve.

God does not empower the church to punish the immoral people of the world. God does, however, call the church to discipline its members. This means to help them become stronger Christians who will make godly, holy choices. Our judgmental feelings of anger and resentment must never get in the way of this objective. Forgiveness is a key.

THOUGHT TO REMEMBER

When forgiveness is needed, we must give it.

Discovery Learning

This page contains an alternative lesson plan emphasizing learning activities. Classes desiring such student involvement will find these suggestions helpful. The next page is a reproducible activity page to further enhance discovery learning.

LEARNING GOALS

After participating in this lesson, each student will be able to:

1. Tell how Paul responded to the evidence of repentance in the Corinthian church and what he urged them to do.

2. Explain why full forgiveness is essential when repentance has taken place.

3. Identify one person to whom he or she needs to extend forgiveness or from whom forgiveness should be asked.

INTO THE LESSON

Prepare four opaque cards, each with a large numeral 4 on one side. Fold each card so that the numeral is on the inside. Hand out the four cards randomly to class members as they arrive. Give the following instruction: "Look at your card but don't let others see what is printed on it."

At the beginning of class, say, "I want those with a card to hand your card to another class member. Be sure to give that person the same directions that I gave you when I handed you the card." Continue in this manner until all have seen a card.

Say, "This activity represents the theme of today's lesson. Who can identify the relationship?" When someone notes that you have been "*four*-giving to others," accept the chuckles and groans, then launch into today's text.

INTO THE WORD

Provide paper for the following agree/disagree activity (or use the activity as it appears in the student book). Say, "As you look at today's text in 2 Corinthians 2:5-11; 7:2-15, decide if you agree or disagree with each of the following statements:"

1. A Christian's sin is an affront to those who have taught him or her.

2. Church discipline is designed to make an example of the wayward brother or sister.

3. Correction must come out of a heart of love, not one of vengeance.

4. Obedience is the only sure indication of respect for authority.

5. Satan revels in an unforgiving spirit.

6. Bold speech in the face of sin can elicit a good response.

7. Few things cheer up a parent more than correction received graciously.

8. There is real joy in seeing a sinner repent in tears.

9. Sorrow over sin can have a harmful effect for the sinner.

10. Sometimes the good of the church as a whole is more significant than the good of an individual.

11. Boasting is an appropriate response for one who has met high expectations.

12. True affection for someone will increase as that person acts in obedience to God's truth.

After allowing time for students to record their answers, say, "Now let's go back and match these statements to the Bible verses in today's text to see whether we should agree or disagree with each one."

Ask a volunteer to read aloud the Key Verse for today, 2 Corinthians 7:10. This verse sharply contrasts godly sorrow and worldly sorrow. Ask, "What are the foundational differences between godly sorrow and worldly sorrow?" Allow for a variety of responses but expect answers to the effect that worldly sorrow remains essentially selfish.

INTO LIFE

Display the following three-word sentences on the board. Ask your class to rank them as to which is most difficult to say: "I was wrong." "Please forgive me." "I forgive you." "We are brothers/sisters." "Christ forgave me." "You were wrong."

Next say, "If one of these statements were on the outside of a greeting card asking for someone's forgiveness, what could the inside of the card say?" If the class needs an example, say, "For the 'We are brothers/sisters' statement, you could write, 'Our love must be greater than my foolishness; please forgive my offense toward you.'"

After brief discussion, hand each class member half of an 8-1/2" by 11" sheet of paper folded to resemble a card. Say, "Write *Forgiveness Card* on the back bottom of this folded sheet. Then create a forgiveness card using one of the six phrases. Someone you know needs your forgiveness. Use this forgiveness card to remind you this week to seek that reconciliation." [Alternative Into Life exercises are found on the reproducible page.]

Unrepented Sin and Unforgiven Sin

Below are some potential results of allowing unrepented or unforgiven sin to fester. *How likely* is each to happen? *How serious* is each? (Answers should be from the viewpoint of one who has sinned and needs to repent as well as from the viewpoint of the one who needs to extend forgiveness to someone who has repented.)

- Avoiding others socially:

- Restless and interrupted sleep:

- Gossip and other forms of vengeance:

- Deteriorating physical health:

- Bouts of depression and guilt:

- Anger and impatience toward others:

- [Add one of your own]:

Covered!

In the areas labeled SIN, write in three personal sins that Christ has forgiven you or for which you need to seek his forgiveness. Clip the FORGIVENESS strip into three pieces, and affix each piece over one of your sins as a symbol of how God has covered your sins with Christ's blood. For added symbolism, change the exclamation point to a cross.

Sin   Sin   Sin

| For- | -give- | -ness! |

GIVING GENEROUSLY

LESSON 11

WHY TEACH THIS LESSON?

A few years ago an eye-opening book was published with the title, *Rich Christians in an Age of Hunger.* The author, Ron Sider, challenged the Christians of the world's wealthy countries (particularly America) to consider the reality of millions of people who live in abject poverty and hunger every day.

Paul dealt with similar themes in 2 Corinthians. At the time he wrote, the citizens of Jerusalem were suffering from famine conditions. Paul spearheaded a campaign for certain churches to raise funds for the relief of their brothers and sisters in need. Some of the churches had completed their offerings. The Corinthians, however, had not. In his encouragement to them to finish, Paul laid out essential principles of stewardship and giving. These timeless teachings still ring true today. This lesson presents crucial information to guide Christians in a duty that is often avoided or neglected: giving for the Lord's work. We have an obligation to learn how God expects us to be people of generosity and concern for those in need.

INTRODUCTION

A. AMISH INSURANCE

The Amish are a people known for industry and thrift. Their farms and businesses are models of cleanliness and order. They are regarded widely for their ethical business practices and the quality of their workmanship. As a result many Amish families enjoy financial prosperity.

A real estate agent once visited an Amish man to discuss the acquisition of a neighboring piece of land. As they spoke, the agent realized that the man had accumulated a great deal of wealth, with a large farm and several herds of dairy cows. He asked the farmer who provided his insurance. The man replied, "God."

The agent, taken aback, pointed out that even very godly people sometimes lose their properties to theft or disasters. What if the man's barn were struck by fire or a tornado? The farmer explained that God would take care of him, because other members of the community would rebuild the barn for him and help him replace his equipment. That was the kind of insurance he relied on.

This commendable outlook reflects the conditions in Paul's day. Christians could not depend on the government or insurance companies in times of need. They could depend only on God. In our passage for today, Paul discusses God's insurance plan: Christians sharing their wealth to help one another get through tough times.

B. LESSON BACKGROUND

During his second and third missionary journeys, Paul expended much effort organizing a collection for the needs of the impoverished Christians in Jerusalem. Palestine is a dry region, and during New Testament times there were several major droughts in that area (compare Acts 11:27, 28). Further, there

DEVOTIONAL READING:
LUKE 20:45–21:4
BACKGROUND SCRIPTURE:
2 CORINTHIANS 8:1-15
PRINTED TEXT:
2 CORINTHIANS 8:1-15

LESSON AIMS

After participating in this lesson, each student will be able to:

1. List reasons that Paul cites for why the Corinthians should have felt compelled to give.

2. Explain how a benevolent gift is an appropriate response to God's grace.

3. Examine his or her personal motives for giving or not giving to those in need.

Aug
13

KEY VERSE

For you know the grace of our Lord Jesus Christ, that though he was rich, yet for your sakes he became poor, so that you through his poverty might become rich.
—*2 Corinthians 8:9*

LESSON 11 NOTES

were continual rumblings of rebellion against Rome throughout the A.D. 50s and 60s. These frequently disrupted the economy of the region. (Note that 2 Corinthians was written in A.D. 57.)

Paul saw this situation as a prime opportunity for his congregations, composed primarily of Gentile believers, to extend a gesture of goodwill to the parent church in Judea (see Romans 15:25-27). In our passage for today, Paul instructs the Corinthians on preparations for their gift. In the process he offers the most extended discussion of benevolent giving found anywhere in the Bible.

I. EXAMPLE OF GIVING (2 CORINTHIANS 8:1-5)

A. PAIN (vv. 1-3)

1, 2. And now, brothers, we want you to know about the grace that God has given the Macedonian churches. Out of the most severe trial, their overflowing joy and their extreme poverty welled up in rich generosity.

Paul begins with a kind of paradox that sets the tone for the rest of the chapter. Normally, we would think of a *grace* that is bestowed as a gift that someone receives. *God*, Paul says, gave the *churches* of Macedonia a gift. But he immediately clarifies that the gift they received was the desire to give something to someone else. What they received from God, then, was a passionate desire to help others.

This fact is especially remarkable in view of their circumstances. Each of the three major churches in Macedonia—namely, Philippi, Thessalonica, and Berea—was born into persecution (Acts 16:16–17:15). These people had suffered adverse circumstances from the day they accepted Christ. Yet, amazingly, this led them to give even more generously. (Corinth itself is part of Achaia, to the south of Macedonia.)

Paul points out two more apparent paradoxes in their situation. First, in a time of great suffering the Macedonians were filled with *overflowing joy*. This is certainly not the normal, worldly response to such a situation! Second, their poverty abounded *in rich generosity*. Through God's power they actually were thankful to give from their limited resources to help other Christians who were in need, even people they had never met.

3. For I testify that they gave as much as they were able, and even beyond their ability. Entirely on their own,

Technically speaking, it is obvious that no one can give more than he or she is able to give since credit cards don't exist in Paul's day. The question is how much we think we can afford to give. That essentially becomes an issue of how much we trust God to provide for us in the future if we give now. The Macedonians not only *gave* what they could afford, they also gave more than they could afford, to a point where it hurt. In this sense their giving was *beyond their ability*. This kind of giving takes faith. This kind of giving hurts!

WHAT DO YOU THINK?

Under which condition are we most likely to learn more about giving: while being rich, while living on a tight budget, or while struggling under severe circumstances? Explain.

GLORIOUS GIVING

There is an old story of a medieval monk who found a precious jewel and kept it. The monk had taken a vow of poverty, so he had no thought of redeeming the jewel for money. He enjoyed it for its beauty and radiance. It reminded him of the glory of God in creation.

One day the monk met a traveler. As the monk opened his bag to share his provisions, the stranger saw the jewel. Knowing that the monk had taken a vow always to help those in need, he asked the monk to give him the jewel.

The monk asked, "Do you really need the gem, my son?" The stranger replied, "Yes, I do." To the man's astonishment, the monk readily gave him the jewel.

The traveler departed, overjoyed with his unexpected stroke of luck. A few days later, though, he came back in search of the monk. Finding him, he gave him back the precious jewel and made a request: "I want to ask you for something even more precious than this jewel. Please give to me that which enabled you to give me the jewel."

The traveler had discerned a great truth: the ability to give is one of the greatest blessings in life. May God grant to us the joyous ability to be gracious in our giving.

—T. B.

B. PRIVILEGE (v. 4)

4. . . . they urgently pleaded with us for the privilege of sharing in this service to the saints.

The key concept in this verse, and in this entire chapter, is fellowship. This refers to a complete *sharing* of life with another. Similar terminology is used to describe the earliest life of the church in Acts 2:42-47. There we see the believers constantly worshiping together, sharing meals, and providing for one another's financial needs.

As Jesus said, God has promised to provide for every person who seeks his kingdom (Matthew 6:33). But that provision can come in many different forms. It may come in the form of a new job, an unexpected bonus, or a financial gift. Sometimes God provides for someone else's needs through your prosperity, as you share with them what God has given you. Later on you may be on the receiving end when you are in need.

This sense of communion with other believers allows the Macedonians not only to give money but actually to plead with Paul to be able to share the gift. They are confident that their Judean brothers and sisters will also help them if the need ever arises.

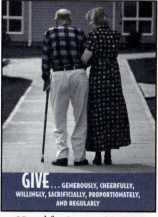

Visual for Lesson 11. *Point to this visual as you ask, "In what ways can we give in non-monetary ways?"*

C. PRIORITIES (v. 5)

5. And they did not do as we expected, but they gave themselves first to the Lord and then to us in keeping with God's will.

Godly stewardship is not just a matter of money but rather is a matter of our very lives. The Macedonians *first* gave their own selves to God in the sense that they placed complete trust in his provision. That was their top priority. This, in turn, enabled them to share their financial resources to the maximum extent. When we give to help God's people, we are only sharing what belongs to God anyway; literally, we are spending someone else's money—God's.

WHAT WE LEAVE BEHIND

Funerals are a time of reflection in which we remember the most redeeming qualities of those who have departed this life. But what if we heard the following at a funeral?

"This fellow had the finest set of golf clubs that money could buy."

"I will really miss seeing his beautiful, weed-free yard."

"The thing that I will always remember about ol' Bob is the way he could get that extra 10 horsepower out of his car's engine."

"I will always appreciate the fact that he made well over $100,000 a year and that his stocks always performed well."

If we did hear those statements at a funeral, we would pity the shallow lives of the people who made them (not to mention the empty life of the deceased). U.S. President Calvin Coolidge (1872–1933) once said, "No person was ever honored for what he received. Honor has been the reward for what he gave."

Coolidge was giving us a formula for successful living. Yet God is the original source and example of this formula. Giving is inseparably connected to the gracious character of God. We live because God is generous. He gave us his Son. One of the greatest traits of those redeemed by Christ is the ability to become like our heavenly Father in generosity. —T. B.

II. GRACE OF SHARING (2 CORINTHIANS 8:6-15)

A. CORINTHIANS' START (vv. 6-8)

6. So we urged Titus, since he had earlier made a beginning, to bring also to completion this act of grace on your part.

Paul now turns from the example of the Macedonian churches to urge the Corinthians to prepare a generous gift for the needy in Jerusalem. He begins with a discussion of the ministry of *Titus*.

After delivering a progress report that brought Paul great joy and relief (see 2 Corinthians 7:5-15), Titus is to go to Corinth ahead of Paul. The reason for the return trip possibly is to deliver the letter of 2 Corinthians. Thus Titus will prepare the Corinthians for Paul's arrival. Primary among his list of things to do, Titus is to encourage the Corinthians to have their offering for Jerusalem ready to go. That way Paul can take it along with him (2 Corinthians 9:3-5).

The *act of grace* refers specifically to the financial gifts of the Corinthians. But it also continues the theme of the previous verses and flows into verse 7. God graciously has given many things to his people, including salvation and spiritual gifts; the Corinthians are to exhibit godly graciousness in turn by giving to their needy brethren. God showed favor to us even before we knew him by sending Christ. The Corinthians should show favor to their brothers and sisters in Judea, even though they have never met them.

7. But just as you excel in everything—in faith, in speech, in knowledge, in complete earnestness and in your love for us—see that you also excel in this grace of giving.

Paul reminds the Corinthians of the spiritual gifts that God had given for their edification and in which they sometimes take too much pride (1 Corinthians 12:14-31). *Faith* as used here is not "saving faith" but rather has the sense of a gift of especially effective faith, perhaps relating to prayer (see 1 Corinthians 12:9; 13:2). *Speech* refers to spiritual gifts that involve the proclamation of God's will, such as prophecy and tongues. *Knowledge* is the gift of insight into God's nature and plans. The Corinthians, having received such marvelous spiritual gifts, should be motivated in turn to share their material possessions with others.

But their diligence in the offering will not show only their appreciation for God's benevolence, it will also demonstrate their love for Paul. The Corinthians already have shown their loyalty by heeding at least some of Paul's warnings (example: 2 Corinthians 7:9). Can he count on them once again? Since they have already received so much, Paul is confident that God will now bestow upon them, like the Macedonians, yet another gracious gift: the willingness to share with those in need.

8. I am not commanding you, but I want to test the sincerity of your love by comparing it with the earnestness of others.

Giving is the right thing to do. But giving ultimately is a personal expression of faith, a private matter between the giver and God. Paul therefore stresses that he is not ordering them to give. Indeed, such a command could lead to suspicions and accusations about his motives, similar to the skepticism many of us feel toward TV evangelists today.

WHAT DO YOU THINK?

How would a Christian know if he or she really had learned the grace of giving?

DAILY BIBLE READINGS

Monday, Aug. 7—The Widow's Offering (Luke 20:45–21:4)

Tuesday, Aug. 8—Chosen to Serve the Poor (Acts 6:1-6)

Wednesday, Aug. 9—Generosity, a Gift from God (Romans 12:3-8)

Thursday, Aug. 10—The Collection for the Saints (1 Corinthians 15:58–16:4)

Friday, Aug. 11—A Fruit of the Spirit (Galatians 5:16-26)

Saturday, Aug. 12—Excel in Generosity (2 Corinthians 8:1-7)

Sunday, Aug. 13—Rules for Giving (2 Corinthians 8:8-15)

At the same time, however, Paul makes clear that the Corinthians should feel very ashamed if they fail to give. In the first place they haven't suffered nearly as much as the Macedonians, the others who have been so generous. In the second place Paul will have to wonder about the Corinthians' *love* if they don't contribute. It is not clear whether Paul is referring to love for the needy saints in Jerusalem, love for himself as an apostle, or love for Christ who has given them such grace. Perhaps all three are in mind, since a generous gift will help the poor, will validate Paul's confidence in them, and will show trust in God's future provision all at once.

B. CHRIST'S EXAMPLE (v. 9)

9. *For you know the grace of our Lord Jesus Christ, that though he was rich, yet for your sakes he became poor, so that you through his poverty might become rich.*

Here as elsewhere, Paul appeals to *Christ* as the ultimate example. Christ, as God, was more than *rich* in human terms. He owns everything in the universe! Yet his love for us led him to give up this privileged position and come to earth in the form of a servant to die for our sins (Philippians 2:5-8). Jesus' suffering led to our blessing—*through his poverty* we have come to possess all the spiritual riches of salvation. The Corinthians can imitate Christ by sharing.

C. PAUL'S ADVICE (vv. 10, 11)

10. *And here is my advice about what is best for you in this matter: Last year you were the first not only to give but also to have the desire to do so.*

Having set the example of Christ before them, Paul now challenges the Corinthians to reflect on their own reputations. They apparently had begun to organize a collection for Jerusalem *last year.* As such, they seem to have been one of *the first* churches to answer Paul's call for aid. But their benevolence program had been sidetracked for some reason.

In the meantime the churches of Macedonia, which probably had fewer resources, had started and completed their giving campaign. Since the Jerusalem offering is a cooperative effort involving many churches in several regions, the Corinthians are in danger of becoming an international spectacle. When someone is absent from a family photo, people will ask why!

11. *Now finish the work, so that your eager willingness to do it may be matched by your completion of it, according to your means.*

Talk is cheap. It is easy to say that we want to help others but quite another thing actually to do something for them. Christ did not save us from our sins by saying that he felt sorry for us; he saved us by dying on the cross. The Corinthians need to *finish* what they started and actually come up with the money they pledged, lest it become obvious to everyone that their mouths are bigger than their hearts (compare James 2:14-17).

D. PAUL'S DESIRE (vv. 12-15)

12. *For if the willingness is there, the gift is acceptable according to what one has, not according to what he does not have.*

On one occasion Jesus and his disciples were watching people drop money into an offering urn in the temple. As people gave their gifts, he noticed one elderly woman who could offer only two small copper coins worth a few pennies. This woman's contribution was greater than all the others because, he said, she had given all that she had. The others had simply shared a small portion of their wealth (Mark 12:41-44).

HOW TO SAY IT

Achaia. Uh-KAY-uh.
Berea. Buh-REE-uh.
Corinth. KOR-inth.
Corinthians. Ko-RIN-thee-unz.
Macedonia. Mass-eh-DOE-nee-uh.
Philippi. Fih-LIP-pie or FIL-ih-pie.
Philippians. Fih-LIP-ee-unz.
Thessalonica. THESS-uh-lo-NYE-kuh.

WHAT DO YOU THINK?

Some Christians need to be reminded repeatedly to give generously. What are some good ways to encourage all of us in the grace of giving without sounding as if money is the only issue to be discussed?

PRAYER

Heavenly Father, help us to overcome our greed. Lead us to recognize selfishness and not rationalize. Fill us with hearts of compassion, and give us the stewardship to manage the resources you have given us in a way that will please you. In everything we do, help us to imitate the example of Christ. In his name, amen.

Paul appeals to this principle to assure the Corinthians that what he has been saying is not intended to make them feel guilty. Perhaps they feel ashamed of the amount they can provide, especially when compared with the Macedonians. So Paul clarifies: What is important is not the size of the gift but rather the fulfillment of the pledge to give. God is more concerned with our motives than with the amount of money in our wallets. (See also Proverbs 3:27, 28.)

13, 14. Our desire is not that others might be relieved while you are hard pressed, but that there might be equality. At the present time your plenty will supply what they need, so that in turn their plenty will supply what you need. Then there will be equality,

Some could look at Paul's efforts to raise money for Jerusalem and conclude that he cared more for that church than for the Corinthians. Paul therefore assures them that he does not wish to seem unfair. The issue is one of *equality*. Even so, these verses should not be taken as an endorsement of a socialist economic program. Paul never states a plan for a government redistribution of wealth so that everyone has the same amount of money.

The real point is that the Corinthians have been blessed with *plenty* while those in the Jerusalem church are suffering. Next year the reverse may be true. In that case Paul will expect the Jerusalem believers to be generous *in turn*. This mutual support in times of need will thus create a sort of godly insurance policy. By this all Christians everywhere can be confident that their needs will be met through the generosity of others.

15. . . . as it is written: "He who gathered much did not have too much, and he who gathered little did not have too little."

Paul now quotes Exodus 16:18, a passage that is particularly relevant to the topic at hand. It refers to the days when the Israelites wandered in the wilderness for 40 years under Moses. During that period, the Jews did not have a stable source of food from the land about them, so God sent them bread from Heaven miraculously. Each person was to take a certain amount of manna for the household. God provided enough for everyone to be satisfied, whether they gathered *much* or *little*.

CONCLUSION

People often claim that they cannot believe in God because of the problem of evil. When asked to explain this argument, they often reply that a good God could not let children in Haiti die of starvation. Since there are, in fact, children in Haiti who are dying of starvation, then God must not exist; if he did exist, so the argument goes, then he surely would do something about this problem.

Notably, however, many people who would cite this argument are doing nothing to help these starving children themselves. Does the fact that they are not helping such children also mean that they do not exist?

God most certainly exists, and he has provided sufficient material resources to sustain every person who lives on this planet. Even today, with a world population of over six billion, there are more than enough resources for the human race to survive—people simply are not willing to share their wealth. And whether we want to admit it or not, God has provided his people with plenty of money to support one another, his church, and the proclamation of the gospel.

If needs are not being met, it is not because God has not provided; it is because we have not provided. If people judged our existence by whether or not we help with the needs of others, could we prove that we exist? To the person in need, we may as well not exist if we are unwilling to share.

Discovery Learning

This page contains an alternative lesson plan emphasizing learning activities. Classes desiring such student involvement will find these suggestions helpful. The next page is a reproducible activity page to further enhance discovery learning.

LEARNING GOALS

After this lesson, each student will be able to:

1. List reasons that Paul cites for why the Corinthians should have felt compelled to give.

2. Explain how a benevolent gift is an appropriate response to God's grace.

3. Examine his or her personal motives for giving or not giving to those in need.

INTO THE LESSON

Display the following puzzle for your class.

R	I	C	H
—	—	—	—
—	**—**	—	—
—	—	**—**	—
—	**—**	—	—
P	O	O	R

Say, "Today's Key Verse, 2 Corinthians 8:9, reveals the change of status that Jesus willingly chose in order to become our Savior." Have a good reader read this verse aloud. Next say, "Can you change RICH to POOR in this puzzle by changing only one letter per line? The bolded blanks are the letters that need changed."

Allow a few minutes before giving the following clues, row by row: "A covered stack of hay or straw" (RICK); "Another word for a stone" (ROCK); "A type of bird or chess piece" (ROOK); "A library's special loan" (BOOK); "A rude or insensitive person" (BOOR).

Write, "Our Ultimate Example of Generous Giving" on a piece of poster board. Under this title write today's Key Verse. Highlight the following words in the verse: *Jesus Christ/was rich/ yet/became poor/that you.*

[Alternative or additional activity: distribute the "How's My Giving?" exercise on the reproducible page for students to work on as they arrive.]

INTO THE WORD

Divide the class into small groups of four to six. Say, "Today's text reveals key truths about the money we return to the Lord for the church's work. I want us to meditate on those truths."

If your congregation has a meditation before the offering is collected during the worship service, introduce the following activity. (If there is no such element in your worship service, say, "Many churches have a brief offering meditation before the offering is collected. For this activity let's pretend that this were true here.")

Introduce this activity by saying: "I am going to give each group member a sheet of paper with a title and a portion of Scripture from today's lesson text printed on it. In your groups you will be writing simple offering meditations based on the titles and Bible passages printed on the top of your sheets. When you get your papers don't do anything, but wait for my instructions."

Ahead of time, print the following offering meditation titles and corresponding Bible references on sheets of paper, one title and Bible reference per sheet. "Poor Man, Rich Man" (vv. 1, 2); "Possible Impossibility" (v. 3); "Reverse Beggars" (v. 4); "First Things First" (v. 5); "Unmerited Giving" (v. 6); "Abundance Begets Abundance" (v. 7); "Love, Sincerely Yours" (v. 8); "Rich . . . Poor . . . Rich" (v. 9); "Add the Bow and Gift Card" (v. 10); "Talk Is Cheap" (v. 11); "No Less, No More" (v. 12); "Reciprocity" (vv. 13, 14); "Manna" (v. 15).

Give each group member one sheet. Say, "Look at the title and Bible verse at the top of your sheet. Then write the first sentence of an offering meditation based on that title and verse. After you have written your one sentence, stop and wait for further instructions."

Allow time for students to work and then say, "Now pass your sheet to the person on your right. Once you get a new sheet, look at the title and verse at the top of your sheet and read the one sentence your classmate has written. Continue the mediation by writing a second sentence of your own." Repeat this process four or five times. Then collect all the sheets, shuffle them, and redistribute them to class members. Allow volunteers to read verses and offering meditations. Include a brief discussion of the meditation titles for each verse.

INTO LIFE

For each student make a list in advance of the offering meditation titles from the preceding activity. Ask students to carry their lists with them or post them in a conspicuous place as daily reminders of the principles of Christian giving. Suggest that they use one title from the list each week as their personal giving guideline for that week.

How's My Giving?

For the questions below that you can answer *yes*, place the indicated letter in the appropriate box.

Q. Do you return to God an amount proportional to your income? Put an *E* in box 4.

Q. Do you give small token gifts to the people around you for no particular reason? Put an *O* in box 6.

Q. Did you make a special monetary gift to a Christian relief agency the last time you heard of a natural disaster? Put an *I* in box 8.

Q. Do you ever find yourself thinking, "I wish I had more to give"? Put an *R* in box 5.

Q. Do you give to God sacrificially? Put a *Y* in box 10.

Q. Do you get more delight from giving gifts than you do from receiving them? Put a *T* in box 9.

Q. At church potluck dinners do you contribute more food than most people do? Put an *E* in box 2.

Q. Do you give to God cheerfully and willingly? Put an *S* in box 7.

Q. If you receive a bonus or other unexpected income, do you return part of the amount to God? Put an *N* in box 3.

Q. In tipping for service rendered to you, do you generally give a greater percent than most people do? Put a *G* in box 1.

Q. Do you ever give in the name of Christ to relief agencies collecting funds in public settings? Put in one of the letters you didn't use earlier into an empty box.

Q. For social occasions such as weddings and graduations, do you cheerfully present a gift to the ones being honored? Put one of the letters that you didn't use earlier into an empty box.

Q. Do you give up personal time to help others who need your presence? Put one of the letters that you didn't use earlier into an empty box.

1	2	3	4	5	6	7	8	9	10

How close do you come to being characterized by *generosity*? How will you move closer?

Called to Be a Christian Community
Unit 3: The Spirit of Giving
(Lessons 10-13)

GIVING IS A WITNESS

WHY TEACH THIS LESSON?

Do we give for a need, or do we need to give? Paul taught the Corinthians that both are true. When we give, we desire that our gift be useful and not squandered, and this is reasonable. Yet there is a spiritual principle involved that is very personal. This lesson teaches that giving is intended to benefit not only the recipient but also the giver.

The spiritual principles taught here go against many of the trends of society. We witness people who give for recognition, to advance a social agenda, or because they are coerced into giving. The Bible teaches that sharing is part of God's plan to take care of the needy and hungry in our world. When we give in this manner, we are truly acting in a godly fashion, and God promises that we will receive joy from our sacrifice. The lesson includes the famous teaching that if we "sow" (give) generously, we will "reap" (receive) abundant blessings. As the lesson points out, giving is not an option. Learning to give is part of the path toward Christian maturity.

INTRODUCTION

A. BENEFITS OF SHARING

For a recent Thanksgiving, my wife and I volunteered to deliver baskets of food from the church to needy families. After spending hours loading and unloading the car and trying to locate addresses on dark houses on a cold evening, we were tired and ready to go home. As we carried our heavy baskets from the car to the last house on our list, I commented wearily that we should perhaps leave this particular service opportunity to others until the time when we did not have two small children to drag around with us.

We knocked on the door and were greeted by a woman in her fifties. With her was a host of children, ranging from infants to girls in high school. She immediately invited us in and asked us to sit. Each child was introduced, and she told us that her eldest daughter had died recently and that another child had moved back in after losing a job. As a result, the lady was working two jobs herself, desperately trying to support her eight children and grandchildren.

We sat speechless, humbled by her testimony and her faith. Before we left she insisted that we all pray together. After we did she burst into tears and thanked us profusely for the food. We told her that she should not thank us; we were only delivering a gift from the church. But as we went out the door, she pressed a letter into our hands expressing deep gratitude for our visit and asking for God's continued blessing on our home. As we walked back to the car, my wife and I decided that perhaps we should volunteer to deliver baskets again next year.

Jesus said, "It is more blessed to give than to receive" (Acts 20:35). This is the case not just because it's better to be able to help than to need help. It is better to give because when we give to meet another's need, we act as God's hand for his sustenance. The food we left at that home was worth perhaps $300; the prayers

DEVOTIONAL READING:
PSALM 37:16-24

BACKGROUND SCRIPTURE:
2 CORINTHIANS 9:1-15

PRINTED TEXT:
2 CORINTHIANS 9:3-15

LESSON AIMS

After participating in this lesson, each student will be able to:

1. Restate Paul's reasons for the need of Christians to be generous givers.

2. Explain how God makes it possible to be generous.

3. Make a personal giving plan.

KEY VERSE

And God is able to make all grace abound to you, so that in all things at all times, having all that you need, you will abound in every good work.

—2 Corinthians 9:8

Aug 20

we took with us were priceless. The benefit of sharing is not a material benefit. The benefit is the chance to participate in God's plan to provide for his people.

B. LESSON BACKGROUND

As noted in our last lesson, Paul wrote 2 Corinthians at a time when the people of the churches in Judea were suffering through a financial crisis. The Roman government did not have a consistent "federal aid policy" to address such situations. Unemployment insurance did not exist.

The situation was especially bad for Christians of Jewish descent who were not able to receive support from synagogues. Fortunately, God has a plan to help Christians in need, but it does not involve miraculous provisions of food or money. Manna no longer falls from the sky. Instead, God provides through the generosity of other believers.

I. READY AND WILLING? (2 CORINTHIANS 9:3-7)

A. PAUL'S BOASTING (vv. 3, 4)

3. But I am sending the brothers in order that our boasting about you in this matter should not prove hollow, but that you may be ready, as I said you would be.

In chapter 8 Paul urged the Corinthians to rise to the example of the Macedonian churches by giving generously to the relief effort for Jerusalem. Paul had sent Titus to Corinth to prepare the church for his own upcoming visit and to collect their offering for the Judean churches (2 Corinthians 8:16-21). But he had also sent along several representatives of the Macedonian churches. They would go with him to Jerusalem as ambassadors of the Gentiles (8:22-24).

Paul's purpose in using this procedure probably is at least twofold. First, it will ensure that the funds will be managed in a proper and ethical way (8:20).

Second, it will allow the Jewish Christians in Jerusalem a chance to meet Gentile believers from a variety of different places. These representatives could then report back to their home churches about their experiences in Jerusalem. Hopefully, this will secure a greater sense of unity between the Jewish and Gentile segments of the first-century church.

4. For if any Macedonians come with me and find you unprepared, we—not to say anything about you—would be ashamed of having been so confident.

Paul now lays out the first reason why the Corinthians should get serious about preparing their gift. In 2 Corinthians 8:1-5, he bragged about the generosity of the Macedonian churches, but it appears he also has been bragging about the Corinthians. How embarrassed he would be if some of the Macedonian Christians were to travel to Corinth with him only to discover that the stewardship campaign was in disarray! And not only Paul would be embarrassed—the Corinthians themselves would surely be even more humiliated. Paul therefore urges them to fulfill their pledges so that his confidence will be confirmed.

B. CORINTHIANS' GENEROSITY (vv. 5, 6)

5. So I thought it necessary to urge the brothers to visit you in advance and finish the arrangements for the generous gift you had promised. Then it will be ready as a generous gift, not as one grudgingly given.

The Corinthians apparently had responded quickly to a previous call for aid. But for some reason almost an entire year passed without any focused efforts to bring this program to a successful conclusion (2 Corinthians 8:10, 11).

Paul assumes that they will be faithful to their pledge. But he goes on to state a key principle about giving: the motive is just as important as the gift. From a fi-

WHAT DO YOU THINK?

How do we handle contributions to reduce temptation or minimize suspicion of misuse?

WHAT DO YOU THINK?

Some may think that Paul's boasting about the Corinthians' intention to give was an attempt to raise a larger offering through guilt. How did Paul guard against the accusation of being manipulative? How can we do the same?

nancial perspective, money is money; a starving person can buy food with it whether it is given with good motives or poor motives. But giving is intended to benefit not only the recipient but also the giver.

A *gift* that is well planned and thoughtfully bestowed allows the giver to share in the joy of the fellowship. But a gift that is rushed or given from a sense of guilt does not provide this joy. Instead, it often creates feelings of resentment, either toward the needy, toward the one who points out the need, or toward God himself, who calls us to give. Thoughtful consideration in advance will make giving a blessing to all involved. Paul urges the Corinthians to plan their giving carefully. *Not as one grudgingly given* speaks of the need to avoid giving a gift that you would really rather keep for yourself.

6. Remember this: Whoever sows sparingly will also reap sparingly, and whoever sows generously will also reap generously.

The imagery here is drawn from agriculture: common sense says that a person who plants more seed will reap a larger harvest. But Paul cannot mean that God is more impressed with a larger gift. As we noted last week, Jesus says that the size of the donation makes no difference (Mark 12:41-44).

In this context the terms *sparingly* and *generously* are proportionate to an individual's ability to give. God does not expect a person who makes $30,000 a year to give as much as a person who makes $100,000; he does, however, expect both to be willing to share when others are in need. God is concerned with one's motive for giving. Any gift given without sincere love is worth nothing in God's sight (1 Corinthians 13:3).

With this in mind Paul's reference to reaping probably should be taken to refer to spiritual blessings. Experience teaches us that people who give a lot of money to Christian causes don't automatically become wealthy in a worldly sense. They do, however, enjoy a wealth of peace and satisfaction because they know that they have done the right thing. They know that God will always provide for those who focus on his service. They know that they are rich toward God (Luke 12:21; compare Proverbs 11:24; 22:9).

C. EVERYONE'S CHOICE (v. 7)

7. Each man should give what he has decided in his heart to give, not reluctantly or under compulsion, for God loves a cheerful giver.

Giving is not an option, and Paul does not present it as an option to the Corinthians. Some of God's people are clearly in need, and God is going to use the financial resources of the Corinthians to meet that need. The Corinthians can, however, choose the kind of attitude they will exhibit in fulfilling this obligation. They can give begrudgingly, out of a sense of duty and guilt, or they can give cheerfully, thanking God that they have the means to help other people. God is pleased with such gifts because they reveal a heart that is in line with his own.

The amount of money each will give is up to the individual heart (compare Acts 5:4). Even so, Paul is not saying that we can give nothing if we feel like giving nothing. Going back to verse 2, the Corinthians already have pledged to give a certain amount, and Paul seems to be aware of that figure. At least part of the issue is that once we are aware of a need and determine the extent to which we can help, we should not go back on our word.

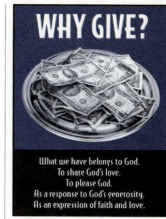

Visual for Lesson 12. *Challenge your students to answer the question "Why give?" as they add to the answers already on this visual.*

WHAT DO YOU THINK?

How will we be affected in the long run if we give grudgingly instead of deciding freely what we want to give?

BAPTIZED POCKETBOOKS

It was a strange statement. But upon reflection, it was quite profound. "Baptized pocketbooks," said the preacher. "We need more baptized pocketbooks!"

When someone's faith in Jesus leads him or her to respond in Christian baptism, it's natural for the person to remove all the items that would be ruined by the water. This includes watches, shoes, pens, and wallets. Although it's not useful for wallets to become literally immersed in the waters of baptism, it is essential that our pocketbooks be baptized symbolically. This doesn't mean that we should have some kind of ceremony in that regard. It does mean that a Christian's pocketbook is part of his or her Christianity.

Sadly, however, the pocketbooks of many Christians seem to be unbaptized. Often people trust God with every area of their lives except their finances. When a person comes to Christ, every aspect of life is to be brought under the lordship of Christ. Everything from our moral standards to our giving should be a proclamation of the Breastplate of Patrick: "Christ with me / Christ in the front / Christ in the rear / Christ within me / Christ below me / Christ above me / Christ at my right hand / Christ at my left."   —T. B.

II. SOURCE AND RESULT (2 CORINTHIANS 9:8-15)

A. GOD'S PROVISIONS (vv. 8, 9)

8. And God is able to make all grace abound to you, so that in all things at all times, having all that you need, you will abound in every good work.

Grace in this context does not refer to "saving grace" but rather to God's gracious provision of spiritual gifts (see Romans 12:3-8). As the Corinthians well know, God has blessed them with every spiritual gift that they would ever need to complete the mission, empowering them to abound in doing good works for the gospel. If God can empower a person to prophesy or miraculously heal the sick, should we doubt that he will secure a sufficient income for those choosing to give a little extra money?

9. As it is written:

> *"He has scattered abroad his gifts to the poor;*
> *his righteousness endures forever."*

Paul emphasizes his point by quoting Psalm 112:9. That psalm describes the character of the person who fears the Lord (112:1), noting the blessings that this person enjoys as a result of God's favor. Such a person gives *gifts to the poor* liberally. As a result, God ensures that this person's *righteousness endures forever.*

The Corinthians similarly should demonstrate their righteousness by giving liberally to the needy believers in Judea. God himself has dispersed liberally gracious gifts to his church, a testimony to his eternally righteous nature. Those who give generously are thus imitating God.

B. CORINTHIANS' FRUITS (vv. 10, 11)

10. Now he who supplies seed to the sower and bread for food will also supply and increase your store of seed and will enlarge the harvest of your righteousness.

Paul now reminds the Corinthians that God provides not only for our spiritual needs but also for our physical needs. Everything comes from him. The farmer buys *seed* by God's grace; the seed grows by God's grace; *the harvest* is preserved by God's grace; the *bread* is baked by God's grace; the money we earn to buy the bread is earned by God's grace. Every bite of food that we put into our mouths is thus the final step in a long series of events that reveal God's care.

This physical provision can be a reflection of the abundant spiritual provision that we enjoy in Christ if we allow it to be. Trusting in such care, we should be able to give generously (compare Isaiah 55:10).

11. You will be made rich in every way so that you can be generous on every occasion, and through us your generosity will result in thanksgiving to God.

WHAT DO YOU THINK?

Before an offering is taken, many worship services feature an offering meditation and prayer. How can these help all to see the possibility of giving more than first thought possible?

Every thing refers to both the physical and spiritual blessings mentioned in verse 10. When we give, God promises to provide and to provide abundantly. The Corinthians should therefore have no hesitation about meeting their pledge. If they do meet it, God will be glorified because the Jerusalem Christians will praise him for providing for their needs in this way.

Through us refers specifically to Paul, Titus, and the representatives of the Macedonian churches who are assigned to deliver the gifts to Jerusalem (2 Corinthians 8:16-23; 9:3-5). But in a more general sense, *us* would include the Corinthians as well. God will provide the money to the Corinthians, who will give it to Paul and companions, who will give it to the needy in Jerusalem. The Corinthians will thus be God's hand to the needy, directly causing this *thanksgiving* to take place.

C. OTHERS' THANKS (vv. 12-14)

12. This service that you perform is not only supplying the needs of God's people but is also overflowing in many expressions of thanks to God.

Any benevolent gift to any charitable cause can help meet *the needs* of a poor person. In this respect it does not make much difference whether we give money to a Christian relief organization or to a secular benevolent group such as the United Way. But a gift given in the name of Christ has a further effect: it brings glory to God because it allows other people to see his hand at work in the world.

This is, ultimately, much more important than the actual physical relief that the gift may bring, for it leads people to a greater trust in God. This has eternal implications. The Corinthians should not give merely as though they are helping some starving people whom they have never met. Rather, they should give as though they are bringing honor to the God who gave them everything they have.

13. Because of the service by which you have proved yourselves, men will praise God for the obedience that accompanies your confession of the gospel of Christ, and for your generosity in sharing with them and with everyone else.

Paul notes two things that the Corinthians have done and one thing that other people will do when they see the results. First, they have professed their faith in *Christ,* submitting themselves to him. Second, they have demonstrated their faith actively by pledging to help the Jerusalem saints. If they are now faithful and live up to their pledge, then others will see Christ at work in them and will glorify God for their *generosity.* In this way a simple act of service—as simple as opening your wallet or writing a check—takes on eternal spiritual significance.

LIBERAL DISTRIBUTION IN DISGUISE

She looked like the cleaning lady from a TV comedy skit. At least that was the first thought that crossed my mind when the director of development at our Bible college introduced me to this humble visitor to our campus. The sweet little lady had arrived to witness the dedication of a new building.

I smiled and introduced myself as one of the professors and made small talk about her home and church family. Then I quickly excused myself to hurry off to my next class. Later that week, I found myself in the school cafeteria and had the opportunity to sit next to my colleague who had introduced me to the older woman.

"Do you remember that nice little lady I introduced you to earlier this week?" she asked.

"Oh, yes," I replied.

"She wasn't very pretentious, was she?"

WHAT DO YOU THINK?

Some who preach a "health and wealth" doctrine would use 2 Corinthians 9:6-11 as proof of their belief. How would you respond to them?

DAILY BIBLE READINGS

Monday, Aug. 14—*Every Good Gift Is from God (James 1:12-17)*

Tuesday, Aug. 15—*Give and You Shall Receive (Luke 6:32-38)*

Wednesday, Aug. 16—*Do Your Giving Quietly (Matthew 6:1-6)*

Thursday, Aug. 17—*Pleased to Share Their Resources (Romans 15:25-29)*

Friday, Aug. 18—*Arrangements for the Jerusalem Collection (2 Corinthians 9:1-5)*

Saturday, Aug. 19—*A Cheerful Giver (2 Corinthians 9:6-10)*

Sunday, Aug. 20—*Generosity Glorifies God (2 Corinthians 9:11-15)*

HOW TO SAY IT

Corinth. KOR-inth.
Corinthians. Ko-RIN-thee-unz.
Gentiles. JEN-tiles.
Isaiah. Eye-ZAY-uh.
Jerusalem. Juh-ROO-suh-lem.
Macedonia. Mass-eh-DOE-nee-uh.
synagogue. SIN-uh-gog.
Titus. TY-tus.

THOUGHT TO REMEMBER

Witness through your giving today!

"No, not at all." And I thought that that was an awfully nice way of putting it. "Very plain and common were the words that would have come to my mind."

"Well, later that day," the director continued, "that very plain and common woman wrote the college a check for $75,000."

Of course, it would have been a great blessing to receive whatever gift she would have generously offered. But God taught me a lesson that day. That very simple lady was one of the most extravagant people I have ever met. Some people choose to live very simple lives in order to be extravagant givers. Only God knows the true nature of each gift. We look on the outer appearance, but God looks upon the heart.   —T. B.

14. And in their prayers for you their hearts will go out to you, because of the surpassing grace God has given you.

Paul indicates that the Jerusalem Christians will return the favor done for them by praying for the Corinthians as they thank God for providing the help. These prayers are, in a sense, the return on the Corinthians' investment. If such prayers seem to have less worth than the money we give, then we clearly have misunderstood how God operates.

D. GOD'S GREAT GIFT (v. 15)

15. Thanks be to God for his indescribable gift!

This verse is foundational to all Christian stewardship. Paul shifts from the narrower discussion of grace as the gifts and financial blessings that the Corinthians have received (v. 14) to a general prayer of thanksgiving. The *gift* of God noted here must be the wonderful grace evident in salvation through Christ. If God loved the world so much that he gave his only Son (John 3:16), then surely we can give a portion of our material blessings to help other believers.

CONCLUSION

Stewardship is not an optional feature of the Christian life. God has given us many wonderful things—salvation, material blessings, spiritual gifts—and he expects us to use these for his purposes. Thoughtful stewardship not only brings relief to those in need but also ultimately brings glory to God.

Of course, when Paul wrote this letter he had no idea whether the Corinthians would come through with their gift. Perhaps they would back out and embarrass him. But the evidence suggests that they did the right thing. Later in the letter, Paul tells them that he is about to visit them once more to check on their progress (2 Corinthians 12:14; 13:1). Paul did travel to Corinth, and he and the representatives from Macedonia spent the winter with the believers there before going on to Jerusalem (see Acts 20:2, 3).

During this layover, Paul wrote the letter to the Romans. At the end of that epistle, he mentions that the churches in Macedonia and Achaia had made contributions for the needy in Palestine. Achaia is the district in which Corinth was located, suggesting that he found things ready as requested (Romans 15:25-28). When Paul and companions arrived in Jerusalem, the gift was received warmly just as Paul anticipated. Further, also as Paul had predicted, the leaders of the Judean church praised God for the grace given to the Gentiles (Acts 21:17-20a).

The Corinthian church was beset with many serious problems, and it is easy to criticize them for their immorality and immaturity. Yet in this instance the church responded to Paul's warnings. They ultimately did the right thing. As such, they stand as a model not only of generosity but also of willingness to repent. May we be so as well.

Discovery Learning

This page contains an alternative lesson plan emphasizing learning activities. Classes desiring such student involvement will find these suggestions helpful. The next page is a reproducible activity page to further enhance discovery learning.

LEARNING GOALS

After this lesson, each student will be able to:

1. Restate Paul's reasons for the need of Christians to be generous givers.

2. Explain how God makes it possible to be generous.

3. Make a personal giving plan.

INTO THE LESSON

Write *Why Give?* on the board. Include two columns underneath for answers. Divide the class in half and assign each half one answer column. Alternate back and forth between the two sides of the class as they give their answers and you record them in the appropriate column. Expect responses such as the following: "Because giving is like God," "Because people have needs," "So that the church can do its work." Continue until no additional answers are suggested.

Say, "In today's text, 2 Corinthians 9:3-15, Paul gives reasons why the Christians in Corinth should give generously to the needy churches in Judea." Ask a volunteer to read the Bible text aloud. Say, "Listen to the text and make a mental checklist of the reasons Paul cites for generous giving. How closely does our list compare with Paul's?" After the text has been read, ask, "Which of the reasons in your group's list did you hear represented in the text? What verses correspond?" Let several students respond. [Option: distribute the "Grace or _____?" exercise from the reproducible page for students to work on as they arrive.]

INTO THE WORD

For this activity students will mingle among themselves wearing a name tag with one of the statements about giving listed below. Some of the statements are true and some are false. Direct the class to circulate and greet one another, noting what each other's name tags have to say about giving. After a time direct everyone to be seated. Ask students to turn to today's text to confirm or refute the statements they have read on the lapels.

Use the following statements or others of your own creation. (Additional statements can also be found in the student book in the "Paul Says" activity.) Note: The true statements have Bible verse numbers in parentheses for your reference. Do not write these verse numbers on the name tags.

Statements: 1. Give because you know that God will make you rich, both in this world and in the next. 2. Give so that God will give to you. 3. Selfishness will prove embarrassing to the Christian (v. 3). 4. Give to encourage others (v. 4). 5. Special giving projects that are well planned honor God (v. 5). 6. Giving helps relieve guilt. 7. Stingy givers reap few benefits (v. 6). 8. Gifts that are given grudgingly are no gifts at all (v. 7). 9. God loves it when people give, regardless of their motives. 10. God provides abundance so that the receiver can do good works (v. 8). 11. The origin of all gifts is God (v. 10). 12. Generosity ultimately brings praise to God (v. 11). 13. A gift given in the name of Christ brings glory to God (v. 12). 14. Generous giving is an indication of submission to the gospel (v. 13). 15. Generous giving elicits prayers for the giver from the recipient (v. 14). 16. All giving should be in response to God's gift of redemptive grace (v. 15). 17. God expects us to give a specific amount.

As an alternative activity, introduce students to several ongoing financial needs of people or organizations, such as support for a missionary school, evangelistic training in another culture, or support of a short-term missions team. Ask the class to pick one month-long project to support with a special offering by collecting their spare change and pooling it together for a month. Be sure to give the class weekly reminders.

INTO LIFE

Help your students develop a giving plan with a "treasure hunt" through Matthew. Provide them with a list of the following Scripture references from that book: 6:19-21; 12:35; 13:44; 13:52; 19:21. If you have an artistic class member, ask that person to create a treasure map on parchment paper titled "Matthew's Island" with the Scripture references printed on it. For example, the map could state, "Go five paces to Matthew 6:19."

Suggest to students that they post their list (or map) where they will see it for the next five days, finding one of the "treasures" each day. Tell them that as they read each Scripture they will be discovering real treasure that they can hide in their hearts. Challenge them to think of giving in other than just monetary terms. [Option: use the "How Hot Is Your Giving?" exercise on the reproducible page as a take-home enhancement this activity; the passages from Matthew can suggest commitments.]

Grace or ____?

God gives to us graciously. His grace, therefore, should be our model for how we deal with others. Unscramble the following words to reveal ungodly alternatives to grace that should be avoided. (Answers are at the bottom of the page.)

Christians should treat others with grace instead of . . .

aceeegnnv

beiinorrttu

beeinrsstt

aegnr

eeemnnrstt

ceijstu

ehimnnpstu

ceeijnort

How Hot Is Your Giving?

Use a red pen to mark the thermometer at the level you believe characterizes your current level of giving.

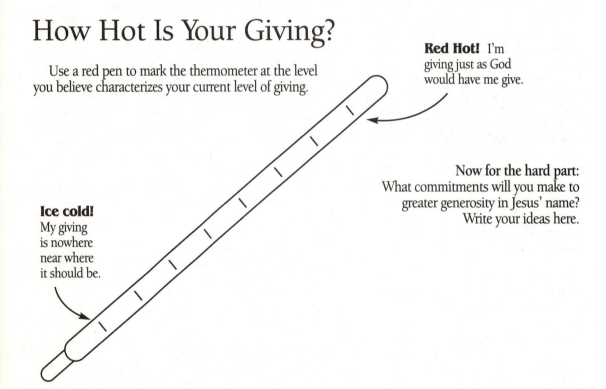

Red Hot! I'm giving just as God would have me give.

Now for the hard part: What commitments will you make to greater generosity in Jesus' name? Write your ideas here.

Ice cold! My giving is nowhere near where it should be.

Called to Be a Christian Community

Unit 3: The Spirit of Giving
(Lessons 10-13)

GIVING SUFFICIENT GRACE

LESSON 13

WHY TEACH THIS LESSON?

"He is my thorn in the flesh." A discouraged person might use such a statement to refer to a frustrating coworker, spouse, or child. The text for today's lesson is the source of the expression, "thorn in the flesh." But Paul did not intend it in the way that it is commonly used now. For Paul, the "thorn in the flesh" was a physical infirmity that limited his personal ability to do ministry.

This lesson, drawn from 2 Corinthians 12, still speaks loudly today. How can we meet the expectations of ministry when we are physically or emotionally limited? Shouldn't the burden of ministering fall on the shoulders of the strong ones in our church, like the preacher and his staff?

Paul answers this with one of the great paradoxes of the Christian faith: we are strongest when we are weak. The victories of the Christian life are not won by our strength but by the power of our God. Learning and applying this lesson will help us understand how God works through us, even in the infirmities of illness or age.

INTRODUCTION

A. ANSWERING THE BURNING BUSH

Moses and Paul both had remarkable calls to ministry. Paul saw the risen Christ in a flash of light on the road to Damascus; Moses heard the voice of God from a burning bush in the desert. Paul responded to God's calling immediately by setting out to preach the gospel. His Christian life was beset with hardships and persecution from the beginning (see Acts 9:17-26).

Moses, however, responded in a very different way. When God told Moses that he would use him to deliver the Jews from Egypt, Moses balked. He first pointed out that he was a nobody; why should people listen to him? He then demanded some sort of evidence that God had really spoken to him. God replied by empowering him with the ability to do several attesting miracles. Moses then declined the invitation on the basis of his lack of skill in public speaking. He even asked God whether the Jews would know which "god" he was talking about! (See Exodus 3:1–4:17.)

Moses, in other words, resisted God's call by pointing out all of the personal weaknesses that would make it impossible for him to complete the task. Paul, by contrast, refused this path. He too labored under serious personal shortcomings, including the painful "thorn in the flesh" discussed in our passage for today. Yet he was determined to fulfill his calling (as Moses eventually was as well). Paul was confident that God would provide the tools he needed to finish the job.

B. LESSON BACKGROUND

Paul wrote 2 Corinthians in A.D. 57 at the conclusion of a very tense period between himself and that church. In the letter of 1 Corinthians, Paul had rebuked them sharply for sectarian divisions and a number of serious spiritual and

DEVOTIONAL READING:
JAMES 4:1-10
BACKGROUND SCRIPTURE:
2 CORINTHIANS 12:1-10
PRINTED TEXT:
2 CORINTHIANS 12:1-10

LESSON AIMS

After participating in this lesson, each student will be able to:

1. Summarize how Paul's vision relates to his "thorn."

2. Contrast the world's view of power through strength with Paul's view of power through weakness.

3. Commit to God's grace one area of weakness in his or her life, seeking his power to overcome that weakness.

KEY VERSE

He said to me, "My grace is sufficient for you, for my power is made perfect in weakness." Therefore I will boast all the more gladly about my weaknesses, so that Christ's power may rest on me.
—2 Corinthians 12:9

Aug
27

moral failures. But that letter, even though supported by a visit from Timothy, was not as effective as Paul had hoped.

Paul, therefore, left Ephesus to make an emergency visit to Corinth, one characterized by confrontation. The trip was successful, but while there Paul apparently was slandered by some of his enemies. These accusations must have continued after he left (see 2 Corinthians 1:23–2:1; 3:1; 10:1–11:33).

All this placed Paul in a difficult situation. Obviously, he needed to defend his credibility by responding to these attacks. Yet at the same time, he did not want to fall into arrogant boasting about his accomplishments or enter the trap of comparing résumés. He avoided these problems by emphasizing his weaknesses as proof that God was working through him in a unique and powerful way.

I. VISION OF GLORY (2 CORINTHIANS 12:1-4)

A. Undesired Talking Point (v. 1)

1. I must go on boasting. Although there is nothing to be gained, I will go on to visions and revelations from the Lord.

Paul begins by stressing that he wishes he didn't have to say any of what he is about to say. Back in 2 Corinthians 10:12-18; 11:5, 6, Paul was clear that he didn't want to rehearse his credentials, yet he felt compelled to do so in view of his enemies' slander.

Paul especially feared that the accusations of enemies would lead the Corinthians to doubt the validity of the gospel that he had preached to them (11:4). As such, he determined to boast only about his own weaknesses and thereby emphasize the power of God working through his ministry (11:30).

B. Unexpected Event (vv. 2-4)

2. I know a man in Christ who fourteen years ago was caught up to the third heaven. Whether it was in the body or out of the body I do not know—God knows.

The *man* in consideration here is clearly Paul himself. If Paul writes 2 Corinthians in A.D. 57, then *fourteen years ago* would date the experience in question to around A.D. 43. This is near the time of the brief visit to Jerusalem mentioned at Acts 11:27-30; 12:25. It is possible that Paul is referring to a vision that occurred in conjunction with his special commission to preach in Acts 13:1-3.

The biblical Hebrew word for *heaven* actually is plural: *heavens* (compare Genesis 2:1, 4). In some schools of thought in ancient Judaism, there are seven heavens that make up a complicated scheme. Paul here alludes to a much more basic line of thinking: the first heaven is the sky (where the birds fly), the second heaven is the universe (home to sun, moon, and stars), and *the third heaven* is the realm where God dwells.

The latter is what we call Heaven today. Paul, then, actually was caught up directly into God's own presence on one particular occasion. What an experience!

3. And I know that this man—whether in the body or apart from the body I do not know, but God knows—

Paul's uncertainty about *the body* emphasizes the spiritual nature of the event. We may conjecture that this event involved a suspension of consciousness. Is it possible for someone to enter God's presence while still in the flesh (Exodus 33:20)? Paul does *not know,* and it makes no difference to his point.

4. . . . was caught up to paradise. He heard inexpressible things, things that man is not permitted to tell.

Paradise, the "third heaven" of verse 2, is the place of God's dwelling (compare Luke 23:43; Revelation 2:7). Paul, in whatever form, had been in God's

What Do You Think?

Paul hesitated to resort to boasting. What makes boasting so potentially destructive, both in Paul's day and now? Under what circumstances, if any, could boasting be appropriate today?

presence. But he cannot talk about what he heard and saw there for two reasons. In the first place no person is *permitted to* reveal these things. That probably means that the vision was for Paul and Paul alone. This fact emphasizes the unique nature of Paul's ministry.

In the second place human language cannot express what Paul witnessed—there are no words to describe it. God's glory far exceeds what the human mind can comprehend or what the human tongue can report.

PAUL'S VISION, OUR VISION

Said Alice to the Cheshire Cat, "Would you tell me please, which way I ought to go from here?"

Said the Cat, "That depends a good deal on where you want to get to."

"I don't much care where . . . " said Alice.

"Then," said the Cat, "it doesn't much matter which way you go" (Lewis Carroll, *Through the Looking Glass*).

This humorous little exchange from the realm of "Wonderland" displays the essential nature of having a vision for the future. It also brings to light a certain confusion regarding how we use the word *vision* today versus how Paul used that concept in 2 Corinthians.

Paul's vision was miraculous in nature. A modern understanding of vision, however, is more along the lines of "a clear mental image of a preferable future. . . . It is based on an accurate understanding of God, yourself, and your circumstances" (George Barna, *The Power of Vision: How You Can Capture and Apply God's Vision for Your Ministry*). We should not expect that God will repeat Paul's vision in the lives of Christians today. Even so, every follower of Jesus must have a vision for a preferable future, as controlled by the Word of God.

Paul's vision of the risen Christ on the Damascus Road and subsequent visions of God's will shaped not only his destiny but also the destiny of the church. May God grant us the courage to embrace God's vision for our own lives as it is drawn from his Word daily. —T. B.

II. GLORY OF WEAKNESS (2 CORINTHIANS 12:5-10)

A. GOD'S DEEDS (vv. 5, 6)

5. I will boast about a man like that, but I will not boast about myself, except about my weaknesses.

Paul now shifts gears to discuss a particularly difficult problem that hinders his ministry. This statement is intentionally ironic, because Paul himself is the very person he has been talking about.

Paul's point is to say that any boasting that he may do will be about things that God has done for him and through him, not about things that he himself has accomplished by personal ability. Specifically, he would defend himself by reminding his detractors that God had given him a vision of Heaven, but he would also remind them that he received this vision as a gracious gift from God. It was not as payment for work Paul had done. If Paul were to speak about things he has accomplished on his own, the discussion would be much less useful.

6. Even if I should choose to boast, I would not be a fool, because I would be speaking the truth. But I refrain, so no one will think more of me than is warranted by what I do or say.

In point of fact, Paul had built an impressive set of credentials by this time in his "career," as both a Jewish and a Christian leader (see 2 Corinthians 11:21b-28). Should it come down to a bragging session, he will not be ashamed (compare 2 Corinthians 10:8; 11:16).

DAILY BIBLE READINGS

Monday, Aug. 21—*Grace Abounds All the More (Romans 5:12-21)*

Tuesday, Aug. 22—*Grace for the Humble (James 4:1-10)*

Wednesday, Aug. 23—*The God of Grace Will Restore (1 Peter 5:5-10)*

Thursday, Aug. 24—*Paul Receives God's Grace (1 Corinthians 15:3-10)*

Friday, Aug. 25—*Paul Experiences Many Difficulties (2 Corinthians 11:23-29)*

Saturday, Aug. 26—*Paul's Deep Spiritual Experience (2 Corinthians 12:1-6)*

Sunday, Aug. 27—*God's Grace Is Sufficient (2 Corinthians 12:7-13)*

Paul further discusses his credentials in Philippians 3:4b-7, especially those that would impress Jewish Christians. "If anyone thinks he has reasons to put confidence in the flesh, I have more: circumcised on the eighth day, of the people of Israel, of the tribe of Benjamin, a Hebrew of Hebrews; in regard to the law, a Pharisee; as for zeal, persecuting the church; as for legalistic righteousness, faultless." But all these things must be counted as a loss when compared with the glories of knowing and serving Christ. As such, Paul will *not be a fool*, rambling on and on about his own accomplishments. Instead, he will stress the things that God has accomplished through him.

B. PAUL'S THORN (vv. 7-9a)

7. To keep me from becoming conceited because of these surpassingly great revelations, there was given me a thorn in my flesh, a messenger of Satan, to torment me.

The flow of this passage suggests that verse 7 is somehow related to the experience described in verses 1-4. Paul's unique vision certainly could make anyone feel special. But his joy was marred by the fact that it was followed by *a thorn in the flesh*. The position of the verb *given* implies that it was God who gave Paul both the miraculous vision and the painful consequence. The purpose of the thorn, Paul says, is to keep him humble. Thus he will not feel undue pride about the special work God has in store for him.

The specific identity of Paul's thorn has long been a subject of speculation. The term *thorn* and the references to the *torment* that it brings suggest that Paul is referring to a chronic physical ailment. Because this vision of Christ, and presumably the thorn also, came to Paul just before the first missionary journey to Galatia, many scholars have sought the key to this puzzle in Galatians 4:13-15. Paul there mentions a serious illness that befell him at that time, one that possibly affected his eyes in some way.

Whether this or some other problem, the thorn threatened Paul's ministry. Although it came from God, he refers to it as *a messenger of Satan* because from a human perspective it hindered his ability to proclaim the gospel. Yet God knows how to turn such things for the good, as the next verses show. (An alternative view is that Satan initiated the thorn, but the thorn is given by God in the sense that God allowed it, as in Job's case of torment.)

8. Three times I pleaded with the Lord to take it away from me.

This verse reveals that it took Paul a while to appreciate God's purposes in the thorn. At first, he viewed it only as a burden. On several occasions Paul asked God to relieve him of it. Doubtless Paul prayed about the issue often, but he recalls at least *three* occasions in particular when he pleaded with God about this troubling issue. Perhaps he accompanied his pleading with fasting.

Paul's example highlights the fact that it's right to ask God for help with our problems. It is acceptable to ask him for help more than once when we don't receive a clear answer. We remember that Jesus prayed the same prayer several times in the garden (Matthew 26:36-44).

9a. But he said to me, "My grace is sufficient for you, for my power is made perfect in weakness."

It is unclear whether God said this to Paul after each of his three periods of supplication or only sometime after the third. It is also unclear whether God revealed this insight in yet another vision of some sort or whether Paul gradually came to this conclusion through God's continued rejections of his request.

Either way, the point is clear: no matter how often or how urgently we ask, God reserves the right to say no. But he does not say no simply because he wants

WHAT DO YOU THINK?

When something significant happens in your life, spiritual or otherwise, what steps do you take to avoid becoming conceited or prideful? What are some thorns that God may give us (or allow us to have) to forestall pride?

WHAT DO YOU THINK?

How can we avoid the temptation of drawing false conclusions about God, self, or life when we have to deal continually with a difficult "thorn in the flesh"?

WHAT DO YOU THINK?

Some might say that Paul was self-centered by praying for an easier life, thus showing a lack of faith. Why and under what circumstances is it OK for us to pray for ourselves?

[Note: James 4:3 should be part of your answer.]

us to suffer and worry. Our weaknesses serve God's purpose, even if that purpose is only that we should remain humble and dependent on him.

This perspective gives Paul the strength to bear his burden without becoming discouraged and to continue to serve despite its limitations. *Perfect* can be understood as "complete." This highlights the contrast between God's *power* and our *weakness:* where our strength is lacking, Christ still empowers us to serve.

STRENGTH IN WEAKNESS

The life of Joni Eareckson changed forever on July 30, 1967. She was a young girl full of promise and hope for the future. While on a family outing, she dived into the waters of Chesapeake Bay and struck an object hidden just below the surface. She became paralyzed from the neck down.

She had planned to be an artist. She had planned to have a family. She had planned to live a normal life. But all those dreams and plans seemingly ended in the lonely confines of a wheelchair. And yet Joni is one of the most celebrated Christian speakers and writers of our day.

In her autobiography Joni writes of the power of the Lord Jesus Christ to make any life wonderful and exciting. "Jesus is alive and his power is available to you. He proves himself daily in my life, and what more couldn't he do in your life!" (*Joni*, Zondervan).

Some may argue that had it not been for the debilitating accident, Joni Eareckson Tada would never have become such an international influence for the cause of Christ. Only the Lord knows if this is so. One thing is for certain: Joni allowed the Lord to work through her weaknesses to display his strength and power.

God is able to work though our weaknesses and trials today. He only asks that we approach each hardship with the eyes of faith. That means trusting that "in all things God works for the good of those who love him, who have been called according to his purpose" (Romans 8:28).   —T. B.

C. GOD'S STRENGTH (vv. 9b, 10)

9b. Therefore I will boast all the more gladly about my weaknesses, so that Christ's power may rest on me.

We normally try to hide our shortcomings from other people. Sometimes we try to hide them from ourselves and from God as well. Paul, however, had said earlier that he would *boast* about his *weaknesses* (2 Corinthians 11:30). So now he does just that. He can do this because he is confident that God will make up for what he lacks.

When God calls us to a specific task, he does so with full awareness of our inabilities and limitations. In fact he may call us because of those very limitations. That way it will be clear to everyone that his *power* is at work when we succeed, not just our own natural ability.

Paul learned to accept his thorn because he realized that ultimately it could not stop him from accomplishing God's mission. In fact the thorn became the primary evidence of God's power at work in him, because his success makes it clear that he must be empowered by God's support. Paul's thorn, even though it remains painful and embarrassing, reminds him that God provides the strength.

10. That is why, for Christ's sake, I delight in weaknesses, in insults, in hardships, in persecutions, in difficulties. For when I am weak, then I am strong.

No one likes to be persecuted or insulted, of course. No one likes to feel inadequate to the task at hand. But Paul delights in these things for Christ's sake. That phrase must mean that Paul is willing to suffer, if need be, in order to fulfill

HOW TO SAY IT

Corinth. KOR-inth.
Corinthians. Ko-RIN-thee-unz.
Damascus. Duh-MASS-kus.
Ephesus. EF-uh-sus.
Galatia. Guh-LAY-shuh.
Galatians. Guh-LAY-shunz.
Moses. MO-zes or MO-zez.
Niebuhr. NEE-burr.
Philippians. Fih-LIP-ee-unz.

PRAYER

Father, many times we feel weak and inadequate, and we don't understand the problems in our lives. But we know that you understand our problems. You know us better than we know ourselves.

We ask for the faith to trust you no matter what happens. Help us find the strength that only you can provide so that we can always do what you have called us to do. In Jesus' name, amen.

God's commission for his life. Paul's Christian life is characterized by hardship (2 Corinthians 11:23-28). It will eventually end with his execution in Rome (2 Timothy 4:6).

Yet the attacks of his enemies do not stop him because, ironically, he becomes stronger and stronger the more harm they inflict. This is not in the sense that "whatever doesn't kill me makes me stronger." Rather, it is in the sense that God provides him with more and more power the weaker and less capable he feels.

CONCLUSION

A. OUR LIMITATIONS

We can easily become discouraged in the face of our limitations. So often we feel that we could be much happier and much more effective if God only would resolve certain persistent problems for us.

These thorns can threaten our faith if we allow them to raise questions of God's care for us. At the same time, however, the fact that we are able to keep pressing forward despite these obstacles reveals God's power and sufficient grace working through our inadequacies. Viewed from this angle, we can embrace hardship with the confidence that everything that happens to us can serve a long-term benefit within God's larger plan for our lives. This is part of what it means to live by faith, not by sight.

B. OUR SERENITY

Reinhold Niebuhr (1892–1971) penned what has become one of the most famous prayers of all time: "God, give us the grace to accept with serenity the things that cannot be changed, courage to change the things which should be changed, and the wisdom to distinguish one from the other."

This simple request is powerful for its combination of faith and resolve. Many difficulties in life are within our power to overcome, and in such cases, we ask God for the courage to fight the battle. He is the one who is able to strengthen us! But we must also realize that some obstacles may never be taken out of our way in this life. Some weaknesses may plague us until we are at home with the Lord.

Things that hinder our bodies must not, however, hinder our faith. We do not abandon God over these struggles. Rather, we ask him to give us calm in the midst of the storm. The challenge is in the last line of the prayer: learning to know when to fight and when to let go. It is not surprising that the Prayer of Serenity has been adopted by Alcoholics Anonymous and other recovery groups.

Some problems that we face disappear almost before we really have time to worry about them; others last long enough to distract us; some become ongoing struggles that threaten our peace of mind and our faith. Paul underwent many temporary trials, and our passage today reveals that he also labored under the pain of a persistent thorn in the flesh. He makes no bones about the fact that God refused to lift this burden and never planned to do so. Remarkably, that fact did not cripple Paul's progress. It did not stop him from fulfilling his calling. The thorn ultimately made him stronger by forcing him to rely upon God's power.

Sometimes we need to ask God for relief from problems. Sometimes we need to ask God repeatedly for relief from problems. Sometimes we need his strength to overcome obstacles. Sometimes we need his peace to live with those obstacles. In all circumstances we need the wisdom and faith to trust in his grace. That grace truly is sufficient for us.

WHAT DO YOU THINK?

What do you do to remain strong when you feel weak? How do you use Philippians 4:11 in this regard?

Visual for Lesson 13. *Use this visual to introduce the question above.*

THOUGHT TO REMEMBER

Allow God's grace to shine through your weakness.

Discovery Learning

This page contains an alternative lesson plan emphasizing learning activities. Classes desiring such student involvement will find these suggestions helpful. The next page is a reproducible activity page to further enhance discovery learning.

LEARNING GOALS

After this lesson, each student will be able to:

1. Summarize how Paul's vision relates to his "thorn."

2. Contrast the world's view of power through strength with Paul's view of power through weakness.

3. Commit to God's grace one area of weakness in his or her life, seeking his power to overcome that weakness.

INTO THE LESSON

Prepare eight large cards with letters from the two words *WEAKNESS* and *STRENGTH*. The first card should have the letter *W* written on the front and the letter *S* on the back. The next card should have the letter *E* written on the front and the letter *T* on the back. (The letters on the backside of the cards should be upside down to the letters on the front of the cards.) Continue in like manner for the remaining cards.

Affix the eight cards to the wall using masking tape on the top of each card so that they can be lifted to show the letter on the back. The letters for the word *WEAKNESS* should face outward.

Also prepare 26 small slips of paper in advance. Each slip should contain one letter of the alphabet. Give each class member one of the slips. (Give more than one slip per student if your class is smaller than 26 students.)

Say to the class, "Ask me a question in this manner regarding your letter(s): 'Is an *A* [or whatever letter that you hold] sufficient?' If your letter is not concealed behind the flaps, I will answer: 'No, that letter is not sufficient.' If your letter is one of the concealed letters, I will say, 'Yes, your letter is sufficient, and then I will lift that flap."

Continue until all letters of *STRENGTH* are revealed. Then affirm, "God turns our weakness into strength, and that is the theme today. God's grace is sufficient for our weakness." [Option: distribute the "Humble Me, Lord" activity from the reproducible page for your early arrivers to work on before class begins.]

INTO THE WORD

A week ahead of time, recruit a volunteer to play the role of Paul for a dramatized interview. Give your volunteer a copy of the questions based on 2 Corinthians 12:1-10 that follow. Ask him to word his own answers based on the verses. One sample answer is given.

Remind the class that Paul repeatedly expresses his reluctance to talk about himself and his authority and power. Say, "But today Paul has agreed to come and answer questions about his qualifications and ministry."

Randomly hand out the interview questions (without any answers) to members of your class. Have class members ask Paul their questions in numerical order. (The sequence of questions is related to the verses of today's lesson text.) Introduce the apostle Paul to your class with flair, noting your appreciation for his willingness to talk about his God-given authority and power.

Questions: 1. Paul, why do you consider it appropriate to talk about yourself? [*Sample answer: "I certainly should not brag. But perhaps you would let me say a few things about special visions that God gave a trusted servant"* (v. 1).] 2. Trusted servant, you say? Who is that servant? (v. 2) 3. How did this vision come to this Christian brother? (v. 2) 4. What was the nature of his vision? What did he see and what did God say? (vv. 2, 4). 5. What's this brother's experience got to do with you? (v. 5) 6. Don't you ever want to brag a bit about all the things you have done? (v. 6) 7. Do all the great spiritual privileges you have been granted ever tempt you to pride? (v. 7) 8. Paul, I have often wondered: if you are God's special messenger, why hasn't God taken your disability away? (vv. 8, 9) 9. Have you never questioned God's wisdom in this matter? (v. 9) 10. Paul, it sounds to me like you're bragging about being weak. Isn't that a strange approach to life and ministry? (v. 9) 11. What are the greatest joys of your apostleship? (v. 10).

INTO LIFE

Distribute a rose with thorns to each class member or display a large picture of a rose. Say, "Paul's Christian life was occasionally hindered because of his 'thorn in the flesh.' Yet the aroma of his beautiful life 'rose' to God in praise."

Ask the class, "Do thorns deter people from growing roses? Do they deter people from enjoying their aroma? Do they deter people from marveling in their beauty?" Ask students to use their roses as reminders that life in Christ is beautiful in spite of the thorns. Encourage class members to be honest about self-inflicted thorns. [Option: expand this rose/thorn imagery by using the second exercise from the reproducible page.]

Humble Me, Lord

Throughout Bible history God used a variety of strategies to keep people humble. Write the letters of the individuals humbled by God in the blanks to the left of the appropriate Scripture texts. On the lines in the middle column, identify the manner of God's humbling hand.

Text	Device	Person Affected
___ Exodus 10:28–11:6	_____	A. Balaam
___ Numbers 22:18-31	_____	B. Nebuchadnezzar
___ Judges 16:20-30	_____	C. Pharaoh
___ 1 Samuel 15:10-23	_____	D. the apostle Paul
___ Daniel 4:28-34	_____	E. Samson
___ 2 Corinthians 12:7-9	_____	F. King Saul

Roses and Thorns

Develop the analogy "My Christian life is like a rose . . ." on the lines below. Ask yourself the following questions to stimulate your thinking: Who are the people who have been wounded by my thorns when they drew close? Who are those who have delighted in the sweet aroma of my righteousness? How do the thorns in my life help me to be the person God wants me to be? How will the "fallen petals" of my life be a blessing after I am gone?

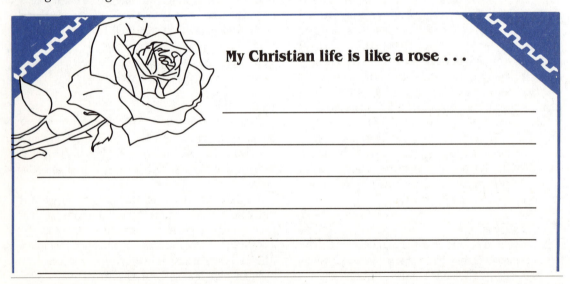

My Christian life is like a rose . . .